THE AME

A CRITIC

THE AMERICAN COURTS
A CRITICAL ASSESSMENT

Edited by

John B. Gates
University of California, Davis

Charles A. Johnson
Texas A&M University

PRESS

A Division of Congressional Quarterly Inc.

Printed in the United States of America

Cover design by Carol Crosby Black

Library of Congress Cataloging-in-Publication Data

The American courts: a critical assessment / edited by John B. Gates, Charles A. Johnson.
    p.   cm.
    Includes bibliographical references and index.
    ISBN 0-87187-541-1
    1. Courts—United States. 2. Justice, Administration of—United States. 3. Judicial process--United States. 4. Judges--United States. I. Gates, John Boatner. II. Johnson, Charles A., 1948-.
KF8719.A2A454   1990
347.73'1--dc20   90-2260
[347.3071]   CIP

To
J. B. and Johnnie Gates
and
Barbara Johnson

CONTENTS

PREFACE

American Courts: A Critical Assessment was prepared with several objectives in mind. First, we wanted to offer leading judicial scholars an opportunity to write about research areas with which they are thoroughly familiar. Second, for classes in the judicial process we wanted to offer a book that highlights important areas of judicial research. And, third, for both students and judicial scholars we wanted to offer a collection of essays that critically assesses contemporary research on the American judiciary.

The scope of the book is broad. The chapters encompass state and federal courts as well as trial and appellate courts. In addition, several theoretical perspectives are represented, although the authors generally assess the development of empirical theory.

The chapters in this book have been written by judicial scholars who have made substantial contributions to the literature, especially on the topics in their respective chapters. They were asked to review contemporary theoretical developments regarding the chapter topic, discuss relevant empirical findings, and describe what future research might be done in the area. Although the authors provide extensive bibliographic information, the chapters primarily offer an analysis of recent work and a critique of the state of knowledge in the field. These essays should be an excellent source of information about where current judicial research is to be found, what the important issues for the field are, and what direction research might take in the 1990s.

Organizing a volume such as this is not without risks. As editors, we recognized that only a limited number of authors on a limited number of topics could be a part of this endeavor. Our list of potential authors and topics was large, and we had to make difficult choices. We are confident, however, that the contributions of many contemporary judicial scholars are reflected in the chapters. The chapter authors also assumed some risk because we actively encouraged speculation and critical assessment. We believe that they have been fair and are confident that their evaluations will be helpful to the discipline.

A project of this type requires contributions from many sources. First and foremost, our heartfelt thanks go to the authors who contributed to this volume; they were very cooperative. Indeed, we had long telephone conversations with one contributor in the hospital; he had a draft of his chapter at his bedside. Another contributor discussed revisions between intense negotiations with a governor and several unions.

We have also been encouraged by our colleagues as the book has taken shape. Supportive comments and substantive evaluations were invaluable during the editing process. In particular, Philip Dubois of the University of California, Davis, contributed his time, encouragement, and advice with his usual grace and good humor.

Joanne Daniels, director of CQ Press until the final manuscript was written, encouraged the development of this book. Joanne has the sense of humor to be supportive, the professional sense to be direct, and the rare ability to combine both in phone messages that can make the most jaded pale. We appreciated her advice and sound counsel as we moved through the various stages of the project. Nola Healy Lynch, as copy editor, provided valuable comments as well. Jerry Orvedahl of Congressional Quarterly skillfully saw the book through its production stages.

We also would like to thank the University of California, Davis, and Texas A&M University, which provided the support necessary to enable a long distance coeditorship. The Committee on Research of the Davis Division of the Academic Senate of the University of California provided much-appreciated financial support. Thank goodness for WATS lines, fax machines, overnight mail services, and understanding chairs and deans.

A special thanks also goes to Micki Eagle, Kathi Miller, Linda Potoski, and Roberta Anderson at the University of California, Davis, and Mary Ann Smith at Texas A&M, who provided secretarial support for this project. Administrative support is often acknowledged, but we doubt that it has been more appreciated than in this endeavor. Finally, we gratefully acknowledge the support and understanding of our families. They did not read the manuscript, but they heard all of the stories about its development.

Part I

JUDICIAL POLICY MAKING: AN OVERVIEW

Scarcely any political question arises in the United States that is not resolved, sooner or later, into a judicial question.

—Alexis de Tocqueville
Democracy in America, 1832

I may give a clue to my thesis by reporting an incident in a debate in the United States Senate. Senator Spooner of Wisconsin had been citing Supreme Court decisions to his purpose. When Senator Tillman of South Carolina was recognized, he complained: "I am tired of hearing what the Supreme Court says. What I want to get at is the common sense of the matter." To which Senator Spooner rejoined: "I too am seeking the common sense of the matter. But as for me, I prefer the common sense of the Supreme Court to that of the Senator from South Carolina."

—Thomas Reed Powell
"The Logic and Rhetoric of
Constitutional Law," 1918

Most Americans perceive of policy making in the United States as a legislative or administrative activity. The public readily associates the making of public policy with committee and floor deliberations of legislatures and the activities of executive officials and their agencies. Yet American courts do make public policy, and as the following chapters remind us, much of this policy is politically significant and enduring. Regardless of the type of court (trial or appellate) or its level in the federal system (state or federal), judicial bodies make authoritative decisions that allocate societal resources, values, and costs.

Political scientists working at the beginning of this century clearly understood the policy making of judicial bodies, especially the U.S. Supreme Court, the apex of the American judicial system. Writing in 1918, Thomas Reed Powell observed in his usual wry tone how courts, and the Supreme Court specifically, must make choices; these choices constitute judgments with significant consequences for the policies guiding a political system. Since the inception of political science, this recognition was clear. Indeed, the early years in the professional study of courts was consumed with understanding the rules laid down by courts. Absent from these early investigations was a concern for explaining the policy-making process outside of the overall structure of legal reasoning, precedent, and the Anglo-Saxon standard for consistent and objective adjudication.

Jack Peltason's *Federal Courts in the Political Process* (1955) marked a major scholarly departure from the approach to judicial institutions as rule-laden, mechanistic, and concerned with the resolution of conflicts over rules. Instead, Peltason's book portrayed the federal courts as political institutions and part of a larger process of political conflict.

In this vein, scholars began to devote most of their energies to understanding the policy-making process of courts; they focused for many years on the federal courts. Fortunately, there has been a growing interest in state court policy making over the last fifteen years. State courts are the forums for the vast majority of litigation in the United States. And although they are subservient to federal courts, state courts make most of the policy that directly affects the daily lives and behavior of individuals.

Both state and federal courts within their respective spheres of policy are important political and legal institutions engaged in policy making. Understanding the range and significance of the policies made by judicial bodies often touches upon questions of what underlies judicial choices. The chapters below illustrate this linkage between understanding policy making and the process of decision making.

Part I addresses the question, To what extent and with what consequences do various types of courts make public policy? The primary focus is on how courts offer their "common sense" judgments on difficult questions of public policy and the implications for the role of courts in a democratic society. David Adamany (Chapter 1) examines the U.S. Supreme Court and the tensions between its policy making and democratic values. Donald R. Songer, in Chapter 2, provides an overview of policy making by U.S. circuit courts of appeal, including their policy agenda, judicial discretion, and variation in policy making among the courts of appeal. In Chapter 3, C. K. Rowland shows the policy-making capabilities of the federal district courts and assesses the policy judgments of the federal trial courts.

Two chapters focus on state courts and their policy making. First, Henry R. Glick (Chapter 4) considers the range of opportunities for policy making by the state courts of last resort. In Chapter 5, Lynn Mather assesses the state trial courts, portraying how the many state trial courts contribute to the making of public policy.

The five chapters in Part I provide an overview of policy making by American courts. Although the chapters discuss a range of issues, analyze and assess the available evidence, and suggest new avenues of research, the chapters emphasize the important role of courts as policy makers in the American political system.

1. THE SUPREME COURT

David Adamany

Every discussion of the Supreme Court refers to the central tension between the Court as a political institution making national policy and the basic principles of representative government. Justice Lewis F. Powell, Jr., stated the problem well: "We should be ever mindful of the contradictions that would arise if a democracy were to permit general oversight of the elected branches of government by a nonrepresentative, and in large measure insulated, judicial branch" (*United States v. Richardson*, 418 U.S. 166, at 188 [1974]). Indeed, this contradiction was planted in the Constitution, which "set up a legislative and an executive branch, each in a large degree representative of the popular will" and "created on the other hand an appointive Court, whose Justices are chosen for life, and thus set up an overriding legal authority completely independent of the popular will" (Jackson 1941, viii). Alexander Bickel (1962, 16-23) has defined this contradiction as the "countermajoritarian difficulty" inherent in judicial review. "When the Supreme Court declares unconstitutional a legislative act or the action of an elected executive, it thwarts the will of representatives of the actual people. . . ; it exercises control, not in behalf of the prevailing majority, but against it" (Bickel 1962, 16-17).

No one ever doubted that the judiciary would interpret the meaning of laws and treaties. And the Judiciary Act of 1789, adopted by the First Congress—in which the framers of the Constitution played a leading role—made clear that the Supreme Court had the power to decide whether state laws or constitutions contradicted the Constitution, laws, and treaties of the United States.

In *Marbury v. Madison* (1 Cranch 137 [1803]), the Supreme Court went a step farther, asserting that its duty was to declare what the law, including the Constitution, means. When there is a conflict between the Constitution and federal laws, as each is defined by the Supreme Court, the justices have a sworn duty to uphold the Constitution by striking down laws approved by Congress and the president. In *Marbury,* Chief Justice Marshall's opinion stated that the judiciary, in declaring the meaning of the Constitution and laws, could order officials of the other branches of government to conform to the

Constitution as interpreted by the justices. Americans are now accustomed to judges invalidating decisions by executive officers and legislative bodies and ordering them to perform duties that conform to the judges' definitions of the Constitution. In 1803, however, this scope of judicial power was shocking; it appeared to breach the separation of powers by subordinating the executive and legislative branches to the judicial branch.

Through American history Congress and the presidency have become more representative. The Senate and members of the Electoral College, once appointed by state legislatures, are now elected by the people. And popular voting in presidential primaries plays a large role in nominating presidential candidates. Moreover, the vote itself has been broadened successively by constitutional amendment and law to include those who own no property and cannot pay poll taxes; women; blacks and members of other racial minorities; and persons eighteen or more years of age. Ironically, even the House of Representatives has become more fully representative, as a result of Supreme Court decisions requiring congressional districts to be of nearly equal population.[1]

On the other hand, there has been no change in the method of selection or the term of service of the Supreme Court to make the justices more responsive either to the people or to their elected representatives. Moreover, the Court is more active now in striking down federal, state, and local laws than it was historically (Caldeira and McCrone 1982, 111-122). In the years since 1933, about one-quarter of the Court's history, the justices have struck down 69 (56 percent) of the 124 federal laws that have been invalidated throughout the nation's history, 603 (57 percent) of the 1,059 state laws, and 65 (56 percent) of the 117 municipal ordinances.[2]

There appears little justification for the Court's heightened activity in striking down laws enacted by elected officials whose accountability to the public has grown through time. As subsequent sections in this chapter will show, the justices have wide discretion in selecting and deciding cases. And in the modern period, these decisions are based principally on the justices' ideological preferences. Traditions of "judicial restraint," if they ever existed, have fallen away; structural checks on the Court by the popular branches, such as constitutional amendments and changes in the Court's authority or membership, have become more and more difficult to use. Moreover, the Court's record in history scarcely justifies judicial review. The Court has only sporadically been the defender of minority rights portrayed by its defenders. Its public visibility and prestige have been vastly overrated by claims that it can confer constitutional blessings on unpopular policies of elected officials. And it has often been a barrier to reform movements at crisis points in American history when voters elect new leaders to alter the nation's course. Consequently, "the basic inconsistency between popular government and judicial supremacy" (Jackson 1941, viii) has persisted throughout history and has grown more difficult to resolve in the modern period than in the past.

Judicial Policy Making and Judicial Discretion

The Supreme Court's role has often been described functionally. The justices interpret federal laws and treaties, both to clarify them and to ensure that they have uniform meaning throughout the nation. The Court also preserves the federal system by settling disputes between the national government and the states about the powers of each. The Court is sometimes said also to maintain the separation of powers by resolving conflicts between the president and Congress. In the modern era, the Court has often been described as the protector of individual rights, striking down both federal and state laws that violate liberties guaranteed by the Constitution.

All of these functions entail policy making by the judiciary. First, the Supreme Court makes policy "not as a matter of choice but of function" (Peltason 1955, 3). If politics is characterized as conflict between various groups, and if lawsuits are seen as ways for these competing interests to pursue their goals, the decisions of judges hand victories to some claimants and defeats to others. It makes no difference how judges interpret the law or whether judges defer to the decisions of elected officials; some interests will be advanced and some set back by court decisions (Peltason 1955, 2-3).

But the Supreme Court makes policy by choice as well as function. In most cases, there is room for judges to exercise discretion in making judgments. Alexander Bickel (1975, 29) has characterized the Constitution as two documents: the "manifest constitution" made up of specific provisions that allow little discretion to judges, and the "open-textured constitution" of broad phrases that can be interpreted in many different ways. Most of the Constitution's provisions establishing the process of government are part of the manifest constitution. The allocation of two senators to each state, the requirement of a two-thirds vote in each house to override a presidential veto or initiate a constitutional amendment, and similar procedural rules leave only slight room for judicial policy making. But there is wide opportunity for judges to interpret the open-textured constitution. The justices may imprint their own meaning on broadly worded safeguards of individual rights, such as the constitutional guarantees of equal protection of the law or due process of law (Fourteenth Amendment). Even in defining the powers of government, the Supreme Court may shape the meaning of the Constitution; the Article I, section 8, powers to "regulate commerce with foreign nations, and among the several states" and to "lay and collect taxes . . . to pay the debts and provide for the common defense and general welfare of the United States" have been subject to extensive and conflicting interpretations by the Court. Most constitutional litigation throughout history has involved the open-textured constitution. And in these cases, not only have the justices made policy by performing the function of judging, they have made discretionary choices to carry out their own preferences.

Like the interpretation of the Constitution, decisions about the meaning of laws are a form of judicial policy making. Although laws are sometimes precisely written, many are worded broadly to allow the executive branch and the courts leeway to interpret and enforce them. Justice Byron White has recently argued that Congress should write laws more clearly to guide judges in interpreting statutes (*Washington Post*, August 6, 1989, A5).

A difference between constitutional decisions and statutory interpretation is that the elected branches can more easily rewrite laws to change unwanted statutory interpretations. One study found that between 1945 and 1957, Congress rewrote the laws to reverse twenty-six Supreme Court decisions on federal taxation and twenty-one decisions on other subjects (*Harvard Law Review* 1958, 1324-1326; Stumpf 1965, 382-383). Another reported eleven instances between 1957 and 1961 when both houses passed legislation to overrule Court decisions in a wide variety of fields (Stumpf 1965, 385-388). A third reported, however, that of 222 Supreme Court interpretations of labor and antitrust laws between 1950 and 1972, only 27 were subject to any congressional action, and only 9 bills overturning the Court's decisions were actually passed (Henschen 1983). The structure and political realities of the lawmaking process make reversal of unwanted Supreme Court interpretations of federal statutes very difficult.

The Justices as Policy Makers

The "countermajoritarian" role of the Supreme Court is especially troubling because most judicial actions in setting the court's agenda and in deciding cases are the result of the justices' individual preferences about policy.

Setting the Policy Agenda

The Supreme Court's policy-making role is sometimes downplayed by observers who argue that the other branches can initiate policy while the justices are limited to deciding cases that others bring to them. Whether this characterization was ever true in American history, it has had little meaning since the Judges Bill of 1925 and has even less meaning today.[3]

Since Congress adopted the Judges Bill of 1925, most cases on the appellate and miscellaneous dockets have been by writ of certiorari—a request for the justices to hear cases that they may, but are not required, to hear. Under Supreme Court Rule 17, which gives broad categories of cases that the Court may hear, at least four justices must agree to hear a case before it is considered by the Court. Some cases on the appellate docket have been "appeals by right," certain cases involving the constitutionality of state or federal laws or state constitutional provisions. By law, the Court was required to hear these cases; but the justices developed broad discretion by rejecting cases that failed to pose a substantial federal question as defined by the justices. In 1988, Congress revised the law virtually to eliminate appeals by right, thus giving the justices almost complete choice about which cases to decide.

With more than 5,000 cases pending annually, the Supreme Court can almost always find a case to raise any policy issue that the justices wish to decide. Chief Justice Earl Warren apparently asked his law clerks to find a case on the Court's docket that would allow the justices to overrule a previous decision holding that there was no right for the poor to have an attorney in every criminal trial. The clerks found such a case, and the Court used it to announce a new constitutional rule guaranteeing the right to counsel (Danelski and Danelski 1989, 508).

The Court has sometimes gone to great lengths to find the issue it wants to decide. In the landmark case of *Mapp v. Ohio* (367 U.S. 617 [1961]), the Court held that illegally seized evidence could not be used in state criminal trials. But the dissenting justices accused the majority of "reaching out" to find that issue in the brief of amicus curiae, because the jurisdictional statements, briefs, and oral arguments of the parties had all been devoted to First Amendment free speech issues.

Where the Court cannot find an issue on its docket, it may order parties to argue an issue that the justices want to consider. Over the strong objection of four justices that the majority was raising "a question not presented" by the parties, five justices ordered the parties in *Patterson v. McLean Credit Union* (485 U.S. 617 [1988]) to reargue the case to determine whether the Court's 1976 interpretation of a federal civil rights statute should be reconsidered and changed.[4] The majority pointed out four previous cases within the past twenty years when the Court had also ordered reargument to determine whether an earlier decision should be reconsidered and changed.

Ordinarily, however, the justices can find cases they want to decide without making special efforts. In those instances, justices' votes on certiorari often reflect their views on how cases should be decided (Ulmer 1972; Ulmer 1983; Ulmer 1984). A study of cases from 1947 to 1956 showed that justices whose final vote in a case was to overrule the lower court also voted to grant certiorari. Justices who voted to affirm the lower court decision had been against certiorari (Ulmer 1972). The Supreme Court has often granted certiorari to "correct" an ideologically unacceptable decision in the lower courts: the liberal justices who dominated the Supreme Court in 1941 and 1961 granted certiorari most often when lower courts produced conservative results, while the conservative justices who were influential on the Court in 1935 and 1972 granted certiorari most often when lower courts handed down liberal decisions (Songer 1979a). Finally, justices who disapprove of lower court decisions will often vote to grant certiorari, even when they are uncertain whether a majority of justices will join them in overruling the lower courts. But justices who favor lower court decisions avoid risking a Supreme Court rejection of those decisions by voting for certiorari only if they are confident they can mobilize a majority in the Supreme Court (Brenner 1979).

Even after the justices have considered cases, major policy issues may still be avoided. The Supreme Court has developed substantive access doctrines that define the conditions that must be present before a decision will be rendered on the issues presented by the parties. One study (Taggart and DeZee 1985, 85) identified nine of these access doctrines addressing such issues as whether there were proper parties to the lawsuit, whether the courts below had jurisdiction, whether the case was moot and its facts fully enough developed to be ripe for decision, and whether the federal courts should abstain from deciding a case out of respect for other branches of the government or for state courts.

During the Burger Court denials of access almost always allowed conservative decisions in the lower courts to stand. Moreover, justices tended to vote for or against access depending on the ideological result: "Denial of access produced conservative effects, which effects correlated extremely highly with the individual justice's ideological preferences" (Rathjen and Spaeth 1983, 84).[5] Justices' attitudes toward access on the Burger Court have also been explained as a combination of administrative factors, such as managing the Court's workload; legal attitudes, such as the proper conditions required to hear cases; and political factors, such as promoting liberal or conservative policies (Rathjen and Spaeth 1979). The number of access decisions and the number of cases in which access was rejected rose very steeply during the Burger Court (Taggart and DeZee 1985, 87-90). Plainly, political access doctrines are often used to achieve policy results.

Policy Decisions on the Merits

The justices generally decide cases in accordance with their own policy views. This is at odds with a vision that the Supreme Court simply interprets the Constitution by following well-developed methods of legal reasoning. Instead, the evidence supports the statement of Charles Evans Hughes, who served as associate justice and later as chief justice: "We are under the Constitution, but the Constitution is what the judges say it is" (1908, 139-140). And most often, what the judges say the Constitution is conforms to their own attitudes about policy.

In the pre-Civil War era, the justices were highly consistent in voting along party and regional lines on cases related to slavery, federal power over interstate commerce, and corporations (Schmidhauser 1961). During the New Deal, and in subsequent Courts, the justices divided into clearly defined groups on economic and social welfare issues (Pritchett 1954, 180-192). In the late Vinson and early Warren Courts, the justices divided consistently along liberal and conservative lines in cases involving economic liberalism, civil liberties, business regulation, and government fiscal claims (Schubert 1962; Schubert 1965, chap. 5; Ulmer 1960a, 647-652; Ulmer 1960b; Ulmer 1961; Spaeth 1963). During the late Warren Court and in the Burger Court, thirteen of the seventeen justices voted consistently as liberals or conservatives in cases involving freedom (civil liberties), equality (political, economic, or racial discrimination), and New Dealism (economic issues, especially government regulation). Two of the remaining four justices were ideologically consistent on some of these issues (Rohde and Spaeth 1976, 137-145). Periodic studies of the Supreme Court in the 1980s continued to show highly consistent ideological voting and clear ideological divisions on freedom, equality, and economic issues (Goldman and Jahnige 1985, 140-146) and on civil liberties (Baum 1989, 140-141).

Groups of justices who share ideological perspectives tend to vote together. Distinct liberal and conservative blocs were identified in the Roosevelt Court (Pritchett 1948). During the Vinson Court, the liberal bloc was larger in the early years and a conservative bloc became more prominent in the later period (Schubert 1959, 91-99; Pritchett 1954, 181-184). The early Warren Court was characterized by stable liberal, moderate, and conservative voting blocs until 1962 (Schubert 1959, 99-129; Ulmer 1965). With the appointments of Justices Marshall, Goldberg, and Fortas, a strong liberal bloc dominated the Supreme Court until the end of the Warren years. President Nixon's appointment of Chief Justice Warren Burger and Justices Harry Blackmun,

Lewis Powell, and William Rehnquist added weight to the conservative bloc, which became the dominant force from 1972 into the early 1980s (Goldman and Jahnige 1985, 137-140). Bloc voting in the Rehnquist Court has not yet been fully analyzed, but a bloc of five conservative justices voted together in seven of the twelve five-to-four decisions in the 1987 term and the same bloc voted together in nineteen of the thirty-two five-to-four decisions in the 1988 term (*Harvard Law Review* 1988, 353; Coyle 1989). This does not imply that partisan or ideological caucuses operated in the Supreme Court or that some system of organized blocs worked to conduct judicial business. Rather, it illustrates that much of the Supreme Court's work is ideological and that justices sharing policy preferences vote together.

Although justices occasionally change their minds during deliberations on cases (Howard 1968), the degree of such fluidity is quite small. During four years of the Vinson Court and two early years of the Warren Court, only 9 percent of justices' votes changed from one side of a case to another between the Court's conferences, at which justices initially discuss and vote on cases, and the Court's final written decisions (Brenner 1980). A similar lack of fluidity was found in the later Warren Court and the early Burger Court, with 87 percent of votes being consistent between conference and final decision (Brenner 1982). Although fluidity sometimes changed the size of the majority, in only 1 percent of cases did it change the result.

Finally, fragmentary evidence shows a strong connection between justices' attitudes before they are appointed to the Supreme Court and their votes on the Court. Speeches made by Pierce Butler and Louis Brandeis in 1915 and 1916 revealed values that were strongly correlated with their votes on the Supreme Court during 1935 and 1936 (Danelski 1966). Editorial descriptions of the ideology (liberal, moderate, conservative) of eighteen Supreme Court justices, ranging from Earl Warren to Anthony Kennedy, during their nomination hearings, correlated very highly with the votes the justices later cast in civil liberties cases (Segal and Cover 1989).

Overall, the evidence is compelling that policy making on the Supreme Court is a reflection of the ideological preferences of the justices, that such attitudes are formed before justices are appointed to the Court, and that justices are highly consistent in casting ideologically oriented votes in most types of cases and from term to term of the Supreme Court. If Supreme Court policy making is largely a reflection of the justices' values, rather than a closely circumscribed rendering of constitutional or statutory language, the inherent contradiction between policy making by nonelected, life-term justices and representative government is heightened.

The Controversy over Judicial Review

History

History provides little guidance in assessing judicial review. Edward S. Corwin, one of this century's leading constitutional scholars, said of judicial review: "The people who say the framers [of the Constitution] intended it are talking nonsense, and the people who say they did not intend it are talking nonsense." [6] The judicial power to strike down acts of the president and Congress is not explicitly stated in the Constitution. Indeed, the Constitutional Convention rejected a proposed Council of Revision, including judges, to reject or revise laws that did not conform to the Constitution. In only a handful of instances before the Constitution was adopted did state courts strike down state laws, and the outrage that followed some of those decisions showed that judicial review was not widely accepted.

On the other hand, the *Federalist Papers*, the most important document explaining and justifying the proposed Constitution, clearly stated that judges would strike down unconstitutional laws. And there was some prior history of the British Privy Council and similar bodies striking down laws in the colonies that contradicted colonial charters or English law. Quite a number of the framers were quoted at one time or another as favoring judicial review, but few did so in the Constitutional Convention, leaving the intent of the document itself uncertain.

Judicial Restraint

Similarly, the idea of judicial self-restraint does not support judicial review. Justices have talked throughout history about their obligation to avoid conflicts with Congress and the president by exercising the power of judicial review rarely and only in the clearest cases of conflict between laws and the Constitution. Some justices do seem consistently to take a narrow view in the small number of cases that involve only the scope of judicial power (Spaeth 1962). On the other hand, justices vote their attitudes rather than exercising self-restraint when reviewing state and federal laws on civil liberties and the regulation of labor and business by state and federal agencies. There is little sign of greater deference to the nationally elected president and Congress than to state governments (Spaeth and Teger 1982; Spaeth 1964).

Democratic Checks on the Court

The Supreme Court is sometimes defended not because it is directly accountable to the voters but because it is subject to potential checks by the elected branches. The best known check on the Supreme

Court is the amendment power. The Constitution has been amended at least three times explicitly to overrule Supreme Court decisions: the Eleventh Amendment in 1793 reversed the Court's decision that individuals could bring lawsuits against the states in federal courts; the Sixteenth Amendment in 1913 reversed the Court's ruling that a federal income tax was unconstitutional; and the Twenty-sixth Amendment in 1970 reversed the Court's rejection of a federal law extending the vote to eighteen-year-olds in state as well as federal elections. The Civil War Amendments (the Thirteenth, Fourteenth, and Fifteenth)—or at least the first clause of the Thirteenth Amendment abolishing slavery—are sometimes counted as overruling the Supreme Court's decisions holding that slaves were not persons within the protection of the Constitution. The amendment power has been used only rarely, as was intended. It falls far short of being a majoritarian check on the Supreme Court because of the required two-thirds vote in each house and ratification in three-quarters of the states.

The elected branches can also change the size of the Court to add justices with different views, as they have three times in American history—during the Jackson, Lincoln, and Grant administrations. Since 1870, however, the Court has remained at nine, despite Franklin D. Roosevelt's massive effort, at the height of his political power in 1937, to bring the Court into line with the New Deal by increasing its size.

The elected branches once, in 1802, delayed the opening of the Court's term to block temporarily judicial review of federal laws; and once, in 1869, they removed the Court's appellate jurisdiction in specific circumstances to prevent Supreme Court consideration of a federal law.[7] Some contemporary legal scholars and judges have challenged the constitutionality of these actions. More persuasive is the failure of Congress to use either of these devices for more than a century. Sometimes discussed, but never adopted, has been legislation to require the vote of an extraordinary majority of justices to strike down laws.

The failure of the elected branches regularly to use these devices to check the Court is not a failure of will only. A distinction must be made between decision-curbing and Court-curbing measures. The former overrule only a particular decision of the Supreme Court, while the latter affect the authority of the Court itself. Altering the Court's calendar, internal voting rules, appellate jurisdiction, and number of justices curbs the Court, and these actions may well stir opposition in Congress and the country from those who disagree with the Court's specific rulings but are reluctant to alter it as an institution. Moreover, on major national policy, where a legislative consensus is unlikely, politically active minorities that favor the Court's policies can usually block either decision-curbing or Court-curbing legislation at one or more strategic spots in the lawmaking process.[8]

The power to make judicial appointments is an important check on the Supreme Court, but only in the long term. On average, a Supreme Court seat becomes available every two years; hence, it would ordinarily take a decade to replace a majority of the justices. Change on the Court can often be achieved more rapidly, however, because some sitting justices usually share the views of new appointees. Presidents nominate justices who share their views. A study (Hulbary and Walker 1980, 190) of eighty-four nominations concluded that in seventy-six instances the president intentionally nominated someone whose political philosophy was similar to his own. Another study (Tate 1981) showed that the appointing president and a justice's ideology were powerful predictors of how justices vote on civil liberties. A third (Rohde and Spaeth 1976, 107-108) reported that justices appointed by Democratic presidents generally compiled liberal voting records, while Republican appointees were by and large conservatives.

There is strong historical evidence that the Senate was expected to consider the policy views of Supreme Court nominees, thus allowing the senators to shape judicial policy (Gauch 1989). Until 1894, the Senate rejected twenty of eighty-one nominations to the Supreme Court, many for partisan reasons. From 1894 to 1968, the Senate assumed a more limited role, rejecting only four of fifty-four. Since 1968, the Senate has again taken a more aggressive part in selection: of fourteen nominations, including those of Abe Fortas and William Rehnquist as chief justice, four have been rejected. Voting on controversial nominations has been along ideological and party lines (Sulfridge 1980; Songer 1979b), but rejection of nominees has most often occurred when concerns about a nominee's qualifications were also raised (Sulfridge 1980, 563-564). The 1987 rejection of Robert Bork, almost solely for ideological reasons, may signal a renewal of more searching Senate review of nominations on the basis of policy.

Protection of Minority Rights

The most widely expressed modern justification for judicial review is that the Supreme Court protects minority rights. It is difficult to specify just what minorities the Court should protect. And there has arisen a conflict in the affirmative action cases between assisting minority groups who have suffered long discrimination and protecting individual members of racial majorities who may be disadvantaged by the remedies to eliminate past discrimination against the minorities.

In general, it has been easiest to justify judicial protection of those rights that allow individuals to pursue their goals through the political process, such as the freedoms of speech, assembly, association, and petition and the rights to vote and to candidacy. There are also strong justifications for judicial protection of groups subject to historical prejudice, such as disfavored religious, nationality, and racial groups; women; and aliens. Judicial protection of the procedural rights of criminal defendants has been justified both because the loss of liberty is such a grave deprivation in a free society and because the resources of the government and the accused in criminal cases are so unequal. The most controversial judicial policies are those protecting rights not mentioned in the Constitution, such as the rights to contract, economic liberty, and privacy, including abortion and contraception.

Although the modern Supreme Court is viewed as a defender of minority rights, the Court's record in history is much less clear.[9] In 1943, Henry Steele Commager said the Supreme Court's record of striking down congressional acts

> discloses not a single case, in a century and a half, where the Supreme Court has protected freedom of speech, press, assembly, or petition against congressional attack. It reveals no instance (with [one] possible exception . . .) where the court has intervened on behalf of the underprivileged—the Negro, the alien, women, children, workers, tenant-farmers. It reveals, on the contrary, that the court has effectively intervened again and again to defeat congressional efforts to free slaves, guarantee civil rights to Negroes, to protect workingmen, outlaw child labor, assist hard-pressed farmers, and to democratize the tax system. (Commager 1958, 55)

Robert Dahl (1958) reached similar conclusions in the mid-1950s. Of twenty-three major congressional policies overruled by the Supreme Court within four years of enactment, Dahl discovered only two cases—both involving the rights of former Confederates—that could be described even by the most generous measure as protecting individual rights. Turning to forty other cases in which the judicial veto was applied more than four years after congressional action, Dahl found fewer than ten instances in which the justices acted to protect minorities under the Bill of Rights. On the other hand, in a large number of cases, the Court struck down federal laws "to preserve the rights and liberties of a relatively privileged group at the expense of the rights and liberties of a submerged group" (292).

In the modern period, civil liberties issues have constituted half or more of the Supreme Court's agenda, compared with a quarter or less in the 1930s and 1940s (Baum 1989, 172). More important, the direction of the Warren Court on civil liberties was fundamentally different. Jonathan Casper reported that of twenty-eight provisions of federal law struck down between 1958 and 1974, Congress either changed the law to conform to the Court's decisions or simply acquiesced in them. With only one exception, the Court's decisions

> were based upon provisions of the Bill of Rights (primarily the First and Fifth Amendments) and the Fourteenth Amendment. In addition to furthering the interests of all society in greater freedom of expression, equal application of the laws, and procedural fairness, the decisions had special impact upon such groups as aliens, communists and other alleged subversives, criminal defendants, war protesters, and poor people. The Court attempted to extend to these groups rights and privileges that the law-making majorities had not chosen to extend. (Casper 1976, 53-54)

The Burger Court began the erosion of criminal defendants' rights by creating substantial exceptions to the warrant requirement for searches and seizures, by permitting illegally obtained evidence to be admitted into court if police officers believed in good faith that they had a valid warrant, and by allowing the use in court of a defendant's statements made when warnings about the rights to remain silent and to have counsel were incomplete. The Burger Court also restored the death penalty.

The Rehnquist Court, especially since the addition of Justice Anthony Kennedy, is further restricting liberties established during the Warren Court. In the 1988 term, the states were allowed to apply the death penalty to sixteen- and seventeen-year-old murderers and to the mentally retarded.[10] The Court found no illegal search or seizure in mandatory drug testing of certain government employees, even in the absence of probable cause that individuals were using drugs.[11] The rights to remain silent and to have counsel were weakened when the justices allowed use of a defendant's statement obtained when a suitable warning was followed by comments suggesting that no lawyer was available and that one could be made available only at trial.[12] Earlier, the Court had limited the right of privacy by holding that it did not extend to homosexual acts between consenting adults in private.[13] In 1989 the justices weakened existing privacy rights by approving extensive new state regulations of a woman's choice to have an abortion.[14]

The new conservative majority also limited rights for minority persons. State and local government contract set-asides for minority vendors were limited to situations where there was past documented discrimination, and these programs were subject to a "strict scrutiny" test to determine if they met equal protection standards.[15] Moreover,

white workers who believed themselves hurt by court-approved affirmative action plans were permitted to bring lawsuits alleging racial
discrimination.[16] The burden of proof was shifted to employees to show
that there was no valid business reason for employers' policies that had
an unequal impact on some racial groups.[17] Finally, the Court held
that a Reconstruction era civil rights law protecting the right to engage
in contracts did not apply to workplace conditions, such as sexual
harassment, after an employment contract was signed.[18]

In the early Warren Court, civil liberties claimants won 58
percent of their cases in the Supreme Court; this rose to 74 percent
when the Warren Court's liberal majority became firmly established
from 1962 to 1968. In the Burger and Rehnquist Courts, between 37
and 49 percent of civil liberties claims were successful (Baum 1989,
146). The early decisions of a newly dominant conservative majority on
the Rehnquist Court suggest the substantial curtailment rather than the
expansion of rights. First Amendment freedoms may be an exception;
in the 1988 term the Court extended the free speech doctrine to
encompass burning the American flag when done for symbolic or
expressive purposes.[19] A continuing retreat on individual rights by the
Rehnquist Court would affirm that the Warren Court was an anomaly
in a long history of judicial indifference or hostility to disadvantaged
minorities. The minority rights justification for judicial review is
supported only by ambiguous evidence, at best.

Public Opinion and the Court

Two broad propositions about public opinion are advanced by
proponents of judicial review. First, the Court's decisions are usually in
line with public opinion. The justices, it appears, follow the election
returns. Second, the Court is said to represent the Constitution and
share the enormous prestige of that American symbol. Consequently,
when the Court declares challenged laws constitutional, as it usually
does, the prestige of the Constitution and the Court wins widespread
acceptance for policies of the elected branches among those who had
opposed those policies. This is the so-called legitimacy-conferring
function.

There is growing evidence that many Supreme Court decisions are
in harmony with public opinion. Moreover, the justices tend over time
to harmonize judicial doctrine with public opinion when the two clash.
Either at the time of the Supreme Court's decisions or soon afterward,
public sentiment favored policies embodied in the Court's controversial
rulings favoring access to birth control information, eliminating school
segregation, supporting an equal role for women in society, and
protecting interracial marriages (Barnum 1985). The Burger Court

either overruled or retreated from Warren Court positions rejecting the death penalty and favoring defendant's rights, affirmative action, and school busing—all of which had been strongly disapproved in public opinion polls.

A comprehensive study identified 146 issues between 1935 and 1986 that were the subject of a Supreme Court decision and which, within five years of Supreme Court action, were also the subject of a public opinion poll (Marshall 1989, esp. chap. 4). On 56 percent of these issues the Supreme Court's decision was consistent with public opinion; on 33 percent the decision was inconsistent; and on 11 percent public opinion was "unclear" because polls were very closely divided or several polls reached different conclusions. The Court's record of *approving* federal laws was especially strong: it upheld 56 (76 percent) of 74 federal laws among the 146 issues studied. And it upheld 81 percent of federal laws that were consistent with public opinion. The Court was much more aggressive in reviewing state laws: it upheld only 47 percent of those challenged and only 56 percent of state laws that were consistent with public opinion.

Although the Supreme Court's decisions are usually consistent with public attitudes, there are a substantial number of issues on which the Court is countermajoritarian. Does a 56 percent record of success in representing public opinion (or 69 percent if the unclear cases are omitted) meet a standard of representative government? In addition, not all issues are of equal importance to the public. National and regional surveys from the mid-1960s to the mid-1970s specifically asking people what they liked and disliked about the Supreme Court showed that two-thirds or more of all responses were negative reactions to specific Court decisions.[20] The Court's decisions favoring defendant's rights, barring the death penalty, prohibiting school prayers, and initiating school busing were very strongly opposed. Its abortion rulings were opposed to varying degrees, and its civil rights decisions were approved in the 1960s but then strongly disapproved in the 1970s as affirmative action and school busing became prominent. Even the studies showing most Supreme Court decisions to be in harmony with public opinion recognize public opposition or very closely divided sentiment on such highly visible issues as school prayers, privacy (for example, morality and abortion), school busing, and criminal justice (Marshall 1989, 89; Barnum 1985, 656-660). Overall, Supreme Court decisions appear to be consistent with public opinion. But in a substantial minority of cases, including many controversial issues about which the public has strong sentiments, the Court is countermajoritarian.

The evidence is much stronger that the Supreme Court does not have a legitimacy-conferring function that would justify judicial review.

If the Supreme Court were to confer legitimacy when it approved policies of the elected branches, the public would need to be knowledgeable about the Court's decisions, to be aware of the Court's constitutional role, and to be so highly respectful toward the Court as an institution that they would accept the propriety of Court decisions that were contrary to their own views (Murphy and Tanenhaus 1968, 359).

Three separate studies (Murphy and Tanenhaus 1968; Adamany 1973; Marshall 1989) conclude that the conditions are not present for the Supreme Court to confer legitimacy on the policies of the elected branches.[21] Fewer than half of Americans polled knew about the Supreme Court's decisions, and a majority of those knew of only a single case (Murphy and Tanenhaus 1968, 363; Dolbeare 1967, 194-212; Casey 1976, 14; Adamany and Grossman 1983, 411). The Court's role as a constitutional decision maker was known to just under 40 percent of survey respondents, even if all answers touching on the Court's work as a constitutional body, interpreter of law, protector of minority rights, and reviewer of executive and legislative power were taken into account (Murphy and Tanenhaus 1968, 365; Casey 1974, 392-394).[22] Finally, only 37 percent of respondents in one survey favorably evaluated the Supreme Court for being nonpolitical and doing its job well (Murphy and Tanenhaus 1968, 373-374). Respondents in a 1976 survey indicated greater confidence in the presidency than in the Supreme Court and believed that national policy disputes would be settled better by Congress than by the Court (Adamany and Grossman 1983, 411). Other survey questions have shown that the Supreme Court commands somewhat greater confidence than the presidency or Congress, but confidence in the Court was expressed by fewer than 50 percent of respondents (Marshall 1989, 138-141).

Supreme Court endorsement of policies does not appear to broaden their acceptance. An experimental study (Baas and Thomas 1984) involving students showed no greater support for specific policies that were described as rulings of the Supreme Court or as Supreme Court interpretations of the Constitution than for those same policies when they were not identified with an institutional source. Polls taken before and after Supreme Court decisions did not show substantial shifts of public opinion toward the Court's positions in either the short or the long term (Marshall 1989, 145-156).

Judicial review cannot be justified as conferring legitimacy on policies of the elected branches. The Court's decisions and its constitutional role are not widely enough known and confidence in the Court is not high enough to legitimate policies. Its endorsement does not seem to change opinion, either in experimental situations or in public opinion polls.

The Supreme Court in History

If most justifications fall short of reconciling the power of judicial review with representative government, some explanations of the Supreme Court's role in history may do so. Dahl (1958, 293-294) has suggested that the Court should be understood in the context of American election cycles. National politics consists of long-term political alliances—the Jeffersonian party system, the Jacksonian party system, the Republican coalition from the Civil War to Franklin D. Roosevelt, and the New Deal coalition. Presidential appointments within each historical period assure that the Court is mainly composed of members of the dominant political alliance, and the justices will therefore support the policies of the national government. Because of the Court's unique prestige, its approval of national policies adds legitimacy to them and to the dominant political coalition. The Court's legitimacy-conferring function now seems dubious. But Dahl's suggestion that the Court is part of the majority coalition, as a result of the appointment process, seems plausible enough.

The reverse side of this argument, however, is that the Court will be out of step with the nation's lawmaking majority when voters, in what are generally referred to as critical elections, replace one long-term political coalition with another.[23] Eventually, of course, the president will replace the justices appointed under the old regime with justices who are part of the new national political coalition. But during the lag time between the election of new political leadership and its appointment of a majority to the Supreme Court, the Court may well stand against the policies of the new lawmaking majority.

Two kinds of critical elections are generally identified: realigning elections, in which the national voting majority changes and a new party takes control of government; and converting elections, in which the same party remains dominant in government but there is a fundamental change in the voting groups that support it and thus a change in the coalition's policies. Although scholars evaluate election cycles differently, the election of Thomas Jefferson in 1800, Andrew Jackson in 1928, Abraham Lincoln in 1860, and Franklin D. Roosevelt in 1932 clearly installed new party majorities in power, following several elections in which the older political coalition foundered over emerging issues that it failed to address successfully. Converting elections occurred in 1836, when Jacksonian democracy shifted from a southern to a northern coalition; 1876, when the Republican party abandoned its base in the South and became almost exclusively a northern party; 1896, when the pro-business wing of the Republican party finally won its twenty-year struggle against the western, populist elements for control within the GOP coalition; and 1964, when southern whites began their transition to the Republican party, leaving the Democratic party more northern and liberal.

There is very little numerical evidence that the Supreme Court was more active in striking down federal laws during the lag periods following realigning elections than at other times.[24] Historical narrative shows, however, that conflict between the elected branches and the Court occurred during these periods (Adamany 1973, 825-843). Moreover, hostility toward the Court, as evidenced by sharp increases in the number of court-curbing bills introduced, was apparent following the realignments of 1800, 1828, 1860, and 1932.[25] Finally, in three historical periods, but not two others, the Supreme Court disproportionately invalidated state policies involving critical election issues from states dominated by the opposition party or associated with the minority wing of the dominant party (Gates 1987; 1989).

The Supreme Court may also shape national policies by supporting the policies of one wing of the majority party on sharply divisive issues that ultimately lead to critical elections. The Court played virtually no role in shaping issues that led to the realigning election of 1800 or the converting elections of 1836 and 1876. But it adopted policies that supported one wing within the majority party, usually the presidential wing, as that party faced the realigning elections of 1828, 1860, and 1932 and the converting elections of 1896 and 1964 (Adamany 1980, 249-257).

The Supreme Court's role in election cycles is largely countermajoritarian. In the lag periods following the realigning elections of 1800, 1828, 1860, and 1932, the justices of the old regime were in conflict with the president and Congress of the new dominant political coalition. Sometimes the Court invalidated laws or policies of the new lawmaking majority; on the whole, these invalidations were soon overruled when the lawmaking majority appointed new justices. But the conflict itself, whether or not it involved invalidations of policy, tended to blunt and weaken the new majority coalition. As conflict unfolded, the most reform-minded wing of the new majority party coalition, usually headed by the president, set about to curb the Supreme Court.

> Elements of the [new lawmaking] coalition's elected elite and of its electoral base now hold back in reverence to a constitutional institution, whose actions and function they may or may not fully understand or approve. The coalition is thus divided over an issue of constitutional structure; the energies, resources, and zeal of the reformist wing of the coalition are diverted to that struggle; the leadership's hold over the loosely joined alliance is weakened; and

the momentum for substantive policy change is slowed or stopped. (Adamany 1973, 845)

In the brief time between a realigning election and the new lawmaking majority's appointment of likeminded justices, the Supreme Court plays a powerful countermajoritarian role in American politics. It may block policy temporarily. More important, it diverts and dissipates reform energies in a struggle over the relationship between the elected branches and the judiciary. In history, therefore, "The judiciary is . . . the check of a preceding generation on the present one; a check of conservative legal philosophy upon a dynamic people, and nearly always the check of a rejected regime on the one in being" (Jackson 1941, 315).

The Modern Supreme Court: The Third Lawmaking Branch

The modern Supreme Court has emerged as a powerful lawmaking department, behaving much like a legislative body, and without substantial intellectual justifications for its sweeping exercise of the power of judicial review. Established checks on the Court have fallen into disuse, and the erosion of majority party coalitions has opened a wide field for judicial policy making. Since 1960, the Supreme Court has been striking down laws passed by Congress and the president at an average of two each year, more than double the rate of the earlier part of this century and four times the rate since 1790.[26] The work of state and local lawmakers has fallen at a much faster rate: the Court has invalidated an average of seventeen state and local laws each year since 1960, more than four times the rate during all of the Court's previous history.

The modern Supreme Court in many ways bears a closer resemblance to a legislative body than to the Supreme Court of the nation's first century and a half. During the chief justiceship of Harlan F. Stone (1941-1946), and perhaps because of Stone's leadership style (Walker, Epstein, and Dixon 1988), the number of cases in which dissents were filed rose dramatically. The dissent rate from the Court's founding to Stone's chief justiceship was 13.3 percent.[27] Even in the tumultuous era of the "Old Court" that blocked the New Deal, the dissent rate was 17 percent. The dissent rate rose to 49 percent in the Stone Court, then to 75 percent in the Vinson Court (1946-1953) and 69 percent during Earl Warren's chief justiceship (1953-1969). The average dissent rate for the 1976 to the 1988 terms was 66.5 percent (Coyle 1989).

In filing frequent dissents, the justices have emulated legislative behavior, casting votes on each issue and entering statements into the record to explain their policy commitments. This reflects a disintegration of the Court's historical role as a collegial body in which justices discussed cases to arrive at decisions justified by common understandings about the development of the law and the methods of legal reasoning. A recent Supreme Court law clerk has said, "It's really nine separate courts. The Justices lead separate, even isolated lives. They deal with each other only in quite formalized settings. They vote the way they want to and then retreat to their own chambers" (Greenhouse 1989a, A6). In this setting, policy disputes among justices become highly personalized, as they sometimes do among legislators. One commentator (Greenhouse 1989a) described the 1988 term as "the nastiest in years." A leading newspaper (*New York Times,* July 9, 1989, E26) introduced an editorial on the justices' behavior with the headline "Supremely Surly." Some justices make public statements critical of the Court's doctrines.[28] And the formerly recognized responsibility of the chief justice to mobilize a unanimous Court to give force to constitutional doctrine appears to have disappeared entirely.[29]

Since the early 1960s, the Supreme Court has also operated in a political setting that gives wide policy-making latitude to the justices. Observing that the Court is normally part of the national lawmaking coalition, Dahl (1958, 294) also points out that the Court may step in to establish policy when a lawmaking majority is unstable or in conflict with respect to key policies. For more than a quarter century, the United States has, according to some commentators, been undergoing a process of electoral "dealignment." The division of voters between the two major parties has become closer, and there has been a substantial increase in the number of independent voters. The Republicans have captured the presidency in five of the seven elections in the past twenty-five years, but the Democrats have controlled the Senate for all but six years and the House of Representatives without interruption. No dominant majority party coalition has emerged.

With the lawmaking branches divided by partisanship and policy, there has been unusual latitude for the Supreme Court to establish policy. The absence of firm majority party control of government has allowed supporters of the Court and its policies to find key points in the legislative process to block both Court-curbing and decision-curbing proposals. Finally, even if strong majorities could be galvanized in the lawmaking process, they would find it difficult to reverse unwanted judicial policies because many of the historical checks on the Court— such as control of jurisdiction and court packing—have fallen into disuse and disrepute.

With the justices' shift away from protection of minority rights during the Burger and Rehnquist Courts, the modern policy activism of the Supreme Court cannot be defended as a protection of rights that are essential for the operation of democratic government. On the other hand, the Court has played a revitalized role in controversies over the separation of powers. The justices have protected the president's appointment power against congressional intrusion (in *Buckley v. Valeo,* 424 U.S. 1 [1976]), and they have rejected the delegation of executive authority to a federal official subject to congressional dismissal (*Bowsher v. Synar,* 478 U.S. 714 [1986]). In a dramatic decision affecting provisions of more than 200 federal laws (*Immigration and Naturalization Service v. Chadha,* 462 U.S. 919 [1983]), the Court struck down the so-called legislative veto which had allowed Congress to reject regulations issued by executive agencies. This greatly strengthened the power of the executive to issue legally binding regulations without congressional approval. The justices also inferred very broad foreign affairs authority for the president, without direct congressional authorization, to settle the Iran hostage crisis by suspending lawsuits in American courts and limiting the financial claims of American citizens (*Dames and Moore v. Regan,* 453 U.S. 654 [1981]).

The president did not fare as well in conflicts with the judiciary itself, however. The justices rejected President Nixon's claim of executive privilege in the Watergate case, *United States v. Nixon* (418 U.S. 683 [1974]). And they sustained the authority of a panel of judges, upon recommendation of the attorney general, to appoint independent counsel to investigate and prosecute officials of the executive branch. In *Morrison v. Olson* (108 S.Ct. 2597 [1988]), they rejected the claim that both the appointive authority and law enforcement authority were executive rather than judicial functions.

Even the important role of the Supreme Court in the separation of powers is policy making with a special tilt. In cases of conflict between the legislative and executive branches, the Court has generally supported the executive. Robert Scigliano (1971, 197-201) has pointed out that the executive and judicial branches "have had a special relationship to each other that neither has had with Congress," and this has inclined judicial policy making to favor executive power.

In the modern period, then, the Supreme Court has expanded its role as a national policy maker. The justices have been more aggressive in invalidating federal, state, and local laws. The Court's decision-making process has begun to resemble a legislative body—with less collegial deliberation, highly consistent ideological voting in setting agendas and deciding cases, and much greater levels of dissent both on and off the Court. At the same time, the lawmaking branches have less ability to reject judicial policies. Traditional checking devices are no longer credible. The complexity of the legislative process allows minority blocs to protect Supreme Court decisions from reversal. And dealignment in American electoral politics has left no strong and cohesive lawmaking majority to set limits on judicial policy making.

Following Franklin Roosevelt's unsuccessful proposal in 1937 to pack the Court with ideologically acceptable justices, Attorney General Robert H. Jackson, later associate justice of the Supreme Court, observed that struggles between elected officials and the Court throughout history had "produced no permanent reconciliation between the principles of representative government and the opposing principle of judicial authority" (1941, vi). That conflict, heightened by the modern Supreme Court's vigorous policy making, remains unreconciled to this day.

Into the Future

The tension between judicial review and representative government will continue to be the central focus of research about the Supreme Court. First, prescriptive specifications remain incomplete of those conditions necessary for the Supreme Court's policy making to be consonant with representative government. Second, new or revised prescriptive specifications require further empirical studies to determine the extent to which the Supreme Court's policy making conforms to these requirements for representative government. Third, established lines of inquiry showing the political nature of judicial policy making should be extended, using both historical and contemporary data. Historical studies can provide insight into whether the Court ever functioned—and thus could again perform—less politically than it does today. Studies employing additional data from the contemporary period and new data resulting from the Court's future work may enlighten public officials and the attentive public about the political character of modern judicial review. So informed, they may be less hesitant to engage in decision-curbing behavior, even when reluctant to undertake court curbing.

Judicial power is most difficult to justify when representative government is conceptualized entirely in terms of public accountability, in which officials' actions are expected to conform to public opinion of the moment. Thomas Marshall (1989, 79-80) has found that the justices' decisions mirror public opinion, as reflected in polls, about as often as do the decisions of state and federal elected officials. This casts the Supreme Court in a more "democratic" light than is suggested by its lack of electoral accountability. Hence, this finding should rigorously be retested. And it should be reevaluated in light of formulations of representative government that reject the significance of short-term congruence between public opinion and official action.

The effectiveness of longer term popular checks on the Supreme Court also requires continuing investigation. Roger Handberg and

Harold Hill, Jr. (1980) found that the federal government was more successful as a litigant before and after periods of high congressional court-curbing activity than during such periods. And Gregory Caldeira (1987, 1149-1150) has shown that public opinion turned strongly against FDR's court-packing plan only after Justice Roberts shifted his vote to favor New Deal measures, thus heading off court-curbing legislation by reversing the Court's policies. If these studies reflect only increases in court-curbing activity provoked by judicial opposition to regime policies during the lag periods following critical elections, they add little to already understood restraints on judicial power.

On the other hand, if it were found that the Court generally responds to high levels of legislative threat, even when unfulfilled, this would suggest a greater degree of elected branch influence over judicial policy than is acknowledged by most modern scholarship. Case studies, such as Walter Murphy's (1962) analysis of congressional and Court conflict in the 1950s over national security issues, could provide insight into judicial response to congressional threats. Since party and ideology are significant factors in congressional voting on court-curbing measures (Schmidhauser and Berg 1972, chap. 7), the Court may most readily reshape judicial policies when its decisions are attacked by elected officials who are part of the same national political coalition as a majority of the justices.

The claim that judicial power lies in democratic functions performed by the Supreme Court is more easily tested. The Court's protection of minority rights through statutory as well as constitutional interpretation, as suggested by Casper (1976, 56-57), calls for systematic investigation. Recently, for instance, the justices have interpreted campaign finance statutes and labor laws to conform to constitutional free speech principles.[30] The frequent amendment or repeal by Congress of its statutes to recognize judicially crafted minority rights decisions (Casper 1976, 53) would suggest the endorsement of judicial protection of minority rights by lawmaking majorities. An examination of such interactions between the Court and Congress would shed light on both the Court's protection of minority rights and the checking function of the elected departments.

Similarly, with respect to the legitimacy-conferring function, the evidence is strongly against judicial power. But there is not yet a comprehensive study, using experimental techniques, to test the impact of the Court's imprimatur on public opinion toward specific policies.

Finally, although the evidence is strong that justices cast consistently ideological votes, no major empirical study tests justices' claims that their decisions are guided by plain constitutional or statutory language, the framers' intent, historical evidence, or precedent. Content analysis and factor analysis could show the consistency with which a justice relies on these decision-making criteria.

Since the beginning of the Republic, judicial policy making has been heatedly criticized and defended. New or reshaped justifications for judicial power have been advanced in every political era. Continued testing of these propositions sheds light on the central question of whether the Supreme Court's exercise of judicial review can be squared with a system of representative government.

Notes

1. *Wesberry v. Sanders*, 376 U.S. 1 (1964). Subsequent cases have insisted on a high degree of mathematical equality in the population of congressional districts. See, for instance, *Kirkpatrick v. Preisler*, 394 U.S. 526 (1969); *White v. Weiser*, 412 U.S. 783 (1973); *Wells v. Rockefeller*, 394 U.S. 542 (1969); and *Karcher v. Daggett*, 462 U.S. 725 (1983).
2. These numbers are complete through 1988 and are reported in Library of Congress (1987, 1883-2133; 1988, 187-206).
3. For illustrative statistics, see *Harvard Law Review* (1988, 354).
4. Ultimately the Court severely limited the reach of the civil rights statute but did not overrule its own earlier decision, in *Patterson v. McLean Credit Union*, 109 S.Ct. 2363 (1989).
5. For further analysis of these access and ideological voting patterns, see Spaeth and Teger (1982, 294-296).
6. U.S. Congress, Senate, Committee on the Judiciary, *Hearings on S. 1392*, 75th Cong., 1st Sess., 1937, 176. The confusing historical arguments are thoroughly summarized in Levy (1967, 1-12).
7. *Ex parte McCardle*, 74. U.S. 506 (1869).
8. The interplay between liberal political activists and liberals in Congress to protect Court rulings is discussed in Adamany and Grossman (1983, 426-431). See also Henschen (1983, 453-454).
9. I have presented this argument in detail previously (Adamany 1977, 284-285).
10. *Stanford v. Kentucky; Wilkins v. Missouri*, 109 S.Ct. 2969 (1989); *Penry v. Lynaugh*, 109 S.Ct. 2934 (1989).
11. *Skinner v. Railway Labor Executive Association*, 109 S.Ct. 1402 (1989); *National Treasury Employees Union v. Von Raab*, 109 S.Ct. 1384 (1989).
12. *Duckworth v. Eagan*, 109 S.Ct. 2875 (1989).
13. *Bowers v. Hardwick*, 478 U.S. 186 (1986).
14. *Webster v. Reproductive Health Services*, 109 S.Ct. 3040 (1989).
15. *City of Richmond v. Croson*, 109 S.Ct. 706 (1989).
16. *Martin v. Wilks*, 109 S.Ct. 2180 (1989).
17. *Wards Cove Packing Co. v. Atonio*, 109 S.Ct. 2115 (1989).
18. *Patterson v. McLean Credit Union*, 109 S.Ct. 2363 (1989).

19. *Texas v. Johnson*, 109 S.Ct. 2533 (1989).
20. These surveys are gathered and summarized in Adamany and Grossman (1983, 421-422).
21. Marshall (1989, 136-147) has also exhaustively cited the other literature that inferentially bears on this issue.
22. For a retabulation of Casey's data confirming this point, see Adamany (1980, 231).
23. For my previous formulation of the Supreme Court's role in critical election periods, see Adamany (1973, 820-843; 1980).
24. For a mathematical analysis suggesting a correlation between judicial invalidation of federal laws and realigning periods, see Funston (1975). But Funston's selection of "lag periods" for analysis and his mathematical calculations have been sharply and persuasively criticized in Beck (1976) and Canon and Ulmer (1976).
25. The data have been persuasively arrayed in Gates (1984, 283). The data on court-curbing bills were developed by Nagel (1969, 261-263).
26. Calculations of Supreme Court invalidations of federal, state, and local laws are based on data reported in Baum (1989, 177-180).
27. Data on dissent rates through the Warren Court are derived from Ulmer (1986, 53).
28. See, for example, Greenhouse (1989b, A6).
29. A notable exception was Earl Warren's patient building of unanimous support for the elimination of school segregation in *Brown v. Board of Education*, 347 U.S. 483 (1954). See Ulmer (1971).
30. With respect to the Court's interpretation of campaign finance legislation, see *Buckley v. Valeo*, 424 U.S. 1 (1976). The Court's interpretation of labor laws is illustrated in *Abood v. Detroit Board of Education*, 431 U.S. 209 (1977); *Chicago Teachers Union v. Hudson*, 475 U.S. 292 (1986); *Communications Workers of America v. Beck*, 198 S.Ct. 2641 (1988).

References

Adamany, David. 1973. Legitimacy, realigning elections, and the Supreme Court. *Wisconsin Law Review*, 790-846.

———. 1977. Book review, *The morality of consent. Wisconsin Law Review*, 271-292.

———. 1980. The Supreme Court's role in critical elections. In *Realignment in American politics,* ed. Bruce Campbell and Richard Trilling. Austin: University of Texas Press.

Adamany, David, and Joel Grossman. 1983. Support for the Supreme Court as a national policy maker. *Law and Policy Quarterly* 5:405-437.

Baas, Larry, and Dan Thomas. 1984. The Supreme Court and policy legitimation. *American Politics Quarterly* 12:355-360.

Barnum, David. 1985. The Supreme Court and public opinion: Judicial decision making in the post-New Deal period. *Journal of Politics* 47:651-666.

Baum, Lawrence. 1989. *The Supreme Court.* 3d ed., rev. Washington, D.C.: CQ Press.

Beck, Paul Allen. 1976. Critical elections and the Supreme Court: Putting the cart after the horse. *American Political Science Review* 70:930-932.

Bickel, Alexander. 1962. *The least dangerous branch.* Indianapolis: Bobbs-Merrill.

_____. 1975. *The morality of consent.* New Haven: Yale University Press.

Brenner, Saul. 1979. The new certiorari game. *Journal of Politics* 41:649-655.

_____. 1980. Fluidity on the United States Supreme Court: A reexamination. *American Journal of Political Science* 24:526-535.

_____. 1982. Fluidity on the Supreme Court: 1956-1976. *American Journal of Political Science* 26:388-390.

Caldeira, Gregory. 1987. Public opinion and the U.S. Supreme Court: FDR's court-packing plan. *American Political Science Review* 81:1139-1153.

Caldeira, Gregory A., and Donald J. McCrone. 1982. Of time and judicial activism: A study of the U.S. Supreme Court, 1800-1973. In *Supreme Court activism and restraint*, ed. Stephen Halpern and Charles Lamb. Lexington, Mass.: Lexington Books.

Canon, Bradley, and S. Sidney Ulmer. 1976. The Supreme Court and critical elections: A dissent. *American Political Science Review* 70:1215-1218.

Casey, Gregory. 1974. The Supreme Court and myth: An empirical investigation. *Law and Society Review* 8:385-419.

_____. 1976. Popular perceptions of Supreme Court rulings. *American Politics Quarterly* 4:3-43.

Casper, Jonathan. 1976. The Supreme Court and national policy making. *American Political Science Review* 70:50-63.

Commager, Henry Steele. 1958. *Majority rule and minority rights.* Gloucester, Mass.: Peter Smith.

Coyle, Marcia. 1989. Court blazes a new trail. *National Law Journal*, August 21, S3.

Dahl, Robert. 1958. Decision-making in a democracy: The Supreme Court as a national policy-maker. *Journal of Public Law* 6:279-295.

Danelski, David. 1966. Values as a variable in judicial decision-making: Notes toward a theory. *Vanderbilt Law Review* 19:721-740.

Danelski, David, and Jeanne Danelski. 1989. Leadership in the Warren Court. In *American court systems*, 2d ed., rev., ed. Sheldon Goldman and Austin Sarat. New York: Longman.

Dolbeare, Kenneth. 1967. The public views the Supreme Court. In *Law, politics, and the federal courts*, ed. Herbert Jacob. Boston: Little, Brown.

Funston, Richard. 1975. The Supreme Court and critical elections. *American Political Science Review* 69:795-811.

Gates, John. 1984. The American Supreme Court and electoral realignment: A critical review. *Social Science History* 8:267-290.

———. 1987. Partisan realignment, unconstitutional state policies, and the U.S. Supreme Court, 1837-1964. *American Journal of Political Science* 31:259-280.

———. 1989. Supreme Court voting and realigning issues: A microlevel analysis of Supreme Court policy making and electoral realignment. *Social Science History* 13:255-283.

Gauch, James E. 1989. The intended role of the Senate in Supreme Court appointments. *University of Chicago Law Review* 56:337-365.

Goldman, Sheldon, and Thomas Jahnige. 1985. *The federal court as a political system*. 3d ed., rev. New York: Harper and Row.

Greenhouse, Linda. 1989a. At the bar. *New York Times*, July 28.

———. 1989b. Marshall says Court's rulings imperil rights. *New York Times*, September 9.

Handberg, Roger, and Harold Hill, Jr. 1980. Court curbing, Court reversals, and judicial review: The Supreme Court versus Congress. *Law and Society Review* 14:309-322.

Harvard Law Review. 1958. Note. Congressional reversal of Supreme Court decisions: 1945-1957. *Harvard Law Review* 77:1324-1337.

———. 1988. The Supreme Court, 1987 term. *Harvard Law Review* 102:4-358.

Henschen, Beth. 1983. Statutory interpretations of the Supreme Court: Congressional response. *American Politics Quarterly* 11:441-458.

Howard, J. Woodford. 1968. On the fluidity of judicial choice. *American Political Science Review* 62:43-56.

Hughes, Charles Evans. 1908. *Addresses and papers of Charles Evans Hughes*. New York and London: G. P. Putnam's Sons.

Hulbary, William, and Thomas Walker. 1980. The Supreme Court selection process: Presidential motivations and judicial performance. *Western Political Quarterly* 33:183-196.

Jackson, Robert H. 1941. *The struggle for judicial supremacy*. New York: Vintage.

Levy, Leonard. 1967. Judicial review, history, and democracy: An introduction. In *Judicial review and the Supreme Court*, ed. Leonard Levy. New York: Harper and Row.

Library of Congress. 1987. *The Constitution of the United States of America: Analysis and interpretation*. Washington, D.C.: Government Printing Office.

———. 1988. *The Constitution of the United States of America: Analysis and interpretation, 1988 supplement*. Washington, D.C.: Government Printing Office.

Marshall, Thomas. 1989. *Public opinion and the Supreme Court*. Boston: Unwin Hyman.

Murphy, Walter. 1962. *Congress and the Court*. Chicago: University of Chicago Press.

Murphy, Walter, and Joseph Tanenhaus. 1968. Public opinion and the United States Supreme Court. *Law and Society Review* 5:357-384.

Nagel, Stuart. 1969. *The legal process from a behavioral perspective.* Homewood, Ill.: Dorsey Press.

Peltason, Jack. 1955. *Federal courts in the political process.* New York: Random House.

Pritchett, C. Herman. 1948. *The Roosevelt Court.* New York: Macmillan.

———. 1954. *Civil liberties and the Vinson Court.* Chicago: University of Chicago Press.

Rathjen, Gregory, and Harold Spaeth. 1979. Access to the federal courts: An analysis of Burger Court policy making. *American Journal of Political Science* 23:360-382.

———. 1983. Denial of access and ideological preferences: An analysis of the voting behavior of the Burger Court justices, 1969-1976. *Western Political Quarterly* 36:71-87.

Rohde, David, and Harold Spaeth. 1976. *Supreme Court decision making.* San Francisco: W. H. Freeman.

Schmidhauser, John. 1961. Judicial behavior and the sectional crisis of 1837-1860. *Journal of Politics* 23:615-639.

Schmidhauser, John, and Larry Berg. 1972. *The Supreme Court and Congress.* New York: Free Press.

Schubert, Glendon. 1959. *Quantitative analysis of judicial behavior.* Glencoe, Ill.: Free Press.

———. 1962. The 1960-61 term of the Supreme Court: A psychological analysis. *American Political Science Review* 56:90-107.

———. 1965. *The judicial mind.* Evanston, Ill.: Northwestern University Press.

Scigliano, Robert. 1971. *The Supreme Court and the presidency.* New York: Free Press.

Segal, Jeffrey, and Albert Cover. 1989. Ideological values and the votes of Supreme Court justices. *American Political Science Review* 83:557-565.

Songer, Donald. 1979a. Concern for policy outputs as a cue for Supreme Court decisions on certiorari. *Journal of Politics* 41:1185-1194.

———. 1979b. The relevance of policy values for the confirmation of Supreme Court nominees. *Law and Society Review* 13:929-948.

Spaeth, Harold. 1962. Judicial power as a variable motivating Supreme Court behavior. *Midwest Journal of Political Science* 6:54-82.

———. 1963. Warren Court attitudes toward business: The "B" scale. In *Judicial decision-making,* ed. Glendon Schubert. New York: Free Press.

———. 1964. The judicial restraint of Mr. Justice Frankfurter—Myth or reality? *Midwest Journal of Political Science* 8:22-38.

Spaeth, Harold, and Stuart Teger. 1982. Activism and restraint: A cloak for the justices' policy references [*sic*]. In *Supreme Court activism and restraint,* ed. Stephen Halpern and Charles Lamb. Lexington, Mass.: Lexington Books.

Stumpf, Harry. 1965. Congressional response to Supreme Court rulings: The interaction of law and politics. *Journal of Public Law* 14:377-395.

Sulfridge, Wayne. 1980. Ideology as a factor in Senate consideration of Supreme Court nominations. *Journal of Politics* 42:560-567.

Taggart, William, and Matthew DeZee. 1985. A note on substantive access doctrines in the U.S. Supreme Court: A comparative analysis of the Warren and Burger Courts. *Western Political Quarterly* 38:84-93.

Tate, Neal. 1981. Personal attribute models of the voting behavior of U.S. Supreme Court justices: Liberalism in civil liberties and economic decisions, 1946-1978. *American Political Science Review* 75:355-367.

Ulmer, S. Sidney. 1960a. The analysis of behavior patterns on the United States Supreme Court. *Journal of Politics* 22:629-653.

––––––. 1960b. Supreme Court behavior and civil rights. *Western Political Quarterly* 13:288-311.

––––––. 1961. Scaling judicial cases: A methodological note. *American Behavioral Scientist* 4:31-34.

––––––. 1965. Toward a theory of sub-group formation in the United States Supreme Court. *Journal of Politics* 27:133-152.

––––––. 1971. Earl Warren and the *Brown* decision. *Journal of Politics* 33:689-702.

––––––. 1972. The decision to grant certiorari as an indicator of decision "on the merits." *Polity* 4:429-447.

––––––. 1983. Conflict with Supreme Court precedent and the granting of plenary review. *Journal of Politics* 45:474-478.

––––––. 1984. The Supreme Court's certiorari decisions: Conflict as a predictive variable. *American Political Science Review* 78:901-911.

––––––. 1986. Exploring the dissent patterns of the chief justices: John Marshall to Warren Burger. In *Judicial conflict and consensus*, ed. Sheldon Goldman and Charles Lamb. Lexington: University of Kentucky Press.

Walker, Thomas, Lee Epstein, and William Dixon. 1988. On the mysterious demise of consensual norms in the United States Supreme Court. *Journal of Politics* 50:361-389.

2. THE CIRCUIT COURTS OF APPEALS

Donald R. Songer

The courts of appeals occupy a pivotal position in our political system, the "vital center of the federal judicial system" according to J. Woodford Howard (1981, 8). Their traditional role of ensuring the uniformity of national law within their respective geographical regions has been important since their creation in the 1890s; it has become vital in an era in which the Supreme Court is able to review fewer than one of every two thousand decisions of the district courts. Their traditional role of supervising federal regulatory agencies grows in importance as federal regulation of the economy continues to become ever more pervasive and as cases with major economic impact are no longer framed exclusively as constitutional issues but increasingly as issues of regulatory detail which are not at the center of the Supreme Court's agenda. Moreover, as the number of cases litigated in the federal courts grows both quantitatively and in complexity while the number of cases reviewed by the Supreme Court remains static, the role of the courts of appeals as the final authoritative policy makers in the interpretation of many areas of federal law expands apace. They are now major political institutions that function not only as norm enforcers but also as important creators of public policy. Finally, the courts of appeals continue to play a pivotal role as mediators between pressures for national policy coherence and the centrifugal forces inherent in a decentralized political system.

The role the courts play in the making of public policy is heavily dependent on the nature of their business. The courts of appeals in the nineteenth century, with caseloads dominated by tort cases, were hardly likely to make policy regarding the constitutional rights of individuals. Conversely, appellate courts that dispose of a large number of criminal appeals inevitably make policy regarding the rights of the accused. Thus, an understanding of the business of the courts is the first step in an assessment of their policy-making role.

To have a significant impact on policy making, judges must have substantial discretion in their decision making. If traditional notions of mechanical jurisprudence were accurate, appeals court judges' effect on policy would be trivial. Therefore, the second step in the assessment of judges' policy-making role is to assess the evidence on the amount of discretion possessed by them.

The policy-making role of the courts of appeals will be enhanced to the extent to which they have in practice the final word on the important cases in various policy areas. Their impact will be maximized if a significant number of cases are brought to them for review, their decisions on these cases are faithfully implemented by courts and administrative agencies below, and their decisions are infrequently disturbed by subsequent review by the Supreme Court. Thus, it is necessary to examine the rate and the success of appeals of the decisions of the courts of appeals.

Finally, the significance of these courts' policy-making role will be shaped in part by the nature and the identity of the players who appear in their cases and by the relative success of different parties. Thus, a full understanding of the policy role of the courts of appeals requires an analysis of the traditional question at the heart of politics: Who wins and who loses?

The Business of the Courts of Appeals

The business of the courts of appeals has changed dramatically over the past century. The most obvious change has been the dramatic increase in the volume of cases, especially in the past two decades. A recent study noted that the caseload of the courts of appeals doubled between 1895 and 1925, then doubled again by 1960 (to 3,899). Then the real explosion began as the number of docketed cases tripled in the decade after 1960 to a total of 11,662 in 1970 (Baum, Goldman, and Sarat 1981). Since 1970 the flood has continued, although at a slightly slower rate of increase, reaching 23,200 cases by 1980 and 35,176 in 1987. Cumulatively, then, there has been a sixty-seven-fold increase since 1895 and a ninefold increase just in the twenty-seven years from 1960 to 1987.

The substance of the cases heard by the courts of appeals has also changed significantly over time. Lawrence Baum, Sheldon Goldman, and Austin Sarat (1981) have shown that during the period of their study (1895-1975), the proportion of the docket of the courts of appeals devoted to the resolution of private economic disputes declined substantially. The relative frequency of real property cases declined most precipitously, dropping from a high of over 25 percent of the cases before 1910 in one of the circuits studied to under 1 percent by 1975 in all three circuits in the study. The proportion of tort and business cases on the appeals courts' agendas also declined, though not as sharply (but it should be noted that since the total volume of cases increased so dramatically, the absolute number of business cases did increase over

Table 2-1   Nature of Cases Decided by the Fourth, Seventh, Eleventh, and District of Columbia Circuits in 1986

Case type	Frequency	Proportion of docket[a]
Criminal appeals	1,071	21.4%
Prisoner petitions	468	9.4
Civil rights (nonprisoners)	569	11.4
Labor	203	4.0
Economic regulation/tax	624	12.5
Social security/welfare	235	4.7
Diversity of citizenship	357	7.2
Procedural questions	898	18.1
Other	567	11.3
Total	4,992	100.0%

[a] Based on all cases, both published and unpublished, terminated by judicial action after submission of briefs or oral argument in calendar year 1986.

Source: Data collected by the author.

time). In contrast, the researchers found substantial increases in the proportion of public law cases (those involving government economic regulation, taxation, patents, labor relations, regulation of aliens, and so on) in two of the three circuits and noted at least a sixfold increase in the proportion of criminal cases in each circuit. Using a different group of three circuits, Howard (1981) found similarly dramatic growth in criminal appeals. From 1961 to 1979, the number of criminal appeals increased by 507 percent while the number of private civil cases and civil cases involving the U.S. government doubled. By 1979, criminal cases comprised 34.1 percent of the docket of the courts of appeals.

But more recent analysis demonstrates that although the number of criminal appeals continues to increase, the explosive growth rates of the 1960s and 1970s have moderated. Between 1979 and 1984, the number of criminal cases increased 54 percent while the number of administrative appeals increased 176 percent and civil cases involving the U.S. government increased 138 percent (Davis and Songer 1988). My own recent analysis of criminal cases in the Fourth, Seventh, Eleventh, and District of Columbia Circuits reveals that criminal cases remain a primary component of the docket of the courts of appeals, comprising more than a fifth of the cases heard in 1986. In addition, a significant proportion of the court's time is now devoted to the resolution of civil rights claims, prisoners' petitions, and government economic regulation (see Table 2-1). Economic disputes involving private parties (especially in the context of diversity suits and labor-

Table 2-2 Parties in the Courts of Appeals in 1986

Party	Appellant		Respondent		
	No.	%	No.	%	*Total*
Business	756	15.3	1,070	21.7	1,826
Nonprofit	79	1.6	86	1.7	165
United States	152	3.0	1,825	37.0	1,977
Local government	61	1.2	532	10.8	593
State government	58	1.2	945	19.2	1,003
Individual	3,830	77.6	468	9.5	4,298
Total	4,936	99.9	4,926	99.9	9,862

Source: Sheehan and Songer 1989, Table 2.

management conflict) have declined in importance relative to their earlier status but still constitute a sizable absolute number of cases (about 600 in the four circuits in 1986).

Both the nature of the issues and the nature of the parties contesting the issues are integral to the picture. Unfortunately, scholarship on the courts of appeals has shed little light on the parties. Howard (1981) noted that in the 1960s, the federal government was a party in more than half of the cases in the three circuits he studied, but he provided little detail on the nature of the other parties and did not differentiate between the appellant and respondent roles. Recently, Reginald S. Sheehan and Donald R. Songer (1989) have shown that the profile of appellants is very different from that of the respondents in the courts of appeals. As can be seen from Table 2-2, the overwhelming majority of cases are brought to the courts of appeals by individuals who have lost in the district courts. A much smaller, but nontrivial, number of appeals are brought by businesses, while governments at all levels are infrequent appellants. In contrast, governments are the respondents in two-thirds of the cases and businesses in the majority of the remaining cases.

When the appearance rates of governments as appellant and respondent are combined and the duplications (one government versus another government) removed, it appears that 71.6 percent of all cases decided by the courts of appeals involved the participation of some level of government. In 40 percent of the cases, the national government participated. These recent findings reinforce the earlier conclusion of Baum, Goldman, and Sarat that the business of the courts of appeals, "once dominated by private economic disputes, now emphasizes disputes involving government activity" (1981, 306). Still, the extent to which the agenda of the courts of appeals is determined by the issues raised in appeals brought by individuals is noteworthy. Even if only civil cases are examined, 69 percent of the appellants are individuals. Sheehan and Songer (1989, 7) interpret these findings as suggesting that the courts of appeals have become an avenue for those with limited resources to involve themselves in the public policy arena. In contrast, individuals not affiliated with organized groups or major institutions appear to have much less impact on the agenda of the legislative and executive branches.

A consideration of the nature of the cases heard by the courts of appeals suggests the potential for substantial impact on the formation and implementation of public policy. Large numbers of cases directly deal with questions of public law, especially the enforcement of criminal law; the treatment and rights of prisoners; a wide array of civil rights issues including claims of race, sex, and age discrimination; the distribution of government benefits; taxation; and a broad range of challenges to a variety of government regulations of economic activity. More than 70 percent of all the cases directly involve some level of government, most frequently the national government. Some of these cases appear to represent little more than the routine affirmance of the denial by the district court of some benefit or claim of a procedural irregularity in an individual case with no clear significance to anyone other than the aggrieved party. Others result in opinions that spend pages explaining the meaning of statutory (or less frequently, constitutional) rules in terms which on their face appear to shape the meaning of the law for broad publics. In addition, cases that settle disputes between private parties often entail the resolution of issues related to core political controversies of interest to the general public. For example, my recent analysis of 1986 appeals court decisions shows that 86.7 percent of the claims brought under consumer protection laws, 29.6 percent of the civil rights issues, 76.5 percent of the antitrust cases, and 62.6 percent of the labor disputes formally involved only private parties even though their resolutions were part of the ongoing political conflict in the nation. Even the remaining cases that deal with more narrowly defined economic issues between private parties (for example, the real property, contract, and tort cases which now make up a much smaller portion of the court's agenda than they did at the beginning of the century) often have political significance if politics is understood as the authoritative allocation of financial and other valued resources among competing groups and individuals in society. These allocative decisions of the courts may particularly be thought to have political significance if the amount of money involved or the degree of economic control at issue is large. There have been no good empirical studies to provide a reliable quantitative assessment of the size of the stakes involved, but my impression, based on my reading of many cases pitting businesses against each other, is that the appeals courts hear few disputes involving trivial amounts of money. Most likely, the costs of litigation provide substantial incentives, particularly in purely economic disputes, to settle most cases before they reach the courts of appeals unless the stakes are high and the outcome is in doubt.

The courts of appeals may also play a role in policy making even in private economic cases if they engage in "cumulative policy making." Henry Robert Glick and Kenneth Vines (1973) suggest that when judges make decisions on the same subjects over and over again, they often adopt a consistent point of view in dealing with certain conflicts. Over time, a series of decisions which viewed individually may appear to have little broad significance may be seen to reflect a bias that establishes an allocation pattern representing a de facto policy of distributional or even redistributional politics.[1]

In summary, the nature of the cases decided by the courts of appeals suggests at least the potential for the courts to have a substantial impact on public policy. Admittedly, it is the potential for impact on only a portion of the full range of policy issues in the political system. A number of policy domains, including foreign policy, national security, monetary policy, and national budget allocations—along with a host of the bread and butter issues of state and local politics—appear infrequently, if ever, on the dockets of the courts of appeals. But the range and significance of the policy issues remaining on their dockets are substantial.

The descriptive studies summarized above outline changes in the caseload of the courts of appeals and examine the nature of the cases heard by the courts (that is, the agenda of the courts) and how this agenda has changed over time. These descriptive studies clearly demonstrate the potential for significant policy making by the courts of appeals. But what is lacking is a solid analysis of the factors that determine the agenda of the courts, and particularly of those factors that explain the changes in its agenda over time.

Early judicial scholarship on agenda setting concentrated on the factors that influenced the certiorari decisions of the Supreme Court (for example, Tanenhaus et al. 1963; Ulmer 1972, 1984; Ulmer, Hintze, and Kirklosky 1972). Since then, others have begun to address wider issues relating to agenda power, including the relative influence of policy goals (Baum 1977), types of dockets (Hall 1985), role perception (Flango 1987), interest groups (Caldeira and Wright 1988), and institutional structure and issue cycles (Provine 1980; Caldeira 1981) on the composition of court dockets or agendas and how these decisions are related to the policy making of the courts. But most of these studies focus on either the U.S. Supreme Court or the appellate courts of states. Comparable studies on the courts of appeals are needed.

In particular, research is needed to evaluate the impact of the entry of new groups and new categories of litigants into the judicial arena on the agenda of the courts. In addition, we need to explore the relationship between changes in the agenda, changes in the balance of political forces in the larger political system, and changes on the courts of appeals. In particular, what is the impact of the Supreme Court on the agenda of the courts of appeals? Do new types of litigants and new issues come to the courts of appeals in response to policy changes announced by the Supreme Court, or do new issues arise first in the lower courts and then bubble up to the High Court? Although a few studies examine the impact of changes in public opinion on the substantive decisions of the courts, we still need an examination of how changes in public opinion, partisan changes reflected in election outcomes, and changes in the partisan composition of the courts affect the agenda of the courts. For example, we know little about how such changes affect the perceptions of litigants and how these perceptions are in turn related to decisions to raise new issues in the courts.

Another line of useful research would be to explore more systematically the effects of the increasing volume of cases heard by the courts of appeals. A number of studies have documented responses of the courts to these increasing caseloads, including the adoption of expedited procedures and the nonpublication of decisions. But little is yet known about the impact these new procedures have on policy making or on the pattern of decisional outcomes. For example, we need to know whether expedited procedures change who wins and who loses on appeal and whether nonpublication increases intra- and intercircuit conflict or leads to the successful hiding of noncompliance with Supreme Court or circuit precedent.

Judicial Discretion as a Prerequisite of Policy Impact

Although the nature of the business of the courts of appeals establishes the potential for a significant role in policy making, the resolution of numerous challenges to government action is not enough by itself to establish an active public policy role (Baum, Goldman, and Sarat 1981, 307). Such activity may simply involve the routine application and enforcement of clear statutes and precedents by a consensual process that adds little to the development of public policy. Judges cannot be said to be significant policy makers unless they have substantial discretion to choose among a range of options when deciding their cases.

At least since the ground-breaking work of C. Herman Pritchett (1948) it has been generally conceded that the agenda of the Supreme Court, with divided decisions in more than half of its cases, provides the justices with extensive discretion to vote in favor of outcomes that are compatible with their policy preferences. The very existence of publicly recorded dissent is taken as an objective indicator that the justices were free to vote in favor of either side. But if the rate of dissent is taken as the indicator of the extent of discretion possessed by judges, then the judges on the courts of appeals would appear to have very little. Goldman's (1975) study of appeals court decisions in the 1960s and 1970s discovered a dissent rate of only 6 percent. My own more recent studies of four circuits indicated that nonunanimous decisions were rendered in only 3.6 percent of the 1986 cases.

However, a number of indicators suggest that discretion actually exceeds the limited magnitude suggested by these dissent rates. One way to gauge the extent of discretion is to ask judges directly about their perceptions. The most systematic exploration of the decision- and policy-making orientations of appeals court judges was undertaken by Howard (1981). Based on interviews with thirty-five judges from three circuits, he estimated that the proportion of cases in which judges had an opportunity to fashion legal rules consistent with their personal preferences seldom exceeded 10 percent. However, virtually all of the judges admitted that lawmaking was inherent in their jobs; they disagreed only over the matter of degree. And although almost all of the judges indicated that they considered precedent "very important" in reaching their decisions, 48 percent said personal views on justice were also "very important" and an additional 40 percent said such values were "moderately important." Thus, although traditional norms of adherence to precedence may inhibit their willingness to acknowledge discretionary decision making, the judges admitted having discretion to engage in policy making more than twice as often as might be supposed from an examination of dissent rates. Moreover, the willingness of the overwhelming majority of judges to admit that they frequently considered the implications of their personal values for the cases before them rather than relying solely on precedent supports an inference that the actual incidence of at least partially discretionary decision making may be substantially higher than the 10 percent estimate offered by the judges.

As an alternative to asking judges how much discretion they have, one might attempt to draw inferences from the patterns of decision making by groups of judges with differing values. By examining the differences in the proportion of decisions in which panels with Democratic and Republican majorities supported the liberal position in unanimous decisions and the frequency of reversals of the district court,

I (Songer 1982) came up with a conservative estimate that courts of appeals were free to support the preferred policy position of the panel majority in between one-fifth and one-third of their cases. More recent work (Songer 1988) supports the conclusion that judges are free to make decisions consistent with their policy values in at least a substantial minority of their decisions.[2] Even in the unpublished decisions of the courts, which according to the rules regulating publication should be characterized by the straightforward application of clear, binding precedent, there were differences of as much as 20 percent in some circuits between panels with Democratic and Republican majorities with regard to support for the liberal position.

Another perspective on the degree of discretion judges have in policy making may be gained from studies of the impact of the Supreme Court on the decisions of judges below. Formally, when the Court announces a change in policy, the new precedent is legally binding on the courts below. Yet a number of studies, especially those examining the response of state courts to the controversial civil liberties decisions of the Warren Court, found instances in which lower courts either overtly defied the Supreme Court "mandate" or found more subtle ways to undermine the practical effect of the policy inherent in the new precedent while appearing to comply with the precedent on the surface. The overall extent and frequency of such noncompliance and evasion are unclear. Yet the extent to which courts succeed in such overt defiance or subversion suggests a degree of independence in policy making by the lower courts.

Although there has been no comprehensive study of the impact of the Supreme Court on the courts of appeals, a few studies (Baum 1980; Gruhl 1980; Songer 1987; Songer and Sheehan 1990; Songer and Reid 1989) make some tentative generalizations possible. First, in the six policy areas examined (antitrust, criminal rights, economic regulation, labor, libel, and patents), no clearly defiant or overtly noncompliant decisions by the courts of appeals have been found. For example, John Gruhl carefully examined the twenty-seven appeals court libel decisions in the decade following the Supreme Court decision in *New York Times v. Sullivan* to determine whether they faithfully applied the new actual malice test mandated by the Supreme Court.[3] He found that the lower courts consistently complied with the new precedent and in fact so accepted the basic thrust of the Supreme Court mandate that they often extended it in anticipation of the direction that the High Court appeared to be moving. These findings support the devotion to precedent claimed by the judges interviewed by Howard (1981).

However, studies of compliance provide a mixed picture of the impact or significance of new precedents announced by the Supreme

Court for the decisions of the courts below. Lower courts may fail to support the basic policy of the Supreme Court without being overtly noncompliant with any specific decision (see Wasby 1970, chap. 2). Baum (1977) argues that appellate court leadership is largely exercised through the establishment of decisional trends that signal its inclination without creating a complete set of explicit rules of law. Therefore, to obtain a more complete understanding of the impact of the Court, we need to examine the extent to which the decisional trends of the courts below change in response to significant changes in precedent. The recent Songer and Sheehan (1990) study shows that the picture of Supreme Court impact provided by studies restricted to compliance analysis is incomplete. First, the study replicated Gruhl's (1980) analysis of compliance with the *New York Times* libel decision and compared those results with an analysis of compliance by the courts of appeals with the *Miranda* decision on the use of coerced confessions.[4] For both decisions there were high levels of compliance. When compliance was used as the only measure of impact, it appeared that the impact of the Court was the same for both the *New York Times* and the *Miranda* decisions. *However*, when the decisional trends of the courts of appeals were examined, different responses were discovered. In the area of libel, the pattern of appeals court decisions changed sharply to reflect the new Supreme Court policy. But there was no significant change in the decisional trends of the appeals courts in cases involving the admissibility of confessions.

Other studies (Baum 1980; Songer 1987; Songer and Reid 1989) have found similar patterns of Supreme Court impact. In the areas of antitrust, economic regulation, labor, First Amendment, and patent policy, after the Supreme Court made a major shift in policy, the decisional trends of the courts of appeals moved in the same direction to a statistically significant degree. Changes in decisional trends were generally evident in the votes of judges of both parties. Thus, it appears that in most policy areas, the judges of the courts of appeals do feel significant constraint imposed by precedent which limits their autonomy in policy making.

Nevertheless, most of the changes in the courts of appeals, while in the same direction as the new policy supported by the Supreme Court, were modest in magnitude (and in one area, criminal rights, there was no measurable change at all). Moreover, although judges of both parties shifted toward the new policy, differences between Democratic and Republican judges remained. It should also be noted that there are many ways to "avoid, mitigate, or nullify the ruling or advice of the Court" which stop short of overt noncompliance (Beatty 1972, 261). For example, judges may adhere to the letter of the rules announced in the new precedent but still achieve their ideologically preferred outcome in at least some of their cases by creatively interpreting the fact situation or by giving a narrow, literal interpretation to the precedent. Gruhl (1980) has labeled such attempts "narrow compliance." A recent examination of the response of the courts of appeals to the Supreme Court's *New York Times* libel decision and *Miranda* confession decision (Songer and Sheehan 1990) found such narrow compliance in 16.7 percent of the libel decisions and 5.2 percent of the confession decisions of the courts of appeals. Finally, it must be kept in mind that the *New York Times* and *Miranda* decisions were clear new precedents and that the cases examined for compliance were only those in which the precedent clearly applied. In the many cases in which there is no clear precedent, it may be presumed that the appeals court judges have more perceived freedom to attempt to fashion policy consistent with their private preferences. It appears, therefore, that although judges do feel constrained in practice to some degree by precedent, they also retain significant independence in a number of cases.

The available evidence, as summarized, suggests that precedent provides real constraints on the policy-making proclivities of the judges of the courts of appeals. Perhaps in as many as two-thirds of their cases, and certainly in at least a substantial minority of cases, their decisions appear to be largely routine enforcement of laws and clear precedent for which there is consensus on the meaning. In these cases there is little opportunity for the policy values of the judges to influence the outcome. But there remains at least a substantial minority of cases spanning a broad spectrum of policy domains in which the judges appear to have the discretion necessary to write their policy preferences into law.

It remains difficult to obtain completely satisfactory measures of the effect of precedent. The examinations of how the decisional trends of the courts of appeals changed in response to changes in precedent announced by the Supreme Court are useful as rough approximations, but these studies have several shortcomings. Typically, only fairly broad issue areas have been examined. Therefore, at least some of the appeals court cases examined are probably ones for which the new Supreme Court precedent may be of doubtful relevance. To the extent that this is true, the effect of precedent may be underestimated. In addition, for many appeals court cases it is difficult, or perhaps impossible, to objectively identify which precedents should apply. In many of these cases the crucial question may be which precedent should be followed rather than whether the judges should follow precedent or their personal sense of justice in the case. Unless the applicable precedent can be identified with some certainty, empirical tests of the effect of precedent are not possible.

It would be helpful to have additional studies which would first select cases from narrow issue categories and then within those issue categories select cases with similar fact situations.[5] An analysis of the extent of change in appeals court decisions in these more carefully matched categories of cases in response to changes in narrowly focused precedent and an analysis of the voting differences in these cases among judges who have been carefully identified as having different political values would then provide a more refined estimate of the effect of precedent versus the effect of judicial values.[6]

Additional interview data would also be helpful. Past interviews about the impact of precedent (such as Howard 1981) have usually been limited to judges, and the questions about precedent have dealt with broad generalizations on the role or significance of precedent. Such interviews have provided a useful first approximation of the significance of precedent. But it would now be helpful to move past these generalizations to questions with a sharper focus. A good place to begin might be to pattern interviews with participants in the judicial process after those of John W. Kingdon (1981). Instead of asking representatives generic questions about the influence of constituents, and so on, Kingdon began by asking how they went about making up their mind on a particular bill. He followed this up by asking them about the impact of particular parties (such as constituents and lobbyists) on that single bill. Such a focus on specific decisions, Kingdon argued, provided a more realistic and more specific measure of the influence of different actors in the legislative process. Similarly, judges might be asked either about actual cases they had decided or about hypothetical cases that closely paralleled actual cases from other circuits. For these cases judges could be asked how tightly they felt constrained by precedent and how likely they believed it would be for judges with different values to reach the same conclusion. Additional insight might be gathered from interviews with attorneys who had argued similar cases before the given circuit and from present and former law clerks of the judges.

The Finality of Appeals Court Policy Making

In theory, all decisions of the courts of appeals are reviewable by the Supreme Court. If the Court actually did review a large percentage of their decisions, then the role of the courts of appeals in policy making would be slight. But a basic condition of our judicial system is that the Supreme Court exerts very little direct supervision over any of the lower courts (Howard 1981, 57).

Even in the 1960s, when the number of cases heard by the courts of appeals was much smaller, Supreme Court review of their decisions was infrequent. For one thing, most litigants who lose do not seek Supreme Court review. Howard (1981) found that only 20 percent of the losing litigants in the courts of appeals in the period 1965-1968 petitioned for certiorari. Further, petitions for review are granted only infrequently. Of the 1,004 cases in which review was requested, the Supreme Court heard only 92 and rendered full opinions in only 62. The Court thus gave full review to only 1.3 percent of the 4,945 cases decided by the three circuits in the period studied by Howard (1981, 57).

In the 1970s and 1980s, the caseload of the courts of appeals increased dramatically, but the number of decisions handed down each year by the Supreme Court remained relatively constant. As a result, it might be expected that the proportion of appeals court decisions reviewed by the Supreme Court would decline even further. Recent research undertaken by Sue Davis and I confirms this expectation. As can be seen from Table 2-3, the Supreme Court reviewed only 19 of the nearly 4,000 decisions from three circuits in 1986; the rate of review was under one-half of 1 percent. Of those cases accepted for review, the Supreme Court reversed the lower court's decision about two-thirds of the time. But since so few cases were reviewed at all, the net result was that the decisions of the courts of appeals were left undisturbed in 99.7 percent of their cases.

Further examination of the data in Table 2-3 reveals that the Supreme Court was quite selective in the types of cases it reviewed. More than two-thirds of the cases reviewed were either civil rights decisions or labor and economic regulation cases, even though these two categories accounted for less than a quarter of all appeals court decisions. Not a single diversity or individual benefits case (such as Social Security disability claims) was reviewed. But even in the most frequently reviewed category, civil rights cases, the decision of the court of appeals stood as the final authoritative resolution of the dispute in more than 98 percent of the cases.

Further evidence of the finality of appeals court decisions comes from the recent research on the impact of the Supreme Court decisions on libel and confession cases heard by the courts of appeals. Of the fifteen cases identified as being in narrow compliance, decisions that appeared to be contrary to the basic policy of the Supreme Court, only one was subsequently reversed by the Supreme Court. None of the others was even reviewed. More broadly, of the sixty-four confession cases and eleven libel cases in which the court of appeals' decision went against the general policy trend of the Supreme Court, only one was reversed (Songer and Sheehan 1990).

The net result is broad autonomy for the courts of appeals. In some areas, such as diversity of citizenship cases, the Supreme Court

Table 2-3 Proportion of 1986 Decisions from Three Circuits of the U.S. Courts of Appeals Reviewed by the Supreme Court

Policy area	Appeals court decisions	Decisions reviewed by Supreme Court	
		No.	%
Civil rights	341	6	1.76
Criminal and prisoner petitions	1,219	4	0.33
Individual government benefits	197	0	0
Labor and economic	589	7	1.19
Diversity	177	0	0
Other	1,411	2	0.14
Total	3,934	19	0.48

Source: Data collected by the author.

has in effect delegated the role of final appellate decision maker to the courts of appeals. In a few selected areas, most notably civil rights in recent years, the Supreme Court maintains an active interest and devotes a substantial portion of its docket to reviewing the decisions of the courts of appeals. But even in these areas, the overwhelming majority of appeals court decisions are left undisturbed, even when the policy interests supported below seem to be contrary to the general thrust of Supreme Court preferences. In between are thousands of appeals court decisions each year in policy areas in which Supreme Court attention is sporadic and in which the odds that any given decision will be reviewed are so low that it seems safe to assume that the consequences of review are not likely to weigh heavily on the minds of the appeals court decision makers. In these areas, the decisions of the courts of appeals generally stand as the policy of their circuit.

It would be helpful to know more about the perceptions of finality held by the judges and by the litigants and how these perceptions affect their behavior. For example, to what extent do perceptions about the chances of victory on appeal versus limitations on resources affect the decisions of litigants to seek review of adverse decisions from either the district courts or the courts of appeals? Similarly, how do judges' estimates of the chances of reversal and their sense of being bound by precedent affect their decisions when these factors conflict with their value preferences?

Winners and Losers in the Courts of Appeals

Politics is defined in many texts as the process that determines who wins and who loses; yet there has been surprisingly little study of winners and losers in the context of courts. The seminal study by Marc Galanter (1974) suggested that the "haves" should usually be expected to come out ahead in litigation. He argued that "repeat players" (those who frequently use the courts and are usually also "haves" in the sense of being advantaged economically, socially, and in terms of institutional position) have a number of advantages. First, they will be more likely to engage in planning to conform their behavior to the requirements of the law than will less experienced "one-shotters." Second, the haves can more easily afford the delays and expenses associated with litigation and because of their superior financial position and their more extensive experience are less likely to accept unfavorable pretrial settlements. Third, they have strategic advantages in shaping the evolution of legal doctrine through their involvement in multiple cases; they can pick and choose which cases to settle and which to push to the limits of the appellate process in the hopes of gaining favorable new precedent. Finally, their greater experience, their case selecting advantages, and the resources that allow them to hire first-rate counsel allow the repeat players to win more frequently than one-shotters when cases are fully litigated.

Although Galanter's ideas are provocative, most of his data to test these propositions came from trial courts. Stanton Wheeler and his colleagues (1987) provided the first comprehensive attempt to test these hypotheses in an appellate court context when they examined the success of different classes of litigants in sixteen state supreme courts. Their findings suggested that the haves won more often than the have nots, but the relationship was not as strong as would have been expected given the trial court findings of Galanter. For example, as predicted from the Galanter framework, city and state governments won more often than both business organizations and individuals, and business organizations won more often than individuals. But while these differences were statistically significant, their magnitude was quite modest: an 8.4 percent "net advantage" for governments over individuals, 6.9 percent for government over business organizations, and 1.8 percent for business organizations over individuals.

Unfortunately, there has been little analysis of who wins and who loses in the courts of appeals. A recent paper by Sheehan and Songer (1989) attempted to apply the Galanter framework by replicating the Wheeler et al. study with data from four circuits of the courts of appeals, but more analysis is clearly needed. For their analysis, Sheehan and Songer examined all of the decisions (both published and unpublished) from four circuits for 1986. Parties were grouped into six general categories which were rank ordered using the logic of the

Wheeler et al. (1987) study by the average resources (such as money, legal talent, and legal experience) each would be expected to have available to influence litigation. In order to control for the tendency of the courts of appeals to affirm the decision below, and to make the findings comparable to the Wheeler et al. study, an index of "net advantage" was created.

There was a strong relationship between resources assumed to be available and success in the courts of appeals. The more advantaged parties consistently won more frequently than those with fewer resources. The most successful litigant was the national government, with an overall success rate of 84.4 percent and a net advantage of +43.4 percent. State governments and local governments were close behind. At the other extreme were individuals, with an overall success rate of only 18.3 percent and an index of net advantage of -18.1 percent. Business interests fell in the middle, with an overall success rate of 56.1 percent and an index of net advantage of +1.7 percent. In cases pitting business interests against individuals, the businesses had a net advantage of +9.1 percent. These relative success rates were essentially unchanged when controls for different policy issues were introduced. When the general category of individuals was subdivided by race, it was discovered that blacks had essentially the same success rate as other individuals, but that identifiably poor people won only one-third as often as individuals in general. These results appear to provide strong support for the Galanter thesis and suggest that the advantages enjoyed by the "haves" are substantially greater in the courts of appeals than they are in state supreme courts.

When combined with the data on participation rates noted above, this first look at who wins and who loses in the courts of appeals suggests that although individuals appear to have greater success in the courts than in other forums in getting their concerns on the agenda of government, they have had little success in converting that access into substantive gains. The traditional normative views that the courts are and ought to be defenders of the weak and that they are blind in regard to the wealth and status of litigants do not appear to be supported. Instead, the data suggest that an important consequence of the policy-making role of the courts of appeals has been to support the status quo. The gains achieved by interests that are well positioned to influence the other branches of government are not often disturbed by adverse decisions from these courts. Moreover, in contests between private parties, those who are relatively disadvantaged usually lose. The large differentials in the success of different categories of litigants also suggest that the concept of cumulative policy making noted above may accurately describe at least some of the areas of appeals court involvement. For example, the consistent success (71.8 percent) of businesses against individuals in private economic cases (cases which may not always be thought of as having policy-making significance) suggests that when the pattern of outcomes in these cases is examined more closely there may in fact be politically significant distributional consequences.

Although the Sheehan and Songer study provides a useful beginning point for analysis, much remains to be learned about the allocation of benefits by the courts of appeals. Clearly, data from all circuits are needed and more refined categories of litigants and issues need to be examined. Refined categories of litigants would aid understanding by permitting analysis of the effects of actual variation in the nature and extent of resources. (Is more money important only up to some threshold amount? What is the relative impact of money versus litigation experience?) In addition, it would be important to analyze trends over time and across circuits or regions to determine the extent to which success in the courts is related to political forces that affect the fortunes of similar interests in other political contexts. More generally, the nature of the litigants needs to be included as a crucial variable in attempts to provide multivariate analyses of the factors that influence policy making in the courts.

A useful beginning is provided by Lettie McSpadden Wenner and Lee E. Dutter's (1989) analysis of environmental policy making, which found a differential impact of contextual variables on the success of three types of litigants in one policy area. The researchers assessed the effects on the success of three types of litigants of different contexts present in the twelve circuits, with controls for the specific federal agency involved in the suit, the specific law used as the basis of the case, and the identity of the presidential administration. Although no circuit context had a significant impact on the success of business litigants, four circuits were significant for the success of environmental groups and two other circuits were important for the success of government. Additionally, business appellants had lower success rates when they faced the Environmental Protection Agency, Coast Guard, or the Departments of Interior and Agriculture, while the presence of these agencies had no significant effect on the success of environmental groups.

In addition to applying this type of analysis to other substantive areas, there is a need for much more analysis of the role of different types of litigants over time. Little is known about how changes in the party system, changes in public opinion, or the rise or fall of social movements affect the movement of different types of litigants or of organized groups into and out of litigation or how these changes affect the relative success of different types of litigants. For example, did the arrival of or end of the Depression affect the success of bankrupts in court and did the civil rights movement affect the success of blacks? Nor is much known about the interaction of such forces with the ideology of the judges on the success of different types of litigants. Finally, little is known about how the provision of additional resources to have nots or one-shotters by means such as the filing of amicus briefs, group sponsorship of litigation, or the provision of free counsel by legal aid programs affects the success of such groups.

Regional Variation versus National Integration

The discussion above has treated the courts of appeals as if they were a single policy-making body. But the courts of appeals do not comprise a single institution for the creation of national policy; rather they are twelve different courts that are marked by wide diversity in their business and behavior. Unfortunately, there has been only limited systematic analysis to date of the extent or nature of that diversity or of the relationship of that variation to differences in state or regional political culture, political party systems, or other environmental or contextual influences.

The present structure of the courts of appeals was the culmination of a century and a half of conflict between nationalist interests demanding the uniform application of national law and the centrifugal tugs emanating from diverse regional political cultures. Although the basic structure and organization of the courts of appeals have remained essentially intact since 1925, the basic conflict between regional and national forces persists.

Several recent analyses have begun to address the extent and nature of regional variation in the courts of appeals. When Howard examined the decisions of three circuits in the 1960s he found substantial variation among the circuits in the nature of their business, the type of litigants, the rates of dissent and reversal, and the nature of decisions. He interpreted this circuit variation as regional variation (since his three circuits were in different regions). Regional diversity, in fact, became a theme of his discussion of the courts of appeals, leading him to conclude that "regionalization of appellate structures, for some subjects at least, may well spawn regional specialization and regional- ized national law" (1981, 33). Yet his interviews discovered that in spite of this diversity, judges in all three circuits strongly embraced an institutional obligation to be an agent of the national government. The judges, he found, were "acutely aware" of their obligation to maintain national supremacy. Most of the judges expressed national rather than regional loyalties without hesitation or qualification (1981, 145-147).

Some light is shed on this seemingly paradoxical finding by more recent analyses. Davis and Songer (1988) updated some of Howard's findings by examining the business of the courts in 1984. When data for all twelve circuits were examined they found that the extent of variation was even greater than that reported by Howard for his three circuits in the 1960s. For eight of the eleven substantive issue areas examined, the circuit with the highest percentage of cases had at least twice the proportion of cases observed in the circuit with the lowest proportion of cases. Some of the variation was extreme. For example, the Fourth Circuit had over four times the proportion of prisoner petitions of the Second Circuit, the Sixth Circuit had four times the proportion of Social Security cases of the D.C. Circuit, and the Second Circuit had over five times the proportion of patent and copyright cases heard in the Tenth Circuit. However, the variation was completely unrelated to geographic region. No systematic pattern among circuits was apparent at all except that the circuits were different. Similarly, substantial variation in reversal rates and in the tendencies to reverse district court decisions in particular issue areas was evident among circuits but the variation did not follow regional lines.

Several recent studies of decisional tendencies in the courts of appeals have also found variation among circuits but few consistent regional effects. Using the presence or absence of each circuit as an independent variable in a multivariate analysis of appeals court environmental decisions, Wenner and Dutter (1989) found that only four circuits had a statistically significant impact on success of environmental groups, two circuits were significant for government outcomes, and no circuits were significantly related to the success of business groups. No consistent regional patterns were found in any of the three analyses. Similarly, Songer and Davis (1988) found no consistent regional effects across the four time periods they examined for antitrust, labor, criminal, First Amendment, or civil rights cases. For the most recent period (1983-1986), region was related to the proportion of liberal votes only in the antitrust area (the South made 9 percent fewer liberal decisions than the non-South).

When policy making is defined through the use of doctrinal analysis instead of quantitative analysis of outcomes, a similar pattern is discovered. Michael W. Combs (1982) found that in the absence of clear Supreme Court standards, the courts of appeals played a prominent role in the development of desegregation policy outside the South. Two distinct patterns were discovered. The most prodesegregation standards were adopted by a group of circuits including two from the East (the First and Second) and two which combine states from the South and Midwest (the Sixth and Eighth).

Table 2-4 Proportion of Liberal Decisions in All 1986 Decisions of Three Circuits

Issue	Fourth Circuit	Seventh Circuit	Eleventh Circuit
Civil rights	8.6%	19.6%	35.0% *
Labor	33.8	51.4	41.2*
Criminal	8.3	8.4	11.3
Prisoner petitions	2.1	13.3	27.5*
Individual benefits	28.1	23.7	50.7*
Diversity	11.1	8.9	20.7*

* Difference between Seventh and Eleventh Circuits significant at the .01 level.

Source: Data collected by the author.

Less rigorous standards were adopted by the Far West's Ninth Circuit and the midwestern Seventh. There were no clear patterns in the Third (East) or Tenth (West) Circuits.

We know that the partisan balance in each circuit has more to do with when vacancies occur on each circuit than with any regional factors. And if judges have national orientations, as Howard found, then they are likely to reflect the values of the national party that controlled the presidency at the time of their appointment. The circuits' policy tendencies may thus vary with the proportion of appointments attributable to presidents of a given party. Some support is provided for this speculation by the finding from my recent reanalysis of the Songer and Davis (1988) data, which demonstrated that partisan effects on voting were not affected to a statistically significant degree by the addition of a control for region. Similarly, a recent analysis of three circuits, reported in Table 2-4, adds some support. The analysis was based on all 1986 decisions of two southern circuits, the Fourth and Eleventh, and one midwestern circuit, the Seventh. Due to chance retirements and the politics surrounding the split of the old Fifth Circuit, Carter was able to make seven appointments to the Eleventh Circuit while Reagan was able to appoint only one judge by 1986. In contrast, both the Fourth and Seventh Circuits were more heavily Republican.

As can be seen from Table 2-4, the Eleventh Circuit was the most liberal in five of the six policy areas. Moreover, in its policy orientation the Fourth Circuit was more similar to the geographically distant but partisanly similar Seventh Circuit than it was to the geographically adjoining Eleventh Circuit in all but one policy area. Complementary results are reported by Sheehan and Songer (1989). They found that poor individuals and labor unions won more frequently and business interests lost more frequently in the Eleventh Circuit than in either the Fourth or Seventh Circuits.

Conclusion

The courts of appeals are clearly established as important policy makers in the American federal system. Their agenda now spans a broad array of issues which includes many of the most important and controversial concerns of domestic politics. As they tackle the highly charged political issues inherent in many of their cases they frequently possess substantial discretion to establish new rules or shade the meaning of existing policies. For most of their decisions, the objective probability of reversal is slight and grows steadily smaller as their caseload continues to grow.

But in spite of our growing understanding of the policy-making role of the courts of appeals, many questions remain unanswered. There is a critical need for good longitudinal studies over significant time periods. We know little about the relationship of the role of the courts to changes over time in the nature of the party system, in public opinion, and in the larger social and economic context of American politics. Do changes in policy making in the courts of appeals follow or lead changes in public opinion and/or policy changes in other institutions, or are the courts autonomous? It would be useful to know whether the courts respond in some direct way to such changes or whether policy change in the courts is influenced only indirectly through personnel change, which may follow changes in the larger political and social systems.

Although there is considerable literature on agenda setting and its relationship to policy making in other subfields of political science, little work has been done in public law. First, there is a need to describe in more detail when and how the agenda of the courts of appeals has changed; the longitudinal study by Baum, Goldman, and Sarat (1981) is a good start. Then there is a need to attempt to link agenda change in the courts to agenda changes in other institutions and to broader social forces. For example, to what extent does the effect of partisan realignment affect the nature of the issues brought to the courts? Do changing electoral fortunes, which change partisan control of Congress, the White House, or states, change the perspectives of potential litigants about the relative gains from pursuing legal rather than more traditional political strategies and thus change the nature or relative frequency of issues that are brought to court?

A better understanding of the relationship of agenda change and the change in policy outputs to elite and mass opinion would have important normative implications. Most broadly, concerns about democratic theory make it relevant to know whether the agenda as well as the substantive outputs of the courts are responsive to public demands. We need to know how frequently the broad sweep of policy making by the courts goes against the policy preferences of the public. When courts do oppose public policy preferences, are they trying to fulfill the normative role often prescribed for them of protecting the liberties of unpopular minorities? In addition, more detailed analysis of the success and failure of different types of litigants is quite relevant for normative concerns with distributive justice and fairness.

Likewise, we need to investigate circuit variation in more detail (and over time) with particular attention to the relationship of that variation to the broader social and political context. For example, do policy differences among circuits produce measurable differences in overall patterns of allocation of benefits within the circuits, and do variations in the business of the circuits result from differences in the generation of issues due to differences in the socioeconomic contexts of the circuits or from more conscious choices (such as forum shopping)?

This review of scholarship on the courts of appeals has shown that considerable evidence exists to establish that the courts of appeals are significant policy makers in the federal system. The courts hear a wide variety of cases that impinge on many of the important disputes that are central to political conflict in the United States; the judges appear to have significant discretion in the resolution of many of those disputes; and the decisions of the courts of appeals are seldom disturbed by the Supreme Court. But many gaps remain in our knowledge, particularly in our understanding of changes over time and of the relationship between change on the courts of appeals and changes in the larger political system.

Notes

1. Distributional policies are those that establish patterns of allocating benefits, most typically discrete material goods, directly to one or more groups without in any direct way imposing a cost on groups not receiving the benefits. Redistributional policies are those that are perceived to take benefits from some broadly defined group or class in society and to confer those benefits on other broadly defined groups or classes (see Lowi 1964).
2. Since judges are randomly grouped on panels and cases are randomly assigned to those panels, it may be assumed that both those cases heard by panels with a Democratic majority and those heard by panels with a

Republican majority are random samples of the universe of cases. Therefore, differences in the proportion of liberal decisions made by these two sets of panels, if statistically significant, support the hypothesis that the values of the judges influenced their decisions.

3. In the case of *New York Times v. Sullivan*, 376 U.S. 254 (1964), the Supreme Court ruled that in order for public officials to collect damages for a statement about them alleged to be libelous, the officials must prove that the statement was untrue, that it injured their reputation, and that it was made with actual malice.

4. In the case of *Miranda v. Arizona*, 384 U.S. 436 (1966), the Supreme Court ruled that no incriminating statement elicited during custodial interrogation could be introduced in a felony trial unless the prosecution met the burden of proving that the statement had been made only after the defendant had been warned of four specific rights (the right to remain silent, that anything said would be used against the defendant in court, the right to consult an attorney before questioning, and that an attorney would be provided free of charge if the defendant could not afford an attorney) and had waived those rights voluntarily and knowingly.

5. See Segal (1984) for a useful illustration of the fact analysis of cases, which results in the identification of narrow categories of cases that could be used for the analysis of precedent suggested here.

6. Instead of simply using the partisan identification of the judge or the party of the appointing president of the judge as an indicator of the political values of the judge, as many previous studies have done, it should be possible to develop a more refined indicator. Two possibilities appear most fruitful. First, one might create an index by combining knowledge of differences in the voting patterns of cohorts of judges appointed by individual presidents with some measure (for example, the measure computed by Americans for Democratic Action) of the ideology of the home state senator of the president's party who was presumably consulted on the appointment of a given judge. Alternatively, one might compute a general ideological support score based on the votes of the judge in the nonconsensual cases outside of the particular issue area used in the analysis of the effect of precedent.

References

Baum, Lawrence. 1977. Judicial impact as a form of policy implementation. In *Public law and public policy*, ed. John A. Gardiner. New York: Praeger.

———. 1980. Responses of federal district judges to courts of appeals policies: An exploration. *Western Political Quarterly* 33:217-224.

Baum, Lawrence, Sheldon Goldman, and Austin Sarat. 1981. The evolution of litigation in the federal courts of appeals, 1895-1975. *Law and Society Review* 16:291-309.

Beatty, Jerry K. 1972. State court evasion of United States Supreme Court mandates during the last decade of the Warren Court. *Valparaiso Law Review* 6:260-285.

Caldeira, Gregory A. 1981. The United States Supreme Court and criminal cases, 1935-1976: Alternative models of agenda building. *British Journal of Political Science* 11:449-470.

Caldeira, Gregory A., and John R. Wright. 1988. Organized interests and agenda setting in the U.S. Supreme Court. *American Political Science Review* 82:1109-1127.

Combs, Michael W. 1982. The policy-making role of the courts of appeals in northern school desegregation: Ambiguity and judicial policy-making. *Western Political Quarterly* 35:359-375.

Davis, Sue, and Donald R. Songer. 1988. The changing role of the United States courts of appeals: The flow of litigation revisited. Vail, Colo.: Law and Society Association.

Flango, Victor E. 1987. Case selection in the Georgia and Illinois supreme courts. *Justice System Journal* 12:384-404.

Galanter, Marc. 1974. Why the haves come out ahead: Speculations on the limits of social change. *Law and Society Review* 9:95-160.

Glick, Henry Robert, and Kenneth N. Vines. 1973. *State court systems.* Englewood Cliffs, N.J.: Prentice-Hall.

Goldman, Sheldon. 1975. Voting behavior on the U.S. courts of appeals revisited. *American Political Science Review* 69:491-506.

Gruhl, John. 1980. The Supreme Court's impact on the law of libel: Compliance by lower federal courts. *Western Political Quarterly* 33:502-519.

Hall, Melinda Gann. 1985. Docket control as an influence on judicial voting. *Justice System Journal* 10:243-255.

Howard, J. Woodford. 1981. *Courts of appeals in the federal judicial system: A study of the Second, Fifth, and District of Columbia Circuits.* Princeton, N.J.: Princeton University Press.

Kingdon, John W. 1981. *Congressmen's voting decisions,* 2d ed. New York: Harper and Row.

Lowi, T. J. 1964. American business, public policy, case studies, and political theory. *World Politics* 16:677-715.

Pritchett, C. Herman. 1948. *The Roosevelt Court: A study of judicial votes and values.* New York: Macmillan.

Provine, Doris Marie. 1980. *Case selection in the United States Supreme Court.* Chicago: University of Chicago Press.

Segal, Jeffrey A. 1984. Predicting Supreme Court cases probabilistically: The search and seizure cases, 1962-1981. *American Political Science Review* 29:451-479.

Sheehan, Reginald S., and Donald R. Songer. 1989. Parties before the United States courts of appeals in the 1980's. Chicago: Midwest Political Science Association.

Songer, Donald R. 1982. Consensual and nonconsensual decisions in unanimous opinions of the United States courts of appeals. *American Journal of Political Science* 26:225-239.

———. 1987. The impact of the Supreme Court on trends in economic policy making in the United States courts of appeals. *Journal of Politics* 49:830-844.

———. 1988. Are the unpublished opinions of the courts of appeals legally trivial and politically insignificant? An empirical analysis. Atlanta: Southern Political Science Association.

Songer, Donald R., and Sue Davis. 1988. The impact of party and region on voting decisions in the United States courts of appeals, 1955-1986. Washington, D.C.: American Political Science Association.

Songer, Donald R., and Susan Reid. 1989. Policy change on the U.S. courts of appeals: Exploring the contribution of the legal and democratic subcultures. Paper presented at the annual meeting of the American Political Science Association, Atlanta.

Songer, Donald R., and Reginald S. Sheehan. 1990. Supreme Court impact on compliance and outcomes: *Miranda* and *New York Times* in the United States courts of appeals. *Western Political Quarterly,* forthcoming.

Tanenhaus, Joseph, Marvin Schick, Matthew Muraskin, and Daniel Rosen. 1963. The Supreme Court's certiorari jurisdiction: Cue theory. In *Judicial decision making*, ed. Glendon Schubert. New York: Free Press.

Ulmer, S. Sidney. 1972. The decision to grant certiorari as an indicator to decision "on the merits." *Polity* 4:429-448.

———. 1984. The Supreme Court's certiorari decisions: Conflict as a predictive variable. *American Political Science Review* 78:901-911.

Ulmer, S. Sidney, William Hintze, and Louise Kirklosky. 1972. The decision to grant or deny certiorari: Further consideration of cue theory. *Law and Society Review* 6:637-644.

Wasby, Stephen L. 1970. *The impact of the United States Supreme Court: Some perspectives.* Homewood, Ill.: Dorsey Press.

Wenner, Lettie McSpadden, and Lee E. Dutter. 1989. Contextual influences on court outcomes. *Western Political Quarterly* 41:113-134.

Wheeler, Stanton, Bliss Cartwright, Robert Kagan, and Lawrence Friedman. 1987. Do the "haves" come out ahead? Winning and losing in state supreme courts, 1870-1970. *Law and Society Review* 21:403-445.

3. THE FEDERAL DISTRICT COURTS

C. K. Rowland

Federal district courts are trial courts presided over by trial judges; as such, they enforce legal norms by resolving individual disputes. In many cases dispute resolution is largely administrative, as when trial judges facilitate out-of-court settlements. In others, it approximates the traditional, mechanical model of judicial norm enforcement—that is, the trial judge "finds" the law, "fits" the law to the facts, and rules in favor of the litigant whose facts fit the law.

But federal district courts do more than enforce norms promulgated by their legislative or judicial superiors. These trial courts are also policy-making institutions that allocate social value and privilege. When judges hear cases of first impression they establish precedent; in a common law system this is the essence of policy formulation. When opinions are codified and published they become policy statements; in a common law system these statements become the rules of the litigation game. When trial judges apply general statutes to individual cases they implement legislative policies. And when federal trial judges devise and supervise equitable remedies to correct or prevent legal harm, they often impose their own policy judgments on administrators and elected officials.

Judicial policy making in the federal trial courts assumes many overlapping forms. Many traditional distinctions, such as the difference between formulation and implementation, are obviated when the trial judge formulates specific policies in the process of implementing general legislative, administrative, or constitutional policies. Policy making in the federal trial courts can, however, be divided analytically into two functions—legal interpretation and equitable remediation—that parallel closely the traditional distinction between "law courts" and "equity courts" and require federal trial judges to involve themselves simultaneously in the formulation and implementation of public policy.

The overlap among legal interpretation, policy formulation, and policy implementation can be illustrated by reference to the model of judicial policy implementation developed by Charles Johnson and Bradley Canon. In the context of this model, federal district judges are part of the "interpreting population"—that is, the trial court "responds

to the policy decisions of a higher court . . . interprets the meaning of
the policy and develops the rules for matters not addressed in the
original decision. . . . Interpretations of lower courts are distinguished
from the interpretations of [others in the interpreting population] since
theirs are viewed as authoritative in a legal sense by others in the
political system" (1984, 16).

As part of the interpreting population district judges are key
components in the implementation process. However, when judges
interpret the law they are also formulating policy. Indeed, absent clear
legal guidelines, judges may actually *create* policy in the process of
implementing vague legal guidelines and fitting the facts of an instant
dispute to the interstices of extant law. When, for example, a federal
trial judge reaches a legal judgment in a case of first impression that
obesity is not a handicap covered by federal antidiscrimination statutes,
the judge is formulating policy to guide other judges and, more
importantly, potential litigants. Even when they are asked to resolve an
intensely personal dispute—for example, whether an unemancipated
minor is mature enough to have an abortion without notifying her
parents—their judgment becomes part of the common law and defines
maturity for potential litigants in that jurisdiction.

Thus, legal interpretations are judicial policy formulations, which
are important links in the chain of policy implementation. When trial
judges interpret the facts and law to mean that a legal harm has
occurred—that is, when they assign legal liability to one or more
parties to a dispute—they may be required to devise a legal remedy for
that harm. To do so, they must participate in the formulation and
implementation of equitable remediation policies designed to correct the
causes of that harm and prevent its recurrence. When, for example, a
federal district judge finds that a state's overcrowded prisons violate
prisoners' Eighth and Fourteenth Amendment rights, not only can the
judge order state officials to correct the overcrowding, he or she can
participate actively in the formulation and administration of policies
designed to correct this legal harm and prevent its recurrence.

Because equitable remediation involves district judges in the
supervision of elected officials, it involves judges directly in the highly
politicized, authoritative allocation of social value and privilege. When,
for example, a federal district judge orders busing to correct illegal
segregation, the judge is allocating social value just as surely as if he
were a legislator or school board member. Thus, equity judgments have
important implications, not only for judicial policy making but for the
intergovernmental policy process. As such they are important links
between the states and the federal government and between the
judiciary and other policy-making institutions.

Despite the useful legal distinction between interpretation and remediation, all forms of judicial policy making give individual district judges the discretion and power to exercise judicial judgment—"the act of determining, as in courts, what is comfortable to law and courts" (*Webster's* 1978). This responsibility is most apparent when judges interpret law and apply these rules to the facts of the case. However, it is equally characteristic of the formulation and implementation of remediation policies that require the judge to estimate the scope of legal harm, whether a proposed remedial decree is commensurate with that perceived harm, whether local officials exercise "good faith" in the remediation process, and a host of other determinations about "what is comfortable to law and courts."

This relationship between judicial discretion, judicial judgment, judicial outcomes, and public policy was encapsulated nicely in district judge C. J. Wyzanski's decision to remain on the trial bench and reject an offer of "promotion" to the appellate bench from Senator Saltonstall (R-Mass.) in 1959: "The district court gives more scope to a judge's initiative and discretion. The district judge so often has the last word. Even where he does not, heed is given to his estimates of credibility, his determination of the facts, his discretion in framing or denying relief upon the facts he found" (reprinted in Murphy and Pritchett 1979, 956-957).

Thus, to the extent facts and laws are ambiguous, federal trial judges' policies are the product of judicial judgment, even when the judges are "simply" evaluating facts, law, and the fit between the two. This is, after all, why we call them judges and why district judges perceive themselves as important policy makers.

The institutional capacity of district courts to authoritatively allocate social value and privilege and the discretion of individual district judges to shape these allocations has attracted substantial scholarly attention. In this chapter, I will evaluate the picture of district court policy making painted by this research. To do so I will first describe the legal parameters of judicial judgment defined by contemporary trial court jurisprudence. Then I will review recent and current research designed to identify the correlates and consequences of trial judges' policy judgments. I will conclude by criticizing the theoretical foundations of current research and calling for a paradigmatic shift from behavioral models of trial court outcomes to cognitive models of trial judges' policy judgments.

Contemporary District Court Jurisprudence

Although district judges exercise substantial discretion, they do so within boundaries defined by formal and informal legal constraints.

The quantity and quality of legal constraints on judicial judgment have varied over time in tandem with diachronic change in the parameters of American jurisprudence and, indirectly, American politics. Most recently, these constraints have been redefined by a shift in the balance between contractual and fiduciary definitions of legal rights and duties (Lieberman 1981). Under the contractual model, rights and duties were assigned contractually; as such they were assumed to be explicit and specific, and a judge should be able to "find" them by fitting relatively specific, explicit laws to individual disputes. That is, one has a right because a specific contractlike agreement exists between two or more parties. The right to Social Security payments or other entitlements upon meeting specific qualifications is an example of such a right. Under the fiduciary model, by contrast, rights are based on trust and confidence among the parties. Because they are established by vague standards of care and equally ill-defined standards of trust, they must be inferred from the fiduciary relationship between litigants or, more important, between the state and its citizens.

Fiduciary jurisprudence has been characterized by legislation (for example, that establishing the Occupational Safety and Health Administration) that assigns a standard of care rather than creates specific obligations and by judicial policies (such as constitutional standing) that create an ill-defined, fiduciary balance between rights and obligations, rather than specify this balance contractually. It has also been characterized by the delegation of substantial authority to federal trial judges to devise and supervise remedies for legal harms (for example, segregation by law) when public officials do not meet their fiduciary obligations.

A cause and a consequence of this shift toward fiduciary jurisprudence has been a dramatic increase in the "fact freedom" and "equity freedom" of judges who preside over disputes engendered by fiduciary ambiguity. Examples of the judicial discretion inherent in fiduciary jurisprudence on federal trial courts could be drawn from cases having to do with the environment (Wenner 1982), prison reform (Taggart 1989), abortion policy (Rubin 1987), and a variety of other policy arenas. But whatever the policy arena, the effect of fiduciary jurisprudence on legal interpretation and equitable remediation is the same. Because it responds to ill-defined rights and obligations that cannot be fit mechanically to individual disputes or narrow dispute categories, fiduciary jurisprudence inevitably assigns federal judges tremendous discretion to infer the contractual specificity omitted by their legislative and judicial superiors. Thus, as an ironic parallel to the evolution of fiduciary rights and duties, we have in the federal courts an analogous change in the responsibility of federal judges to specify the authoritative allocation of value and privilege.

Nowhere have the causes and consequences of fiduciary jurisprudence been more apparent than in the federal trial courts. Its effects are perhaps most obvious in the quantity of litigation (Posner 1985). In 1960, 79,200 cases were filed in the federal district courts; in 1983, 277,031 cases were filed. The increase in twenty-three years was more than 350 percent; moreover, the increase of 198,000 cases was almost three times the increase recorded for the previous 171 years! However, changes in the quality of litigation have been even more dramatic. For example, of the new filings in 1960, only 306 were classified by the Federal Judicial Center as civil rights cases. By 1983, 19,735 civil rights cases were filed, an increase of more than 6,000 percent!

Changes in the quantity and quality of litigation indicate an increase in the district courts' policy-making responsibilities. But what about appellate review? Given their position at the bottom of the federal judicial hierarchy, one might argue that, even when their policy-making *responsibilities* are maximized, the policy-making *powers* of federal trial judges are constrained by the power of appellate courts to reverse their judgments. To some degree this is true. Certainly the legal judgments of appellate courts and the prospect of appellate review constrain the interpretative and remedial discretion of trial judges. However, these institutional constraints are mitigated by several factors

First, only about 20 percent of contested district court judgments are appealed (Howard 1981) Second, most appeals are unsuccessful, and, as anticipated by the expanded fact freedom inherent in the evolution of fiduciary jurisprudence, the reversal rate is declining. For example, the reversal rate in 1960 was almost 25 percent; by 1983 it had declined to less than 16 percent (Todd 1989). In combination, the low rates of appeal and reversal ensure that less than 5 percent of the district courts' contested judgments will be reversed on appeal (.16 x .20 = .03). Finally, even when judicial superiors reverse trial judges' decisions, these reversals impose no sanctions on the district judge. Indeed, for some trial judges controversial reversals may become badges of distinction (Posner 1985).

It should be noted that rates of appeal and reversal are higher for some litigation categories than for others. Remedial decrees, for example, are routinely appealed (Cooper 1988). And rates of appeal and reversal vary substantially among circuits and among dispute categories within circuits (Howard 1981). Nonetheless, the surprisingly low rates of appeal and reversal suggest that the relative independence inherent in fiduciary jurisprudence is hardly vitiated by the threat of appellate review. This suggestion is buttressed by the response of a noted federal trial judge to this writer's question about the susceptibility of district judges' factual judgments to appellate review:

> The power [of the trial judge] is maximized when the outcome hinges on questions of fact. The judge can rely on those facts that persuade him and explain his decision in light of those facts. Legal truth, like beauty, is in the eye of the beholder. If there is an evidentiary basis for the judge's interpretation of the facts, this interpretation, unlike interpretations of law, is virtually immune from appellate review. (Motley 1986)

To point out that fiduciary jurisprudence makes the federal district courts important policy-making institutions and increases the policy-making discretion of individual district judges is not to argue that these courts are necessarily the most *appropriate* policy-making institutions or that district judges are always competent policy makers. Indeed, many sociolegal scholars argue that contemporary jurisprudence has "politicized" the federal courts, that the scope of policy making by trial judges far exceeds the judicial role envisioned by the Constitution (Glazer 1978; Feeley 1989), and that courts often lack the capacity and judges the competence to fulfill the obligations inherent in fiduciary jurisprudence (Horowitz 1977; Feeley 1989; but see Wasby 1981).

Normative criticisms of political jurisprudence have important implications for all levels of the federal judiciary and for the larger political system. However, although the debates over activism and competence are fueled by empirical *evidence* of judicial policy making, I would argue that such criticisms are largely irrelevant for the empirical *study* of policy making in the district courts. District judges do not initiate cases of first impression. They do not travel their districts looking for overcrowded prisons. They do not write the ambiguous statutes they must interpret. Rather, as federal judicial officials in a local setting they are *required* to resolve controversial disputes between local majoritarian values and national, constitutional values. Thus, for those who study the federal trial courts as highly politicized policy-making institutions, the immediate task is not to decide whether federal trial judges *should* do what they are doing, but to understand the politicization of policy making within the legal parameters defined by fiduciary jurisprudence. Fortunately, political scientists and others interested in understanding public policy have devoted substantial attention to these courts as policy-making institutions and to the influence of the political subculture on district judges' fiduciary policy judgments.

Extralegal Correlates
of Federal Trial Judges' Policy Judgments

The seminal study of federal trial courts as political institutions was Jack W. Peltason's *Federal Courts in the Political Process* (1955). Working from the pluralist perspective that dominated political studies at the time, Peltason rejected the legal fiction that federal judges, including district judges, simply enforce norms promulgated from above. His observation that trial judges, like other political actors, "had to choose between conflicting interests" (p. 15) attracted political scientists and other sociolegal scholars to the study of federal trial courts as political, policy-making institutions. The resultant scholarship has tended to focus on the relative and interactive influence of the legal and political subcultures on trial judges (Richardson and Vines 1970). Although these studies span more than thirty years, all are the product of political scientists' desire to understand the unique influence of the political subculture on federal judicial institutions presided over by judges who are the political products of that subculture. A complete review of this work is beyond the scope of a single chapter; however, its flavor can be gleaned from a brief survey of two sets of exemplar studies. The first focuses primarily on the effects of the local and national political environments on judicial selection and judges' subsequent interpretations of ambiguous facts and laws. The second focuses on a nascent research program concerned primarily with the interactive effects of local legal and political environments and judges' formulation and administration of equitable remediation.

Environmental Effects on Legal Interpretation

Much of the early work on environmental effects focused on relatively specific policy questions evoked by unique local environments. An important example is Kenneth M. Dolbeare's (1969) finding that variation in the judicial agendas of urban federal trial courts was positively correlated with variation in local political environments and the agendas of local political institutions.

More typical were studies of the nexus between local subcultures and judicial implementation of desegregation and other civil rights policies (Peltason 1961; Vines 1964; Giles and Walker 1975). These studies found that desegregation was correlated with local environments and the ties of presiding judges to those environments. For example, Micheal W. Giles and Thomas Walker found that desegregation in southern school districts was correlated with the size of the district, the size of the district's black population, whether the district court was located within the school district's boundaries, and whether the judge presiding over the desegregation effort had been educated outside of the South.

During the Vietnam era scholarly attention shifted to the influence of spatial and temporal environments on the conviction and sentencing of draft resisters (Cook 1973; Kritzer 1978). Researchers found significant correlations between temporal and spatial variation in public support for the war and the severity of sentences imposed upon resisters.

Most recently, work on environmental effects has been extended to topical policy categories and to legal environments defined explicitly by political jurisdiction. This effort is best exemplified by Lettie M. Wenner and Lee E. Dutter's (1988) study of differences among circuits in federal district judges' support for environmental regulation. They found, as anticipated by previous work, that support for environmental regulation varied significantly among circuits and that the level of judicial support coincided with the level of legislative support by members of Congress from states in that circuit. This led them to conclude that district judges, like legislators, were responsive to the political context of environmental disputes.

Politicized Judicial Appointments

A second research path focuses on the relative influence of legal and political subcultures in the selection of district judges and the link between politicized selection criteria and policy making in the federal trial courts. Studies of judicial selection are unanimous in their conclusion that, despite the role of home state senators in identifying candidates for judicial vacancies and the role of the Senate Judiciary Committee in screening nominees, the appointment of district judges is primarily a presidential prerogative. Therefore, virtually all such studies are organized by presidential administration.

One approach to the study of judicial selection is qualitative and somewhat historical. As exemplified by Neil McFeeley's study of the Johnson administration (1987), this approach uses interviews with participants and original sources available in presidential libraries to delineate the procedures and selection criteria that define a president's appointment strategy. This qualitative methodology enables researchers to describe in detail the criteria and strategies, such as negotiations with home state senators, surrounding individual appointments.

Other scholars have focused their efforts on judicial recruitment by sitting presidents and supplemented qualitative descriptions of recruitment strategies with quantified descriptions of the judicial and political backgrounds of that president's judicial recruits. This work is best exemplified by the ongoing endeavors of Sheldon Goldman (1989).

Goldman's work on judicial recruitment during the Reagan administration is valuable, among other reasons, because it documents the unprecedented success of Attorney General Edwin Meese and the Justice Department's Office of Legal Policy in reconstructing the partisan and ideological balance of the lower federal courts.

An important recent addition to the study of judicial recruitment is Elliot Slotnick's (1988) review of research in this area. In addition to summarizing his own work on the Carter administration, Slotnick has synthesized recent work, including Goldman's, and placed it in a perspective that helps us understand the historical relationship between jurisprudence and the politics of recruitment. Slotnick's compilation reinforces the conclusions of others that, with few exceptions, presidents appoint judges who share the president's party affiliation, judicial philosophy, and basic policy predilections. Moreover, his perspective makes it clear that the importance of these extralegal appointment criteria is increasing in tandem with the evolution of fiduciary jurisprudence:

> Presidents Carter and Reagan have enjoyed unique opportunities to re-make the lower federal bench.... Both presidents treated their lower court judicial selection responsibilities as primary domestic policy making opportunities, and both presidents generated public controversy over the clear ideological bent in their appointments. (1988, 318)

The obvious question implicit in these findings is whether presidents' partisan, ideological appointment criteria are reflected in their appointees' subsequent policy judgments. A predictable proliferation of research has examined this link by comparing the published opinions of cohorts appointed under the same president.

Appointment Effects in Legal Interpretation

Using as its data source published judgments, which are assumed to be policy formulations that explain and defend the exercise of judicial discretion (Carp and Rowland 1983; Dolbeare 1969), this work finds a strong, consistent link between politicized appointment criteria and appointment cohorts' subsequent policy judgments.[1] Moreover, this link has grown stronger as extralegal policy predilections have become more important appointment criteria and fiduciary jurisprudence has increased judicial discretion.

For example, Robert Carp and I looked at more than 25,000 opinions published by district judges between 1936 and 1977 (Carp and Rowland 1983). We found that judgment differences among presidential appointment cohorts were relatively small and insignificant before 1968, but that their growth after the inauguration of President

Nixon and the appointment of Chief Justice Burger was dramatic. Johnson and Kennedy appointees were much more supportive of economic regulation, civil rights, civil liberties, and the rights of the accused than were Nixon appointees. Moreover, the Johnson cohort was much more supportive of civil rights than was the Kennedy cohort, a difference that reflects the inordinate influence of Senator Eastland, the segregationist chairman of the Senate Judiciary Committee, over Kennedy's trial court appointments in the South (Navasky 1974).

Given the continued growth of fiduciary jurisprudence and the increased politicization of judicial appointment during the Carter and Reagan administrations, it is hardly surprising that the polarization of policy judgments between these two appointment cohorts is significantly greater than the differences among previous presidential appointment cohorts. Separate studies found Carter appointees twice as likely as Reagan appointees to support the claims of criminal defendants (Rowland, Carp, and Songer 1988) or civil rights claims (Stidham and Carp 1987). Moreover, as with the Kennedy and Johnson cohorts, these differences are much more pronounced in the South than in the North.

The research depicts a consistent pattern of fiduciary judgments shaped by the decision-making environment, politicized judicial recruitment, and the judicial policy propensities selected in that recruitment process. The importance of appointing presidents and presidential appointment criteria is buttressed by evidence of consistency within appointment cohorts. For example, President Carter's black and female appointees were not significantly more supportive of civil rights claims than were his white male appointees (Walker and Barrow 1985). And the judgments of Carter appointees recruited by selection commissions were indistinguishable from the judgments of his more traditional recruits (Todd 1985). It is, however, a picture painted with broad strokes. As such, it leaves unanswered many interstitial questions about the interactive influence of the legal and political subcultures on district judges' interpretations of laws and facts. Current research that expands and refines this picture continues to focus primarily on the causes and consequences of politicized recruitment.

Current Research on Recruitment

Researchers are adding to our understanding of recruitment politics by exploring details not addressed by previous research. Particularly interesting, and somewhat ironic, is Christopher Smith's work on the recruitment of federal magistrates *by* federal district judges (1987, 1989). Noting that the quantity and quality of magistrates' responsibilities are expanding rapidly, Smith outlines the important role of district judges in recruiting magistrates and in creating their job descriptions. He does so by delineating district-by-district variation in selection criteria, the recruitment process, and in the quantity and quality of judicial responsibility assigned to magistrates. Although Smith's research program is relatively new, its significance increases in tandem with the responsibilities of magistrates.

My own work carries the examination of recruitment in another direction. Most studies of judicial selection ignore questions about the home state recruitment of candidates for district court vacancies. Who is responsible for selecting the candidates for presidential consideration? What are the legal and political criteria that guide this recruitment process? Are home state recruiters guided by their own political and legal priorities, or are they deferential to perceived presidential preferences? I have addressed these and other questions by interviewing senate staffers and others with responsibility for home state judicial recruitment during the Reagan administration. Although the work is incomplete, initial analysis indicates that substantial variation exists in the degree to which senators consider the selection of district judges a presidential or a senatorial prerogative and the degree to which senators rely on policy predilections as recruitment criteria. Furthermore, the involvement of other organizations, such as local bar associations, from the legal subculture varies idiosyncratically from state to state. The extent to which this variation in criteria and procedures affects the link between selection and policy making remains a topic for future research.

Current Research on Appointment Effects

Another current of ongoing research concentrates on comparisons between the Carter and Reagan appointees' policy judgments, but refines our understanding of these differences by using the new computerized legal information sources (such as Westlaw, Lexis) to go beyond the broad policy categories (such as civil rights) looked at by previous research and focus on relatively specific, highly politicized dispute categories (such as abortion). Although this work builds on previous findings, it also expands previous efforts in two important ways. First, it is much more attentive to legal constraints and the qualitative interaction between legal and extralegal influences. Second, several of these studies pay careful attention not only to political links but to nonpolitical background characteristics, such as religion, that are theoretically linked to the category of disputes under investigation.

Steve Alumbaugh (forthcoming) compared the effects of appointing president and religion on district judges' support for abortion rights. He found, as anticipated by the Republican platform's criticism of *Roe v. Wade*, that the Carter appointment cohort was more supportive of abortion rights than was the Reagan cohort; in fact, Carter appointees ruled in favor of abortion rights 88 percent of the time while Reagan appointees supported such claims only 23 percent of the time. However, he also found that Carter's Catholic appointees were substantially less supportive of these rights than were his Protestant appointees.

Robert Dudley (1989) isolated district judges' obscenity decisions and examined the relative effects of appointing president and religion on these judgments. He found, among other things, that Johnson appointees were much less likely than Nixon appointees to place allegedly obscene materials outside the protection of the First Amendment, but that Catholics in both appointment cohorts were less supportive of this form of expression than were Protestants.

The persistent link between politicized appointment and judgments in a variety of relatively specific dispute categories raises an interesting question about selection effects on disputants' pretrial judgments. To what extent do appointment politics influence indirectly the decisions of attorneys and their clients to settle or litigate disputes? Bridget Todd and I are currently addressing this question in the Western District of Missouri (Kansas City) by drawing a sample of cases from the docket book and asking the attorneys of record to re-create their decisions to settle or litigate specific cases. Although our analysis is incomplete, findings to this point suggest that attorneys' settlement judgments are extremely sensitive to their perceptions of the presiding judge's personal stare decisis and that, for many types of cases, these perceived predilections parallel closely the extralegal criteria that secured the judge's appointment. For example, defendants in civil rights cases are prone to settle when their case is to be tried by one of the three Carter appointees in this district. Thus it appears that presidential appointment effects extend not only to judicial policy judgments but to attorney/client judgments in the shadow of the law as well.

Exceptions to Appointment Effects on Legal Interpretation

Although most work on appointment effects depicts a highly politicized jurisprudence, an interesting subset of studies has identified three important exceptions to this pattern. First, when appropriate legal variables are included in models of legal interpretation they sometimes displace political predictors. An important example of this exception is Charles Johnson's (1987) examination of the congruence between Supreme Court policy formulation and the implementation of these policies by the lower federal courts. To measure this congruence Johnson combined legal (such as specificity of Supreme Court guidelines) and political (such as trial judge's political party) variables in a statistical model of trial (and appellate) judges' responsiveness to Supreme Court precedent. He found that judges at both levels are more responsive to legal than political cues; however, the explanatory power of cues from the legal *and* political subcultures is substantially greater for district courts than for courts of appeals.

The second exception to the pattern of politicized policy judgments is limited to noncontroversial policy categories. Specific examples of this exception include Ronald Stidham and Robert Carp's study of labor and economic regulation judgments (1987) and the exploration of voting rights judgments by Rowland, Carp, and Todd (*Washington Post* 1989). Both studies find that for these relatively settled, unambiguous policy categories differences between Reagan and Carter appointees are trivial and statistically insignificant. But the most interesting exception to the pattern of appointment effects was identified by Craig R. Ducat and Robert L. Dudley (1989). They found that the "two presidencies" thesis extended to appointment effects on district judges—that is, although federal trial judges are much more supportive of *domestic* policy initiatives from their appointing president than from other presidents, these appointment-based disparities do not extend to *foreign* or *military* policy initiatives. Thus, district judges, like members of Congress and Supreme Court justices, are much more deferential to presidential prerogatives when the president is acting as chief of state or commander-in-chief.

A final exception to the link between appointment politics and district judges' decisions has been identified by Bridget Todd (1989). Responding to the fact that extant research has been based entirely upon published opinions, which are assumed to exclude the courts' routine, norm enforcement decisions, Todd has looked at the effects of presidential appointment and unspecified environmental influences on unpublished decisions in the Detroit, Houston, and Kansas City district courts. Her analysis is in progress, but interim results suggest that, although patterns of support for civil litigants vary significantly *among* the three courts, differences among presidential appointment cohorts *within* each court are small and statistically insignificant. These results lead her to conclude that appointment effects did not extend to the routine, unambiguous judgments that did not need to be explained and codified.

Theory-based Explanations of Extralegal Effects

To explain the aggregate patterns of politicized jurisprudence, and the exceptions to these patterns, one must fit these aggregate research findings to theories of individual judicial behavior. Most of the work summarized above has been guided, explicitly or implicitly, by adaptations of preference-based, psychometric models of appellate judicial "votes" to the behavior of federal trial judges (Kritzer 1978; Rowland and Carp 1983). Adopted from the social psychological theories that dominated the study of political behavior during the 1960s and 1970s, these models rest explicitly on the axiomatic assumption that political actors, including judges, are motivated primarily by their personal beliefs: "There is, according to the [psychometric] model, complete isomorphism between the configuration of ideal points in the psychological space and the belief systems of the justices that *motivate* their voting in Supreme Court decisions" (Schubert 1975, 18; emphasis added).

James Gibson (1983) succinctly generalized this model to all levels of the federal judiciary: "Judges' decisions are a function of what they prefer to do, tempered by what they think they ought to do, but constrained by what they perceive is feasible to do" (p. 9). Thus trial judges, like their appellate colleagues, are motivated primarily by personal policy preferences. Legal norms and the law are relegated to secondary and tertiary constraints on these preferences.

In trial court settings it is difficult to test preference-based models. Unlike the values of appellate judges on collegial courts, trial judges' preferences cannot be inferred from different responses to the same stimuli. But they can be inferred when, for example, presidential appointment cohorts respond differently to similar legal stimuli. Thus, trial court adaptations of psychometric models interpret differences among judges from different political subcultures as aggregate evidence that federal trial judges, like other political actors motivated by their policy preferences, impose these preferences on disputes when the imposition can be accommodated by the norms of the judicial role and the ambiguity of factual and legal stimuli. The absence of extralegal effects is assumed axiomatically to indicate the presence of secondary and tertiary legal constraints that negate these preferences.

The Legalistic Process of Judicial Remediation

Social scientists in general and political scientists in particular have devoted much less attention to equitable remediation than to the politics of legal interpretation. Moreover, as noted in the introduction, much of the scholarly attention to remediation has been rather polemical, using case studies to focus on the normative question of whether fiduciary remediation is properly within the bounds of the judicial role, or to ask whether the resources and competence of trial judges qualify them to formulate, promulgate, and implement such decrees. Most exceptions to these evaluative case studies have focused not on the process of remediation but on the impact of controversial decrees on target populations and other policy makers (Johnson and Canon 1984; Bullock and Lamb 1984; Rosenbloom 1987; Taggart 1989; Feeley 1989).

Given the fiduciary discretion inherent in equitable remediation, the dearth of systematic social scientific attention to the judicial formulation and implementation of remediation policies is surprising and unfortunate. Most of what we know about remediation per se must be gleaned from impact studies. For example, although it is primarily a study of the impact of a district judge's decrees and the legal and political conflicts between the judge and state and local officials, Anthony Champagne's study (1983) of the Dallas (Texas) County jail reform also paints a rather vivid picture of the remediation process and the political, social, and legal cross-pressures that shape that process. Fortunately, however, recent work by Phillip Cooper (1988) has initiated systematic comparative inquiry that promises to tell us a great deal about the formulation and implementation of remedial decrees by district judges.

Cooper's work parallels traditional legal approaches in that it focuses on the policy-making process from the judge's perspective, asking "what a judge saw at the time of the decision, what options were available to the decision maker, and what forces constrained the judge's choice among options" (1988, 18). To understand the judge's perspective Cooper relies primarily on qualitative, textual analysis of judicial opinions and briefs, and secondarily on newspaper accounts and interviews with attorneys and other observers of the process. However, two important aspects of Cooper's work are unique. First, rather than rely on individual case studies, he systematically compares five remediation cases. Second, to facilitate this comparison, he develops a "decree-litigation" model that conceptualizes the diachronic nexus between remediation and the legal and political subcultures.

According to Cooper's legal-decree model, the remediation process is characterized by four stages: an action that triggers litigation, a judicial response in which the judge must assess liability, the formulation and implementation of a remedy, and the refinement or abandonment of that remedy. Each of these steps is fraught with opportunities for judges to impose their personal policy preferences on policy judgments. Which expert witness was qualified to estimate the educational impact of proposed policies? What scope of remediation would be commensurate with the perceived scope of legal harm? Would local policy makers exercise good faith?

Yet Cooper rejects emphatically the notion that the judges were actively imposing their own policy preferences on legal disputes:

The notion that the controversial remedial decree cases are simply manifestations of a liberal federal judiciary intent upon playing guardian . . . simply does not withstand empirical analysis . . . this study indicates that the judges in these cases were by and large more defensive in approach, more interested in resolving cases than reforming the ills of American society. (1988, 328)

Cooper's conclusions seem at first blush to contradict explicitly the findings and conclusions of most research summarized in this chapter. His cases epitomize fiduciary jurisprudence. Most are rooted in politicized policy disputes. All require district judges to make a series of highly politicized policy judgments. Yet he finds little or none of the "activism" usually associated with political jurisprudence.

How do we reconcile Cooper's conclusions with the aggregate evidence that district judges' policy judgments are highly politicized? To some degree his findings may be an artifact of his methods; certainly, if one relies on secondary sources of legal documentation to recreate the remediation process from the judge's perspective, one is unlikely to discover a highly politicized process. Likewise, Cooper's commitment to the judge's perspective eliminates important variables, such as the preferences of significant others in the political subculture (Johnson and Canon 1984), which might lead to different conclusions. These criticisms notwithstanding, I think the stark contrast between Cooper's picture of the remediation process and the picture of interpretive outcomes painted by most social scientific research is indicative of a fundamental anomaly that must be resolved if we are to move beyond the quasi-journalistic accumulation of information and increase significantly our understanding of policy making in the federal district courts.[2]

Where We Need to Go

At this point one is always tempted to conclude by extolling the virtues of extant research programs (especially one's own) and calling for incremental advances in these efforts. Certainly there is much to praise in the accumulation of information about the district courts' policy-making function and district judges' politicized policy judgments over the last twenty years. And future research *should* extend these research programs incrementally to new questions engendered by changes (for example, the election of President Bush) in the legal and political subcultures. However, if future research is to be more than a quasi-journalistic chronicle of incremental changes, it must first address more fundamental questions about the nexus between appointment politics and political jurisprudence. Therefore, I conclude this chapter with a critical look at some theoretical and methodological shortcomings of current research programs and a proposal for fundamental, paradigmatic changes designed to overcome these limitations.

The shortcomings of current research are manifest in the persistent anomaly between quantitative evidence that district judges' policy judgments are driven by their personal policy preferences and qualitative evidence that trial judges do *not* consciously impose their personal preferences on the resolution of legal disputes. Moreover, this anomaly is symptomatic of a more fundamental failure to synthesize quantitative and qualitative research and focus our attention on the fundamental question that must be resolved if we are to move beyond the quasi-journalistic accumulation of information to an enhanced understanding of politics and policy making in the federal district courts: How do trial judges bound by the legalistic norms of judicial procedure consistently transform legal information into politicized policy judgments?

Why have we not come to grips with this question? I believe that the answer may be traced to the fact that the extant research programs are bifurcated by theoretical and methodological differences that derive from irreconcilable assumptions about the individual judicial behaviors that produce trial judges' policy judgments. Traditional qualitative approaches assume implicitly that trial judges are motivated by an ill-defined justice motive and that this legal motive overrides any temptation to impose personal preferences on legal disputes; as a result, traditionalists cannot accommodate quantitative evidence that judicial judgments are influenced by extralegal environments and judges' personal policy preferences. Quantitative approaches, derived from behavioral theories of appellate judges' behavior, assume axiomatically that judges are motivated primarily by their personal policy preferences; as a result, behaviorists cannot accept qualitative evidence that judges' politicized judgments are not necessarily motivated by the judges' politicized personal preferences.

The inability of either research paradigm to accommodate the other's findings and the roots of this failure in irreconcilable, axiomatic assumptions about the motivational foundations of judicial behaviors elucidates implicitly the major barrier to understanding policy making in the federal district courts. The traditional and behavioral paradigms are bifurcated and irreconcilable because neither is grounded in a viable theory of human behavior that accommodates parallel evidence of a legalistic judgment process *and* evidence of highly politicized judicial judgments.

As political scientists we can respond to the theoretical lacuna that plagues current research in one of two ways. The easy path would be to continue down the bifurcated path by committing ourselves to the development of preference-based adaptations of psychometric models and denigrating the findings of Cooper and other students of remediation as the product of a naive legal paradigm that accepts legal argumentation at face value. The temptation to follow this path is great. Certainly the assumptions of traditional methods cannot be reconciled with mounting evidence of politicized trial judgments. And the contributions of psychometric models to the study of policy making in appellate courts is impressive.

But to follow this path of least resistance is to leave intact the deleterious theoretical, methodological, and empirical bifurcation that burdens current research. Moreover, it would leave us committed axiomatically to unvalidated, indeed naive, assumptions about judicial behavior. Why should we be constrained by the assumption that all trial judges have the same motives? Why should we be saddled with the assumption that the same judge is always driven by the same motive?

These assumptions are contrary to what we know about human motives in other judgment settings (Arkes and Hammond 1986) and to self-reported differences in trial judges' perceptions of their role (Sarat 1977; Carp and Wheeler 1972). Moreover, if we accept them uncritically we can never resolve the anomalies that plague current research. Therefore, if we are to understand how legal procedures engender political outcomes, we must abandon extant models and develop a theoretical framework that obviates unvalidated assumptions about judges' motivations, takes seriously the cognitive process of human judgment, and encourages qualitative attention to the informational foundations of fiduciary jurisprudence. Models derived from this framework must conceptualize judgment as a cognitive process by which judges, whatever their motives, rely on perception, memory, and inference to interpret imperfect, ambiguous information and transform this information into acceptable decision criteria. The development of this framework is well beyond the scope of this chapter. Fortunately, however, the conceptual foundation for such a framework can be gleaned from cognate social psychological theories of social cognition and social judgment.

A Cognitive Conceptualization of Judicial Judgment

Although social cognition is not itself a theory, it has become a dominant approach to the social psychological study of social judgments—that is, judgments in which the judge has little personal stake. Its fundamental assumption, derived from basic research on human cognition (Glass and Holyoke 1986), is that all humans, even those who wear robes and are called "your honor," are cognitively limited thinkers with quite limited information processing capabilities but quite capacious long-term memory capacities (Fiske and Taylor 1984; Lau and

Sears 1988). These cognitive limitations force them to become "cognitive misers." When asked to judge on the basis of information that is unmanageably complex or ambiguous, cognitive misers rely on experience-based perception, memory, and inference as cognitive shortcuts to transform that information into mental representations that serve as manageable, acceptable decision criteria.

When making policy, judges may act as cognitive misers by responding not to objective decision criteria but to the subjective criteria created by their own judgment process. Most important for our purposes, "For the cognitively limited, [judgment] errors and biases stem from inherent features of the cognitive system, not necessarily from motivations . . . the role of motivation has vanished almost entirely from the cognitive miser model" (Fiske and Linville 1980, 120).

If the role of motivation has virtually vanished from the model of human judges as cognitive misers, how can such models account for the politicized pattern of policy judgments identified by quantitative research? The hypothetical answer lies in the influence of experience-based mental structures—usually referred to as social schemata or psychological anchors—on the processing and evaluation of imperfect information. These mental structures are conceptualized as *unconscious* cognitive representations of organized prior knowledge, abstracted from experience with specific instances, that determine "whether information is processed or ignored, how information is encoded and retrieved from memory, perceived and evaluated" (Taylor and Crocker 1981). Functionally, they enable cognitive misers to process new information and incorporate it into working memory by filtering estimates of missing or ambiguous information through the judge's experience and existing knowledge (Conover and Feldman 1984).

Thus, regardless of their motives, to the extent that judges have different legal and political experiences—the kind of differences that distinguish presidential appointment cohorts and extralegal environments—they will often see similar evidence differently, remember evidence that fits their relevant mental constructs more vividly and accurately than evidence that does not, and interpret ambiguous information in ways consistent with their schematic predilections. More important, because cognitive misers must rely on long-term memory to represent imperfect information, no contradiction exists between a neutral, legalistic processing of ambiguous legal information and a cognitive representation of that information that leads to highly politicized judgment outcomes. Thus, given this conceptualization of unmotivated human judgment, no anomaly exists between an apolitical judgment process and what appears to be highly politicized responses to the evidence as perceived, remembered, and interpreted.

The extension of general social cognition concepts to judicial settings is straightforward; indeed, the most influential contemporary work on juror behavior is guided by models of jurors as cognitive misers (Hastie, Penrod, and Pennington 1983). But, as Herbert Simon reminds students of economic choice, the study of judgment as a cognitive process will be characterized by the tedium of molecular biology rather than the elegance of physics (Simon 1986). Thus, the development and implementation of such models in trial court settings will be challenging. It will require innovative methodologies that combine quantitative, qualitative, and, ultimately, experimental approaches to specify the informational and cognitive determinants of the process by which trial judges transform ambiguous legal information into politicized judicial policies. Nonetheless, if judicial policies are the products of judicial judgment and judgment is a cognitive process, we must understand judicial cognition if we are to understand policy making in the federal trial courts and the policy judgments of federal trial judges.

Notes

1. At the trial court level, published opinions are the exception, not the rule. Indeed, less than 5 percent of federal trial judges' opinions are published. Thus, we cannot treat these published decisions as an unbiased sample and generalize from them to the universe of decisions. On the other hand, codification and publication are indicative of "law creation" (Posner 1985) or policy making (Carp and Rowland 1983), which makes them important indicators of jurisprudential change and ideal subjects for the influence of presidential appointment on individual policy judgments and the evolution of jurisprudence (Dolbeare 1969).
2. How does one explain these anomalies? The temptation is great to respond that remediation and legal interpretation, like courts of law and courts of equality, serve disparate legal functions; thus it is not surprising that one is linked to the political system more strongly than the other. It is also tempting to argue from the assumptions of the psychometric model that remediation policies, like certain categories of policy judgments, are not politicized because they do not afford district judges the discretion to impose their personal policy preferences on remedial disputes. Unfortunately, however, neither of these arguments holds up under close scrutiny. Although equitable remediation and legal interpretation may be distinguished analytically, each requires multiple policy judgments by the presiding judge. Moreover, equity judgments typically offer the trial judge *more* discretion than do questions of legal interpretation. Thus, one would expect to find individual examples of aggregate politicization in the remediation process.

A more persuasive argument can be made that the differences are simply methodological artifacts. At first blush this argument is not without merit. No matter how rigorous the research design, no matter how diligent the researcher, a qualitative focus on remediation from the judge's perspective is unlikely to reveal extralegal motives contrary to the norms of trial judging. Indeed, the reliance on legal documents, such as opinions and briefs, ensures that findings will be framed by the judicious language of legal interpretation. By contrast, a quantitative focus on aggregates of highly politicized policy judgments maximizes the probability that one would find aggregate disparities between presidential appointment cohorts.

Perhaps, then, these anomalous conclusions would be reconciled if each program were to incorporate the other's methods. Again, there is merit to this suggestion. It is certainly true, for example, that remediation studies should supplement their traditional textual analysis with rigorous, quantitative content analysis (Segal and Cover 1989; Gates 1987). It is also true that aggregate quantitative studies should utilize textual analysis of legal documents to estimate ambiguity of legal disputes. On reflection, however, it is clear that these anomalies are more than methodological artifacts. Assume that every aggregate study included qualitative attention to the legal process of remediation; assume, moreover, that this approach revealed no explicit evidence of extralegal motivation. The aggregate evidence of political jurisprudence would remain. Or assume that students of remediation aggregated judgment points across cases and found evidence that appointees of different presidents interpreted similar disputes differently, we would still be without evidence of the assumed motives that explain the aggregate differences identified by quantitative research.

Thus, we are left with a classic anomaly in which the dominate research paradigm cannot accommodate evidence contrary to its fundamental, axiomatic assumption—that is, absent individual decisions motivated by personal policy preferences, how can the legalistic judgment process described by Cooper engender the politicized policy outcomes identified by aggregate studies of judicial policy making?

References

Alumbaugh, Steve, and C. K. Rowland. n.d. Federal district judges' abortion judgments. *Judicature,* forthcoming.

Arkes, Hal R., and Kenneth R. Hammond, eds. 1986. *Judgment and decision making.* New York: Cambridge University Press.

Bullock, Charles S. III, and Charles S. Lamb, eds. 1984. *Implementation of civil rights policy.* Monterey, Calif.: Brooks-Cole.

Carp, Robert A., and C. K. Rowland. 1983. *Politics and policy making in the federal district courts.* Knoxville: University of Tennessee Press.

Carp, Robert A., and Russell Wheeler. 1972. Sink or swim: The socialization of a federal district judge. *Journal of Public Law* 21:359-390.

Cavanagh, Ralph, and Austin Sarat. 1980. Thinking about courts: Toward and beyond a jurisprudence of judicial competence. *Law and Society Review* 14:371-420.

Champagne, Anthony. 1983. The theory of limited judicial impact: Reforming the Dallas County jail as a case study. In *The political science of criminal justice*, ed. S. Nagel and E. Fairchild. Springfield, Ill.: C. C. Thomas.

Conover, Pamela S., and Stanley Feldman. 1984. How people organize the political world: A schematic model. *American Journal of Political Science* 28:95-126.

Cook, Beverly B. 1973. Sentencing behavior of federal judges: Draft cases, 1972. *Cincinnati Law Review* 42:597-633.

Cooper, Phillip. 1988. *Hard judicial choices*. New York: Oxford University Press.

Dolbeare, Kenneth M. 1969. The federal district courts and urban public policy: An exploratory study (1960-67). In *Frontiers of judicial research*, ed. J. Grossman and J. Tanenhaus. New York: Wiley.

Ducat, Craig R., and Robert L. Dudley. 1989. Federal district judges and presidential power. *Journal of Politics* 51:98-118.

Dudley, Robert L. 1989. Lower court decision-making in pornography cases: Do we know it when we see it? Paper presented at the annual meeting of the Midwest Political Science Association, Chicago.

Feeley, Malcolm M. 1989. The significance of prison condition cases: Budgets and regions. *Law and Society Review* 23:273-282.

Fiske, Susan, and Patricia Linville. 1980. What does the schema concept buy us? *Personality Bulletin* 6:543-561.

Fiske, Susan, and Shelley Taylor. 1984. *Social cognition*. New York: Addison-Wesley.

Gates, John B. 1987. Partisan realignment, unconstitutional state policies, and the U.S. Supreme Court, 1837-1964. *American Journal of Political Science* 31:259-280.

Gibson, James. 1983. From simplicity to complexity: The development of theory in the study of judicial behavior. *Political Behavior* 5:7-49.

Giles, Micheal W., and Thomas Walker. 1975. Judicial policy making and southern school segregation. *Journal of Politics* 37:917-937.

Glass, A. L., and K. J. Holyoke. 1986. *Cognition*, 2d ed. New York: Random House.

Glazer, Nathan. 1978. Should courts administer social services? *Public Interest* 50:64-80.

Goldman, Sheldon. 1981. Carter's judicial appointments: A lasting legacy. *Judicature* 64:344-355.

———. 1989. Reagan's judicial legacy: Completing the puzzle and summing up. *Judicature* 72:318-330.

Hastie, Reid, S. Penrod, and Nancy Pennington. 1983. *Inside the jury*. Cambridge, Mass.: Harvard University Press.

Horowitz, Donald L. 1977. *The courts and social policy.* Washington, D.C.: Brookings Institution.

Howard, J. Woodford, Jr. 1981. *Courts of appeals in the federal judicial system: A study of the Second, Fifth and District of Columbia Circuits.* Princeton: Princeton University Press.

Johnson, Charles. 1987. Law, politics and judicial decision making: Lower federal court uses of Supreme Court decisions. *Law and Society Review* 21:325-342.

Johnson, Charles, and Bradley C. Canon. 1984. *Judicial policies: Implementation and impact.* Washington, D.C.: Congressional Quarterly.

Johnson, Frank. 1976. The Constitution and the federal district judge. *Texas Law Review* 54:903-916.

Kritzer, Herbert. 1978. Political correlates of the behavior of federal district judges: A best case analysis. *Journal of Politics* 40:25-58.

Lau, Richard, and David Sears. 1988. An introduction to political cognition. In *Political cognition,* ed. Richard Lau and David Sears. Hillsdale, N.J.: Erlbaum.

Lieberman, Jethro. 1981. *The litigious society.* New York: Basic Books.

Lodge, Milton, and Ruth Hamill. 1986. A partisan schema for political information processing. *American Political Science Review* 80:505-519.

McFeeley, Neil. 1987. *Appointment of judges: The Johnson presidency.* Austin: University of Texas Press.

Motley, Constance Baker. Interview. Lawrence, Kansas. October 13, 1986.

Murphy, Walter F., and Joseph Tanenhaus. 1972. *The study of public law.* New York: Random House.

Murphy, Walter F., and C. Herman Pritchett. 1979. *Courts, judges and politics: An introduction to the judicial process,* 3d ed. New York: Random House.

Navasky, Victor. 1974. *Kennedy justice.* New York: Atheneum.

New York Times. 1989. Judge in abortion case is calm in the limelight. April 21, A21.

Peltason, Jack W. 1955. *Federal courts in the political process.* New York: Random House.

———. 1961. *Fifty-eight lonely men: Southern federal judges and school desegregation.* Urbana: University of Illinois Press.

Posner, Richard. 1985. *The federal courts.* Cambridge, Mass.: Harvard University Press.

Richardson, Richard J., and Kenneth Vines. 1970. *The politics of federal courts.* Boston: Little, Brown.

Rosenbloom, David H. 1987. Public administrators and the judiciary: The new partnership. *Public Administration Review* 47:75-101.

Rowland, C. K., and Robert Carp. 1983. The relative effects of maturation, time period, and appointing president on district judges' policy choices: A cohort analysis. *Political Behavior* 5:109-133.

Rowland, C. K., Robert Carp, and Donald R. Songer. 1988. The effect of presidential appointment, group identification and fact-law ambiguity on lower federal judges' policy judgements: The case of Reagan and Carter appointees. Paper presented at the annual meeting of the American Political Science Association, New Orleans.

Rowland, C. K., Robert Carp, and Ronald A. Stidham. 1984. Judges' policy choices and the value basis of judicial appointments: A comparison of support for criminal defendants among Nixon, Johnson, and Kennedy appointees to the federal district courts. *Journal of Politics* 46:886-902.

Rubin, Eva. 1987. *Abortion, politics and the courts*. New York: Greenwood Press.

Sarat, Austin. 1977. Judging in trial courts: An exploratory study. *Journal of Politics* 39:368-398.

Schubert, Glendon. 1975. *The judicial mind revisited: Psychometric analysis of Supreme Court ideology*. New York: Cambridge University Press.

Segal, Jeffrey A., and Albert D. Cover. 1989. Ideological values and votes of U.S. Supreme Court justices. *American Political Science Review* 83:557-566.

Simon, Herbert A. 1986. Rationality in psychology and economics. In *Rational choice: The contrast between economics and psychology*, ed. R. M. Hogarth and M. W. Reder. Chicago: University of Chicago Press.

Slotnick, Elliot E. 1988. Federal judicial recruitment and selection research: A review essay. *Judicature* 71:317-324.

Smith, Christopher. 1987. Merit selection committees and the politics of appointing U.S. magistrates. *Justice System Journal* 12:210-231.

_____. 1989. Factors underlying the development of U.S. magistrates' diverse roles within the federal district courts. Paper presented at annual meeting of the Midwest Political Science Association, Chicago.

Stidham, Ronald, and Robert Carp. 1987. Judges, presidents and policy choices: Exploring the linkage. *Social Science Quarterly* 68:395-407.

Taggart, W. A. 1989. Redefining the power of the federal judiciary: The impact of court-ordered prison reform on state expenditures for corrections. *Law and Society Review* 23:241-272.

Taylor, Shelley E., and Jennifer Crocker. 1981. Schematic bases of social information processing. In *Social cognition: The Ontario symposium*, ed. E. T. Higgins, C. P. Herman, and M. P. Zanna. Hillsdale, N.J.: Erlbaum.

Todd, Bridget. 1985. A comparison of President Carter's traditional and non-traditional nominees to the federal district courts: What difference does the difference make? Masters thesis, University of Kansas.

_____. 1989. The relative effects of legal environment and appointing president on district judges' unpublished decisions. Paper presented at the annual meeting of the Southwest Political Science Association, Little Rock.

Vines, Kenneth. 1964. Federal district judges and race relations cases in the South. *Journal of Politics* 26:337-357.

Walker, Thomas, and Deborah Barrow. 1985. Diversification of the federal bench: Policy and process ramifications. *Journal of Politics* 47:596-617.

Wasby, Stephen L. 1981. Arrogation of power or responsibility: Judicial imperialism revisited. *Judicature* 65:208-221.

Washington Post. 1989. A chance to deepen stamp on courts. January 29, A1.

Webster's third international dictionary. 1978. Springfield, Mass.: G. and C. Merriam.

Wenner, Lettie M. 1982. *The environmental decade in court.* Bloomington: Indiana University Press.

Wenner, Lettie M., and Lee E. Dutter. 1988. Contextual influences on court outcomes. *Western Political Quarterly* 41:115-137.

Wyzanski, C. J. 1959. Letter to Senator Saltonstall. Reprinted in *Courts, judges and politics*, 4th ed., ed. W. F. Murphy and C. H. Pritchett. New York: Random House.

4. POLICY MAKING AND STATE SUPREME COURTS

Henry R. Glick

Many Americans are aware of the important policy-making role of the U.S. Supreme Court. Cases involving civil rights and liberties, the rights of criminal defendants, abortion, and other issues receive prominent attention in the news media and arouse deep emotions and often hostile reaction among the public and elected officials alike. A recent Supreme Court case involving flag burning as political protest demonstrates how a single Court decision can arouse the nation with promises of new legislation and constitutional amendments to follow. It is rare, however, for the state supreme courts to achieve such visibility or to stimulate as much citizen reaction. At first appearance, state court decisions seem to involve routine and less volatile issues that do not affect basic values and beliefs or important policy. But this is a misperception due in part to less news coverage of the state courts and the tendency of most citizens to be more interested and aware of national political events. Yet state courts make many important decisions that affect a wide range of policies directly relevant to the lives of most citizens.

This chapter examines the ways that political scientists have explored state supreme courts as policy-making institutions. First, I describe the range of opportunities and avenues of state supreme court policy making, briefly review past policy research, and suggest new directions for future investigation. Then I turn to two examples of recent policy research. The first investigates the role of state supreme courts in judicial review, an area that has been widely explored and understood for the U.S. Supreme Court but that has received very little attention in the states. This is followed by an examination of judicial innovation in a new field of policy—the right to die.

Opportunities and Avenues of Policy Making

State supreme courts have many opportunities to make policy. First, state supreme courts are courts of last resort. Win, lose, or draw, their decisions end litigation in most cases. In one sample of nearly 6,000 state supreme court decisions, only 2 percent were appealed to the U.S. Supreme Court and only a few were the subject of opinions of the Court (Kagan et al. 1977). Second, the volume of state supreme court decisions is huge. In the early 1980s, the fifty courts decided over 53,000 cases per year, and the volume is rising (U.S. Department of Justice 1983). Even if relatively few of the thousands of decisions were to make new policy or have an impact beyond the immediate litigants, the finality and volume of state supreme court decisions provide a huge potential for the courts to have a substantial impact on state government and its citizens.

State supreme courts also generally have distinctive but socially important agendas. The main categories of cases include: appeals in major felonies; state regulation of business and professions; a wide range of private economic disputes, including business contracts and real estate; wills, trusts, and estates; divorce, child custody, and child support; and personal injury suits involving automobile accidents, medical malpractice, job-related injuries, and the like.

State supreme court decisions generally are less visible and salient than decisions of the U.S. Supreme Court, especially those involving civil rights and liberties, but by any standard state court decisions are important ones. For instance, millions of people are directly and deeply affected by state policy regarding divorce and child support and directly or indirectly (through the cost of insurance and medical care) by court rules concerning liability and financial recovery in medical malpractice, faulty products, and automobile and other accident cases. State courts will continue to be important in newly emerging social problems. As the United States becomes a more technological and urban society, and people increasingly depend on large organizations and strangers for their work, health, and other of life's necessities, novel problems and disputes will arise. State supreme courts will confront new demands and have opportunities to set new public policy.

Judicial Activism

Discussions of judicial policy making usually focus on judicial activism, which is often considered to be at work when courts render decisions requiring actions by other parts of the government or instituting new policy for a political system. To many observers, judicial activism is synonymous with judicial policy making.[1] Interest in judicial activism is part of a very old debate concerning the proper role of the judiciary, particularly the U.S. Supreme Court, in American politics. The traditional view is that courts ought to act with restraint, meaning that they ought to follow prior decisions (judicial precedents) and defer to the policy-making prerogatives of democratically elected officials and institutions—Congress, the president, and state legislatures. Courts are also to avoid imaginative and expansive interpretations of law which support judicial innovation (making novel policy where none currently exists).

There are a number of problems with this debate and with the use of judicial activism as a surrogate for policy making. One difficulty is that calls for judicial restraint conflict with another core role for the U.S. Supreme Court (and of other courts): the power of judicial review, in which courts have the authority to review acts of Congress and state legislatures to determine their fit with the Constitution. Second, certain dimensions of judicial activism contradict each other and create more confusion than clarity about the role of courts (Canon 1982, 1983). In particular, when courts declare acts of a legislature unconstitutional or when they interpret legislative acts in novel ways—thus appearing to be activist—they may claim that they really are acting with restraint because they are merely interpreting the Constitution or adhering to well-established judicial precedent.

Debate about judicial activism and restraint often has partisan overtones, which further limits the concepts' usefulness as a basis for research. We usually find that those who call for judicial restraint and condemn judges for going beyond their proper judicial role really object to the policy content and direction of certain Court decisions. Supporters of the policy, however, laud the Court for correctly interpreting the Constitution. In the 1960s, conservatives railed against the liberal Warren Court while advocates of broadened civil rights believed the Court was doing the right thing. Under today's increasingly conservative Rehnquist Court, liberals are shocked and dismayed at interpreta tions given the law in civil rights and liberties, abortion, and other matters; conservatives, on the other hand, are pleased that the Court has returned to the "true" meaning of the Constitution.

Finally, judicial activism is an incomplete basis for understanding the role of courts. Activism is synonymous with change and ignores policies that maintain the status quo or reject cases for decision in order to keep an issue off the judicial agenda. Policy maintenance and agenda or gate-keeping decisions (judicial restraint in the activism-restraint debate) are crucial policy decisions also, but they are underplayed in discussions of judicial policy making.

The concept of judicial activism as a research tool has additional pitfalls when applied to the state supreme courts. The states exist as co-equal and parallel policy makers (under the system of horizontal federalism). A state supreme court that creates a totally new policy surely would be seen as an activist court. But it is less clear how we should classify other supreme courts that become aware of and adopt— or reject—the innovative policy of the first state. Are the later adopters also activist courts, since the decision is new to their states, or are they merely followers who get on a rising curve of change in national policy? How are later decisions to be classified if a following state adds a policy twist of its own to the previous decision? If a state supreme court explicitly rejects a new policy developed in other states, is this too a form of activism? Or is it restraint, especially if the court adheres to its own precedents or other interpretations of law? A decision to reject a widely adopted policy also fails to meet one of the criteria of activism: rejection does not eliminate the precedent. It has no effect on the jurisprudence of innovative and adoptive courts.

Avenues and Substance

Ambiguity and contradiction with activism as policy making, especially in parallel state supreme courts, suggest that it probably is more useful to focus on the avenues through which courts make policy and to learn more about the substance of particular judicial policies and their impact on people and politics. There is no counterpart in state judicial literature to the enormous knowledge generated over the last forty years concerning the policy-making processes, policy content, and impact of U.S. Supreme Court decisions. Understanding the dimensions of state supreme court policy making and the content of judicial decisions will enable us to map more completely the roles of state supreme courts in state political systems and across the nation, and to explore the effect of courts on the daily lives of millions of Americans.

There are four main avenues through which courts make policy: (1) judicial review of legislation, involving state and federal constitutions as the basis for rulings; (2) interpretation of frequently vague and general legislation and administrative rules; (3) interpretation, application, and possible rejection of precedents in most cases that do not involve legislation or executive rules; and (4) judicial innovation, in which courts create new policies that have no clear or explicit basis in existing legislation, administrative rules, or court precedent.

Judicial innovation requires some additional explanation. Courts typically cite precedents as part of the expected judicial role, but in the process of innovation, linking old and new decisions often requires as much judicial imagination as forming the new decision itself. Judicial innovation also distinguishes a special type of judicial decision from routine and repetitive ones made in most cases and distinguishes the role of appellate courts from that of the trial courts. Routine decisions frequently are classified as norm enforcement decisions in which trial courts apply community values, standards, and customs and law to common disputes. Although many appellate decisions are also routine, trial courts in particular are thought to have limited leeway in most civil and criminal cases and judges are not expected to produce novel solutions to problems. They impose typical sentences in criminal cases, routinely grant divorces, and award custody of children to mothers, and so on. In contrast, innovation occurs when new problems arise and judges receive little or no guidance from existing law and community standards are not yet established or are in conflict (Jacob 1984, chaps. 2 and 3; Glick 1988, 292-299). Innovation, which occurs mostly in appellate courts, may be required in cases involving surrogate parenting, removal of life-sustaining medical treatment from the terminally ill (discussed later in this chapter), new opportunities for consumers to recover damages through tort action, and many other once-novel situations. Even though judges frequently refer to precedents and the cases may involve statutes and constitutions, the distinctive feature of innovative decisions is that judges create novel solutions to social problems.

Research on State Supreme Court Policy Making

The Policy-making Process

Recognizing that appellate judges have substantial discretion, early research focused on the potential for policy making by examining judges' role orientations toward a fundamental dimension of policy making: whether judges should be lawmakers or law interpreters. Lawmakers embrace opportunities to create new and often broad policy applicable to many similar cases, while law interpreters call for judges to restrict their decisions to clarifying the meaning of existing law and applying that law to specific disputes. Law interpreters do not believe it is their role to fashion sweeping or general solutions to social problems. Previous research in the 1960s demonstrated that judges adopted the traditional law interpreter role and most who saw themselves as lawmakers were more likely to innovate in the liberal direction (Glick 1971, 93-99; Wold 1974).

Opportunities for policy making have also been revealed in early research on court dockets, in which state socioeconomic and political environments and judicial structure affect the composition of court agendas. Supreme courts in socially and economically diverse states, and especially those with intermediate appellate courts below, generally have greater opportunities to decide a larger proportion of civil liberties and economically complex litigation and are less loaded with routine private economic disputes (Atkins and Glick 1976; Kagan et al. 1977). However, some supreme courts in states with high crime rates and with intermediate appellate courts below have tended to become heavily loaded with appeals in major felony criminal cases.

This research established that, in addition to state socioeconomic and political environments, which generate different types of litigation, judicial structure makes a significant difference in the potential of state supreme courts to make policy. Approximately 60 percent of the states have both intermediate appellate and supreme courts. In these states, 80 percent of the intermediate appellate courts hear more cases than the state supreme court. A few hear the bulk of all cases: the California and Florida intermediate appellate courts, for example, hear approximately 80 to 90 percent of all appellate cases (U.S. Department of Justice 1983). The jurisdiction of intermediate appellate courts tends to screen a large volume of mostly routine personal and private economic disputes out of the judicial system, leaving supreme court judges more time for thinking, researching, and writing about the larger number of complex and socially significant issues that reach them. Such opportunities are important when we recall that it is through written judicial opinions that courts express and transmit their policy to the legal community, the mass media, and society as a whole. Indications are that intermediate appellate courts are so loaded with cases that judges rarely have time for thoughtful written opinions, thereby generally precluding the opportunity to make judicial policy on matters that come before them (Wold 1978).

Recent research in the policy-making process has focused on judicial leadership among state supreme courts, using the frequency of case citation among the courts as an indicator of their relative reputation and probable innovation. Gregory A. Caldeira argues that citation almost always means approval (high reputation) of the cited court and that courts that are cited most often probably produce liberal, innovative policies (Caldeira 1983, 1985, 1988; Harris 1982). Table 4-1 presents the reputation scores and ranks for state supreme courts based on 1975 data (Caldeira 1983). It is derived from subtracting the expected percentage of references for each court (one-fiftieth of each state's total citations of other courts) from the actual percentage of references to other states. Both positive and negative deviations from the expected percentage of references are possible. Table 4-1 shows that California leads the other states by a huge margin in citation rates and the Wyoming Supreme Court is cited least often. California is followed by New York and then by New Jersey and other northeastern states. However, some midwestern and western states also rank high in reputation. All states with negative scores receive fewer citations than expected based on the assumption of equal citation of each court. Caldeira has discovered through multiple regression analysis that several variables largely account for variations in judicial reputation. The population of a state, measures of legal professionalism, and measures of state policy liberalism are largely responsible for increasing a supreme court's reputation among other courts.

Table 4-1 Reputational Scores and Ranks for State Supreme Courts, 1975

Rank	State	Reputational score	Rank	State	Reputational score
1	California	354.6	26	Alabama	− 28.0
2	New York	215.4	27	Arkansas	− 32.4
3	New Jersey	104.2	28	New Mexico	− 34.1
4	Pennsylvania	91.7	29	Mississippi	− 34.6
5	Massachusetts	91.6	30	Virginia	− 35.6
6	Wisconsin	87.4	31	Utah	− 35.9
7	Illinois	86.3	32	Delaware	− 38.7
8	Washington	65.4	33	New Hampshire	− 38.9
9	Iowa	54.6	34	Georgia	− 41.8
10	Michigan	54.1	35	Idaho	− 43.3
11	Minnesota	43.8	36	Alaska	− 45.0
12	Colorado	4? ?	37	Tennessee	− 46.0
13	Kansas	24.4	38	Texas	− 49.1
14	Florida	21.6	39	Louisiana	− 52.4
15	Oregon	19.7	40	Montana	− 54.9
16	Oklahoma	17.9	41	Maine	− 55.4
17	Kentucky	16.2	42	South Carolina	− 56.2
18	Maryland	13.1	43	West Virginia	− 56.6
19	Arizona	9.8	44	Nevada	− 59.1
20	North Carolina	8.3	45	North Dakota	− 63.1
21	Ohio	5.3	46	Rhode Island	− 63.5
22	Nebraska	− 3.9	47	Vermont	− 66.7
23	Missouri	− 7.9	48	Hawaii	− 68.0
24	Connecticut	− 11.0	49	South Dakota	− 68.5
25	Indiana	− 21.0	50	Wyoming	− 74.7

Source: Gregory A. Caldeira, "On the Reputation of State Supreme Courts," *Political Behavior* 5 (1983): 89. Reprinted with permission.

Caldeira's research is significant because it systematically measures and analyzes the treatment that the fifty supreme courts give each other's decisions and the variables that account for differences in judicial stature. His research also demonstrates that the fifty state supreme courts do not exist as separate, isolated institutions within their own state political systems (although a few courts cite only their own decisions), but interact as part of a larger network of parallel organizations, using each other's decisions in different ways as part of their own policy-making processes.

Caldeira also believes that states that are cited most often provide policy models for other states to adopt in their own decisions and that certain courts are more influential than others in judicial policy making. However, caution is needed here. Variation in citation indicates that certain courts provide more legal ammunition for other courts to use in their own legal opinions, and it is possible that, in the aggregate, states that are cited most often also produce a larger number of policy models for other states. But this has not yet been established, and other research suggests that citation alone is an insufficient indicator of a policy leadership hierarchy among state supreme courts (Tarr and Porter 1988, 33). For instance, in examining twenty-three different tort policies, Bradley C. Canon and Lawrence Baum (1981) discovered that policy leadership in one policy does not necessarily mean leadership in others and that discrete policies diffuse in a variety of ways. Moreover, certain courts that are generally cited heavily by others were not innovators in tort law. In contradiction to Caldeira's findings, explanatory factors—including legislative innovation, ideology, population size, urbanization and industrialization, political culture, judicial professionalism, and regionalism—generally were found to be poor predictors of cumulative innovation scores. These researchers suggest that since courts are dependent upon litigants to bring cases, there is a high degree of idiosyncracy in opportunities to decide cases and, consequently, in the resulting diffusion of policies among the states.

Policy Content

Political scientists have placed heavy emphasis on the process of policy making, but they have begun to examine as well the content of state supreme court policies. Research has focused on two major areas: recent state supreme court innovation in civil liberties, a role dominated in recent decades by the federal courts; and the content of other policies that are most typical of state political systems.

During a twenty-year period from the mid-1950s to the early 1970s, the U.S. Supreme Court vastly liberalized the nation's conception of civil rights and liberties. But according to some analysts, the recent conservative turn of the Burger and Rehnquist Courts has prompted a "new judicial federalism," in which liberal state supreme courts rely on state constitutions to expand constitutional rights beyond recent conservative U.S. Supreme Court policy.[2] There are many examples of the new judicial federalism. In the mid-1970s, the California, New Jersey, Alaska, and Michigan supreme courts created standards for police interrogation and search and seizure that went beyond the weakened requirements created by Burger Court reinterpretations of earlier Supreme Court policies. Also in the 1970s, the Illinois and Pennsylvania supreme courts banned distinctions based on sex in child support and adoption cases that went beyond Supreme

Court policies in sexual discrimination (Porter 1982; Friedelbaum 1982).

The number of such cases is growing. From 1950 to 1974, the fifty state supreme courts produced 46 such decisions, an average of less than 2 per year. However, from 1975 to 1979, the number of decisions was 88, or nearly 18 per year, and from 1980 to 1986, the number had risen to 177, or approximately 25 per year. These cases were not evenly distributed throughout the country, which suggests that certain courts have cast themselves in a new role but that many others have not. About one-quarter of the cases were decided in the Northeast, one-half in the West, and the remaining one-quarter in the Midwest and South (Collins, Galie, and Kincaid 1986). Supreme courts in California, New Jersey, Michigan, Alaska, and a few others stand out.[3] Given the conservative history and content of most state politics, and the unequal distribution of cases, it seems unlikely that most courts will follow the liberal leaders.

Significant as individual rights and liberties are in American democracy, state supreme courts make larger contributions to public policies in traditional areas of state regulation and economic and family life. An important example is the changing law of torts (Canon and Baum 1981; Baum and Canon 1982). Torts deal with "civil wrongs"— financial recovery for damages and personal injury and death caused by negligence or possibly criminal actions of others. Generally, in recent decades, state supreme courts have liberalized opportunities for individuals to recover for injuries and damages caused by government agencies and their employees; have permitted suits against nonprofit organizations, mainly hospitals, for injuries; and have provided opportunities for the injured to hold manufacturers directly liable for faulty products. The trend toward greater opportunities for the injured to sue for damages has become a major political issue in the states, with insurance companies, hospitals, doctors, and manufacturers lobbying state legislatures to limit access to the courts or impose financial caps on the amounts that can be recovered. Research on tort policy is significant because it explores substantive changes in judicial policy distinctive to the states and seeks to account for the adoption of similar state judicial policies throughout the nation. However, as discussed above, Canon and Baum have been unable to account for patterns of diffusion, calling attention to the great amount of work that is yet to be done in explaining how judicial policies spread among the fifty states.

Finally, in addition to examining the content and diffusion of particular policies, researchers have recorded the win/lose ratios of classes of litigants in a wide array of state supreme court cases. Landlords, employers, and the state win most of the time, presumably reflecting and reinforcing judicial values and law which allow the "haves" to come out ahead (Wheeler et al. 1987). This is not judicial policy making in the usual sense because it does not involve clear changes in policy found in separate, individual cases and written opinions. But winning and losing also change over time and it is clear, for example, that the same groups that dominated the courts in tort policy a half century ago are no longer in control.

An intriguing research problem still on the agenda is to correlate substantive changes in judicial policy, and perhaps other law, with changes in the win/lose ratios of particular classes of litigants. If the law has its anticipated cumulative impact, we should see positive relationships between liberal changes, for example, in tort or divorce and child custody policy and aggregate measures of who wins and loses in court (accident victims versus employers or insurance companies; husbands/fathers versus wives/mothers). Individual decisions, of course, will vary. However, a lag may be found between changes in appellate policy and patterns of subsequent decisions until current and future judges fully embrace the policy and lawyers and litigants reorient litigation strategy to take full advantage of changes in the law. But the new losers also can be expected to devote themselves to promoting new interpretations of law and lobbying efforts to shift the thrust of lawmaking back to their own advantage. But generally, if proof of the policy is in the winning (or losing), it is important to learn how the state supreme courts treat classes of litigants routinely in cases. Judicial policy frequently is broad and general and permits much discretion in case-by-case application, and we need to know how the courts use their policies every day. Differences in the aggregate win/lose ratios of different classes of litigants over time may provide a clue.

New Directions in Policy Research

Confronting the study of state supreme court policy making are special data problems that require strategic choices in research design. A choice may seem to be required between large, aggregate studies of the fifty states, which provide a broad overview, and case studies of individual states which examine the content of individual policies more closely. It is difficult to do both in a single integrated study.

Aggregate or Case Studies

To obtain a full panorama of state judicial policy, new aggregate studies on the work of the fifty state supreme courts need to be done. The previous work in this area is out of date, and it is unclear whether and how current cases compare with the old. It is probable that the content of supreme court dockets has changed. For example, it appears that the work of certain state supreme courts has become heavily loaded with death penalty cases and that the decisions of the courts may be different from those of years ago. State supreme court decisions in capital cases clearly are extremely controversial and have figured heavily in recent state judicial elections, especially the defeat of Chief Justice Rose Bird and two associate justices of the California Supreme Court. Justice Bird and her colleagues were targeted by conservatives for defeat in a nonpartisan, merit-type retention election because they had consistently overturned death sentences (Wold and Culver 1987). It would be very useful to know how contemporary judicial policies vary in these and other cases, the variables related to policies, and the consequences for state judicial politics.

However, large aggregate studies cannot provide much detail about judicial policy in particular subject areas, nor can they be the basis for the analysis of agenda setting and policy diffusion. And, given the huge amounts of data that are required for a comprehensive study, fifty-state aggregate studies may not be practical. Various commentators have suggested other focuses for the study of state supreme court policy making. One approach is to select one or a few state supreme courts as case studies for comprehensive analysis. Such research could examine changes in workload over time and identify notable judicial contributions to policy. It also could describe the political context of the courts, the history of the courts, and how courts fit into their states' politics. A related approach is to examine the interrelationships of all courts within a particular state. This task would require massive data gathering from county and district court records and mapping the flow of litigation through judicial hierarchies. Flows of litigation and differences in dockets would provide a comprehensive picture of the potential for policy making by different state supreme courts and the roles they play in comparison with lower courts in their state. Advocates of the state-by-state approach believe that the intricacies of local and state processes influence courts differently in each state, a factor that multistate studies overlook, and that detailed case studies can provide hidden clues needed to develop more complete and subtle theories about the policy-making roles of state supreme courts (Daniels 1988; Tarr and Porter 1988).

A prominent recent example of the case study approach is the work by G. Alan Tarr and Mary Cornelia Porter on the supreme courts of Alabama, Ohio, and New Jersey (1988). The authors orient their study around three sets of political relationships that are important for state supreme courts: vertical federalism (relations with the U.S. Supreme Court); horizontal federalism (mainly citation among courts); and intrastate political relationships (links between supreme courts and other state political institutions and the development of judicial policy). However, these themes are not explicitly applied to the three courts, possibly because they are too general and broad without the development of additional, more specific theory and sets of testable hypotheses. Instead, the research concentrates on the characteristics of each supreme court and the individuals who have contributed the most to notable court decisions and trends in policy. The study concludes by offering a new concept of institutional identity, which reinforces the view that each court is a separate and distinct political entity.

The general problem with this approach to the study of state supreme courts is that, however interesting the intricacies of a particular court or state judicial system may be, detailed case studies tend to emphasize the uniqueness of particular states or courts and generally fail to produce theory, hypotheses, or a research agenda to be applied comparatively. If the comparative fifty-state aggregate studies lack detail and overlook certain variables that might account for some additional—but frequently small—variance among the states, case studies tend to go far in the opposite direction—focusing heavily on events and personalities on particular courts while failing to provide a basis for generalizing about state courts. For the case study approach to contribute to knowledge of state supreme court policy making, an explicit theory of policy making must be developed in advance to guide data gathering and analysis so that genuine comparisons among the few selected states can be made and new theory developed to enhance general knowledge of the judicial process.

A Policy Focus

Instead of choosing between large aggregate or narrow case studies of judicial institutions, new research might begin by selecting a particular policy and proceed to examine the behavior of all state supreme courts regarding that policy. In-depth case studies of particular states that represent different models or streams of policy might also be done in order to illustrate local or regional variations in the avenues of policy making and the content of policy.

Increased emphasis also needs to be placed on the various avenues of policy making and bringing state judicial policy making into the broader realm of policy research and state politics. Attention needs to be paid to how and which issues become and do not become court cases (agenda setting) and the diffusion of innovations of judicial policy among state supreme courts. In addition, research needs to link the content of state judicial policy to legislative and executive policy. For example, although state supreme courts have been largely responsible for the revolution in tort policy, state legislatures have also been active in this area, frequently in response to lobbying by defendants' groups that see themselves as recently disadvantaged in court (Baum 1989). The adoption of no-fault divorce legislation was also partly a response to the cumulative results of litigation, particularly the legal fictions and perjury needed to satisfy statutory requirements for proof of adultery as the sole basis for divorce (Jacob 1988, 33-34). Thus, students of state courts need to be students of state politics so that the courts are cast as integral parts of the total state political process. In the remainder of this chapter, I report on new research under way on the avenues and content of state supreme court policy making, in an effort to illustrate new approaches to state supreme court policy analysis.

State Supreme Courts and Judicial Review

There is wide consensus among legal scholars and political scientists that judicial review is the clearest, most dramatic, and most salient element of judicial policy making. Generally, when we think of judicial review, we think of the U.S. Supreme Court, but state courts engage in judicial review as well and may employ both state and federal constitutions as grounds for their decisions. Recall also that very few state supreme court cases are taken to the U.S. Supreme Court, so that in effect state supreme courts have final authority. However, despite new interest in state judicial review, until recently we have lacked basic and comprehensive information about this avenue of policy making. Craig F. Emmert has examined all cases in which acts of state legislatures were challenged before state supreme courts from 1981 to 1985.[4] Emmert identified nearly 3,250 cases, an average of 650 per year for all fifty courts and approximately 13 per court per year. This figure is much larger than the number of civil rights cases reported by Ronald Collins, Peter Galie, and John Kincaid (1986) (177 decisions from 1980 to 1986) and gives a much more complete picture of the judicial review potential of the courts.

Opportunities and Issues

There is considerable variation in the exercise of judicial review among state supreme courts. Table 4-2 presents the rank ordering of the courts according to the number of laws challenged, the number of laws overturned, and the percentage of laws overturned. The number of laws challenged provides a baseline indicating the relative opportunity for judicial review. The data show that there is substantial opportunity for state supreme courts to engage in judicial review. In the five-year period, only a few courts had fewer than twenty-five such cases. There is a high correlation between the number of challenges and number of laws over-

Table 4-2 Number of State Laws Challenged and Number and Percent Declared Unconstitutional, 1981-1985

State	Number challenged		Number unconstitutional		Percent unconstitutional	
	Rank	N	Rank	N	Rank	%
Georgia	1	165	4	25	41.5	15.2
Louisiana	2	111	3	28	20	25.2
Colorado	3	107	13.5	15	44	14.0
Florida	4	104	6	22	24	21.2
Illinois	5	91	11	18	26	19.8
Arkansas	6	87	5	23	17	26.4
New York	7.5	80	8.5	20	22	25.0
Washington	7.5	80	1.5	29	6	36.3
Kansas	9	76	20.5	12	39.5	15.8
Massachusetts	10	75	13.5	15	25	20.0
Missouri	11	72	18	13	33	18.1
Iowa	12.5	64	48	2	49	3.1
Minnesota	12.5	64	20.5	12	28	18.8
South Carolina	14	63	1.5	29	1	46.0
Montana	15	61	11	18	12	31.1
Utah	16	59	26	10	36	16.9
Alabama	17	58	8.5	20	8	34.5
Nebraska	18	57	30.5	9	39.5	15.8
Connecticut	19	56	34.5	8	43	14.3
New Hampshire	20.5	54	15.5	14	19	25.9
West Virginia	20.5	54	7	21	3	38.9
Indiana	22	51	30.5	9	34	17.6
California	23	50	18	13	18	26.0
Pennsylvania	24	46	11	18	2	39.1
South Dakota	25.5	44	18	13	13	29.1
Tennessee	25.5	44	34.5	8	31.5	18.2
Idaho	28	43	38	7	37	16.3
Maine	28	43	34.5	8	31.5	18.2
Wyoming	28	43	48	2	48	4.7
Kentucky	30.5	42	15.5	14	9	33.3
Rhode Island	30.5	42	34.5	8	27	19.0
New Jersey	32.5	40	26	10	22	25.0
Ohio	32.5	40	38	7	35	17.5
Michigan	34	38	38	7	30	18.4
Nevada	35	36	26	10	15	27.8
North Dakota	36.5	34	30.5	9	22	25.0
North Carolina	36.5	34	50	1	50	2.9
Mississippi	38.5	33	41.5	5	41.5	15.2
Oregon	38.5	33	30.5	9	16	27.3
Arizona	40	32	44	4	45	12.5
Oklahoma[a]	41.5	31	26	10	10.5	32.3
Wisconsin	41.5	31	26	10	10.5	32.3

continued

Table 4-2 (continued)

State	Number challenged		Number unconstitutional		Percent unconstitutional	
	Rank	N	Rank	N	Rank	%
Alaska	43	30	22.5	11	5	36.7
Maryland	44	29	22.5	11	4	37.9
New Mexico	45	27	46	3	46	11.1
Vermont	46	25	44	4	38	16.0
Virginia	47	22	44	4	31.5	18.2
Delaware	48.5	21	48	2	47	9.5
Hawaii	48.5	21	40	6	14	28.6
Texas[a]	50	14	41.5	5	7	35.7
	Mean = 53.2		Mean = 11.8		Mean = 22.7	
	S.D. = 28.2		S.D. = 7.3		S.D. = 9.8	
		$r = .72$				
		$p = .001$				

[a] Court of Civil Appeals only.

Source: Adapted from Craig Emmert, "Judicial Review in State Supreme Courts: Opportunity and Activism." Paper presented at the annual meeting of the Midwest Political Science Association, Chicago, April 13-16, 1988. Used with permission.

turned ($r = .72$). However, there is not a close relationship between the number of opportunities and the percentage of laws overturned. Some courts overturn a fairly high percentage of the laws which they rule on, despite relatively few opportunities to exercise judicial review (for example, Alaska, Kentucky, and Maryland). In state supreme courts, unlike the U.S. Supreme Court, the percentage of court dockets devoted to judicial review of legislation is not large—the average is 6.3 percent, with a range (not reported in Table 4-2) of nearly 15 percent down to 2.6 percent. However, as will be discussed, state supreme courts are equally or more active in reversing legislation than the Supreme Court.

Several states that normally are perceived as leaders in judicial innovation and the new federalism, and that rank high on measures of prestige developed in other research, do not rank high on any of the measures in Table 4-2. In number of laws challenged, New York shares rank 7.5 with Washington; Massachusetts is 10th, but California ranks 23d, New Jersey 32.5, and Alaska 43d. Perhaps more important, none of these states ranks high in the number or percentage of laws declared unconstitutional. In contrast, many southern states rank high in the number of laws challenged and reversed. To a large extent, opportunities for judicial review—like opportunities for innovation—probably are embedded in the social and political fabric of the states and are only partially controlled by state supreme courts. It certainly appears that innovative courts do not rely on judicial review extensively as an avenue to their innovative role. But courts that are not normally ranked among the innovators may nevertheless perform important and controversial political functions within their state political systems by more frequently overturning legislation. This discovery should lead to a broadening of our perspective of the avenues of policy making and the political functions of state supreme courts. National leadership in innovation is not everything.

In the five years studied, state supreme courts overturned nearly 23 percent of all laws challenged. The average number of laws overturned by each state supreme court is 2.4 per year, very similar to the average of 2 congressional laws overturned annually by the U.S. Supreme Court. Recently, the U.S. Supreme Court has overturned approximately 22 state laws per year, but collectively the fifty state supreme courts have rejected an average of nearly 120 laws per year. In sum, the quantity of state supreme court judicial review activity is as great as or greater than that of the U.S. Supreme Court.

There are important distinctions between state judicial review and U.S. Supreme Court judicial review that these numbers do not reveal. For instance, some individual U.S. Supreme Court decisions overturn a group of similar state laws at the same time, either directly, by combining cases for decision, or implicitly, by ruling on legislation which is similar to that in other states. Few, if any, state court decisions address more than one law in each case. Certain U.S. Supreme Court decisions also have the potential for widespread national impact that cannot be achieved by a single state—and by a group of states only if they take similar action over a long period. Nevertheless, within the boundaries of their own political systems, state supreme courts perform a substantial judicial review function, and combined, the fifty state supreme courts have a considerable impact on state law.

State supreme courts also generally deal with recent state legislation and active lawmaking majorities. In contrast to Robert A. Dahl's and Jonathan D. Casper's observations regarding the great time lag between the passage of a majority of national laws and U.S. Supreme Court reversal—suggesting that much judicial review does not challenge a current or active lawmaking majority in Congress (Dahl 1958; Casper 1976)—over 55 percent of laws challenged and nearly 60 percent of laws overturned by state supreme courts had been enacted within five years of state supreme court decisions. State supreme court rejection of recently elected legislatures could foster significant political conflict in the states and should heighten our interest in the reactions of state legislatures and the interplay between the two branches.

There are no obvious reasons for the difference between the date of enactment and judicial review in the U.S. and the state supreme courts. However, we can speculate that the structure of state law, constitutions, and court systems may account for some of the difference. State constitutions are long and detailed documents, addressing many areas of public policy much more precisely and narrowly than does the U.S. Constitution; their nature may encourage constitutional litigation on specific points of law in the states. Many laws challenged before state supreme courts also are specifically tied to particular groups of citizens and state officials; in this smaller political arena, litigation may be generated more quickly.

Probably more important are the relative hurdles and uncertainty in getting a case before the U.S. Supreme Court compared with the state supreme courts. The U.S. Supreme Court grants certiorari to very few cases; therefore, potential litigants have to weigh carefully the importance of the law and their interests in litigation. Interest groups that sponsor most cases brought by convicted criminals and by blacks and others in civil rights cases must choose their cases and opportunities well, or they risk expending enormous amounts of time and money on cases that may not reach the Supreme Court or that do not adequately address the issue they wish to contest. Conceivably, they seek other ways to resolve conflict or to obtain their goals or they endure mounting disadvantages before taking the arduous, expensive, and risky road to the U.S. Supreme Court. The state courts, in contrast, have far more expansive jurisdictions and are required to hear many cases involving the state constitution so that litigation is a much more routine consideration and a likely alternative in the state political process. Finally, cases considered especially important by the lower courts in certain states may be certified to the state supreme courts, meaning that the trial and intermediate appellate courts immediately pass on some cases to the highest court for decision. This too may make constitutional litigation more quickly available and encourage groups and individuals to take frequent challenges before the state's highest court. Since state judicial review is a relatively new field of research for political scientists, these and other propositions require investigation before we can accept them as explanations for the rapidity of state constitutional litigation.

The issues contained in state judicial review cases run the gamut of state court dockets (Table 4-3). Criminal cases contribute the most, followed by economic regulation. Civil liberties and intergovernmental disputes each contribute the least. However, the percentage of laws

Table 4-3 Types of Judicial Review Cases Heard and Overturned

Type of case (N = 3,248)	Percent heard	Percent overturned *
Criminal	41	9
Economic regulation	24	23
Private disputes	15	23
Civil rights/liberties	8	34
Intergovernmental	8	39
Other	4	— [a]

* $p < .01$.

[a] Not reported.

Source: Adapted from Craig Emmert, "Judicial Review in State Supreme Courts: Opportunity and Activism." Paper presented at the annual meeting of the Midwest Political Science Association, Chicago, April 13-16, 1988. Used with permission.

declared unconstitutional produces a very different ranking. As indicated above, overall, the fifty state supreme courts reverse approximately 23 percent of laws challenged. As might be expected, criminal cases, which often involve last-ditch efforts to overturn convictions and sentences, produce judicial reversals in only 9 percent of the cases. However, courts overturn 39 and 34 percent of laws, respectively, in intergovernmental and civil liberties cases. Clearly, while contributing a small portion of the judicial review caseload, intergovernmental and civil rights issues apparently are the most controversial ones. The higher rates of reversal in these two issue areas merit additional in-depth analysis of the content of these issues and the different roles that various courts play in establishing state policy.

Accounting for Variation

Building on much previous state court research, Emmert accounts for variations in opportunities for judicial review and laws overturned. He examines the effects of state socioeconomic and political variables, region, and court structure on judicial review. Through a series of path analyses, he finds overall that the length of state constitutions contributes heavily to the size of a court's caseload, which, in turn, increases the number of cases challenging state laws. Court control over its own jurisdiction (or, equally, the presence of an intermediate appellate court) also increases opportunities for judicial review. The number and percentage of laws overturned is strongly related to the number of cases on the docket, but also to the length of state constitutions, which provide many opportunities for courts to find constitutional conflicts in state law.

Table 4-2 reveals that there is a South — non-South differential in opportunities for judicial review, which suggests that different variables affect judicial review in different regions. Emmert finds that in the nonsouthern states, caseload and discretionary jurisdiction are significantly related to the number and percentage of laws challenged and overturned. Discretion in selecting cases may lead judges to choose those in which they are inclined to overturn legislation. In the southern states, effects on judicial review are different. There, caseload is positively related to the number of laws challenged, which, in turn, correlates with the number of laws overturned. However, the length of state constitutions (long constitutions are found more often in the South) is related significantly only to the number and percentage of laws overturned. This suggests that heavy caseloads contain substantial opportunities to review legislation, but that the length and complexity of southern constitutions account for the tendency of courts to declare laws unconstitutional. Court jurisdiction plays a much less important role in the South due to the limited docket control exercised by southern courts.

The New Federalism

Emmert has also examined the types of constitutional grounds raised by litigants and the grounds used by the courts for their decisions. He finds some support for the view that independent and adequate state grounds (the new federalism) are important in state supreme courts, but that other bases for constitutional decision making are more plentiful. State constitutions are used as the sole basis for decisions in only 16 percent of all cases. In contrast, the federal constitution is used in 33 percent of cases, and state and federal grounds together are used in 42 percent of cases. No grounds were specified in the remaining cases. The reactions of courts differed somewhat depending on the grounds for decisions presented to the courts. When litigants employed state grounds only, they were used 80 percent of the time by courts. But when either federal grounds only or a combination of state and federal grounds were offered by litigants, courts relied on these grounds in nearly 100 percent of the cases. Thus, state constitutions as the sole basis sometimes were rejected by state supreme courts. Moreover, state grounds were used differently in various types of cases. State grounds became the basis for decision in 56 percent of intergovernmental disputes, 29 percent of economic regulation cases, and 20 percent of private disputes, all instances in which the federal constitution may be least relevant. In contrast, state grounds were used in only 9 percent of criminal cases and 15 percent of civil liberties cases. Thus, independent and adequate state grounds are used *least* often in the areas which have been stressed most heavily in the new federalism literature and most often in traditional areas of state policy making.

It is clear that state supreme courts have a significant part in judicial review—the most visible and controversial area of judicial policy making. This research on judicial review should impel future work into other avenues of judicial policy making, such as the role of state supreme courts in interpreting state legislation, interpreting and reversing court precedent, and policy innovation. It would be very useful to know, for example, the relative importance of each of these in court decisions and the kinds of policies affected by them. Such research could be addressed using either aggregate fifty-state studies or comparative studies of regional or representative groups of courts.

Judicial Innovation and Streams of Policy Making: The Case of the Right to Die

The life-prolonging power of medical technology, coupled with medical ethics that require the maintenance of life and doctors' fears of liability for disconnecting life support systems, have generated growing political demand for new legal policy to establish the rights of individuals to determine the course of their own treatment. The galvanizing event that stimulated the rising chorus of concern is the Karen Quinlan case (*In the Matter of Karen Quinlan,* 355 A.2d 647 [1976]).[5] Until this case was decided, there was no policy at any level of government dealing with the rights of the terminally ill or seriously injured and permanently comatose patients and their families to end life-prolonging medical treatment. Faced with a novel problem and willing to decide the case, the New Jersey Supreme Court began a rising wave of judicial innovation in this policy field.

By the end of 1988, dozens of appellate court cases had been decided in fifteen states addressing the use of life support systems and other treatment for the terminally ill, and thirty-eight states and the District of Columbia had enacted living will legislation to allow people to specify in advance of a terminal illness the kind of medical treatment they wish to receive. The court cases generally deal with terminally ill or permanently comatose patients who have not left legal instructions about what should happen in such circumstances (living wills), when there is doubt concerning a patient's wishes, or when doctors insist on a court order before disconnecting equipment. As part of a comprehensive examination of state policy making concerning medical treatment for terminally ill and seriously injured patients, I have examined all state supreme court decisions and the decisions of intermediate appellate courts in states in which the highest court has not heard a case in this field.[6]

The research has two primary purposes. First, I wish to explore the substance of this policy, which is an important and controversial issue. Second, the litigation provides an opportunity to expand research on judicial innovation. In particular, most researchers have assumed that states or other political units that embrace a particular innovation over time adopt uniform policies; that assumption permits them to aggregate adoption scores on many different policies without concern for the details of individual legislation or court cases. As important as the chronology of innovations may be, other researchers of innovation suggest that the content of policy and the way that it changes over time—or is *reinvented* by later adopters—is an equally or even more important aspect of innovation (Rogers 1983). Unlike most previous studies, research on the right to die is sufficiently focused so that it is possible to determine whether there are important differences in policy innovations within this single field of policy, the extent to which different versions of the innovation are adopted by other state courts, and whether and how the innovations change over time.

Three themes in this research relate to past innovation research and offer suggestions for future work. First, certain familiar states appear as the early innovators in right-to-die cases, but the pattern of later adoptions does not follow that of other judicial innovations. Second, instead of a single, uniform innovation, state supreme courts soon produced several different streams of policy and substantially reinvented the policy during the diffusion process, with very different impacts on later adopting courts. Consequently, since the states have had several policy options, citation rates alone are not adequate indicators of policy leadership in this field. Third, the research demonstrates that judicial innovation is but a part of state policy innovation and that research on the courts must be linked to similar research on state legislatures, and probably on the executive as well, in order for us to obtain a complete perspective on particular state policies and the contributing role of courts as policy-making institutions.

The core elements of judicial policy in the right-to-die cases are presented in Table 4-4. The cases are listed in chronological order. The table includes the substantive issue in each case, the direction of the decision (for or against withdrawal or withholding treatment), the key precedent relied upon by the court, and the major policy content of the opinion. Reliance on precedent was coded as an explicit statement in the majority opinion that the court was following a particular precedent. "Cited" and "Cited 1%+" indicate the extent to which each of the cases has been cited subsequently by other courts.

There is an important distinction between the "Cited" and "Cited 1%+" categories. The first indicates the percentage of later cases in

Table 4-4 Elements of Right-to-Die Judicial Policy

Case	Substantive issue [a]	Decision [b]	Key precedents	Cited	Cited 1% +	Major policy content [c]
Quinlan, N.J. 1976	withdraw respirator	+	Griswold v. Conn., Roe v. Wade; new	80.0%	66.7%	I. extends constitutional right to privacy; no judicial intervention required
Saikewicz, Mass. 1977	withhold treatment	+	Quinlan; new	72.4	41.4	I. accepts right to privacy, but judicial supervision required
Perlmutter, Fla. 1/80	withdraw respirator	+	Saikewicz; partly	51.8	25.9	F. accepts constitutional right to privacy for competent patients; extensive call for legislation
Spring, Mass. 5/80	withdraw treatment	+	Saikewicz; modified	46.1	7.7	F. interprets Saikewicz; court approval not required in some cases, but policy left unclear
Severns, Del. 9/80	withdraw respirator	+	Quinlan	32.0	4.0	F. grants authority to trial court; no general policy; extensive call for legislation
Storar, N.Y. 3/81	withhold respirator	−	none	58.3	25.0	F. limits decision to a case by case approach; court approval required
Eichner, N.Y. 3/81	withdraw respirator	+	none	39.1	26.1	F. facts in each case will determine outcome; requires unequivocal evidence of patient's wishes
Colyer, Wash. 3/83	withdraw respirator	+	Quinlan	63.6	36.4	F. endorses Quinlan; guardian required
Barber, Calif. [d] 10/83	withdraw respirator and food/hydration	+	none	23.8	14.3	I. extends basis beyond State Nat. death Act for terminating life support systems

Case	Action	+	Precedents				Holding
Leach, Ohio [d] 5/2/84	withdraw respirator	+	*Saikewicz*	52.9	0.0	F.	endorses *Saikewicz*
Bludworth, Fla. 5/24/84	withdraw respirator	+	*Colyer; Quinlan*	66.7	27.8	F.	endorses *Quinlan* and *Colyer* but allows family decision making; validates living wills
LHR, Ga. 10/84	withdraw respirator	+	*Quinlan*	29.4	0.0	F.	endorses *Quinlan* but allows family decision making
Hamlin, Wash. 11/1/84	withdraw respirator	+	*Colyer* modified	63.6	36.4	F.	interprets *Colyer*; no guardian
Torres, Minn. 11/2/84	withdraw respirator	+	*Quinlan*	53.3	6.7	F.	endorses *Quinlan*
Bartling, Calif. [d] 12/84	withdraw respirator	+	*Barber; Quinlan*	57.1	35.7	F.	endorses *Barber* and *Quinlan*
Conroy, N.J. 11/85	withdraw food/hydration	+	*Quinlan*; new	76.9	69.2	I.	no distinction between "ordinary" and "extraordinary" procedures; provides rules; extensive call for legislation
Bouvia, Calif. [d] 6/86	withdraw food/hydration	+	*Bartling*	54.5	22.2	F.	endorses *Bartling*
Brophy, Mass. 9/86	withdraw food/hydration	+	*Conroy*	90.0	40.0	F.	endorses *Conroy*
Farrell, N.J. 6/24/87	withdraw respirator	+	*Conroy; Quinlan*	77.7	22.2	F.	endorses *Quinlan* and *Conroy*
Jobes, N.J. 6/24/87	withdraw food/hydration	+	*Conroy; Quinlan*; new	57.1	28.6	F.	endorses *Quinlan* and *Conroy*
Peter, N.J. 6/24/87	withdraw food/hydration	+	*Quinlan; Conroy*	62.5	12.5	F.	endorses *Quinlan* and *Conroy*

continued

Table 4-4 (continued)

Case	Substantive issue [a]	decision [b]	Key precedents	Cited	Cited 1% +	Major policy content [c]
Rasmussen, Ariz. 7/87	withdraw food/hydration	+	Hamlin; Quinlan; Torres	66.7	50.0	F. endorses *Hamlin, Torres,* and *Quinlan*
Gardner, Maine 12/3/87	withdraw food/hydration	+	Storar	40.0	0.0	F. limits decision to case by case; living will does not apply
Grant, Wash. 12/10/87	withdraw respirator and food/hydration	+	Colyer	50.0	0.0	F. endorses *Colyer*
Prange, Ill. [d] 2/88	withdraw food/hydration	+	Rasmussen	25.0	0.0	F. endorses several other decisions
Dradick, Calif. [d] 4/88	withdraw food/hydration	+	Barber	50.0	0.0	F. endorses numerous other decisions
Westchester, N.Y. 10/88	withdraw food/hydration	–	Storar	100.0	0.0	F. endorses *Storar*
Cruzan, Md. 11/88	withdraw food/hydration	–	none	–	–	I. rejects other states' decisions

[a] Withdraw or withhold respirator, other treatment, or food and hydration.
[b] + = In favor of request to withdraw or withhold.
 – = Against request to withdraw or withhold.
[c] I. = Innovative.
 F. = Follows own or other state's precedent.
[d] Intermediate court of appeals decision.

which the listed case was later cited. The second indicates the percentage of later cases in which the opinion received 1 percent or more of the lines of the citing court's majority opinions. One percent of a majority opinion was the natural breaking point in the amount of an opinion devoted to a particular precedent. These figures distinguish between the mere mention of a case, often among a long list of citations—in which courts cite many or even all other cases in the policy area—and in-depth consideration of a policy by other courts.

Early Innovators

The earliest innovators in right-to-die judicial policy were New Jersey and Massachusetts. This is perhaps not surprising, since these two states also placed high in Caldeira's aggregate measures of judicial reputation and were two of the several courts cited most often by others (Caldeira 1983, 1988). However, innovation in the right to die does not closely relate to innovations in other fields of law. For example, Canon and Baum (1981) found that New Jersey was first in tort innovations, but Massachusetts ranked forty-eighth.

Despite the lack of close parallels between innovation in the right to die and other aggregate studies of innovation and leadership, most of the fifteen states that decided right-to-die cases during the relatively short period between 1976 and 1988 generally are among the policy leaders identified by Caldeira and Canon and Baum. It probably is not a coincidence that supreme courts in New Jersey and Massachusetts produced distinctive policies early in the process—especially New Jersey, which appears on every list of innovative or prestigious courts. Moreover, a majority of the cases (sixteen of twenty-nine, or 55 percent) decided in this period were decided in just five states (New Jersey, Massachusetts, Illinois, California, and New York), all of which are ranked among the top eight in reputation by Caldeira.[7] Florida and Minnesota, which also had cases in this field, are ranked among the top fifteen in reputation, producing a combined total of nineteen of twenty-nine cases (66 percent).

I speculate that early innovation is more predictable than later adoption. A small group of states with large populations, diverse societies and economies, and perhaps with certain government-structure and cultural characteristics are more likely to produce novel litigation and judicial (and legislative) policies; but later adoption is more dependent upon the random or idiosyncratic movement of litigation through appellate courts. Thus, once we look beyond the first dozen states, which often have high scores as early innovators and adopters, we may find little consistency in the ordering of the remaining states from one policy arena to another.

Streams of Policy and Reinvention

The earliest leading courts in the right to die did not produce a uniform policy that was embraced by following courts. Instead, New Jersey and Massachusetts produced two distinctive streams of policy with different impacts. In addition to expanding the right to privacy and the power of families to act as guardians (in consultation with doctors), the New Jersey Supreme Court permitted the future withdrawal of a respirator without prior judicial approval. As Table 4-4 shows, this policy has been embraced by most other courts. However, in *Superintendent of Belchertown State School, et al. v. Joseph Saikewicz* (370 N.E.2d 417, 1977), the Massachusetts Supreme Judicial Court adopted New Jersey's right-to-privacy view, but required prior judicial approval before medical treatment could be withheld. The distinction between the courts on this point is important. The Massachusetts decision was greeted with great confusion and concern among lawyers and doctors who worried that the court intended that prior court approval be required in *all* cases involving the removal or withholding of life-sustaining treatment. Numerous articles in legal and medical journals focused on the anticipated financial and emotional burdens that the decision would impose on patients, families, and medical institutions and personnel (Doudera and Peters 1982). The Massachusetts court later modified but never fully abandoned this policy. Most important from the perspective of innovation research, its policy has been followed by only one other court.

Other states also produced distinctive policies within the broad context of earlier rulings, but with little impact on other courts. The New York Court of Appeals produced its own unique policy and contributed two of the three court cases decided against patients. Its policy is to require extensive proof of a patient's prior wishes before life-sustaining treatment can be withdrawn or withheld. This policy has been followed only by the Maine Supreme Court. The California decisions all were produced by intermediate courts of appeals and relied solely upon California precedent. They have not been cited heavily or relied upon by other courts, even though the policies of these courts are very similar to those in other states. Finally, the Missouri Supreme Court recently deviated from all others by flatly refusing to grant permission for the withdrawal of artificially administered food and hydration from a permanently comatose patient. (The United States Supreme Court heard oral arguments in this case in the 1989-1990 term; the decision is pending.)

Not only have several state supreme courts differed from the policy established by New Jersey, the issues and policy in the right to die were substantially reinvented as later litigants used essentially the same medical facts but focused on different dimensions of treatment. Significantly, major changes in policy once again followed New Jersey's lead. *In re Conroy* (486 A.2d 1209, 1985) presented the issue of defining artificial feeding and hydration as medical treatment rather than ordinary care.[8] The court ruled that artificial food and hydration was part of medical treatment and, therefore, could be withdrawn, allowing a terminally ill or permanently comatose patient to die. The New Jersey court relied heavily on its prior *Quinlan* decision and expanded the policy in that case to apply to artificial food and hydration.

Conroy may have stimulated additional litigation concerning identical issues and, with few exceptions, courts reached similar conclusions. However, many courts did not rely explicitly on *Conroy* as the key precedent but rested on several cases instead of or in addition to *Conroy*, which probably reflects the greater number of available precedents as more litigation was produced.

Citation Rates

The presence of multiple streams of policy in the early period of diffusion and the substantial enlargement and reinvention of the issue in the *Conroy* case strongly suggest that citation rates among state supreme courts cannot adequately account for policy leadership since courts have many options to choose from in formulating their own policy. They might cite many relevant cases but rely heavily on one or two in crafting their own majority opinions. Consequently, citation rates might exaggerate the amount of influence that a particular court has on others in one or more specific areas of policy.

Table 4-4 indicates the precedents that are adopted by later innovating courts and the frequency with which a particular court's precedents are cited by the later adopters. Together, they are indicators of the policy leadership role of the state supreme courts in this field of policy. Both the early New Jersey and Massachusetts decisions are cited heavily by other courts. The Massachusetts court cited the *Quinlan* case seven times and devoted fully 12.7 percent of its majority opinion to discussion and quotation of this decision—the greatest attention given by any court to the *Quinlan* decision. Of course, it was the only clearly relevant precedent available at the time. If we were to infer leadership in terms of frequency of citation, the Massachusetts court's heavy use of the *Quinlan* decision would lead us to classify Massachusetts as following New Jersey. It did, in part, but the content of Massachusetts policy also differed in important ways, suggesting that even very heavy citation may not indicate clear policy direction or the influence of one court on another. The Massachusetts decisions have been cited in nearly three-quarters of other opinions, but the policy generally has been rejected: only the Ohio Supreme Court has endorsed the Massachusetts policy in the right to die.

Courts and State Policy Making

Finally, it is important to note that the right-to-die decisions have moved the issue beyond the judicial arena to become part of a larger policy-making process in state politics. No living will legislation has been enacted in New Jersey, Massachusetts, or New York, states with powerful political and religious organizations opposed to such legislation. Nevertheless, these three states have led in the creation of distinctive judicial policies in this field.

An examination of legislative documents and hearings relating to the enactment of living will legislation in the states and intensive case studies conducted in California, Florida, and Massachusetts reveal that opposition by Catholic and right-to-life organizations has almost always blocked legislation until it appeared that the legislation might finally pass despite their opposition and they wished to influence the content of the law. Some Catholic leaders also now favor legislation as a means of curtailing court decisions which, in their view, go well beyond existing legislation and promote euthanasia (Paris and McCormick 1981).

Implications for Innovation Research

Although this research is limited to a specific set of cases, making generalization risky, it relates to previous research on innovation and leadership and future approaches to this subject. First, certain familiar courts appear as early innovators, but there is no predictable and familiar path in the diffusion of innovations. This research also reveals greater complexity in judicial policy making than generally has been assumed in state judicial politics. There are variations on the central theme of patients' rights which create important differences in how similar social problems are solved or managed in the states. Consequently, it may be hazardous to oversimplify the process of the diffusion of innovations and the content of policies created by courts. Also, the scope of judicial policy has expanded over time regarding similar factual circumstances, and courts reinvent their earlier innovations. The medical facts in most of the cases have remained the same, but the issues brought and the responses of courts have enlarged in a short period.

This research also underscores the need to identify policy leadership in ways other than mutual court citation. In the aggregate, courts that are cited most often may be the policy leaders, but this and other research suggests that citation does not always mean approval. Clearly, the failure of Massachusetts to influence the policy of most other courts would not be discovered through an analysis of citations alone.

Finally, the research suggests important political relationships between courts and legislatures and underscores the multiple avenues to judicial policy making. Unlike what was shown in the previous discussion of judicial review, none of the court decisions in the right-to-die cases overturned state laws. All of the decisions were produced through interpretation and application of precedent, and half interpreted existing state law. In addition, judicial and legislative policies dealt with somewhat different issues and there is evidence that the substantial political insulation of state courts enables them to produce policy that is unpopular with the powerful interest groups that influence state legislatures. Moreover, judicial policies that go beyond the policy preferences of interest groups and legislators may encourage state legislatures to act to limit the courts. Clearly, much more research needs to be done to elaborate on the political relationships among the branches of state government in determining the content of state policy.

Conclusion

Previous research and recent work on state supreme court judicial review and right-to-die policy have a number of implications. It is clear that we need to know much more about the avenues and means of state judicial policy making and the content of state supreme court policy. Clearly, state supreme courts are important political institutions within their own political systems, and combined, they contribute importantly to public policy nationwide. Although the existence of fifty courts makes the job more difficult, we need to produce knowledge about state supreme courts comparable to our knowledge of the U.S. Supreme Court.

But research also needs to link state supreme courts to the policy-making and political roles of other state political institutions. As important as the new federalism may be in the area of civil rights and liberties, state supreme courts have greater roles to play in traditional areas of state regulation and social and economic life, and we need to map them more fully. It would be valuable to know, for example, how state legislatures respond to state supreme court decisions overturning recent legislation and the impact of both institutions on political and social life in the states. Right-to-die policy is a new field for the courts, but also for state legislatures; as research on the law of torts has discovered, other policies have been dealt with by both institutions. We need to explore more fully the distinctive roles of each institution, their interactions in formulating policy, and their effects on the states.

Notes

1. See the various essays and research reported in Halpern and Lamb (1982). For a recent example of such treatment dealing with state supreme courts, see Baum (1989).
2. There is a revival of interest in state constitutional law and the role of state supreme courts in relying on state constitutions particularly as they pertain to individual rights. See Williams (1983, 1988). Also see the discussions of state courts and state constitutions in Porter and Tarr (1982); Tarr and Porter (1988, chap. 1); Collins, Galie, and Kincaid (1986), and the entire issue of *Intergovernmental Perspective* devoted to judicial federalism (1989).
3. See the various chapters in Porter and Tarr (1982).
4. Emmert (1988a, 1988b, 1989a, 1989b). The discussion of state judicial review in this chapter relies on Emmert and is used by permission. Professor Emmert is due the credit but not the blame, for my interpretation of various data. For additional work on state supreme court judicial review, see Fino (1984).
5. Karen Quinlan was a young woman in a coma, but not brain dead, who had been placed on a respirator in "an altered state of consciousness" with no hope of recovery. Her parents pressed attending physicians to remove the respirator so that she could die, but were refused. After much delay and litigation, the New Jersey Supreme Court, relying on an expansive interpretation of the constitutional right to privacy and the right of parents to act as guardians, ordered the respirator removed. Although the respirator was disconnected, Karen Quinlan was fed artificially and lived for another ten years.
6. The cases studied include all state supreme court and several intermediate appellate court cases involving adult right-to-die litigation decided from 1976 to 1988. The list of cases was provided by the Society for the Right to Die and confirmed through additional Lexis analysis.
7. However, the California decisions were at the intermediate appellate level.
8. The removal of artificial food and hydration first appeared in *Barber v. Superior Court* (195 Cal. Rptr. 484, 1983). However, unlike all other cases, this was a criminal case involving two doctors who removed all life support systems as well as artificial food and hydration from a terminal patient. It also is an intermediate appellate court decision and is less likely to be used by other courts.

References

Atkins, Burton M., and Henry R. Glick. 1976. Environmental and structural variables as determinants of issues in state courts of last resort. *American Journal of Political Science* 20:97-115.

Baum, Lawrence. 1989. State supreme courts: Activism and accountability. In *The state of the states,* ed. Carl E. Van Horn. Washington, D.C.: CQ Press.

Baum, Lawrence, and Bradley C. Canon. 1982. State supreme courts as activists: New doctrines in the law of torts. In *State supreme courts: Policymakers in the federal system,* ed. Mary Cornelia Porter and G. Alan Tarr. Westport, Conn.: Greenwood Press.

Caldeira, Gregory A. 1983. On the reputation of state supreme courts. *Political Behavior* 5:83-108.

———. 1985. The transmission of legal precedent: A study of state supreme courts. *American Political Science Review* 79:178-193.

———. 1988. Legal precedent: Structures of communication between state supreme courts. *Social Networks* 10:29-55.

Canon, Bradley C. 1982. A framework for the analysis of judicial activism. In *Supreme Court activism and restraint,* ed. Stephen C. Halpern and Charles M. Lamb. Lexington, Mass.: Lexington Books.

———. 1983. Defining the dimensions of judicial activism. *Judicature* 66:236-247.

Canon, Bradley C., and Lawrence Baum. 1981. Patterns of tort law innovations: An application of diffusion theory to judicial doctrines. *American Political Science Review* 75:975-987.

Casper, Jonathan D. 1976. The Supreme Court and national policy making. *American Political Science Review* 70:50-63.

Collins, Ronald K. L., Peter J. Galie, and John Kincaid. 1986. State high courts, state constitutions and individual rights litigation since 1980: A judicial survey. *Publius* 16:141-161.

Dahl, Robert A. 1958. Decision-making in a democracy: The Supreme Court as a national policy-maker. *Journal of Public Law* 6:279-295.

Daniels, Stephen. 1988. A tangled tale: Studying state supreme courts. *Law and Society Review* 22:854-861.

Doudera, A. Edward, and J. Douglas Peters, eds. 1982. *Legal and ethical aspects of treating critically and terminally ill patients.* Ann Arbor, Mich.: AUPHA Press.

Emmert, Craig F. 1988a. Issues in state supreme court judicial review cases. Paper presented at the annual meeting of the Southern Political Science Association. Atlanta, November 3-5.

———. 1988b. Judicial review in state supreme courts: Opportunity and activism. Paper presented at the annual meeting of the Midwest Political Science Association. Chicago, April 13-16.

———. 1989a. Factors affecting state supreme court decisions in judicial review cases: A multivariate analysis. Paper presented at the annual meeting of the American Political Science Association. Atlanta, August 31-September 3.

———. 1989b. *Judicial review in state supreme courts: 1981-1985.* Ph.D. dissertation, The Florida State University.

Fino, Susan P. 1984. State supreme courts and the new judicial federalism. Ph.D. dissertation, Rutgers University.

Friedelbaum, Stanley H. 1982. Independent state grounds. In *State supreme courts: Policymakers in the federal system,* ed. Mary Cornelia Porter and G. Alan Tarr. Westport, Conn.: Greenwood Press.

Glick, Henry R. 1971. *Supreme courts in state politics.* New York: Basic Books.

———. 1988. *Courts, politics and justice,* 2d ed. New York: McGraw-Hill.

Halpern, Stephen C., and Charles M. Lamb, eds. 1982. *Supreme Court activism and restraint.* Lexington, Mass.: Lexington Books.

Harris, Peter. 1982. Structural change in the communication of precedent among state supreme courts, 1870-1970. *Social Networks* 4:201-212.

Intergovernmental Perspective. 1989. Judicial federalism 16:8-32.

Jacob, Herbert. 1984. *Justice in America,* 4th ed. Boston: Little, Brown.

———. 1988. *Silent revolution: The transformation of divorce law in the United States.* Chicago: University of Chicago Press.

Kagan, Robert, Bliss Cartwright, Lawrence M. Friedman, and Stanton Wheeler. 1977. The business of state supreme courts, 1870-1970. *Stanford Law Review* 30:121-156.

———. 1978. The evolution of state supreme courts. *Michigan Law Review* 76:961-1001.

Paris, John J., and Richard A. McCormick. 1981. Living-will legislation, reconsidered. *America,* September 5, 86-89.

Porter, Mary Cornelia. 1982. State supreme courts and the legacy of the Warren Court. In *State supreme courts: Policymakers in the federal system,* ed. Mary Cornelia Porter and G. Alan Tarr. Westport, Conn.: Greenwood Press.

Porter, Mary Cornelia, and G. Alan Tarr, eds. 1982. *State supreme courts: Policymakers in the federal system.* Westport, Conn.: Greenwood Press.

Rogers, Everett. 1983. *Diffusion of innovations,* 3d ed. New York: Free Press.

Tarr, G. Alan, and Mary Cornelia Porter. 1988. *State supreme courts in state and nation.* New Haven: Yale University Press.

U.S. Department of Justice, Bureau of Justice Statistics. 1983. *State court caseload statistics.* Washington, D.C.: Government Printing Office.

Wheeler, Stanton, Bliss Cartwright, Lawrence M. Friedman, and Robert Kagan. 1987. Do the "haves" come out ahead? Winning and losing in state supreme courts, 1870-1970. *Law and Society Review* 21:403-445.

Williams, Robert F. 1983. State constitutional law processes. *William and Mary Law Review* 24:169-228.

———. 1988. *State constitutional law: Cases and materials.* Washington, D.C.: Advisory Commission on Intergovernmental Relations.

Wold, John T. 1974. Political orientations, social backgrounds, and role perceptions of state supreme court judges. *Western Political Quarterly* 27:239-248.

———. 1978. Going through the motions. *Judicature* 62:58-65.

Wold, John T., and John H. Culver. 1987. The defeat of the California justices. *Judicature* 70:348-355.

5. POLICY MAKING IN STATE TRIAL COURTS

Lynn Mather

The conventional wisdom in political science holds that appellate courts make policy and that trial courts generally do not. Trial judges, especially at the state level, are seen simply as administrators or bureaucrats who routinely process thousands of individual, private disputes and petty criminal cases. Trial judges are not, except on very rare occasions, considered to be policy makers. Despite the frequency with which this view is argued, I think it is fundamentally misguided both for its incomplete portrayal of trial court activity and for its narrow understanding of the process of policy making.

My aim in this chapter is to construct a view of state trial courts that emphasizes their political functions and highlights their role in shaping public policies.[1] To develop this perspective I first review the conventional wisdom on trial courts as administrators or norm enforcers and then discuss criticism of that view. Next I draw on the public policy literature and research on dispute transformation to expand our thinking about trial courts as policy makers. This broader view of trial courts attends to the behavior of litigants, lawyers, clerks, juries, and audiences to litigation rather than just focusing on the decisions of trial judges. In suggesting the various ways in which trial courts make public policy, I review some of the sociolegal research on litigation strategies, lawyer/client interaction, dispute transformation, pretrial negotiation, the media and trial courts, judicial decision making, and the politics of juries. The last part of the chapter illustrates my argument on trial court policy making through an analysis of changing public policy on employment contracts and the particular events in a recent lawsuit brought by a fired football coach.

I am grateful to Elizabeth Day, Gregory Garre, and Barbara Ucasz for their research assistance and to the Dartmouth Faculty Research Committee for their support. I also wish to thank John Gates, Charles Johnson, Deborah Stone, and Barbara Yngvesson for their helpful comments on an earlier draft.

Trial Courts and Policy Making

By the mid-1960s there was a major shift in the paradigm used for the analysis of courts as political scientists convincingly argued for a behavioral or political view of judicial decision making to replace the formal or legalistic view of the judicial process. While most of the new research centered on the Supreme Court, it also engendered a revival of interest in state trial courts. Studies of the politics of criminal courts from the 1920s and 1930s which had been ignored for decades were reread by a second generation of trial court scholars who, like their predecessors, were fighting against the "myth that upper courts are the heart of court-house government" (Frank 1949, 222). Research of the late 1960s and 1970s on trial courts yielded a large body of material on the politics of local criminal justice, and a smaller set of studies about civil courts.[2] Criminal court studies described and explained how charging and plea bargaining decisions were made by prosecutors, defense lawyers, and judges and what factors influenced those decisions.[3] These works revealed a great deal about court processes, but few of them explicitly considered the criminal justice policies that resulted from local patterns of discretion and plea negotiation. Similarly, studies of civil courts explored factors involved in the decision to litigate and described the processes of settlement negotiation, but they rarely analyzed civil court outcomes.[4]

Given the focus of empirical work on the processing of individual disputes (whether criminal or civil), it is not surprising that the initial theoretical conception of trial courts was one of process, not of policy. Thus, Herbert Jacob (1965) first distinguished between the *norm enforcement functions of trial courts* and the *policy-making functions of appellate courts* and, although rejecting a "mechanical" view of norm enforcement, he wrote that "it would exaggerate the process to say that trial judges make policy when they exercise their discretion in the administration of justice" (p. 24). Trial courts do not make policy, in his view, because they do not declare a general rule for handling cases, because even where there is a consistent trend in their decisions, trial judges are often not aware of it, and because few trial court cases challenge an existing norm—"Only when a norm is itself challenged can the courts engage in policy-making" (p. 26). Jacob reiterated this position in his most recent (1984) edition of *Justice in America*.[5] Moreover, this distinction between norm enforcement and policy making for trial and appellate courts has been followed recently in widely read judicial process texts such as Ball (1987), Baum (1986), Carp and Stidham (1990), and Glick (1983). For example, Baum (1986) writes that "the work of the trial courts generally involves rule application, while the creation of new rules becomes more common at successively higher levels of the court system" (p. 7). The view of trial courts as norm enforcers has been called the "dominant view" in political science (Glick 1983, 277), but a dissenting perspective has also been proposed.

The alternative conception of trial courts gives them a much greater policy-making role. Argued first by Schubert (1965) and Wells and Grossman (1966) and developed recently by Shapiro (1981) and Stumpf (1988), this view rejects the distinction between norm enforcement and policy making. For one thing, these critics challenge any notion of policy making that is defined only in terms of making "new" law: "It makes no sense to say that policy cannot be made through the application of settled law, for the mere decision to apply that law—or to depart from it—is a policy decision" (Wells and Grossman 1966, 294). Another problem is found in the distinction between policy-making decisions—said to require intent and awareness by judges as to their precedential value—and norm enforcement decisions that may also result in legal change ("slowly through judicial usage" [Jacob 1965, 26]) but without the requisite judicial consciousness. This insistence on judicial intent for policy making has been contradicted by a picture of appellate court decision making as incremental and without rational planning. Surely if appellate courts engage in policy making without their realizing it (as all judicial scholars agree they do), then the same can be said of trial courts. Instead of asking what judges are thinking about their decisions, we should simply look at the decisions themselves.

Henry R. Glick (1983, 278) presents the idea of "cumulative policy making" as an "alternative to viewing trial courts mainly as norm enforcers." [6] In this view, trial judges engage in policy making whenever they take a consistent point of view in their decisions, regardless of whether the judges are consciously aware of the policies they create. Thus, for example, when judges exercise their discretion to dismiss routinely certain kinds of cases or issue particular court orders, or when they consistently sentence criminal offenders in certain ways, they are creating policies for their communities (see Stumpf 1988). Harold J. Spaeth also argues that trial court judges make public policy through their authoritative allocation of society's resources:

> The local judge who invariably sends drunken drivers to jail, the judge in the next county who throws the book only at youthful drug offenders, and the judge who sits in the courthouse making life miserable for errant spouses who have fallen behind in their child support and alimony payments—all are making policy. (1979, 6-7)

The extensive literature on variation in criminal sentencing provides perhaps the best illustration of this kind of state trial court policy making, showing clear differences in the sentencing decisions of various urban criminal courts (see Levin 1977; Eisenstein and Jacob 1977). Sentencing behavior has also been analyzed for patterns of individual variation among judges, for example, in the study "Women as Policymakers: The Case of Trial Judges" (Gruhl, Spohn, and Welch 1981).

The identification of policy making through aggregate study of individual court decisions demonstrates a fundamental similarity between appellate and trial courts. That is, the cumulative policy making of trial courts parallels Supreme Court decision making as described by Martin Shapiro:

> The Supreme Court's contributions to policy-making in such fields as labor and tax law are not made by sweeping judicial gestures but by the patterns and overall effects of numerous decisions, none of which is individually very striking. In short, as with most administrators or decision-makers, *it is the day-to-day power over small decisions rather than the ability to change dramatically the whole course of government that often constitutes the key to judicial policy-making.* (1964, 41-42; emphasis added)

In a later work on judicial decision making, Shapiro (1970) includes trial judges and juries along with appellate courts as policy makers in the area of tort law, and he faults most efforts to identify judicial policy making for their use of "the single court decision or the single opinion of the single judge as the basic unit of analysis" and their consequent inattention to the accumulation of individual decisions that constitute the "massive, central bodies of judicial activity" (Shapiro 1970, 44). Michael Lipsky (1980) makes a similar point in his discussion of "street-level bureaucrats"—local officials (specifically including trial judges) with high discretion and relative autonomy from authority who regularly make policy through their repeated interactions with citizens.

In sum, there are strong reasons for conceptualizing trial courts as policy makers: the distinction between norm enforcement and policy making is difficult to maintain; there are clear parallels between the incremental processes that characterize trial court and appellate court decision making; and empirical evidence on cumulative policy making suggests consistent patterns in trial judges' decisions. Even though these arguments have expanded our understanding of trial courts as policy makers, they still remain incomplete. A look at two different fields of inquiry—public policy and dispute processing—will suggest still other ways in which trial courts make policy besides through the cumulative decisions of judges.

The Concept of Policy Making

In the final analysis, the answer to the question, Do trial courts make policy? depends simply on the definition of *policy making* used in the discussion, since a narrow definition tends to deny trial courts a significant policy-making role while a broader one does not.[7] When policy making is defined as the expressed declaration of a general standard for handling cases or as the establishment and use of authoritative rules (Jacob 1965, 24; Baum 1986, 6), then indeed the correct conclusion is that trial courts do not make policy. But in contrast, when one views policy making more broadly as "a problem-solving endeavor or enterprise" (Wells and Grossman 1966, 293), then the natural conclusion is that trial courts do engage in policy making. Additional support for cumulative policy making by trial judges comes from a conceptualization of policy as the "patterns of impact created by the aggregate of decisions" made by those who implement general principles (Davis and Dolbeare 1968, 242). Alternatively, Spaeth (1979) offers a broad view of policy making as the authoritative allocation of resources and then emphasizes the ways in which judicial decisions allocate resources between competing litigants. With any of these more inclusive definitions in mind, clearly trial courts make policy.

It would be nice at this point if we could turn to the public policy literature for guidance on the definitive view of policy making, but unfortunately there is no consensus there. As one book wryly notes, textbooks "traditionally give three or four definitions [of public policy], which are then shown to be inadequate. After showing the inadequacy of other definitions, the author's own definition is then put forward" (Bullock, Anderson, and Brady 1983, 2). Rather than follow this approach, I will summarize certain key ideas from the policy literature and then, in the next section, proceed inductively to show the various ways in which state trial courts make policy.

Central to any recent treatment of the concept of policy making is an insistence on including the entire policy process, rather than limiting consideration to any one stage of the process. In particular, policy is not made only at the moment a new rule or decision is announced, but instead begins from the initial point of problem definition, through the formulation of alternative solutions, to the adoption of a course of action and its final implementation. Thus, policy analysts typically define the policy-making process as a *series of different stages*. As phrased by Bullock, Anderson, and Brady (1983, 5), these stages include "problem formation, policy agenda, policy formulation, policy adoption, policy implementation, [and] policy evaluation." Although I question whether the process is as neat and orderly as conveyed by this sequence of stages, a real strength of this approach is its broad view of the policy process and rejection of definitions limited solely to the stage of policy adoption.

Second, by recognizing the differentiated nature of policy making, we can avoid the mistake of even imagining that any single political actor or institution could command the entire policy process. That is, public policy is made through the actions and interaction of different political players at different points in the process. Just as Congress may be stronger or weaker than the president on certain issues or at certain stages of policy making (Price 1985), so may the courts be most influential at particular points. Thus the question is not, Do trial courts make policy? but rather, How (or, in what ways and at what stage in the process) do trial courts make policy? Although trial courts rarely establish new legal rules, they do play an important role in the definition of policy problems, in the formulation of alternatives, and certainly in the implementation and evaluation stages of the policy process.

Third, the policy process is not unidirectional and linear such that one begins with problems and ends with solutions (or the evaluation of those solutions). Feedback loops, interactional effects, and the reverse notion of solutions creating problems must all be included in any model of policy making. That is, problems that are on policy makers' agenda for action do not arrive full blown; instead they are socially and politically constructed, and solutions may in fact produce problems. Malcolm Spector and John I. Kitsuse (1977) show how solutions lead to problems "by providing the framework within which those problems can be stated" (p. 84) and how "a prospective solution makes possible the existence of a problem by proposing that some obnoxious aspect of life, heretofore thought to be unalterable ('nothing can be done'), might be alleviated" (p. 128). Trial court outcomes, whether the result of trial or a negotiated settlement, may alert others with a similar "unperceived injurious experience" (Felstiner, Abel, and Sarat 1981, 633) to voice their grievance, with either legal or political action. Likewise, awareness of the potential clout inherent in a trial court order may lead one to search for an appropriate legal claim to obtain that clout, a process that parallels occasions of policy making in which, as Deborah A. Stone (1988) points out, one sees "a solution first and then formulate[s] a problem to require the solution" (p. 9). Further, even just hearing about someone else's legal claim can change how people view their own problems and, through these changed perceptions, contribute to the collective formulation and identification of a problem for public policy.

Finally, it is important to remember that policy making is fundamentally a "struggle over ideas" (Stone 1988, 7), a dynamic process in which political actors do more than just establish standards, solve problems, or allocate resources (though they do all of these as well). That is, they construct, maintain, and change the political order of communities through continual processes of negotiation over the identification and solution of problems. Making policy involves a competition over a normative framework for understanding events and relationships and for shaping identities and expectations, as much as it provides the resources and rules for responding to competing claims. In other words, as Stone (1988, 7) defines policy making, it is "a constant struggle over the criteria for classification, the boundaries of categories, and the definition of ideals that guide the way people behave."

Dispute Transformation in Trial Courts

Just as appellate courts make policy by creating categories (such as "fair trial," "clear and present danger," or "fundamental rights") and defining those categories through the classification of various fact situations as in or out, so do trial courts make policy by defining the categories of "reasonable man," "unfit parent," or "normal burglary" through their repeated disposition of cases. Note that it is in the disposition or handling of cases—not only in the trial judges' decisions—that we should look for this policy activity, since over 90 percent of state court cases are settled without trial; consequently, it makes little sense to exclude from consideration the bulk of what occurs in trial courts. Moreover, given that lawyers play a central role in case negotiations, we must broaden our investigation of trial court activity beyond the judge to include lawyers, litigants, juries, and others. Richard S. Wells and Joel B. Grossman (1966) first noted that most notions of judicial policy making were too judge-centered, and since then considerable research on dispute processing and legal mobilization has demonstrated the importance of nonjudicial participants in trial courts. However, current political science treatments that do acknowledge trial court policy making still limit the discussion to judicial decisions.

Instead of starting with trial court outcomes, we should begin with a disputant's choice to commence legal action. By invoking legal norms, citizens actively participate in the making and implementation of public policy (Zemans 1983). Going to court can be seen as simply one of several political alternatives for asserting a claim, and indeed, historically litigation has been an alternative form of political activity (McIntosh 1983). When voicing and responding to claims in trial court, disputants rephrase their concerns to take advantage of the leverage provided by law. Or, as Edward H. Levi (1949) describes the legal process, parties in a lawsuit argue the similarity or difference between fact situations in an effort to bring the law to their side; legal rules are created out of the process of comparing examples; consequently, it is the parties and their lawyers as much as the court who participate in the lawmaking.

A court case is not an objective event or thing, but is itself a social and political construct. Disputes that enter court have been reformulated or transformed into legal language (for example, a car crash becomes a "tort," a beating becomes an "assault") to facilitate their resolution (Mather and Yngvesson 1981).[8] Dispute transformation changes a conflict in form or content from its initial perception by the parties. Moreover, dispute transformation inevitably involves values and legal norms, as fact situations are defined in terms of one or more particular normative frameworks. The political significance of changes that occur in the disputing process lies not in the *number* of grievances that do or do not become claims, disputes, or court cases (Miller and Sarat 1981), but in the *systems of meaning* used to define those claims, disputes, and court cases.

Courts typically transform cases by imposing conventional categories for classification on events in dispute, that is, by *narrowing*. For instance, lawyers and judges narrow cases by classifying them according to their own folk system of "normal crime," "routine debt," or "ordinary divorce." With the classification comes an expected mode for handling and a typical outcome. Consistent patterns of case outcome in local courts (referred to earlier as cumulative policy making) result from this narrowing of cases. Sometimes, however, courts expand or shift the framework of argument to challenge conventional understandings. Dispute *expansion* changes the normative framework used to interpret events by rephrasing them in terms of a new system of meaning. Thus, an "ordinary" case of parental child abuse is reinterpreted as a case of family discipline based on strong religious faith; or a "routine" firing of an incompetent employee is transformed into an instance of discrimination; or a "typical" hired-gun murder becomes self-defense by a battered wife. Cases may be expanded through the efforts of litigants, their supporters or lawyers, judges or juries, or an audience to the litigation; legal change is linked to social change in part through the expansion of individual disputes (Mather and Yngvesson 1981).

As others besides the litigants become involved in a case, they bring their own interests, perspectives, and agendas to bear on it. Throughout the court process, the definition (as well as resolution) of a case is negotiated and renegotiated by various parties. A central problem becomes how to assert and maintain control over the object in dispute. Clearly the power to transform cases is not equally distributed in court, and tensions frequently arise between lawyer and client, opposing lawyers, lawyer and judge, judge and jury, or even between the court and the wider community. Understanding policy making as it occurs in trial courts involves attention to struggles over the nature and meaning of a case.

The language used to define disputes is of particular importance. The language of law provides the framework in which to present arguments and fix the meaning of disputes. Further, through imaginative use of the linguistic framework, new juxtapositions can be arranged that may change the meaning of old terms. The language in which a case is phrased not only affects its outcome but also connects directly to the political order. For instance, calling an incident a "family fight" suggests the inappropriateness of court action and likely dismissal of charges, but defining the same event as "domestic violence" indicates a serious problem both for the individuals involved and for the polity. Attempts to create new orderings require linguistic as well as political strategies, as those who wish to expand a dispute for the purpose of stimulating policy change must consider public reactions to their formulation. In considering how problems come to be viewed as important and appropriate for political action, Roger W. Cobb and Charles D. Elder (1983) observe that the language of the disputants is "a crucial element in determining the likelihood of an issue attaining access to the political agenda" (p. 38). Another crucial element in agenda building is the scope of the conflict. By enlarging the audience to a particular case, lawyers or interest groups, for example, can change the balance of power in the courtroom (see Schattschneider 1960). Issues that might otherwise be narrowed in conventional ways have greater potential to be redefined through the implicit participation of a wider audience.

By combining these ideas about public policy, dispute transformation, and agenda building, we can see numerous ways in which trial courts contribute to policy making (see also Gambitta 1981). Table 5-1 summarizes and illustrates how trial courts make policy. Clearly a judicial decision to adopt a new law is only one out of a wide range of policy activities that occur in trial courts. Other important aspects of court policy making include the definition of political problems (including the attention, legitimacy, and support for dealing with problems), the construction of solutions to problems (through the creation of local norms and the implementation of law), and the feedback and evaluation of policy (through the response to litigation and the filing of new legal claims). Note that court cases can contribute to policy making at any stage of the litigation and at any stage of the policy process. Thus Table 5-1 does not necessarily reflect a develop-

Table 5-1   How Trial Courts Make Public Policy

Aspect of policy making	Examples
Agenda setting	Case screening defines what is a "legal" matter and what is not; what is "serious" and what is not.
	Litigation encourages others to file similar claims in same court and elsewhere.
	Interest groups file "test cases" to place issue on agenda of courts.
Forum for political argument	Courts provide public arena for discussion of political issues.
	Cases contribute to definition of policy problem and formulation of alternatives.
	Litigation offers occasion to explain ideas and express beliefs.
Agenda building	Particulars of case publicize issue and attract audience.
	Court hearing gives legitimacy to issue and to litigants.
	Court cases influence agenda of other political actors (appellate courts, legislatures, etc.).
	Media devotes attention to problem through news analyses, talk shows, docudramas, etc.
Mobilization of support or opposition	Litigation arouses sympathy or aversion in mass public.
	Cases spur interest groups to act (for example, with money, time, political and legal advice).
	New interest groups are formed to lobby issue.
	Political participation increases to address problem.
Definition of local legal norms	Judicial and jury "fact-finding" leads to construction of local legal categories.
	Norms are set through routine classification of cases (dispute narrowing) in legal negotiation.
	Appellate and statutory law is adapted and implemented for local community.
Definition of new legal norms	Judicial activism leads to new case law.
	Juries substitute their own norms for the formal law (for example, jury nullification).
	Novel legal issue forces judges to create new law.
	Legal framework for interpreting events or relationships changes through dispute expansion.
Political symbolism	Cases act as metaphors for broader problem.
	Individuals and groups associated with litigation attract wider coalitions or cleavages.
	Language of case shapes debate on the policy issues.
Provision of political or legal resources	Groups and individuals are advantaged by the publicity and legitimacy given their cause.
	Use of legal "rights" provides bargaining leverage in conflicts.
	People change their behavior to avoid potential litigation.

mental sequence of policy making whereby every case begins with "agenda setting" and concludes with the "provision of political or legal resources," although such a sequence could happen.

State Trial Court Policy Making

To illustrate how state trial courts make policy, I next review some previous research and present an extended case study of my own. Drawing first on the literature about state trial courts, I provide examples of how courts contribute to problem definition, the formulation of alternatives, and the adoption and implementation of policy. The discussion is organized according to conventional steps in the trial court process: filing a legal claim, negotiation, adjudication, and impact of the case. In the last section of the chapter I analyze the events and policy consequences of *Yukica v. Leland*, a recent New Hampshire lawsuit over a broken contract brought by a college football coach after he was fired.

Filing a Legal Claim

The initial decision to file a lawsuit is highly problematic, as sociolegal research has clearly shown. Whether someone with a grievance will even seek a lawyer depends upon factors such as perceptions of the law, of the court, and of the issues in conflict; the alternatives to law for resolving the dispute; the relationship between disputants; the goals and resources of disputants; and cultural attitudes toward law and conflict.[9] Lawyers then play a critical role in translating issues and events into legal discourse and in adding their own concerns, interests, and beliefs to those of their client (Cain 1979; Mather and Yngvesson 1981). The dynamics of interaction between lawyer and client act as one influence on the final construction of the legal claim (Rosenthal 1974; Sarat and Felstiner 1986), while economic concerns (Johnson 1981), cultural norms (Engel 1984), and political interests (Olson 1984) may act as others.

In "Sander County," a small rural county in Illinois, David M. Engel (1984) reports that relatively few personal injury claims were filed in the civil court.[10] Reluctance to use tort law for injuries was due primarily to deeply ingrained attitudes among most of the residents, attitudes that were reflected—and reinforced—by the local lawyers of the county and by the decisions of trial judges and juries (very low awards and suspicion of personal injury plaintiffs). Engel writes that traditional values of individual responsibility, hard work, and self-sufficiency help to explain community pressures against personal injury litigation. That is, most residents felt that transforming a personal injury (even when the fault of another) into a financial and legal claim was an attempt to avoid personal responsibility and an inappropriate effort to cash in on misfortune. However, in contrast to these negative attitudes and infrequent use of tort law for injuries, litigation over broken contracts (even for "routine" debt collection) was quite common (nearly ten times as frequent as personal injury litigation) and met with wide approval. Engel explains that contract litigation "was seen as enforcing a core value of the traditional culture of Sander County: that promises should be kept and people should be held responsible when they broke their word" (p. 577).

If we try to evaluate the Sander County civil court using the framework of norm enforcement, we quickly run into the question of which norms are being enforced—the legal norms established by the Illinois supreme court and legislature, or the norms of Sander County? By Engel's account it is clearly the latter. In effect, the public policy in Sander County on personal injuries was adopted and implemented through a complex process—in and around the state trial court—involving an aversion by most victims to define their problems as legal ones due to the social meaning of personal injuries, stigmatization of those few victims who did file legal claims, a reluctance of local lawyers to bring personal injury actions, and hostility toward personal injury plaintiffs by local juries.

The role of civil litigants and private lawyers in shaping civil law is similar to that of victims of crime, police, and prosecutors in shaping criminal law. In particular, police and prosecutors establish criminal law norms for their local communities through their routine policies on arrest and case screening. For example, in the early 1970s the district attorney's office in Los Angeles had an official policy of filing misdemeanor, rather than felony, charges for all offenses with particular fact situations: possession of dangerous drugs if ten pills or less; possession of marijuana if five cigarettes or less; assault if between family members; statutory rape if the defendant had no prior felony; bookmaking if no suspicion of organized crime involvement; and so forth (Mather 1979). This policy was written and circulated within the office after use for several years as a set of informal guidelines. Other district attorney's offices in California defined their own—and often very different—policies for prosecution on the level of charge and on dismissal of (or refusal to file) charges.[11] Consequently, although the California legislature had adopted general criminal statutes for the entire state, the actual criminal law policies for a given area were determined by prosecutors who set criteria such as these for classifying and assigning meaning to various behaviors. Prosecutors are not entirely free in constructing criteria for case screening, however, since they operate in a close working environment with police, defense attorneys, and judges, and are constrained as well by the political and social context of their communities (see Cole 1970; Eisenstein and Jacob 1977).

In some communities the decision to issue a criminal complaint is made by a lay magistrate, the court clerk, to whom both private citizens and police (if there has been no arrest) must apply. Barbara Yngvesson (1988) describes the politics of this process in neighbor and family conflicts in the "Jefferson County" district court in Massachusetts. When citizens come to court with their complaints and disputes, the clerk's role is to act as watchdog, distinguishing between "real" criminal conflicts that are worthy of the court's time, and "garbage" cases that require mediation or advice by the clerk but do not merit the issuance of a complaint. The clerk typically dominates the hearings, Yngvesson reports,

> by controlling the language in which issues are framed, the range of evidence presented, and the sequence of presentation. He silences some interpretations and privileges others, constructing the official definition of what constitutes order and disorder in the lives of local citizens. (p. 410)

For instance, a complaint by one citizen of assault and threats by another child on her daughter was transformed by the clerk into normal behavior among children ("Kids push kids," pp. 434-435). But even while the clerk is helping to define norms and construct the community, community residents are using the clerk and the power of the courthouse to further their own interests in various social and political conflicts, and it is by this interaction that "court and community are mutually shaped" (p. 410).

In these examples, the cumulative acts of filing a legal claim, filing criminal charges, or issuing a criminal complaint defined the issues for consideration by the trial courts of Sander County, Los Angeles County, and Jefferson County. This "routine" agenda setting involved important political decisions to define some conflicts as legal matters and others as essentially private. Even where certain public policies (such as personal injury law or felony statutes) were clearly established by other branches of the government, they could not be implemented unless claims on those policies were voiced and then admitted into court by private lawyers, public prosecutors, or court clerks. Moreover, given that "whoever decides what the game is about decides also who can get into the game" (Schattschneider 1960, 195), it is clear that such case screening significantly affects not only the problems to be considered but also the balance of power among different groups and individuals.

Control over the agenda of trial courts is not entirely in the hands of lawyers and legal officials, however; citizen participation in voicing their grievances also plays a role. At a very basic level, lawyers need clients to stay in business and prosecutors need public support to stay in office. But even further, there is an interaction between citizens bringing their demands to legal officials and the ability of those officials to transform those demands into public discourse. For example, when many rape victims had their complaints summarily rejected by prosecutors as not involving "real" crimes, women victims were effectively denied access to the "game" of the criminal courts. The modest improvement that has occurred in the courts' response to rape complaints is only partly due to increased sensitivity and changed consciousness of legal officials. It has also resulted from women's willingness to pursue their grievances in court; the readiness of those at support centers to act as advocates for victims; pressure exerted on officials from political leaders, interest groups, and the courts themselves; and change in state laws and in ideas about rape and its social meaning.[12]

Customary frameworks for classifying certain disputes as "legal" and rejecting others develop their strength through repeated use, but they also change—usually in slow, incremental ways—through their imposition on new and different disputes. Sometimes such change results from an otherwise uneventful case, for example, through publicity that attracts an audience and influences the actions of regular court participants. At other times, litigants or their lawyers consciously seek such change and plan their litigation strategy accordingly: to raise new arguments, obtain publicity, gain supporters, and, if not to achieve actual policy change, at least to gain greater legitimacy for their views.

Test cases sponsored by social reform organizations are a classic example of policy making in state trial courts through the filing of legal claims. Beginning with the National Association for the Advancement of Colored People's (NAACP) litigation campaign on behalf of desegregation, and continuing through later use of courts by consumer and environmental organizations, interest groups have used state trial courts for the express purpose of defining issues, arguing their cause, formulating solutions, and working generally toward a change in public policy (Handler 1978; Vose 1959). Social reform litigation has increased in frequency in recent years, and has also shifted somewhat in style and strategy as a result of greater "rights consciousness," expansion of statutory and regulatory remedies, and easier access to the judicial process for articulating group interests (Olson 1984, 4-5). In her study of lawsuits brought by disability rights groups to gain access to mass transit, Susan M. Olson shows how litigation merges with political activity outside the courts and how conscious political strategies shape decisions about the form and content of litigation. For example, she describes interest groups "stacking the plaintiffs," a process of choosing the most appealing representative of their claim and also of enlarging the class of plaintiffs to increase their size and their diversity (a kind of "ticket balancing" of plaintiffs) (Olson 1984, 13-16). The disability rights organizations in the lawsuits for accessible transit were especially active clients in the litigation, participating significantly in decisions about case filing and settlement strategy.

In contrast, litigation strategy in class action lawsuits tends to be determined almost exclusively by lawyers. Class actions, an alternative to organizational lawsuits for aggregating large numbers of plaintiffs, are fascinating legal devices that depend on the initiative of a lawyer for their creation. In effect, an entrepreneurial lawyer can create a class, an abstract, formal entity for the purpose of litigation, and, through the class action, could conceivably enforce legal rights against the wishes of class members (Garth 1982). The most successful class actions, however, are likely to be those in which the lawyer not only facilitates access to the courts, but also engages in political education and organization of the class members (Paul-Shaheen and Perlstadt 1982). Class actions that both achieve and sustain some kind of policy change tend to combine political and legal strategies; that is, using litigation as a political resource can facilitate the mobilization of the class, attract supporters to the cause, and change the normative framework of the wider policy debate (Mather 1982; Scheingold 1974).

In sum, the simple act of filing a legal claim in a state trial court can have enormous political—and policy—significance. It may constitute a step in creating new ways of thinking about a problem or it may reaffirm conventional norms. Merely by bringing their demands to the court, litigants participate in the maintenance and development of law; lawyers aid in this enterprise and frequently dominate it. Moreover, the court, as an institution, is defined by the cases filed with it, a definition that shapes in turn how future disputants will view and use the court.

Negotiation

The predominant mode of dispute processing in state trial courts is negotiation, usually just between opposing lawyers, but sometimes with the participation of the judge. Although I distinguish between the negotiation and adjudication phases for purposes of discussion here, it is important to realize that they are not entirely distinct. When negotiation occurs in the context of its alternative—adversary trial—then the issues, norms, and principles of trial enter into and influence the course of negotiations. That is, as Robert H. Mnookin and Lewis Kornhauser (1979) write, bargaining occurs within "the shadow of the law." Marc Galanter (1984) notes that negotiation and litigation really comprise a single process—"litigotiation" it might be called—in which parties negotiate through mobilization of the court. Since most case outcomes emerge from negotiations between lawyers and not from trial, more research should be devoted to understanding the normative content and policy implications of the negotiation process.

One reason that political scientists tend to ignore out-of-court bargaining processes could be the belief that such bargaining is shaped solely by individual interests and negotiating skill without reference to norms. Yet this view lacks support in empirical and theoretical studies of dispute negotiation.[13] Melvin A. Eisenberg (1976), for example, reminds us that observations of negotiations reveal that they proceed largely by the "invocation, elaboration, and distinction of principles, rules, and precedents" (p. 639). He suggests that by treating the verbal content of negotiation as meaningful, we find a norm-centered process that is quite similar for both dispute negotiation and adjudication. Note that even where bargaining involves compromise based on differing strength and interests, there is usually an effort to phrase the compromise in normative terms; significantly, such a transformation reinforces the power of those norms and ideas independent of individual interests that gave rise to the rephrasing.

Most of the empirical research on case negotiation in American courts centers on the plea bargaining process in criminal court. What emerges from this research is a picture of case dispositions shaped by local understandings and values of the courtroom work group.[14] Attorneys who work regularly with one another develop shared notions of the criteria for distinguishing between cases and informal norms for applying the categories of the criminal statutes to the individual cases. For example, while the penal code does not differentiate between the amount of money or stolen goods involved in a felony theft case, in a local courthouse "everyone knows" that the more stolen, the more serious the case is. This working knowledge is shaped in part by patterns of judge and jury behavior: perceptions of likely trial outcomes thus constitute the law that influences plea bargaining in its shadow. But defense and prosecuting lawyers also create the law themselves through their own criteria for classifying cases and ideas about "what a case is worth." For instance, attorneys in Los Angeles explained plea bargaining in first degree robbery cases as narrowing cases in terms of whether they involve "real" first degree robberies or not. "We look at the background of the individuals, how much involvement they've had with the law, and the circumstances of the case," as described by one prosecutor; put more simply by a public defender, a "real" first degree robbery involves "the meanest guys ... the least going for them. They're really vicious ... terrible S.O.B.s ... backgrounds going way back to childhood with crimes of violence. Hostile, very aggressive acts"

(Mather 1979, 106, 102). When lawyers engage in plea bargaining, they are negotiating identities and events and transforming them into particular categories of case outcomes. This is an active, political process quite in contrast to passive, administrative enforcement. Or, as Joseph R. Gusfield (1981) describes the disposition of drunk drivers in a local court, it involves a process of negotiating meaning rather than a "consistent, direct implementation of a clearly stated rule and a clearly perceived instance of its violation" (p. 161).

Those few empirical studies we have of out-of-court bargaining in civil cases also show the narrowing of disputes into conventional categories and the use of norms in settlement. In his classic study of personal injury negotiations, H. Laurence Ross (1970) describes the principal issue between attorney and insurance adjuster as whether the case should be considered routine or serious. While each side used various bargaining tactics, he notes, they also each tried to frame their positions in terms of general, mutually shared principles. Recent research by James B. Atleson (1989) describes the transformation of labor disputes in settlement negotiations between attorneys and judge in Buffalo, New York. In cases of labor union picketing where employers seek injunctions against the picketing, Atleson asks why most actions are settled despite strong statutory law against such injunctions. He finds lawyers (who work regularly together in a relatively small community representing employers and unions) creating their own standards for compromise, standards that are influenced by their perceptions of the role of police, of the unpredictability of judicial decisions, and of appellate case law. Interestingly, although certain aspects of the formal law were potentially ambiguous, both company and union lawyers acted as if the law were clear; indeed it *was* clear for the lawyers, as Atleson (p. 61) argues, because they had implicitly created it themselves. Using these shared norms and understandings, lawyers typically transformed a dispute over the union's right to picket into a conflict over interests that could be settled by agreement to limit the number or location of picketers or both.

Negotiation to settle cases without formal legal action thus operates with lawyers in center stage and often reveals lawyers to be the creators as well as the enforcers of legal norms. Consistent patterns of criminal court sentencing, viewed in one sense as cumulative policy making by trial court judges, may actually be more reflective of routine dispute transformation by attorneys. Central to the negotiation process is the construction of disputes as particular kinds of cases where each kind has a well-known path for resolution, or where there is potential to negotiate a new resolution. Other parties (such as clients, their supporters, or the trial judge) can actively affect this bargaining process. Although most judges do not participate in plea negotiations in criminal cases, they do play a significant role in the settlement of civil cases. In a nationwide survey, 68.7 percent of state court judges responded that they typically did not attend plea negotiations; in contrast, 78.2 percent reported that they normally did intervene in civil settlement discussions, either through the use of cues or suggestions or through the use of direct pressure (Ryan et al. 1980, 175-177). It would be interesting to know more about the nature of such judicial intervention, not just about its style but about its normative content as well.

Adjudication

Discussion of cumulative policy making in trial courts usually centers on judicial actions in adjudication. Trial court researchers have sought to identify and then explain variation in judicial decision making by factors such as role orientation and attitudes (Gibson 1978), method of judicial recruitment and social background of the judge (Levin 1977), environmental context (Gibson 1980), public opinion (Kuklinski and Stanga 1979), and gender of the judge (Gruhl, Spohn, and Welch 1981). These empirical studies have yielded some extremely interesting results about individual decision making by local judges and about the cumulative policies from routine decision making, but these studies have all examined sentencing in criminal cases. What about judicial decisions on pretrial motions or on bail, or about motions or judgments in civil law cases? We need to know more about how judges formally and informally define the local meaning of a broad range of legal norms, especially in civil cases.

Trial judges routinely construct local operating policies in state courts, and they also participate in changing policy by defining entirely new legal norms. The creation of new law happens infrequently in both trial and appellate courts, but it is still useful to consider how and when such lawmaking occurs. On the one hand, some trial judges assume a particularly expansive and creative style that may result in innovation, and on the other hand, litigants or their lawyers may raise challenges in a case in an attempt to force a judge to develop new precedent, regardless of the judge's predisposition toward lawmaking.

Although most research on judicial activism has been done on appellate courts, a few studies have looked at state trial judges. Trial judges vary individually and from one locality to another in their willingness to depart from precedent. That some judges believe the judicial role to be highly creative and discretionary while others favor strict adherence to precedent has been explained by Austin Sarat (1977) and Gregory A. Caldeira (1977) in terms of incentive theory. That is, the personal incentives or motivations of judges are said to explain their role orientations (which in theory should explain their behavior).[15] In a different approach to identifying variation in trial judges, anthropologists John M. Conley and William M. O'Barr (1988) applied conversational analysis to the texts of hearings in small claims courts. Their analysis of judicial speech revealed several judicial types. One of these was the "lawmaker," a judge who uses legal principles primarily as resources rather than constraints and who adapts or invents law in order to pursue justice. Another type of activist judge was the "mediator," a judge who manipulates procedure and exerts his or her own view of a case in order to conciliate the disputants.

Just as judicial activism has many different meanings at the appellate level (Canon 1982), so it does at the trial level. Marc Galanter, Frank S. Palen, and John M. Thomas (1979) outline a number of independent activist dimensions along which trial judges may deviate from the prototype of the passive arbiter bound by precedent. For some of these dimensions, it is easy to see how an active judge can contribute significantly to creating new policies. For example, judges who are doctrinally innovative (not precedent bound), assertive (not deferential) toward other political actors, or managerial (not the passive umpire) are more likely to shape cases before them in dynamic and political ways. Two other dimensions also suggest strong potential for proactive policy making by trial judges: substantive policy orientation (rather than formal or legalistic approach) and a broad view of cases (rather than seeing them one by one). Interestingly, the last two dimensions are similarly identified in two separate studies (Caldeira 1977; Galanter, Palen, and Thomas 1979) and both consider the combination of traits to be policy making. In their view, then, judicial policy makers are those who use the law to advance policy goals and whose consideration of issues goes beyond the individual case to the community.

In some trial court cases, new law is created not because of a particularly active judge but because litigants and lawyers present arguments that compel judicial lawmaking. With changing social, economic, and technological conditions, people are forever fighting over new problems that were not foreseen by existing law. As lawyers expand legal frameworks to address such conflicts, they force judges to choose between competing interpretations and thus to invent new law. The recent *Baby M* case illustrates this point well. Lawyers representing the biological father and mother of a baby conceived by a surrogate arrangement debated the child custody dispute in terms of conflicting expanded frameworks. The New Jersey trial judge in the case had to define a new legal norm simply to settle the dispute. Other examples of new issues for trial judges include the custody determination of frozen embryos in a divorce case, the prosecution for manslaughter of a woman who had used cocaine before delivering a stillborn fetus, or the right of family members and their doctor to disconnect life support for a terminally ill patient. Note that even if the judge's decision at trial is ultimately overturned by an appellate court (as it was in the *Baby M* case), it has still contributed to the creation of new policy. Judges in other states faced with a similar case may prefer the reasoning and original trial judgment over the views of the appellate court.

The initial court case on a novel issue may also come to symbolize and define the problem for public policy. Given its symbolic importance and media attention, the case becomes an arena for advancing ideas and interpretations of events not just in the confines of the courtroom but to a broader public as well. In such a setting the trial judge must fashion a decision for the particular case yet also be aware of how the decision will be used by others to build political support or opposition. The policy consequences of a decision at trial may thus depend less on the judge and more on the actions of others—the media, lawyers, interest groups, political leaders, or an interested audience.

Another kind of case that forces trial judges into a more active policy role is complex, multiparty litigation such as a lawsuit over school desegregation, conditions in a public mental hospital or prison, or responsibility for environmental pollution. While these cases most frequently appear in federal district courts, they are also brought in state trial courts. By virtue of the very nature of such a lawsuit, judges are forced to define problems, preside over and mediate between important actors, and construct the appropriate law for dealing with controversial social and political conflicts. The diffuse scope of issues and parties and the continuous interplay of factual and legal issues require that the trial judge actively shape the litigation (Chayes 1976). In a recent environmental pollution trial in San Bruno, California, proceedings were moved from the courthouse to a former school auditorium (remodeled at a cost of $661,000) to accommodate the huge number of lawyers involved. The Shell Oil Company was suing 250 of its insurance carriers for the costs of cleaning up hazardous waste sites, while the insurance companies had brought in the federal government and the state governments of Colorado and California on their behalf (Labaton 1987). Because of the multiple parties and complex issues of insurance liability and environmental law, the California judge was compelled to construct policy for the case.

Juries as well as judges preside over adjudication and also play an important role in trial court policy making. Although the petit jury has a long and rich political history, discussion of juries frequently ignores their political features and concentrates instead on their decision-making processes. Exceptions in this regard are Gary J. Jacobsohn's (1977) and James P. Levine's (1983a, 1983b) explicit investigations of the ways in which juries participate in the formulation of public policy. Juries make policy through the routine process of fact finding and through the occasional substitution of their own legal norms for those of the legislative or appellate courts.

Ostensibly juries only establish the facts in dispute and apply the law as given to them by the trial judge, but it is well known that a clear distinction between facts and law is difficult to maintain. For example in a negligence case, the jury must evaluate the facts of a defendant's actions to conclude whether or not "reasonable care" was exercised; simply by resolving the facts, the jury is also interpreting the law, that is, the jury is defining what legally constitutes reasonable care. Jacobsohn quotes the comment of one legal scholar on such cases: "The jury makes policy in the guise of 'finding the facts'" (1977, 80). Interestingly, one can examine trends in jury behavior for the implicit policies they reveal, for example, toward criminal defendants. Research in the 1950s suggested that juries were more lenient than judges in criminal cases (Kalven and Zeisel 1966), but more recent data point to "jury toughness," an increase in the conviction rate by juries over that of judges (Levine 1983a).[16] Levine compares conviction rates for state judges and juries over time with public opinion data on criminal justice to conclude that the current severity of juries reflects prevailing conservative ideology.

A second form of jury policy making occurs when juries in effect create their own legal norms for resolving a case. Jury nullification, the most commonly cited example of such independent jury action, occurs when juries ignore the formally stated law to reach a verdict based on their particular sense of justice. For instance, juries frequently acquitted obviously guilty offenders of liquor violations during Prohibition to express their hostility to the law, and juries of the late 1960s sometimes did the same for defendants charged with possessing small amounts of marijuana. In another example, from Canada, abortion in Quebec was effectively legalized as a result of jury nullification; believing that abortion should not be a criminal offense, three separate juries between 1973 and 1976 refused to convict a doctor charged with performing illegal abortions. As a result the Quebec government stopped enforcing the federal law.[17] Rather than invalidating a law, juries may also modify it in particular ways through the informal development of their own substantive rules. Although juries do not officially communicate with each other, they do reflect the norms or attitudes of a local community (as illustrated by jury actions in personal injury cases described by Engel [1984] in Sander County). In a study of jury verdicts in medical malpractice cases in California, James L. Croyle (1979) suggests how the development of substantive jury norms may provide an explanation for the divergence of jury verdicts from appellate court doctrine. As an example, he cites an interesting decision rule of juries that seemed to emerge in his analysis of verdicts:

> If the plaintiff goes to a medical practitioner, hospital or clinic with a relatively minor medical problem and comes away from that practitioner or institution with a relatively serious medical problem he will most likely be given a jury verdict regardless of the rules relating to malpractice. Similarly, if he is marginally worse off, or simply bad off in a different way, he is unlikely to win a jury verdict regardless of the question of negligence. (p. 11)

That is to say, juries appear to ignore formal liability doctrine and construct their own policy of compensation.

Impact of Litigation

The very process of litigation operates to define problems, identities, and relationships; to adapt formal state law to local beliefs and conditions; and to create local legal norms that may, at some future point, influence state policy. The immediate impact of any particular case is generally restricted to the local community, although occasionally the case may have broader policy ramifications (for example, in test cases brought by interest groups, the introduction of new issues at trial, the broad construction of a case by a policy-making judge, or instances of jury nullification). Also, some cases that are framed as narrow legal claims and decided accordingly may actually represent far wider interests so that the case outcome will also have a broader meaning. For instance, Katherine Bishop (1989) reports from northern California on the recent use of small claims courts to fight drug dealers. In one of the cases, fifteen neighbors filed individual claims (for the court maximum of $2,000 each) against the owner of a house used for drug use and sale. The plaintiffs argued that the owner was negligent for maintaining a public nuisance. They won a favorable judgment and award of $30,000 from the court. Subsequently, the owner evicted the drug-dealing tenants and the city boarded up the house. Thus, although phrased as a narrow legal claim, the case had wide ramifications.[18]

Beyond the local court and community, cases can influence how others in similar situations think about and react to disputes. Regardless of the nature of the final case outcome, the very fact of raising and resolving a claim in court legitimizes the grievance and may encourage others to pursue similar complaints. Informal communications networks among likeminded litigants or lawyers can heighten the impact of litigation. For example, insurance companies, environmentalists, asbestos manufacturers, women's activists, and a host of other groups closely watch the progress of certain lawsuits and attend to the language and strategies used. Specialized groups of lawyers (such as prisoners' rights specialists, the personal injury bar, employment law experts) devote even more attention to relevant litigation and, when accompanied by political strategies (Scheingold 1974), can be effective in helping to change policy. Note that the policy influence of a lawsuit may occur even for parties who lose in court. Gambitta (1981) compared the impact of several lawsuits that challenged school financing laws and found that the "winning" litigants failed to obtain full policy reform, while the "losing" litigants in a separate challenge ultimately succeeded despite their defeat in court.

The most dramatic way in which a trial court case can lead to widespread policy change is by its role in the process of agenda building. A controversial trial, particularly with extensive media coverage, can lead to the identification of an important public issue and propel its consideration onto the agenda of political decision makers. There are two ways we can think about this process. On the one hand, research on agenda building suggests how to conceptualize the process as a sequence of different stages, with pressure for expansion or contraction of conflict depending on the nature of the issues, the groups involved, the type of media coverage, and so forth (Cobb and Elder 1983; Cook 1981; Nelson 1984). A controversial trial initially provides a forum for debate over the definition and solution of a conflict and calls attention to the importance of the dispute. Influenced by the trial, supporters and opponents may organize on their own, or in connection with established interest groups. Political leaders may respond to this political mobilization by issuing public statements of concern or by initiating legislative change.

For example, immediately after the highly publicized custody trial over Baby M, the following events occurred to help place surrogate motherhood on the popular agenda: national polls were conducted to gauge public response; newspapers were flooded with letters and editorials; and comments on the dispute were made by President Reagan, Pope John Paul II, and scores of elected officials. Interest groups were formed on both sides of the issue, and leaders of organizations such as the American Civil Liberties Union and the National Organization for Women met to consider their response. Organized moves for policy change occurred in the appellate court of New Jersey (with the filing of numerous amicus curiae briefs), through newly created task forces, and within legislative arenas and public hearings. By December 1987, less than nine months after the trial court's decision in *Baby M,* seventy bills seeking to ban, regulate, or study surrogacy had been introduced in twenty-seven states, three bills had been introduced in Congress, and Louisiana had enacted the country's first law against surrogacy (Peterson 1987).

Instead of looking at the policy impact of a trial in a chronological or sequential way, we could focus on its symbolic dimensions. Drawing on ideas about drama, language, and symbolic politics, we could investigate the ways in which trials act as metaphors for larger social or political concerns. Depending on the elements of a case and the way it is presented by the media, a particular lawsuit may reveal or exacerbate deep social cleavages. When Bernard Goetz shot four black youths in a New York subway several years ago, the case threw into sharp relief the city's conflicts over racial tension, crime, and violence. Indeed, the real import of a court or jury trial lies not in the rule that is enforced, but in the ritualized acting out of popular beliefs. Trials generally function as a series of object lessons and examples (Arnold 1935), but they also provide an arena for the dramatization of conflicting ideas. To understand more about how trial courts shape public policy, we should explore how they create expectations and influence perceptions of right and wrong. That is, we should include trial courts in our study of what Murray Edelman (1964) calls the symbolic uses of politics.

The following New Hampshire lawsuit provides another example of the politics of litigation and the ways in which trial courts participate in the formation of public policy as exemplified by the categories of Table 5-1.

Case Study: *Yukica v. Leland*

On November 29, 1985, after a disappointing football season, the head football coach at Dartmouth College, Joseph Yukica, was fired.[19] Three days later, Yukica filed suit in Grafton County, New Hampshire, Superior Court against Edward Leland, Dartmouth's athletic director, charging a breach of contract and seeking a temporary injunction to halt the termination and to prevent Dartmouth from taking steps to hire a new coach. Judge Walter Murphy granted the temporary injunction, but prior to a full hearing on the merits of Yukica's claim the parties negotiated a settlement out of court. Although the law had clearly favored Dartmouth, Yukica succeeded in continuing as head coach for one more Dartmouth football season.

On the face of it, there is little to commend this case to the student of public policy making. It was a suit involving private law, filed in a New Hampshire county court, that never even went to trial. Although the judge's order to grant a temporary injunction surprised observers, the order had been carefully tailored to the facts of Yukica's contract and no new law was made. Yet, through its arguments, ideas, media coverage, and impact, this case contributed significantly to the politics and law of employment policy, especially in the sports field. *Yukica v. Leland* also illustrates that the "contracts questions that matter, aren't just contracts questions" (Wisconsin Contracts Group 1989, 568).

Joe Yukica became coach at Dartmouth in 1978 with a contract that was renewed every two years. During Yukica's early tenure, the team did extremely well (winning or tying for the Ivy League title three times) but then the team fell into a slump, winning only two games each in the 1984 and 1985 seasons. Just before the 1985 season, Leland sent Yukica a contract renewal letter with warm praise for his coaching, but after the last game of the 1985 season Leland suggested to Yukica that he resign as head coach. Yukica refused to resign and contacted Michael Slive, a good friend and local lawyer who was also a nationally known expert in sports law and former university athletic director. Four days later Yukica received an official letter of termination from Leland. Slive and Yukica hired David Nixon to be the trial lawyer; Nixon then initiated the lawsuit on Yukica's behalf.

In brief, Yukica claimed that he should be allowed to continue for another year as head coach as outlined in his contract. He also charged procedural irregularities in the way Dartmouth had handled the termination. And he sought a temporary injunction on the basis that he was in danger of "irreparable harm" were he to be fired, due to the damage to his professional reputation and career opportunities. These arguments were unusual, seeking to stretch principles of equity in a novel way. In response, Dartmouth College and its athletic director narrowed the case into well-established legal categories with the law weighted to their side. They argued that they had every right to reassign Yukica to other duties within the college as long as they paid his salary and benefits for the remaining eighteen months of the contract. Moreover, Dartmouth argued that the court could not force it to accept Yukica as its football coach; that is, the court could not order the specific performance of Yukica's contract. To do so would contradict the legal precedents on personal services contracts which have held that compensation ("pay-off"), and not specific performance, is the appropriate legal remedy for a breach of contract.

In firing Yukica while offering money damages, Dartmouth had simply done what colleges around the country had traditionally done when they wanted to change coaches. But Yukica and his lawyers were able to draw support from prominent sports figures who agreed with their view that coaching was in some ways unique, that a broken coaching contract could not be repaired simply through the payment of money. At the December 13 preliminary hearing, Yukica called on numerous witnesses, including Pennsylvania State University coach Joe Paterno, Boston College coach Jack Bicknell, and former Dartmouth football coach Bob Blackman. Their testimony furthered the already growing public interest in the case and attracted national media attention. The case was transformed from a fairly routine dismissal into a dispute over the quality of Yukica's twenty-year record of coaching football, over the importance of not breaking contracts, and over the relative power of institutions vis-à-vis coaches.

A week after the hearing, Judge Murphy granted the temporary restraining order preventing Yukica's dismissal and the college's efforts to replace him. In his order, the judge (himself a former football coach) indicated the likelihood that Yukica would win on the merits in part because of procedural irregularities in the dismissal. The procedural question was whether Leland had the sole authority to dismiss Yukica or whether the contract required approval of the dismissal by the sixteen-member athletic council. The judge held that such approval was necessary and offered Dartmouth the chance to obtain it and return to court. That happened in January, as the college brought a motion to dismiss the case based on the minutes of the council meeting in which Yukica's termination was approved. However, Yukica raised additional procedural issues about the council meeting and the judge refused to dismiss the case. In addition to the judicial orders, time was clearly on Yukica's side in negotiations, since football recruitment was under way and the college was operating in effect without a head coach. Further, public opinion was behind Yukica based on the media coverage of the case. As a result, Dartmouth finally settled out of court with an agreement to let Yukica coach another season.[20]

Yukica had succeeded in shifting the framework of argument, not just in legal terms but in the wider public debate. National publications reported the case through Yukica's views ("A deal is a deal"; "All we're asking is that the college honor a contract") rather than as a dispute over the legal remedy for a breach of a personal services contract. For example, the headlines read:

"It's a Matter of 'Principle' for Coach Fighting Ouster"
New York Times, December 11, 1985
"Technicalities and Ideals"
Sports Illustrated, January 6, 1986
"Hell No, He Won't Go! Dartmouth's Joe Yukica Fights
for his Right to Coach Football"
People, January 20, 1986

The story in *People* most graphically defined the case in Yukica's terms. The conflict was between a loyal, hard-working coach, fifty-four years old, son of an immigrant steelworker (pictured in one photo with the caption "Alone in the Dartmouth locker room") and the athletic director of a powerful Ivy League institution, a thirty-six-year-old "resolute young man and maybe brash as well" (Mano 1986). The images and text of this and other articles tapped deeply held cultural values on the sanctity of contract (see the earlier discussion of Sander County), on the ideals of college athletics (rather than an emphasis on winning games), and on the struggle of the powerless underdog.

Interestingly, reports on the case seemed to indicate its precedential value despite the limits in the judge's ruling to the particular facts of the contract and despite the fact that it was a negotiated outcome. The president of the American Football Coaches Association, Vince Dooley, was widely quoted calling *Yukica v. Leland* "a landmark case," and the *Boston Globe* called the judge's initial order a "resounding court victory . . . that could have far-reaching ramifications for the collegiate coaching profession" (Singelais 1985). The *Los Angeles Times*, in a long story about the case that was reprinted in newspapers around the country, described the doctrine of irreparable harm as "a theory that will be mentioned often from now on, no doubt, when coaches challenge the right of employers to pay them off" (Oates 1986, 3). Some might fault the newspapers for oversimplifying and exaggerating the case's import, yet in another sense the accounts were quite accurate.

That is, the lawsuit was highly significant in terms of raising people's consciousness about the issues and symbolizing the problems of a fired coach. Also, through the court hearing and the mass media, Yukica articulated a set of legal ideas—ideas that, in the words of one of his lawyers, challenged "established law and conventional thinking" (Oates 1986). And the fact that the college ultimately did not succeed in dismissing Yukica (albeit through its own agreement to allow him to continue) reinforced the legitimacy of the coach's claim. In addition, the case clearly provided a potential bargaining chip for coaches who might find themselves in conflict with their employers. And employers were forced to pay greater attention to how and when they terminated their employees.

Finally, and perhaps of most importance, it affected how coaching contracts are written, as athletic administrators and coaches began to look more closely at the contract language. Yukica himself published a detailed account of his case in the 1986 Manual of the American Football Coaches Association and provided a fourteen-point listing of "Joe Yukica's Thoughts on Contracts" (Yukica 1986, 56). And administrators made comments such as, "Contracts obviously are going to be more carefully written by the institution" and "I think it [the case] means when you make contracts with a coach, you better know what you've done" (Asher 1986). It is important to remember that contract law is constituted in part by the way people think about and write their contracts, not just by what happens when a contract is breached. If we think of the contracting process as a sequence of legally significant stages (Tomain 1987), then it seems clear that change has occurred in the early stages involving assumptions, negotiations, and formulation of coaching contracts—even without definitive change at the stage of legal remedy.

Rather than being a completely isolated or aberrant case, *Yukica v. Leland* is one of a number of recent lawsuits filed by coaches dismissed by their employers. Instead of filing for specific performance, most of the plaintiffs have sought (and some have won) large financial awards not only for compensatory damages but also for the loss of "collateral opportunities" (the perquisites of being a coach beyond salary and benefits). Graves (1986) analyzes these cases (with a footnote on *Yukica*) in a recent law review article, "Coaches in the Courtroom," that he subtitled "How an Unlikely Group of College and University Figures Is Causing Lawyers and Judges to Reexamine the Traditional Limitations on Recovery in Actions for Breach of Employment Contracts." Indeed, another way to understand the policy importance of *Yukica* is to place it in the larger context of current American employment law. In recent decades the legal rights of employees have been greatly expanded through changes in statutory and case law, but the question of how far to expand those rights is still hotly debated. Cases like this one promote a particular normative interpretation of the issues in ways that distinctly favor employees and encourage legal change.

American legal doctrine on employment has traditionally reflected laissez faire economics in which employers were free to run their business without government interference. More specifically, by the doctrine of "employment at will," employers have been legally entitled to dismiss their employees for any reason, a bad reason, or no reason at all. The "at will" doctrine developed at the end of the nineteenth century as a response to particular social and economic conditions and expressed the dominant political ideology of the times (Feinman 1976; Moskowitz 1988). With some exceptions, this doctrine still governs the majority of the American work force (Moskowitz 1988). The exceptions are important, however, because they show the at-will doctrine eroding through political pressure and legal change. First, certain categories of employees are protected from arbitrary dismissal: unionized employees with collective bargaining agreements; government and civil service employees; and those with written contracts of fixed terms. Second, employers are prohibited by federal statute from dismissing employees based on race, sex, national origin, handicap, or age. Third, case law developments have given employees leverage to fight their termination through court rulings on implied contract, the tort of wrongful discharge, and the public policy exception (*Harvard Law Review* 1980; Tobias 1988). As a result of these statutory and appellate legal changes, there are now limits on the ability of private employers to terminate employees at will.

A second way in which employers have been limited in employee dismissals is through the remedies that have been provided to those employees who have been wrongly discharged. Litigation in this area has grown enormously in recent years with increasing monetary awards to victorious plaintiffs. A study of jury verdicts in California between 1980 and 1984 found that plaintiffs won almost 60 percent of reported wrongful termination suits, with an average award of $173,050 for compensatory damages and $396,650 for punitive damages (Greenan 1984). Juries are thus helping to shape the law in this area through the pattern of their verdicts. The sympathetic response by juries to employee challenges of arbitrary dismissal is not surprising in view of popular attitudes. As one survey revealed, less than 20 percent of those polled knew that employers have the right to fire an employee without giving a reason, and close to 90 percent felt that such employer action was not ethical (quoted in Wisconsin Contracts Group 1989, 564). For employees working with an employment contract (such as Yukica), rather than at the simple discretion of their employer, the legal recourse for an unfair termination is to sue for breach of contract and the conventional remedy is monetary compensation. In recent years, however, legal scholars have advocated specific performance as a remedy for breach of contract (Schwartz 1979; compare Bishop 1985). Specific performance has also been authorized by civil rights statutes that mandate job reinstatement for employees fired due to illegal discrimination. Lawyers for Yukica were thus attempting to accomplish judicially for coaches what had already been done by statute for other groups of employees. Just as Congress made policy when it passed the Civil Rights Act to protect minority employees, so do state trial courts make policy when they extend common law and equitable remedies to protect employees from arbitrary dismissals.

Conclusion

While the concept of policy making includes the adoption of a new rule or remedy, it also involves the definition of problems, agenda setting, the formulation of alternatives, and implementation. Most important, policy making involves conflict over ideas and struggle over a normative framework for interpreting events. State trial courts provide a public arena for citizen participation and lawyer influence on that struggle, as events are transformed into legal categories and law is expanded to resolve individual disputes. Whether through informal negotiations or through the adversary proceedings of trial, lawyers debate the nature and normative meaning of a case. On occasion, as occurred in the cases of *Baby M* and *Yukica v. Leland,* the debate widens to include new meanings as interest groups, the media, or others become involved. Trial courts thus contribute significantly to the formation of public policy through struggles over the use of law in the definition and resolution of conflict.

The norm enforcement view of American state trial courts has stubbornly persisted in the literature on judicial processes. Over twenty years of research on the political dimensions of trial courts and dispute processing seem not to have dislodged the paradigm of the trial court as an institution whose sole occupant is a largely passive arbiter of private conflict. By shifting perspectives, political scientists can observe a wide range of policy-making activities in state trial courts: the judge is not the only political actor in court, and formal decisions are not the only vehicle for making policy. Thus, when litigants and lawyers file legal claims and present arguments, they are defining problems and formulating policy alternatives. Interest groups incorporate litigation as part of their political strategy for changing policy, and the mass media use individual cases to dramatize political conflict and set an agenda for action by others. Lawyers implement state law and define local policies through their routine negotiation and classification of cases. Juries create policies through their fact finding at trial and through their modification (and occasional nullification) of formal law. And, finally, judges too make policy—not just by the substance of their decisions at trial, but also by the way in which they frame issues, by their consistent patterns of action (in motions, hearings, or sentencing), and by their interactions with lawyers in case negotiation.

Notes

1. Although my argument applies to federal—as well as state—trial courts, I have confined my literature review to state courts in view of Rowland's discussion of the federal district courts in chapter 3 of this book. I suspect, however, that my argument on trial court policy making is considerably broader than that of Rowland, at least based upon his discussion in Carp and Rowland (1983). Note that even those authors who deny trial courts much of a policy-making role acknowledge that federal trial courts make more policy than state trial courts (see Ball 1987; Jacob 1965).

2. Civil courts have received much less scholarly attention than criminal courts in part due to the bias that says that "private law" matters are somehow inappropriate for study by "public law" oriented political scientists. For a critique of the private law/public law distinction, see Shapiro (1972) and Zemans (1983). Even in studies with explicit focus on the politics of civil litigation, such as Dolbeare's (1967) *Trial Courts in Urban Politics,* there is a reluctance to claim much of public policy import in the civil trial court. For example, Dolbeare begins by criticizing political scientists for their neglect of state trial courts, arguing that these courts are "as important or in some respects *more* important" than the U.S. Supreme Court (1967, 2), but then he limits his analysis of cases to those involving "public policy problems"—which, by his prior definition, comprised only 17 percent of the civil caseload of the court (Dolbeare 1967, 35).

3. For example, see Cole (1970); Heumann (1978); *Law and Society Review* (1979); Mather (1979); and Neubauer (1974).

4. Exceptions to this point are Dolbeare's (1967) and Wanner's (1974, 1975) studies of civil case outcomes. On the decision to litigate, see Miller and Sarat (1981) and Zemans (1982); on processes of settlement negotiation, see Mnookin and Kornhauser (1979) and Ross (1970). In Jacob's (1983) review of the literature on trial courts he also notes the paucity of civil court studies and especially encourages attention to case outcomes and the timing of court actions.

5. I find it surprising that Jacob would continue with this early (1965) formulation in view of his own detailed research on the politics (although not policies) of both civil (Jacob 1969) and criminal (Eisenstein and Jacob 1977) trial courts. I think that these works implicitly speak against a norm enforcement view of trial courts.

6. In his book, Glick (1983) discusses "cumulative policymaking" as a possible alternative to the dominant view that trial courts do not make policy. However, in a more recent article on state courts, Glick (1987) assumes trial courts to be policy makers and presents judges' cumulative policies as one illustration of policy making by state trial courts.

7. Casper (1976) makes this point about Supreme Court policy making in his influential critique of Dahl (1957). Casper argues that Dahl misrepresents the Supreme Court's contribution to policy because he has adopted an overly narrow definition of policy making.

8. Barbara Yngvesson and I use the concept of dispute transformation as an analytic framework for comparing dispute processing cross-culturally and for linking the processing of individual disputes to the maintenance and change of political order (Mather and Yngvesson 1981; Yngvesson and Mather 1983; see also Emerson and Messinger 1977; Santos 1977). I draw on that framework here to extend policy making in trial courts to include the normative changes in cases that occur during court processing. For a slightly different view of dispute transformation, see Felstiner, Abel, and Sarat (1981).

9. For discussion of influences on the decision to file a legal claim, see Boyum (1983); Felstiner, Abel, and Sarat (1981); Miller and Sarat (1981); Silberman (1985); and Zemans (1982, 1983).

10. Personal injury claims were few both relative to other types of legal claims in Sander County and relative to personal injury claims in other areas (Engel 1984, 552-553).

11. For discussion of prosecutorial filing policies in various California counties, see Mather (1979) on Los Angeles; Utz (1978) on Alameda and San Diego; and Carter (1974) on "Vario County" in northern California.

12. Treatment of rape by trial courts remains an enormous problem. Despite rape law reform and feminist political pressure on the courts, it is not clear how much improvement has actually occurred. See Estrich (1987); Henderson (1987); and Marsh, Geist, and Kaplan (1982).

13. In addition to the work cited in the text below, see Cartwright and Schwartz (1973); Comaroff and Roberts (1981); Shapiro (1981); and Yngvesson and Mather (1983).

14. The literature on this point is enormous. See, for example, Eisenstein, Flemming, and Nardulli (1988); Eisenstein and Jacob (1977); Feeley (1979); Heumann (1978); Mather (1979); Neubauer (1974); and Sudnow (1965).

15. Although Sarat (1977) found incentive theory useful for explaining Wisconsin judges' role orientation, he found the theory much less helpful in explaining and predicting judicial behavior (as measured by judicial response to hypothetical sentencing problems). Caldeira (1977) examined only the incentives and role orientations of trial judges in New Jersey, not their behavior.

16. The methodology of these two studies was different, however. Kalven and Zeisel (1966) asked judges at the conclusion of a trial (but before the jury had reached its verdict) their view of the proper verdict. The study then compared the judges' view with the actual jury decision for identical cases. In contrast, Levine (1983a) compared aggregate data on judge and jury verdicts in a large set of cases, with the explicit assumption that judges and juries heard similar cases. I question that assumption. During my research in 1970 I found that defense lawyers in Los Angeles routinely recommended jury (rather than judge) trials to their clients in those cases where the evidence was most incriminating and the charges and defendant's prior record most severe. A higher conviction rate for juries could thus be explained by the strategy of jury selection rather than by actual differences between judge and jury behavior. Levine's conclusion on "jury toughness" may still be correct but it would be more convincing with greater attention to the nature of cases heard by judges and juries.

17. After Dr. Henry Morgantaler's successful battle to legalize abortion in Quebec, he opened an abortion clinic in Toronto in 1983. Again he was charged by provincial authorities with breaking the federal law, and again he was acquitted by a jury—his fourth acquittal on abortion charges. The

Crown appealed Dr. Morgantaler's acquittal in Toronto and the case led to a landmark policy change for the entire country. On January 28, 1988, the Supreme Court of Canada declared the federal abortion law unconstitutional under the new Canadian Charter of Rights and Freedoms (see *MacLean*'s 1988).

18. In another example, Canan and Pring (1988) examined a set of civil tort lawsuits that were strategic attempts to retaliate against individuals or groups because of their political activity. In these cases, plaintiffs alleged injury in trial court in order to intimidate and stifle public expression. The lawsuits were directed against such citizen action as circulating petitions, writing letters, complaining to government, or organizing a boycott. The lawsuits functioned initially to transform political conflict (for example, overzoning, police brutality, consumer rights, water resources) into a narrow legal case, but the defendants were usually able to transform the tort issue back into the larger conflict by raising a First Amendment defense of freedom to petition. At times the lawsuits served to weaken the defendants, due to the cost and time involved in litigation, but some lawsuits also acted as important agents of political mobilization and garnered sympathetic support for the defendants.

19. Information on this case comes from articles in the local newspaper (the *Valley News*), and other newspapers and magazines; from the pleadings, memoranda, and judicial orders filed in the Grafton County Superior Court; and from personal interviews with the litigants and lawyers conducted by Gregory Garre in fall 1986, and follow-up calls by the author in fall 1989. Gregory Garre also aided in the analysis of the case, while Stewart Macaulay and Jack McCrory provided useful background on contract law.

20. During Yukica's final football season, tensions surfaced between the coach and Athletic Director Ted Leland over a number of minor issues such as the making of the team's highlights film and removal of Yukica's parking space. These conflicts illustrate why specific performance is rarely ordered in cases involving breach of employment contract: courts do not want to force parties to stay together in an unpleasant personal relationship (Wisconsin Contracts Group 1989). As a final aside, the Dartmouth football team had a 3-6-1 record in fall 1986, and Joe Yukica retired from coaching at the end of the season. Yukica still lives in the Hanover area, however, where he works in real estate and hosts a weekly radio show on sports. Since the case, he has been contacted by a number of prominent sports figures for advice on their contract disputes. One of Yukica's lawyers, Mike Slive, joined a large Chicago law firm and now specializes in representing colleges on issues of sports law. Dartmouth's president resigned less than a year after the college's settlement with Yukica, amidst criticism that included the president's handling of this case. Several years later Ted Leland left Dartmouth to become athletic director of the University of the Pacific.

References

Arnold, Thurman W. 1935. *The symbols of government.* New York: Harcourt, Brace and World.

Asher, Mark. 1986. Yukica-Dartmouth case raises contract questions. *Washington Post,* February 16, E3.

Atleson, James B. 1989. The legal community and the transformation of disputes: The settlement of injunction actions. *Law and Society Review* 23:41-73.

Ball, Howard. 1987. *Courts and politics: The federal judicial system.* Englewood Cliffs, N.J.: Prentice-Hall.

Baum, Lawrence. 1986. *American courts.* Boston: Houghton Mifflin.

Bishop, Katherine. 1989. Neighbors in West use small claims court to combat drugs. *New York Times,* October 17, A16.

Bishop, William. 1985. The choice of remedy for breach of contract. *Journal of Legal Studies* 14:299-319.

Boyum, Keith O. 1983. The etiology of claims: Sketches for a theoretical mapping of the claim-definition process. In *Empirical theories about courts,* ed. Keith O. Boyum and Lynn Mather. New York: Longman.

Bullock, Charles S. III, James E. Anderson, and David W. Brady. 1983. *Public policy in the eighties.* Monterey, Calif.: Brooks/Cole.

Cain, Maureen. 1979. The general practice lawyer and the client: Towards a radical conception. *International Journal of the Sociology of Law* 7:331-354.

Caldeira, Gregory A. 1977. Judicial incentives: Some evidence from urban trial courts. *Iustitia* 4:1-28.

Canan, Penelope, and George W. Pring. 1988. Strategic lawsuits against public participation. *Social Problems* 35:506-519.

Canon, Bradley C. 1982. A framework for the analysis of judicial activism. In *Supreme Court activism and restraint,* ed. Stephen C. Halpern and Charles M. Lamb. Lexington, Mass.: Lexington Books.

Carp, Robert A., and C. K. Rowland. 1983. *Policymaking and politics in the federal district courts.* Knoxville: University of Tennessee Press.

Carp, Robert A., and Ronald A. Stidham. 1990. *Judicial process in America.* Washington, D.C.: CQ Press.

Carter, Lief H. 1974. *The limits of order.* Lexington, Mass.: Lexington Books.

Cartwright, B. C., and R. D. Schwartz. 1973. The invocation of legal norms: An empirical investigation of Durkheim and Weber. *American Sociological Review* 38:340-354.

Casper, Jonathan D. 1976. The Supreme Court and national policy-making. *American Political Science Review* 70:50-63.

Chayes, Abram. 1976. The role of the judge in public law litigation. *Harvard Law Review* 89:1281-1316.

Cobb, Roger W., and Charles D. Elder. 1983. *Participation in American politics: The dynamics of agenda-building,* 2d ed. Baltimore: Johns Hopkins University Press.

Cole, George F. 1970. The decision to prosecute. *Law and Society Review* 4:331-343.

Comaroff, John L., and Simon Roberts. 1981. *Rules and processes.* Chicago: University of Chicago Press.

Conley, John M., and William M. O'Barr. 1988. Fundamentals of jurisprudence: An ethnography of judicial decision making in informal courts. *North Carolina Law Review* 66:467-507.

Cook, Fay Lomax. 1981. Crime and the elderly: The emergence of a policy issue. In *Reactions to crime,* ed. Dan A. Lewis. Beverly Hills, Calif.: Sage.

Croyle, James L. 1979. The impact of trial courts on the public policy of private law: Medical malpractice jury verdicts in California. Paper delivered at meeting of the Western Political Science Association, Portland, Oregon.

Dahl, Robert A. 1957. Decision-making in a democracy: The Supreme Court as a national policy-maker. *Journal of Public Law* 6:279-295

Davis, James R., and Kenneth M. Dolbeare. 1968. *Little groups of neighbors: The selective service system.* Chicago: Markham.

Dolbeare, Kenneth M. 1967. *Trial courts in urban politics.* New York: Wiley.

Edelman, Murray. 1964. *The symbolic uses of politics.* Urbana: University of Illinois Press.

Eisenberg, Melvin A. 1976. Private ordering through negotiation: Dispute settling and rulemaking. *Harvard Law Review* 89:637-681.

Eisenstein, James, and Herbert Jacob. 1977. *Felony justice: An organizational analysis of criminal courts.* Boston: Little, Brown.

Eisenstein, James, Roy B. Flemming, and Peter F. Nardulli. 1988. *The contours of justice: Communities and their courts.* Boston: Little, Brown.

Emerson, Robert M., and Sheldon L. Messinger. 1977. The micro-politics of trouble. *Social Problems* 25:121-134.

Engel, David M. 1984. The oven bird's song: Insiders, outsiders, and personal injuries in an American community. *Law and Society Review* 18:551-582.

Estrich, Susan. 1987. *Real rape.* Cambridge, Mass.: Harvard University Press.

Feeley, Malcolm M. 1979. *The process is the punishment.* New York: Russell Sage Foundation.

Feinman, Jay M. 1976. The development of the employment at will rule. *American Journal of Legal History* 20:118-135.

Felstiner, William L. F., Richard L. Abel, and Austin Sarat. 1981. The emergence and transformation of disputes: Naming, blaming, claiming. . . . *Law and Society Review* 15:631-654.

Frank, Jerome. 1949. *Courts on trial: Myth and reality in American justice.* Princeton: Princeton University Press.

Galanter, Marc. 1984. Words of deals: Using negotiation to teach about legal process. *Journal of Legal Education* 34:268-276.

Galanter, Marc, Frank S. Palen, and John M. Thomas. 1979. The crusading judge: Judicial activism in trial courts. *Southern California Law Review* 52:699-741.

Gambitta, Richard A. L. 1981. Litigation, judicial deference, and policy change. In *Governing through courts,* ed. Richard A. L. Gambitta, Marlynn L. May, and James C. Foster. Beverly Hills, Calif.: Sage.

Garth, Bryant G. 1982. Introduction: Toward a sociology of the class action. *Indiana Law Journal* 57:371-383.

Gibson, James L. 1978. Judges' role orientations, attitudes, and decisions: An interactive model. *American Political Science Review* 72:911-924.

———. 1980. Environmental constraints on the behavior of judges: A representational model of judicial decision making. *Law and Society Review* 14:343-370.

Glick, Henry R. 1983. *Courts, politics, and justice.* New York: McGraw-Hill.

———. 1987. State court systems. In *Encyclopedia of the American judicial system,* ed. Robert J. Janosik. New York: Charles Scribner's Sons.

Graves, Judson. 1986. Coaches in the courtroom: Recovery in actions for breach of employment contracts. *Journal of College and University Law* 12:545-558.

Greenan, James S. 1984. The problems of wrongful termination. *California Lawyer* 4:29-31.

Gruhl, John, Cassia Spohn, and Susan Welch. 1981. Women as policymakers: The case of trial judges. *American Journal of Political Science* 25:308-322.

Gusfield, Joseph R. 1981. *The culture of public problems.* Chicago: University of Chicago Press.

Handler, Joel F. 1978. *Social movements and the legal system: A theory of law reform and social change.* New York: Academic Press.

Harvard Law Review. 1980. Protecting at will employees against wrongful discharge: The duty to terminate only in good faith. *Harvard Law Review* 93:1816-1844.

Henderson, Lynne N. 1987. Review essay: What makes rape a crime? *Berkeley Women's Law Journal* 3:193-229.

Heumann, Milton. 1978. *Plea bargaining: The experiences of prosecutors, judges, and defense attorneys.* Chicago: University of Chicago Press.

Jacob, Herbert. 1965. *Justice in America.* Boston: Little, Brown.

———. 1969. *Debtors in court: The consumption of government services.* Chicago: Rand McNally.

———. 1983. Trial courts in the United States: The travails of exploration. *Law and Society Review* 17:407-423.

———. 1984. *Justice in America,* 4th ed. Boston: Little, Brown.

Jacobsohn, Gary J. 1977. Citizen participation in policy-making: The role of the jury. *Journal of Politics* 39:73-96.

Johnson, Earl, Jr. 1981. Lawyers' choice: A theoretical appraisal of litigation investment decisions. *Law and Society Review* 15:567-610.

Kalven, Harry, Jr., and Hans Zeisel. 1966. *The American jury.* Chicago: University of Chicago Press.

Kuklinski, James H., and John E. Stanga. 1979. Political participation and government responsiveness: The behavior of California superior courts. *American Political Science Review* 73:1090-1099.

Labaton, Stephen. 1987. Big courtroom for toxic web. *New York Times,* November 16, D2.

Law and Society Review. 1979. Special issue on plea bargaining, 13:189-687.

Levi, Edward H. 1949. *An introduction to legal reasoning.* Chicago: University of Chicago Press.

Levin, Martin A. 1977. *Urban politics and the criminal courts.* Chicago: University of Chicago Press.

Levine, James P. 1983a. Jury toughness: The impact of conservatism on criminal court verdicts. *Crime and Delinquency* 29:71-87.

———. 1983b. Using jury verdict forecasts in criminal defense strategy. *Judicature* 66:448-461.

Lipsky, Michael. 1980. *Street-level bureaucracy.* New York: Russell Sage Foundation.

McIntosh, Wayne. 1983. Private use of a public forum: A long range view of the dispute processing role of courts. *American Political Science Review* 77:991-1010.

MacLean's. 1988. Abortion. February 8, 8-16.

Mano, D. Keith. 1986. Hell no, he won't go! Dartmouth's Joe Yukica fights for his right to coach football. *People,* January 20, 1986, 36-38.

Marsh, Jeanne C., Alison Geist, and Nathan Caplan. 1982. *Rape and the limits of law reform.* Boston: Auburn House.

Mather, Lynn M. 1979. *Plea bargaining or trial? The process of criminal case disposition.* Lexington, Mass.: Lexington Books.

———. 1982. Conclusion: The mobilizing potential of class actions. *Indiana Law Journal* 57:451-458.

Mather, Lynn, and Barbara Yngvesson. 1981. Language, audience, and the transformation of disputes. *Law and Society Review* 15:775-821.

Miller, Richard E., and Austin Sarat. 1981. Grievances, claims, and disputes: Assessing the adversary culture. *Law and Society Review* 15:525-566.

Mnookin, Robert H., and Lewis Kornhauser. 1979. Bargaining in the shadow of the law: The case of divorce. *Yale Law Journal* 88:950-997.

Moskowitz, Seymour. 1988. Employment-at-will and codes of ethics: The professional's dilemma. *Valparaiso Law Review* 23:33-73.

Nelson, Barbara J. 1984. *Making an issue of child abuse: Political agenda setting for social problems.* Chicago: University of Chicago Press.

Neubauer, David W. 1974. *Criminal justice in middle America.* Morristown, N.J.: General Learning Press.

Oates, Bob. 1986. He fought the system . . . and won. *Los Angeles Times,* March 30, III 3, III 14.

Olson, Susan M. 1984. *Clients and lawyers: Securing the rights of disabled persons.* Westport, Conn.: Greenwood Press.

Paul-Shaheen, P. A., and Harry Perlstadt. 1982. Class action suits and social change: The organization and impact of the Hill-Burton cases. *Indiana Law Journal* 57:385-423.

Peterson, Iver. 1987. States assess surrogate motherhood. *New York Times,* December 13, A42.

Price, David E. 1985. Congressional committees in the policy process. In *Congress reconsidered,* 3d ed., Lawrence C. Dodd and Bruce I. Oppenheimer. Washington, D.C.: CQ Press.

Rosenthal, Douglas E. 1974. *Lawyer and client: Who's in charge?* New York: Russell Sage Foundation.

Ross, H. Laurence. 1970. *Settled out of court: The social process of insurance claims adjustments.* Chicago: Aldine.

Ryan, John Paul, et al. 1980. *American trial judges.* New York: Free Press.

Santos, Boaventura de Sousa. 1977. The law of the oppressed: The construction and reproduction of legality in Pasargada. *Law and Society Review* 12:5-105.

Sarat, Austin. 1977. Judging in trial courts: An exploratory study. *Journal of Politics* 39:368-398.

Sarat, Austin, and William L. F. Felstiner. 1986. Law and strategy in the divorce lawyer's office. *Law and Society Review* 20:93-134.

Schattschneider, E. E. 1960. *The semisovereign people.* New York: Holt, Rinehart and Winston.

Scheingold, Stuart A. 1974. *The politics of rights: Lawyers, public policy, and political change.* New Haven: Yale University Press.

Schubert, Glendon. 1965. Book Review of *Justice in America. American Political Science Review* 59:1038-1040.

Schwartz, Alan. 1979. The case for specific performance. *Yale Law Journal* 89:271-306.

Shapiro, Martin. 1964. *Law and politics in the Supreme Court.* New York: Free Press.

_____. 1970. Decentralized decision-making in the law of torts. In *Political decision-making,* ed. S. Sidney Ulmer. New York: Van Nostrand Reinhold.

_____. 1972. From public law to public policy, or the "public" in "public law." *PS* 5:410-418.

_____. 1981. *Courts: A comparative and political analysis.* Chicago: University of Chicago Press.

Silberman, Matthew. 1985. *The civil justice process.* Orlando, Fla.: Academic Press.

Singelais, Neil. 1985. Yukica gets job back. *Boston Globe,* December 21, 33, 38.

Spaeth, Harold J. 1979. *Supreme Court policy making.* San Francisco: W. H. Freeman.

Spector, Malcolm, and John I. Kitsuse. 1977. *Constructing social problems.* New York: Adline DeGruyter.

Stone, Deborah A. 1988. *Policy paradox and political reason.* Glenview, Ill.: Scott, Foresman.

Stumpf, Harry P. 1988. *American judicial politics.* San Diego: Harcourt Brace Jovanovich.

Sudnow, David. 1965. Normal crimes: Sociological features of the penal code in a public defender office. *Social Problems* 12:255-276.

Tobias, Paul H. 1988. Current trends in employment dismissal law: The plaintiff's perspective. *Nebraska Law Review* 67:178-192.

Tomain, Joseph P. 1987. Contracts. In *Encyclopedia of the American judicial system,* ed. Robert J. Janosik. New York: Scribner's.

Utz, Pamela J. 1978. *Setting the facts: Discretion and negotiation in criminal court.* Lexington, Mass.: Lexington Books.

Vose, Clement E. 1959. *Caucasians only: The Supreme Court, the NAACP, and the restrictive covenant cases.* Berkeley: University of California Press.

Wanner, Craig. 1974. The public ordering of private relations. Pt. 1: Initiating civil cases in urban trial courts. *Law and Society Review* 8:421-440.

_____. 1975. The public ordering of private relations. Pt. 2: Winning civil court cases. *Law and Society Review* 9:293-306.

Wells, Richard S., and Joel B. Grossman. 1966. The concept of judicial policy-making: A critique. *Journal of Public Law* 15:286-310.

Wisconsin Contracts Group. 1989. *Contracts: Law in Action (Contracts I, Pt. B).* Madison: University of Wisconsin Law School.

Yngvesson, Barbara. 1988. Making law at the doorway: The clerk, the court, and the construction of community in a New England town. *Law and Society Review* 22:409-448.

Yngvesson, Barbara, and Lynn Mather. 1983. Courts, moots, and the disputing process. In *Empirical theories about courts,* ed. Keith O. Boyum and Lynn Mather. New York: Longman.

Yukica, Joe. 1986. A deal is a deal. *1986 Summer Manual.* American Football Coaches Association.

Zemans, Frances Kahn. 1982. Framework for analysis of legal mobilization: A decision-making model. *American Bar Foundation Research Journal* (Fall): 989-1071.

_____. 1983. Legal mobilization: The neglected role of the law in the political system. *American Political Science Review* 77:690-703.

Part II

JUDICIAL SELECTION

Even if he were mediocre, there are a lot of mediocre judges and people
and lawyers, and they are entitled to a little representation aren't they?
We can't have all Brandeises, Frankfurters, and Cardozos.

—Sen. Roman L. Hruska (R-Neb.)
Defending the nomination of
Judge G. Harrold Carswell to the U.S. Supreme Court
New York Times, March 17, 1970

We do not seek to put on the Court nine men who will represent, in ratio,
the adequacies and inadequacies of our society.

—Sen. Phillip Hart (D-Mich.)
Responding to Senator Hruska's comments
New York Times, March 17, 1970

Perhaps no other office in the American political system offers a greater diversity in selection mechanisms than that of judge. Judges are selected differently in virtually each state, and sometimes differently within a state, depending on the type of court; a federal judge is selected in yet another way. Yet persons selected to serve as judges in American courts are not as varied as the American population or the federal and state political systems. The backgrounds of judges serving in North Dakota and Texas and New York are not dissimilar; and the backgrounds of U.S. Supreme Court justices do not differ greatly from those of federal judges in Florida or state supreme court justices in Tennessee. By and large, judges in America are white, male, Protestant, and well educated. They differ in political party backgrounds and in political opinions, but they often share significant political experience prior to joining the bench.

If selection and recruitment patterns yield judges who are generally more similar than dissimilar, the question arises why selection and recruitment issues warrant discussion. One answer is that although selection systems do not produce judges with widely varying backgrounds, the systems themselves may influence the decision making of judges and their relationship to the political system.

The two key concepts that focus our attention on the potential impact of judicial selection systems are judicial independence and political accountability. The independence of judges, freedom from the influence of anyone except the litigants in cases before them, is thought to be an important characteristic of jurists in America. That independence is assured by cultural expectations of judges (for example, noninvolvement in political activities while on the bench), of citizens (extralegal lobbying is usually frowned upon), and of fellow politicians (turning to judges for political favors is viewed as unethical). The independent judge is expected to be uninfluenced by swings in public opinion, threats of mob opinion, or pressures from other branches of government. Do any selection systems effectively maintain judicial independence?

Part I demonstrated that courts, and thus judges, are active participants in policy making in the United States. A fundamental principle in our democracy is that officials who make policies should be politically accountable. Clearly, political accountability is at cross purposes with the notion of judicial independence. If judges are truly independent, then they will be unaccountable, and thus out of step with democratic expectations regarding officials who make public policy. To what extent, then, do selection systems enforce accountability? And how do selection systems strike an appropriate balance between the objectives of judicial independence and political accountability?

The next two chapters are devoted to judicial selection and recruitment offering analyses of state and federal systems, respectively. Chapter 6, by Charles H. Sheldon and Nicholas P. Lovrich, Jr., both of whom have extensively researched state judicial selection systems, directly addresses the issue of judicial independence and political accountability. They offer a model to evaluate the potential independence of state judicial systems and discuss the implications of movement toward one extreme or another. Sheldon Goldman, a leading scholar on the federal judiciary, offers an overview of the federal selection procedures and a portrait of the results of those procedures (Chapter 7). He clearly describes the potential consequences of changes in the executive administrations. Because federal judges, having life tenure, are usually considered among the most independent judges, there are clear implications for the development of politically unaccountable decision makers in the American political system.

6. STATE JUDICIAL RECRUITMENT

Charles H. Sheldon and Nicholas P. Lovrich, Jr.

Democratic Theory and Judicial Selection

Constitutional Dimensions

How judges are selected to sit on state benches bears heavily on whether the reality of American state and local politics coincides with the theory of constitutional democracy. State governments are all products of a constitutional compact between the governors and the governed (Lutz 1980; Elazar and Kincaid 1987). Popular consent is one dimension of the ubiquitous compact, designated public offices is another, and authoritative limitations on those public officials is the third. Government by consent assures sufficient public support for those who govern, permitting them to perform their assigned duties with the authority of duly vested agents of the citizenry; the compact clearly circumscribes, however, the extent of that authority. Indeed, the essence of all American constitutional thought is the maintenance of a government based on popular consent, constitutionally separated powers, and written limits placed on those conducting the public's business (Wood 1969).

It is the several types of public officials who serve the people—legislators, executives, administrators, and judges—who execute the governmental powers. Of course, the constitutional limits placed on the powers of these officials are not self-executing, and the competitive struggle for power among public officials is specifically intended to check abuses in this regard. Ultimately, however, it is the people who determine whether important governmental duties have been neglected or constitutional limits exceeded by any particular branch of government or office. Should the built-in checks and balances fail, the public removes or threatens to remove the non-, mis-, or malfeasant officials from public office by means of the ballot box. Consent is withdrawn, and public officials are reminded that the ultimate voice in American government rests with the voters; majoritarian democracy means no less.

The internal constitutional checks and balances generally serve their purpose of policing errant officials. On occasion the constitutional system fails to produce a consensual understanding of official prerogatives despite the intent of the original design. For example, in the matters of an anti-capital punishment supreme court justice in California, a governor who demonstrated racial insensitivity in Arizona with his off-the-cuff remarks, and the pro-choice pressures on the governor of Idaho to veto strong anti-abortion legislation, the popular consent foundation of American government came strongly to the fore.

Judicial Responsibilities within the Constitutional Framework

Judges perforce play a leading role in this American constitutional framework. Like other public officials they can be responsible for abusing as well as neutralizing political power. However, their role is in some sense more sensitive to power than that of other officials. Judges carry both the shield and the sword of government. In the process of resolving disputes between private parties, judges on occasion make significant public policy. Karl Llewellyn proposed that judges are involved with policy decisions when they think "in terms of prospective [public] consequences of the rule under consideration" (1960, 36). Whenever judges contemplate the impact of a decision on the public or a significant segment thereof, they are contemplating a public policy. In commenting on Alexis de Tocqueville's oft-quoted statement— "Scarcely any political question arises in the United States that is not resolved, sooner or later, into a judicial question"—James Gibson wrote:

> It is difficult to imagine a more appropriate way of describing the relationship between courts and public policy in modern day America. Many, if not most, of the pressing political issues of the last few decades have been the object of judicial involvement and pronouncement. (1978, 115)

Courts make public policy and, consequently, are clearly among those actors in society who wield the governmental sword.

Judges are given two primary opportunities to exercise power from the bench. First, in applying the law to the resolution of a dispute, judges most commonly are called upon to construe the law. Does the law, as interpreted by the judges, provide an answer to the legal issue? Even in those cases where they must contemplate the public conse-quences of their rulings, judges must attempt to reach a fair resolution of the issue. Objectivity, independence, and balancing must be blended into the resolution. And, when the community is to be affected by the decision, the concerns of the public must be part of the blend as well. On occasion, public concerns can run counter to the interests of the parties to the dispute; in such cases the demands placed on judging are indeed great.

State judges have a second opportunity to enhance their ability to exercise power, an aspect of their work which may extend their governing responsibilities or thwart another's aggrandizing efforts. Since before the celebrated U.S. Supreme Court case of *Marbury v. Madison* (1803) state jurists have exercised the ultimate in judicial power—judicial review (Sheldon 1987). The power to determine the constitutional propriety of statutes, ordinances, and administrative practices often provides state justices with the final say in fundamental issues.[1] In addition, judges are the primary enforcers of state bills of rights, constitutional provisions designed to prevent governmental (and sometimes private) intrusions upon individual and minority affairs (Utter 1989). Although constitutional rights cases are not the everyday disputes confronting judges, for better or worse, decisions rendered in these cases often have a profound policy impact on the state system and on the practice of individual freedom.

The historically pivotal governing role played by state judges in the development of state politics highlights the fact that American-style constitutionalism permits them either to contribute to an abuse of power or to place limits on other officials who may contemplate or attempt an unwarranted extension of power. Because of the sensitivity of this role—both in historical and contemporary aspects—we must understand the process that places the black robes of office on the shoulders of some but not others. Despite the long history with various selection methods (Haynes 1944; Volcansek and Lafon 1988; Winters 1973), the almost continuous debate over which is the best system (Wasmann, Lovrich, and Sheldon 1986), and the volumes of research on judicial recruitment (Slotnick 1988), the process remains largely a mystery to both scholars and practitioners. Our purpose here is not to solve this mystery, but rather to propose a means by which a fuller understanding of this important aspect of state politics might be reached. We must begin with a brief review of democratic political theory as it bears on the judging function.

Democratic Theory and Judicial Recruitment

Over the turbulent history of judicial selection, arguments concerning how judges were to be recruited to state benches centered on the tradeoff between *public accountability* and *judicial independence* (Wasby 1978). Those making decisions about which selection procedures to employ knew well the kinds of effects they were seeking but were not altogether sure of the proper procedures to ensure those effects. For example, the selection method that limited access to law firm members, bar association activists, corporate attorneys, Republicans, and nonpolitical lawyers would likely be one that enhanced judicial independence. The method that promoted partisan lawyers with political backgrounds, general practitioners, low status attorneys, those from the working class, and Democrats would place on the state benches jurists who would likely lean toward public accountability in their dispositions. Of course, selection methods that require judges to renew periodically their mandates to serve the people through elections will tend to encourage judges to pay more attention to those who participate in their selection and retention. On the other hand, long terms of office with infrequent accountings give judges the opportunity to remain independent of prevailing public sentiment.

Although the accountability versus independence issue largely dominated the historical debates over judicial selection, American democratic practice brings to the fore other equally important value tradeoffs to be considered in the assessment of methods of judicial recruitment. One aspect of democratic theory bears on the *representativeness* of public officials, including judges (DeGrazia 1951; Pitkin 1967). Should not jurists reflect a cross-section of the American people? Should they not mix freely with the community they serve? Perhaps both of these aspects of representativeness are required in order for judges to be in tune with the values of the community (Lovrich, Sheldon, and Wasmann 1988). *Access* to positions of power and the opportunity to be among those who formulate public policy clearly is a tenet of American democratic theory as well (Smith 1989). Are minorities and women systematically excluded from judicial office by the selection process obtaining in most jurisdictions? Fair access to judicial office, then, is an important aspect of the assessment of judicial recruitment systems. Finally, a government based on majority rule should be the product of an explicit outpouring of the citizens. Citizen *participation* in government—in elections and in interest group politics—should be high. Widespread participation adds to the legitimacy of the government (Pateman 1970; Verba and Nie 1972; Milbrath and Gael 1977). Because those participating in their selection are few, do the decisions of unelected judges have the same legitimacy as those handed down by elected jurists (Slotnick 1988, 110)? Considered in this broader framework, then, judicial recruitment is a complicated process that ought to reflect varied aspects of democratic governance.

Accountability versus Judicial Independence

In the process of resolving disputes, judges are on occasion called upon to confirm or reject legal precedent and legislative enactments and thereby establish public policy. As we have seen, when judges must contemplate the effect of their decisions on the community or a large part thereof, they are in fact making public policy decisions. The principles of majoritarian democracy require that those who make public policy, including judges, be accountable to the public.

Accountability is a term in common usage applied to a complex concept of government based on popular consent. We adopt here Stephen Wasby's definition: "Generally . . . accountability . . . mean[s] keeping an institution's decisions in line with community political or social values." Constraints are placed on a "court's exercise of discretion" which could lead the court away from prevailing societal values (1978, 145). Public officials are held accountable to the public (or publics) by means of elections, recall, impeachment, limited tenure, political party loyalty, pressure group activities, expressions of public opinion, investigative reporting, ethics commissions, and any number of more subtle techniques such as withholding endorsements, refusing campaign contributions, or extracting campaign promises. Many of these constraints apply to state judges as directly as they apply to other servants of the public, and they are present in some form or another no matter what the formal process by which the jurists are selected.

It is generally assumed among scholars of judicial recruitment that partisan elections of judges,[2] where the political parties act as surrogates for the public in the selection and retention of judges, maximizes judicial accountability. The party nominates, underwrites, and manages electoral campaigns, and the party presents to the voters at least a general picture of what its judicial candidates stand for as public officials. For some scholars legislative selection[3] also represents a formal method for electing judges that places a high premium on accountability—at least to the legislative version of the public good.

Although it is widely recognized that judges are public officials who are intimately involved in the making of policy decisions, most court observers—professional as well as laypersons—would argue that judges are nonetheless different from their more political counterparts. Unlike legislators, county commissioners, or executives, judges are compelled by training, inclination, theory, and practice to endeavor to ignore political or economic interests in resolving disputes. In the ideal case, judicial decisions are based upon objective and independent appraisals of the law determined without regard to what interests the litigants represent and how the decision may affect society (Hamilton 1961, 466). Should judges be unable to perform their duty objectively, they are obligated to excuse themselves and turn the resolution of the dispute over to other jurists. Judges also must be isolated from the political pressures and prejudices of society in order to protect individuals and minorities from the tyranny of the majority. A substantial degree of judicial independence is necessary for any viable legal system.

Judicial independence is assumed to be enhanced when selection is controlled by the legal profession itself. The organized bar has been regarded as the professional antithesis to the political party with respect to judicial selection (Jacob and Vines 1976, 251). Lawyers emphasize the need for judicial discretion constrained by law, precedent, due process, self-restraint, and traditions of the bench. As newly designated Chief Justice Keith Callow of the Washington Supreme Court told the audience at his swearing-in ceremony in 1989: "The judicial branch ... must not legislate. Neither should the legislative or executive branch adjudicate" (Seattle-King County Bar Association 1989). Only under such conditions, many believe, can the rule of law be faithfully observed.

The Missouri plan and the several versions of merit selection processes inspired by that plan have been regarded by selection advocates as an effective means of maintaining judicial independence.[4] Under such arrangements, the selection of judges is largely removed from political party influence and, for that matter, from the influence of voters. Retention elections are the sole means of popular accountability. Nomination to judicial office is decided upon by a blue ribbon commission of experts, and appointment is by a governor required to draw exclusively from only those nominated by the commission. The voters are limited to a yes or no response as to whether the judge's record warrants his or her retention. Once selected, then, the judge possesses considerable independence.

The process of nonpartisan election has been advocated as a balance between the pressures of accountability evident in partisan elections and the relative judicial freedoms enjoyed by products of appointments or the Missouri plan.[5] Gubernatorial or executive appointment, perhaps tempered by some legislative intervention, is also widely presumed to allow the appointee a high degree of isolation from politics.[6]

Although majoritarian democracy demands that when judges make policy they ought to be answerable to the public, the rule of law also requires that judges be largely free from the pressures of politics.[7] Ideally, a balance between these two necessary elements of the state political system must be struck. Most often, the tradeoff between judicial independence and public accountability has remained at the center of the never ending struggle for judicial reform; however, it is important to know that judicial selection embraces other important aspects of democratic theory as well (Slotnick 1988, 110).

Participation in Judicial Recruitment

Constitutional democracy rests upon the foundation of popular consent. Although the contractarian myth holds that popular consent was formally given when people voted to approve original state constitutions, a periodic renewal of this expression of consent adds further to the legitimacy of those chosen to perform the duties assigned by the constitutions. The amendment process is one means of renewing consent, and periodic elections of those who govern is another. The wider the participation in the selection and retention of those who govern, the deeper the legitimacy of government.

Elections of some sort should allow for the necessary participation to legitimate the decisions of the judges. Partisan elections have the attribute of generating the highest level of voter participation (Dubois 1979). The political party label continues to provide some guidance to voters, increasing their confidence in making meaningful choices in the election of judges. Partisan elections also encourage contested judicial elections, providing voters an element of choice that attracts their attention. Nonpartisan elections, in contrast, attract the more attentive voter; the numbers participating are considerably lower than in partisan elections, especially in primaries wherein most contested races are decided (Lovrich and Sheldon 1984). The Missouri plan involves voters at the retention phase of the process alone (Griffin and Horan 1979, 1983). But even in those states that allow a challenger to file against incumbent judges, voters often stop voting on a given ballot before reaching less salient elections such as those involving judges. Citizen participation is present in such electoral settings, but at a negligible level. For many observers of judicial recruitment processes such weak involvement of the public raises serious concerns for the state of democratic values.

Representativeness and Judicial Recruitment

American state governments take pride in claiming to be representative of their people. Representativeness means that those making decisions in the state for the people ought to reflect the wide array of types of citizens of the state. Representativeness can be accomplished by having the representatives reflect a cross section or microcosm of the social, economic, and political characteristics of the state or jurisdiction. It is assumed that with this common background, those in government can better appreciate the values, interests, needs, and concerns of the citizenry. Representativeness can also be achieved by judges who—though they may not possess community characteristics—closely monitor public needs and wants and, within the limits of the law, seek to reflect those perceptions. Such monitoring reflects the belief that jurists ought to be closely attuned to changes in societal values.

Residency requirements can to some extent ensure that the judges have some familiarity with their jurisdictions. A well-known name, ethnic and gender clues, and small enough electoral districts can promote representativeness of candidates for judicial office (Sherman 1989). Additionally, judges who are active in community affairs participate in state civic events and frequently travel about their jurisdictions, are generally more in tune with state happenings than jurists who are not. Those who follow political and social events, attend public forums, and listen to attentive voters during election campaigns can also remain representative (MacManus 1988, 187).

Although contested partisan, nonpartisan, and retention elections give judges the opportunity to talk and listen to the public, it is important to note that the canons of judicial conduct forbid candidates from answering many of the sensitive questions voters would ask.[8] Gubernatorial and legislative appointment, as opposed to electoral systems of recruitment, tends to draw political, social, and civic activists to the governor's attention when a vacancy is to be filled.

Access in Judicial Recruitment

For adequate access to state judicial positions, all of those eligible—namely, lawyers—must have a chance to be among the judiciary, and the pool of eligibles ought to be as deep as possible. Nearly every lawyer ought to possess or be able to acquire the formal requirements to be a judge. Of course, only a few will survive the recruitment process and be awarded the robes of office, but none should be excluded—or for that matter, be chosen—primarily because of factors such as status, class, race, gender, or religion. These consider-ations have precious little to do with the technical requirements of judging, although such factors might be considered in order to redress a history of narrow access and inadequate representativeness. Of course, other prerequisites can be imposed by those active in the recruitment process. For example, rarely will Democratic governors appoint Republicans to fill vacancies. There is evidence that women and ethnic minorities stand a better chance of being promoted to the state bench under an appointment system than in elective recruitment settings. Those without legislative experience would be at a disadvantage in the four states that rely on legislative selection. Nonetheless, democratic theory dictates that an equal chance to become a judge be afforded those who possess the minimum educational and experience qualifications.

Requirements of a Viable Judicial Recruitment System

In summary, judicial recruitment in a democracy must blend these conflicting requirements—accountability, independence, partici-pation, representativeness, and access—into a balanced mix. The attainment of a balanced mix is complicated by the interactive effect

Figure 6-1 A Model of Democratic Judicial Recruitment

each has on the others. For example, more accountability means less independence. Limited access means poor representativeness. Wide participation may come at the expense of independence, with high involvement serving to overwhelm those relatively few citizens who have a greater interest in and knowledge of the benefits of judicial independence. A delicate balancing is required. Thus, a democratic system of judicial recruitment should look something like that portrayed in Figure 6-1.

Judicial recruitment must be so structured as to maintain balanced levels of access, representation, and participation which then will bring about an equilibrium between accountability and independence. However, low levels of access, participation, and representation will result in a judicial system skewed in the direction of independence. High levels of the three prerequisites will result in a system which remains closely accountable to the people. To accomplish a balance among the five elements of democratic recruitment is, in practice, not an easy task.

The Practice of Judicial Selection

The State of Selection Research

What has judicial selection research revealed regarding these dimensions of the democratic model? The empirical research on judicial selection has focused primarily on two areas. Most commonly, students of judicial selection have compared and contrasted the backgrounds of the judicial survivors of each of the selection methods (see Canon 1972; Glick and Emmert 1986). The underlying assumption is that if judges' backgrounds are known, their competence can be known and most likely their decisional tendencies can be predicted. Because of the selectivity involved in the various selection methods, those possessing certain traits will be excluded and those with the desirable characteristics will survive the process.

A second and more difficult approach to selection research is to compare and contrast the behavior of those selected by different methods (as done by Atkins and Glick 1974; Levin 1977). For example, do products of executive appointments give stronger sentences than judges selected by the legislature? Again, the assumption is that certain selection criteria will exclude those who will be, for example, "soft on crime" or sympathetic toward plaintiffs in civil cases. Some studies have attempted to combine these two general approaches by appraising both backgrounds and decisional tendencies and attributing the differences to how the jurists were selected (for example, Nagel 1973).

Judicial selection has stimulated a good deal of research by social scientists (Flango and Ducat 1979). Some studies have concerned themselves with the accountability/independence issue, but usually without empirical evidence to support their conclusion regarding the contribution of one or another selection method to the issue (Jacob and Vines 1976, 251; but see Dubois 1980). Most studies have ignored broader theoretical issues and focused on the details of the recruitment experience of but one or two states. These limited studies have not produced agreement regarding whether particular background characteristics can be associated with a particular selection system. In 1972, Bradley Canon's review of state judicial selection research led him to observe:

> While proponents of various judicial selection systems have been quite vocal about why their favorite will produce more meritorious judges, few of them (or more neutral researchers, for that matter) have come up with hard data about just what kinds of differences do in fact result from the adoption of alternative systems. (p. 580)

Seven years later, Gene Flango and Craig Ducat concluded their comprehensive review of selection research with words equally as discouraging: "Despite extensive research, no one has been able to show that different selection procedures produce differences in the characteristics of judges[,] decisions or courts" (1979, 39).[9] Later, Mary Volcansek was not much more sanguine about the research: "The methodological difficulties in cross-state research have resulted in a minimal contribution to our knowledge about the different effects of different selection systems" (1982, 88). Elliot Slotnick's most recent review of the judicial recruitment literature led him to express disappointment with the limited theoretical development in this area:

> Clearly, from the perspective of the academic social sciences, while many research approaches and diverse methodologies have been utilized by analysts to examine judicial recruitment concerns, this is not an area where great theoretical advances of broad interest and applicability are likely to be made. Studies have te..ded to take place in limited research contexts where analysts have viewed the trees but not the forest. (1988, 121)

Does this mean that research on judicial recruitment should be abandoned? Because of our failure to discover what characteristics are possessed by products of different recruitment methods and because we have been unable to isolate any consistent decisional patterns among judges selected in particular ways, must we turn our attention to other research concerns? The answer is emphatically no. As we have tried to show, the recruitment of judges to state benches is simply too important a subject not to continue the search for better understanding. Rather than building on studies that have failed to produce the answers we seek, the focus should be on new methodologies and different approaches. The third part of this chapter is devoted to describing such an exploratory model to accomplish what heretofore has eluded us.

An Articulation Model for Research on Judicial Recruitment

A New Look at Recruitment Processes and Results

The hypothesis remains that different selection methods result in different kinds of judges. The problem with previous research is that selection has been wrongly viewed. Nearly all studies have compared the *formal* methods by which judges are placed on state benches. A few examples will suggest the fallacy of such comparisons. For instance, since both Washington and Oregon employ nonpartisan elections to recruit judges, it is generally assumed that the process in those two neighboring states produces like results. Similarly, Mississippi (Coyle 1972; Alfini 1981) and Pennsylvania (Keefe 1959; Levin 1972; Bolton 1975) use partisan elections; consequently, successful candidates are expected to share many characteristics and to behave in similar ways. Even casual observation, however, reveals that these states produce very different judges, leading to an unwarranted view that how judges are selected makes little difference. The problem is that we have not yet succeeded in isolating the dimensions that constitute the most meaningful aspects of judicial selection and that lend themselves to comparative analysis. We must reappraise the recruitment *process,* casting a more sensitive theoretical net. We must abandon the polemics of judicial selection that focus on which system produces the "best" judge or the most restrained decisions and concentrate instead on what factors constitute measurable results of the recruitment process that comport with democratic theory.

To make a systematic comparison of state judicial recruitment processes, we must find a common denominator in the states under investigation. What do the processes used by Oregon and Washington, New Mexico and New York, and, for that matter, virtually all states have in common? Then, after variations of degree in the commonality are discovered, the effects of accountability, independence, access, participation, and representativeness can be compared.

The Recruitment Process: Participants and Structures

All state judicial recruitment systems attract a variety of participants who at one time or another have been intimately involved in bringing judges to all levels of the state benches. The *candidates,* either through their own efforts or upon the urgings of others, test the waters and perhaps file for available judicial seats or submit their names to the appointing authorities (Crowe 1963; Sheldon 1988). The *bar associations* or groups of attorneys seek out and recommend or endorse candidates and provide the infrastructure for campaigning (Sheldon 1977; Goldstein 1980; Martin 1936). On occasion lawyers may informally agree among themselves who should be the next judge. *Political parties* nominate and endorse candidates and fund and organize campaigns (Moos 1941; Hall 1984). *Interested groups,* such as municipal leagues, good government associations, business interests, or labor unions participate throughout the selection process, providing candidates, funds, campaign resources, and political persuasion which may succeed in getting their person appointed or elected. Ad hoc groups may also be involved at the local level. The *electorate* commonly verifies incumbents or retains appointees through the ballot box (Dubois 1980). The state's *chief executive* or a city's mayor appoints candidates to temporary vacancies in most states or to permanent posts in some states (Herndon 1962; Schneider and Maughan 1979). The official making the appointment is often advised by a member or members of the bar or special commissions. Church organizations, insurance companies, prosecutors' groups, women lawyers' caucuses, or Mothers Against Drunk Driving have been known to participate in some cases of judicial selection, either during election campaigns or in the process of advising the appointment authorities (Sheldon 1986). Although the listing of participants here may be incomplete, common to every method of selection, whether appointment or election, whether Missouri plan or legislative selection, is the predictable *interaction of various participants* resulting in the retention, defeat, or elevation of candidates to the state benches.

The structure in which these participants interact is also common to all recruitment systems. All successful aspirants to state benches pass through three distinct recruitment stages: initiation, screening, and affirmation (Richardson and Vines 1970). In *initiation* the participants either volunteer themselves or push, entice, or persuade others to pursue a judicial position. Initiation is the step that draws the few aspirants from the many who are eligible. One, few, or many participants may be involved in this beginning stage—some successfully in initiating a candidacy, and others not.

Screening constitutes a competitive stage in which candidates are compared with one another and each with the standards set by the screening participants. Again, in any particular judicial contest, one, a few, or many actors may participate in the screening. The initiation and screening may well have all taken place before candidates formally file for office or send in their names to the appointing authorities. Nonetheless, at these early stages they are being recruited for judicial office.

In the final *affirmation* stage the candidates are awarded their robes of office. The actors who are responsible for the final decision—the appointment or the election victory—are affirming participants. The affirmation stage is structured by constitutional and statutory requirements that constitute the formal methods of selection. A focus on these formal methods may neglect the crucial initiation and screening stages. The entire recruitment sequence is inextricably mixed, and the activities that occur in one stage affect the others (Lovrich and Sheldon 1985).

Thus, all state judicial recruitment processes experience the involvement of significant participants, of which the numbers and types of groups can vary. Additionally, all recruitment structures display identical sequences from initiation through screening to affirmation. Upon these commonalities a comparative judicial recruitment model can be constructed. How do these two factors—participants and sequence—fit together to provide us with a framework for gathering data?

Figure 6-2   An Articulation Model of the Recruitment Process

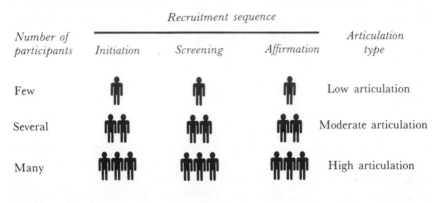

| Number of participants | *Recruitment sequence* | | | Articulation type |
	Initiation	*Screening*	*Affirmation*	
Few				Low articulation
Several				Moderate articulation
Many				High articulation

The Recruitment Process Model

Information on the two common dimensions of judicial recruitment can be gathered to highlight the differences in degree between and among states. The number of participants actively engaged in the three stages of the recruitment structure does vary widely, permitting a meaningful search for explanations for those variances. The number of participants involved throughout the recruitment sequence determines the type of recruitment system predominating in a particular jurisdiction.

A considerable number of actors could be involved in initiation, screening, and affirmation, pushing for competing candidates or urging common standards. Conversely, only a few actors could participate in one or another of the stages in the recruitment sequence, presenting a simple version of recruitment. With this information, state recruitment systems can be placed along an articulation continuum. At one extreme of the continuum is a *high articulation* recruitment system (Lovrich and Sheldon 1985). In such a system a great number of participants or actors are actively involved in all three stages of judicial recruitment. At the other end of the articulation continuum is the *low articulation* system in which very few actors dominate in each of the three stages in the process; in the extreme case, one actor predominates in all three stages. A *moderate articulation* recruitment type obtains when a moderate number of actors are engaged in two or three of the stages. Of course, a state's recruitment could be located anywhere along the continuum between the two extremes. Figure 6-2 outlines articulation types.

The research advantages of the articulation model are many. First, the informal stages of recruitment, namely initiation and screening,

Figure 6-3 Level of Articulation and Balanced Democratic Recruitment

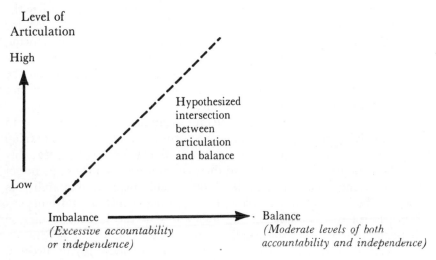

Level of
Articulation

High

Hypothesized
intersection
between
articulation
and balance

Low

Imbalance ⟶ Balance
(Excessive accountability *(Moderate levels of both*
or independence) *accountability and independence)*

dictate much of what transpires at the formal stage of affirmation. To neglect them is to neglect two-thirds of the process. Second, the concept of articulation—with its concentration on the numbers of participants throughout the recruitment sequence—captures the recruitment commonalities shared by all states or jurisdictions, making instructive comparisons possible. Third, the gathering of pertinent data to flesh out the model is not an altogether onerous task. Finally, the model will tell us much about whether one system or another comes closer to an equilibrium among access, participation, and representation—and consequently between accountability and independence, the requisites of a democratic recruitment system.

The Effects of the Process on Democratic Theory

The degree of articulation identified by the data collected within the framework of the research model produces a hypothesized link with the balanced democratic judicial recruitment system. The link can be visualized as in Figure 6-3.

Possible explanations for the association between level of articulation and democratic balance relate to the likely consequences of the frequency and intensity of the interactions among the many participants in the judicial recruitment process. Candidates interact with individuals and groups representing a wide range of interests and different public policy perspectives. Candidates seeking to be elected or appointed often must seek support in quarters beyond the narrow confines of the legal community. In doing so they both learn of the views and perspectives of those active subpopulations and teach the others something about the functioning of courts and the need for judicial independence. This exchange is mutually beneficial, enhancing the level of appreciation for a need to balance the accountability expressed by the subpopulations and for independence expressed by the candidate and the legal profession. As judicial aspirants experience highly articulated initiation, screening, and affirmation environments it is likely that they are inclined to attempt to enhance their empathy with and sensitivity to the public and activist group interests, and to develop a capacity to work with a broad range of interests. They arguably should be better able to represent their community as a consequence of the experience with a high level of articulation. Accountability is softened because of the diversity of the publics involved, and independence is softened because of the awareness of the legitimate diverse demands placed upon the candidate by constituents of the court.

With a number of diverse participants involved in the process, access likely will be open but tempered with a reluctance on the part of many to suffer the ordeal of campaigning, which involves—even in nonelection systems—considerable time, money, and effort. Initiation and screening may exist away from the ordinary scrutiny of the public, but they exist nonetheless, and necessitate some form of "campaigning." Access remains open, but few attorneys are being pushed or are jumping forward to become judges.

Further reasons to suppose a connection between articulation and achieving a balance between accountability and independence could be suggested. However, the crucial questions to be considered at this point are whether the articulation model is researchable, and whether evidence exists to support the relationship hypothesized in Figure 6-3.

Empirical Application of the Articulation Model

Complete data have yet to be collected within the framework of the articulation model. However, a review of data collected from 1984 and 1986 surveys of judicial voters and attorneys in Washington and Oregon provides some tantalizing clues that indicate potential for fruitful research. Our purpose here is not to test the model directly, but rather to present some suggestive findings to stimulate further thinking on the articulation-democratic balance model's potential. Our empirical findings are limited to work on the nonpartisan election system (with gubernatorial appointment to fill vacancies) of Washington and Oregon. As we have argued, however, the model itself is applicable to any system of judicial selection regardless of the formal methods of bringing lawyers to the state bench. Those methods of formal selection constitute but a small part of what should be studied to truly understand state judicial recruitment.

One of the leading concerns of those involved in the study and operation of judicial recruitment at the state level has been the paucity of women and ethnic and racial minorities selected to state benches. If our assumptions about the relationship between articulation and democratic recruitment are correct in Oregon or Washington, we would expect that as the activities of more recruitment actors intensified throughout the recruitment sequence, a more balanced concern for access, representation, and participation of women and minorities would develop. Ultimately, accountability and independence would reach an equilibrium.

Recruitment Roles and Balance
between Accountability and Independence

The results of a balanced recruitment system or, from our empirical perspective, those who have survived a high articulation situation—should be judges who give equal attention to the needs of judicial independence and the demands of public accountability. Having successfully passed the tests of initiation, screening, and affirmation in which a considerable number of recruitment actors participated, the survivors of such travails should be judges who have accepted a particular orientation toward accountability or independence. For our purposes, we have designated this viewpoint "recruitment role orientation" (Lovrich and Sheldon 1984, 1985). In this regard, at least three primary role alternatives are possible. A *trustee* recruitment role orientation, which emphasizes judicial independence and which in our survey studies was defined this way: "Elections should support those judges who are independent of public opinion and remain *unaffected* by the people's demands." In contrast, a "balanced" intermediate *stewardship* recruitment role is accepted by those judges who feel "elections should only *inform* the judges of the general feelings of the people so that judges don't become too isolated." Judges who accept a *delegate* role orientation—in favor of strict accountability—strongly agree that "elections should tell the judges what the people want, and the judges *should follow* the people's desires."

Our expectation is that judges who are products of a low articulation recruitment environment will tend to accept an orientation that favors either accountability or independence over the intermediate balanced position. It is further expected that judges who experience a highly articulated recruitment process will tend to adopt the balanced stewardship role, the role that best reflects the democratic ideal of a balanced recruitment system.

On the assumption that both lawyers and voters are among the leading actors in a nonpartisan election recruitment process, their respective views toward access, representation, participation, independence, and accountability are of considerable interest. In this brief case study, then, we will: (1) allocate the candidates', lawyers', and voters' preferences among the three role orientation categories; (2) determine whether those role orientations are associated with a high or low articulation situation; and (3) contrast the views of those actors found in a high articulation situation with those in a low articulation system regarding aspects of access, participation, and representativeness. Should the persons who are separated into the three role orientations come from different articulation situations and display contrasting views, the articulation model would appear to hold potential for understanding much of what heretofore has eluded scholars of judicial selection—namely, the relationship between methods of recruitment and kinds of judges who come to occupy the state and local benches of American government.

Attorneys who have observed that many participants are involved in the three stages of recruitment in their county or jurisdiction and voters who use more sources of information on candidates—the result of the increased involvement of recruiters—are taken to represent individuals experiencing a high articulation recruitment system. Of course, if lawyers felt that very few groups and individuals were involved in the selection of a judge in their counties and if the voters had little access to information on candidates, both would be experiencing a low articulation system. How do the participants in the two contrasting systems compare in their respective views of the three ideal type recruitment role orientations?

A review of our 1984 and 1986 survey data from the May and September primaries in Oregon and Washington, respectively, regarding the hypothesized relationships is reported in Table 6-1.[10]

Indeed, there is a close relationship between articulation and role orientation. As anticipated, for both attorneys and voters when the level of articulation increases, support for the stewardship role tends to increase, and support for the trustee and delegate roles (the extremes in independence and accountability, respectively) tends to decrease. (Somewhat of an anomaly occurs among the attorneys in Washington, where support for the delegate role tends to grow as the level of articulation increases.) Among Oregon attorneys, the trustee role gains support from among those in a moderately articulated environment, but returns to the same level experienced among attorneys in both the low and high articulation situations. Overall, it can be said that articulation and role orientations indeed appear to be related in the manner hypothesized.

Table 6-1 Articulation and Recruitment Role Orientation

Level of articulation	*Delegate*		*Steward*		*Trustee*	
	Wash.	Ore.	Wash.	Ore.	Wash.	Ore.
Attorneys						
Low	34%	10%	46%	59%	61%	39%
Medium	47	6	64	57	49	51
High	52	6	67	64	39	39
Voters						
Low	—	52	—	39	—	32
High	—	42	—	52	—	24

Source: Data are from the authors' 1984 survey of Oregon attorneys and voters and 1986 survey of Washington attorneys.

Representation of Women and Minorities on the Bench

How closely does the Oregon and Washington judiciary mirror the presence of women and minorities in the general population and in the legal profession? Out of an Oregon population of 2,687,000 in 1985, women constituted 51 percent. Minorities (blacks, Asians, native Americans, and Hispanics) constituted 6.2 percent. Complete representativeness should result in similar percentages in the legal profession and in the judiciary. Of the 8,759 active Oregon attorneys in 1989, 1,647 (19 percent) were women and 177 (2 percent) were minorities. In the judiciary of 163, 13 (8 percent) were women and 4 (2 percent) were minorities. The Oregon judiciary was representative of minorities in the legal profession but lacked a representative number of women. The Washington figures are quite similar to those reported for Oregon. The 1988 population of Washington was 4,565,000, of which women constituted 50 percent and minorities 10.6 percent. Out of 14,750 active attorneys, approximately 4,130 (28 percent) were females and 525 (3.6 percent) were minorities. Three hundred sixty judges constituted the Washington judiciary, but only 42 (12 percent) were women and 15 (4 percent) were minorities. Although the percentage of minority judges approximated the percentage among lawyers, clearly women remained underrepresented. However, Washington failed adequately to represent the numbers of women or minorities in the general population. Is this state of affairs recognized as a problem, and if so by whom? If the model is viable, those recruitment participants within high articulation systems would more readily recognize an imbalance in representativeness than would those recruitment actors in low articula-

Table 6-2 Need for More Representative Bench: High versus Low Articulation

| | Add women to bench | | | | Add ethnics to bench | | | |
| Level of articulation | Need more effort | | Need less effort | | Need more effort | | Need less effort | |
	Wash.	Ore.	Wash.	Ore.	Wash.	Ore.	Wash.	Ore.
Attorneys								
Low	30%	42%	34%	34%	30%	31%	38%	33%
Medium	34	39	22	18	32	35	22	16
High	39	47	15	15	39	46	16	15
Voters								
Low	—	39	—	26	—	22	—	36
High	—	40	—	23	—	31	—	26

Source: Data are from the authors' 1984 survey of Oregon attorneys and voters and 1986 survey of Washington attorneys.

tion jurisdictions. Table 6-2 contrasts the views of lawyers and voters in a high articulation environment with those in a low articulation situation with respect to whether they think the courts should be more representative of the public. Each respondent in our surveys was asked: "To what extent do you agree that more women (ethnic and racial minorities) ought to be selected to Oregon (Washington) courts?" The resulting breakdown is presented in Table 6-2.

The findings suggest that, indeed, those participants within a highly articulated recruitment situation were more sensitive to the imbalance in representativeness in Oregon and Washington courts. Among the attorneys, the concern for better representation among women and minorities increases as the level of articulation increases, and those who saw less need for more women or minorities on the Washington and Oregon benches were found mostly in a low articulation situation.[11]

The Oregon voters found in a high articulation environment make a stronger case for more representatives of ethnic minorities than do those in the low articulation situation. It is likely that some meaningful adjustments in access will be required to increase the representativeness of the Oregon judiciary beyond its current state.

Access and Women and Minorities on the Washington Benches

The disparity between women and minorities present in the general population and found in the legal profession can, of course, be

Table 6-3 Reasons for Not Running for a Judicial Position: High
versus Low Articulation and Male versus Female

Reasons	High articulation	Low articulation	Male	Female
Costs of campaigning	77%	69%	73%	82%
Dictates of Canon 7 [a]	8	13	11	16
Retaliation by a challenged incumbent	30	30	30	60
Personal efforts needed for a public campaign	77	62	68	73
Time lost from practice	80	71	74	85
Raising money for campaign	84	77	78	88
Problems of organizing	67	53	59	70
Insecurity of short elected term	32	32	34	34

[a] Code of Judicial Conduct, which prohibits "inappropriate" political activity.
Note. Percentage designating reason as a "very important" or "important" deterrent against
running for judicial office.
Source: Data are from the authors' 1986 survey of Washington attorneys.

explained by the requirement of a legal education, unavailable to many
because of cost. Nonetheless, the disparity between women and
minorities in the legal profession and on the bench is not as easily
explained. Fortunately, our survey work within the Washington setting
highlights some aspects of access that might account for the disparity.

In response to a question asking the sample of attorneys why they
had not given serious consideration to filing for a judicial office in
Washington, those from the high articulation environments tended to
agree with the views of those from the low articulation situation, but
with interesting differences in degree of attention given to a range of
concerns. These responses are reported in Table 6-3.

The financial aspects of running for the bench are the primary
concern for Washington attorneys; that is, the costs of campaigning,
problems of raising money, and time lost from practice deter most
attorneys. Financial considerations appear to be a greater deterrent for
those attorneys from high articulation environments than those from
low articulation settings. This should be expected simply because of the
higher costs most likely involved in a multimedia and widespread high
articulation campaign. Women attorneys agreed with their male
counterparts in most regards, but fear of "retaliation" from incumbents
should their challenge fail was more troublesome for them than for
men. The problems of raising money, taking time from practice to

campaign, and the costs of campaigning were viewed as primary deterrents by women.

The survey findings suggest that a better balance between access and representativeness could be achieved if campaign costs were brought under control. Some form of public financing or voluntary or legal limits placed on campaign contributions would likely contribute to bettering this balance. During a hotly contested statewide race for the supreme court in Washington in 1984, one losing candidate spent nearly $140,000. A total of $258,860 was expended by three candidates for the one position which, at the time, had an annual salary of $51,500. The same year in Oregon in a three-way race for a supreme court spot $230,645 was spent on campaigning for a position that paid $53,308 a year. We suspect that the fears expressed in Table 6-3 are well founded. However, if the news media covered judicial campaigns more thoroughly, the requirements of a high articulation system could be partially met without additional costs to candidates.[12]

Participation for Women and Minorities in the Oregon Judiciary

The level of electoral participation can be measured in a number of ways, including calculating the number of judicial candidates filing, the number of active supporters backing the candidates, and the number of citizens who vote in the judicial races. In the 1984 primary election in Washington 2,267,432 citizens were registered to vote, and of those only 932,820 (41 percent) cast ballots in the September primary. Of these voters, 656,249 (70 percent) voted in one of the statewide supreme court races. Thus, the roll off between those who voted in the primary and those who cast a ballot for a judge was 30 percent. In 1984, Oregon had 1,457,067 registered voters, of whom 767,565 (53 percent) participated in the May primary. Of these, 552,296 (72 percent) cast ballots in a statewide supreme court race. Oregon's roll-off vote was only slightly lower than in Washington, registering 28 percent. In light of the low turnout and the high roll off in the decisive primary balloting, participation in the recruitment of judges in both states was fairly low.

However, was the level of participation higher in the high articulation systems than in the low articulation situation? Sixty-three percent of the voter respondents in the low articulation setting said they voted in the 1984 May primary in Oregon; 52 percent of the total said they also voted for a judicial candidate. Participation was greater in the high articulation environment. Seventy-four percent cast a ballot in the primary, and 67 percent of the respondents voted in a judicial race. Although these percentages are higher than in the general voting population, the differences indicate that the high articulation environs do spark more participation.[13] Although in our survey the male voting population exceeded slightly the female, women tended to increase their participation over the men as the articulation level was raised.

It is apparent that the level of articulation has an effect on the level of participation of the underrepresented voters. Women voters are more active in the high articulation environment than in low articulation settings. In the high articulation environment, 68 percent of the women voted for judges, while in the low articulation environment 49 percent voted. Previously published research has also made it clear that black voters in Oregon (Portland) disproportionately cast their ballots for black candidates, and that the roll off in predominantly black precincts is lower when a black person is on the ballot (Lovrich, Sheldon, and Wasmann 1989, 809).

Conclusion

If these few factors relevant to the various dimensions of our empirical model are any indication, studying the degree of articulation in judicial recruitment will lead us to a greater understanding of judicial selection. Looking beyond the formal affirmation methods and constructing a model that possesses all the important elements of judicial recruitment appears to be a fruitful approach. Initiation, screening, and affirmation take place in all selection systems—a fact that provides the necessary common denominator for comparative research. The sequence differs across jurisdictions in terms of how many active participants are involved in each of those three steps in the process. Consequently, a common recruitment ingredient varies enough to permit meaningful comparative analysis.

It would seem clear that the level of articulation is important in judicial recruitment, for it is apparent that this aspect of judicial election processes has something to do with the orientations the selection process actors wish the winning candidates to possess regarding accountability and independence. Why wouldn't surviving candidates share these orientations and, on occasion, reflect the sharing in their rulings? It would seem as well that access, participation, and representativeness—the independent variables in our ideal model— appear also to be associated with levels of articulation. Quite consistently across the several dimensions of our concern, the higher the level of articulation, the greater the approximation of balance among the major components of the recruitment scheme. Of course, what we have presented here is only a beginning, but perhaps an exciting new approach is in the offing for research into judicial selection at the state level.

Notes

1. Judge Theodore Stiles, one of the first members of the Washington Supreme Court, in 1889 expressed the then prevailing view which, if anything, has been reinforced in modern times. In an address to the state bar he argued that "the courts are, and in the nature of things, must be the appellate body, and their power to review extends over the entire domain of public and private rights. Once it is conceded, as it now universally [is], that a statute may be declared void as unconstitutional, there is no denying the proposition of judicial supremacy. . . . There is no power except that of the people in constitutional convention that can reverse [a court decision]" (1899, 66).
2. As in Alabama, Arkansas, Illinois, Mississippi, North Carolina, Pennsylvania, Tennessee, Texas, and West Virginia.
3. Legislative selection is used in Connecticut, Rhode Island, South Carolina, and Virginia.
4. States using some form of the Missouri plan for the selection of some or all their judges are Alaska, Arizona, Colorado, Delaware, Florida, Hawaii, Indiana, Iowa, Kansas, Maryland, Massachusetts, Missouri, Nebraska, New Mexico, New York, Oklahoma, South Dakota, Utah, Vermont, and Wyoming.
5. States selecting judges by nonpartisan elections are Georgia, Idaho, Kentucky, Louisiana, Michigan, Minnesota, Montana, Nevada, North Dakota, Ohio, Oregon, Washington, and Wisconsin.
6. As in California, Maine, New Hampshire, New Jersey, and Rhode Island.
7. Wasby identifies two kinds of accountability: internal and political (Wasby 1978, 155, 165; see also *Harvard Journal of Law and Public Policy* 1983).
8. Canon 7 of Washington's Code of Judicial Conduct is titled "A Judge Should Refrain from Political Activity Inappropriate to his [her] Judicial Office" and reads in part, a judge "should not make pledges or promises of conduct in office other than the faithful and impartial performance of the duties of the office; [or] announce his [her] views of disputed legal or political issues."
9. An extensive test of whether elective judges differ in their decision making from nonelected judges was conducted by Philip Dubois (1980). He found few differences in the decision making of Democratic and Republican judges in states with different selection methods; albeit, partisan ballots in state elective systems provide for greater accountability (compare Nagel 1973).
10. Oregon holds its primary election in May. Judicial candidates who garner 51 percent of the vote are designated as winners and go to the November ballot unopposed; otherwise, the top two finishers compete for the votes in the general election. Fifty-seven percent (or 313) of the sample of Oregon voters (1984) responded to the survey. The same year, 201 attorneys (70

percent answered the questionnaire. The Washington 1986 response rate involved 299 attorneys, which was 58 percent of the original 520 sample.

11. As might be expected, Washington women attorneys sensed a greater need for increased representation of women (86 percent) and minorities (77 percent) than their male counterparts (28 percent and 26 percent, respectively). Nearly the same percentages held for Oregon: 82 percent of the female lawyers saw a need for more women and 79 percent for a greater representation of minorities. Among the male lawyers in Oregon the percentages were only 35 percent and 30 percent, respectively.

12. For a discussion of voter knowledge, activism, and media responsibility see Lovrich, Pierce, and Sheldon 1989.

13. The registered voter respondents undoubtedly were mostly among those who had voted in the Oregon primary, and those who failed to return their surveys had not participated in the election. Nonetheless, the crucial aspect of our measure of participation is the difference between respondents in high and low articulation situations.

References

Alfini, James J. 1981. Mississippi judicial selection: Election, appointment and bar anointment. In *Courts and judges,* ed. James E. Cramer. Beverly Hills, Calif.: Sage.

Atkins, Burton M., and Henry R. Glick. 1974. Formal judicial recruitment and state supreme court decisions. *American Politics Quarterly* 2:427-419.

Barber, Kathleen. 1971. Ohio judicial elections—Nonpartisan premises with partisan results. *Ohio State Law Journal* 32:762-789.

Bolton, F. 1975. House of Delegates appellate courts judicial poll. *Pennsylvania Bar Association Quarterly* 4.

Canon, Bradley C. 1972. The impact of formal selection process on the characteristics of judges, reconsidered. *Law and Society Review* 6:579-593.

Coyle, Arlen B. 1972. Judicial selection and tenure in Mississippi. *Mississippi Law Journal* 43:90-107.

Crowe, John E. 1963. Subterranean politics: A judge is chosen. *Journal of Public Law* 12:275-289.

DeGrazia, Alfred. 1951. *Public and republic: Political representation in America.* New York: Knopf.

Dubois, Philip. 1979. Voter turnout in state judicial elections: An analysis of the tail on the electoral kite. *Journal of Politics* 41:865-885.

———. 1980. *From ballot to bench: Judicial elections and the quest for accountability.* Austin: University of Texas Press.

Elazar, Daniel, and John Kincaid. 1987. *Covenant, polity and constitutionalism.* Lanham, Md.: University Press of America.

Flango, Victor, and Craig Ducat. 1979. What difference does the method of judicial selection make? Selection procedures in state courts of last resort. *Justice System Journal* 5:25-44.

Gibson, James L. 1978. Performance indicators in the court system. In *Accountability in urban society,* ed. Scott Greer, Ronald Hedlund, and James Gibson. Beverly Hills, Calif.: Sage.

Glick, Henry R., and Craig F. Emmert. 1986. Selection systems and judicial characteristics: The recruitment of state supreme court judges. *Judicature* 70:228-235.

Goldstein, Joel H. 1980. Bar poll ratings as the leading influence on a nonpartisan judicial election. *Judicature* 63:377-384.

Griffin, Kenyon, and Michael J. Horan. 1979, Merit retention elections: What influences the voters? *Judicature* 63:78-88.

———. 1983. Patterns of voting behavior in judicial retention elections for supreme court justices in Wyoming. *Judicature* 67:68-77.

Hall, Kermit. 1984. Progressive reform and the decline of democratic accountability: The popular election of state supreme court judges, 1850-1920. *American Bar Foundation Research Journal* 1984:345-369.

Hamilton, Alexander. 1961. Federalist no. 78. *The Federalist Papers.* New York: Mentor.

Harvard Journal of Law and Public Policy. 1983. Symposium: Politicization of the courts: Balancing the need for judicial independence against the need for judicial accountability. *Harvard Journal of Law and Public Policy* 6:295-340.

Haynes, Evan. 1944. *The selection and tenure of judges.* Newark, N.J.: National Conference of Judicial Councils.

Herndon, James. 1962. Appointment as a means of initial accession to elective state courts of last resort. *North Dakota Law Review* 38:60-73.

Jacob, Herbert, and Kenneth Vines. 1976. *Politics in the American states: A comparative analysis.* Boston: Little, Brown.

Keefe, William J. 1959. Judges and politics: The Pennsylvania plan of judicial selection. *University of Pittsburgh Law Review* 20:621-631.

Levin, Martin A. 1977. *Urban politics and the criminal courts.* Chicago: University of Chicago Press.

Llewellyn, Karl. 1960. *The common law tradition.* Boston: Little, Brown.

Lovrich, Nicholas P., Jr., and Charles H. Sheldon. 1984. Voters in judicial elections: An attentive public or an uninformed electorate? *Justice System Journal* 9:23-39.

———. 1985. Assessing judicial elections: Effects upon the electorate of high and low articulation systems. *Western Political Quarterly* 38:276-293.

Lovrich, Nicholas P., Jr., John C. Pierce, and Charles H. Sheldon. 1989. Citizen knowledge and voting in judicial elections. *Judicature* 73:28-33.

Lovrich, Nicholas P., Jr., Charles H. Sheldon, and Erik Wasmann. 1988. The racial factor in nonpartisan judicial elections: A research note. *Western Political Quarterly* 41:807-816.

Lutz, Donald S. 1980. From covenant to constitution in American political thought. *Publius* 10(4):101-133.

MacManus, Sheila. 1988. Focus. *Judicature* 72:185-188.

Martin, Edward M. 1936. *The role of the bar in electing the bench in Chicago.* Chicago: University of Chicago Press.

Milbrath, Lester, and M. L. Gael. 1977. *Political participation.* Chicago: Rand McNally.

Moos, Malcolm. 1941. Judicial election and partisan endorsement of judicial candidates in Minnesota. *American Political Science Review* 35:69-75.

Nagel, Stuart S. 1973. *Comparing elected and appointed judicial systems.* Beverly Hills, Calif.: Sage.

Pateman, Carole. 1970. *Participation and democratic theory: The logic of political analysis.* Cambridge: Cambridge University Press.

Pitkin, Hanna. 1967. *The concept of representation.* Berkeley: University of California Press.

Richardson, Richard J., and Kenneth Vines. 1970. *The politics of federal courts.* Boston: Little, Brown.

Schneider, Ronald, and Robert Maughan. 1979. Does the appointment of judges lead to a more conservative bench? *Justice System Journal* 5:45-57.

Seattle—King County Bar Association. 1989. Chief Justice Callow's inaugural remarks. *Bar Bulletin* 7:1.

Sheldon, Charles H. 1977. Influencing the selection of judges: The variety and effectiveness of state bar activities. *Western Political Quarterly* 30:397-400.

_____. 1986. The recruitment of judges to the Washington Supreme Court: Past and present. *Willamette Law Review* 22:85-128.

_____. 1987. Judicial review and the supreme court of Washington, 1890-1986. *Publius* 17:69-90.

_____. 1988. *A century of judging: A political history of the Washington Supreme Court.* Seattle: University of Washington Press.

Sherman, Roie. 1989. Is Mississippi turning? *National Law Journal* 11:1.

Slotnick, Elliot E. 1988. Review essay on judicial recruitment and selection. *Justice System Journal* 13:109-124.

Smith, Hedrick. 1989. *The power game: How Washington works.* New York: Ballantine.

Stiles, Theodore Lamme. 1899. Legislative encroachments upon private right. *Proceedings of the Washington State Bar Association,* 59-75.

Utter, Robert F. 1989. Interpreting state constitutions: An independent path. *Intergovernmental Perspective* 15:30-32.

Verba, Sidney, and Norman H. Nie. 1972. *Participation in America.* New York: Harper and Row.

Volcansek, Mary L. 1982. The effects of judicial selection reform: What we know and what we do not. In *The analysis of judicial reform,* ed. Philip L. Dubois. Lexington, Mass.: Lexington Books.

Volcansek, Mary L., and Jacqueline Lucienne Lafon. 1988. *Judicial selection: The cross evolution of French and American practices.* New York: Wiley.

Wasby, Stephen. 1978. Accountability of courts. In *Accountability in urban society,* ed. Scott Greer, Ronald Hedlund, and James Gibson. Beverly Hills, Calif.: Sage.

Wasmann, Erik, Nicholas P. Lovrich, Jr., and Charles H. Sheldon. 1986. Perceptions of state and local courts: A comparison across selection systems. *Justice System Journal* 11:168-185.

Winters, Glenn R., ed. 1973. *Judicial selection and tenure: Selected readings.* Chicago: American Judicature Society.

Wood, Gordon S. 1969. *The creation of the American republic, 1776-1787.* New York: W. W. Norton.

7. FEDERAL JUDICIAL RECRUITMENT

Sheldon Goldman

In recent years increased popular attention has been paid to the issue of the recruitment of federal judges. A high point of this interest occurred in 1987 with the nomination of Robert H. Bork to fill an associate justiceship on the Supreme Court. The nomination proved controversial and ultimately unsuccessful, as did the aborted nomination of Douglas H. Ginsburg following Bork's defeat. (Anthony Kennedy was eventually confirmed for this seat on the Court.) But media and public attention were sharply focused on judicial recruitment, and it was widely recognized that the selection of Supreme Court justices as well as lower federal court judges constitutes a significant political event. This chapter addresses five broad questions associated with recruitment: Why is it important to know about judicial recruitment and the backgrounds of the judges selected? What do we know about how federal judges are selected? Who are the persons chosen for judgeships? How do we assess the recruitment process? Are we asking the right questions, and are there new avenues of research that should be considered?

The Importance of Recruitment and Background

At the outset, it should be made clear why it is important to know about federal judicial recruitment and the judges who are selected. This means that we are concerned with what difference it makes how we select judges and who is chosen.

As we shall explore in greater detail shortly, federal judicial recruitment is a political process, that is, judges are chosen by politicians (the president and senators) who are given formal appointment authority by the Constitution. Judges are not recruited through the civil service, as is common in European legal systems. Our method of selecting judges has links with democratic theory in that the

This chapter was written while on leave as a faculty fellow at the University of Massachusetts at Amherst. I would like to thank the Research Council and Dean Samuel F. Conti of the Graduate School for the award.

judiciary, a branch of government not directly responsible to the people through the electoral process, is kept in touch with popular sentiment by being selected by politicians who have been directly elected by the people and who presumably represent that sentiment. Judges chosen by a democratically elected president can be expected in a general sense to reflect the values and policy outlook of the appointing administration and in turn the majority that elected the president. Senators, also democratically elected, represent, in theory, further links between the judiciary and public opinion. Federal judicial recruitment thus provides the opportunity for party responsibility in accord with democratic theory. People who vote for president and senator, in theory, know what these officials stand for, share their values and policy goals, and expect that the appointment power will be exercised consistent with those views. Study of federal judicial recruitment shows us the extent to which it reflects party responsibility and the democratic theory assumptions underlying that theory.

Representative government is the implementation of democratic theory and suggests not only that government consists of representatives of the people but that they are *representative* of the people, at least in terms of some personal attributes. Extended to the judiciary, the question becomes the extent to which the judiciary mirrors the population as a whole in such matters as gender, race, ethnicity, and religion.

Because recruitment is a political process, study of the process and those who are chosen by it shows us the extent to which appointments made by different administrations produce diversity on the bench in terms of legal, economic, and other backgrounds or attributes such as gender, race, and age.

A recruitment process rooted in politics has been thought to encourage talented people who aspire to federal judgeships to participate in politics. Study of the recruitment process can shed light on when and how judgeships are used as political rewards. Study of the process can also highlight the problem areas of the misuse of patronage with the appointment of marginally qualified or unqualified people.

Once on the bench, judges have opportunities to use judicial discretion. As a result they may disagree about how a case should be decided. They differ because they may have different political values or different priorities among their values; they have different ways of perceiving and evaluating reality; and they have conflicting views of their role as judge. Differences in backgrounds and experiences may well account for why judges decide cases the way they do. Thus it is widely accepted that the type of justice that is dispensed is intimately connected with the judges who do the dispensing. This is another reason why judicial backgrounds are important and why scholars of the judiciary study them.

Recruitment

The process of becoming a federal judge involves five stages. Initially, *the administration selects an individual to be recommended to the president to fill a judicial vacancy.* Studies of the selection process suggest that historically and through the present this stage has been complex and typically intensely political. The selection of a particular individual for a judgeship is the climax of a series of interrelated transactions that lead to one individual rather than another among many qualified individuals. David Danelski (1964) conducted a study of the selection in 1923 of Pierce Butler to the Supreme Court. By a thorough search of archival materials he was able to piece together the series of interrelated events and interpersonal exchanges that resulted in Butler and not someone else receiving the nomination. Danelski's research makes it clear that no *one* appointment can be adequately explained without knowledge of the unique set of transactions propelling one candidacy and stalling the others.

The second stage in the process is when *the president formally nominates the individual and the White House sends the nomination to the U.S. Senate.* This is thought to be routine, but that is not always the case. For example, during the Reagan presidency, after Robert H. Bork's nomination to the Supreme Court was defeated on the floor of the Senate, President Reagan announced his intention to nominate Douglas H. Ginsburg. Shortly thereafter, newspaper reporters published stories alleging that at social events while he was a Harvard Law School professor, Ginsburg had smoked marijuana. When Ginsburg admitted that he had experimented with marijuana, his prospective nomination was attacked by conservative Republicans, and the White House never sent the nomination to the Senate (see, for example, Cohodas 1987). There are also examples concerning prospective lower court nominations. For example, the Reagan administration had decided upon a well-regarded Republican lawyer from Missouri, Judith Whittaker, for an Eighth Circuit court of appeals judgeship when right-winger Richard Viguerie unleashed a campaign against her charging her with being "a strong feminist." The Reagan administration soon dropped Whittaker, and her name was never sent to the Senate (see *New York Times* 1981, 1982).

Stage three is when *the Senate Judiciary Committee considers the nomination and votes whether to approve and to send the nomination to the full Senate.* With lower court nominees this stage has been considered routine, provided that the senator or senators of the president's party from the state of the nominee cleared (that is, approved or offered no objection to) the nomination.[1] It is unusual for an administration to ignore senators from the president's party when making nominations for judgeships; as a consequence, the Senate Judiciary Committee rarely has before it a judicial nomination opposed by a senator of the president's party. Since 1979, however, the Senate Judiciary Committee has played a more active role in the process and no longer rubber stamps all nominations.[2] Over the past three decades, Supreme Court nominees have been carefully scrutinized by the committee, and the evidence suggests that ideology has been a major factor in the voting of senators (Weisberg and Felice 1988).

Sometimes stage four, when *the Senate votes to confirm by a simple majority vote,* can also be politically complex. This has been most prominent historically with Supreme Court nominations. During the nineteenth century about one in three Supreme Court nominees failed to win approval by the Senate. During the twentieth century, the rate has been one in ten. Fewer lower court nominees have been controversial enough to trigger a debate on the Senate floor; however, several Reagan nominees were among those historically select few. The politics of Senate confirmation, particularly of Supreme Court nominees, has attracted scholarly attention. Much of this work has focused on an analysis of roll call votes. In determining the relevant variable related to confirmation or rejection of Supreme Court nominees, Jeffrey A. Segal (1987) found most important whether the president's party controlled the Senate, whether the nominee was a senator or cabinet member, and whether the nomination was made during the president's last year of his term. Analyses of senatorial voting behavior have shown that the policy positions (Songer 1979) or ideological stance of senators are strongly related to their confirmation votes (Sulfridge 1980; Weisberg and Felice 1988).[3]

If any stage in the recruitment process should be considered a routine bureaucratic one, it is stage five, when *the president signs the commission which is delivered to the individual who then takes the judicial oath of office.* But even here we have one famous historical precedent to the contrary: in 1801 the new Jefferson administration refused to deliver certain judicial commissions signed by outgoing President Adams. The nondelivery of the commissions led to the famous case of *Marbury v. Madison* (1 Cranch 137 [1803]).

A variety of participants are involved in judicial recruitment. From selecting a Supreme Court justice to picking a district judge nominee, the president and his closest White House advisers may be involved, along with officials in the Justice Department, especially the attorney general, the deputy attorney general, and their assistants (Chase 1972). The American Bar Association's Standing Committee on Federal Judiciary rates nominees and provides the ratings to the Justice Department and to the Senate Judiciary Committee.[4] With lower court nominations, senators of the president's party from the state where the potential nominee resides play a role, as can various others from the state, such as members of Congress, the state party chairperson, the governor, members of the national party committee, and mayors of large cities. Those who aspire to federal judgeships should also be considered participants—particularly those who campaign for these positions. The campaigning is usually done behind the scenes as the individual contacts political figures, bar association leaders and groups, and friends and acquaintances among the bar and the bench to back his or her candidacy.[5]

The actual process of judicial recruitment varies from administration to administration (Chase 1972; McFeeley 1987; O'Brien 1988). For example, during the Carter administration, judicial selection commissions were used for appeals court nominations. The commissions were charged with actively seeking out well-qualified women and members of minority groups (see Berkson and Carbon 1980). Although President Carter wanted similar commissions for the selection of district court judges, it was politically impossible to get Democratic senators to surrender their prerogatives. However, senators were encouraged to (and many did) create their own commissions (Neff 1981). The Reagan administration dropped the commissions and instead created the Office of Legal Policy in the Justice Department to recruit persons whose judicial philosophy meshed with that of the administration (Goldman 1989b). The Bush administration, however, abolished the Office of Legal Policy and returned the locus of judicial recruiting activity to the deputy attorney general's office. For all administrations, however, the Justice Department plays a major role in selecting the person to be recommended to the president.

Senators of the president's party expect to play an influential role in picking district judges and even, to some extent, appeals judges. Although traditionally Justice Department officials have had more leeway in filling courts of appeals positions than in filling district court judgeships, even with district judgeships the senators' wishes have not been granted automatically. This has meant that judicial recruitment frequently becomes a negotiations process that includes senators and other party leaders. Sometimes there are long delays, a factor seen by critics of federal judicial recruitment as a serious flaw in the process.

Several variables come into play in judicial recruitment across administrations. First and most important are the political party credentials of potential nominees. Historically, the large majority of appointments have gone to members of the president's party. Nine out of ten appointments to members of the president's party is typical (Evans 1948; Committee on the Judiciary 1972; O'Brien 1988, 37). Not only are partisans nominated, but those with a background of previous party activity tend to be favored.

A second recruitment variable is the professional qualifications of the candidates for judicial office. As a general rule incompetents are not nominated to lifetime positions on the federal bench. Indeed, Justice Department officials have a special interest in not sabotaging the courts. The federal government is the major litigant in the federal courts, and Justice Department lawyers will be arguing cases before these same judges.[6] This parenthetically raises the question whether there is a conflict of interest on the part of the Justice Department in selecting judges before whom department lawyers will be arguing cases.

Also coming into play in judicial recruitment are the judicial philosophical views or policy views or overall ideology of the nominees. At times in our history this has been particularly important for Supreme Court appointments and to a lesser extent for the lower federal courts (Solomon 1984; Abraham 1985; McFeeley 1987; Goldman 1989a). President Franklin D. Roosevelt's administration was concerned with placing economic liberals on the courts, and both the White House and the Justice Department were sensitive to the policy views of judicial nominees. President Richard Nixon was committed to naming law-and-order conservatives to the courts, and there were some efforts at ideological screening; however, the administration usually went along with the choices of Republican senators even when the nominees were politically moderate. The Carter administration placed greater emphasis on affirmative action appointments than on ideological or policy views. The Reagan administration, however, asserted the primacy of judicial philosophy and instituted a systematic screening process unprecedented in American history.

In general, political party considerations have taken priority over the ideological or policy views of the candidates, which in turn have tended to be more important than their legal scholarship. The Carter administration in a number of instances put affirmative action considerations at the head of the list. The Reagan administration elevated ideology and legal policy to the highest concern. It is too early to determine the priorities of the Bush administration, although some see a continuity with the Reagan regime (*New York Times* 1990).

Backgrounds

Who are the people recruited for judicial office? Have they shared similar socialization experiences? Are there differences in the demographic and attribute profiles of appointees of different administrations? These are some of the questions that have interested political scientists who study the judiciary. This interest is fueled by evidence suggesting that the values of judicial decision makers influence their decisions and that attitudes and values are associated with certain backgrounds and experiences (see discussion and citations in Goldman and Jahnige 1985, 146-149).

Studies of family backgrounds have revealed that historically, high social status and wealth have been greatly overrepresented on the federal bench. John Schmidhauser's (1979) authoritative study of the backgrounds of Supreme Court justices found that close to 90 percent of the justices came from economically comfortable families (pp. 49-55). Interestingly, with only four exceptions all of the Supreme Court justices through the present with humble backgrounds were Democrats.[7] In all, 25 percent of the justices appointed by Democratic presidents (nine out of thirty-six) were from humble backgrounds, while only 10 percent of the justices appointed by Republicans (five out of fifty, two of whom were Democrats) were from such backgrounds.[8] These findings seem to highlight the differences in socioeconomic groups to which each party has traditionally had its greatest appeal. The available data concerning lower court judges indicate much the same pattern (Goldman and Jahnige 1985, 52). However, it must be emphasized that the majority of those appointed by both Democratic and Republican presidents came from economically well off backgrounds.

Close to 85 percent of those appointed to the Supreme Court attended the best law schools or (as was typical of legal education in the nineteenth century) served apprenticeships with prominent lawyers and judges. Findings for the Eisenhower and Kennedy administrations were that about one-third of the judges graduated from state-supported law schools (Goldman 1965, 757). This proportion has increased somewhat, as seen in Table 7-1: note that over 48 percent of the Carter appointees attended state-supported law schools. Many state-supported law schools are, of course, distinguished, but they are also less expensive to attend than private schools. It is possible that the gradual increase in the proportion of appointees who attended state law schools reflects an increase in the proportion of judges who come from lower middle class or even lower class backgrounds. Another interesting finding in Table 7-1 is that the proportion of appointees who attended Ivy League law schools, among the most distinguished in the nation, fell from the high of almost one in four during the Nixon administration to the low point during the Reagan administration of about one in seven. This was the lowest proportion of all administrations from the

Table 7-1 Selected Backgrounds of Johnson through Reagan Appointees to Lifetime Positions on the Lower Federal Courts of General Jurisdiction (U.S. District and Appeals Courts)

	Appointing administration								
	Johnson		Nixon		Ford		Carter		Reagan	
	%	N	%	N	%	N	%	N	%	N
Law school education										
Public-supported	40.1	65	41.1	92	45.3	29	48.1	124	41.8	154
Private (not Ivy)	35.8	58	34.8	78	35.9	23	29.5	76	43.8	161
Ivy League	22.8	37	24.1	54	18.8	12	22.5	58	14.4	53
Experience										
Judicial	41.9	68	39.7	89	48.4	31	54.3	140	49.5	182
Prosecutorial	46.3	75	42.9	96	45.3	29	37.2	96	40.8	150
Neither	30.2	49	32.6	73	29.7	19	30.2	78	29.6	109
Occupation										
Politics/government	18.5	30	9.4	21	18.8	12	4.7	12	11.4	42
Judiciary	37.7	61	33.5	75	42.2	27	44.9	116	41.0	151
Large law firm	3.1	5	9.8	22	9.4	6	13.2	34	16.6	61
Moderate-size law firm	18.5	30	26.8	60	21.9	14	18.9	49	17.4	64
Small law firm	9.3	15	12.9	29	6.2	4	9.7	25	6.2	23
Solo practice	9.9	16	3.6	8	1.6	1	2.3	6	2.2	8
Law professor	3.1	5	2.7	6	—	—	5.4	14	4.4	16
Other	—	—	1.3	3	—	—	0.8	2	0.8	3
ABA ratings										
Exceptionally well qualified	12.4	20	7.1	16	3.1	2	6.6	17	7.1	26
Well qualified	42.9	69	43.8	98	45.3	29	49.6	128	48.1	177
Qualified	42.2	68	49.1	110	50.0	32	42.6	110	44.8	165
Not qualified	2.5	4	—	—	1.7	1	1.2	3	—	—

	%	N	%	N	%	N	%	N	%	N
Party										
Democratic	94.4	153	7.1	16	18.8	12	90.3	233	3.8	14
Republican	5.6	9	92.9	208	81.2	52	5.0	13	94.3	347
Independent	—	—	—	—	—	—	4.7	12	1.6	6
Past party activism	51.2	83	50.9	114	51.6	33	63.6	164	60.9	224
Religious origin or affiliation										
Protestant	58.6	95	73.7	165	70.3	45	60.5	156	59.2	218
Catholic	29.6	48	17.9	40	20.3	13	26.7	69	30.2	111
Jewish	11.7	19	8.5	19	9.4	6	12.8	33	10.3	38
xo										
Gender										
Male	98.1	159	99.6	223	98.4	63	84.5	218	92.4	340
Female	1.9	3	0.4	1	1.6	1	15.5	40	7.6	28
Ethnicity/race										
White	93.8	152	95.9	215	90.6	58	78.7	203	93.5	344
Black	4.3	7	2.7	6	4.7	3	14.3	37	1.9	7
Hispanic	1.9	3	0.9	2	1.6	1	6.2	16	4.1	15
Asian	—	—	0.5	1	3.1	2	0.8	2	0.5	2
Total number of appointees	—	162	—	224	—	64	—	258	—	368
Average age at nomination	51.6 years		50.0 years		49.7 years		50.2 years		48.9 years	

Note: Two Johnson appointees to the district courts studied law privately and did not attend law school and are therefore not included in the statistics. There was also no ABA rating for one Johnson appointee to the courts of appeals because the administration did not request a rating.

Reagan appointed one person to the appeals courts who was a member of the Conservative Party of New York. There was also one Reagan appointee who was self-classified as nondenominational in religion. These appointees are not included in the statistics.

Source: Data collected by the author.

Eisenhower administration on. The Reagan administration was charged with appointing marginally qualified ideologues to the lower courts (Schwartz 1988), and the findings in Table 7-1 provide a basis for comparison in terms of law school education.

Looking at the professional background of federal judges—in particular, previous judicial experience—we find that of the eighteen Supreme Court appointments from the Eisenhower through Reagan administrations, two-thirds had judicial experience. A substantial proportion of lower court federal judges have been drawn from the state judiciary and in some instances from the ranks of federal magistrates and federal bankruptcy judges. The trend since the Eisenhower administration has been for larger proportions of district court appointees to come to the federal bench with previous judicial experience. Table 7-1 shows the figures for the district and appeals court appointees combined from the Johnson through the Reagan presidencies.[9]

When a candidate for a judgeship has previous judicial experience, he or she has a track record that can be examined by the appointing administration. If there is a concern with one or more policy areas, the administration can determine whether that track record conforms to the administration's positions. The trend of appointing those with judicial experience, including those whose occupation at time of appointment is in the judiciary, can be seen as evidence of growing concern by administrations with policy or ideology. It can also be seen as contributing to the professionalization of the judiciary.[10] Table 7-1 also shows the trend away from prosecutorial experience. During the Ford, Carter, and Reagan administrations a larger proportion of appointees had judicial experience than prosecutorial experience. The reverse was true for previous administrations. For Supreme Court appointees from Eisenhower through Reagan, we find that of the total of eighteen, eleven (61 percent) were members of the judiciary when receiving their Supreme Court appointment, five were government officials, and two were in private practice in large law firms.[11]

Age is an attribute that is associated with professional experience and also with an administration's attempt to leave a judicial legacy by appointing younger judges who will remain on the bench long after the president has left office. Table 7-1 shows the average age of lower court judges; the trend is toward a younger judiciary, with the Reagan appointees having the lowest average age at time of nomination. This was particularly true for courts of appeals judges: the Reagan appointees were on the average about two years younger than the Carter, Ford, and Johnson appointees and close to four years younger than the Nixon appointees. Historically, the Reagan appeals court appointees were the youngest group of appointees since the modern courts of appeals were established in 1891 (Goldman 1987; 1989b, 324-327).

Ratings of the American Bar Association's Standing Committee on Federal Judiciary play a role in the recruitment process and are taken as indicators of the quality of the appointees. Although there are serious issues in evaluating quality and major questions whether the ABA can objectively do such an evaluation, its ratings continue to be relied on. We see in Table 7-1 the ABA ratings of the lower court appointees of five administrations. If the top two ratings are combined it appears that about the same proportions of the Carter, Johnson, and Reagan appointees were given such high ratings. This also suggests that charges that the Reagan administration was lowering the quality of the bench were not well founded.

Moving from professional backgrounds to political backgrounds, we can observe that presidents tend to make the large proportion of their appointments from members of their own party. From the Roosevelt through the Reagan administrations, 84 percent of Supreme Court appointments were made from the president's party. In fact, Kennedy, Johnson, and Reagan did not appoint anyone from the opposition party to the Supreme Court. The figures for the lower federal courts are presented in Table 7-1 and show the high level of partisanship that surrounds judicial recruitment. It should be noted that all of the Democrats appointed by the Reagan administration were appointed to the district bench. At least half of all lower court appointees have had a record of prominent partisan activism.

Personal attributes have also been considered of interest by students of the Judiciary. Religious origin or affiliation is one such attribute. When we look at the Supreme Court we find that close to nine out of ten Supreme Court justices have been affiliated with a Protestant denomination, and of these about eight out of ten belonged to high-status Protestant sects (Schmidhauser 1979, 62-68).[12] Low-status Protestants as well as the Catholic and Jewish appointees have typically been Democrats. The same has been true for lower court judges. It would appear that differing ethnic and class support given to the major parties is reflected in the appointments. When there are changes in that support, we can anticipate corresponding changes in the backgrounds of the appointees. This is precisely what happened with Catholics and the Republican party. As the Republican party has won over more Catholics, larger proportions of Catholics have been selected for the judiciary by Republican presidents. Of Reagan's four appointments to the Supreme Court, two are Catholic. The proportion of Catholics named by Reagan to the lower federal courts exceeded that of Democratic presidents, as seen in Table 7-1.

Women have faced gender discrimination in the professions, including law, and this was historically reflected in the lack of women on the bench. Franklin D. Roosevelt placed one woman on the bench, Florence E. Allen, the first on an appeals court. Not until some three decades later, in the administration of Lyndon B. Johnson, was another woman so named. On the federal district bench the first woman, Burnita Shelton Matthews, was appointed by Harry S Truman. Ronald Reagan broke the sex bar on the Supreme Court with his appointment of Sandra Day O'Connor, but he lagged behind Jimmy Carter in his appointments of women to the lower federal bench, as Table 7-1 indicates.

Democratic presidents have been largely responsible for the black Americans who have served on the federal bench. Truman named the first, William Henry Hastie, to the appeals courts; Kennedy named the first to the federal district bench, James Parsons; and Johnson made the historic appointment of Thurgood Marshall to the Supreme Court. Democrat Jimmy Carter achieved a quantitative breakthrough for black access to federal judgeships, as seen in Table 7-1. Carter named a total of thirty-seven blacks to the two principal lower courts (twenty-eight to the federal district bench and nine to the appeals courts). Ronald Reagan, however, appointed the smallest proportion of blacks to the federal courts since the Eisenhower administration (which appointed none). The Reagan record in absolute numbers was seven blacks (six to district courts and one to an appeals court). The record of appointments to Hispanic-Americans and Asian-Americans is also presented in Table 7-1.

Assessing the Recruitment Process

We have examined briefly federal judicial selection and the backgrounds of judges so recruited. These are areas of ongoing research activity. Less research attention has been focused on assessing the process itself. In part this reluctance on the part of scholars (but not judicial reformers) to assess the process can be attributed to the difficulty of generating hard data to analyze. An important exception is the research that has considered the decisional behavior of judges from the standpoint of the success presidents have had in placing on the federal courts judges who have shared the president's policy or philosophical orientation.

Empirical analyses of district judge decisional behavior by Robert Carp and C. K. Rowland (1983) revealed that decisional behavior was most closely linked to appointing administration. The judges appointed by conservative Republican presidents tended to be more conservative than the judges appointed by liberal Democratic presidents. Ronald

Stidham and Robert Carp (1987) also studied district court behavior and found that the Reagan appointees gave the least support and the Carter and other Democratic presidents' appointees gave the most support to the claims of disadvantaged minorities and other civil rights and civil liberties claims; the appointees of other Republican presidents fell between the two extremes. C. K. Rowland, Donald Songer, and Robert Carp (1988) examined both district and appeals courts in cases concerning criminal justice policy and found that the Reagan appointees decided cases in a more conservative fashion than did the Carter appointees, and, unexpectedly, even the Nixon appointees. Studies focusing on the appeals courts have also found a strong relationship between appointing president and decisional behavior, suggesting that the federal recruitment process does make it possible for a president to use his powers of appointment to shape the course of American law (see, for example, Davis 1986; Gottschall 1986; Hensley and Baugh 1987; and, in general, Murphy 1989). At the Supreme Court level there is persuasive evidence that presidents can and have used appointments to further their policy agendas (see Rohde and Spaeth 1976; Abraham 1985; Tribe 1985; Gates and Cohen 1988; Goldman 1989a).

Assessment of the recruitment process focusing on presidential success in appointing "likeminded" judges is rooted in empiricism and generally avoids more normative considerations of whether it is desirable for presidents to be able to shape the course of law. There are exceptions (see, for example, Schwartz 1988), and it is worth noting that Laurence Tribe (1985) is concerned with this and urges greater senatorial scrutiny and independence of judgment in the confirmation stage. But assessment of federal judicial recruitment suggests a more fundamental although normative research direction geared to answering the deceptively simple question whether the process produces the best qualified people. To answer this question it is necessary first to specify the criteria to be used in determining who is qualified for judicial office. This also means that researchers must confront issues of applying those criteria to specific individuals. This further requires inquiry into what aspects of the process appear to create obstacles to the recruitment of the most qualified people.

It is useful to consider what traits are desirable in a federal judge and then how to evaluate those traits in particular individuals in order to determine who is qualified for a judicial position. It is not difficult to come up with a list (see, for example, Goldman 1982, 113-114; Abraham 1985, 4). Such a list includes: impartiality toward the parties in litigation; fairness in the conduct of judicial proceedings, with a special concern for procedural due process; knowledge of and experience in the law; a talent for thinking, writing, and speaking clearly and logically; impeccable honesty and integrity; good physical and mental health; and a judicial temperament that includes being even-tempered, courteous, patient, reflective, and not impulsive. It is extraordinarily difficult, however, to take this list or any other and apply it to specific individuals. It is hard to establish an objective indicator with precise measurement for most of these criteria (exceptions may be physical health, which can be measured by objective standards, and possibly experience in the law, which can be tied to certain kinds of experience and the amount of time spent in each law-related activity). At best, applying most of these criteria to individuals is likely to be a subjective endeavor, but thus far researchers have neglected to examine whether this must be so.

Assuming that applying these criteria to individuals involves subjective determination, the question then becomes: Whose subjectivity? It is possible to survey the bar, former clients, and judges before whom the judicial candidate practiced. A candidate's legal briefs and other legal writings can be analyzed. If the candidate is already a lower court judge or has previous judicial experience, a qualitative and quantitative analysis of the judicial record can be conducted. Such examination of the criteria suggested earlier can at the very least eliminate those who are not suitable for a judgeship and at the very best identify the best prospects for the judgeship. Determination of who is *best* qualified from among a group of similar candidates will likely be a result of subjective evaluation.

Are these or similar criteria a part of existing federal judicial recruitment? The answer appears to be yes, in part, but in a somewhat haphazard fashion. The American Bar Association's Standing Committee on Federal Judiciary takes it upon itself to determine the professional qualifications of candidates for judgeships and has been participating in the selection process beginning with the Eisenhower administration. It is unusual for an administration to go ahead with a judicial nominee who is rated "not qualified" by the ABA committee. Table 7-1 showed how few these instances are. Yet the ABA committee has been controversial in carrying out its mission.

Joel Grossman's study (1965) of the ABA committee during the Kennedy administration found that evaluations of judicial candidates were made primarily by wealthy corporate lawyers whose inclinations were conservative and Republican (pp. 250-251). By the 1970s the ABA had responded to criticism by expanding the range of lawyer and bar group contacts and by the placement of female and minority lawyers on the committee. Nevertheless, Elliot Slotnick's study (1983) of the ABA committee during the Carter years found that the committee tended to give higher ratings to higher income white males and lower ratings to women and nonwhites. By the late 1980s, the ABA committee was attacked by conservative groups for being too liberal and for allegedly giving poor ratings to some Reagan appointees because of their right-wing views. The ABA committee does not offer reasons for its ratings of specific individuals. Its meetings and minutes are confidential. Serious questions have been raised about whether a private group should play such a role in judicial recruitment.[13] Should other bar groups and public interest groups have an equal voice in the process? Is the very subjectivity of the evaluation enterprise a sufficient reason to add other groups to the evaluation process?

Assuming that highly qualified individuals can be identified using the criteria suggested earlier, even though there is imprecision and subjectivity involved, what aspects of the process *appear* to place obstacles to the recruitment of the most qualified people?

First, it should be noted that the organized bar and the American Judicature Society have long argued that partisanship has an overriding and deleterious influence on recruitment. These groups argue that party affiliation and political connections should be irrelevant to the administration of justice and that it is demeaning for those with judicial ambitions to have to court party influentials and to otherwise play the political game. The best selection process, they insist, is one that minimizes party affiliation and party connections and maximizes professional qualifications.

There is a counterargument, however, that emphasizes that for every judicial vacancy there are many qualified persons who could be selected. According to this view, party affiliation and party activism are legitimate variables to take into account when sorting through a group of approximately equally qualified candidates. To ignore party considerations would remove an incentive for talented men and women to participate actively in politics. Bar association reformers typically want the bar associations to have a more influential role in judicial selection. But that would substitute bar association politics for party politics. Instead of politicians' associates having the inside track for judgeships we would have bar leaders' associates in that position. On a more positive note, it is argued that by choosing partisans, voters on election day can hold the party responsible for the judges' decisional behavior. Whether this actually occurs is an empirical question that can be explored.

A second obstacle that is seen as preventing the recruitment of the best available persons for the federal bench is the policy or ideological screening that an administration might undertake. This was particularly an issue with the Reagan administration, which was quite open in its goal of recruiting individuals who shared the president's philosophy.

Critics argue that it is not right to use an ideological or policy litmus test for prospective judges. An individual's personal views on controversial questions of public policy should play no part in the decisions that an individual will make as a judge. To suggest otherwise is to undermine the professional integrity of the judiciary. But acknowledging that in close cases a judge's personal preferences will influence the decisions he or she makes, selecting only those who lean toward one side of controversial issues means that the courts are being stacked with one set of biases. Even if the individuals selected act in a thoroughly professional manner, they will come to the bench with an image of being biased.

The counterargument is that federal courts cannot help but make policy by their interpretations of precedents, statutes, and the Constitution. Where there is room for judicial discretion, a judge's personal values and judicial philosophy come to the forefront. A concern with a future judge's policy or ideological orientation is then a concern with how that judge will use the very discretion that is inevitable and inherent in the judicial function. It is therefore reasonable for an administration to recruit judges who will use their judicial discretion in general to further the president's policy agenda. Surely it makes little sense for a president to appoint judges whose policy views and philosophy are contrary to the president's.

A complicating factor, of course, is the role of the Senate in the confirmation process, when the Senate is controlled by the party in opposition to the president, as was the case during the last two years of the Reagan administration and into the Bush administration. With the Reagan administration screening its judicial candidates for policy and ideology, the Senate Democrats became more alert to the more extreme among the nominees and offered opposition to some of them. The tip of the iceberg appeared with the Robert Bork nomination to the Supreme Court and the subsequent hearings of the Senate Judiciary Committee. The use of policy and ideological screening, if the conditions are ripe, can lead to confrontation, if not delay or defeat.

A third obstacle in the process that is seen as preventing the recruitment of talented people who could bring strength to the judiciary is the lack of affirmative action and the perpetuation of subtle racial and sexual biases. We have previously discussed the low numbers of women and minorities on the bench before the Carter administration. The concept of affirmative action for the judiciary was introduced by the Carter administration in order "to seek out and identify well-qualified women and members of minority groups as potential nominees." These words were contained in Carter's executive order establishing the circuit judge nominating commissions (Berkson and Carbon

1980, 215). Carter's selection commission panels contained substantial proportions of women and minority members and were thought to be a particularly effective way of eliminating racial and sexual barriers (Berkson and Carbon 1980, 41-55).

Affirmative action for the judiciary has met with criticism, including the charge that in practice affirmative action means the use of quotas, which is incompatible with the selection of the "best" person available. Furthermore, if quotas are used, reverse discrimination results in that persons of the "wrong" race or sex are not seriously considered. Critics further argue that affirmative action is inappropriate for the judiciary not only because there is a need for the most highly skilled legal practitioners available but because a person's race and gender are totally irrelevant to the performance of judicial duties.

The counterargument is that affirmative action for the judiciary during the Carter administration did not include the use of quotas but rather widened the recruitment net. Rather than being incompatible with the selection of the best people available, affirmative action ensures that all potential candidates will be considered on their individual merits. White males were not discriminated against during the Carter administration and constituted the large majority of appointments. Defenders of affirmative action point out that race and sex *are* relevant to the judicial process. Issues of sexual and racial discrimination have frequently come before the federal courts since the enactment of civil rights legislation in the 1960s. Women and minorities personally familiar with discrimination bring to the bench experiences and sensitivities that white males may not. When this is brought to issues of discrimination before the courts, the participation of women and minorities on the bench may add a new dimension of justice to the courts (but see Walker and Barrow 1985). Their visibility on the bench may inspire greater confidence in the courts on the part of women and minorities. Furthermore, once on the bench these judges cannot help but educate and sensitize their colleagues about discrimination. Given the wide range of factors and personal attributes associated with judicial selection, the recruitment of professionally qualified women and minorities may indeed result in the "best" people to fill certain judgeships.

New Questions, New Research

There is always more to be known about federal judicial recruitment. Each administration has its own nuances in the recruitment process, and there are a variety of background and attribute variables of judicial appointees that could be studied. Valuable historical research on the appointment process and judicial backgrounds by Kermit Hall (1979) and Rayman Solomon (1984) suggests that such research can yield rich findings. Likewise, the monitoring of new administrations is important in determining new trends.

But there is a need for going beyond more of the same. Elliot Slotnick, after reviewing the judicial recruitment literature, observed:

> Studies of judicial selection have implications that go well beyond the primary concern of who gets chosen to fill judgeship vacancies. Rather, research in the area of federal judicial recruitment has clear implications for a broader understanding of political participation, executive-legislative relations, elite governmental recruitment and ultimately, questions about the very nature of representative democracy and the requirements of democratic theory. (1988, 324)

Aside from the usefulness of more broadly focused research and analyses with a larger theoretical and comparative perspective, there could well be new research exploring ways of quantifying the professional selection criteria (Goldman 1982). Researchers and students of the judiciary might want to ponder whether alternative methods for judicial selection authorized by the Constitution would be more desirable than the existing process. Article II of the Constitution suggests that lower court judges could be appointed by the president alone if Congress so provided. Article II also suggests that Congress could authorize the Supreme Court or another court of law or the attorney general to appoint lower court judges. One major implication of this provision is that Congress could, in effect, establish merit selection by creating a new court, specifying that the judges appointed be equally drawn from the two major parties, and vest that court with responsibility for judicial selection. Were Congress so inclined it could even use this method to establish a European type civil service process whereby would-be judges would be required to complete a special course of study, take special examinations, and work their way up the judicial hierarchy—all outside the political appointment process.

Whether analysis of federal judicial recruitment focuses on broader theoretical issues, consideration of alternative processes, or study and evaluation of the process by current and past administrations, it is necessary for the research to be as empirically based as possible. But in the final analysis determination of how well federal judicial recruitment is functioning will depend upon a subjective evaluation no doubt filtered through a political lens.

Notes

1. The Senate Judiciary Committee until 1979 allowed a senator from the state of the nominee to place a permanent hold on the nomination by not

returning the official blue slip sent by the committee chair to such senators soliciting their comments on the nominee. In 1979, when Senator Edward Kennedy became head of the committee, he changed the process in that the committee would now consider the nomination of an individual for whom the blue slip had not been returned.

2. Both the majority and minority party on the committee have their own investigatory staff that conducts separate investigations of certain nominees. Several Reagan nominees, particularly during the last two years of the Reagan presidency, were stopped primarily by Senate Democrats on the Judiciary Committee.

3. Weisberg and Felice (1988) conducted a multiple regression analysis of controversial confirmation votes from 1955 to 1988 and concluded: "Ideology is the only one of these predictors with a consistent large effect on all of the confirmation votes. Region and party each affected only a few nominations, and presidential support was even less of a factor" (p. 9).

4. The ratings are: exceptionally well qualified, well qualified, qualified, and not qualified. For an assessment of the ABA committee during the 1970s and early 1980s, see Slotnick 1983.

5. It might be noted that one does not campaign for the Supreme Court in quite the same way in large part because vacancies are so few, occur so unexpectedly, and are so visible. However, those who aspire to serve on the Court have been known to seek a high legal profile with the hope that it will attract the attention of the administration when there is a vacancy on the Court.

6. There is another incentive for an administration to avoid unqualified nominations—such nominations bring down the wrath of the organized bar and editorial writers.

7. The exceptions were: Federalist James Wilson and Republicans Samuel Miller, Earl Warren, and Warren Burger.

8. These figures include the Reagan appointees.

9. During the Eisenhower administration, about 26 percent of the district court appointees had previous judicial experience. With the Carter administration over 54 percent had such experience, although during the Reagan years that proportion dropped for the first time in more than thirty years to about 47 percent. However, for appeals court appointments, over half of all appointees from every administration starting with Eisenhower had previous judicial experience.

10. This trend is further accented when we consider that 28 percent of the Eisenhower and 32 percent of the Kennedy appointees were judges at the time of their appointments.

11. For a historical perspective see Schmidhauser 1979, 79-83, 92-95.

12. High-status Protestant denominations include Episcopalian, Presbyterian, Congregational, and Unitarian (Demarath 1965).

13. A coalition of right- and left-wing groups challenged the ABA committee in court, arguing that it was a governmental advisory agency and subject to the open meeting law. The case came up to the Supreme Court, which

unanimously ruled in favor of the ABA committee (*Public Citizen v. U.S. Dept. of Justice*, 109 S.Ct. 2558 [1989]). The question nevertheless remains whether the ABA, regardless of the makeup of the committee, has too much influence in the process, and whether it is capable of objectively determining, insofar as it is possible, the professional qualifications of judicial candidates.

References

Abraham, Henry J. 1985. *Justice and presidents,* 2d ed. New York: Oxford University Press.

Berkson, Larry C., and Susan B. Carbon. 1980. *The United States Circuit Judge Nominating Commission: Its members, procedures and candidates.* Chicago: American Judicature Society.

Carp, Robert A., and C. K. Rowland. 1983. *Policymaking and politics in the federal district courts.* Knoxville: University of Tennessee Press.

Chase, Harold W. 1972. *Federal judges.* Minneapolis: University of Minnesota Press.

Cohodas, Nadine. 1987. Ginsburg hurt badly by marijuana admission. *Congressional Quarterly Weekly Report,* November 7, 2714-2716.

Committee on the Judiciary, 92d Congress. 1972. *Legislative history of the United States Circuit Court of Appeals and the judges who served during the period 1801 through May 1972.* Washington, D.C.: Government Printing Office.

Danelski, David J. 1964. *A Supreme Court justice is appointed.* New York: Random House.

Davis, Sue. 1986. President Carter's selection reforms and judicial policymaking. *American Politics Quarterly* 14:328-344.

Demarath, Nicholas Jay, III. 1965. *Social class in American Protestantism.* Skokie, Ill.: Rand McNally.

Evans, Evan A. 1948. Political influences in the selection of federal judges. *Wisconsin Law Review* 1948:330-351.

Gates, John B., and Jeffrey E. Cohen. 1988. Presidents, justices and racial equality cases, 1954-1984. *Political Behavior* 10:22-36.

Goldman, Sheldon. 1965. Characteristics of Eisenhower and Kennedy appointees to the lower federal courts. *Western Political Quarterly* 18:755-762.

_____. 1982. Judicial selection and the qualities that make a "good" judge. *Annals of the American Academy of Social and Political Science* 462 (July 1982):112-124.

_____. 1987. The age of judges: Reagan's second term appeals court appointees compared to the appointees of presidents since 1891. *American Bar Association Journal* 73:94-98.

_____. 1989a. Judicial appointments and the presidential agenda. In *The presidency in American politics,* ed. Paul Brace, Christine B. Harrington, and Gary King. New York: New York University Press.

_____. 1989b. Reagan's judicial legacy: Completing the puzzle and summing up. *Judicature* 72:318-330.

Goldman, Sheldon, and Thomas P. Jahnige. 1985. *The federal courts as a political system,* 3d ed. New York: Harper and Row.

Gottschall, Jon. 1986. Reagan's appointments to the U.S. courts of appeals. *Judicature* 70:48-54.

Grossman, Joel B. 1965. *Lawyers and judges.* New York: Wiley.

Hall, Kermit L. 1979. *The politics of justice: Lower federal judicial selection and the second party system, 1829-61.* Lincoln: University of Nebraska Press.

Hensley, Thomas, and Joyce Baugh. 1987. The impact of the 1978 Omnibus Judgeships Act. In *Research in law and policy studies,* ed. Stuart Nagel. Greenwich, Conn.: JAI Press.

McFeeley, Neil D. 1987. *Appointment of judges.* Austin: University of Texas Press.

Murphy, Walter F. 1989. The legacy of Reagan's judicial strategy. In *The Reagan imprint,* ed. Larry Berman. Baltimore: Johns Hopkins University Press.

Neff, Alan. 1981. *The United States District Judge Nominating Commissions: Their members, procedures and candidates.* Chicago: American Judicature Society.

New York Times. 1981. December 24, B4.

_____. 1982. January 7, A26.

_____. 1990. April 10, A19.

O'Brien, David M. 1988. *Judicial roulette.* New York: Priority Press.

Rohde, David W., and Harold J. Spaeth. 1976. *Supreme Court decision making.* San Francisco: W. H. Freeman.

Rowland, C. K., Donald R. Songer, and Robert A. Carp. 1988. Presidential effects on criminal justice in the lower federal courts: The Reagan judges. *Law and Society Review* 22:191-200.

Schmidhauser, John. 1979. *Judges and justices.* Boston: Little, Brown.

Schwartz, Herman. 1988. *Packing the courts: The conservative campaign to rewrite the Constitution.* New York: Scribner's.

Segal, Jeffrey A. 1987. Senate confirmation of Supreme Court justices: Partisan and institutional politics. *Journal of Politics* 49:998-1015.

Slotnick, Elliot E. 1983. The ABA Standing Committee on Federal Judiciary: A contemporary assessment. *Judicature* 66:348-362, 385-393.

_____. 1988. Federal judicial recruitment and selection research: A review essay. *Judicature* 71:317-324.

Solomon, Rayman L. 1984. The politics of appointment and the federal courts' role in regulating America: U.S. courts of appeals judgeships from T. R. to F. D. R. *American Bar Foundation Research Journal* 1984:285-343.

Songer, Donald R. 1979. The relevance of policy values for the confirmation of Supreme Court nominees. *Law and Society Review* 13:927-948.

Stidham, Ronald, and Robert A. Carp. 1987. Judges, presidents, and policy choices: Exploring the linkages. *Social Science Quarterly* 68:395-404.

Sulfridge, Wayne. 1980. Ideology as a factor in Senate consideration of Supreme Court nominations. *Journal of Politics* 42:560-567.

Tribe, Laurence H. 1985. *God save this honorable court: How the choice of Supreme Court justices shapes our history.* New York: Random House.

Walker, Thomas G., and Deborah J. Barrow. 1985. The diversification of the federal bench: Policy and process ramifications. *Journal of Politics* 47:596-617.

Weisberg, Herbert F., and John Felice. 1988. An ideological model of Senate voting on Supreme Court nominations, 1955-1988. Paper presented at the annual meeting of the Midwest Political Science Association, Chicago.

Part III

JUDICIAL DECISION MAKING

Courts are the mere instruments of the law, and can will nothing. When they are said to exercise discretion, it is a mere legal discretion, a discretion to be exercised in discerning the course prescribed by law; and, when that is discerned, it is the duty of the court to follow it. Judicial power is never exercised for the purpose of giving effect to the will of the judge; always for the purpose of giving effect to the will of the legislature; or in other words, to the will of the law.

—Chief Justice John Marshall
Osborn v. Bank of the United States (1824)

I had thought of the law in terms of Moses—principles chiseled in granite. I knew judges had predilections. I knew that their moods as well as their minds were ingredients of their decisions. But I had never been willing to admit to myself that the "gut" reaction of a judge at the level of constitutional adjudication, dealing with vagaries of due process, freedom of speech and the like, was the main ingredient of his decision. . . . No judge at the level I speak of was neutral.

—Justice William O. Douglas
The Court Years: 1939-1975, 1980

The three chapters that follow move beyond examining the policy making of courts and the recruitment of judges to address some of the most enduring questions in the study of legal institutions: How can we come to understand the range and diversity of choices available to judges? How can we explain their ultimate decision?

The legal model of how courts hear and decide cases suggests that the choices available to judges in any particular case are determined by rules: Chief Justice Marshall's description of judicial choice is a classic statement of the "mechanical" application of the law to the facts of a case. This perspective suggests that judges merely apply the law after the legally relevant facts are clearly ascertained through judicial proceedings. These facts are weighed, not through the judge's eyes, but according to precedent and a system of rules.

A major turning point in addressing judicial decision making was the publication of C. Herman Pritchett's *The Roosevelt Court: A Study* in *Judicial Votes and Values* in 1948. Pritchett was also seeking to understand the choices made by judges, but his concern was not with legal rules but with the attitudes and values of the individual justices of the U.S. Supreme Court. Pritchett inferred political attitudes from the votes of the justices and found that the justices could be consistently ranked in their support for policies dealing with such areas as criminal justice and economic regulation. Soon Pritchett added another element: the judge's perspective on proper judicial behavior. Judicial choices appeared to reflect the political goals of the justices shaped by what the justice thought was appropriate judicial behavior *(Civil Liberties and the Vinson Court)*. From the 1950s, judicial scholars, influenced by a disciplinewide movement toward measurement and precision, began to map the individual element in judicial choice.

The chapters in Part III assess our knowledge of judicial decision making and how future research could enhance our understanding of the availability and exercise of judicial choices. Collectively, the chapters provide insight into the range of perspectives brought to bear on the individual element in decision making. Herbert Jacob (Chapter 8) emphasizes the trial judge as one element in a complex organization. In Chapter 9, H. W. Perry, Jr., stresses the rules and procedures that set some boundaries on the scope of court agendas and the control of agendas by judges. James Gibson, in Chapter 10, presents the complexities of viewing the individual judge as a political actor who has attitudes regarding law, courts, and politics and who must confront multifaceted issues.

The study of judicial decision making has one primary question: What factors explain the availability and exercise of judicial choice? Although these chapters discuss various perspectives on judicial decision making, it appears that the correct answer may be more in keeping with the words of Associate Justice William O. Douglas than with those of Chief Justice John Marshall.

8. DECISION MAKING IN TRIAL COURTS

Herbert Jacob

The past forty years have marked an unprecedented exploration of trial courts. Although they had always been the principal point of contact for ordinary litigants and many lawyers, they were terra incognita to sociolegal scholars. Until the 1960s most researchers were under the spell of the "upper court myth" and remained fixated on the Supreme Court. That was true even for the venturesome band of political scientists who pioneered the study of judicial behavior, for they used that term to describe the behavioral study of the U.S. Supreme Court. Since the early 1960s, however, scholars from many disciplines have explored the vast intellectual swamp occupied by trial courts. The boundaries of this swamp have been mapped and become familiar. The ecosystem thriving there, however, remains beyond our ken.

In 1960, observers knew trial courts as the domain of judges. Everyone else who worked in trial courts or appeared before them was thought to be subordinate to the judge and responding to his or her preferences (see, for example, Peltason 1955). It was assumed that trials were the dominant mode of decision making and that juries played a prominent role. Although it was apparent that prosecutors and defense counsel played a prominent role in criminal trials, little was known about them. Even less was known about decision making in civil courts.

In the ensuing years, a large body of scholarship developed around criminal courts. This research was promoted by grants from U.S. Department of Justice units that Congress had established to undertake the "war on crime." The studies were often motivated by a desire to propose or evaluate reforms aimed at increasing the effectiveness of the criminal justice process. In these efforts, prosecutors and defense counsel became the central objects of concern; defendants and their attributes were also studied. Trials faded into the background of research, jury research became a highly specialized endeavor, and judges became dethroned. Yet as I shall make clear, we have learned an enormous amount only to discover how limited our understanding of trial court decision making remains.

To a much lesser extent, the same process of elaboration characterized research on civil courts. However, the efforts to analyze civil courts did not enjoy similar federal beneficence. Although during this period there was interest in such issues as the overuse of litigation and consequent court delays, inequities arising from dependence on jury decisions, and difficulties inherent in complex litigation, these concerns generated relatively little empirical research on decision making in civil courts.

In the following pages, I shall examine the ways in which the explorers of the trial court swamp in the 1960s and 1970s conceptualized their enterprise. Then I shall analyze the organizational model of trial courts, which promises to provide a more comprehensive understanding of trial proceedings. Finally, I will outline some of the tasks that the next generation of explorers might undertake.

Focusing on Individual Participants

The first stage of the rediscovery of trial courts was marked by an elaboration of the characteristics of the participants in the trial process.[1] To a considerable extent, the research was motivated by Supreme Court decisions and government funding. The rulings of the Warren Court focused attention on both policy and prosecutors. In a series of controversial cases that reflected an awareness of the findings of a previous generation of legal realists about the shape of law in action, the Court held that defendants in serious cases had to be represented by counsel (*Gideon v. Wainwright*, 372 U.S. 335 [1963]) and that confessions could not be used in trials unless the defendant had been offered a defense attorney (*Miranda v. Arizona*, 384 U.S. 436 [1966]). These decisions highlighted the roles of the police, prosecutors, and defense attorneys in criminal trials. At about the same time, the Law Enforcement Assistance Administration of the Department of Justice began funding empirical studies which examined these participants in much greater detail than ever before.

A series of studies of policing accented the immense discretion exercised by the police and the consequent screening performed by them in deciding which cases to bring to prosecutors (Bittner 1970; Rubenstein 1973; Black 1980; Brown 1981). Ethnographic in design, these studies exposed the normal routines of police work and the pressures brought to bear on patrol officers' decisions. They stressed the discretionary character of their work. However, by focusing narrowly on the police, they paid little attention to the consequences of these discretionary acts upon the remainder of the criminal justice process. Nevertheless, these studies and others made it clear that cases that go to court are the product of both criminal behavior and decisions by the police to focus on some criminal violations while overlooking others.

Researchers also focused on discretion among prosecutors. Concentrating on the ubiquity of plea bargaining, a series of studies of prosecutors exposed the discretion wielded by prosecutors when they chose whether to prosecute, what particular charges to bring, and whether to accept a guilty plea either to a reduced charge or for a less than maximal sentence (Alschuler 1965; Cole 1970; NILECJ 1975). Indeed, an entire cottage industry grew around the study of plea bargaining (see *Law and Society Review* 1979). Some of the studies explored why the practice existed and rejected the hypothesis that plea bargaining was a response to the high case loads characteristic of the 1960s (Feeley 1975; Heumann 1975; Schulhofer 1984). Malcolm Feeley and Milton Heumann looked at historical data; Stephen J. Schulhofer examined the contemporary practices in Philadelphia, which suggested that plea bargaining was not a necessary concomitant of case load pressure. Other studies sought to show that plea bargaining was arbitrary and a denial of due process rights because it effectively made the constitutional right to a jury trial contingent on the risk of an exceptionally harsh sentence should the defendant be found guilty (Brunk 1979; McDonald 1979).

Researchers also scrutinized defense attorneys, although they concentrated most of their attention on the work of public defenders, who during the 1970s came to handle the majority of cases in many large jurisdictions; the work of private defense attorneys was never the object of the ethnographic or statistical analysis that characterized research on the other participants in the criminal justice process. Several studies found that services supplied by publicly provided defense attorneys were on average as good as those of privately retained counsel (*Stanford Law Review* 1961; Taylor 1972, 1973; summarized by Flemming 1989). Jonathan D. Casper (1972), however, reported that publicly paid defense attorneys did not inspire the trust of their clients; clients believed that they got what they paid for.

Another set of studies examined the work of juries. The landmark study of American juries was published by Harry Kalven, Jr., and Hans Zeisel in 1966; it provided information on many aspects of jury practice and suggested that in only a small proportion of cases did juries make decisions contrary to those that judges would have reached. However, others did not replicate the work by Kalven and Zeisel or extend it because their method—recording actual jury deliberations— was outlawed when it became known that the privacy of jury deliberations had been breached. Nevertheless, within a decade psychological researchers began simulating jury behavior with subjects drawn from a variety of sources including actual jury pools. Much of this research sought to refute assumptions made by the Supreme Court when it ruled in *Williams v. Florida* (399 U.S. 510 [1968]) that juries with six members behaved similarly to those with twelve and that this difference in size made no difference in their decision-making procedures. Other cases involving so-called death-qualified jurors (for example, *Lockhart v. McCree*, 106 S.Ct. 1758 [1986]) also stimulated research on the dynamics of jury decision making.[2] In both instances, the researchers built a substantial empirical case against the Supreme Court's assumptions only to have the Court ignore or reject their findings (Roper 1980; Zeisel 1982; Hans 1988; Ellsworth 1988). The findings on juries had little impact on other researchers of trial court decision making because juries are used in only a very small percentage of cases that go to trial and the questions driving jury research were directed to relatively narrow issues in the development of criminal law and constitutional jurisprudence.

The role of judges also became the object of research. This research focused to a large extent on the degree to which so-called extralegal characteristics of defendants and/or judges, such as their race or socioeconomic background, were associated with sentences imposed by judges (Hagan 1974; Gibson 1978; Uhlman 1978; Kleck 1985). The recruitment of judges captured the attention of other scholars who were often motivated by claims of judicial reformers that so-called merit selection produced better judges than traditional elective or appointive processes. Few of these scholars, however, focused on trial judges (but see Ryan et al., 1980; Goldman 1987, 1989) and some, such as Bradley C. Canon (1972) and Philip L. Dubois (1980), spoke of the recruitment of judges when their data referred almost entirely to state supreme court justices. If the pattern revealed for supreme court justices may be used as a guide, few differences exist in the formal qualifications possessed by judges selected by merit and other processes; nor does the public view merit-selected judges more favorably (Wasmann, Lovrich, and Sheldon 1986). Moreover, the most extensive examination of a "merit" system revealed that private bar association politics had replaced public partisan politics (Watson and Downing 1969). Unlike other areas of trial court scholarship, research into the selection of federal trial judges attracted considerable attention; the results clearly indicated that different administrations appoint judges with different social backgrounds and ideological commitments (Slotnick 1988; Goldman 1989).

For both state and federal trial judges, the degree to which their decisions are affected by the manner in which they were selected remains unknown. In large part this is because judges do not make decisions alone (see below), but it is also the result of difficulties in coding judges' decisions in a manner that permits systematic analysis. It does not suffice to characterize them simply in terms of who won or lost because many judicial decisions are compromises or partial victories; nor can litigants be easily coded according to their social class or purported interest.

In contrast to the research discussed so far, research on judicial recruitment rarely distinguished between judges sitting in criminal courts and those working in civil courts. Nor could such a distinction be easily made because a large number of the nation's trial judges rotate between the two kinds of cases (Ryan et al. 1980). Moreover, these studies were generally unsuccessful in linking recruiting procedures to patterns of decision making.

Although many of the studies of individual participants revealed their social background, important organizational traits of their office, and details of their work, they failed to explain how the criminal justice process worked. It became increasingly evident that none of the participants—not even the judge—acted autonomously. In some instances, it appeared that the most influential person in criminal courts was not the judge but the prosecutor; but in most instances, it appeared that each participant depended on the others and could act only in concert with them. To capture that reality, studies needed larger resources because they had to look at entire court *systems* and do so comparatively in several jurisdictions.

The same developments proceeded more slowly and less completely with regard to the work of civil trial courts. No Supreme Court decisions spurred research on the civil side, and little federal money enticed researchers to turn their attention from the criminal courts. Moreover, civil proceedings seemed more amorphous than criminal trials; they involved a larger set of issues over a broader range of participants. While criminal courts at least shared the common concern with criminal acts, civil courts handled disputes (and some nondisputes) over the entire range of social interaction. Not even such legal categories as "contracts" or "torts" proved to be useful classifications because of their breadth. Torts, for instance, may concern personal injury cases in which ordinary citizens are the litigants, and the amounts may be very small or very large; but torts also encompass multibillion dollar suits such as those involving the asbestos industry and other businesses that handle toxic substances as well as claims arising from product liability cases, medical malpractice, and the like. These large claims are handled by specialized attorneys and attract much more public attention than do ordinary personal injury cases. Moreover, the social scope of civil cases is broader than that of the criminal justice process. Whereas criminal proceedings are dominated by the poor who constitute the majority of both defendants and victims, civil proceedings involve the wealthy and the middle class, as well as the poor.

The easiest handle on the study of civil litigation proved to be the attorneys involved in such cases. However, the study of attorneys in civil cases proceeded from a different launching point than was the case for prosecutors and criminal defense attorneys. The intellectual stimulus in this category was the sociological study of professions. Thus the first studies of attorneys in civil cases were embedded in concerns over the structure of the legal profession, an environment from which such research has generally not emerged. Jerome E. Carlin's classic study of solo lawyers in Chicago (1962) was soon followed by similarly rooted studies of lawyers in Wall Street law firms (Smigel 1964) and New York divorce lawyers (O'Gorman 1963). The apotheosis of such analysis was reached by John P. Heinz and Edward O. Laumann (1982) in their examination of the entire legal profession in Chicago. Others took a different tack, looking not just at the characteristics of attorneys and their work environment but also at the legal needs of the public and how they were met (Mayhew and Reiss 1969; Curran 1977). However, unlike the studies of prosecutors and criminal defense counsel, these studies of attorneys had relatively little to say about their work in trial courts. In large measure that was because many attorneys spent little time in or around the courtroom.

The realization that little of the work of civil attorneys centered on the courtroom was accompanied by the recognition that much of the work of lawyers, even when it involved disputes, entailed the avoidance rather than pursuit of trials. This was true in personal injury cases (Ross 1970; Rosenthal 1974) as well as in many others (Cartwright, Galanter, and Kidder 1974; Merry 1979). By the 1980s, these findings spilled over into an entirely new enterprise, the examination of the many alternative dispute resolution processes which exist to avoid litigation (Miller and Sarat 1981; Lempert 1981). The most important result for the study of trial court decision making is the emerging understanding that as complex a series of screening devices exists for civil courts as for criminal tribunals and that disputes coming to court constitute only a small fraction of the universe of quarrels which might under other circumstances become the focus of litigation. It became apparent that attorneys serve not merely as advocates in court but also as gatekeepers to the court hearings (Jacob 1986, 123-151).

The study of the work of judges in civil proceedings has had a constricted domain. Judges' contribution to and participation in the pretrial conferences that forge many settlements was an early focus (Zeisel, Kalven, and Buchholz 1959) which has not been much expanded. No studies parallel to those of sentencing in the criminal justice process exist. However, in the mid-1980s some scholars began examining the role of judges in court hearings by using transcripts of their interactions with attorneys and witnesses (O'Barr and Conley 1985). Analysis of the transcripts led John M. Conley and William M. O'Barr (1988) to suggest that some judges behave as strict law applicators while others are proceduralists, mediators, or lawmakers. Such styles may be related to litigants' satisfaction with the outcome. As such transcripts and videotapes become more readily available from the routine coverage of court proceedings by television and as courtroom personnel become less hostile to the use of recording devices, more such research may be possible in the future.

A few particular courts have attracted the special attention of researchers. Curiously, the largest amount of research has been done on small claims courts, which handle cases involving the smallest monetary amounts, because of their accessibility and the apparent simplicity of the claims presented to them (such as Yngvesson and Hennessey 1975; Sarat 1976; McEwen and Maiman 1984, Vidmar 1984). However, it is difficult to summarize the research findings because they have not been organized around a single paradigm or central set of ideas. Some of this research showed that small claims courts gave a special advantage to interests who routinely appear before them, such as collection agents, even though they were originally established to make it easier for ordinary citizens to process claims. Moreover, although their procedures are simplified, they still require proofs that necessitate more recordkeeping than the common person is accustomed to. Other court actions have also attracted some attention, such as those dealing with housing disputes (Jones 1985). Other special kinds of cases, such as school desegregation cases and claims of civil rights violations, have been the object of considerable scrutiny. Some studies examined the particular role of judges in those cases (see Peltason 1961/1971) while others examined the entire litigation process (Sheehan 1984). However, most of these studies were used not as windows on the trial decision-making process but rather to illuminate the particular disputes that were central to these cases.

Finally, some researchers have attempted to distinguish between policy making and the routine application of well-established legal principles by trial courts. The application of this distinction to the difference between the Supreme Court and trial courts is relatively simple since the researcher can perhaps assume that most Supreme Court decisions are policy decisions while trial court decisions are norm enforcement decisions (Jacob 1965). However, when applied to trial courts, the distinction is difficult to operationalize. For instance, in their examination of federal district courts, Robert A. Carp and C. K.

Rowland (1983) seek to identify policy decisions by the amount of discretion exercised by district court judges and by the novelty of the issues that they decide. However, they establish no procedure for measuring discretion or novelty, and it is unlikely that all of the 27,772 cases they examine would qualify under some such criterion. No scholar has persuasively demonstrated that it is possible to distinguish consistently between the routine and the novel at the time cases are being processed or that the actions of a trial court systematically vary according to which kind of case it hears.

Organizational Paradigms for Understanding Trial Courts

Informative as studies of individual participants in trial courts have been, they have left us far short of understanding decision making in trial courts. No single set of participants, not even judges, is so powerful in American trial courts that comprehending all the nuances of their behavior allows one to understand what occurs in their courtrooms. Rather, we have become aware that all the participants are linked to one another in complex relationships.

One of the first to conceptualize criminal justice in explicit organizational terms was Abraham Blumberg (1967). Blumberg emphasized the interdependence of all of the participants in criminal proceedings. Working in a sociological tradition that saw organizations as bureaucracies, Blumberg viewed criminal courts as bureaucratic mechanisms in which the quest for efficiency drove participants to maximize the number of convictions they produced. Blumberg stressed informal mechanisms that linked participants in the criminal court and made them dependent upon one another. Prosecutors, judges, defense counsel, and defendants all had well-defined roles in the drama enacted in courtrooms. That drama bore only a faint resemblance to the adversarial model proclaimed by the formal law. Most particularly, defense attorneys, rather than being vigorous advocates for their clients, usually acted as agent-mediators so that "the lawyer must then be sure to manipulate the client and stage manage the case so that help and service at least *appear* to be rendered" (Blumberg 1967, 111; italics in original). In a phrase destined to be much quoted, Blumberg characterized the work of defense attorneys as "the practice of law as a confidence game" (p. 110).

David Neubauer's (1974) study of a whole criminal court system in a small midwestern city repeated the main thrust of Blumberg's description of criminal justice as a process dominated by interdependent players. In some ways, Neubauer went even further than Blumberg by including an analysis of crime and the work of the police in his description of the criminal justice process. He saw plea bargaining as "shaped by the social network of legal actors" (p. 217) and "the judge's main source of power in sentencing is anticipation by others. . . . The judge in most cases can only reject agreements reached by opposing counsel" (p. 103). Neubauer, as a political scientist, attempted to place the criminal court in the context of the local political arena. Echoing Harold Lasswell's (1936) phrase, Neubauer aimed at who gets what, when, and how. He viewed the criminal justice process as allocating significant values in the local community. Although Neubauer did not reject Blumberg's use of the organizational image, he also did not build upon it by detailing the ways in which organizational imperatives motivate participants in criminal justice.

James Eisenstein and Herbert Jacob (1977) went a step further by using an organizational model that was explicitly nonbureaucratic. Rather than focusing on the criminal court as an abstract entity, they concentrated on work groups operating in the courthouse. They noted the loosely linked structure of these work groups; each of their participants belongs to a sponsoring organization but spends much of the day in the work group. Thus prosecutors are hired, fired, and controlled by the district attorney's office; defense counsel come from the public defender's office or from private law offices; judges come from the pool of judges in the county. But each of these participants needs to accommodate the requirements of the others; they manage to collaborate because they share common instrumental goals (disposing of their case load and reducing uncertainty) and expressive goals (doing justice and maintaining group cohesion). The authors attempted to use this framework to explain differential outcomes in three large cities. Unfortunately, their research was not well designed to operationalize their variables. For instance, they had no measurements of work group cohesion, nor did they include confirming evidence of the goals they believed to motivate work group participants. Although plausible, their theoretical structure was not confirmed by the data they presented.

Eisenstein, Roy Flemming, and Peter Nardulli, in the most recent of these efforts (1987; Nardulli, Eisenstein, and Flemming 1988), opted for a different vocabulary to describe criminal courts in nine moderate to small communities. While they speak of the "courthouse community" rather than its work groups and organizational structure, they seem to mean much the same thing, although they encompass the entire set of work groups in a courthouse in their scheme rather than focusing on discrete courtroom work groups. Having directly measured attitudes of participants and organizational characteristics, they are able to show how these courthouse organizations vary from place to place and the kinds of constraints they impose on the principals in the criminal justice process.

Thus the study of criminal courts has moved from intensive description of individual actors to the analysis of their interactions, the constraints that those interactions impose on them, and the outcomes that flow from these different kinds of situations. It has become clear that the work of individual decision makers can be understood only in the context of their organizational relationships. No single official makes criminal court decisions; decision making is shared by many.

For civil litigation, no comparable descriptions of the interactions of the principal actors exist. A 1989 paper by Marc Galanter, for instance, implicitly recognizes that settlements are the result of an interactional process in which clients, attorneys, and judges play important roles; however, he does not specify those roles, and he can find no empirical basis in the existing research literature for delineating the shape of such interactions. The best we can say at this point is that clients sometimes exert considerable control over the course of litigation, particularly when they are extremely knowledgeable (as in the case of corporations with their own legal departments) and when the issue is extremely salient to them (see Stewart 1983). Some attorneys vigorously seek to wrest control from clients because it threatens their professional judgment about the optimal course of action and because client control may lead to decisions that reduce their fee (Rosenthal 1974). The role that judges play and how they react to litigants and attorneys is poorly understood. We know of extreme cases where a judge has excluded an attorney from his courtroom because of his personal distaste for the attorney's actions (*New York Times*, August 14, 1989, 1). We also know of judges' efforts to control their dockets (Ryan et al. 1980). However, we have little information about the informal relationships that mold the routine of civil courts.

Tasks for the Future

Two major tasks face the next generation of researchers of trial court decision making. First, they need to develop more general models of trial court processes and operational instrumentation for them; this requires an exercise in theory building and application. Second, they need to bring civil proceedings into the core of our research agenda; this requires extensive new field work.

Theory Building and Application

Past studies of trial court decision making have often been imaginatively designed, but they have had little cumulative effect because each researcher formulated a new theoretical framework. No consensus exists about which questions are the most important and promising to pursue; instead, much research is driven by the whims of operating agencies and by chance opportunities. The result is that many of the energies of researchers are wasted on peripheral questions. As every research design text argues, research should be driven by theory.

Perhaps the most promising set of theoretical propositions centers on the organizational paradigm. That paradigm explicitly recognizes relationships between participants in trial court proceedings. It acknowledges the importance of both formal structure and informal arrangements that characterize all trial courts. It links court research with a body of investigation into many other organizations operating in the private and public sphere. Moreover, it allows researchers to build on a considerable base of prior scholarship specifically on courts. It needs to be exploited far more systematically and self-consciously than in the past, yet with discretion.

Such an endeavor might begin by looking at the links between the internal processes of court organizations and their external environment. All organizations engage in continuous exchanges between themselves and their environment, and they struggle to manage the environment so that they may govern their own destiny. From their environment, organizations extract the resources they require to survive: most notably, legitimacy and money to purchase staff, equipment, and other resources. The environment also supplies the needs the organization is to address; just as the demand for cars justifies an automobile manufacturer, so the desire for justice justifies the courts. Some organizations face relatively placid or malleable environments; others encounter turbulent and intractable surroundings.

The environment of criminal courts is full of uncertainties. There is little consensus about what the product of the courts should be; the possibilities include a flow of convictions, evenhanded justice, harsh sentences, or sanctions carefully targeted on the most threatening offenses. The flow of cases to them is largely beyond their direct control; they must constantly adapt themselves to the actions of external forces that operate autonomously whether they be the criminals engaging in illegal activity, the police in making arrests, or prosecutors deciding to invoke the legal process. Media campaigns about crime also place pressure on the criminal courts. Resources available to the courts cannot be simply exchanged with the courts' product as a manufacturer exchanges output for more supplies. Rather, resources must be negotiated gingerly with other public officials since court officials are not supposed to engage in politics. At the other end of the process, courts have little or no control over the amount of space that jails and prisons have to accommodate those whom they sentence to incarceration.

Civil trial courts face an even greater array of external forces over which they have little influence. The incidence of disputing is the result of inchoate social forces. For instance, while the number of bankruptcies is a function of economic conditions, personal injury suits are a consequence of the number of accidents, the actions of insurance companies, the kinds of protective devices built into cars, the willingness of people to use them, and many other factors. Civil courts have even less ability to monitor the flow of business than do criminal courts. No public body like the police and the prosecutor's office screens civil cases; that function is performed by a host of private attorneys who respond to their own need for fees and their own feelings of professional propriety. Nor are there data on disputing comparable to victimization and crime statistics which would allow court personnel to develop empirically grounded plans for the future. Finally, like their criminal counterparts, civil courts face an ambivalent demand for justice with little consensus about what that entails.

The lack of control over the external environment alerts the court researcher to look for the many ways in which these organizations adapt themselves to the resulting uncertainties. Many decision-making routines are likely to be motivated by environmental threats. Examine, for instance, the use by courts of allocative procedures to ration access. Differential access to courtroom time controls the flow of cases because it erects a price barrier. Allocative procedures will force some potential litigants to seek alternative remedies and the price of litigation will motivate others to avoid it. In addition, allocative procedures may also be designed to extract legitimacy and support from those who are influential in the external environment by favoring their demands for court time. Thus an organizational perspective makes it easier to understand why certain dockets are given preference in many courts.

Although agenda control may often be motivated by external forces, it plays an enormously important role in decision making. Agendas not only allocate time for the consideration of alternatives but they influence the presence of participants, the resources they bring with them, the information at their disposal, and the alternatives they are willing (or able) to consider. Docketing has been given little attention in this light. Yet we have every reason to believe that it is as important as agenda setting in other organizational contexts. Delay acts as a rationing device, forcing some litigants out of the courts. The need to be in court on a particular day leaves other litigants without all the information they would like to display, with an ill-prepared attorney, or with circumstances that preclude their consideration of alternative remedies that they might otherwise find acceptable.

Finally, we may shed light on the trial courts' information policies by examining them from the perspective of the courts' struggle to control their external environment. Many courts are not simply passive onlookers as journalists come and go. Rather they actively seek to mold media portrayals by guiding reporters to some stories while attempting to keep others hidden in obscurity. Manipulation of good feelings toward courts is an important component of their attempt to maintain a hospitable environment which will contribute the material and symbolic resources required for their operation. Little is yet known about the prerequisites for such an environment, but much significant research has recently focused on the consequences of the perceived legitimacy of courts. These investigations have shown that people place more importance on their being treated fairly than on their obtaining the results that brought them to court (Tyler 1984, 1988).

The organizational paradigm also points to other variables that are important to understanding trial court decision making. The interaction of formal authority with informal influence patterns has been shown to be central to understanding courts. Formally, judges are in charge; informally, they share authority with all the other participants. Judges rely on attorneys for information about the case before the court; they count on attorneys and litigants to maintain an efficient flow of business through the courtroom. Judges may embarrass, cajole, and threaten to have their way, but they cannot dismiss the attorneys or litigants as if they were subordinates. The imposition of penalties on attorneys or unfavorable rulings on litigants is subject to review by other agencies; their arbitrary use will make a judge's work more difficult as his or her victims retaliate using their resources from the informal influence network. Much intensive ethnographic research is required to flesh out these interactions in the organizational context, so that we can specify the conditions under which the judge, prosecutor, or defense attorney is likely to prevail and understand the character of likely coalitions or compromises between them. This remains a challenging task, but the paradigm provides some guidance.

Information flows play a large role in organizational theory and provide further guidance to the study of court decision-making. Almost all courtroom technologies center on the distribution and evaluation of information. Legal scholars lavish attention on evidentiary rules and processes, but these are only a small part of the information processing that occurs in trial courts. Information moves not only through formal channels, such as at hearings, but also through informal paths in corridors, offices, chambers, and telephone messages. Moreover, information is conveyed not just in verbal exchanges but also by gestures, facial expressions, and body movement. Control over information is one of the principal sources of informal influence. The examination of the entire range of communication in trial courts is just beginning as the technology for recording interactions has improved to permit the researcher to replay video recordings as often as needed in order to expose the many layers of the communication process.

Leadership skills are the focus of some organizational studies; in others skilled operatives are taken for granted. In the court context, leadership may be less significant, but the relative skills of participants has attracted much attention from legal scholars, although less from empirical investigators. Given what we know from the observation of decision making in other organizational contexts, however, we should expect skill in framing issues to be particularly important for influencing judicial decisions. This is revealed in the legal literature, which emphasizes the importance of asking for particular remedies in the original court filing, making the correct pretrial motions, and emphasizing a favorable characterization of a claim in informal and formal court hearings.

Finally, courts produce highly visible decisions upon which the researcher can focus. In many organizations, decisions emerge with so little formality that it is difficult to discern when and by whom they have been made. In others, it is difficult to distinguish between the formal decision (the award of a contract, for instance, or the decision to fire an employee) and the informal decision that preceded it. Those difficulties are not as significant in trial courts. Although courts sometimes only ratify decisions that have been made elsewhere, in many instances the decision point is the one observed in the courtroom. Thus a decision on a motion comes after argument; a trial verdict comes at the end of a trial; a decision on a plea recommendation comes after informal negotiations.

However, researchers cannot slavishly apply organizational theory to the study of trial court decision making. While the organizational model may be helpful in sorting out many elements of the trial decision making process, much of what occurs inside courts differs from the life of most other organizations, for trial courts are in many ways unlike most other organizations. For instance, they do not control many of the processes that lie at the heart of organizational maintenance. Thus they do not recruit their own staff but rather rely on what Eisenstein and Jacob (1977) called sponsoring organizations. They also do not control their own procedures but rather rely on other external organizations like the legislature or the state's supreme court for many of their procedural rules (Grau 1978).

Yet as Lawrence B. Mohr (1976) suggested, organizational models emphasizing different goals seem to have some applicability to trial court decision making. Among the organizational processes Mohr discusses are the conventional rational model, in which organizational participants seek to make decisions that best achieve their goals; satisficing, in which the organization seeks to obtain the most accept- able objective rather than an optimal solution; and strategic agglomera- tion, in which the decision is the result of several coincidental streams of decisions that happen to come together.[3] A fourth model Mohr labels political in the sense that the actor who wins a contest imposes his or her will over others; this model resembles the conventional (but as we have seen, misleading) understanding of trials as contests that are won by some and lost by others. As Mohr points out, the mechanical application of such organizational concepts will not do for the courts. Much of the organizational literature examines the ways in which authority is imposed and sanctions are used; hierarchical authority and formal sanctions play relatively small roles in the ordering of relation- ships in courtrooms. Trials are complex interactions rather than simple contests. Courtrooms and courthouses are not bureaucracies in the sense that sociologists working in the Weberian tradition use that term. Researchers seeking to use organizational paradigms need to be eclectic. They also need to develop a typology of organizational forms that courts exhibit in varying circumstances.

Investigating the Civil Courtroom

One place to begin the application of a more general theoretical model such as the organizational one is in the study of decision making in civil courts. However, that task poses some special problems. One of the difficulties that must be overcome is obtaining the cooperation of clients, attorneys, and judges in this effort. Unlike criminal courtrooms, civil courtrooms have as participants many private citizens rather than public officials, and they hesitate to share their dispute with outside observers. It is easier for researchers to stalk prosecutors and public defenders because these are public officials accustomed to dealing with requests from outsiders; moreover, the time they give to researchers does not directly cost them money. Not so for the private attorneys encountered in most civil courtrooms. Their time is money; they perceive themselves and their clients as private parties who need not respond to the snooping of outside researchers. The same contrast holds for clients in the two courtrooms. In criminal courts, defendants frequently perceive themselves as powerless and often have little else to do with their time when a researcher approaches them. Moreover, the activity that brought them to court has already been made public through their arrest. Not so for many clients in civil courts. They do not necessarily see themselves as powerless; they do not understand that using the courts has made their dispute public property; their time is not without value.

Moreover, researchers in civil courts must overcome the apparent formlessness of interactions among courtroom regulars. In many civil courtrooms, there is a larger set of regulars who are more specialized according to type of case than in criminal courts. Their interactions occur more frequently outside the courthouse, often on the telephone, and thus they are more difficult to observe. The public hearings in courtrooms are like the surfacing of whales; they denote something of importance but their exact significance cannot be determined without further examination of the many actions that take place beneath the surface.

Several strategies may overcome these difficulties. One is to emulate Neubauer's (1974) examination of the work of criminal courts in a middle-sized city. Although civil courts in the Middletowns of the United States do not operate identically to those in Manhattan, Los Angeles, Chicago, or Washington, D.C., they are likely to provide clues that will enable others to tackle more complex court systems. Alternatively, it might be fruitful to divide decision making in civil courts into instances involving individual clients and those involving private and governmental organizations. Such a distinction recognizes the vast differences in resources participants bring to their organizational roles. Moreover, prior research on attorneys indicates that the bar is divided into these two worlds, and it roughly corresponds to the distinction that Galanter (1974) made between those who use the courts infrequently (one-shotters) and those who do so routinely in the course of the normal work (repeat-players). We may well discover that trial court decision making varies systematically with these distinctions.

Conclusion

Advances in research are more than responses to the scholar's innocent curiosity. They also echo external stimuli, such as Supreme Court decisions and prominent social problems. They respond to the allocation of resources. They react to technology.

I have no crystal ball to indicate where resources will flow or what external stimuli will capture the imagination of the next generation of court researchers. However, it is possible to perceive some technological changes that are beginning to affect research on court decision making.

One change is the growing tendency of courts to permit television coverage of court proceedings. Of course, what happens in open court reveals only a small part of the decision-making process, but it is a portion that formerly was relatively inaccessible for research purposes. The more routine television coverage becomes, the more likely it is that videotaped archives can be developed for court researchers to use. No longer will it be necessary for researchers to strain to hear what is going on and to attempt to record what they hear and see on the fly. Instead, videotapes can be played and replayed until all elements of the proceedings have been analyzed.

Moreover, computer technologies are being developed to analyze verbal communications. Such software will not substitute for painstaking reading and rereading of transcripts. However, it makes it possible for the researcher to examine text more systematically. For an organization in which the communication of information is central, such analyses are especially appropriate.

The exploration of trial court decision making is still in its infancy. Having established the perimeters of the phenomenon we wish to comprehend, researchers are now able to move forward with greater confidence that their efforts will deepen our understanding of the complexities involved in trial court decision making. Twenty years from now not only may we be able to chart the perimeters of judicial decision making, we may also understand some of its central processes.

Notes

1. The evolution of the research described here is not quite as orderly as I imply; some studies of individual participants persist into the 1980s while the first examinations of entire court systems date back to the late 1960s. However, the most active research streams are as I have described them.
2. This term refers to the practice of excluding from juries that might consider the death penalty those men and women who are opposed to the death penalty on principle. For a further examination of this issue, see Ellsworth 1988, 189-204.
3. This model is also called the garbage can model of decision making. Its developers are James G. March and Johan Olsen (1976).

References

Alschuler, Albert W. 1965. The prosecutor's role in plea bargaining. *University of Chicago Law Review* 36:50-112.
Bittner, Egon. 1970. *The functions of the police in modern society.* Washington, D.C.: National Institute of Mental Health.
Black, Donald. 1980. *The manners and customs of the police.* New York: Longman.
Blumberg, Abraham S. 1967. *Criminal justice.* Chicago: Quadrangle.

Brown, Michael K. 1981. *Working the street: Police discretion and the dilemmas of reform.* New York: Russell Sage Foundation.

Brunk, Conrad G. 1979. The problem of voluntariness and coercion in the negotiated plea. *Law and Society Review* 13:527-554.

Canon, Bradley C. 1972. The impact of formal selection processes on the characteristics of judges. *Law and Society Review* 6:579-594.

Carlin, Jerome E. 1962. *Lawyers on their own: A study of individual practitioners in Chicago.* New Brunswick, N.J.: Rutgers University Press.

Carp, Robert A., and C. K. Rowland. 1983. *Policymaking and politics in the federal district courts.* Knoxville: University of Tennessee Press.

Cartwright, Bliss, Marc Galanter, and Robert Kidder. 1974. Introduction: Litigation and dispute processing. *Law and Society Review* 9:5-8.

Casper, Jonathan D. 1972. *American criminal justice: The defendant's perspective.* Englewood Cliffs, N.J.: Prentice-Hall.

Cole, George F. 1970. The decision to prosecute. *Law and Society Review.* 4:331-344.

Conley, John M., and William M. O'Barr. 1988. Fundamentals of jurisprudence: An ethnography of judicial decision making in informal courts. *North Carolina Law Review* 66:467-507.

Curran, Barbara A. 1977. *The legal needs of the public: The final report of a national survey.* Chicago: American Bar Foundation.

Dubois, Philip L. 1980. *From bench to ballot: Judicial elections and the quest for accountability.* Austin: University of Texas Press.

Eisenstein, James, Roy B. Flemming, and Peter F. Nardulli. 1987. *The contours of justice: Communities and their courts.* Boston: Little, Brown.

Eisenstein, James, and Herbert Jacob. 1977. *Felony justice: An organizational analysis of criminal courts.* Boston: Little, Brown.

Ellsworth, Phoebe C. 1988. Unpleasant facts: The Supreme Court's response to empirical research on capital punishment. In *Challenging capital punishment: Legal and social science approaches,* ed. Kenneth C. Haas and James A. Inciardi. Beverly Hills, Calif.: Sage.

Feeley, Malcolm. 1975. The effects of heavy caseloads. Paper presented to the annual meeting of the American Political Science Association, San Francisco.

Flemming, Roy B. 1989. If you pay the piper, do you call the tune? Public defenders in America's criminal courts. *Law and Social Inquiry* 14:393-414.

Galanter, Marc. 1974. Why the "haves" come out ahead: Speculations on the limits of legal change. *Law and Society Review* 9:95-160.

———. 1989. Judges and the quality of settlements. Typescript.

Gibson, James L. 1978. Race as a determinant of criminal sentences: A methodological critique and a case study. *Law and Society Review* 12:455-478.

Goldman, Sheldon. 1987. Reagan's second term judicial appointments: The battle at midway. *Judicature* 70:324-339.

_____. 1989. Reagan's judicial legacy: Completing the puzzle and summing up. *Judicature.* 72:318-330.

Grau, Charles W. 1978. *Judicial rulemaking: Administration, access, and accountability.* Chicago: American Judicature Society.

Hagan, John. 1974. Extra-legal attributes and criminal sentencing: An assessment of a sociological viewpoint. *Law and Society Review* 8:357-384.

Hans, Valerie P. 1988. Death by jury. In *Challenging capital punishment: Legal and social science approaches,* ed. Kenneth C. Haas and James A. Inciardi. Beverly Hills, Calif.: Sage.

Heinz, John P., and Edward O. Laumann. 1982. *Chicago lawyers: The social structure of the bar.* New York: Russell Sage Foundation.

Heumann, Milton. 1975. A note on plea bargaining and case pressure. *Law and Society Review* 9:515-528.

Jacob, Herbert. 1965. *Justice in America.* Boston: Little, Brown.

_____. 1986. *Law and politics in the United States.* Boston: Little, Brown.

Jones, Bryan D. 1985. *Governing buildings and building government: A new perspective on the old party.* University: University of Alabama Press.

Kalven, Harry, Jr., and Hans Zeisel. 1966. *The American jury.* Boston: Little, Brown.

Kleck, Gary. 1985. Life support for ailing hypotheses: Modes of summarizing the evidence for racial discrimination in sentencing. *Law and Human Behavior* 9:271-285.

Lasswell, Harold Dwight. 1936. *Politics: Who gets what, when, how.* New York: P. Smith.

Law and Society Review. 1979. Special issue on plea bargaining. 13:199-687.

Lempert, Richard O. 1981. Grievances and legitimacy: The beginnings and end of dispute settlement. *Law and Society Review* 15:707-716.

McDonald, William F. 1979. From plea negotiation to coercive justice: Notes on the respecification of a concept. *Law and Society Review* 13:385-392.

McEwen, Craig A., and Richard J. Maiman. 1984. Mediation in small claims court: Achieving compliance through consent. *Law and Society Review* 18:11-50.

March, James G., and Johan P. Olsen. 1976. *Ambiguity and choice in organizations.* Bergen, Norway: Harald Lyche.

Mayhew, Leon, and Albert J. Reiss, Jr. 1969. The social organization of legal contacts. *American Sociological Review* 34:309-318.

Merry, Sally Engle. 1979. Going to court: Strategies of dispute management in an American urban neighborhood. *Law and Society Review* 13:891-926.

Miller, Richard E., and Austin Sarat. 1981. Grievances, claims, and disputes: Assessing the adversary culture. *Law and Society Review* 15:525-566.

Mohr, Lawrence B. 1976. Organizations, decisions, and courts. *Law and Society Review* 10:621-642.

Nardulli, Peter F., James Eisenstein, and Roy B. Flemming. 1988. *The tenor of justice: Criminal courts and the guilty plea process.* Urbana: University of Illinois Press.

Neubauer, David W. 1974. *Criminal justice in middle America.* Morristown, N.J.: General Learning Press.

NILECJ (National Institute of Law Enforcement and Criminal Justice). 1975. *Prosecutorial discretion: The decision to charge, an annotated bibliography.* Washington, D.C.: Law Enforcement Assistance Administration.

O'Barr, William M., and John M. Conley. 1985. Litigant satisfaction versus legal adequacy in small claims court narratives. *Law and Society Review.* 19:661-702.

O'Gorman, Hubert J. 1963. *Lawyers and matrimonial cases.* New York: Free Press.

Peltason, Jack W. 1955. *Federal courts in the political process.* New York: Random House.

———. 1961/1971. *Fifty-eight lonely men: Southern federal judges and school desegregation.* Urbana: University of Illinois Press.

Roper, Robert T. 1980. Jury size and verdict consistency: "A line has to be drawn somewhere"? *Law and Society Review* 14:977-995.

Rosenthal, Douglas E. 1974. *Lawyer and client: Who's in charge?* New York: Russell Sage Foundation.

Ross, H. Laurence. 1970. *Settled out of court: The social process of insurance claims adjustment.* Chicago: Aldine.

Rubenstein, Jonathan. 1973. *City police.* New York: Ballantine.

Ryan, John Paul, Allan Ashman, Bruce D. Sales, and Sandra Shane-DuBow. 1980. *American trial judges: Their work styles and performance.* New York: Free Press.

Sarat, Austin. 1976. Alternatives in dispute processing: Litigation in a small claims court. *Law and Society Review* 10:339-376.

Schulhofer, Stephen J. 1984. Is plea bargaining inevitable? *Harvard Law Review* 97:1037-1107.

Sheehan, J. Brian. 1984. *The Boston school integration dispute: Social change and legal maneuvers.* New York: Columbia University Press.

Slotnick, Elliot E. 1988. Federal judicial recruitment and selection research: A review essay. *Judicature* 71:317-324.

Smigel, Erwin O. 1964. *The Wall Street lawyer: Professional organization man?* New York: Free Press.

Stanford Law Review. 1961. Representation of indigents in California: A field study of the public defender and assigned counsel systems. 13:522-565.

Stewart, James B. 1983. *The partners: Inside America's most powerful law firms.* New York: Simon and Schuster.

Taylor, Jean. 1972. An analysis of defense counsel in the processing of felony defendants in San Diego. *Denver Law Journal* 49:233.

———. 1973. An analysis of defense counsel in the processing of felony defendants in Denver, Colorado. *Denver Law Journal* 50:36.

Tyler, Tom R. 1984. The role of perceived injustice in defendants' evaluations of their courtroom experience. *Law and Society Review* 18:51-74.

_____. 1988. What is procedural justice? Criteria used by citizens to assess the fairness of legal procedures. *Law and Society Review* 22:103-136.

Uhlman, Thomas M. 1978. Black elite decision making: The case of trial judges. *American Journal of Political Science* 22:884-904.

Vidmar, Neil. 1984. The small claims court: A reconceptualization of disputes and an empirical investigation. *Law and Society Review* 18:515-550.

Wasmann, Erik, Nicholas P. Lovrich, Jr., and Charles H. Sheldon. 1986. Perceptions of state and local courts: A comparison across selection systems. *Justice System Journal* 11:168-185.

Watson, Richard A., and Rondal G. Downing. 1969. *The politics of the bench and bar: Judicial selection under the Missouri nonpartisan court plan.* New York: Wiley.

Yngvesson, Barbara, and Patricia Hennessey. 1975. Small claims, complex disputes: A review of the small claims literature. *Law and Society Review* 9:219-274.

Zeisel, Hans. 1982. The verdict of five out of six civil jurors. *American Bar Foundation Research Journal* 1982:141-156.

Zeisel, Hans, Harry Kalven, Jr., and Bernard Buchholz. 1959. *Delay in the court.* Boston: Little, Brown.

9. AGENDA SETTING AND CASE SELECTION

H. W. Perry, Jr.

Deciding to decide is one of the most important tasks performed by any political institution. Setting the agenda defines and orders alternatives, and scholars have long noted that outcomes—for example, legislation, an executive action, or a judicial opinion—are dependent upon the availability and ordering of alternatives (Kingdon 1984; Levine and Plott 1977). To understand an institution fully, then, we must understand how its agenda is set. But beyond interest in an institution per se, many normative questions central to democratic theory require understanding something about who sets agendas, how they are set, and how access to this process is achieved. Scholars generally have not studied agenda setting to an extent that is commensurate with its importance.[1] Relative to other institutions, however, a fair amount of work has been done on agenda setting in courts—or, more precisely, on one significant aspect of agenda setting, case selection.

This chapter begins with a brief discussion of the rudiments of case selection in the U.S. Supreme Court, proceeds to evaluate political science research on the topic, and concludes by suggesting directions for future research. Discussion is devoted primarily to case selection in the U.S. Supreme Court because that has been the object of most research by political scientists.[2] The focus is understandable. Federal courts of appeals are not afforded much discretion in setting their agenda. And in state courts, there are as many different systems of case selection as there are states.

Case Selection in the U.S. Supreme Court

Cases are granted review by the Supreme Court solely at the discretion of the justices. Each year, review is sought for over 5,000 cases, but fewer than 5 percent are actually taken.[3] When the Court agrees to take a case, it grants certiorari, or cert.[4] The cert. decision process is significantly different from the decision process on the merits (deciding who wins the case and why). Actually, it is misleading to talk about *the* cert. process. There are at least nine separate processes—one for each chamber. The description here is generic and therefore much oversimplified.[5]

Each chamber receives a copy of every cert. petition. The chief justice prepares a list of cases he believes to be worthy of discussion at conference, though any justice can add a case to this list simply by informing the chief's chambers. All cases not making this "discuss list" are denied cert. automatically. Prior to the conference, each justice develops a fairly firm idea of how he or she will vote. Justices rarely change their minds (Perry 1991). In conference, the cases are discussed, and if a case receives four votes—"the rule of four"—it is granted cert. For most cases, there is usually just a vote with very little discussion, and contrary to lore, votes are taken in order of seniority (Perry 1991).[6] If cert. is granted, the case is set for argument.[7]

The role of law clerks in the cert. process is important. For most petitioned cases, justices read only their clerk's memo. Justices vary in their reliance on clerks, and within a chamber, reliance varies with the confidence that a justice has in an individual clerk. Clerks certainly are not powers behind the throne; there are controls, not the least of which is that clerks are diligently trying to please their bosses, whose confidence must be earned. Nevertheless, it is unwise to understate the crucial role played by clerks in the cert. process as much research has done.

Justice Murphy, speaking for the Court in *Wade v. Mayo* (334 U.S. 680 [1948]), declared, "Writs of certiorari are matters of grace." The concept of grace alleviates a lot of theological dilemmas, but it is not a very satisfactory explanation for case selection. We continue to look for justification. The justices offer little guidance or encouragement in our search. In the "Rules of the Supreme Court of the United States," Rule 17 is the only official information that the justices give on what they consider important when evaluating a petition for certiorari. Rule 17, however, is extremely vague (I have added the italics):

> A review on writ of certiorari is not a matter of right, but of judicial discretion, and will be granted *only when there are special and important reasons therefor. The following, while neither controlling nor fully measuring the Court's discretion, indicate the character of reasons that will be considered.*
>
> (a) When a federal court of appeals has rendered a decision in conflict with the decision of another federal court of appeals on the same matter; or has decided a federal question in a way in conflict with a state court of last resort; or has so far departed from the accepted and usual course of judicial proceedings, or so far sanctioned such a departure by a lower court, as to call for an exercise of this Court's power of supervision.
>
> (b) When a state court of last resort has decided a federal question in a way in conflict with the decision of another state court of last resort or of a federal court of appeals.

(c) When a state court or federal court of appeals has decided an important question of federal law which has not been, but should be, settled by this Court, or has decided a federal question in a way in conflict with applicable decision of this Court. . . .

Note that the Court says that the above conditions are not "controlling" and only "indicate the character of the reasons that will be considered." With the exception of specifying certain types of conflicts, they have essentially defined certworthiness tautologically; that is, what makes a case important enough to be certworthy is a case that they consider important enough to be certworthy. The existence of such vague standards, of course, whets the curiosity of the political scientist, and most of our research has been an attempt to discover what determines certworthiness, or more precisely, what factors enhance a petition's chance for a full hearing by the Court.

Case Selection Research in Political Science

Two early studies set the agenda for most subsequent research.[8] To my knowledge, Glendon Schubert (1959, 1962) was the first social scientist to deal specifically with the certiorari process. He used game theory to try to predict how certain justices voted on cert. for Federal Employers' Liability Act cases, arguing that a bloc of justices voted strategically. In other words, cert. votes were cast strategically to effect desired outcomes on the merits. There was no rigorous way to test Schubert's assertions, however, because certiorari votes are secret.[9] The next major study on certiorari was conducted by Joseph Tanenhaus and several colleagues (1963). Upon examination of the 1956-1958 terms of the Court, Tanenhaus developed the "cue theory of certiorari." He argued that the presence of certain cues increased the likelihood that a case would be selected. Given the large number of cases that justices must sift through, Tanenhaus posited that the presence of certain cues would cause a case to be scrutinized more closely and ultimately lead to a greater likelihood of selection. He hypothesized that the following cues would increase the likelihood of a grant: (1) when the federal government seeks review; (2) when dissension has been indicated among the judges of the court immediately below, or between two or more courts and agencies in a given case; (3) when a civil liberties issue is present; and (4) when an economic issue is present. Tanenhaus found support for the first three. As discussed below, however, many of his findings have since been challenged.[10]

For some time, Tanenhaus's and Schubert's studies stood as the premier works on case selection by social scientists. Because certiorari votes are secret, the testing of hypotheses has been very difficult. This frustrating situation was eased when the papers of Justice Harold H.

Burton (1945-1957) were made public after his death in 1965. Burton kept copious notes of conference proceedings, including records of how each justice voted on certiorari. These voting records have made statistical analysis possible and have served as the data base for many subsequent studies on case selection.[11]

Despite some instability in results and some contradictory findings and explanations, we have lifted the veil of secrecy surrounding case selection to some degree. We have learned that the presence or absence of certain characteristics of a case increases the likelihood that cert. will be granted. For example, we know with a high degree of certainty that when the federal government seeks review, the chances that a case will be taken are quite high. Tanenhaus's finding has been confirmed repeatedly in several different types of studies (Ulmer 1972; Armstrong and Johnson 1982; Perry 1986b). This finding is not surprising, because without knowing anything about the Court's decision process or criteria, we know that the solicitor general's petitions are accepted at rates in the neighborhood of 80 percent. The importance of other cues is less conclusive. Ulmer and colleagues did not find support for any Tanenhaus cue except when the United States was a party. Armstrong and Johnson, however, found Tanenhaus's cues to be "alive and well" in studies of both the Warren and Burger courts.[12] Using the Burton data, Marie Provine (1980) demonstrated that justices did not use cue theory, as formulated by Tanenhaus, to be dispositive in sorting petitions into those that would and would not be further discussed. I have argued (Perry 1986b), however, that notwithstanding the convincing argument by Provine that cue theory as described by Tanenhaus was disproved by the Burton data, the idea of cues has been discarded too quickly. Few cues will be sufficiently important by themselves to place a case on the discuss list or predict case selection with any degree of impressiveness. Nonetheless, Tanenhaus's basic idea of cues still has validity in describing a decision process, through not precisely as Tanenhaus envisioned it. Like Provine, I have argued that the justices do not rely on such cursory information to sort petitions; however, I see the cues as sending important information to the law clerks, and to some extent to the justices. I have likened the process to signaling as discussed in economics and international relations (Spence 1974; Jervis 1970).

Beyond the cues offered to us by Tanenhaus, we have learned that other characteristics increase the likelihood that a case will be selected. We know with some certainty that conflict in the courts below is a very important criterion in assessing the certworthiness of a petition (Estreicher 1986; Feeney 1975; Perry 1986b; Ulmer 1983, 1984). This, of course, is one criterion that the Court had told us was important in Rule 17. Still, it was important to verify it empirically. We have also learned that the presence of an amicus brief increases the likelihood of a grant (Caldeira and Wright 1988; Perry 1986b). Others have suggested that at a macro level there is some life cycle to issues and responsiveness on the part of the Court (Caldeira 1981; McLauchlan 1980; Pacelle 1985).

Scholars have persuasively demonstrated that cert. votes are frequently related to votes on the merits (Baum 1976, 1977, 1979; Perry 1986a, 1991; Ulmer 1972). Similarly, though not precisely the same thing, we know that justices sometimes cast cert. votes on an ideological basis and are more likely to vote to reverse lower court decisions that they feel to be wrongly decided (see Armstrong and Johnson 1982; Baum 1977, 1979; Palmer 1982; Perry 1986a; Provine 1980; Songer 1979; Ulmer 1978). Likewise, there is evidence that cert. votes are sometimes strategic; that is, not only are they related to the votes on the merits, but calculations of likely outcomes on the merits drive the cert. vote (see Brenner 1979; Schubert 1959, 1962; Ulmer 1978). Notice, however, the qualifications in the preceding three sentences. Our understanding of how and when cert. votes are strategic or proxies for votes on the merits is problematic. There is a fair amount of instability in our findings. I have argued elsewhere (Perry 1991) that sometimes justices cast cert. votes as this literature describes and sometimes they do not, depending upon their interest in the outcome of a case. I am not alone in this assessment. Using the Burton data, Provine persuasively demonstrated problems with Schubert's concepts of strategic blocs, and she also raised serious problems with some of the findings that related votes on cert. to votes on the merits. But the findings are mixed. For example, Armstrong and Johnson found that there is an interaction between the presence of a Tanenhaus cue and the ideological direction of the lower court decision such that if the lower court decision is "erroneous," that is, the ruling is in the wrong ideological direction, the Court was more likely to take the case, at least in some areas of law. Findings by various scholars are consistent enough to know that cert. votes are related to votes on the merits, but results have not been stable enough, or studies have not measured the same things in such a way as to be able to say definitively, how the cert. vote and merits vote are related.

In sum, we have progressed a great deal from what we could learn by reading Rule 17. Cases may come before the Court by grace, but research has demonstrated that grace is dispensed in nonrandom ways.

Limitations and Difficulties
with Current Research

I offer two types of criticism of the research on case selection, though the types are not neatly separable.[13] The first is the perspective of one person who works in the field quibbling with current findings and research efforts. Though I try to be fair, I make no pretense to being disinterested. The second line of criticism suggests a general broadening and refocusing of research on case selection implicit in the next section, "New Directions in Agenda Research."

As previously stated, I believe that Schubert and Tanenhaus set the agenda for case selection research. Most studies that followed were in many ways building upon their research, trying to determine the extent to which a justice's cert. vote was a preliminary and/or strategic vote on the merits; or attempting to see whether the presence of certain variables increased the likelihood of review; or positing some combination of the two. This has proved to be a blessing and a curse. It gave research a direction and helped it to be cumulative, but it sometimes restricted our vision, discouraging us from thinking about the process in different ways.

For example, I believe that strategic behavior by the justices has been overemphasized, resulting in a distortion of our understanding of the cert. process specifically and of the Supreme Court as an institution. Provine makes a similar argument (1980; see also Baum 1979). She posits that perceptions of the judicial role "significantly limit the range of case selection behavior that the justices might otherwise exhibit" (Provine 1980, 6). Elsewhere (Perry 1991) I have carried the argument further, suggesting that it is not only that judges would act strategically but for constraints on strategic behavior such as perception of the proper role of the Court; rather many decisions on cert. are made without any inclination to calculate an expected outcome on the merits. It is not so much an issue of being constrained; a conflict between strategy and role may never arise. At some times the justices are highly strategic; at other times they are not. Whether they are, I argue, depends upon how much they care about the outcome of a case on the merits. And the concern with outcome on the merits may have little to do with ideology.

Political scientists have always acknowledged that strategic voting may not occur for some types of issues—whether on cert. or the merits—or that "political" behavior may from time to time be mitigated by other factors. But by focusing almost exclusively on strategic voting situations, scholars have failed to draw a complete picture of the process. Regardless of whether more or fewer decisions involve strategic behavior, if issues differentiate decision-making behavior, then focusing exclusively on one is likely to lead to a misunderstanding of both strategic and nonstrategic decision processes. Justices make cert. decisions, and they design decision rules to help them in this burdensome task. Even if they have different decision strategies for different kinds of cases, it is important to have a complete view of the process so that we know when one set of decision criteria is being used as opposed to another. Students of Congress have developed sophisticated empirical explanations of congressional decision making precisely because their models incorporate the broad range of factors that actually influence the actions of members in many different settings.

A related criticism involves our general lack of interest in those things "legalistic." There are two separate aspects of case selection: (1) jurisdiction and procedure; and (2) the discretionary decision processes of the justices. The two are not entirely separate—justices have the discretion to evaluate jurisdiction, and they may run roughshod over jurisdictional and procedural requirements or they may hide behind them. But, usually, cases must be jurisdictionally and procedurally acceptable before the discretionary decision process begins. Political scientists have focused heavily on the discretionary stage, but by giving short shrift to the jurisdictional and procedural requirements, we have often understated their importance. As Professor Felix Frankfurter noted:

> The role of procedure in the evolution and activity of political institutions has been little heeded by political scientists. . . . The story of . . . momentous political and economic issues lies concealed beneath the surface technicalities governing the jurisdiction of the Federal Courts. (Frankfurter and Landis 1928)

Professor Frankfurter's criticism of political scientists is a little unfair, particularly for 1928. One of our own, C. Herman Pritchett (1969), has also admonished us:

> Again political scientists who have done so much to put the "political" in "political jurisprudence" need to emphasize that it is still "jurisprudence.". . . Judges make choices, but they are not the "free" choices of Congressmen. . . . Any accurate analysis of judicial behavior must have as a major purpose a full clarification of the unique limiting conditions under which judicial policy making proceeds.

Jurisdiction and procedure are two such limiting conditions. Issues of jurisdiction and procedure can be very complex and highly technical. Treatises, law review articles—indeed, entire courses in law school—are devoted to these issues and the subtleties that surround them.[14] The political scientist need not become an expert in procedure, but if the justices care much about these "technical" issues—and they do—so should we. Jurisdictional and procedural issues are crucial for understanding why certain cases are accepted and why others are not. For example, the Supreme Court worries a great deal about things such as standing, mootness, and collateral consequences. Problems in these areas will quickly eliminate a particular case regardless of policy predispositions. The Supreme Court has developed rather elaborate (if confusing) doctrines in these areas and expects lower courts to adhere to certain strictures. Though the Supreme Court is capable of modifying its restrictions—or, as it does sometimes, ignoring them without satisfactory explanation—it generally takes such barriers to review quite seriously. Moreover, it is the presumption of justices that if an issue is important, it will come back in another case, so there is no need to take a case that is jurisprudentially unsound (Perry 1991).

Another example of an important jurisdictional consideration is the role of "appeals." [15] Though some scholars note the difference between cert. and appeals, much of the research on case selection has treated the two as the same or has excluded appeals from the analysis altogether. Treating appeals like certs. in research is a problem because the justices do not treat appeals as if they were certs. On the other hand, to ignore appeals eliminates an important part of the Court's docket. Moreover, appellate jurisdiction can have an effect on which cert. cases are or are not taken. Frequently an issue can arise on cert. or appeal. In such instances, justices almost always take the case on appeal.

Legal constraints need not be thought of only in terms of jurisdiction and procedure. They also involve issues such as resolving circuit conflicts, clarifying the law, and easing the burden on lower courts. The types of questions being adjudicated by the U.S. Supreme Court are frequently of this sort. A large part of what goes on in the agenda setting of the Court has little to do with strategic maneuvering to further policy goals and has a lot to do with legalistic, jurisprudential concerns. All too often we tend to think of the Court's work as involving mostly major issues of societal importance, or legal issues that can be characterized ideologically and for which justices have strong preferences for a desired outcome. For every *Brown v. Board,* however, there is a *Brown v. Allen.*[16]

Political scientists are certainly aware that there are legalistic, non-policy-oriented considerations, and some research has examined them explicitly. An excellent example is Ulmer's work (1984) on circuit conflicts. More work with greater attention to such legal variables would be highly desirable. The problem is not that scholars have focused on one aspect of the Court's work, for that would be defensible. Once again, the problem is that the focus distorts our understanding of the portion that properly interests us. The decision process that has evolved in the Court is one to handle all cases, and we cannot ignore the legalistic constraints.

One final observation about current scholarship serves as a bridge to suggestions for new directions in research. It is an old saw: we have been more interested in predicting than in explaining. That, of course, is a problem for much of social science; and too often when the criticism is lodged, it is simply an attempt to derogate empiricism. That is not the intention here. It has been important to learn which factors increase the likelihood of a grant of cert. and which seem to be unrelated, and to know that there is a correlation between a justice's vote on cert. and the merits. And we want to know this from empirical as well as other forms of research. But if we stop there, we will invariably have instability in results.[17] For the research to have staying power, we must begin to explain why the predictions work, and the best way to do this is to develop theory, or to relate the work to decision theories that already exist.

Short of developing theory, however, there are other things to be done. Much of social science is about reducing premises to testable hypotheses, but the generation of hypotheses should reflect as much sophistication as possible. One way to do this is by broadening our concept of what is interesting to learn, and by exploiting the full range of our discipline's methodological and substantive expertise.

As an example, let us return for a moment to the enigmatic Rule 17. In addition to characteristics that predict selection, what should also intrigue us—and it seems not to have—is the ambiguity of the justices about being ambiguous. The vagueness of Rule 17 is not some unfortunate oversight by the justices. They have intentionally enunciated murky criteria because they do not want attorneys to know precisely what they consider to be a certworthy petition. Yet justices are always complaining—indeed, at times scolding the bar for petitioning cases that do not belong in the Supreme Court—all the while refusing to give more guidance. What is going on in this communication between the bar and the bench? Do the justices really believe attorneys ought to be better able to discern what type of case belongs in the Supreme Court? Or are the justices simply trying to police the bar by periodic exhortations when they know full well that because they have issued no real sanctions, attorneys will continue to petition cases that in the eyes of the justices do not belong in the Supreme Court? Or are the justices themselves confused about what is certworthy? Answering these questions involves examining the justices' attitudes on communication specifically, and on case selection generally. To do this may require, in Richard Fenno's terms, "a little soaking and poking"—something we have done too little of. Ideally we would like to talk to the justices, but there are other opportunities. We might, for example, try to learn how the receivers of the justices' signals interpret them even if we cannot ask the justices. Moreover, such signal sending and receiving is not unique to bench and bar, and we might turn to other political actors to generate hypotheses and explanations. Determining factors that correlate with certworthiness, though useful in understanding important things about case selection, should be supplemented with a better understanding of how actors in the process see their role. In sum, a broadening of what interests us and a broadening of our methodology would, at the least, help us develop better hypotheses, and it might lead toward theory building.

New Directions in Agenda Research

The most promising path for the future of agenda-setting studies of courts lies not with finding new variables, or demonstrating higher correlations, or even expanding our research questions and methodologies, though surely some effort along those lines is desirable. Rather it lies in finding ways to link work on court agenda setting with broader work in the discipline. We should try to learn from, and integrate our studies with, non-court-related agenda-setting studies. It goes without saying that the very special nature of courts or the role of "the law" cannot be ignored. However, neither should all comparisons with other institutions be immediately suspect.

One way to become broader and more theoretical, and to tie in more directly with other political science research, is to expand the horizon from case selection to the broader concept of agenda setting.[18] Much of John Kingdon's (1984) important work on agenda setting is applicable to courts. For example, he makes much of the distinction between agenda setting and alternative specification. The "agenda" for Kingdon is the list of subjects to which people are giving serious attention. Alternatives refer to different real possibilities for action. That distinction is generally applicable to courts. Picking among cases is really alternative specification. This is not the place to summarize Kingdon except to say that he finds the distinction quite helpful. For example, who sets agendas and who specifies alternatives may be very different players. The business of the Court is determined in far more complex ways, and by more players than simply the cases offered to it for review. We should work to specify who the players are and to what extent they can shape agendas and alternatives. The normative import of this is obvious, but distinguishing among players also affects how we might choose to formulate and test hypotheses. Kingdon also discusses policy entrepreneurs; so does much of the literature on courts.[19] He discusses the conditions under which such entrepreneurs are more and less effective in getting items on the agenda (or specifying alternatives). We, too, could probably develop a better understanding of contextual situations in which legal policy entrepreneurs would have greater likelihood of success. The idea is not simply to cite literature from other areas, but to test theories and hypotheses generated in that literature, or if not testing hypotheses, at least to play out some of the analogies to other institutions so as to generate hypotheses. Research on the role of interest groups in public law has done this well. This research has consciously attempted to fit into the broader research on interest groups in the discipline. Both sides have benefited as a result.

It might also be profitable to step back from agenda setting per se and examine the theoretical literature. There is both the behavioral and formal decision theory literature. Decision theory about strategies of maximizing versus satisficing is rarely applied to courts generally, let alone agenda studies.[20] Do justices engage in different types of decision-making behavior (such as satisficing, maximizing) depending upon context and goals, as Richard Cyert and James March (1963) suggest? If they do, then it would be profitable to try to specify goals and decision contexts. Much of the current discussion in social science literature involves formal modeling and rational choice theory. This method of analysis is probably as applicable to the courts as it is to Congress. Formal modelers are frequently concerned with the structuring of agendas. Much of the work on cert. already has involved taking a simple assumption to see how far it can go in explaining outcomes. The work, however, has been empirical rather than an attempt to model. There is no reason to believe that some of the insights provided by rational choice theory to other decision processes would not also be applicable to the cert. process. For example, modelers have shown quite convincingly how the difference in outcome is dependent upon the ordering of alternatives. The order of when cases come before the Court for selection may well influence decision outcomes on cert., let alone the merits. The advantage of formal modeling is that the theories are more easily generalizable and can often draw on a developed theoretical heritage. Concomitantly, the importance of rules and procedures is reemerging, especially among those engaged in formal theory and the "new institutionalism" (see, for example, Shepsle and Weingast 1984a, 1984b). I have already argued the importance of such considerations.

Broadening our scope need not mean that we must constantly be repairing to theory, be it agenda-setting theory or decision theory. We could do a better job simply by showing an awareness of agenda-setting studies of other institutions. For example, Jack Walker (1977) has talked about agendas in the legislative branch. One of his arguments is that issues can be arrayed along a continuum of required to discretionary. Certain measures, such as funding the government, must be placed on the agenda; they are required. Other issues are discretionary and may or may not make the agenda. This, it seems to me, might be quite similar to issues resolved by the Supreme Court. Certain cases are such that refusal to decide them might throw the legal system into havoc, and notwithstanding the preferences of justices, the issue must be decided for system maintenance. Examples might be whether or not a rule of some sort was to be retroactive, and the lack of ruling one way or the other would cause chaos; or where a department has to apply one set of rules in one circuit and another in a different circuit such that until a uniform rule is issued, the process is costing the government thousands of dollars a day. Other issues, while important, might be seen as discretionary, and would bring about a different decision behavior. The Court might feel free to reject many cases over a long period in order to wait for the best case to resolve the issue.

So, by broadening our focus, we might be led to ask a different question: Are decision-making criteria evoked by the issue at hand, or by the goals of the decision maker? Of course, this question is implicit in much of the work already. But putting the question this way ties us to the literature of organization theory as well as to Fenno's congressmen in their committees (Fenno 1973). Trying to understand agenda setting along these lines allows for sensitivity to the uniqueness of legal institutions, but it allows generalization and comparison at a more meaningful level.

To broaden our perspective, we need not go outside of courts. Most state appellate courts now have discretionary jurisdiction of some sort; and as litigation grows, so does discretion (Baum 1986, 264). With fifty different state court systems, there are wonderful opportunities to make comparisons.[21] Studies should probably be comparative across several systems, but a collection of studies of individual state court systems could be cumulative.

Agenda studies can be informed very profitably by some of the work being done on the legal system generally. Frances Zemans's (1983) work on legal mobilization and Susan Lawrence's on legal services for the poor (forthcoming) are two examples. Zemans suggests that courts are in some ways the ultimate democratic (and not republican) institutions because individuals are the central players. She notes the interactive nature of the law with the individual and argues that it is important to democratic socialization to think of using the law as a form of participation by individuals. Lawrence demonstrates the importance of certain legal policy entrepreneurs, legal service lawyers. She, too, demonstrates the importance of individual litigators in policy making, especially in their ability to get cases before the U.S. Supreme Court. In a different vein, much of the critical legal studies literature involves normative issues of agenda setting. Oversimplifying, the claim of much of that literature is that legal institutions are not responsive to whole categories of needs or perspectives. Does that not invite some testing as it relates to case selection? (See Ulmer 1978.)

Let me be a bit more specific about case selection in the Supreme Court to show how it relates to the literature discussed in the previous paragraph. With a few technical exceptions, if the Court refuses to take a case, the litigant has no further legal recourse.[22] That is it; it is over. The decision of the last highest court to hear the case stands. From the litigant's perspective the decision to review or not review a case is of great consequence—not to decide *is* to decide. From a jurisprudential or precedential perspective, the denial is theoretically without meaning. By refusing to take the case, the Supreme Court is not saying that the decision below was correct—indeed the justices may well believe that the case was incorrectly decided. The justices are saying simply that they will not review the case, that the decision below stands, and that they are making no official judgment on the correctness of the decision or the issues it raises.[23] Lawyers as well as political scientists have questioned this on jurisprudential and strategic grounds, but have tended to stay focused on the jurisprudential or policy implications writ large, not on who can have their day in court.[24] The underlying principle, of course, is that the Supreme Court is there not primarily to do justice in individual cases, but rather to resolve issues of law so that justice can be done in the legal system. But we may have accepted too quickly the concept that individual litigants are not important, that only the policy or the class of people matters. If we take seriously the points made by Zemans, Lawrence, or even Sidney Verba and Norman Nie (1972), who participates and has access to particular kinds of participation matters. Access to the legal system generally may not be the same thing as access to the top appellate courts. And access for classes of individuals may not have the same systematic implications as access for individuals. As Justice Jackson noted:

> Some say denial means nothing, others say it means nothing much. Realistically, the first position is untenable and the second is unintelligible. How can we say that the prisoner must present his case to us and at the same time say that what we do with it means nothing to anybody. . . . Its minimum meaning is that this Court allows the judgment below to stand with whatever consequences it may have upon the litigants. (*Brown v. Allen,* 344 U.S. 542-543 [1952])

In conclusion, if we are willing to become more catholic and less parochial, there is a wealth of hypotheses and interesting ideas in political science awaiting a nexus with agenda studies on courts. Exploiting the link will not only lead us in new and interesting directions and allow us to build more productively on the good work that has been done, it will also allow political scientists to use our work for a better understanding of whatever institution they are studying.

Notes

1. See, however, Cobb and Elder 1972; Kingdon 1984; Light 1982; Polsby 1984; Walker 1977.
2. However, for excellent discussions of a state court and federal courts of appeals, respectively, see Baum 1976, 1977, 1979; Howard 1981.
3. Though reviews are sought for 5,000 cases per year, that is a small proportion of lower court decisions that could be appealed to the U.S. Supreme Court. J. Woodford Howard, Jr. (1981) found that only 30 percent of the Second, Fifth, and D.C. Circuit decisions were appealed to the Supreme Court. The rate of appeals would probably be lower for other circuits.
4. Almost all cases now come to the Supreme Court under its certiorari jurisdiction, which means their selection is completely at the discretion of the justices. A few cases each year come by original jurisdiction as provided for in the Constitution, and cases can also come by appeal, though this route was effectively eliminated in 1988. See note 15 below.
5. For a detailed discussion of the process see Perry 1991.
6. This order of voting is true for votes on the merits as well.
7. Some cases are treated summarily. Different informal rules have developed for these cases. For a description see Perry 1991.
8. Literature reviews can be found elsewhere. See, for example, Provine 1980; Caldeira and Wright 1988.
9. In fact, a major study cast serious doubts upon his findings. See Provine 1980.
10. Several scholars have examined Tanenhaus's cue theory. Though this is not an exhaustive list, see, for example, Armstrong and Johnson 1982; Perry 1986b, 1991; Provine 1980; Songer 1979; Teger and Kosinski 1980; Ulmer 1972.
11. See, for example, Provine 1980; Ulmer 1972, 1978, 1984; Brenner 1979. Another data base has become available that could be of use to political scientists. The New York University Supreme Court Project examined a huge number of petitions for certiorari, *New York University Law Review* 59:823-1003 and 59:1403-1929. Sam Estreicher and John Sexton (1986) use this data in their book. Caldeira and Wright (1988) also use the NYU data.
12. See also, however, Songer 1979; Teger and Kosinski 1980.
13. I focus disproportionately on the problems of case selection research rather ˙ than praise the successes. Moreover, I frequently make general criticisms without systematically noting exceptions. As is often the case, the critic stands on the shoulders of those he criticizes.

14. For a thorough discussion of jurisdiction and procedure that is particularly accessible to the non-legal scholar, see Stern and Gressman 1978.

15. Review is obligatory for "appeals" and prior to 1988 made up about 20 to 25 percent of the cases argued in the Supreme Court. Categories of cases qualify as appeals solely because Congress passes a law deeming them so. Legislation in 1988 removed most of the categories of appeal; only a few categories remain. However, since most studies of case selection preceded this change, and since some mandatory review remains, and though unlikely, Congress could reinstate categories of appeals, it is important to understand that there is a difference between certiorari and appeal. Even prior to 1988, appeals had become effectively discretionary, that is, most appeals were also dismissed; however, justices felt much more constrained in their ability to deny review, and many cases were granted review as appeals that would have been denied as certs. (Perry 1991).

16. *Brown v. Board of Education,* 347 U.S. 483 (1954); *Brown v. Allen,* 344 U.S. 443 (1952), were important cases dealing with technical jurisdictional issues.

17. Larry Mohr has discussed this methodological point at some length in his impressive book, *Explaining Organizational Behavior* (1982). The book contains a sophisticated discussion of methodology drawing from many fields of research, but it is quite accessible. He would describe the research in search of cues as variance models and he elaborates reasons for instability. For an example of statistical research where the author is sensitive to methodological issues and tries to sort out endogenous from exogenous effects, see Caldeira 1981.

18. For efforts along these lines see Caldeira 1981; Caldeira and Wright 1988; McLauchlan 1980; Pacelle 1985; Perry 1991.

19. Some of the concepts developed in literature on interest groups and courts is related to Kingdon's notion of policy entrepreneurs. See, for example, Barker 1967; Caldeira and Wright 1988; Epstein 1985; Hakman 1966; Krislov 1963; much of the work of Karen O'Connor and Lee Epstein, one example being O'Connor and Epstein 1983; Olson 1981; Puro 1971; Wasby 1983.

20. For an example of direct application of this literature to courts, see Mohr 1976.

21. See Larry Baum's several pieces on the California court; see also Flango 1986.

22. As an example of an exception, applications for a writ of habeas corpus may appear more than once; or the Court might refuse to review a state court decision that upholds a criminal conviction, yet the prisoner could apply for a writ of habeas corpus in federal court. See *Brown v. Allen,* 344 U.S. 443 (1952).

23. The classic statement propounding this interpretation of Court denial comes from Justice Frankfurter in a frequently quoted passage from *Maryland v. Baltimore Radio Show,* 338 U.S. 912 at 917-920 (1950). Other justices have made the same argument time and again. See Justice

Brennan, "State Court Decisions and the Supreme Court," 31 *Penn Bar Assn. Q.* 393 at 402-403 (1960); Justice Marshall in *U.S. v. Kras,* 409 U.S. 434 at 460-461 (1973); *Hughes Tool Co. v. Trans World Airlines,* 409 U.S. 363 at 366 (1973). See also Stern and Gressman 1978, 353-360.

24. See Linzer 1979. He argues that one can in fact read more into these denials than the justices suggest. See also Perry 1986b.

References

Armstrong, Virginia, and Charles A. Johnson. 1982. Certiorari decision making by the Warren and Burger Courts: Is cue theory time bound? *Polity* 15:141-150.

Barker, Lucius J. 1967. Third parties in litigation: A systemic view of the judicial function. *Journal of Politics* 29:41-69.

Baum, Lawrence. 1976. Decisions to grant and deny hearings in the California supreme court: Patterns in court and individual behavior. *Santa Clara Law Review* 16:713-744.

_____. 1977. Policy goals in judicial gatekeeping: A proximity model of discretionary jurisdiction. *American Journal of Political Science* 21:13-33.

_____. 1979. Judicial demand—screening and decisions on the merits: A second look. *American Politics Quarterly* 7:109-119.

_____. 1986. *American courts: Process and policy.* Boston: Houghton Mifflin.

Brenner, Saul. 1979. The new certiorari game. *Journal of Politics* 41:649-655.

Caldeira, Gregory A. 1981. The United States Supreme Court and criminal cases, 1935-1976: Alternative models of agenda building. *British Journal of Political Science* 11:449-470.

Caldeira, Gregory A., and John R. Wright. 1988. Organized interests and agenda-setting in the U.S. Supreme Court. *American Political Science Review* 82:1109-1127.

Cobb, Roger W., and Charles D. Elder. 1972. *Participation in American politics: The dynamics of agenda-building.* Boston: Allyn and Bacon.

Cyert, Richard M., and James G. March. 1963. *A behavioral theory of the firm.* Englewood Cliffs, N.J.: Prentice-Hall.

Epstein, Lee. 1985. *Conservatives in court.* Knoxville: University of Tennessee Press.

Estreicher, Samuel, and John Sexton. 1986. *Redefining the Supreme Court's role: A theory of managing the federal judicial process.* New Haven: Yale University Press.

Feeny, Floyd. 1975. Conflicts involving federal law: A review of cases presented to the Supreme Court. In *Structure and internal procedures: Recommendations for change,* ed. Commission on Revision of the Federal Court Appellate System. Washington, D.C.: Government Printing Office.

Fenno, Richard F., Jr. 1973. *Congressmen in committees.* Boston: Little, Brown.

_____. 1978. *Home style: House members in their districts.* Boston: Little, Brown.

Flango, Victor E. 1986. Case selection by courts and by justices in the Georgia and Illinois supreme courts. Paper presented at the annual meeting of the American Political Science Association, Washington, D.C.

Frankfurter, Felix, and James M. Landis. 1928. *The business of the Supreme Court: A study in the federal judicial system.* New York: Macmillan.

Hakman, Nathan. 1966. Lobbying the Supreme Court: An appraisal of political science folklore. *Fordham Law Review* 35:50-75.

Howard, J. Woodford, Jr., 1981. *Courts of appeals in the federal judicial system: A study of the Second, Fifth, and District of Columbia Circuits.* Princeton: Princeton University Press.

Jervis, Robert. 1970. *The logic of images in international relations.* Princeton: Princeton University Press.

Kingdon, John W. 1981. *Congressmen's voting decisions.* 2d ed. New York: Harper and Row.

_____. 1984. *Agendas, alternatives, and public policies.* Boston: Little, Brown.

Krislov, Samuel. 1963. The amicus curiae brief: From friendship to advocacy. *Yale Law Journal* 72:694-721.

Lawrence, Susan. 1990. *The poor in court.* Princeton: Princeton University Press, forthcoming.

Levine, Michael E., and Charles R. Plott. 1977. Agenda influence and its implications. *Virginia Law Review* 63:561-604.

Light, Paul C. 1982. *The president's agenda: Domestic policy choice from Kennedy to Carter.* Baltimore: Johns Hopkins University Press.

Linzer, Peter. 1979. The meaning of certiorari denials. *Columbia Law Review* 79:1227-1305.

McLauchlan, William. 1980. An exploratory analysis of the Supreme Court's caseload from 1880-1976. *Judicature* 64:32.

Mohr, Lawrence B. 1976. Organizations, decisions and courts. *Law and Society Review* 10:621-641.

_____. 1982. *Explaining organizational behavior: The limits and possibilities of theory and research.* San Francisco: Jossey-Bass.

New York University Supreme Court Project. 1984a. Summaries of cases granted certiorari during the 1982 term. *New York University Law Review* 59:823-1003.

New York University Supreme Court Project. 1984b. Appendices. *New York University Law Review* 59:1403-1929.

O'Connor, Karen. 1980. *Women's organizations' use of the courts.* Lexington, Mass.: Lexington Books.

O'Connor, Karen, and Lee Epstein. 1983. The rise of conservative interest group litigation. *Journal of Politics* 45:479-489.

Olson, Susan. 1981. The political evolution of interest group litigation. In *Governing through courts,* ed. J. Gambitta. Beverly Hills, Calif.: Sage.

Pacelle, Richard L., Jr. 1985. The Supreme Court agenda across time: Dynamics and determinants of change. Ph.D. dissertation, Ohio State University.

Palmer, Jan. 1982. An econometric analysis of the U.S. Supreme Court's certiorari decisions. *Public Choice* 39:387-398.

Perry, H. W., Jr. 1986a. Deciding to decide in the U.S. Supreme Court: Bargaining, accommodation, and roses. Paper presented at the annual meeting of the American Political Science Association, Washington, D.C.

———. 1986b. Indices and signals in the certiorari process. Paper presented at the Midwest Political Science Association Meetings, April 9-11, Chicago.

———. 1991. *Deciding to decide: Agenda setting in the United States Supreme Court.* Cambridge: Harvard University Press, forthcoming.

Polsby, Nelson W. 1984. *Political innovation in America.* New Haven: Yale University Press.

Pritchett, C. Herman. 1969. The development of judicial research. In *Frontiers of judicial research,* ed. Joel Grossman and Joseph Tanenhaus. New York: Wiley.

Provine, Doris Marie. 1980. *Case selection in the United States Supreme Court.* Chicago: University of Chicago Press.

Puro, Stephen. 1971. The role of amicus curiae in the United States Supreme Court: 1920-1966. Ph.D. dissertation, State University of New York, Buffalo.

Schubert, Glendon. 1959. The certiorari game. In *Quantitative analysis of judicial behavior.* New York: Free Press.

———. 1962. Policy without law: An extension of the certiorari game. *Stanford Law Review* 14:224-327.

Shepsle, Kenneth A., and Barry R. Weingast. 1984a. Uncovered sets and sophisticated voting outcomes with implications for agenda institutions. *American Journal of Political Science* 28:49-74.

———. 1984b. When do rules of procedure matter? *Journal of Politics* 46:206-221.

Songer, Donald. 1979. Concern for policy outputs as a cue for Supreme Court decisions of certiorari. *Journal of Politics* 41:1185-1194.

Spence, A. Michael. 1974. *Market signaling: Informational transfer in hiring and related screening processes.* Cambridge, Mass.: Harvard University Press.

Stern, Robert L., and Eugene Gressman. 1978. *Supreme Court practice.* 5th ed. Washington, D.C.: Bureau of National Affairs.

Tanenhaus, Joseph, Marvin Schick, Matthew Muraskin, and Daniel Rosen. 1963. The Supreme Court's certiorari jurisdiction: Cue theory. In *Judicial decision making,* ed. Glendon Schubert. New York: Free Press.

Teger, Stuart, and Douglas Kosinski. 1980. The cue theory of Supreme Court certiorari jurisdiction: A reconsideration. *Journal of Politics* 42:834-846.

Ulmer, S. Sidney. 1972. The decision to grant certiorari as an indicator to decision "on the merits." *Polity* 4:429-447.

———. 1978. Selecting cases for Supreme Court review: An underdog model. *American Political Science Review* 72:902-909.

———. 1983. Conflict with Supreme Court precedent and the granting of plenary review. *Journal of Politics* 45:474-477.

———. 1984. The Supreme Court's certiorari decisions: Conflict as a predictive variable. *American Political Science Review* 78:901-911.

Ulmer, S. Sidney, William Hintz, and Louise Kirklosky. 1972. The decision to grant or deny certiorari: Further consideration of cue theory. *Law and Society Review:* 637-643.

Verba, Sidney, and Norman H. Nie. 1972. *Participation in America.* New York: Harper and Row.

Walker, Jack L. 1977. Setting the agenda in the U.S. Senate: A theory of problem selection. *British Journal of Political Science* 7:423-445.

Wasby, Stephen L. 1983. Interest groups in court: Race relations litigation. In *Interest group politics,* ed. Allan Cigler and Burdett Loomis. Washington, D.C.: CQ Press.

Zemans, Frances K. 1983. Legal mobilization: The neglected role of law in the political system. *American Political Science Review* 77:690-703.

10. DECISION MAKING IN APPELLATE COURTS

James L. Gibson

Political scientists have been systematically studying decision making within the United States Supreme Court and other appellate courts since the publication of C. Herman Pritchett's *The Roosevelt Court* in 1948. Indeed, the central problem in the study of judicial behavior and process over the course of the last forty years has been to understand the processes through which decisions are made by the judges sitting on appellate benches. These research efforts have generated a variety of interesting theories and conceptual frameworks.

Most research on appellate court decision making has been directed at understanding the justices of the U.S. Supreme Court. Standing at the pinnacle of the nation's justice system, the U.S. Supreme Court is arguably the most powerful judicial institution in the world, and there are few areas of American public policy that are unaffected by rulings of the Court.[1] Furthermore, few political institutions in the United States wield such politically unaccountable and furtive political power. That political scientists would be interested in the internal dynamics of such an institution is not surprising.

However, because the Supreme Court is shielded behind a "purple curtain," the institution has historically resisted the efforts of scholars to analyze its decision-making processes.[2] This resistance of the Court to scholarly inquiry has slowed progress in developing and testing theories, yet has also contributed to sustained scholarly effort to understand why the justices act as they do. Absent the normal sorts of research tools and access to data, those who would study the Supreme Court have often been forced to travel a rather circuitous, inferential pathway.

Another consequence of the Court's disdain for scholarly scrutiny has been the redirection of research attention to the U.S. courts of appeal and the state "supreme courts."[3] The judges of these courts are frequently more accessible and their decisions less shrouded in secrecy. Thus, though much of our understanding of appellate court decision making is based on research on the U.S. Supreme Court, there are a number of important studies on other appellate courts.

Despite the difficulties of collecting data, great strides have been made in developing theories and models of the decision-making process within appellate courts. Even with the cloak of secrecy, analysts have been able to penetrate these courts, largely through statistical methods. This has produced a series of strong hunches about how decisions get made. The purpose of this chapter is to have a look at these hunches in an effort to understand how the judges who sit on appellate courts reach their decisions.

This chapter will review what social scientists know about decision making on appellate courts (primarily the U.S. Supreme Court), examining both micro-level and macro-level theories of decision making. At the micro level—the level of the individual decision maker—I focus on the influences of values, facts, and role orientations. At the institutional, or macro, level, the focus is on the influence of the group, institution, and environment on the behavior of judges. Perhaps more important, I will try to identify what we *do not* know about decision making on appellate courts. In doing so, I hope to identify a set of theoretical and empirical issues to be addressed in future research.

In an effort to simplify the decision-making process and to provide a structure for thinking about the various influences on decisions, I have earlier summarized judicial decision making as follows: "Judges' decisions are a function of what they prefer to do, tempered by what they think they ought to do, but constrained by what they perceive is feasible to do. Individuals make decisions, but they do so within the context of group, institutional, and environmental constraints" (Gibson 1983, 7). This succinct description of judicial decision making will guide the analysis that follows. I begin with a consideration of the effects of judicial values, case facts, and role orientations on judicial decisions.

Micro-Level Models of Judicial Decision Making

No area of inquiry into judicial decision making is more theoretically and empirically advanced than micro-level analyses.[4] Indeed, the initial impetus for studying Supreme Court decision making came from those interested in micro-level processes. Research over a forty-year period has generated some notable progress.

The Effect of Judicial Values on Decisions

The phenomenon that nearly all micro-level analysis attempts to explain is the vote of the individual judge. Votes are typically conceptualized as favoring one interest or another; most common is the postulation of a liberal-conservative dimension. Judges are said to vote in favor of "liberalism" or in favor of "conservatism" within the context of the individual case. For example, decisions favoring the expansion of rights are typically treated as liberal decisions, while those that would set limits on rights are considered to advance conservative values.

Table 10-1 Variation in Voting Behavior, U.S. Supreme Court Justices, 1953-1986

	Percentage liberal in nonunanimous cases			
Justice	Civil liberties	N	Economics	N
Warren Court				
Reed	12.2	74	40.7	86
Minton	17.5	63	53.3	75
Burton	21.4	159	38.6	145
Harlan	22.1	551	20.9	402
Clark	24.7	485	70.3	380
Whittaker	26.1	184	17.5	166
Frankfurter	37.1	278	20.2	247
Jackson	38.9	18	20.8	24
Stewart	39.6	424	33.8	299
White	44.2	278	62.9	175
Black	74.7	582	83.6	450
Brennan	76.0	509	71.5	382
Warren	77.6	576	79.2	457
Fortas	81.1	159	51.1	90
Marshall	83.5	79	56.0	25
Goldberg	87.3	102	58.3	72
Douglas	96.1	583	86.4	455
Burger Court				
Rehnquist	5.6	959	22.8	285
Burger	17.6	1,099	25.0	328
O'Connor	24.5	318	31.0	87
Harlan	27.6	105	29.6	27
Powell	31.2	940	29.7	256
White	33.7	1,103	50.6	328
Blackmun	39.5	1,056	46.5	310
Stewart	43.6	782	32.1	234
Black	43.9	107	65.4	26
Stevens	61.4	676	52.6	211
Brennan	85.5	1,086	74.2	329
Marshall	88.5	1,078	68.2	321
Douglas	94.1	374	78.4	111

Source: Jeffrey A. Segal and Harold J. Spaeth, "Decisional Trends on the Warren and Burger Courts: Results from the Supreme Court Data Base Project," *Judicature* 73 (1989): 103-107. Reprinted with permission.

Within this conceptualization, Supreme Court justices differ mightily. Considering those who served on the high bench between 1953 and 1986, Table 10-1 reports a description of the behavior of the justices of the Warren and Burger Courts, as developed by Jeffrey Segal and Harold Spaeth (1989). The scores reported are derived from

nonunanimous decisions and are divided by the substance of the case—
either civil liberties/civil rights claims or economic disputes. "Liberal"
decisions in civil liberties/civil rights cases are basically those supporting rights claimants (including minorities and criminal defendants),
while liberal economic decisions favor economic "underdogs" over
economic "upperdogs" (see Segal and Spaeth 1989).[5]

The most notable aspect of Table 10-1 is the variability across
the justices. In civil liberties/civil rights cases, the percentages range
from Justice Douglas during the Warren Court (96.1 percent liberal)
to Justice Rehnquist during the Burger Court (5.6 percent liberal).
In economics cases the range is nearly as wide: 86.4 percent of Justice
Douglas's decisions in the Warren Court were liberal, while only 17.5
percent of Justice Whittaker's decisions were liberal. There could
hardly be more variability in these scores. We should also note
that there is a strong tendency for those who vote to uphold liberal
values on civil liberties/civil rights cases to vote similarly on economics cases.

Just what do these differences mean? After all, each of the
members of the Supreme Court is confronted with the same constitutions, the same statutes, the same precedents. How can they vary so
much? Why do they vary so much? These are central issues to which
political scientists have devoted a great deal of energy.

The first observation to make in formulating an explanation of
differences across judges is that they have enormous discretion when
they make their decisions. The text of constitutions, statutes, and
precedents does not *command* the votes of the judges. Since there is no
"true" or "objective" meaning to constitutional phrases like "due
process of law," judges *cannot* merely follow the law.[6] Indeed, the
texts of these documents provide the clay from which the judges mold
their decisions in individual cases. Like the sculptor's block of clay,
the text does have limitations, but there is a wide variety of
possibilities inherent in the medium.

The most commonly accepted explanation of the exercise of
discretion in decision making is that the judges rely on their own
ideological positions in making their decisions. *Judges' decisions are a
function of what they prefer to do;* judges who hold liberal values tend
to vote in a liberal direction, while those who are conservative tend to
vote conservatively. Liberals and conservatives perceive the world
differently (how much discrimination is there in American society
against African-Americans?), and they weight values differently
(which is more highly valued, freedom or equality?). Thus, conservatives may not believe that burning the U.S. flag is constitutionally
protected freedom of speech because they perceive the social disrup-

tion of such activity as too great, and because they tend to ascribe greater value to social order than to individual liberty (that is, in instances such as this when the two are in conflict). Given basic differences in perceptions and values among individuals, it is hardly surprising that they would act differently, even in the context of interpreting legal documents.

Using only the simple model that claims that political values directly determine votes, the behavior of the justices of the Supreme Court is highly predictable. The evidence for this assertion derives from two sources. First, statistical scaling analysis (see Schubert 1965, 1974; Spaeth 1979) describes a degree of consistency in voting behavior across disparate areas of law that almost certainly is attributable to the political values of the justice.[7] Despite differences in the law, judges act quite consistently. This consistency is not with each other, but is instead *within* each judge—liberal judges appear to vote in favor of liberal interests whether they are in economics, criminal justice, civil rights, or due process cases. The most compelling explanation for this consistency is that the judges are relying on their own values in making their decisions.

A second, less inferential source of evidence of the role of values in decision making is available. Jeffrey Segal and Albert Cover (1989) have shown that journalistic perceptions of the values of the justices at the time of their nominations very strongly predict the subsequent voting behavior of the justices (see also Danelski 1966). They take this to mean that the ideological values of the justices prior to going on the bench (as perceived by the editors of major newspapers) strongly influence the behavior once on the bench. Indeed, Segal and Cover have even gone so far as to suggest that "virtually nothing else directly affects the aggregate decisions of justices" (1989, 562). The votes of the justices strongly reflect the values of those casting the votes.

If the values of individual judges make a difference for their votes, then one would predict that changes in the membership of appellate courts result in changes in the policy outputs of the institution. That is just what social scientists have found: as justices have been replaced over the past two decades, the Supreme Court has become gradually, though markedly, more conservative (Johnson 1981; Baum 1988). This is also probably true of state appellate courts (for example, Dubois 1988). Whether there are conservatives or liberals on the bench makes a difference for the types of decisions made.

Thus, we can be fairly confident that the values of the decision maker are an important part of the decisional calculus—indeed, perhaps even the most important part. Those who wish to understand judicial decision making cannot ignore the role played by the ideological preferences of the judges.[8]

Adding Cases and Facts to the Equation

There can be a large difference, of course, between predicting the average behavior of judges and predicting outcomes in individual cases. Analysis of the sort conducted by Segal and Cover is aimed at accounting for the central tendency in an aggregation of cases. Similarly, those who study decision making in other appellate courts typically focus on measures of the average decision (see Howard 1981). Every distribution of decisions has not only a central tendency (that is, an average) but a dispersion as well (that is, a standard deviation). Indeed, it would not even be surprising to find that central tendencies are well predicted by the values/attitude model while individual decisions are not particularly well predicted. This is because what judges prefer to do is not always feasible to do. Discretion certainly exists in judicial decision making, but there are constraints on the exercise of that discretion, constraints that often emanate from within the cases themselves.

Judges make decisions in cases, not in aggregates. That is, although it is obviously important to attempt to explain decision-making propensities, decisions in individual cases brought before the Court are also important concerns for social scientists.

Psychometric theories of decision making have been employed to explain decision making on the Supreme Court, most notably in the work of Glendon Schubert (see, for example, 1965, 1974).[9] These theories are termed psychometric because they attempt to understand judicial decision making by measuring the psychological distance between cases and values as they exist in the minds of the judges. Beginning by conceptualizing a highly abstract psychological space, psychometric theory posits that decisions reflect the spatial relationship between judges' preferred positions (their i points) and the location of individual cases (j points). Cases are thought of as requiring varying degrees of liberalism to affirm the claim made by the liberal litigant.[10] If a case requires more liberalism than a judge has available, then his or her decision will be a conservative one; otherwise the decision will be liberal.

One stream of analysis considers the ways in which particular configurations of facts structure the decisions of individual judges. For instance, Segal (1986) found that the justices of the Supreme Court are more likely to find a search reasonable in cases in which the search was incident to a lawful arrest, while they are less likely to find reasonableness in searches of private homes. More generally, he found (1984,

1986) that a significant proportion of the variation in decisions could be explained by a small number of discrete facts in the case. Such research strongly suggests that different justices perceive and react to facts in quite different ways.

Cue theory—used to explain certiorari decisions of the Supreme Court—represents a special case of the analysis of facts.[11] Cue theory begins with the assumption that justices cannot process large amounts of information about any single case; the crush of cases simply does not allow it.[12] Consequently, justices rely on cues that signal the presence of a case worthy of more careful scrutiny. The most widely considered cue is the position of the solicitor general. As the justices are scrutinizing the voluminous petitions for certiorari, they seem to rely on the judgment of the solicitor general to tell them whether the case is worthy of further consideration. Cue theory is only a special case of a more general concern with the role of facts in decision making.

There can be little doubt that the facts of cases are an extremely important part of any judicial equation. Yet research in the study of facts has not progressed very far. We are at present unable to locate cases or facts within ideological space using any criteria independent of the decision itself. Our models of the processes of weighting facts in making decisions are often primitive and atheoretical, with most research efforts relying on weights derived from statistical methods (such as regression analysis) rather than from theory. Surely judges assemble information in a much more complex fashion.[13] Finally, little work has been done on perceptions of facts.[14] It is unlikely that all judges perceive facts similarly; models that rely on such assumptions are unlikely to be very successful. Thus, though we all recognize that attitudes alone cannot determine behavior, that before attitudes even become relevant, they must be stimulated, much more research needs to be done to understand the ways in which the facts of cases influence the decisions made.[15]

Translating Votes into Opinions

Despite their prominence in nearly every study of judicial decision making, votes in cases are not the only important aspect of judicial decision making. Political scientists have not made much headway in explaining the *opinions* of the judges; indeed, little headway has been made in even conceptualizing the basic nature of the continua involved. The analysis of opinions is one of the most exciting but uncharted areas for future inquiry into decision making.

Analyzing opinions requires rethinking some basic assumptions of the models of votes. For instance, analysis of judicial votes has traditionally assumed that the votes can be aligned along a single, unidimensional continuum. A vote is either "for" or "against" a particular value—for some it is liberalism-conservatism (see Spaeth 1979), for others it is underdogs versus upperdogs (Ulmer 1978). But one can easily imagine multidimensional disputes. Given differences in perceptions, it is quite possible that the judges perceive the cases on different dimensions and that they are not even voting on the same issues. The simplest example is one raising a jurisdictional issue. A justice may vote against the issue because he or she believes that the case should not even be heard by the Court (as when the issue is moot), while other judges are voting on the substantive dimensions of the dispute. Many state criminal cases raise at least two basic value conflicts: the conflict between order and liberty and the conflict between national and state authority. In a different context, Joel Grossman (1962) was one of the first to argue that some justices on the Court have responded to cases in role-related terms instead of in terms of a substantive dimension (on role theory see below). Spaeth (1979) has also proposed a multidimensional scheme.[16] There are many other instances in which conflicts in cases may be multidimensional. At a minimum, the hypothesis that disputes are unidimensional should be subjected to empirical testing.

Just how widespread is multidimensional conflict? Due to the dearth of analysis of opinions, no one knows. Thus, while much is known about how judges cast their votes, little is understood about the complexities of their opinion writing. Future research should pay a great deal more attention to this problem.

Role-Related Constraints on Judicial Decision Making

Another important constraint on judges' decisions is the expectation that they exercise judicial restraint. This expectation, based on the rather precarious position of unaccountable judges within a democratic polity, basically asks judges to do what is legally proper rather than what they prefer on ideological grounds. This means that judges must on occasion vote against their political values.[17] Judges' ideological preferences are tempered by what they think they ought to do.

Judges differ in the degree to which they accept or subscribe to norms of judicial restraint. Some judges view restraintism as essential to the protection of the right of the majority to rule in a democratic polity. They view the role of the judge as one of last resort: only when the majority becomes abusive of the rights of minorities should the courts intervene. Otherwise, judges should restrain themselves and allow the majority to rule.

Activists, on the other hand, believe that judges have the obligation to right the wrongs perpetuated by majoritarian institutions. The objective to the activist judge is to achieve justice, not just legality. For these judges, it is entirely appropriate, if not essential, for the judiciary to scrutinize the work of legislative and executive institutions very carefully. Thus, it is perhaps simplistic but nonetheless useful to conceptualize decision-making role orientations[18] as ranging from *restraintism*—following precedents, strict construction of constitutions, and deference to legislative "intent"—to *activism*—the subordination of precedents and statutes, and deference to personal attitudes, values, and goals. This conceptualization is consonant with a variety of work on role theory (Becker 1966; Howard 1977, 1981; Gibson 1978; see also Halpern and Lamb 1982).

Kenneth Vines, using quotes from his interviews with state supreme court judges, provides a nice summary of the difference between activists and restraintists. One of his restraintist judges asserted:

> I think that it is terrible that judges interpret the laws or the Constitution in accordance with what they think it should be instead of interpreting the language of the Constitution or the statute. . . . The United States Supreme Court and other state courts, too, have set themselves up as some sort of super-Congress, and they interpret the Constitution to mean what they think it should say. That's a violation of the separation of powers. (1969, 475)

On the other hand, one of his activists asserted:

> Inevitably, a judge makes law as does a legislative body. No matter how you decide a case, you're making law. . . . That whole idea about whether a judge makes law or whether he found what the law always was by looking somewhere up in the blue is not true. Judges always made law and always will. . . . In interpretation you're trying to give answers to problems that were not considered by the legislature, and you try to guess what the legislature would have thought had they thought about this problem. But you get away from this quickly. What do you do when you get a question like this? You can't send it back to the legislature for a decision. . . . The question comes up, and you decide it. (1969, 475-476)

It is extremely difficult (especially when personal interviews cannot be conducted) to devise rigorous measures of the degree of activism of individual judges. One way to think about role orientations is to consider activists as those who tend to rely more on their own values in making decisions, and to consider restraintists as those who rely less on their own values. This conceptualization has been used by several scholars (such as Becker 1966; Jaros and Mendelsohn 1967; Ulmer 1974; Gibson 1977), and basically contends that the degree to

Table 10-2 Variation in Judicial Activism-Restraintism, U.S. Supreme Court Justices, 1953-1988

Justice	Restraintism score[a]	Attitude score[b]	Justice	Restraintism score[a]	Attitude score[b]
Powell	2	−0.67	Blackmun	10	−0.77
Brennan	3	1.00	Rehnquist	11	−0.91
Burger	4	−0.77	Stewart	13	0.50
Kennedy	5	−0.27	Warren	15	0.50
Marshall	5	1.00	O'Connor	17	−0.17
Fortas	6	1.00	Stevens	17	−0.50
Scalia	7	−1.00	Goldberg	27	0.50
White	8	0.00	Harlan	27	0.75
Whittaker	8	0.00			

[a] Large scores indicate greater degrees of judicial restraintism.
[b] Large scores indicate greater degrees of liberalism.

Sources: Restraintism scores from James L. Gibson and James P. Wenzel, "Models of Decision Making in the U.S. Supreme Court" (unpublished manuscript). Houston, Texas: University of Houston. Attitude scores from Jeffrey A. Segal and Albert D. Cover, "Ideological Values and the Votes of the U.S. Supreme Court Justices," *American Political Science Review* 83 (1989): 557-564.

which the votes of judges can be predicted from their values is a measure of activism.[19] Gibson and Wenzel (1989) have developed such a measure, relying on a statistical manipulation of the data reported by Segal and Cover (1989).[20] The activism scores—scores that indicate the degree to which decisions reflect attitudes—of the justices serving in the Warren, Burger, and Rehnquist Courts are shown in Table 10-2.

According to this measure the most activist judges were Justices Powell and Brennan—their decisions were very strongly predictable from their attitudes. On the other hand, Justices Harlan and Goldberg were the most restraintist—their votes diverged the most from their attitudes. Generally, there is considerable variability among the justices in the degree of restraintism, with some justices tending to rely heavily on their values in making decisions and others hardly at all.

Also shown in Table 10-2 is the measure of judicial attitudes derived by Segal and Cover (1989). The correlation between liberalism and restraintism is +.20, indicating that there is a slight tendency for *liberals* to be more *restraintist*. This finding runs contrary to the conventional wisdom that associates liberalism with activism. However, political scientists have long recognized that there is no necessary relationship between ideology and role orientation (Gibson 1977; Howard 1977, 1981), and that the relationship no doubt varies over time. Thus, this finding is not unreasonable. After all, it was the conservative Chief Justice Warren Burger who wrote: "I do not acquiesce in prior holdings that purportedly, but nonetheless erroneously, are based on the Constitution. . . . I am bound to reject categorically [the] thesis that what the Court said lately controls over the Constitution" (*Coleman v. Alabama*, 399 U.S. 22 [1970]).

The influence of these role orientations on decisions is not direct. Instead, role orientations interact with other factors when judges are making decisions. For instance, one implication of the difference between activism and restraintism is that judges will evaluate different facts differently. A restraintist judge may assign great weight to precedents and little weight to the preferences of interest groups. Conversely, an activist might discount the intent of the framers of the Constitution while heavily weighting contemporary social mores and norms. Thus, the major difference between activists and restraintists is in their respective processes of decision making, not their liberalism-conservatism per se. Even if what judges think they ought to do does not perfectly predict what they actually do, these normative orientations are an important influence on decision making.

The utility of role theory is that it describes the decision-making process in contextual terms. Individual judges are seen as constrained by the expectations of their colleagues—they cannot act without regard to their environment. Thus, role theory is more than a micro-level theory; it is a theory that transcends the micro-macro gap. Before considering how role theory accomplishes this purpose, it is important to review some major macro level theories of judicial decision making.

Macro-Level Influences on Decision Making

The analysis above suffers from the tendency to view decision makers as if they were acting within a vacuum, not in an intensely political world filled with individuals and groups pressing demands on the decision makers. Appellate court judges often cannot act as they wish, or even as they think they ought to. Instead, they are constrained by the structures of their institutions and the larger political environments in which they function—they are constrained by what they perceive as feasible to do. What judges prefer to do and what they think they ought to do are not necessarily compatible with what they are encouraged or allowed to do.

Institutional and Organizational Constraints

Political scientists have recently rediscovered the importance of institutions (see Smith 1988). While much of this rediscovery is of little utility for empirical analysis, this movement alerts us to the need to model institutional structure and environmental processes, even within micro-level analyses. Judges of appellate courts cannot make any decision they wish; instead, they must satisfy both formal and informal imperatives. To gain a comprehensive understanding of decision making, it is important to consider how the institutional and organizational attributes of appellate courts affect the decisions that are made there.

Many structural constraints on decision making within the Supreme Court are obvious. The justices cannot decide a case that is not before them;[21] nor can they create cases that do not exist. The "rule of four" governs certiorari decisions; the chief justice speaks and votes first in conference; and there are legal limitations to the sort of solutions a decision can craft (Brigham 1978). That there is a "freshman effect" (see Heck and Hall 1981, for example) suggests that there are informal norms of behavior that are just as powerful at structuring action as the formal legal imperatives. The justices must deal with the law—precedents, statutes, and constitutions—in some fashion (see Johnson 1981), even if the law does not dictate their decisions.

Perhaps the most important structural attribute of the Supreme Court is that it is a collegial decision-making body—the justices must interact as a group prior to voting on most cases, and the assembling of coalitions for the purposes of writing opinions is obviously an interpersonal process of bargaining and negotiation. Political scientists have long been concerned with group dynamics on the Court, beginning with Walter Murphy's masterful *Elements of Judicial Strategy* (1964). Murphy analyzed patterns of interpersonal influence on the High Court, based on the assumption that the justices are motivated to shape public policy. But because so much of this process goes on behind the closed doors of the Court, little headway has been made in analyzing the patterns of interpersonal influence.

Studies of state supreme courts have also identified structural attributes that contribute to processes of decision making. For instance, Melinda Hall and Paul Brace (1988) have shown that such institutional characteristics as judicial salaries, opinion assignment mechanisms, and methods of judicial selection substantially affect state supreme court dissent rates. Though research of this sort is in its infancy, future inquiry will surely uncover a variety of institutional factors that influence how decisions are made.

Structural and institutional analyses in the future should not focus primarily on the formal attributes of judicial institutions. Informal norms and expectations impose substantial constraints on the behavior of members of appellate courts. For instance, at one point in the history of the Supreme Court informal norms strongly discouraged dissent

(Walker, Epstein, and Dixon 1988). There are most likely certain expectations that influence the behavior of newly appointed members of the Court (see Heck and Hall 1981; Scheb and Ailshie 1985). Leadership styles adopted by the chief justice are also of enormous importance (see Danelski 1960; Ulmer 1971a, 1971b). Some chief justices are mainly interested in ensuring collegiality among the justices; others are more task oriented; and still others lead very little at all. Informal institutional attributes may be the most important influences on behavior, even if they are the most difficult to study.

Generally, there have been few investigations of the impact of structural attributes on decision making. One of the most successful such inquiries is that of S. Sidney Ulmer (1978), who discovered that Supreme Court justices occasionally act strategically in order to conceal their motivations in voting on cases. At the most obvious level, a justice seeking to maintain the appearance of restraintism would gain little from authoring a solo dissent because he or she would appear to be voting on the basis of ideology, not on the law. There is also evidence that some justices have been persuaded to change their votes so as to protect the institutional legitimacy of the Court when it is called upon to issue intensely political decisions (Ulmer 1971b). Though the evidence available is often more anecdotal than rigorous, it does seem that the justices act differently within the institutional context than they would if they were alone. The attributes of the institution clearly impinge upon the exercise of individual discretion.

Environmental Constraints

The environment also impinges upon the actions of the judges, limiting the ways in which they can exercise their discretion. Decisions may differ in times of war, for instance, even if the law does not. Political crises in the government, and in the streets, set an important context for decision making. The structure of political, economic, and social conflict within a given period has much to do with the sorts of issues submitted to the judiciary. The need to maintain legitimacy and support, both from other political institutions and from the mass public, clearly affects the behavior of the judges. To ignore this larger political world when thinking about models of decision making is perilous.

On the other hand, there would be little reason to expect the justices of the Supreme Court to respond directly to public opinion, as a representative in a legislature might, or even as elected state supreme court judges might. After all, there are no mechanisms through which the justices can be held politically accountable. Life tenure on the bench, as well as the fact that most justices are not ambitiously seeking higher office, means that the traditional means of ensuring democratic accountability are absent. The two forces that most directly contribute to responsiveness—the fear of electoral accountability and ambition (Gibson 1980)—are minimized for most judges, even at the state supreme court level. And since Supreme Court justices are increasingly selected from the ranks of the lower federal judiciary, it is all the more unlikely that judges with role orientations predisposing them to responsiveness will be elevated to the high bench. Nearly all of the mechanisms that motivate individual responsiveness to constituent preferences are absent on the Supreme Court. Thus, the hypothesis that members of the Court are directly affected by public opinion is not altogether sensible—any relationship between public opinion and the policies of the Court cannot be very strong or direct.

We must recognize, however, that there are other quite legitimate avenues through which public opinion can affect the behavior of judges. For instance, judges may well consider community notions of what is pornographic in making certain free press decisions, just as they may refer to contemporary understandings of what sort of punishment is cruel and unusual. The feasibility of certain remedies—for instance, busing public school children for the purposes of racial integration—is no doubt judged within the context of public opinion. Supreme Court justices might not respond to public opinion in the sense that they try to represent it, but they may nonetheless take public opinion into account in deciding certain kinds of cases (see Barnum 1985). In a sense, then, the proper role of public opinion in a decision-making model is simply that of another fact in the case. Just as with other facts, judges differ in the degree to which they find the fact useful within their decision-making calculus, and in the degree to which they believe it appropriate to rely on the fact in making decisions.[22]

Several studies have found a general correspondence between the policy outputs of the Supreme Court and public opinion. The most systematic assessment of this relationship has been conducted by Thomas Marshall (1989). He found that when a clear majority or plurality existed in public opinion, over three-fifths of the Court's decisions were congruent with the preferences of Americans. One cannot posit a direct causal linkage—it is doubtful that the justices were responding to perceived demands from their constituents. More likely, the factors that move public opinion also move the opinions of the justices. Given the tendency (one that may well be changing) to appoint relatively old men to the high bench, there seems to have been sufficient circulation of members of the Court to ensure that its decisions are not long out of touch with the preferences of the majority (see Dahl 1957).[23]

The justices of the Supreme Court do not react identically to all environmental influences. Though there is not much research on the matter, Marshall has examined the relationship between public opinion and the behavior of the individual justices. He developed a measure of the degree to which each justice has been in agreement with public opinion (in the instances in which public opinion is known through surveys). Though the number of cases on which these scores are based is not great, the data reveal tremendous variability, ranging from Justice Hughes (agreement score of 86 percent, based on fourteen votes) to Rutledge (agreement score of 30 percent, based on ten votes) (Marshall 1989, 106, Table 5.1). Though Marshall had little success in accounting for this variability, he did find that politically "moderate justices, chief justices, justices from prestigious law schools, and justices who had served as close presidential advisors were all somewhat more [in step with public opinion] than their remaining brethren" (Marshall 1989, 124-125).

There are other ways in which appellate court judges are constrained by environmental forces. Political scientists have recently given a great deal of attention to the role that interest groups play in the judicial process (O'Connor 1980; O'Connor and Epstein 1983; Epstein 1985). Interest groups not only sponsor legislation by recruiting litigants and paying for litigation, but they can also play an important role in the deliberations of judges as amicus curiae participants. For instance, Gregory Caldeira and John Wright (1988) have shown that interest groups are influential in building the agenda of the Supreme Court. Although interest groups cannot command the Court, they are certainly instrumental in bringing important issues to the attention of the justices.

Thus, a variety of factors constrain the behavior of Supreme Court justices. What judges prefer to do is limited by what they perceive is feasible to do.

Bridging the Micro-Macro Gap

The most important research on judicial decision making incorporates both micro-level and macro-level factors in its models. No theory of decision making can escape the simple fact that individuals make decisions—it is judges, not courts, that cast votes. But neither can theories be insensitive to the lack of freedom available to individual decision makers. Judges are constrained by their colleagues, by their institutions, by their environments. If we are to have a comprehensive understanding of decision making—one that transcends the limited understandings generated to date—"cross-level" models are essential.

My own preference is to think about the cross-level problem from the perspective of the individual. That is, most contextual processes must be mediated through individual perceptions. Pressures to conform, for instance, are not equally perceived by all people; nor do all acquiesce at the same rate. Reactions to institutional structures, to environmental pressures, vary across individuals (see Gibson 1981). Though this position may be accused of excessive reductionism—an overreliance on the assumption that the "sum" can be reduced to its component "parts"—attempts to model macro-level influences on decision making must at least sketch the micro-level processes presumed to be involved.

Role theory is particularly useful for cross-level analyses. Role theory posits that individuals act differently in different positions, primarily due to differing expectations. That not all role occupants assume the same role orientations—beliefs about what constitutes proper behavior under the circumstances—is evidence of the individual-level forces recognized by role theory. At the same time, there are group-level and environment-level factors—for instance, expectations—that impinge upon the behavior of individual decision makers. The utility of role theory is that it points toward both macro-level and micro-level influences on judges' decisions.

At the same time, role theory has served better as a heuristic device than as a formal theory or model of decision making. Few details of the way in which judges perceive expectations emanating from their context have been worked out, and empirical tests of role-related hypotheses are uncommon. This is in part because the data requirements for testing role-theoretic propositions are so substantial; not only must we be able to conduct personal interviews with the judges, but we must also assemble data on their voting patterns, as well as on relations with their colleagues and various constituencies.[24] Indeed, the data demands of role theory are so substantial that it is unlikely that successful tests can be conducted on institutions as uncooperative as the U.S. Supreme Court. Thus, while we are prepared to extend research in this direction—most of the micro-level and macro-level pieces of the puzzle are already in place—research that bridges the cross-level gap has not yet been conducted.

Conclusion

The factors that influence decision making on appellate courts in the United States are highly varied, and the processes through which they interact are complex. Many influences operate at the micro-level—for instance, the ideological preferences of the judges. Macro-level influences, such as public opinion, also constrain these courts, limiting the discretion available to the judges. The interplay of micro-level and macro-level factors is among the most interesting of unanswered research questions.

A host of important research problems remain. We still understand little about the complex ways in which ideologies and role orientations interact with perceptions of facts to structure decisions. Do liberal judges perceive facts as they are perceived by conservative judges? Are the same facts evaluated similarly? Do different judges rely on different sorts of facts in making their decisions? Do activist and restraintist judges differ in the sorts of facts they find necessary or useful for proper decision making? There are a number of interesting questions concerning the fact-value interaction that require additional analysis.

Nor are the dynamics of interpersonal influence on the Court well understood. Since nearly all of the negotiations over votes and opinions occur behind the purple curtain, we have little insight into patterns and styles of influence. The structure of interactions during oral argument—in cases in which it takes place—provides a few clues to these interpersonal interactions, and further analysis of opinions may provide some useful data, but much additional research is necessary.

Efforts to understand structural influences on decision making will no doubt continue due to a renewed interest in the role of institutions in politics. Appellate courts come in a wide variety of structural manifestations. Figuring out how these various forms influence decision making will certainly be an important item on the research agenda.

The ways in which individual judges react to their larger political environments also require a great deal more study. Judges increasingly work in an environment in which their decisions are recognized as public policy making, not simple legal interpretation. In that environment, demands for political accountability will escalate, as will competition for judgeships. Even if many appellate courts have been relatively insulated from politics in the past, it is unlikely that this state of affairs will continue. The challenge for political scientists is to learn more about the ways that judges interact with, influence, and are influenced by their various constituencies.

Judges' decisions are a function of what they prefer to do, tempered by what they think they ought to do, but constrained by what they perceive is feasible to do. There can be little doubt that this is an accurate but gaunt depiction of decision making within appellate courts. The many factors influencing decision making can be listed, even if specific processes of influence are poorly understood. Fleshing out this simple view of the decision-making process will require a great deal of additional research, but, in light of the advances made to date, there is every reason to be optimistic about theoretical progress.

Notes

1. This is not to deny that there are some important areas of public policy in which the Court is relatively uninvolved. For instance, the Court rarely rules on foreign policy and war-related issues (such as the Vietnam War) and of late has not been much involved in setting or reviewing macroeconomic policy.

2. This is not true of other political institutions like Congress—see, for example, Fenno 1978. Nor is it true of all courts below the U.S. Supreme Court—see, for example, Howard 1981; Nardulli, Eisenstein, and Flemming 1988.

3. I shall refer to these as the state supreme courts, even though many state courts of last resort are not known as supreme courts, and even though the supreme courts of New York State are trial courts. For a fairly recent compilation of research on state supreme courts, see Neubauer 1986.

4. As a heuristic device, I will distinguish between micro-level and macro-level throughout this chapter. By *micro-level* I mean analyses of the decision-making behavior of individual judges. By *macro-level* I mean analyses that focus on institutional or environmental factors. The trickiest part of the analysis, and the most important area for future inquiry, concerns processes that cross the micro- and macro-levels.

5. Civil liberties/civil rights cases include those involving criminal procedure, civil rights, the First Amendment, due process, and privacy. Economic disputes include cases involving unions and general economic activity. Segal and Spaeth have defined liberal civil liberties decisions as those (1) favoring persons accused or convicted of a crime, (2) favoring those making a civil liberties or civil rights claim, (3) favoring indigents, (4) favoring Indians, and (5) opposing the government in due process and privacy disputes (Segal and Spaeth 1989, 561). Similarly, liberal economic decisions (1) favor union interests, (2) oppose business interests, (3) oppose employer interests, (4) favor economic competition, (5) favor a finding of liability, (6) favor injured persons, (7) favor indigents, (8) favor small businesses when in conflict with large businesses, (9) favor debtors, (10) favor those who are bankrupt, (11) favor Indian interests, (12) favor environmental protection, (13) favor the interests of economic underdogs, (14) favor consumers, and (15) favor accountability in governmental corruption disputes.

6. Indeed, one surprisingly common response to unwelcome precedents is simply to ignore them (see Johnson 1981)!

7. For an excellent exposition of scaling analysis, see Murphy and Tanenhaus 1972.

8. An important stream of analysis has used personal attributes of judges (such as party affiliation, region of origin) to predict decisions (see Tate 1981). Since background attributes are typically conceptualized as surrogates for judicial values, and since direct measures of values are occasionally now available, I have not addressed that literature in this chapter.

9. Baum (1988) provides an excellent exposition and test of these theories.

10. Most work using psychometric theories conceptualizes the basic ideological space in liberal-conservative terms. It is not essential to do so, however. Moreover, all research recognizes that this space is multidimensional, not unidimensional, although there is some disagreement over the number of dimensions to be included. For a recent analysis using this sort of theory, see Ducat and Dudley 1987.

11. For recent research within the cue theory tradition see Ulmer 1984; Segal and Reedy 1988; Caldeira and Wright 1988.

12. Research within the judicial context has tended to stress this as a limitation associated with the necessity of making large numbers of decisions within a relatively short period of time. Recent work in cognitive psychology suggests that this may be a more general limitation of the human brain.

13. For instance, I have earlier (Gibson 1983) argued:

> Fact "weights" may be generated from [the values of the judge]. Because values are themselves organized, possibly even in an hierarchical fashion, and because cases rarely stimulate only a single value, some sort of prioritization must occur. As judges sort out the relative importance of their values, it becomes possible to assign weights to the facts. These weights reflect the value hierarchy. In addition, a discount factor may be applied to compensate for the relative unreliability of certain facts. (p. 15)

Little empirical research has addressed this complex process.

14. But for a highly imaginative and successful effort to model facts at the level of the trial court, see Hogarth 1971.

15. Baum's (1988) analysis of the U.S. Supreme Court is one of the few efforts to use this theory to explain changes in the aggregate policy output of the high bench.

16. Care must be taken to distinguish between the dimensionality of a single case and the dimensionality of the caseload of the Court. A group of cases can easily represent a variety of values. For example, Spaeth has argued that three dimensions—Freedom, Equality, and New Dealism—are adequate to characterize the issues addressed by the Court (Spaeth 1979, chap. 5). The sort of multidimensionality I am addressing here concerns not a group of cases but rather a single case. I simply argue that a particular case may stimulate more than a single dimension of value conflict.

17. One of the most poignant statements of this view came from Justice Blackmun's dissent in 1972 from a ruling invalidating the death penalty. See *Furman v. Georgia,* 408 U.S. 405-406, 410-411 (1972).

18. As Wahlke et al. (1962) noted long ago, there are many dimensions to role orientations. My focus in this chapter is on role orientations that directly affect the decision-making process.

19. Similarly, Ulmer has defined activism as indicated by "the ability of political or non-legal factors to explain variation in voting behavior" (Ulmer 1974, 55; see also Gibson 1977). Jaros and Mendelsohn (1967)

also take as evidence of a "nonactivist" role orientation the inability of extralegal criteria to explain variations in role behavior.

20. Their measure of values is based on newspaper editorials assessing the ideology of each justice at the time of his or her nomination. The behavior data are aggregate votes in civil liberties cases. The two variables are quite strongly related ($R^2 = .64$). Most important for my purposes, there is considerable variability in the degree to which the values predict the behavior of the individual justices. By calculating the squared residuals a measure of predictability for each justice can be constructed. The equation used to create the residuals is $Y_i - \hat{Y}_i$, where $\hat{Y}_i$ is defined as equal to $a + bx_i$. Since the term x_i represents the values of the justices (and a is simply a constant that is a statistical adjustment), the $\hat{Y}_i$ term indicates the decisions predicted if values perfectly determined behavior. Thus, the difference between Y_i and $\hat{Y}_i$ indicates the deviation of observed voting behavior from the behavior expected on the basis of attitude alone. The signs of the residuals must be removed in order to create a measure of predictability because it does not matter whether the behavior is more or less liberal than is predicted on the basis of the justice's values. Thus, the measure of restraintism is simply the absolute value of the residuals resulting from regressing votes on the Segal and Cover measure of attitudes. Small residuals indicate that the votes are highly predictable and are thus a sign of activism, while large residuals indicate restraintism. For simplicity I have not followed the practice of Segal and Cover of distinguishing Rehnquist as an associate justice and as chief justice. Thus, the number of cases available for analysis is seventeen. For a discussion of the measurement issues involved with the index, see Gibson and Wenzel 1989.

21. Although it should be noted that the Court occasionally decides issues or points of law that are not technically before the Court. Ulmer (1982) terms this issue fluidity.

22. The alert reader will note the potential connection here to role theory. For an analysis of *representational* role orientations and their impact on judicial decision making, see Gibson 1980.

23. Some important qualifications to this assertion are summarized best in Casper 1976. See also Adamany 1973 and Lasser 1985.

24. For an excellent example of a study that accomplishes this in the legislative context, see Kirkpatrick and McLemore 1977.

References

Adamany, David W. 1973. Legitimacy, realigning elections, and the Supreme Court. *Wisconsin Law Review* 1973:790-846.

Barnum, David G. 1985. The Supreme Court and public opinion: Judicial decision-making in the post-New Deal period. *Journal of Politics* 47:652-666.

Baum, Lawrence. 1988. Measuring policy change in the U.S. Supreme Court. *American Political Science Review* 82:905-912.

Becker, Theodore. 1966. A survey study of Hawaiian judges: The effect on decisions of judicial role variations. *American Political Science Review* 60:677-680.

Brigham, John. 1978. *Constitutional language: An interpretation of judicial decision*. Westport, Conn.: Greenwood Press.

Caldeira, Gregory A., and John R. Wright. 1988. Organized interests and agenda-setting in the U.S. Supreme Court. *American Political Science Review* 82:1109-1128.

Casper, Jonathan D. 1976. The Supreme Court and national policy making. *American Political Science Review* 70:50-63.

Dahl, Robert A. 1957. Decision-making in a democracy: The Supreme Court as a national policy-maker. *Journal of Public Law* 6:279-295.

Danelski, David J. 1960. The influence of the chief justice in the decision process of the Supreme Court. Paper delivered at the annual meeting of the American Political Science Association, Washington, D.C.

_____. 1966. Values as variables in judicial decision-making: Notes toward a theory. *Vanderbilt Law Review* 19:721-740.

Dubois, Philip L. 1988. The illusion of judicial consensus revisited: Partisan conflict on an intermediate state court of appeals. *American Journal of Political Science* 32:946-967.

Ducat, Craig R., and Robert L. Dudley. 1987. Dimensions underlying economic policymaking in the early and later Burger Courts. *Journal of Politics* 49:521-539.

Epstein, Lee. 1985. *Conservatives in court*. Knoxville: University of Tennessee Press.

Fenno, Richard F., Jr. 1978. *Home style: House members in their districts*. Boston: Little, Brown.

Gibson, James L. 1977. Discriminant functions, role orientations and judicial behavior: Theoretical and methodological linkages. *Journal of Politics* 39:984-1007.

_____. 1978. Judges' role orientations, attitudes, and decisions: An interactive model. *American Political Science Review* 72:911-924.

_____. 1980. Environmental constraints on the behavior of judges: A representational model of judicial decision making. *Law and Society Review* 14:343-370.

_____. 1981. Personality and elite political behavior: The influence of self esteem on judicial decision-making. *Journal of Politics* 43:104-125.

_____. 1983. From simplicity to complexity: The development of theory in the study of judicial behavior. *Political Behavior* 5:7-49.

Gibson, James L., and James P. Wenzel. 1989. Models of decision making in the U.S. Supreme Court. Unpublished paper. Houston, Texas: University of Houston.

Grossman, Joel B. 1962. Role playing and the analysis of judicial behavior: The case of Mr. Justice Frankfurter. *Journal of Public Law* 11:285-309.

Hall, Melinda Gann, and Paul Brace. 1988. Institutional arrangements and dissent in state supreme courts: A pooled cross sectional time series analysis. Paper presented at the annual meeting of the Western Political Science Association, San Francisco, March 10-12.

Halpern, Stephen C., and Charles M. Lamb, eds. 1982. *Supreme Court activism and restraint.* Lexington, Mass.: Lexington Books.

Heck, Edward V., and Melinda Gann Hall. 1981. Bloc voting and the freshman justice revisited. *Journal of Politics* 43:852-860.

Hogarth, John. 1971. *Sentencing as a human process.* Toronto: University of Toronto Press.

Howard, J. Woodford, Jr. 1977. Role perceptions and behavior in three U.S. courts of appeals. *Journal of Politics* 39:916-938.

_____. 1981. *Courts of appeals in the federal judicial system: A study of the Second, Fifth, and District of Columbia Circuits.* Princeton: Princeton University Press.

Jaros, Dean, and Robert Mendelsohn. 1967. The judicial role and sentencing behavior. *Midwest Journal of Political Science* 11:471-488.

Johnson, Charles A. 1981. Personnel change and policy change in the U.S. Supreme Court. *Social Science Quarterly* 62:751-758.

Kirkpatrick, Samuel A., and Lelan McLemore. 1977. Perceptual and affective components of legislative norms: A social-psychological analysis of congruity. *Journal of Politics* 39:685-711.

Lasser, William. 1985. The Supreme Court in periods of critical realignment. *Journal of Politics* 47:1174-1189.

Marshall, Thomas R. 1989. *Public opinion and the Supreme Court.* Boston: Unwin Hyman.

Murphy, Walter F. 1964. *Elements of judicial strategy.* Chicago: University of Chicago Press.

Murphy, Walter F., and Joseph Tanenhaus. 1972. *The study of public law.* New York: Random House.

Nardulli, Peter F., James Eisenstein, and Roy B. Flemming. 1988. *Tenor of justice: Criminal courts and the guilty plea process.* Urbana: University of Illinois Press.

Neubauer, David W. 1986. Research on state supreme courts: A bibliography. Paper presented at the annual meeting of the American Political Science Association, Washington, D.C., August 28-31.

O'Connor, Karen. 1980. *Women's organizations' use of the courts.* Lexington, Mass.: Lexington Books.

O'Connor, Karen, and Lee Epstein. 1983. The rise of conservative interest group litigation. *Journal of Politics* 45:479-489.

Pritchett, C. Herman. 1948. *The Roosevelt Court: A study in judicial politics and values, 1937-1947.* New York: Macmillan.

Scheb, John M., and Lee W. Ailshie. 1985. Justice Sandra Day O'Connor and the "freshman effect." *Judicature* 69:9-12.

Schubert, Glendon. 1965. *The judicial mind: Attitudes and ideologies of Supreme Court justices, 1946-1963.* Evanston, Ill.: Northwestern University Press.

_____. 1974. *The judicial mind revisited: Psychometric analysis of Supreme Court ideology.* New York: Oxford University Press.

Segal, Jeffrey A. 1984. Predicting Supreme Court cases probabilistically: The search and seizure cases, 1962-1981. *American Political Science Review* 78:891-900.

_____. 1986. Supreme Court justices as human decision makers: An individual-level analysis of the search and seizure cases. *Journal of Politics* 48:938-955.

Segal, Jeffrey A., and Albert D. Cover. 1989. Ideological values and the votes of U.S. Supreme Court justices. *American Political Science Review* 83:557-564.

Segal, Jeffrey A., and Cheryl D. Reedy. 1988. The Supreme Court and sex discrimination: The role of the solicitor general. *Western Political Quarterly* 41:553-568.

Segal, Jeffrey A., and Harold J. Spaeth. 1989. Decisional trends on the Warren and Burger Courts: Results from the Supreme Court Data Base Project. *Judicature* 73:103-107.

Smith, Rogers M. 1988. Political jurisprudence, the "new institutionalism," and the future of public law. *American Political Science Review* 82:89-108.

Spaeth, Harold J. 1979. *Supreme Court policy making: Explanation and prediction.* San Francisco: W. H. Freeman.

Tate, Neal C. 1981. Personal attribute models of the voting behavior of U.S. Supreme Court justices: Liberalism in civil liberties and economics decisions, 1946-1970. *American Political Science Review* 75:355-367.

Ulmer, S. Sidney. 1971a. *Courts as small and not so small groups.* New York: General Learning Press.

_____. 1971b. Earl Warren and the *Brown* decision. *Journal of Politics* 33:689-702.

_____. 1974. Dimensionality and change in judicial behavior. In *Mathematical applications in political science,* ed. James F. Herndon and Joseph L. Bernd. Charlottesville, Va.: University Press of Virginia, pp. 40-67.

_____. 1978. Selecting cases for Supreme Court review: An underdog model. *American Political Science Review* 72:902-910.

_____. 1982. Issue fluidity in the U.S. Supreme Court: A conceptual analysis. In *Supreme Court activism and restraint,* ed. Stephen C. Halpern and Charles M. Lamb. Lexington, Mass.: Lexington Books, pp. 319-350.

_____. 1984. The Supreme Court's certiorari decisions: Conflict as a predictive variable. *American Political Science Review* 78:901-911.

Vines, Kenneth N. 1969. The judicial role in the American states: An exploration. In *Frontiers of judicial research,* ed. Joel Grossman and Joseph Tanenhaus. New York: Wiley.

Wahlke, John C., Eulau Heinz, William Buchanan, and LeRoy C. Ferguson. 1962. *The legislative systems.* New York: Wiley.

Walker, Thomas G., Lee Epstein, and William J. Dixon. 1988. On the mysterious demise of consensual norms in the United States Supreme Court. *Journal of Politics* 50:361-389.

Part IV

COURTS AND EXTERNAL PRESSURES

Public opinion being what it now is, few will protest the conviction of these Communist petitioners. There is hope, however, that in calmer times, when present pressures, passions, and fears subside, this or some later Court will restore the First Amendment liberties to the high preferred place where they belong in a free society.

—Justice Hugo Black
Dissenting in *Dennis v. U.S.* (1951)

The five chapters of Part IV assess the relationship between courts and environmental forces in a very broad sense. The authors present a variety of perspectives on how the world outside of the courtroom is extremely important to the work of courts. External pressures are significant for understanding the types of claims brought to the judiciary, the individuals, groups, or governments that mobilize the law. In addition, such pressures may be important for understanding the types of policies handed down by courts (Part II) as well as the exercise of judicial choice (Part III).

That courts are subject to pressures and demands from their environment is perhaps a pedestrian notion. Yet their function at the state and federal levels is to serve as one of the arenas for the resolution of societal conflict. Social scientists are interested in determining whether Justice Black's prophetic comments are the exception or the rule. Do judges make certain decisions because of the winds of public opinion? Do judges pay particular attention to whether a case is brought by an individual as opposed to an interest group? How can we come to understand the sources and impact of societal conflict on judicial agendas and decision making?

These are important questions, especially with respect to the impact of environmental forces on judicial decisions. In Chapter 11, Wayne McIntosh examines the connections among broad, long-term socioeconomic change, societal conflict, and court agendas. The chapter provides insight into the external forces that precipitate societal conflict and the implications for courts.

Various elements of the political system have, or attempt to have, an impact on judicial activities. Three chapters examine several of these elements: public opinion, interest groups, and legislative and executive governmental agencies. Gregory A. Caldeira (Chapter 12) pursues the possible impact of public opinion on courts. In addition, he explores public support for courts and how court decisions may affect public opinion.

The chapters by Lee Epstein (Chapter 13) and Jeffrey Segal (Chapter 14) turn to an investigation of the relationship between political actors and the courts. Epstein focuses on courts and interest groups, while Segal examines courts, legislatures, and executives. Each addresses such important questions as: What influence, if any, do interest groups and governmental agencies have on the setting of court agendas? What is their impact on the types of policies and the substance of those judicial policies? And of what influence are external political institutions on the choices made by judges as they attempt to respond to external demands for change or no change?

The courts are also affected by the demand for their decision-making services and by society's determination of what criminal and civil proceedings must be resolved by the courts. Issues concerning such demands often fall to those scholars interested in the pressures of caseloads on courts. William McLauchlan concludes Part IV with a chapter on the caseloads of courts. This chapter (15) discusses the small but growing literature in this area and offers insights into several issues, including the problems surrounding the definition of *caseload*. McLauchlan also points out that it is important to consider differences in the types of cases and the types of courts when discussing caseload.

The five chapters in this part of *American Courts* speak to the reality that judicial institutions do not exist apart from their environment. They are political institutions subject to the same pressures as are other political institutions. Courts are also contributors to political dialogue and to public policy-making processes. The essential questions, therefore, are: What is the character of those relationships, and what factors aid in understanding variations in the relationships?

11. COURTS AND SOCIOECONOMIC CHANGE

Wayne V. McIntosh

This chapter addresses the relationship between courts and the society in which they operate. In what capacities do courts serve their communities as the social and economic mix changes, perhaps even lurches haltingly by stops and starts through various phases? Do they facilitate such changes? Do they serve to mitigate the effects of change? Or are they entirely neutral and passive institutions whose doors are open to whichever parties can gain access to them and for whatever purposes those parties are pursuing?

The study of social change and law has a rich tradition, tracing its roots to nineteenth-century social theory (including Maine 1866; Durkheim 1893/1966; Weber 1904-1905/1958; Marx 1911), and it has attracted the interest of a wide and multidisciplinary group of scholars.[1] In this chapter I shall take a broad look at the place of socioeconomic change within traditional theories of courts, assess our current understanding of these phenomena, and hypothesize about where we are headed in order to further our understanding of courts and the larger environment. Before moving to a discussion of theories and current research effort, we must first consider the question of what is meant by the concepts socioeconomic change and court.

What Is the Research Target?

A variety of issues involved in this area of inquiry divides researchers, and we can break them into two categories. First, what constitutes socioeconomic change? It is clear that few communities remain stagnant for any length of time. Change occurs both gradually, almost unnoticeably, and rapidly in deep-rooted and wide-scale transformations. For the investigator this presents a problem regarding what indicators or indices of socioeconomic change may be useful and reliable measures.

For example, industrialization is a process to which researchers often refer as a source of social change. All aspects of life—social, economic, political—are transformed. Each individual's expectations and aspirations, as well as each person's nexus of relationships, are completely restructured as agrarianism gives way to the forces of industry.[2] Few would argue otherwise. However, it is a nontrivial matter to decide upon empirical observations that will capture accurately the process of industrialization. Moreover, to study social change requires a longitudinal framework, and there is no pat answer to the question of what length of time is sufficiently long. Twenty years is clearly not enough. One hundred years is much more appropriate, but data sources become increasingly less reliable as one goes back in time.

Gradual change obviously takes place all the time and is the consequence of a host of different sources, like technological development, economic diversification and growth (or decline), population diversification and growth (or decline), and changes in the state and state institutions, just to name a few commonly cited ones.[3] Based upon this type of conceptualization of social change, a number of investigators have developed an evolution theory, arguing that all communities go through similar stages of development that inevitably lead toward modernization.[4] Others have, instead, focused upon socioeconomic change that occurs in the wake of transformation episodes that shake the foundations of a community, such as war, economic depression, technological revolution, and the massive influx of population.[5]

A second, equally difficult, problem is how to determine the role courts play in this process. An initial question one must address is what constitutes a court. A court can be defined in several quite different ways. First, one can construct an institutional definition, which would include a statutory description or jurisdiction, rules and access costs, associated staff, and other institutional resources. In other words, a researcher invoking this image of a court would be interested in structure (and structural change) and institutional capacity to perform its assigned tasks, and what happens to structure and capacity when socioeconomic change occurs.

A second court conception would encompass court functions, such as conflict management, norm enforcement, resource and value allocation, administration, and enhancement of the state's political stability (see Shapiro 1975, 1981). An investigator taking this approach would be interested in the nature of claims brought to the system, the court's responses to them, and whether either or both of these are contingent upon a particular socioeconomic context.

A third court vision is an instrumental one, focusing upon how and for what purposes a court is used by members of the community. Under this conception, the investigator would look at the level and mixture of claims as demands (including caseload volume, rate of trials, rate of appeals), and would also want to determine which parties are placing demands, against whom, for what reasons, and how effectively (see Grossman, et al. 1982; Wanner 1974, 1975). These demands might be a way of working out political and economic conflict occurring as the macroenvironment undergoes change. Moreover, certain parties may attempt to use the court as part of a strategy to deal with changes taking place or to direct them in some way.

Our conception of what a court is, therefore, is not only important but necessary to developing a set of expectations regarding the role courts play as their host communities undergo socioeconomic change. Moreover, our target for investigation is contingent upon how we visualize what a court is all about. For example, one could examine judges' decisions for trends in doctrinal development and/or their acknowledgment of the social, economic, and political forces at work in the community. This would follow from Roscoe Pound's (1912; see also Cardozo 1921, 1924) notion that judges are influenced by, and must take into account, the world around them. Their decisions are not crafted in an intellectual vacuum.

Alternatively, one could assess phenomena such as caseload composition, the mix or variation in the issues placed on a court's docket, the level of demands placed upon a court (volume of cases or per capita litigation), the constellations of parties who are involved in court actions, who wins and who loses, and the degree to which the court intervenes in its caseload (rate of trials, rate of written opinions in appeals, rate of settlements). Because conflict, and ultimately court cases, are produced by the deterioration of relationships, a court's docket should provide important clues about what is happening in the community it serves. For example, if a court's business is dominated by debt collection litigation, the likelihood is quite high that the local economy is in distress. Moreover, if these cases are predominantly initiated and won by institutional creditors against individual debtors, the researcher has unearthed significant evidence about the court's role and how it is utilized to reinforce existing political-economic power relationships within the community.

Another point is division about which set of courts warrants attention. The most obvious place to start is with the U.S. Supreme Court and other appeals courts, whose decisions attain the highest degree of visibility, have singular and wide-ranging impact, and lay out principles, guidelines, or benchmarks to which important sectors of the community refer in conducting their business. Perhaps because of these reasons, our appeals courts have been the most studied.[6] Much of the effort in this field has attempted to connect doctrinal development with changes in the larger society.[7]

More recently, a few scholars have shifted gears somewhat to look at things other than doctrine and appeals courts other than the highest one. For example, caseflow and change in the mix of issues have been studied in several U.S. courts of appeals (Baum, Goldman, and Sarat 1982). The investigators in this instance selected three geographically and economically distinct circuits under the expectation that the business conducted by the courts would vary according to differences observable in their respective jurisdictions. Similarly, another research team has examined a sample of sixteen state supreme courts (Kagan et al. 1977), expecting to find common shifts occurring in state litigation that would reflect the most important problems of particular eras over a hundred-year time spread (1870-1970). In addition, they also predicted that structural differences among state court systems would influence the flow of litigation. In general, most of the research effort at the appellate level finds that both doctrinal development and the amalgamation of cases flowing through the system reflect major and recognized changes in the macroenvironment. Indeed, Kagan et al. note that

> the automotive society is reflected in the rise of personal-injury cases stemming from automobile accidents. The number of debt-collection cases in state supreme courts has been sensitive to the rate of business failures and, in the last 30 years, to economic and institutional changes that have put credit on a sounder, less volatile footing. . . . Even that tiny proportion of litigation that reaches state supreme courts reflects social and economic change; the legal system, even at the apex of the judicial system, must reflect what is going on in society. (1977, 153)[8]

Less obvious but equally important are the trial courts that handle the overwhelming majority of all the cases that are filed, are on the front line in facing conflicts arising in a community, and are where pragmatic solutions (rather than abstract principles) must be forged. Indeed, a strong case could be made that we omit the most significant parts of the courts and socioeconomic change saga if the trial courts are ignored. By gazing only at the appeals courts, we might miss a broad and important part of the picture. Only a small fraction of cases, and usually self-selected from the trial level, are subsequently appealed. Moreover, appeals court activities are another step removed from the political-economic environment. In essence, they are insulated from direct contact by the institutional, spatial, and time buffer provided by the set of front-line trial courts.

It is also unclear whether appellate level courts render decisions that are any more definitive and final than do courts whose decisions they review. The literature is full of accounts of appellate court failure to fashion policy with which target populations will properly comply (for example, Johnson and Canon 1984). A number of studies have uncovered a range of compliance problems. Indeed, Supreme Court policies with regard to rights of criminal defendants (Skolnick 1974), prayer in public schools (Muir 1973), and racial desegregation (Peltason 1961; Hochschild 1984), to name only three, have met serious resistance. Finally, nearly all litigation is initiated in the trial courts, and the vast majority of it travels no farther. In fact, much of it ends even before a trial judge has an opportunity to intervene, with the parties and their lawyers determining the outcomes.

For these and other reasons, our trial courts (especially at the state level) have come under greater scrutiny in the last fifteen years, and most of this chapter will be devoted to this research. Before doing so, however, we must first establish and understand the tradition of this field of research and the most important theoretical statements and expectations arising from it.

Traditional Perspectives

The best way to describe the tradition of this field of inquiry is the sociology of law. The general perspective is that law reflects its society. We can readily attribute the founding of this school of thought to Emile Durkheim (for example, 1897/1951, 1893/1966, 1895/1982; Lukes and Scull 1983), a nineteenth-century sociologist who studied a range of social institutions and behaviors and influenced many succeeding generations of scholars. Durkheim's principal idea was that a society can be studied as a single living organism, and the collective behavior of the people in a society characterize the behavior of that society. Hence, a particular community is characterized by a unique culture and certain behavioral tendencies that set it apart from others. A community's behavior can be measured through crime rates, suicide rates, unemployment rates, litigation rates, and so on—and in the Durkheimian tradition, scholars observe that communities in fact do behave quite differently from one another. According to this theoretical perspective, the law and legal institutions directly reflect their host community, and social change inevitably produces change in the law and the business conducted by courts. Courts are influenced by socioeconomic change, therefore, simply as a matter of course.

Another line of argument has roots in the work of Max Weber, another nineteenth-century grand social theorist (see, for example, Weber 1947, 1904-1905/1958; Rheinstein 1954). Weber was concerned about why certain countries had developed diverse economies and were engaged in industrialization while others were not. Upon reflection, Weber concluded that law and legal institutions could serve as agents of change. Once created, courts become semi-autonomous from their community, not merely reflections of them, and their presence has consequences for how people act. The law, and courts by extension, is a purposive institution. It provides a means for formalizing rules that serve as guides in structuring activities and rationalizing relationships throughout a society. This is particularly important in promoting economic growth, because as growth (like industrialization) occurs the world becomes geometrically more complex. Each individual actor becomes involved in an increasingly complex web of interactions and relationships. In order to minimize risks and to maximize predictability, such a community requires a set of authoritative, formal, and rational institutions to which it can refer its conflicts.

A third major theoretical framework and set of expectations was influenced and informed by the writings of Karl Marx, another nineteenth-century scholar interested in uncovering the grand patterns of social and economic development.[9] In Marx's perspective, the primary source of political conflict derives from economic class distinctions which are readily observable in all societies. Within this framework law plays a mediating role between economic classes, and legal institutions (courts) are focal points for legitimization of and challenge to the distribution of political power among classes based upon economic relationships.[10] A variant on this central theme is that courts support the dominant social and economic interests and power structures. Law is seen, then, as a way of influencing behavior in preferred directions and structuring activities in support of the existing governing system. Some have argued that law has been used as a way to suppress unrest in the face of important social or economic changes, as an instrument protective of the status quo and the existing power structure (for example, Horwitz 1977; Kairys 1982; Balbus 1973; Auerbach 1976). Precedent-based decision theory followed by judges not only makes law predictable in situations as they arise, without referring everything to courts, but also serves to insulate the system of law from societal changes. The law, many believed, was and should be autonomous, representing and promoting a social order based upon longstanding principles of fair play.

A wide variety of research has adopted this set of assumptions to investigate and make sense of the relationship between the legal system and broad social change. For example, some have noted that it is the economically powerful entities in our society that not only dominate the agenda of the U.S. Supreme Court but also use the system to engineer legal doctrine that suits their interests (Twiss 1942; Llewellyn 1925). Other investigators have uncovered a similar state of affairs in a variety of the nation's trial courts (Galanter 1974; Stookey 1986). Still others marshal evidence to indicate that the criminal law and delivery of sanctions have a decidedly economic class bias (Balbus 1973; Gorecki 1983; Spitzer 1982, 1983).

Current Research: A General Assessment

As I noted earlier, the body of literature that attempts to place courts in a dynamic historical framework is growing. Much of it accepts the notion that law and legal behavior are heavily influenced by the sweep of environmental conditions. The general idea is that there is a broad evolutionary relationship between law and society that produces a gradual enhancement of courts as the host community develops and modernizes. The act of litigating has been adopted by an increasing number of investigators as a useful indicator of this phenomenon. Thus, a rise in litigation activities suggests that the courts' position in the community has been enhanced. It also suggests that the court system has achieved a high degree of relevance to community life. This would mean that more parties are referring their conflicts there, and that courts have proportionately greater input and intervention in deciding how significant social, economic, and political divisions are resolved. Similarly, a drop in litigation would mean that the courts' role in the community has diminished. In fact, the original argument suggests that there is a linear correlation between litigation and social development. By the mid-1970s a number of observers began to argue that the relationship was more nearly curvilinear, with litigation leveling off or even declining at some point in the developmental history of a community. Figure 11-1 depicts graphically what this prediction looks like. One group, showing its Durkheimian roots, bases its argument largely on anthropological and sociological research regarding disputing behavior and relationship structures (see Sarat and Grossman 1975). Another grounds its expectation on structural-functional analyses of institutions and institutional roles (see Friedman and Percival 1976); a clear Weberian influence is in evidence here. A third perspective (most noticeably influenced by Durkheim and Marx) views litigation as a form of political behavior that may be influenced by the larger political-economic environment. Each of these three is discussed more thoroughly in the paragraphs that follow.

The literature is in basic agreement concerning the effects of early societal development. The quality of life and the face-to-face relationships among members of simple communities promote informal methods of dispute management (Abel 1974; Felstiner 1974). Industrial development, with its correspondingly more complex social and economic interactions, produces greater communal need for a consistent system of legal relationships and legally defined rights. Thus the law and legal institutions become increasingly necessary and relevant to both the day-to-day and long-range activities in an industrializing

Figure 11-1 Generally Accepted Relationship between Litigation and Socioeconomic Development

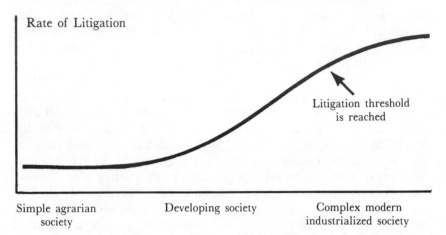

Rate of Litigation

Litigation threshold
is reached

Simple agrarian   Developing society   Complex modern
    society   industrialized society

Socioeconomic Development

community. In addition, the act of invoking law to manage conflict becomes more common. "According to this theory," Sarat and Grossman (1975) state, "as the complexity, differentiation, and scale of a society increase, reliance on courts and other formal-public adjudicators also increases" (p. 1209).

Observers who have examined this proposition empirically support the idea that legal activity and social development are related and that their relationship is not a linear one. That is, the rate of litigation increases to some threshold level, at which point it stabilizes or even declines (Sarat and Grossman 1975). This is true despite continued escalation in the number of legal transactions, such as the formation of corporations or the signing of contractual agreements.

It seems likely that as a society becomes more urban and industrial, social and economic connections that bind people together are more formal, strictly functional, and less personal. The social grouping becomes less a community of relatives, friends, and associates and more nearly a "community of strangers" (see, for example, Merry 1981). Within such a context, informal ways of dealing with conflict break down, and people turn more frequently to the courts for help. At some point, however, "social relationships may become so much more complex and specialized that generalized courts no longer have the expertise, and hence the legitimacy, to intervene effectively" (Sarat and Grossman 1975, 1210). People with specialized problems do not trust generalist judges to be sensitive to their particular status and milieu, and they naturally seek out some alternative.

Societal development, differentiation, and complexity thus affect the stability and structure of networks among and between individuals and organizations. Significant changes in social context tend to produce unstable social and economic relationships and, therefore, lead to the breakdown of informal institutions of conflict management. These changes, in turn, create higher demand for legality and greater need for court services. As a result, litigation escalates. Litigiousness, though, is considered characteristic of communities experiencing the stress of fast-paced development. A litigation threshold is reached when a sufficient number of private parties engaged in ongoing symbiotic relationships avoid litigation, exercising other options to achieve the desired results. This is especially true for people engaged in business relations. Litigation can be counterproductive to their mutual interests, and many prefer specialized arbitration or mediation (see Macaulay 1963; Mentschikoff 1965; Bossy 1983).

An alternate argument states that litigiousness is a function of the availability of judicial resources. It is a perspective based largely upon Weberian notions of organizational rationalization. In particular, Lawrence M. Friedman and Robert V. Percival (1976) suggest that the rate of litigation should exhibit curvilinear behavior over time because the costs associated with going to court have increased prohibitively. According to this view, the demand for court services rises as a society develops; but due to the increased demands, the courts become overburdened and less available to a greater number of potential litigants. Laws and procedural rules become complex and confusing to the lay public. The per capita number of judges is allowed to decrease, and it takes longer to process cases. Dollar costs associated with going to court rise automatically with information costs and time delays. Thus the price of litigating a dispute affects not only the ability of people to enter the court system but also the attractiveness of litigation as an option. That is, high costs produce barriers that make the system literally unavailable to those parties who cannot marshal the necessary resources and unattractive to many of those who can. This also affects the courts' functions. In a developed community a court is no longer a place where people turn to have serious conflicts resolved (but see Lempert 1978). They learn to resolve their problems without the court's help, and the court becomes essentially an administrative forum, where solutions to problems derived elsewhere are merely given an authoritative stamp of approval. Hence most civil cases are negotiated out of court, and the great majority of criminal cases are plea bargained (see, for example, Skolnick 1974; Chayes 1976).

A third line of argument sees a court as one among many points of popular access to government and activity in court as political activity. Indeed, much litigation actually represents demand for definition of the current meaning of public policies, calling for remedies such as a reaffirmation or change of community norms, cessation or performance of some government or private activity, redistribution of values and resources, recognition of rights and obligations, or adjustment in established balances of power between competing interests. Thus litigation is inevitably a political exercise, requiring each party to marshal available resources and to manipulate the legal system in order to create strategic advantages and to protect a set of interests vis-à-vis the opposition (Zemans 1983; Galanter 1974; Scheingold 1974). Winning and losing in court should reveal which interests are winning and losing elsewhere in the social-political system. Litigation ought to reflect the power balances existing in the larger community. Research at all court levels reinforces these expectations. Indeed, it is the resource-rich and politically powerful parties who are most visible and most persuasive at the U.S. Supreme Court during eras of intense nationwide socioeconomic change and dislocation (Twiss 1942; Gawalt 1984; and see Gates 1987; Dahl 1957). Generally speaking, such parties use the court to protect their interests in the wake of changes taking place around them. Such parties also have the means and wherewithal to make the system work to their advantage, utilizing any and all courts to harness the forces of more gradual and long-run socioeconomic change. Indeed, Marc Galanter (1974) theorizes that the "haves" will ultimately win out over the less powerful "have nots," because they employ the courts on an ongoing basis to ensure this result.[11]

Current Research: Some Specifics

In my own research, focusing upon civil case litigation and flow in a state trial court in St. Louis, I have found some merit in all of these approaches. However, none standing alone provides an adequate framework for appraising the relationships between our courts and socioeconomic change. For example, environmental change clearly alters the character of conflict occurring in the community, and the litigation of a particular historical era reflects the problems and conflicts generated from existing conditions.

Changes in Issues

Broadly speaking, the rapid development phase of industrialization and the early period of urban growth in St. Louis (that is, the first half of the nineteenth century), produced high rates of market-oriented litigation. Nearly all cases brought into court involved market transactions and economic matters, such as debt collection, property and land boundary disputes, and commercial contract issues. In contrast, greater emphasis upon individuals, individual rights, and social welfare issues mark the postindustrial era. Indeed, the more recent docket is dominated by cases involving personal injury and dignitary rights of individuals and by domestic relations.[12]

When the population boom struck in the early and mid-1800s, land became a scarce and more valuable commodity, creating a need that had not previously existed. Clearer definition of property boundaries and property rights became a paramount individual and collective concern, and property litigation crowded the court. In addition, in the early and mid-nineteenth century, manufacturing, trading, and merchandizing activities developed at an unheard-of pace. This development produced greater economic diversity and complexity, as well as new market dependencies, coalitions, and competitions. As a consequence, questions concerning contractual rights and obligations poured into the court in unprecedented numbers.

Shortly after the turn of the twentieth century, the local economy moved into another phase, resulting in extensive dislocation in the web of existing relationships. The altered conditions produced a fresh menu of problems, many of which produced litigation, creating a new generation of demands upon the legal system. Labor intensity in the manufacturing industries peaked with the birth of automation. Railroads and other heavy industries experienced a decline in political clout; with the decline, they also lost many government protections against tort liability. Moreover, the invention of the automobile ushered in a new age in transportation. The quake from these economic and political changes and technological innovations produced new relationship sets and magnified questions of communal obligation regarding the impact of machines on individuals. Tort litigation (especially involving rail, industrial, and auto accidents) escalated during this era of transformation. Finally, the period following the Great Depression of the 1930s saw still another transition. The Industrial Revolution had clearly run its course, and the service sector was quickly expanding. The national political agenda had shifted toward consideration of certain perceived human costs of market decisions and social welfare issues and reforms. Divorce and automobile accident litigation rose significantly. Such claims, as issues, are symptomatic of the uncertainties and risks confronting people in the postindustrial environment. Deteriorating domestic relationships reflect the stress felt by people attempting to cope with a competitive and impersonal world over which they exercise minimal and imperfect control. Highway injuries represent random events, unpredicted meetings between total strangers, which also occur in an impersonal environment where people have minimal control over what happens.

The prominent appearance of cases in each category, then, is associated with a particular phase of the societal development process. In fact, litigation in each field has a distinct life cycle, exhibiting similar patterns of growth and decline over a period of years.[13] Each fundamental change disrupts the normal flow of activity, producing new realities to be governed by anachronistic and outmoded custom and legal convention. Routines, habits, observances, and rules must be realigned in congruence with the renovated social conditions. Litigation is part of the adaptation process.

Restructuring Courts

There are also several indications that during different time periods the court has been restructured on a more rationalized model, becoming considerably less accessible to the average potential litigant and performing much more routine administrative tasks. During the first half of the nineteenth century, there was no central location or formal court facilities. In order to facilitate access, the judges and lawyers rode the circuit, literally holding court sessions in saloons and inns at various locations around the district. In fact, these sessions served as a source of popular entertainment; the arrival of the court entourage usually drew a crowd of spectators filled with anticipation.[14] No doubt this atmosphere was less intimidating to potential litigants than the imposing and impersonal, formalized yet chaotic air of the twentieth-century courthouse. Moreover, the rate of trials has steadily declined. Although at one time trial and direct judicial intervention in the case resolution process was quite common, in more recent times this has become rather unusual. The vast majority of cases are resolved by the parties and their lawyers, and judicial intervention ordinarily consists of granting approval of private settlements.[15]

Characteristics of Litigants

Characteristics of litigants are important in determining outcomes. Analysis of litigation in St. Louis over a 150-year period indicates that particular classes of plaintiffs and defendants have established unmistakable track records in court. For example, individual plaintiffs and defendants are comparatively unsuccessful—they lose much more often than they win—suggesting that their status is perennially weak. Wholesale and retail merchants, on the other hand, are more consistently successful, both as plaintiff and as defendant. Transportation and manufacturing companies appear to behave aggressively as litigants and consistently realize profitable results. Although the overall trend is away from trial, with the vast majority of all cases now negotiated well before reaching that stage, these industrial entities, likely to wield considerable influence in political and economic markets, maintain a significant presence in the trial process, and they are disproportionately visible in appeals as well.

James Willard Hurst (1950, 1979, 1982) argues that, given the overlap between the lawmaking process and other markets, we should expect to find such parties very much involved in the judicial system at any given time (also see, for example, Twiss 1942; Horwitz 1977; Llewellyn 1925; Epstein 1985). The evidence here strongly suggests that transportation and manufacturing companies include a number of haves who are not risk averse,[16] but who are interested in using the courts to engineer advances in the law to promote their interests in the current socioeconomic environment.

Limitations and Open Questions

One of the primary limitations of this field of inquiry is that individual cases are deemphasized. Uniqueness is sacrificed in the search for general trends and higher order patterns of decisions and activities. Certainly each court action has its unique aspects; each has a history that perhaps entails a most interesting story of many stages of give and take. The evolution of conflict, the idiosyncratic paths that ultimately lead plaintiffs and defendants to the courthouse, are lost in this kind of research. Clearly, these are important activities to understand.

However, unless a case achieves celebrity status—that is, is extremely unusual—there is no way to reconstruct its history. It is "ordinary" cases that constitute the great mass of courts' business (see Kritzer 1985), and our only evidence regarding their nature is that which appears in the court records. Excluded altogether are the many potentially litigable conflicts that are never logged because the parties find some other means to resolve them.

Nonetheless, there is merit in searching for general trends. For example, when a community witnesses an increase (or decline) in some class of activity, this certainly represents an important community-level behavior that is symptomatic of a phenomenon that extends well beyond the particular individuals involved, no matter how interesting their unique stories might be. This is true when the crime rate escalates. Granted, this would involve many different types of criminal activities and a wide variety of motivations among the lawbreakers. However, an escalated crime rate is also evidence that something more general, more systemic, is happening in the community. A similar argument can be constructed in the event of increases in such indices as the unemployment rate, the suicide rate, and the rate of heart attacks, or when the turnout in presidential elections declines. Such trends represent responses to underlying socioeconomic conditions.

Virtually unexplored are commonalities in many of our community-level symptomatic behavioral trends and patterns. My preliminary research on this question reveals considerable coincidence in a number of such phenomena (Colella and McIntosh 1988). Indeed, homicide, suicide, voter turnout, and litigation trends track very closely in St. Louis history, all increasing and decreasing in specific and overlapping eras. Perhaps these (and others) actually represent varying aspects of a common reaction to socioeconomic change.

These are questions for which we simply do not have adequate answers. The basis for such a line of inquiry draws upon all three of the intellectual traditions I identified earlier. It may be the case that increasing rates of litigation are symptomatic of stress occurring throughout the community. When political-economic conditions create severe dislocations in people's lives and in their expectations for living together, the stress will inevitably be expressed through avenues that people find accessible to them. No doubt Durkheim and his followers would be interested in exploring the similarities and differences among various stress-induced behaviors. What do litigation, suicide, and political activity have in common? How are they different? Is the action directed inwardly (as is the case with many suicides), or is it directed at others (as in litigation)?

A structural approach, using a Weberian framework, leads to a different set of unanswered questions. A rise in the rate of litigation in any particular area (tort law, for example) may reflect a growing need among the population (or at least some subset of the population) to make a disorderly and chaotic world seem more rational and predictable. A similar argument could be constructed to help explain significant rises in the homicide rate. Periods of social change, then, produce demand for forums that enhance stability. Does there exist among such forums a natural division of labor that is enhanced or exaggerated during intervals of serious macroenvironmental change? Similarly, how are the functions performed by, and hence the functional relationships existing among, courts at different levels affected? How are the market structure of and the functions served by the legal profession influenced by such political-economic change and the sets of demands thus created?

Yet another cluster of questions that deserves further exploration derives from Marxist notions that law plays a mediating role in ongoing class conflict. Class conflict is likely to intensify during periods of intense political-economic change. Indeed, most litigation involves interclass problems (landlords versus tenants, creditors versus debtors, accident victims versus insurance companies, employees versus employers) rather than intraclass disputes. Is the process of litigation and adjudication a dialectical system that produces some sort of synthesis when the status quo (or settled principles) is challenged by antithetical questions arising from unanticipated social conditions? Do courts provide a means for safely channeling class conflict (and for reintegrating those who feel alienated from the community), rather than allowing such forces free reign to be expressed more pervasively in completely dysfunctional (from society's perspective) ways, like homicide and suicide?

Examining any of the sets of questions I have presented in the last section of this chapter would carry us into unfamiliar territory. Placing courts and court-related activity in this light certainly calls for rethinking what our courts are all about and what roles they play in our society. The fact is that our understanding of the relationship between law and social change is far from complete.

Notes

1. Indeed, these connections have been aggressively investigated by historians, economists, anthropologists, sociologists, psychologists, linguists, philosophers, and theorists (see R. Clark 1981). Political scientists joined the effort at a relatively late date.
2. For a variety of perspectives on the issue of social change, see Horwitz 1977; Hunt 1958; Schmookler 1984; Sumner 1940; Huntington 1968; Eisenstadt 1966; Homans 1950.
3. A community is also not immune to influence from external sources, such as changes taking place in geographically adjacent or otherwise connected communities.
4. This framework emphasizes the commonalities in all states. All clearly do not pass through the same developmental phases contemporaneously, but the process is seen as inevitable (see Schwartz and Miller 1964; Friedman 1969; Friedman and Percival 1976; Sarat and Grossman 1975). Explicit in this line of argument is that states are all developing in the same direction, albeit at varying paces and in varying sequence. Most of these studies also assume that this direction of development is a positive phenomenon and represents progress. This assumption, as a few have noted, is nothing more than a Western bias crafted to justify industrial and technological developments and to derogate nonindustrial states as backwater, primitive societies (see Ferrarotti 1985).
5. Research in this vein works from a social crisis theory, arguing that serious events create stress in the environment that completely transforms

a society into something different than before (Stookey 1985, 1986; McIntosh 1983, 1990).

6. In addition, appeals courts provide the easier targets of investigation because their opinions are published, thereby lending themselves to assessment. Until fairly recently, in fact, nearly all scholarship dealing with the relationships between American courts and the macroenvironment focused entirely upon appeals courts, especially the U.S. Supreme Court (for example, Holmes 1909; Pound 1921; Twiss 1942; Miller 1968, 1985).

7. See Note 6. This traditional approach continues to be in vogue today (see Gates 1987).

8. Sensitivity to the surrounding environment is more direct at the trial court level. For discussion of these connections in a variety of state court systems, see McIntosh 1990; Friedman and Percival 1976, 1981; Daniels 1986; Munger 1988.

9. See, for example, Marx 1911. Also see Cain and Hunt 1979; Pashukanis 1978; Collins 1982.

10. A significant and growing school of legal thought takes this as a central theme and point of departure. For a thorough discussion of critical legal studies see Unger 1976, 1986; and Kairys 1982.

11. The process of litigation does seem to offer advantages to those parties who possess a wealth of resources and who engage in litigation as a matter of business. Such parties can make legal conflict excessively costly for lesser opponents, and they can sacrifice some cases in playing a longer range strategy. Litigants with fewer resources, however, have to play it safe, taking a settlement if they can get it. In addition, they are generally unable to engage in follow-up legal actions to ensure continued protection of their interests. Also see Scheingold 1974; Wolfskill 1962; Macaulay 1966; Hurst 1982; Horwitz 1977; Caine 1970; Caplovitz 1974; Wanner 1975.

12. These changes in docket composition seem to be universal across the various state court systems. See, for example, Friedman and Percival 1976; Kagan et al. 1977; Friedman 1983.

13. Others have uncovered similar trends in litigation of different types in varying contexts. See Friedman and Percival 1976; Munger 1988a, 1988b; D. Clark 1981.

14. For a full discussion of the practice of law in early St. Louis, see Bay 1878; English 1947; and compare Konig 1979; Silverman 1981.

15. This trend away from trials and toward negotiation seems to be pervasive. See Friedman and Percival 1976; Daniels 1985; Feeley 1979; Chayes 1976, 1982; D. Clark 1981.

16. Allowing one's case to progress to trial is a risky proposition. Outcomes at that stage of the process are unpredictable, determined by outside parties with no interest at stake. For this reason, most litigants and their lawyers prefer to maintain control over their own fates and work toward some agreeable settlement.

References

Abel, Richard L. 1974. A comparative theory of dispute institutions in society. *Law and Society Review* 8:217-230.

Auerbach, Jerold S. 1976. *Unequal justice: Lawyers and social change in modern America.* New York: Oxford University Press.

Balbus, Isaac D. 1973. *The dialectics of legal repression: Black rebels before the American criminal courts.* New Brunswick, N.J.: Transaction.

Baum, Lawrence, Sheldon Goldman, and Austin Sarat. 1982. The evolution of litigation in the federal courts of appeals, 1895-1975. *Law and Society Review* 16:291-309.

Bay, W. V. N. 1878. *Reminiscences of the bench and bar of Missouri.* St. Louis: F. H. Thomas.

Bossy, John, ed. 1983. *Disputes and settlements: Law and human relations in the west.* Cambridge: Cambridge University Press.

Cain, Maureen, and Alan Hunt, eds. 1979. *Marx and Engels on law.* New York: Academic Press.

Caine, Stanley P. 1970. *The myth of a progressive reform: Railroad regulation in Wisconsin, 1903-1910.* Madison: State Historical Society of Wisconsin.

Caplovitz, David. 1974. *Consumers in trouble: A study of debtors in default.* New York: Free Press.

Cardozo, Benjamin N. 1921. *The nature of the judicial process.* New Haven: Yale University Press.

———. 1924. *The growth of the law.* New Haven: Yale University Press.

Chayes, Abram. 1976. The role of the judge in public law litigation. *Harvard Law Review* 89:1281-1337.

———. 1982. Foreword: Public law litigation and the Burger Court. *Harvard Law Review* 96:1-60.

Clark, David S. 1981. Adjudication to administration: A statistical analysis of federal district courts in the twentieth century. *Southern California Law Review* 55:65-152.

Clark, Robert C. 1981. The interdisciplinary study of legal evolution. *Yale Law Journal* 90:1238-1287.

Colella, Cynthia C., and Wayne V. McIntosh. 1988. The social foundations of litigation. Paper presented at the annual meeting of the Law and Society Association, Vail, Colo., June 9-12.

Collins, Hugh. 1982. *Marxism and law.* New York: Oxford University Press.

Dahl, Robert A. 1957. Decision-making in a democracy: The Supreme Court as a national policy-maker. *Journal of Public Law* 6:279-305.

Daniels, Stephen. 1985. Ladders and bushes: The problem of caseloads and studying court activities over time. *American Bar Foundation Research Journal* 1985:751-795.

———. 1986. Continuity and change in patterns of case handling: A case study of two rural counties. *Law and Society Review* 19:381-420.

Durkheim, Emile. 1897/1951. *Suicide.* New York: Free Press.

———. 1893/1966. *The division of labor in society.* New York: Free Press.

_____. 1895/1982. *The rules of sociological method.* W. D. Hills (trans.) and Steven Lukes (ed.) London: Macmillan.

Eisenstadt, Samuel N. 1966. *Modernization: Protest and change.* Englewood Cliffs, N.J.: Prentice-Hall.

English, William Francis. 1947. *The pioneer lawyer and jurist in Missouri.* Columbia: University of Missouri Press.

Epstein, Lee. 1985. *Conservatives in court.* Knoxville: University of Tennessee Press.

Feeley, Malcolm M. 1979. *The process is the punishment.* New York: Russell Sage Foundation.

Felstiner, William L. F. 1974. Influence of social organization on dispute processing. *Law and Society Review* 9:63-94.

Ferrarotti, Franco. 1985. *The myth of inevitable progress.* Westport, Conn.: Greenwood Press.

Friedman, Lawrence M. 1969. Legal culture and social development. *Law and Society Review* 4:29-45.

_____. 1983. Courts over time: A survey of theories and research. In *Empirical theories about courts*, ed. Keith O. Boyum and Lynn Mather. New York: Longman, pp. 7-50.

Friedman, Lawrence M., and Robert V. Percival. 1976. A tale of two courts: Litigation in Alameda and San Benito Counties. *Law and Society Review* 10:267

_____. 1981. *The roots of justice: Crime and punishment in Alameda County, California, 1870-1919.* Chapel Hill: University of North Carolina Press.

Galanter, Marc. 1974. Why the "haves" come out ahead: Speculations on the limits of legal change. *Law and Society Review* 9:95-160.

Gates, John B. 1987. Partisan realignment, unconstitutional state policies, and the U.S. Supreme Court. *American Journal of Political Science* 31:259-280.

Gawalt, Gerard W. 1984. *The new high priests: Lawyers in post Civil War America.* Westport, Conn.: Greenwood Press.

Gorecki, J. 1983. *Capital punishment: Criminal law and social evolution.* New York: Columbia University Press.

Grossman, Joel B., Herbert M. Kritzer, Kristin Bumiller, Stephen McDougal, Richard Miller, and Austin Sarat. 1982. Dimensions of institutional participation: Who uses the courts and how? *Journal of Politics* 44:86-114.

Hochschild, Jennifer L. 1984. *The new American dilemma: Liberal democracy and school desegregation.* New Haven: Yale University Press.

Holmes, Oliver Wendell. 1909. *The common law.* Boston: Little, Brown.

Homans, George C. 1950. *The human group.* New York: Harcourt Brace.

Horwitz, Morton J. 1977. *The transformation of American law: 1780-1860.* Cambridge, Mass.: Harvard University Press.

Hunt, Robert S. 1958. *Laws and locomotives: The impact of the railroad on Wisconsin law in the nineteenth century.* Madison: State Historical Society of Wisconsin.

Huntington, Samuel P. 1968. *Political order in changing societies.* New Haven: Yale University Press.

Hurst, James Willard. 1950. *The growth of American law: The law makers.* Boston: Little, Brown.

_____. 1979. Old and new dimensions of research in United States legal history. *American Journal of Legal History* 23:1-20.

_____. 1982. *Law and markets in United States history.* Madison: University of Wisconsin Press.

Johnson, Charles A., and Bradley C. Canon. 1984. *Judicial policies: Implementation and impact.* Washington, D.C.: CQ Press.

Kagan, Robert A., Bliss Cartwright, Lawrence M. Friedman, and Stanton Wheeler. 1977. The business of state supreme courts, 1870-1970. *Stanford Law Review* 30:121-156.

Kairys, David, ed. 1982. *The politics of law: A progressive critique.* New York: Pantheon.

Konig, David Thomas. 1979. *Law and society in Puritan Massachusetts, Essex County, 1629-1692.* Chapel Hill: University of North Carolina Press.

Kritzer, Herbert M. 1985. The form of negotiation in ordinary litigation. University of Wisconsin Law School, Dispute Processing Research Program. Working Papers, series 7, no. 2.

Lempert, Richard D. 1978. More tales from two courts: Exploring changes in the "dispute settlement function" of trial courts. *Law and Society Review* 13:91-138.

Llewellyn, Karl N. 1925. The effect of legal institutions upon economics. *American Economic Review* 15:665-683.

Lukes, Steven, and Andrew Scull, eds. 1983. *Durkheim and the law.* New York: St. Martin's.

Macaulay, Stewart. 1963. Non-contractual relations in business. *American Sociological Review* 28:55-67.

_____. 1966. *Law and balance of power: The automobile manufacturers and their dealers.* New York: Russell Sage Foundation.

Maine, Henry Sumner. 1866. *Ancient law: Its connection with the early history of society, and its relation to modern ideas.* London: John Murray.

Marx, Karl. 1911. *Critique of political economy.* Chicago: Charles H. Kerr.

McIntosh, Wayne. 1983. Private use of a public forum: A long-range view of the dispute processing role of courts. *American Political Science Review* 77:991-1010.

_____. 1990. *The appeal of civil law: A political-economic analysis of litigation.* Urbana: University of Illinois Press.

Mentschikoff, Soia. 1965. Commercial arbitration. *Columbia Law Review* 61:846-869.

Merry, Sally Engle. 1981. *Urban danger: Life in a neighborhood of strangers.* Philadelphia: Temple University Press.

Miller, Arthur Selwyn. 1968. *The Supreme Court and American capitalism.* New York: Free Press.

———. 1985. *Politics, democracy, and the Supreme Court.* Westport, Conn.: Greenwood Press.

Muir, William K., Jr. 1973. *Law and attitude change.* Chicago: University of Chicago Press.

Munger, Frank. 1988a. Law, change, and litigation: A critical examination of an empirical research tradition. *Law and Society Review* 22:57-83.

———. 1988b. Social change and tort litigation: Industrialization, accidents, and trial courts in southern West Virginia, 1872 to 1940. *Buffalo Law Review* 36:75-115.

Pashukanis, Evgeny B. 1978. *Law and Marxism: A general theory.* London: Ink Links.

Peltason, Jack W. 1961. *Fifty-eight lonely men: Southern federal judges and school desegregation.* Urbana: University of Illinois Press.

Pound, Roscoe. 1912. The scope and purpose of sociological jurisprudence, pt. 3. *Harvard Law Review* 25:489-562.

———. 1921. *The spirit of the common law.* Francestown, N.H.: Marshall Jones.

Rheinstein, Max, ed. 1954. *Max Weber on law and economy in society.* Cambridge, Mass.: Harvard University Press.

Sarat, Austin, and Joel Grossman. 1975. Courts and conflict resolution: Problems in the mobilization of adjudication. *American Political Science Review* 69:1200-1217.

Scheingold, Stuart A. 1974. *The politics of rights.* New Haven: Yale University Press.

Schmookler, Andrew Bard. 1984. *The parable of the tribes: The problem of power in social evolution.* Berkeley: University of California Press.

Schwartz, Richard D., and V. Lee Miller. 1964. Legal evolution and societal complexity. *American Journal of Sociology* 70:159-172.

Shapiro, Martin. 1975. Courts. In *A handbook of political science*, ed. Nelson Polsby and Fred I. Greenstein. Reading, Mass.: Addison-Wesley.

———. 1981. *Courts: A comparative perspective.* Chicago: University of Chicago Press.

Silverman, Robert A. 1981. *Law and urban growth: Civil litigation in the Boston trial courts, 1880-1900.* Princeton: Princeton University Press.

Skolnick, Jerome H. 1974. *Justice without trial: Law enforcement in a democratic society.* New York: Wiley.

Spitzer, Stephen. 1982. The dialectics of formal and informal control. In *The politics of informal justice: The American experience*, ed. Richard Abel. New York: Academic Press.

———. 1983. Marxist perspectives in the sociology of law. *Annual Review of Sociology* 9:103-120.

Stookey, John A. 1985. Capitalism in crisis: Trial courts and the emergence of the positive state. Draft manuscript in author's files.

———. 1986. Economic cycles and civil litigation. *Justice System Journal* 11:282-302.

Sumner, William Graham. 1940. *Folkways: A study of the sociological importances of usages, manners, customs, mores and morals.* New York: Ginn.

Twiss, Benjamin. 1942. *Lawyers and the Constitution: How laissez faire came to the Supreme Court.* Princeton: Princeton University Press.

Unger, Roberto M. 1976. *Law in modern society: Toward a criticism of social theory.* New York: Free Press.

_____. 1986. *The critical legal studies movement.* Cambridge, Mass.: Harvard University Press.

Wanner, Craig. 1974. The public ordering of private relations, pt. one: Initiating civil cases in urban trial courts. *Law and Society Review* 8:421-440.

_____. 1975. The public ordering of private relations, pt. two: Winning civil court cases. *Law and Society Review* 9:293-306.

Weber, Max. 1947. *The theory of social and economic organization.* New York: Free Press.

_____. 1904-5/1958. *The Protestant ethic and the spirit of capitalism.* New York: Scribner's.

Wolfskill, George. 1962. *The revolt of the conservatives: A history of the American Liberty League, 1934-1940.* Boston: Houghton Mifflin.

Zemans, Frances Kahn. 1983. Legal mobilization: The neglected role of the law in the political system. *American Political Science Review,* 77:690-703.

12. COURTS AND PUBLIC OPINION

Gregory A. Caldeira

Early in the summer of 1989, the *Washington Post* (June 23, A21) reported the results of a poll on public knowledge of the U.S. Supreme Court. Less than ten percent of the public could name the chief justice, but more than one-quarter could identify television's famed Judge Wapner. This bit of political trivia illustrates one facet of the Supreme Court's and other courts' ambivalent place in the eyes of the American public: lack of saliency in all but a few situations.[1]

Another event demonstrates a second aspect of the Court's relationship with the public: it is often in the position of taking stands against majority opinion. On June 21, 1989, the Supreme Court handed down a decision in *Texas v. Johnson* (57 L.W. 4770 [1989]), striking down the state of Texas's criminal statute against flag desecration and casting doubt that any such statute could pass constitutional muster. The public hue and cry was spectacular. Polls showed little support for the Supreme Court, even though the deciding majority cut across ideological lines.

Several years ago, a campaign to defeat Rose Bird for reelection as chief justice in California generated a great deal of public interest and a number of scholarly studies of public opinion and the California Supreme Court. This extraordinary example is the exception rather than the rule; pollsters and scholars have paid little attention to the relationship between court and public for the state courts. Consequently, here I shall focus primarily but not solely on the U.S. Supreme Court.

The relationship between public opinion and the Supreme Court has always created both theoretical and practical problems for scholars, politicians, and the justices themselves (Bickel 1962; Black 1960; Dahl 1957). In the American political system, the president and members of Congress exert extraordinary efforts to curry the favor of the public,

---

I acknowledge my intellectual debt to James L. Gibson of the University of Houston, who has collaborated with me on work on public opinion and the judiciary.

but the Court has traditionally done little—despite a reliance on public esteem rather than the purse or sword. If by some chance the members of the Court were to read social science, the justices could take scarce comfort from the scholarly work on the relationship between public opinion and the Court. Citizens know little about the Court and its business; express little concern about its personnel (see Gallup Poll 1987a, 1987b) and policies; and seem to lend support contingent upon agreement with specific policies (Adamany 1973; Daniels 1973; Murphy and Tanenhaus 1968b, 1970; Kessel 1966; Jaros and Roper 1980). Similarly, it is not clear whether and to what extent the Supreme Court can shape public opinion on the issues it decides.

Nevertheless, most political scientists harbor a belief in the ability of the Court to affect public opinion, and in turn in the influence of public opinion on the Court. This important connection may loom even larger today because courts intrude into our daily lives so often and appear in the limelight so much more than before. Scholars and judges have always speculated about this relationship; now, with the tools of modern survey research, we no longer need rely on conjecture.

I divide this chapter into three parts. As I have suggested, much, although not all, of the evidence will come from studies of the U.S. Supreme Court. First, I shall consider the influence of the Court on public opinion. Can the Court shape the public's views; and, if so, under what conditions? Second, does public opinion, as it does at least some of the time in Congress, influence the courts? Third, how much support does the public accord the Court? To what extent does the public distinguish between esteem for the institution and support for specific decisions? What influences public support? And how and why does support for the Court change over time? In each of these sections, I review the major theoretical developments, describe the most important empirical results, criticize the previous work, and highlight the current and potential research with the greatest promise of gains in theoretical and empirical knowledge.[2]

Do Courts Influence Public Opinion?

The justices themselves seem to operate on the premise that the Court can shift the tides of opinion. Opinions often speak of the Court's moral suasion. Some justices have minimized the capacity of the Court to influence public attitudes and behavior. But for the most part the justices have shared a robust view of the Court's persuasive capabilities.

Until quite recently, the empirical basis of the Court's ability to change public opinion has largely gone unexamined. Does the Court truly exert an independent effect on public attitudes? This looms as a difficult question to answer because influence, as any freshman in introduction to government knows, can take on many meanings. Does it mean to shape one's mind about an issue? That is, do we expect the Court to change people from segregationists to integrationists, from right-to-lifers to pro-choicers? In most of the literature of political science, that is what we have in mind when we speak of impact on public opinion. Does it mean to legitimize a policy in the mind of an individual, without changing his or her mind about the policy itself? There is a venerable tradition of writing about the "legitimacy-conferring" capacity of the Supreme Court. The Court, in this view, has the best opportunity to persuade the public of governmental agencies' rights to undertake action—not to shift beliefs in the substantive issue at hand. Might it also mean the encouragement of behavioral compliance with the law and the Court's decision? That is, although the Court might not change the public's attitudes about an issue, it might well be able to discourage active disobedience. The power to encourage compliance, one might argue, could be even more important than the power to change minds.

Surprisingly, we have little systematic empirical research on the important question of judicial impact on public opinion.[3] Most of the best work has come out in recent years. For the most part, scholars have simply compared the distribution of public opinion on particular issues before and after the Supreme Court has made a relevant decision. There is at least one major bar to the study of impact on public opinion: pollsters seldom pose questions to the public on cases before the Court, and when they do the wording often does not match the issues at controversy. For many years, most of the issues before the courts simply did not excite much public interest, so pollsters naturally did not ask about them. Questions on the courts have not become perennials in the regular academic surveys of the nation, such as the General Social Survey and the National Election Study. More recently, with the rise of hot issues such as abortion, affirmative action, and capital punishment, pollsters have begun more carefully to monitor issues of relevance to judicial decisions. Even if a pollster has asked a relevant question, most of the time we have no adequate basis of historical comparison. In other words, we need to know both current and past public attitudes on a given matter. And we probably ought to have multiple observations across time to avoid mistaken inferences of cause and effect.

Even with multiple observations of public attitudes on an issue, we should control for other, rival causes of changes in public opinion; the Court is not the only force for change in society. Our task is complicated because the Court itself changes its positions, incrementally, even as public opinion changes out in society. During the 1950s and 1960s, for example, as the public became acquainted with the meaning of *Brown v. Board of Education* (347 U.S. 483 [1954]), the Court moved forward aggressively against racial segregation and expanded the implications of its initial decision. In the 1970s, the Court waffled from term to term on the rights of the accused. So the Supreme Court does not provide a constant stimulus. Virtually no body of the law in a salient field remains stationary.

Popular and journalistic discussions do not distinguish between the shaping of individuals' opinions and public opinion in the aggregate. Yet stability in aggregate distributions can mask systematic and important shifts in the views of individuals in particular segments of the population. Changes at the level of individuals and in the aggregate can come about in quite different ways. The Court, like Congress and the president, has a set of constituencies, and hidden shifts in the opinions of these constituencies can have important consequences for its ability to function.

Studies in this area come in three basic varieties. First, many scholars have tried to show the connection between the Court's decisions and aggregate shifts in public opinion via historical narrative and marshaling of data from public polls—without any multivariate analysis (that is, consideration of more than one cause or correlate at a time). This variant provides an acute sense of the sweep of history, informed by analysis of case law, together with straightforward presentation of distributions of opinion. Some would argue that it is the best we can do, given the paucity and quality of data at hand.

Second, others have brought multivariate techniques[4] to bear on aggregate data on public opinion matched with the Supreme Court's decisions. This task, as I suggested earlier, is no mean feat, since we have so few good matches between polls and decisions. Here we have two good studies, one on the Supreme Court exclusively, the other a broad analysis of public opinion. Benjamin Page, Robert Shapiro, and Glenn Dempsey (1987) find a significant impact of the federal courts on public opinion; it is, contrary to expectation, a negative relationship: "When their statements and actions push in one direction (e.g., . . . a federal court orders school integration through busing) public opinion tends to move in the opposite direction" (p. 32). It could well be, as they suggest, that "the federal courts served as negative referents in the 1970s and early 1980s because of their unpopular actions on such issues as busing and capital punishment" (p. 32). Unfortunately, Page and his colleagues used television reports of the actions of the federal courts, rather than the decisions themselves, and we see no evidence of the size of the sample of cases relevant to the federal courts. Furthermore, in investigating the sources of change in public opinion, they controlled only for the effects of the *sources of news* (such as experts versus interest groups)—not for other plausible forces.

Of this genre of research, Thomas Marshall's (1987, 1989) holds the greatest and most direct interest for those who study the courts and is the most careful and well conceived. He began with the question of whether "Supreme Court decisions favorably influence mass public opinion" (1987, 147) and anchored the research firmly in the tradition of Charles Black (1960, 34-67) and others who have argued for a legitimizing role for the Court. Marshall compares eighteen decisions of the Supreme Court from the mid-1930s through the present with the aggregate results of polls taken before and after the decisions. Unlike others who have done this sort of investigation, Marshall takes into account a broad array of explanations for the Court's performance, or nonperformance, as a leader of public opinion. Interestingly, although he assembled 144 instances in which he could match one or more polls with a decision of the Supreme Court, in only 18 cases could he obtain data from polls both before and afterward. This should give us an idea of the considerable barriers to rigorous inquiry on the dynamics of the influence of the Court on public opinion. Polls shifted in all directions as a result of the eighteen decisions, but, overall, Marshall reports little evidence of a consistent direction to change (see Figure 12-1). Generally, the evidence in Figure 12-1 seems plausible, although I cannot help but wonder at the similarity in the short-term effects of the decisions on capital punishment (*Furman v. Georgia*) and on payment of foreign debts (*Cummings v. Deutsche Bank*). Sometimes opinion moves against the Court; at other times it follows the Court; and at still others it scarcely moves at all.

For the shifts in opinion he did detect, Marshall examined several different hypotheses. Judicial activism and liberal outcomes significantly moved public opinion in the direction of the Supreme Court's decisions. A lag of time made a difference, too: over time, public opinion shifted in favor of the Court's choices. Decisions taken consensually within the Supreme Court similarly lead the public, but this connection did not reach statistical significance. Somewhat surprisingly, publicity attendant to a decision had little or no effect on the movement of public opinion. Thus, Marshall concludes: "Under limited circumstances . . . Supreme Court decisions are associated with measurable poll shifts. The 'mobilization' explanation seems to fit the data best. When the Court makes liberal, activist decisions, those decisions are accompanied by significant (positive) poll shifts" (1987, 161).

The interpretations Marshall places on the results make a good deal of sense, but, as with the work of Page and Shapiro, one cannot help but wonder about the necessarily restricted nature of the sample.

Figure 12-1 Short-Term Effects of the Supreme Court's Decisions on Public Opinion

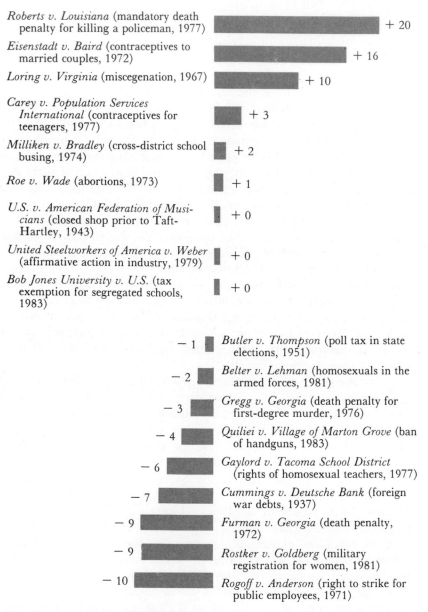

Roberts v. Louisiana (mandatory death penalty for killing a policeman, 1977) + 20

Eisenstadt v. Baird (contraceptives to married couples, 1972) + 16

Loring v. Virginia (miscegenation, 1967) + 10

Carey v. Population Services International (contraceptives for teenagers, 1977) + 3

Milliken v. Bradley (cross-district school busing, 1974) + 2

Roe v. Wade (abortions, 1973) + 1

U.S. v. American Federation of Musicians (closed shop prior to Taft-Hartley, 1943) + 0

United Steelworkers of America v. Weber (affirmative action in industry, 1979) + 0

Bob Jones University v. U.S. (tax exemption for segregated schools, 1983) + 0

− 1 *Butler v. Thompson* (poll tax in state elections, 1951)

− 2 *Belter v. Lehman* (homosexuals in the armed forces, 1981)

− 3 *Gregg v. Georgia* (death penalty for first-degree murder, 1976)

− 4 *Quiliei v. Village of Marton Grove* (ban of handguns, 1983)

− 6 *Gaylord v. Tacoma School District* (rights of homosexual teachers, 1977)

− 7 *Cummings v. Deutsche Bank* (foreign war debts, 1937)

− 9 *Furman v. Georgia* (death penalty, 1972)

− 9 *Rostker v. Goldberg* (military registration for women, 1981)

− 10 *Rogoff v. Anderson* (right to strike for public employees, 1971)

Note: Data represent percentage change.

Source: Adapted from *American Politics Quarterly,* Vol. 15 No. 1, January 1987, 147-168. Copyright © 1987 Sage Publications, Inc. Reprinted by permission of Sage Publications, Inc.

And even in those instances in which pollsters have left a sufficient trail of observations, the wording of the items and the timing of the survey often leave much to be desired. For example, sometimes the phrasing of an item did not adequately reflect the nuances of the Court's decision; and the space between the date of the decision and the taking of the poll varies wildly.

Experimental and quasi-experimental studies of change in the opinions of individuals constitute a third approach to the study of the impact of the Court on public opinion.[5] Here the question is: Do individual opinions on issues change in response to a decision of the Supreme Court, controlled for other relevant forces? The extraordinary advances in the field of social psychology suggest the power of experimental methods in the investigation of the sources of attitudinal change. Political scientists seem to have an instinctive—and undoubtedly proper—suspicion of the results of experimental analysis, always questioning the applicability to the real world of politics, so natural and quasi-experiments probably hold more promise for the development of persuasive evidence about the impact of the Supreme Court on public opinion. Unfortunately for political scientists, the Supreme Court rarely provides the ammunition for a good quasi-experimental design; and, when the justices do cooperate, pollsters and researchers may not have the foresight or resources to do the work necessary for an appropriate design.

To my knowledge, we have only a handful of studies in this line of research; I discuss three of them. Larry Baas and Dan Thomas (1984) published an experimental analysis of the Supreme Court's ability to legitimize controversial policies. It is, as far as I can tell, one of only a few true experimental assessments of this issue (see also Baas and Thomas 1985; Hensley, Baugh, and Brown 1985, 1986). Their evidence, unlike that presented in other quarters (Adamany 1973; Murphy and Tanenhaus 1968b), bears directly on the question of legitimation. As Baas and Thomas (1984, 335) point out, many distinguished scholars have assumed the ability of the Supreme Court to confer legitimacy upon the policies of the other branches of government.

Baas and Thomas conceptualize the Court's legitimizing power as "opinion leadership"; it is the ability to "generate consent," to "create acceptance of policy among those who oppose or who are neutral about its substance and heighten acceptance among those already committed to its content" (Adamany 1973, 804). To detect opinion leadership on the part of the Supreme Court, Baas and Thomas used the split-half ballot technique on a sample of students. In half of the cases, respondents learned nothing about the source of the statement on policy; in the other half, the investigators associated the policy with a particular person or institution. For two of the studies, Baas and Thomas attributed the policy to the Court as well as the Constitution, a condition clearly more favorable to the initial hypothesis. And, yet, on *none* of the sixteen issues in three different experiments did the Supreme Court appear to exercise even minimal abilities to legitimate controversial public policies. These results differ strikingly from those reported in similar studies of presidential leadership of public opinion (see Rosen 1974).[6]

Do we therefore reject the power of the Supreme Court to legitimate policies of the other branches of government? Not yet, I think. First, Baas and Thomas performed only three experiments, none of which comes close to rivaling the complexity and sophistication typical in the best of today's social psychology. We should devote further effort to the development of more and better experiments; experimentalists do not give up after a few tries. Second, quite apart from the technical problems of design, we should look harder at our theoretical account of the Supreme Court's power of legitimation; we may not have included all of the relevant variables in our model of this process. To blame the design or to deliver a verdict of no effect would therefore be a mistake. Third, the usual problems of external validity (that is, accuracy as a representation of the phenomenon in the outside world) in experiments seem especially severe in the context of the Supreme Court's effect in the real world of politics. In the real world, the Supreme Court's decisions have time to sink into people's minds.

Fourth, college students may be the poorest targets for persuasion by an external authority such as the Supreme Court. Students, after all, have already exceeded the average level of educational attainment and possess a level of affluence beyond most of the population by virtue of entry into college. The less well educated, less well informed may prove better subjects for the Supreme Court's powers (see, for example, Zaller 1987). Baas and Thomas themselves raise the issue of generalizability across issues, pools of respondents, and time (1984, 354). Fifth, as Baas and Thomas remark, we need to distinguish between general and specific forms of support. General professions of support for a policy do not predict very well the actions of individuals in specific situations; and attitudes and behaviors often do not coincide. Thus, although the Supreme Court might not change what people say about an issue, the justices could provide legitimation in the form of *behavioral* compliance. The Court might encourage acquiescence. In some sense, it is silly for an individual to change his or her mind about a salient issue simply because the Supreme Court is the source. Even if we could register that kind of response in an experiment, it is unlikely to persist over time if it is simply a function of the source and has nothing more in support of it. For example, public support for the president and his policies goes up during a crisis, but it declines to more realistic levels after time has passed. Opinion must rest on something other than the source. Time, it is often said, is the test of leadership.

More recently, Franklin and Kosaki (1989) have taken advantage of the happy coincidence of excellent survey data and an important decision of the Supreme Court—*Roe v. Wade* (410 U.S. 113 [1973]) (see also Johnson and Canon 1984, 12-13). The Court did indeed influence public attitudes toward abortion, in Franklin and Kosaki's view, but in a manner quite different from what one might anticipate. Their point of departure is that we have made too much of aggregate support for a policy as an indicator of the Supreme Court's influence. Instead, Franklin and Kosaki focus on "which groups support and oppose a position and how intensely. If support rises (or falls) then the decision had an effect. But if the structure of group support and opposition changes, even if the net effect is nil, then we argue that the Court still had an impact" (1989, 753). The Court may increase support for a policy or increase dissension. This they call the "structural response" hypothesis.

Obviously, the Supreme Court can influence only those who have at least some awareness of the decision, so cases of high salience provide especially appropriate places to test the impact on public opinion. But, as Franklin and Kosaki remark, in those situations the Supreme Court has the toughest job, since opinions will probably have taken on some degree of clarity as a result of the salience of the issue. For Franklin and Kosaki, as for others who use quasi-experimental designs, the problem of attribution of effects looms large. Because decisions of the Supreme Court in principle affect all citizens, Franklin and Kosaki do not have a group not exposed to the "experiment." It is therefore difficult to rule out spurious effects. The investigators compensate here by differentiating between those who had heard of *Roe* and those who had not. This solution, as they readily admit, is imperfect, for those who had knowledge of *Roe* will undoubtedly differ from those who had none in important and consequential ways.

The data for the quasi-experiment come from NORC's General Social Survey conducted in the winter and spring of both 1972 and 1973. Thus Franklin and Kosaki have cross-sections both before and after *Roe* at their disposal.[7] In the case of discretionary abortions, the Court's decision did not lead to an increase in overall support and seems to have polarized groups on this issue. Catholics and nonwhites, in particular, became less supportive of discretionary abortions as a result of *Roe v. Wade*. For decisions based on the health of the mother or child, the Supreme Court's decision increased the overall level of support, but it did not exacerbate differences between groups. For those who had no avowed knowledge of *Roe,* Franklin and Kosaki find no evidence of either structural shifts in opinion or changes in the overall level of support for both the discretionary and health scales.[8]

Franklin and Kosaki's research represents a good model of quasi-experimental research on public opinion to emulate; it is carefully and self-consciously designed. The investigators offer a coherent and well-articulated theoretical framework to account for their results; and they entertain alternative explanations. The framework is, as the authors readily admit, imperfect, but it is a good start at understanding how the Supreme Court shapes public opinion.

This brings us back to our initial question: What does the available evidence tell us about the impact of the Supreme Court on public opinion? First, we have relatively few well-documented instances in which the Supreme Court has shaped the aggregate distribution of public support for this or that policy. In many cases, support for a policy has gone up after the Supreme Court has made a decision, but we cannot rule out the possibility of other influences. We suffer from a paucity of observations over time on the public's views of issues on the Court's agenda. So, when the Court announces an important decision, we have no lengthy basis of comparison. Second, in light of the lack of data on aggregate change, we probably do not yet have an adequate test of the Supreme Court's ability to shape this kind of opinion. The evidence in the best studies (such as Marshall 1989) does not provide encouragement for a view of the Court as shaper of aggregate opinion, but other research with better data just might. Third, we set an unrealistic standard for the Supreme Court when we expect it to engender significant movements of aggregate distributions of public opinion in relatively short periods of time. We do better, I think, to look for shifts within segments of the population. The most important of the Supreme Court's decisions, after all, usually engender some controversy both inside and outside the Court. Controversy results from the differential impact of decisions on the various constituencies within the Court and out in the nation. Thus, we should anticipate differences in response across groups. For example, in the controversy over prayer in public schools, the Court's decision should arouse more ire among southerners than New Englanders; and, presumably, southern Catholics and evangelical Protestants will react somewhat differently.

So my answer is: the Supreme Court probably shapes aggregate distributions of public opinion, at least in some highly visible instances, and can move parts of the public depending upon the differential impact of the decision. There are, unfortunately, too few studies to permit me to state this with much confidence. The Supreme Court can shape public opinion in a number of different ways, and we should attempt to reflect that diversity in our designs.

Does Public Opinion Influence the Courts?

Normally, we do not think of courts as representative institutions in the same sense as legislatures, executives, and even bureaucracies. And yet politicians and the public often behave as though they expect the courts to perform at least some representational functions. Thus, for example, on the Supreme Court today we speak of "seats" for Jews, Catholics, blacks, and now women. And, the justices will often refer to and defer to public opinion in making decisions. So, for instance, the Supreme Court has relied heavily on the emergence of broad popular support for capital punishment as a justification for its interpretation of "cruel and unusual punishment" (see Marshall 1989, 31-67; Vidmar and Ellsworth 1974; Sarat and Vidmar 1976). Moreover, although some expect the Supreme Court to stand against the winds of oppression, many—if not most—others express outrage if the justices do not reflect the clearly expressed views of the majority. Robert Dahl (1957) flatly states it: over the long run the Supreme Court takes on the views of the governing coalition. In a 1988 speech at the University of Kentucky, Justice Antonin Scalia made much the same point: public opinion inevitably influences the Court; judges, after all, come from among the people and thus represent public opinion, even if only in the long run.

Dahl and Scalia are undoubtedly correct. But it is much more difficult to speak with precision about the impact of public opinion on the courts in the short run. The truth is, we know virtually nothing systematically about the effect of public opinion on the Supreme Court. Unfortunately, here, as with other parts of this area of research, pollsters have not cooperated by providing sufficiently long-term and comparable sets of data.[9] Most of the work on the Supreme Court deals with the broad concept of "representativeness," without any clear theory of linkage or any explicit attempt to show whether or how public opinion might influence the views of the justices.[10] Thus, in much of this section, contrary to the practice in the rest of the chapter, I rely on studies of public opinion in trial courts.

Perhaps the best example of a study based on data from surveys but uncluttered with any statistical controls is David Barnum's (1985) analysis of the Supreme Court and public opinion on several issues. Working in the tradition of Dahl (1957) and Jonathan Casper (1972, 1976), Barnum contends that the Supreme Court usually reflects trends in public opinion: in other words, over the long run, the Supreme Court follows the election returns. He focuses on several of the most emotional issues of the period after the end of the New Deal and the rise of the modern Supreme Court—including racial integration of schools, birth control, the role of women, and interracial marriage. The criticism of this approach is obvious: it provides for no controls or tests of alternative ideas about the relationships among the Court, public opinion, and public policy. It posits a relationship between the Supreme Court and public opinion unfettered by complications from other sources. This sort of study may well persuade us of the author's interpretation of history, but ultimately we are left with many questions and competing and untested hypotheses. Dahl, of course, had propounded a sophisticated version of Mr. Dooley's dictum: the Supreme Court follows the election returns. Mr. Dooley may well be correct about the Supreme Court following the election returns, but I suspect that the causal linkage may be considerably more complicated than either Dahl or Barnum allows.

Benjamin Page and Robert Shapiro's (1983) project on the relationship between public opinion and public policy from 1935 through 1979 shows much greater awareness and care about precise statistical relationships. It is, to be sure, a study of a whole range of policies, but Page and Shapiro examine many issues of relevance to the courts. Animated for the most part by concerns about political representation, Page and Shapiro wish to assess the degree of congruence between policy and opinion. Strikingly, they report greater congruence between opinion and policy for "salient and large-scale social issues" than for economic or welfare policies. The former issues of high congruence include abortion (100 percent), civil liberties (89 percent), and civil rights (74 percent). On these issues, primarily of a judicial nature, public opinion and public policies tracked together. In light of the lack of an electoral connection between the federal courts and the public, we would anticipate a lesser degree of congruence between opinion and policy for the federal courts than for the executive or Congress. But Page and Shapiro find "little difference between the executive, Congress, [and the] federal courts" (1983, 183). They entertain the possibility that political institutions shape public opinion, and find that in about half of the cases of congruence "policy may affect opinion" (1983, 187; see also Marshall 1988; Monroe 1979).

Unfortunately, Page and Shapiro's study is not clear about congruence as a concept. Congruence tells us only of a similarity between policy and opinion; it tells us nothing about the mechanisms that brought about this state of affairs. Ultimately, we want to unravel the causal linkages between our political institutions and public opinion. This task requires sharp measurements of the variables across time. To report on the congruence of policy and opinion is, to be sure, a valuable contribution, but it tells us little about the central question: Does policy lead to change in opinion, or does change in opinion lead to policy? Unavoidably, Page and Shapiro's sample of matches consists only of issues salient enough to motivate pollsters to ask questions about them. There is, of course, little we can do about this problem.

More recently, Marshall (1989, 68-103) has attempted to estimate and account for the degree to which the Supreme Court's decisions represent American public opinion. As in the study I described earlier (see Marshall 1987), he matched results from national polls and decisions of the Supreme Court in 146 instances from 1935 through 1986.[11] He found consistency between the actions of the Supreme Court and public opinion in a clear majority of the cases. Following Page and Shapiro (1983), he concludes: "The modern Court appears neither markedly more nor less consistent with the polls than are other policy makers" (Marshall 1989, 80; see Page and Shapiro 1983; Monroe 1979). He tests a number of competing explanations of the Court's agreement with public opinion, and some of them do quite well. First, during times of crisis, the Supreme Court reflected public opinion more accurately than at other junctures. Extraordinary, as opposed to narrow, margins of public support for a policy made no difference in the level of agreement. Second, if public preferences conflicted with a challenged federal law, the Court was more likely to agree with the majority's view. Federal laws typically reflected public sentiment, so the Court's normal deference to the federal government translated into greater fidelity to public opinion. Third, state and local policies usually did not agree with national opinion; when the Court confronted a conflict with public views, the justices chose public opinion over the decisions of state and local governments.

Here, as with Page and Shapiro's research, we find problems of data and conceptualization. The bias of the sample of cases in which Marshall could find polls is an obvious one, as he recognizes, and I will not belabor the point. The problem of conceptualization strikes me as a much more serious one. Neither Marshall nor Page and Shapiro—or, for that matter, Barnum, Casper, or Dahl—specify a sophisticated model of representational linkage. Why should we anticipate a relationship between public opinion and the Court's decisions? Should public opinion have a direct impact on the Court, or will other forces mediate? The high level of aggregation poses severe problems for the study of the Court and representation of public opinion. For the Court on most issues, as for other political actors, particular constituencies (such as blacks) will probably loom larger than undifferentiated opinion at the national level. Unless we can move downward to lower levels of aggregation, I think we will continue to have trouble in trying to connect the Court and public opinion. From the literature on legislatures, we have many persuasive models of representation, but scholars of the Supreme Court have paid little heed. It is too bad, for studies of representation in legislatures stand as one of the best developed nodes of research in political science; we could do well to borrow some of these ideas (for citations, see Gibson 1980).

Does the Supreme Court represent public opinion? The answer, I think, is that we do not yet have sufficient evidence on which we can place much confidence. The extant studies, although intriguing and suggestive, lack the conceptualization and measurement to permit us to make a well-considered judgment on this issue. This should not reflect poorly on the scholars working in this arena; the problems of data here are severe, perhaps insuperable, and the enterprise remains young enough to justify exploratory efforts.

Research on representation in trial courts comes much closer to the best work on legislative behavior (see Miller and Stokes 1963). Trial judges, as I suggested earlier, have a much more intimate view of and access to salient constituencies; their districts are bound to be more homogeneous than an appellate court's. By nature, of course, trial courts are local organizations, and so we should expect trial judges to take public opinion into account in making decisions. For state trial judges subject to election and especially in partisan systems, representation of crystallized public opinion might be a matter of survival. Electoral sanctions do not apply to federal district judges, who serve for life during good behavior, but local communities can exact severe informal penalties (see, for example, Peltason 1961); those who populate the bench may well reflect public opinion as a result of socialization and perhaps as a matter of principle.

Here we have several varieties of research.[12] Some have assessed the responsiveness of trial judges to the sociopolitical characteristics of the environment as proxies for public opinion (Gibson 1980; Giles and Walker 1975). Others, in addition, have used data on public opinion in models of representation (Cook 1973, 1977, 1979; Graebner 1973; Kritzer 1978, 1979; Kuklinski and Stanga 1979; Pruet and Glick 1986). Yet others have examined judicial representation of public opinion in a dynamic context (Cook 1977, 1979; Kritzer 1979). In each of these categories we encounter studies of both federal and state trial judges. And in each some measure of sentencing behavior—after all, sentencing is the chief product of trial courts—serves as the dependent variable. Several of the more recent of these pieces set forth impressive attempts to formulate and test alternative theories of representation (for example, Gibson 1980; Pruet and Glick 1986).

Some dispute the findings and interpretations, but Beverly Cook (1973, 1977, 1979) has done important research on this topic and, without doubt, has drawn scholarly interest. For present purposes, Cook's (1977) investigation of the relationship between public opinion and the sentencing decisions of federal district judges from 1967 through 1975 provides a handy exemplar of her work to discuss and criticize. Cook presents a "representational model" as an account of her data, and she tests rival explanations—the "legal," "bureaucratic," and "sociopsychological" models. Federal judges do not face the electorate, so Cook looks for bases of a representational linkage; she finds them in "common socialization" and "role conception" (1977, 568). In part, federal judges represent the public because they come from and live within the local community. In part, federal judges find out about public opinion just as others do, through television, newspapers, and daily conversations.

The model estimated includes a wide variety of controls, including an indicator of elite opinion (such as support for the Vietnam War within Congress). Of the results, Cook concludes: "Public opinion is the most important of the independent variables explaining the sentence. Opinion also works through Congress to add slightly to the explanation of sentence and through [other variables]" (Cook 1977, 585). Cook finds some evidence for rival hypotheses, but public opinion clearly makes a difference.

This research raises a number of concerns, as Cook and others have recognized (see Kritzer 1979 for detail, and, in response, Cook 1979). First, although Cook does explore alternative hypotheses, she admittedly does not test sophisticated theories of the representational linkage. Cook does not, for example, include perception of role as an intervening variable,[13] even though we have good reason to suspect its importance. Second, Cook's simulation of public opinion goes against sound methodological advice (Seidman 1975). To simulate opinion within states via a combination of survey data and demographics makes sense only if public opinion is a linear function of social, political, and economic characteristics. We would have little reason to do survey research in most cases if we could safely make such a heroic assumption. Third, as Herbert Kritzer asks: Do Cook's "impressive correlations . . . actually represent responses of federal judges to public opinion"? The evidence, Kritzer suggests, "casts doubt on the argument that the influencing factor was public opinion rather than something like the judges' own doubts about the war, or their opinion concerning the degree of governmental commitment to the war" (1979, 198). The large correlations observed between public opinion and sentencing decisions might well imply a strong representational linkage; but,

Kritzer notes, other interpretations are equally plausible. To find in favor of the representational linkage that Cook suggests would require additional variables as controls. Ultimately, however, Kritzer and Cook agree on one fundamental: federal judges did respond to the sociopolitical environment in the sentencing of draft offenders (Kritzer 1979).

James Gibson (1980) does not use an explicit indicator of public opinion—an unfortunate flaw—but he does a thorough job of placing trial judges within contemporary understandings of the empirical measurement and analysis of representation. The question he poses is this: Does the "environment" influence the sentencing behavior of judges in criminal cases? He tests two models of representation—"sharing" and "role-playing"—on a sample of state trial judges in Iowa. The dependent variable is the severity of sentences. Quite apart from the "environment," Gibson incorporates three major sets of controls—attributes of cases and defendants, attitudes and values of officials in the criminal justice system, and the policies and practices of pretrial decision makers. The main elements of the model include the seriousness of crime, as measured by the rate of crime within a district; the perception of the seriousness of crime in a district, as indicated by a trial judge's response to a question; and the severity of sentences. Overall, the incidence of crime influences judicial perceptions of the seriousness of crime, which in turn shape sentencing choices. But, then, why do judges respond to environmental conditions? Gibson offers three variables as explanations of the strength of representational linkages. First, if a judge has contact with the local community, he or she will have more information about the local environment, so we should see a stronger linkage between environment and decision. Second, if a judge believes in the appropriateness of public opinion as a criterion in the making of sentencing decisions, we should encounter a strong linkage. Third, if a judge has suffered an electoral defeat in the past, he or she will weigh environmental conditions more heavily in making decisions. Gibson presents strong evidence of the conditional effect of this set of three variables. All of this evidence suggests the sort of representational behavior among trial judges that we normally expect to find among legislators.

I see two problems, perhaps inevitable, in Gibson's adept analysis. First, as I suggested earlier, he has no true measure of public opinion, so he cannot speak of judicial responses to public concerns; he has an indication of how judges' views and decisions reflect the objective reality of crime within a jurisdiction. There is often a tenuous relationship between what people see as a problem and the objective reality of the matter. Thus we know that the rate of crime does not predict public concern about crime very well. Second, although Gibson persuasively shows the impact of role, electoral threat, and local contacts on the strength of linkage, he does not—and perhaps cannot—assess the relative influence of these forces. It would be nice to know which provides the best explanation; it would advance our understanding of judicial representation of public concerns.

George Pruet and Henry Glick (1986) investigate the impact of public opinion on sentencing in criminal cases in Florida's trial courts. Unlike Gibson (1980), Pruet and Glick present a direct measure of public opinion, taken in a survey of the state's citizenry, in addition to indicators of the social and political contexts. Public opinion apparently does not shape sentencing decisions, although high rates of crime and large numbers of nonwhites in a jurisdiction increase popular concern about crime as a problem. Unfortunately, Pruet and Glick have no measure of whether the trial judges saw public opinion as an appropriate criterion in the sentencing of criminals. The lack of this intervening variable, so important in Gibson's analysis, could very well account for the failure to find a significant connection between public opinion and judicial decision making.

Does public opinion influence the choices of trial judges? The answer, based on the handful of studies and what I can divine from them, seems to be yes—under certain conditions. If anything, the design of previous studies—poor or no measures of public opinion, no observations on perceptions of role—has probably worked heavily against the finding of such a connection. The research I have reviewed here is in many respects impressive in conceptualization, measurement, and execution, especially if we take into account the severe limitations of data. Indeed, students of the connection between public opinion and the Supreme Court would do well to emulate the rigor of the work on trial courts. In the future, we should design studies in which we gather information on public opinion *as well as* on those variables likely to condition its influence on judicial decision making in trial courts.

What Shapes the Public's Opinion of Courts?

The Supreme Court and courts in general, like other political institutions, require some minimal—and unknown—level of support among mass and elite publics.[14] Most scholars and judges would assent to some form of this proposition. As Justice Felix Frankfurter put it: "The Court's authority—possessed of neither the purse nor the sword—ultimately rests on sustained public confidence in its moral sanction" (*Baker v. Carr,* 369 U.S. 186 [1962]; see also Lerner 1937; Levinson 1980). For several decades, political scientists have devoted a great deal of time, money, and energy to the assessment of levels and sources of popular support for political institutions (Patterson,

Hedlund, and Boynton 1975; for further references, see Easton 1975; Wahlke 1971), and work on the Supreme Court has figured prominently in this enterprise (see Dennis 1975). Several years ago, at a roundtable on the past and future of research on judicial behavior, one panelist announced, or perhaps encouraged, the demise of research on public evaluations of the courts; it was an "overtilled" area of research (see Arnold 1982; Polsby 1981; Stumpf et al. 1983). To be sure, the bibliography of articles, chapters, and papers on support for courts is bulky, but, as we shall see, size does not necessarily translate into precise knowledge; and at this late date we can state surprisingly little with confidence about this connection.

Empirical analysis of popular support for the Supreme Court traces back to the advent of modern polling. In the 1930s, when the Supreme Court pushed its constitutional warrant to the hilt, President Roosevelt and others proposed major changes in the procedures and roles of the Court. Pollsters took soundings on a number of these proposals (see Caldeira 1987; Cantwell 1946; Dolbeare 1967; Dolbeare and Hammond 1968; Handberg 1984; Alsop and Catledge 1938; Baker 1967). These questions went to the very heart of the matter: Would the respondents support truly radical changes in the nature of the Supreme Court's position in our constitutional polity? For example, during 1935, as the crisis around the Court intensified, Gallup asked a sample of the public: "As a general principle, would you favor limiting the power of the Supreme Court to declare acts of Congress unconstitutional?" (Cantril and Strunk 1951). Even though most of the public opposed the stands the Court had taken against the New Deal, far fewer than half of the sample expressed any degree of approval for a limitation on judicial review. During the early part of 1937, the Gallup Poll queried the public: "Do you think some kind of change is necessary regarding the Supreme Court?" This item presents a weaker stimulus; strong supporters of the Court might favor some kind of change, even if relatively marginal to the main functions of the Court. Yet about 40 percent of the public opposed change. Even many partisans of FDR refused to assent to his plans to "pack" the Supreme Court (see Figure 12-2). In Caldeira (1987) I present a series of observations on public support for FDR's program during the winter and spring of 1937. As Figure 12-2 shows, popular support for the measure declined substantially over the weeks, at least in part in response to several of the Court's decisions. These and other data show the strong resistance among the American public to proposals for large alterations of the Supreme Court and the functions it performs.

Because once again most of the work deals with the U.S. Supreme Court, I direct my attention to it rather than other courts. I pose a

Figure 12-2 Support for President Roosevelt's Court-Packing Plan

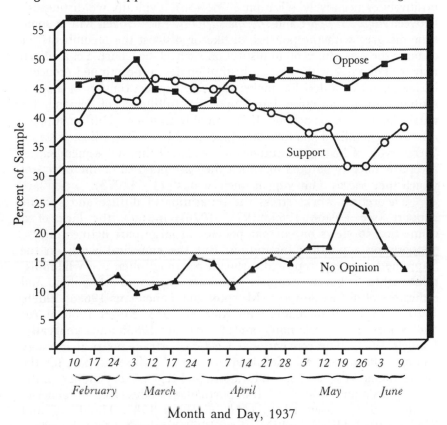

Month and Day, 1937

Source: Gregory A. Caldeira, "Public Opinion and the Supreme Court: FDR's Court Packing Plan," *American Political Science Review* 81 (1987): 1147.

series of issues: How have scholars conceptualized and measured support for the Court? Can we account in a systematic fashion for variations in support within the public? How much support, according to the various definitions, does the Court command? Does support for the Court change over time? If so, why? How does support for the Court compare to that for other courts and political institutions? Does popular support, or lack thereof, actually make a difference in the effective functioning of the Supreme Court?

Scholars have conceptualized and measured support for the Supreme Court in a number of ways. These include specific support, diffuse support, confidence in the Court or the leaders of the Court, and procedural fairness. Support generally refers to "an attitude by which a person orients himself to an object either favorably or unfavorably, positively or negatively" (Easton 1975, 436). Typically we distinguish between *diffuse support* and *specific support*. Each citizen will at some time disagree with the policies, dislike or distrust the incumbents, or criticize the procedures of an institution such as the Court. Yet a citizen may well disagree with what an institution does yet continue to concede its legitimacy as a decision maker. Specific support consists of a set of attitudes toward an object based upon the fulfillment of demands for particular policies or actions. It is probably transient. Diffuse support refers to generalized and firm attachments. It is, as David Easton states, "a reservoir of favorable attitudes or good will that helps members to accept or tolerate outputs to which they are opposed or the effects of which they see as damaging to their wants" (1965, 273).

Theoretical works stress the separation of diffuse and specific support (see Easton 1965, 1975, 1976); in fact, the lack of a connection to views on current policies in large part defines diffuse support for a political institution. But the empirical work on the Supreme Court has repeatedly shown a strong, often overwhelming, relationship between people's opinions on issues of policy and indicators of diffuse support (Murphy and Tanenhaus 1968a, 1968b, 1970; Murphy, Tanenhaus, and Kastner 1973; Kessel 1966; Jaros and Roper 1980; Adamany and Grossman 1983; and, generally, Daniels 1973). The conventional wisdom portrays political ideology and specific support as chief determinants of diffuse support for the Court, along with race, age, education, and region—depending on the time, place, and design of the particular study (see, in general, Daniels 1973; Casey 1974, 1975; Graham 1985; Handberg and Maddox 1982; Hirsch and Donohew 1968; Sigelman 1979). Paradoxically, specific support for the Court, as measured by agreement with its decisions, is a function of partisanship, political ideology, race, and region—more or less the same sources of diffuse support (Murphy and Tanenhaus 1968b; Casey 1976; Jaros and Roper 1980; Secret, Johnson, and Welch 1986).

Consider, for example, Walter Murphy and Joseph Tanenhaus's project on public support for the court—one of the best and most carefully planned of the previous studies.[15] They report a strong relationship between diffuse support and agreement with recent decisions of the Court, general political outlook, and partisanship. For a sample of the mass public, the correlations for several measures of ideology and support run from .45 to .55—very substantial for data on individuals. For samples of elite publics, the correlation goes as high as .80 (Murphy and Tanenhaus 1970) and perhaps suggests no empirical distinction between specific and diffuse support. Should we, accordingly, give up on the distinction between specific and diffuse support, as some would have us do (for example, Loewenberg 1971, 184)?

I think not. First of all, the conceptualization and measurement in previous research leave much to be desired. I leave questions of theoretical and explanatory utility until somewhat later in the text. To construct a scale of diffuse support, Murphy and Tanenhaus (as in 1968b) asked respondents how well the Court was doing its basic job, whether the Court was too involved in partisan politics, whether it was basically fair, and the relative degree of trust in Congress in comparison to the Supreme Court. Similarly, in a more recent project on the Supreme Court, David Adamany and Joel Grossman (1983) rely on a variety of indicators of popular views of the high bench, including how well it is doing its job, the degree of confidence in it as an institution, and comparisons of trust across branches of government. The wording of these items suggests to me a very strong component of specific support (see Easton 1975, 442, for much the same point). These scholars seem to capture transient views rather than firm attachments.[16] Naturally enough, opinions on policy issues and support for specific decisions explain much of the variation in these items and scales.

Partly in response to concerns about flaws in prior conceptualization and measurement, James Gibson and I (Caldeira and Gibson 1989) have designed and tested a new scale of diffuse support. There we tried to tap the more durable elements of popular views of the Court by posing questions to respondents about their willingness to accept, make, or sustain major changes in how the Supreme Court performs its role in our system (see Loewenberg 1971). Unwillingness to make fundamental alterations in the Court goes to the heart of the notion of diffuse support as a commitment to the legitimacy of an institution—that is, the rights to do its appointed tasks. We use the term "institutional commitment" for this dimension of support (see Patterson, Hedlund, and Boynton 1975). Incidentally, quite a number of the items on surveys the Gallup Poll conducted in the 1930s on the public's responses to FDR's threat to the Supreme Court as an institution tapped something akin to our conception of commitment.

We offered the sample tough choices, including items on the elimination of the Court's power to invalidate federal statutes, abolition of the Court, reduction of judicial powers, and Court-stripping measures.[17] These items do not constitute the ideal scale—others will undoubtedly think of better ones—but after careful analyses we are satisfied with the scale's validity and reliability as a measure of commitment to the Supreme Court. We found, in contrast to earlier research, no connection between diffuse support for the Court and indicators of political ideology, partisanship, and specific support.

Instead, we report significant and direct effects of commitment to liberty as opposed to order, support for democratic norms, attentiveness to the Court, educational level, and the use of ideological schema on diffuse support for the Supreme Court among our national sample of white Americans in 1987. The difference in results is fundamental: none of the variables significant in prior research survived in our statistical analysis. So, just as Easton predicted, views on public policy do not condition diffuse support among members of the mass public.

Commentators often posit "opinion leaders" and other elite publics as the last bastions of defense for the Supreme Court against the marauding hordes of the mass public. Yet, for opinion leaders—a moderately elite public—Gibson and I report a set of relationships in striking contrast to those for the mass public. Views on issues of direct relevance to the Court constitute some of the most potent determinants of diffuse support among opinion leaders. Opinion leaders, unlike members of the mass public, apparently condition commitment to the Court as an institution upon agreement with judicial policies. In fact, diffuse support seems to behave much like specific support among this sample.

These results dramatize another problem, to which I alluded earlier, in this line of research: lack of a coherent theoretical framework or even some self-consciousness about the development and testing of theories. In other words, we have no theory of support for the Supreme Court. Studies of public opinion abound with competing theories and explanations, but scholars of the courts have not often drawn on them. For example, Philip Converse (1964) and others have offered persuasive theories about the lack of stability of attitudes among the mass public and the relatively structured opinions of activists, opinion leaders, and elites. That work helps to account for the patterns Gibson and I (Caldeira and Gibson 1989) encountered; Easton's and others' frameworks cannot.

Our theoretical poverty creates even more havoc when we move from cross-sectional studies and attempt to explain change over time in popular support for the Supreme Court. And, if our theoretical problems were not troubling enough, we have no more than a handful of empirical analyses of the dynamics of support. For systematic evidence on the sources of change in support for the Court, we must rely on just two studies (but see Handberg 1984; Cantril and Strunk 1951). From a two-wave panel (1966-1975), Tanenhaus and Murphy report a significant decline in support for the Court but a considerable amount of stability in opinion—a correlation of .53 between support in 1966 and 1975 (Tanenhaus and Murphy 1981). Diffuse support for the Court in 1975 stemmed from diffuse support in 1966, specific support in 1966, change in specific support, attitudes toward civil rights in 1966, and changes in attitudes toward civil rights. Changes in judicial policy produced changes in public support—very much the same argument Tanenhaus and Murphy pursued in their earlier research. But Tanenhaus and Murphy offer a "learning" model, along the lines of James Coleman's theorizing about social change, as an account of the dynamics of diffuse support. It is a rudimentary but welcome start.

In a study of changes in public confidence in the Court from 1966 through 1984, I (Caldeira 1986) offered results broadly consistent with the view of diffuse support as a creature of specific support—but presented no theory of change. Invalidations of state and federal laws, most of which pushed in the same ideological direction, decreased confidence in the Court (see Lehne and Reynolds 1978 for a similar report on a state supreme court). Similarly, the more solicitude the justices showed for the rights of those accused of crime, the less confidence the mass public bestowed on the Court.[18] Confidence in the leaders of the Court differs in important respects from diffuse support, and it probably picks up strong elements of specific support (Lipset and Schneider 1987). It also has a number of more technical flaws as an indicator of popular support for the Court. Indeed, its main virtue is that the National Opinion Research Center and the Harris Survey ask questions about popular confidence in the leaders of a number of institutions on a frequent and regular basis. Nevertheless, both studies (Tanenhaus and Murphy 1981; Caldeira 1986) suggest in a general sense specific support and political ideology as the chief sources of change in diffuse support over both the long and the short haul.

Gibson and I (Caldeira and Gibson 1989) offer speculations about the nature and sources of change in diffuse support. For the mass public, "our findings strongly support the Eastonian model . . . basic political attitudes toward the regime and its institutions reflect fundamental political values acquired through socialization during childhood" (p. 23; see also Easton and Dennis 1969; Caldeira 1977). Yet the Eastonian model does not account for change.

Gibson and I see "perceptions of the institution" as the missing link in this theoretical framework. Socialization will engender predispositions to see institutions in a certain light and to lend them support, but at times other influences will override basic inclinations. So long as the justices maintain a low profile and policies reinforce expectations, basic political values will shape attitudes toward the Supreme Court. Eventually, the Supreme Court upsets expectations, creates controversy, and becomes a more salient target. Some members of the public will come to see a disjuncture between expectation and performance. Diffuse support will therefore weaken, and views toward the Court will reflect opinions on matters of policy more directly. Accordingly, basic inclinations toward the Court will play a smaller role in the structuring of current views. These speculations seem broadly compatible with the experiences of and evidence from the 1960s and the 1970s (Caldeira and Gibson 1989, 24). Naturally, opinion leaders will monitor the Supreme Court more steadily than members of the mass public, so we would not anticipate large changes in salience. Commitments to the Court among opinion leaders will go together with their views of proper public policy rather than stem from basic predispositions. Opinion leaders will move freely from support to opposition as the Supreme Court's policies change (on congressional elites, see Murphy 1962; Schmidhauser and Berg 1972). Obviously, these theoretical speculations currently await testing and evaluation.

No matter how hard we try to avoid it, we who study the sources of popular support inevitably confront the question of whether all of this has any consequences for the performance of our political institutions. For some institutions, such as the presidency, we have fairly strong evidence of the impact of support on political effectiveness. But for most political institutions, we have taken the political consequences of popular support as an article of faith. Does diffuse support for the Supreme Court help the justices to gain compliance within the public? Two studies bear directly on this question. Tom Tyler (forthcoming) shows the significant impact of supportive attitudes toward the police and the courts on compliance with the law. Even in the midst of a multivariate analysis, images of institutional legitimacy influence compliance. Similarly, Gibson (1989) argues for the role of institutions "in insuring citizen compliance with unpopular policy decisions. . . . The results suggest that the legitimizing capacity of judicial institutions exceeds that of legislative institutions" (p. 491).

This pair of studies makes a good start on an issue of central importance to research. Clearly we have more work to do. We should, in addition, give attention to the interconnections among diffuse support, the Court's capacity to confer legitimacy, and representational linkages between judges and the public.

Conclusion

This journey through the highways, byways, and perhaps even dead ends of research on public opinion and American courts should humble even the most bullish of students. The fact is, a quarter of a century after the launching of the first systematic research on public evaluations of the Court (Kessel 1966; Murphy and Tanenhaus 1968a), we have precious few findings and generalizations planted in solid empirical soil. We possess even less theoretical understanding. Now, of course, on some of the issues raised in this chapter we have had much greater success than on others. For example, in studies of the representational roles of trial courts, I can point to admirable attempts to borrow and test theoretical insights from research on legislative behavior. And, sometimes I think that if we were to compare what we know with what other areas of the subfield or discipline can offer in interesting and well-established generalizations, perhaps our work would not look quite as humble as when we judge it in absolute terms.

Despite all of my criticisms and worries, I remain optimistic about progress in the understanding of public opinion and courts. First of all, we have clear maps before us. Students of legislatures and public opinion have gone down these paths before and we can draw important lessons from their experiences. Judicious borrowing and adaptation can yield benefits. Sometimes we can simply import theoretical frameworks or forms of measurement to suit our purposes. On other occasions we will have to make much less mechanical transfers of methods and concepts. Second, the failings and lacunae in this area of research have a pleasant flipside: just about any interesting issue remains wide open to further exploration. In most cases no one has even muddied the waters; there is so little research of any kind. Unlike students of voting behavior, who face a well-developed field of action, we do not have to concoct esoteric designs or launch massive statistical strikes in order to make significant progress. We can go about our business in a more or less ordinary way for years to come. Third, perhaps most important, we should not forget what drew most of us to this subfield in the first place: the substantive importance and interest of law, courts, and judicial behavior. The relationship between the public and American courts affects the quality of our democracy and our lives. It deserves our best efforts at understanding.

Notes

1. Consider another example. During the lengthy and highly visible debate over the nomination of Judge Robert H. Bork to the Supreme Court, polling organizations conducted a number of surveys. Even though the mass media treated the public to a barrage of information about the nomination and the Court, surprisingly few citizens expressed concern or formed opinions on the issue. See, for example, Gallup Poll 1987a, 1987b.
2. I make no pretense here of discussing all or even most of the relevant studies. Marshall 1989 collects and reviews most of the work of direct interest.

3. Of course, the wealth of research on the implementation and impact of judicial decisions relates closely to the discussion in this section. For detailed analysis, see Chapter 17 of this book, by Canon. Accordingly, I do not trace the Court's efficacy vis-à-vis the public as far as I might otherwise.

4. That is, statistical methods designed to take into account more than one independent or explanatory variable at a time. Examples of such techniques applied in the literature include ordinary least squares, logit, and probit.

5. People intentionally create experiments. Thus, for example, psychologists induce various levels of stress in order to assess the reactions of individuals. Occasionally, nature and life cooperate and permit social scientists to do natural or quasi-experiments. For example, prior to the Supreme Court's decision to ban prayer in public schools, Muir 1967 assayed the attitudes of educational personnel within a single district. He then treated the Court's decision as an "experimental" condition and investigated its effects on the staff.

6. This pattern could, of course, reflect greater persuasive powers on the part of the president, or it could stem from problems of measurement and conceptualization.

7. The six items cover the circumstances under which a respondent would permit an abortion and break down into two scales—one on considerations of "health," the other "discretionary."

8. To account for the different reactions across the scales and groups, Franklin and Kosaki (1989) offer a theory based on interpersonal influences: "social interpretation of events drives the differing outcomes." Thus, for example, the Supreme Court's decision increased the salience of abortion among Catholics and heightened interpersonal pressure among those who lived among other Catholics. The evidence for this interpretation is sketchy, of course, but it is extremely appealing.

9. Indeed, as Gibson has remarked, "the basic problem with [research on the representativeness of the Supreme Court] is that data limitations make it quite difficult to unravel the complex chain of causality. These limitations also exist at the trial court level, ... but ... they can be resolved or minimized. At the Supreme Court level, it is unclear that they can be resolved or minimized" (1980, 345).

10. For a detailed discussion of the related issue of whether and how the Supreme Court connects with massive shifts in the system of political parties, see David Adamany's chapter in this book (Chapter 1).

11. See also Marshall's analysis of the relationship between public opinion and the votes of individual justices (1989, 104-130). It is, I am afraid, much less successful than is the investigation of aggregate relationships. For a success here, he would have to develop a comprehensive model of judicial choice—an unreasonable expectation, since no one else has done so. But see Gibson's essay on judicial decision making in this volume (Chapter 10).

12. I make no attempt here to cite this literature exhaustively. For references to the work on trial courts and sentencing decisions as it relates to our concerns, see Gibson 1980; Cook 1977; Pruet and Glick 1986).

13. Role perception probably links two other variables. For example, a judge may have very conservative views on crime and punishment, but if he or she does not believe in the appropriateness of implementing these personal premises, we may not detect a connection between attitudes and sentencing.

14. In the section that follows I borrow some of the ideas presented in Caldeira and Gibson 1989.

15. Lest a reader think I hold myself out as without fault, I should point out that I used Murphy and Tanenhaus's items in research on support for the Court among trial judges. Unfortunately, the same points I make in this chapter apply with equal and perhaps greater force to my own work. There is blame enough to go around for those who have taken part in the work on public opinion and the Court.

16. In all fairness, I should take note of Murphy and Tanenhaus's recent reanalysis of data on support collected back in 1966 and 1975 (forthcoming). It shows once again, as did their earlier work, an awareness of the imperfect nature of these measures

17. We worded the items as follows: (1) the power of the Supreme Court to declare acts of Congress unconstitutional should be eliminated; (2) if the Supreme Court continually makes decisions that the people disagree with, it might be better to do away with the Court altogether; (3) it would not make much difference if the U.S. Constitution were rewritten so as to reduce the powers of the Supreme Court; (4) the right of the Supreme Court to decide certain types of controversial issues should be limited by the Congress; and (5) people should be willing to do everything they can to make sure that any proposal to abolish the Supreme Court is defeated.

18. I examined the relationship between the mass media's coverage of the Supreme Court and the public's confidence and found a positive relationship between visibility and support. We ought to look into this connection in more detail. Unfortunately, in our understanding of the relationship between the mass media and the Court, we have not gone much beyond Newland 1964 and Grey 1972.

References

Adamany, David W. 1973. Legitimacy, realigning elections, and the Supreme Court. *Wisconsin Law Review* 3:790-846.

Adamany, David W., and Joel B. Grossman. 1983. Support for the Supreme Court as a national policymaker. *Law and Policy Quarterly* 5:405-437.

Alsop, Joseph, and Turner Catledge. 1938. *The 168 days*. Garden City, N.Y.: Doubleday.

Arnold, R. Douglas. 1982. Overtilled and undertilled fields in American politics. *Political Science Quarterly* 97:91-103.

Baas, Larry R., and Dan Thomas. 1984. The Supreme Court and policy legitimation: Experimental tests. *American Politics Quarterly* 12:335-360.

———. 1985. The Supreme Court and legitimacy: Opinion and behavioral effects. Paper presented at the annual meeting of the American Political Science Association, New Orleans.

Baker, Leonard. 1967. *Back to back: The duel between FDR and the Supreme Court.* New York: Macmillan.

Barnum, David G. 1985. The Supreme Court and public opinion: Judicial decision making in the post-New Deal period. *Journal of Politics* 47:652-665.

Bickel, Alexander M. 1962. *The least dangerous branch.* Indianapolis: Bobbs-Merrill.

Black, Charles, Jr. 1960. *The people and the Court.* Englewood Cliffs, N.J.: Prentice-Hall.

Caldeira, Gregory A. 1977. Children's images of the Supreme Court: A preliminary analysis. *Law and Society Review* 11:851-871.

———. 1986. Neither the purse nor the sword: The dynamics of public confidence in the United States Supreme Court. *American Political Science Review* 80:1209-1226.

———. 1987. Public opinion and the Supreme Court: FDR's court-packing plan. *American Political Science Review* 81:1139-1154.

Caldeira, Gregory A., and James L. Gibson. 1989. The etiology of public support for the Supreme Court. Paper presented at the annual meeting of the Midwest Political Science Association, Chicago.

Cantril, Hadley, and Mildred Strunk. 1951. *Public opinion, 1935-1946.* Princeton: Princeton University Press.

Cantwell, Frank V. 1946. Public opinion and the legislative process. *American Political Science Review* 40:924-935.

Casey, Gregory. 1974. The Supreme Court and myth: An empirical investigation. *Law and Society Review* 8:385-419.

———. 1975. The theory of presidential association: A replication. *American Journal of Political Science* 19:19-25.

———. 1976. Popular perceptions of Supreme Court rulings. *American Politics Quarterly* 4:3-45.

Casper, Jonathan D. 1972. *The politics of civil liberties.* New York: Harper and Row.

———. 1976. The Supreme Court and national policy making. *American Political Science Review* 70:50-66.

Converse, Philip E. 1964. The nature of belief systems in mass publics. In *Ideology and discontent,* ed. David Apter. Glencoe, Ill.: Free Press.

Cook, Beverly B. 1973. Sentencing behavior of federal judges: Draft cases—1972. *University of Cincinnati Law Review* 42:597-633.

———. 1977. Public opinion and federal judicial policy. *American Journal of Political Science* 21:567-600.

_____. 1979. Judicial policy: Change over time. *American Journal of Political Science* 23:208-214.

Dahl, Robert A. 1957. Decision-making in a democracy: The Supreme Court as a national policy-maker. *Journal of Public Law* 6:279-295.

Daniels, William. 1973. The Supreme Court and its publics. *Albany Law Review* 37:632-661.

Dennis, Jack. 1975. Mass public support for the U.S. Supreme Court. Paper presented at the annual conference of the American Association for Public Opinion Research, Itasca, Ill.

Dolbeare, Kenneth M. 1967. The public views the Supreme Court. In *Law, politics, and the federal courts,* ed. Herbert Jacob. Boston: Little, Brown.

Dolbeare, Kenneth M., and Phillip E. Hammond. 1968. The political party basis of attitudes toward the Supreme Court. *Public Opinion Quarterly* 37:16-30.

Easton, David. 1965. *A systems analysis of political life.* New York: Wiley.

_____. 1975. A re-assessment of the concept of political support. *British Journal of Political Science* 5:435-457.

_____. 1976. Theoretical approaches to political support. *Canadian Journal of Political Science* 9:431-448.

Easton, David, and Jack Dennis. 1969. *Children in the political system: Origins of political legitimacy.* New York: McGraw-Hill.

Franklin, Charles H., and Liane C. Kosaki. 1989. The republican schoolmaster: The Supreme Court, public opinion and abortion. *American Political Science Review* 83:751-772.

Gallup Poll. 1987a. Public backs Senate's rejection of Bork. *Gallup Report* 267:15-17.

_____. 1987b. Public divided on Bork nomination: Many uninformed, uncommitted. *Gallup Report* 264:29-30.

Gibson, James L. 1980. Environmental constraints on the behavior of judges: A representational model of judicial decision-making. *Law and Society Review* 14:343-370.

_____. 1989. Understandings of justice: Institutional legitimacy, procedural justice, and political tolerance. *Law and Society Review* 23:469-496.

Gibson, James L., and Gregory A. Caldeira. 1990. Black support for the American Supreme Court. Paper presented at the annual meeting of the Midwest Political Science Association, Chicago.

Giles, Micheal W., and Thomas G. Walker. 1975. Judicial policy-making and southern school desegregation. *Journal of Politics* 37:917-936.

Graebner, Dianne B. 1973. Judicial activity and public attitudes: A quantitative study of selective service sentencing in the Vietnam War period. *Buffalo Law Review* 23:465-498.

Graham, Barbara Luck. 1985. Institutional popularity of the Supreme Court: A reassessment. Paper presented at the annual meeting of the American Political Science Association, New Orleans.

Grey, David. 1972. *The Supreme Court and the news media.* Evanston, Ill.: Northwestern University Press.

Handberg, Roger. 1984. Public opinion and the United States Supreme Court, 1935-1981. *International Social Science Review* 59:3-13.

Handberg, Roger, and William S. Maddox. 1982. Public support for the Supreme Court in the 1970s. *American Politics Quarterly* 10:333-346.

Hensley, Thomas R., Joyce A. Baugh, and Steven R. Brown. 1985. The Supreme Court and the 1985 "school prayer" case: Testing legitimacy theory. Paper presented at the annual meeting of the American Political Science Association, New Orleans.

———. 1986. Testing Supreme Court legitimacy theory. Paper presented at the annual meeting of the American Political Science Association, Washington, D.C.

Hirsch, Herbert, and Lewis Donohew. 1968. A note on black-white differences in attitudes toward the Supreme Court. *Social Science Quarterly* 49:557-663.

Jaros, Dean, and Robert Roper. 1980. The Supreme Court, myth, diffuse support, specific support, and legitimacy. *American Politics Quarterly* 8:85-105.

Johnson, Charles A., and Bradley C. Canon. 1984. *Judicial policies: Implementation and impact.* Washington, D.C.: CQ Press.

Kessel, John H. 1966. Public perceptions of the Supreme Court. *Midwest Journal of Political Science* 10:167-191.

Kritzer, Herbert M. 1978. Political correlates of the behavior of federal district judges: A "best case" analysis. *Journal of Politics* 40:25-58.

———. 1979. Federal judges and their political environments: The influence of public opinion. *American Journal of Political Science* 23:194-207.

Kuklinski, James H., and John E. Stanga. 1979. Political participation and government responsiveness: The behavior of California superior courts. *American Political Science Review* 73:1090-1099.

Lehne, Richard, and John Reynolds. 1978. The impact of judicial activism on public opinion. *American Journal of Political Science* 22:896-904.

Lerner, Max. 1937. Constitution and court as symbols. *Yale Law Journal* 46:1290-1319.

Levinson, Sanford V. 1980. "The Constitution" in American civil religion. *Supreme Court Review* 1979:123-151.

Lipset, Seymour Martin, and William Schneider. 1987. *The confidence gap: Business, labor, and government in the public mind.* Rev. ed. Baltimore: Johns Hopkins University Press.

Loewenberg, Gerhard. 1971. The influence of parliamentary behavior on regime stability. *Comparative Politics* 3:177-200.

Marshall, Thomas. 1987. The Supreme Court as an opinion leader. *American Politics Quarterly* 15:147-168.

———. 1988. Public opinion, representation, and the modern Supreme Court. *American Politics Quarterly* 17:286-316.

———. 1989. *Public opinion and the Supreme Court.* New York: Longman.

Miller, Warren E., and Donald E. Stokes. 1963. Constituency influence in Congress. *American Political Science Review* 52:45-56.

Monroe, Alan D. 1979. Consistency between public preferences and national policy decisions. *American Politics Quarterly* 7:3-19.

Muir, William K., Jr. 1967. *Law and attitude change.* Chicago: University of Chicago Press.

Murphy, Walter F. 1962. *Congress and the Court: A case study in the American political process.* Chicago: University of Chicago Press.

Murphy, Walter F., and Joseph Tanenhaus. 1968a. Public opinion and the Supreme Court: The Goldwater campaign. *Public Opinion Quarterly* 32:31-50.

————. 1968b. Public opinion and the United States Supreme Court: A preliminary mapping of some prerequisites for Court legitimation of regime changes. *Law and Society Review* 2:357-382.

————. 1970. The Supreme Court and its elite publics: A preliminary report. Paper presented at the meeting of the International Political Science Association, Munich, West Germany.

————. n.d. Publicity, public opinion, and the Supreme Court. *Northwestern University Law Review,* forthcoming.

Murphy, Walter F., Joseph Tanenhaus, and Daniel Kastner. 1973. *Public evaluations of constitutional courts. Alternative explanations.* Beverly Hills, Calif.: Sage.

Newland, Chester A. 1964. Press coverage of the U.S. Supreme Court. *Western Political Quarterly* 17:15-36.

Page, Benjamin I., and Robert Y. Shapiro. 1983. Effects of public opinion on policy. *American Political Science Review* 77:175-190.

Page, Benjamin I., Robert Y. Shapiro, and Glenn Dempsey. 1987. What moves public opinion? *American Political Science Review* 81:23-44.

Patterson, Samuel C., Ronald Hedlund, and G. R. Boynton. 1975. *Representatives and represented: Bases of public support for the American legislatures.* New York. Wiley.

Peltason, Jack. 1961. *Fifty-eight lonely men: Southern federal judges and school desegregation.* New York: Harcourt, Brace, and World.

Polsby, Nelson W. 1981-1982. Contemporary transformations of American politics: Thoughts on the research agendas of political scientists. *Political Science Quarterly* 96:551-570.

Pruet, George W., Jr., and Henry R. Glick. 1986. Social environment, public opinion, and judicial policymaking. *American Politics Quarterly* 14:5-33.

Rosen, Corey M. 1974. A test of presidential leadership of public opinion: The split ballot technique. *Polity* 6:282-290.

Sarat, Austin, and Neil Vidmar. 1976. Public opinion, the death penalty, and the Eighth Amendment: Testing the Marshall hypothesis. *Wisconsin Law Review* 1976:171-197.

Schmidhauser, John, and Larry Berg. 1972. *The Supreme Court and Congress: Conflict and interaction, 1945-1968.* New York: Free Press.

Secret, Philip E., James B. Johnson, and Susan Welch. 1986. Racial differences in attitudes toward the Supreme Court's decision on prayer in public schools. *Social Science Quarterly* 67:877-885.

Seidman, David. 1975. Simulation of public opinion: A caveat. *Public Opinion Quarterly* 39:331-342.

Sigelman, Lee. 1979. Black and white differences in attitudes toward the Supreme Court: A replication in the 1970s. *Social Science Quarterly* 60:113-119.

Stumpf, Harry P., Martin Shapiro, David J. Danelski, Austin Sarat, and David M. O'Brien. 1983. Whither political jurisprudence: A symposium. *Western Political Quarterly* 36:533-569.

Tanenhaus, Joseph, and Walter F. Murphy. 1981. Patterns of public support for the Supreme Court: A panel study. *Journal of Politics* 43:24-39.

Tyler, Tom R. n.d. *Why people follow the law: Procedural justice, legitimacy, and compliance.* New Haven: Yale University Press, forthcoming.

Vidmar, Neil, and Phoebe Ellsworth. 1974. Public opinion and the death penalty. *Stanford Law Review* 26:1245-1270.

Wahlke, John C. 1971. Policy demands and system support: The role of the represented. *British Journal of Political Science* 1:271-290.

Zaller, John R. 1987. Diffusion of political attitudes. *Journal of Personality and Social Psychology* 53:821-833.

13. COURTS AND INTEREST GROUPS

Lee Epstein

In the fall of 1969, Justice Hugo Black received a visit from an old friend, Thomas G. ("Tommy the Cork") Corcoran. Black and Corcoran had known each other since the 1930s when they both were "zealous advocates of the New Deal"; Black had even hired Corcoran's daughter, Margaret, as a law clerk. Lately, though, the relationship had taken a turn for the worse. Black had nothing but disdain for Corcoran's present occupation, as a lobbyist for organizational and corporate interests.

Nevertheless, Black was pleased to see his old acquaintance. At least he was until Corcoran revealed the purpose of his visit—to put in a good word for a corporation seeking a rehearing from the Supreme Court.[1] As the story goes (Woodward and Armstrong 1979, 79-85), Black was shocked and dismayed; he regarded as taboo any mention of a pending case to a sitting justice of the Court. He banished Corcoran from his office and from his life, the relationship irreparably damaged.

What Black's reaction to Corcoran's visit suggests, of course, is that judges consider themselves above the ordinary pressure tactics used by groups to influence elected officials. Though lobbyists line the corridors of the Capitol to converse with members of Congress, such is not the case in the Marble Palace, the Supreme Court building. The rules of the legal game simply prohibit direct encounters.

Hence, if interest groups wish to influence the outcomes of legal disputes, they must find alternative routes of "lobbying," routes that correspond to the norms of the judiciary. In this chapter, we explore the various strategies groups have developed to affect judicial decision making, as well as several related aspects of interest group litigation: the frequency of group participation, the sorts of organizations most typically found in judicial corridors, the types of issues engendering group interest, and the question of efficacy: Are their efforts successful? First, though, we consider several issues endemic to the study of group litigation: the development of this line of inquiry and its place within the larger study of group politics.

The Study of Interest Group Litigation

To scholars studying interest group behavior in the more political institutions of government—the executive and legislative branches—Justice Black's reaction to Corcoran's visit would seem anomalous. After all, members of Congress and the bureaucracy maintain regular contact with representatives of pressure organizations, so-called lobbyists. Indeed, it would be virtually impossible to study the policy-making process in the United States without considering the role of organized pressure groups.

A plethora of research highlights the intensity of pluralism within the elected institutions. In their survey of Washington, D.C.-based organizations, Kay Schlozman and John Tierney (1986) found that 98 percent of their respondents contacted governmental officials directly "to present their point of view" and that 85 percent actually helped draft legislation (p. 150). Jeffrey M. Berry's more contextual work (1989) further describes the extent to which lobbyists are willing to go to make their presence felt. As he notes:

> Contrary to the image of lobbyists as back-room operators, much of their time is taken up trying to be visible. They spend valuable time at congressional hearings even though nothing of great consequence is likely to happen there. Still, it's a chance to touch base with other lobbyists and congressional staffers. They'll make repeated visits to Capitol Hill offices. . . . (p. 79)

By the same token, research by Robert Salisbury and his colleagues (1987) illustrates the depth of pressure group involvement in the governmental process. They asked organizations involved in several discrete policy areas (such as agriculture, the environment) to identify allied and adversarial groups existing within that domain. Each nominating organization listed hundreds of different groups lobbying in the various areas.

That the environment within which the Court works has become increasingly populated by organized interests is undoubtedly true: virtually every case heard by the justices during the past terms has generated some interest within the pressure group community. Consider the Court's recent foray into abortion, *Webster v. Reproductive Health Services* (109 S.Ct. 3040 [1989]), in which more than 400 groups participated, expressing their views on reproductive freedom.[2]

Cases like *Webster* provide substantial proof that groups attempt to influence the outcome of judicial decisions. Surprisingly, though, it took many years and many studies to convince the academic community of this; in fact, only during the past decade has the study of group litigation sparked the imagination of increasing numbers of students of the judicial and group processes.

It is, indeed, surprising that this line of inquiry took so long to reach fruition when we consider that the works of the great pluralists— Arthur Bentley (1908) and David B. Truman (1951)—both included discussions of interest group involvement in the judiciary. Bentley's *The Process of Government,* one of the first studies to acknowledge that organized interests played any role in the policy process, included a chapter on the judiciary.[3] In the book, he argued that there were "numerous instances of the same group pressures which operate through executives and legislatures, operating also through supreme courts" (1908, 338). Truman's (1951, 1971) *The Governmental Process,* an expansion of Bentley's work, reiterated the role organized pressures play in all arenas of government, including the courts. As he claimed, "The activities of the judicial officers of the United States are not exempt from the processes of group politics.... Though myth and legend may argue to the contrary ... the judiciary reflects the play of interests, and few organized groups can afford to be indifferent to its activities" (1971, 479).

These works, particularly Truman's, generated great excitement among academics, many of whom quickly turned their attention to interest group involvement in the legislative and executive branches. In the preface to his revised edition of *The Governmental Process,* Truman (1971) listed scores of works examining group involvement in these institutions. When it came to the judiciary, however, he noted that "academic research" had not been "extensive" (p. xxxvii). In fact, he cited but one work focusing exclusively on organizational involvement in the legal system: Clement E. Vose's (1959) *Caucasians Only,* an examination of the National Association for the Advancement of Colored People's (NAACP's) efforts to end racially based housing discrimination.[4]

This sole exception, though, was an important one: scholars uniformly praised *Caucasians Only* for its meticulous documentation of the NAACP's litigation campaign in the restrictive covenant cases. Virtually every leading textbook of the day on American government, the interest group process, and the judiciary cited Vose's work approvingly. For all this attention, though, that book and Vose's other works (1955, 1957, 1958, 1966) generally failed to spawn broader interest in the subject of group mobilization of the law.

In retrospect, we can point to a number of factors that inhibited the growth of this area of inquiry during the 1950s and 1960s. An important one was that some confusion existed over its appropriate academic classification. Was it a unique phenomenon that was best examined by students of the judicial process, or was "it general enough to be treated profitably by interest group analysts" (Epstein, Kobylka, and Stewart, 1991)? Because scholars, including Truman, could not agree over the answer to this question, the study fell between the cracks. Those exploring pluralism in the elected institutions tended to leave "the courts" to judicial researchers, apparently believing that certain "attributes" of legal lobbying set it "apart from other forums" (Vose 1981, 13). Yet, with only a handful of exceptions (see Barker 1967; Cortner 1964, 1968; Hakman 1966, 1969; Manwaring 1962), students of the law showed little inclination to study group use of the judiciary.

Why did students of the courts, in particular, virtually ignore this area of inquiry? For one thing, the whole idea that interest groups attempt to influence judicial outcomes seemed so counterintuitive as to border on the ludicrous. At that time, many analysts viewed the Court as operating in a wholly different context than Congress or the president, a context that placed it above the ordinary political pressures. As such, they asked why interest groups would even attempt to lobby justices, as their pleas would fall on deaf ears.

The seminal empirical studies of the day reinforced these views. Those conducted by the behavioralists (see Schubert 1959, 1965; Spaeth 1963) argued that justices based "their decisions solely upon personal preferences"; and, because they lacked "electoral accountability," they did not have to cloak those views to satisfy any constituency (see Rohde and Spaeth 1976, 72). Even more damaging were the analyses of Nathan Hakman (1966, 1969). After examining group involvement in Court cases from 1928 through 1966, he concluded that organizational presence in the legal system was virtually nonexistent. His works went so far as to call the entire line of inquiry "scholarly folklore" and to suggest that Vose's study represented the exception, not the rule.[5]

Further repelling scholars from this area was the difficulty of collecting data about group involvement in the Court. Obstacles here were (and continue to be) numerous. For one, unlike students of the legislative and executive processes, who can readily obtain interviews with politicians and their staff, those of the Court are often less successful: justices of the Supreme Court are not inclined to talk to scholars about particular cases, or much else, for that matter. And, when they will talk, the justices limit the kinds of questions they will answer.[6]

Hence, if scholars want to explore interest group involvement in the judiciary, they must rely on two other sources, neither of which is flawless. The first is contact, either through interviews or mail questionnaires, with group representatives. Such data provide researchers with insight into the ways in which groups frame legal arguments, into how they perceive the legal environment, and into more basic issues: why they choose to litigate, the resources they appropriate to court suits, and so forth. Although this is valuable information, it also is one-sided data: we learn a great deal about how groups relate to the judiciary, but not vice versa. Moreover, the use of interview and survey data often raises questions of reliability and validity: Would another researcher evoke the same responses from interviewees? Do all subjects understand and react to questions in the same way? Concomitantly, as we describe later, even identifying a sampling frame can pose complex questions: for example, should we survey all groups or just those that use litigation?

Given these issues, most of those studying group litigation have acknowledged the need to supplement interview data with data from the Court's records. Here, they also face obstacles, albeit of a different ilk. Because the usual sources of Court opinions—the reporter systems—contain incomplete information about group involvement in cases, scholars must turn to legal briefs. Such briefs are readily available to most researchers only in microfiche form, making for a tedious data-collection process. What further complicates matters is that even these legal briefs may not necessarily provide a full picture of group involvement in specific cases; for example, some attorneys fail to list their organizational affiliation on the briefs. It is common knowledge that the NAACP Legal Defense Fund (LDF) sponsored *Brown v. Board of Education of Topeka* (347 U.S. 483 [1954]), but nowhere does the brief mention that group. Even more troublesome is that it is virtually impossible to identify groups that might have assisted lead counsel (that is, provided legal expertise and/or funds), but chose to conceal their involvement. So although legal briefs constitute the primary data sources for those studying group litigation, they are imperfect gauges that tend to underestimate organizational involvement in cases.

In short, during the 1950s and 1960s those who wished to study group participation in the judicial process faced a bumpy road. Not only did the evidence point against widespread pluralism in the legal system, but gathering data to the contrary proved to be most difficult.

The decades of the 1970s and 1980s, though, saw a resurgence of interest in this area of inquiry. In part, this came about because scholars began to marshal a great deal of evidence dismissing the notion that the Court was impervious to outside influences, including interest groups, public opinion, and the like. So too they began to question whether Hakman's data accurately portrayed group involvement in the Court. After publication of Frank J. Sorauf's (1976) investigation of religious establishment suits and Karen O'Connor's (1980) of sex discrimination cases, both of which provided ample evidence of group involvement in the judiciary, some suggested that Hakman's analysis was bound to past Court eras and that pluralism in the judicial process was on the rise.

Indeed, since 1980, scholars have published nearly fifteen books and thirty articles directly on the subject of interest group litigation. Also significant is that textbooks on interest groups (see Hrebenar and Scott 1982; Schlozman and Tierney 1986; Berry 1989) and on the Court (see Baum 1985; Wasby 1988) devote full sections, if not chapters, to the subject, when just a few years earlier a paragraph would have sufficed.

Clearly, difficult problems of data collection remain, but no longer do scholars have to be exhorted to this area of inquiry. A new generation of analysts finds the counterintuitive aspect of group involvement in the judiciary intriguing, rather than bemusing. And their interest has created a new conventional wisdom about group litigation: that "the external environment under which the judiciary operates is, in important respects, similar to that of other governmental institutions" (Epstein, Kobylka, and Stewart 1991, 1).

Needless to say, these recent studies have opened many doors into the world of group litigation. In the next sections, we enter that world, reporting current knowledge of the strategies and tactics of group litigation, the kinds of groups involved in the judiciary, the sorts of issues that attract groups' attention, and the issue of efficacy—do groups matter? We also speculate on some unexplored terrain, areas of interest for future research.

Strategies and Tactics of Group Litigation

In the introduction to this chapter, we told of the story of Justice Black's reaction to his face-to-face lobbying encounter with Tommy Corcoran. If that story carries any moral, it is this: groups and their representatives must avoid direct encounters with justices and judges. This is a reality of the legal system to which virtually all scholars submit; even Truman recognized that direct lobbying of judges would violate the norms of the judiciary. As Truman and others (see Vose 1959) demonstrated, to avoid breaching these traditions while attempting to influence judicial decisions, groups rely on two legal strategies: they sponsor test cases and they file amicus curiae briefs. These practices continue to be the major approaches used by organizations to influence court decisions.[7]

Sponsorship of Test Cases

In general, groups sponsor test cases—those designed to test specific legal arguments—by supplying the attorneys and funds necessary to carry an appeal to the U.S. Supreme Court. Consider the 1988 case of *Bowen v. Kendrick* (108 S.Ct. 2562 [1988]), in which American Civil Liberties Union (ACLU) attorneys helped other organizations, taxpayers, and clergy to challenge the Adolescent Family Life Act (AFLA), a law providing federal grants to agencies and groups, including those with ties to religious organizations, for "services and research in the area of premarital adolescent sexual relations and pregnancy." [8] The alleged purpose of this act was to address the "severe adverse health, social, and economic consequences" associated with adolescent pregnancy, by involving a "wide array of community groups. . ." (42 U.S.C. 300z[a][5]). The law, though, placed several restrictions on potential grantees; most important, they could not use any AFLA funds to promote abortions.

In its legal briefs and in oral argument before the U.S. Supreme Court, the ACLU alleged that the process by which groups obtained funding under the act (and their use of those monies) violated the religious establishment clause of the First Amendment. That is, because some of AFLA's grantees were religious organizations, the ACLU argued that the act permitted too much intermingling of church and state.

To substantiate these claims, ACLU attorneys loaded their briefs with facts about the selection process; for example, they claimed that the director of the program selected grant evaluators who were affiliated with religions and who "understood that the legislation was intended to require religious indoctrination to achieve" its goals. They also presented profiles of some of the organizations that obtained funding and of those that were rejected; indeed, their data indicated that a large proportion of applicants receiving grants were affiliated with religious groups, while those rejected "were told they had not received funding because their programs promised 'no involvement of religious groups.' " Finally, they excerpted sections from successful applications to demonstrate that organizations were, in fact, using government funds to promote religious views. As one applicant, the Southeastern Missouri Association of Public Health Administrators, wrote:

> One of the most obvious tools which can be used to change the attitude of young people toward sexual activity . . . is the use of the religious foundation as a support for sexual education. Most major religions see sexuality as being of God and can therefore . . . help young people to learn about their bodies and the values that relate to their sexual functioning in a context that is consistent with the tenants [sic] of their particular faith.

As *Bowen* highlights, groups often supply litigants with attorneys and present legal arguments to the Court. Previous analyses reveal, though, that direct sponsorship can entail a good deal more (see Wasby

1986). Consider *Muller v. Oregon* (208 U.S. 412 [1908]), a test case sponsored by the National Consumers' League (NCL), one of several organizations founded during the Progressive Era to secure protective legislation for women workers (Vose 1957, 1972). To accomplish this objective, NCL members lobbied state legislators across the country.

At first, this strategy worked quite well: by the early 1900s several states had enacted maximum-hour work laws. The NCL's victory in Oregon, which passed a ten-hour work law for laundresses in 1903, was particularly encouraging. Within two years, though, an employer challenged the Oregon law, arguing that it violated constitutional guarantees. Indeed, his argument rested on solid legal ground: in *Lochner v. New York* (198 U.S. 45 [1905]), the U.S. Supreme Court had ruled that a ten-hour work law for bakers went beyond the state's "police powers."

With nothing but unfavorable precedent on their side, Oregon state attorneys were in a bit of a quandary; after all, they had to find some legal ground on which to defend their state's law. The NCL, too, was troubled; having worked hard to secure passage of the law, it did not wish to see its victory nullified by a court. To safeguard against this possibility, NCL leaders contacted Boston attorney and future Supreme Court justice Louis Brandeis.[9] After considering their predicament, Brandeis agreed to assist NCL leaders under two conditions. First, he demanded sole control over the case, a condition to which Oregon happily acceded. Second, he asked NCL members and volunteers to gather "*facts,* published by anyone with expert knowledge of industry and its relationship to women's hours of labor" (Goldmark 1953, 148-149, italics in original). Given the unfavorable state of the law, Brandeis needed such data to bolster his case.

Within two weeks NCL workers compiled vast statistical evidence indicating that long work hours could be detrimental to women's reproductive systems. Brandeis's resultant legal argument before the U.S. Supreme Court, often called the Brandeis Brief, relied almost exclusively on this "social science" data: the 113-page brief contained but 2 pages of legal argument! Nonetheless, in a unanimous decision, the Court adopted Brandeis's position; in fact, it cited and "actually commended" the Brandeis brief (Vose 1972, 173).

The point of this story is quite simple. Supplying attorneys to needy litigants is insufficient. Rather, we now know that groups seeking to sponsor litigation often prime the Court before they enter its corridors. Like the NCL, many other organizations rely on social science evidence to do just that (see Loh 1984). Most illustrative was the NAACP LDF's legal brief in *McCleskey v. Kemp* (481 U.S. 279 [1987]), which presented statistical evidence indicating that Georgia juries were more likely to give the death penalty to blacks (those who had killed whites) than to whites. Other group attorneys write journal articles to achieve similar ends (Newland 1959). Prior to its litigation involving racial discrimination in housing, the NAACP LDF and its allies "inundated law reviews with articles presenting constitutional justification for their cause," which they later cited in their legal briefs (Epstein 1985, 13; see also Vose 1959).[10] Moreover, interest group preparation for litigation may begin even before a case has crystallized. In *Muller*, the NCL had no choice but to defend the legislation it had initiated. It is often true, though, that groups take offensive postures, initiating challenges to laws, not defending them. In such circumstances, groups must formulate priorities and then select cases best meeting those objectives (Sorauf 1976). Again consider *Bowen v. Kendrick*. If the ACLU wanted to participate, it had no other option but to mount a challenge to the Adolescent Family Life Act. After all, because Congress had already passed the law, the organization was forced into an offensive posture.

Given the complexity involved in directly sponsoring litigation, why do groups even attempt to lobby the judiciary? After all, would it not have been easier for the NCL to have allowed Oregon attorneys to defend their state's laws or for the ACLU to have watched passively as citizens and clergy hired their own counsel to challenge the Adolescent Family Life Act? Groups and scholars offer a number of explanations. First, it is arguably true that many organizations have insufficient status to accomplish their objectives in the more political branches and processes of government. The most obvious example of this was the NAACP's quest to attain equal status for blacks. When that organization formed in 1909, southern state legislatures denied blacks access to their floors, placed barriers to the ballot and to quality education, and so forth. Because such attitudes made it virtually impossible for the NAACP to achieve its objectives in traditional arenas, it turned to the courts. As Richard Cortner (1968) has argued, the NAACP and other *politically disadvantaged* groups

> are highly dependent upon the judicial process as a means of pursuing their policy interests usually because they are temporarily or, even permanently, disadvantaged in terms of their ability to attain successfully their goals in the electoral process, within the elected institution or in the bureaucracy. If they are to succeed at all in the pursuit of their goals they are almost compelled to resort to litigation. (p. 287)

Put in this context, the ACLU was the politically disadvantaged group in the *Bowen* litigation because a majoritarian branch of government, Congress, had enacted the AFLA. To challenge it, then, the ACLU was forced into legal arenas. And, even there, it had to counter the arguments of the U.S. solicitor general, who represents the U.S. government in Court—no small feat for any organization![11]

Many studies conducted in the 1970s and early 1980s (see O'Connor 1980; Wenner 1984) reinforced Cortner's basic conclusion: in general, it is politically disadvantaged groups that seek redress through the legal system. Yet since most of these analyses focused on organizations representing inherently disadvantaged groups (such as blacks, women, environmentalists), such empirical verification was inescapable: studies solely of disadvantaged groups that use the courts are bound to find that such interests do, in fact, litigate.

In the late 1980s, though, when it became apparent that many groups, seemingly representing "advantaged" interests, were using the courts, some began to question seriously the generalizability of Cortner's thesis. Why, for example, were business interests and trade associations turning to court litigation? After all, one could hardly label the Chamber of Commerce or the American Booksellers' Association disadvantaged interests. Consider even the National Consumers' League—that group actually won in state legislatures before moving into the legal system.

As more and more apparent exceptions emerged to Cortner's proposition, scholars (see Gates and McIntosh 1989) began to suggest other motivating factors behind group litigation. Some hypothesized that, like the NCL, many of today's organizations go to court to support laws for which they fought in the elected institutions. After Congress passed legislation limiting Medicaid funding for abortions in 1976, pro-life groups went to court to defend it, fearing that the Carter administration would provide inadequate representation (see Epstein 1985). Others argued that because many groups now perceive the Court as the final arbiter of the law, they believe that a victory there has a degree of permanency often lacking in congressional legislation. To see the wisdom in this belief, we only have to consider the Jehovah's Witnesses' successful litigation campaign to overturn mandatory flag salutes (pledges of allegiance).[12] Despite public opinion, protests, and state legislation to the contrary, it stands as good law. Still another proposition was that organizations found themselves in adversarial relations with groups that were litigating and thus had no choice but to oppose their efforts in the judicial arena. Seen in this light, once the ACLU and other pro-choice groups moved the abortion debate into the legal system, they practically forced pro-life organizations to follow suit (see Rubin 1987).

Recent research has begun to test systematically some of these explanations. Patrick Bruer (1987) surveyed 712 Washington, D.C.-

based organizations, asking them to enumerate their reasons for using litigation (if they did). His results suggest that several factors contribute heavily to the decision to litigate: the policy opposition faced by the group in other arenas, the scope of the group's interests and its policy focus, and the legal environment. Others, such as the group's litigation budget and its constituency (that is, whether it represented minority interests), had no apparent explanatory value.

This and several other attempts at exploring group litigation from a broader perspective are not without problems. In Bruer's case, the source from which he draws his sample—*Washington Representatives*—may help explain his results. This reference contains only Washington, D.C.-based organizations, while many litigating groups, particularly those representing minority interests (such as the NAACP LDF) are located outside of the D.C. area. Thus, Bruer's sample may have been less than reflective of the litigating population.

These issues aside, survey research is an important advancement for this line of inquiry. As Bruer notes:

> Much of the research on use of the courts by organizations to influence public policy has focused on particular types of groups litigating in selected policy areas. The in-depth case studies suggest some broader hypotheses to account for organizational use of litigation to achieve policy goals, *but do not provide the information needed to test the applicability of these possible explanations across groups and issues.* (1987, 35; emphasis added)

Survey research of the sort he conducted can accomplish that objective if researchers take proper care in developing their sampling frame and, as we discuss later, in dealing with other issues related to scientific inquiry.

The Amicus Curiae Brief

Though its benefits are considerable, direct sponsorship also carries significant costs. Not only is it difficult to execute, but it can be extremely expensive to implement, running into hundreds of thousands of dollars. Moreover, just as it can produce extraordinary victories, direct sponsorship can result in devastating losses. Fifteen years after *Muller,* the NCL lost a major case involving minimum wage legislation.[13] Some argue that this defeat ultimately led to the demise of the organization. For these and other reasons (see Barker 1967), many groups file amicus curiae briefs in addition to or in lieu of direct sponsorship.

The translation of the Latin *amicus curiae* is "friend of the court"; but this strategy actually involves befriending a party to a suit, not the Court.[14] That is, nonparties file amicus curiae briefs in support of one of the litigants in a case; filers themselves are not direct participants. Again, consider *Bowen v. Kendrick*. As illustrated in Table 13-1, organized interests filed thirteen amicus curiae briefs onto which more than eighty groups signed. Moreover, interests filed on both sides of the case: eight briefs supported the ACLU's position, while five asked the Court to uphold the act.

Beyond overcoming the deficits of the sponsorship approach, why do so many groups file these briefs? One reason is that they desire input into a case, but are unable to sponsor it. Americans for Effective Law Enforcement (AELE), founded in 1966 to reinforce the efforts of prosecutors in criminal cases, relies exclusively on the amicus curiae strategy. Because U.S. and district attorneys and other governmental litigators "sponsor" its position, this is the most direct way it can accomplish its objectives.

Sometimes groups file briefs at the request of other groups (see Caldeira and Wright 1988; O'Connor 1980). Such coalition building manifests itself in a number of ways; for example, again consider Table 13-1, which depicts briefs filed in *Bowen*. As we can see, almost thirty groups signed onto one brief, written by the National Coalition for Public Education and Religious Liberty.[15]

Finally, many groups believe that a well-crafted brief can influence the outcome of a Court decision. The ACLU holds this policy on amicus curiae activity: "Amicus curiae participation will ordinarily present no problems beyond simple questions whether an appropriate civil liberties question is involved and whether an amicus brief *will be helpful to the court* and generally advance the purpose of the ACLU" [emphasis added].[16] Other group representatives agree, but for different reasons. One suggested that the amicus curiae is more effective than sponsorship because it allows them "to take a broader perspective" by "paring down other issues" of little interest. Another stated that his group thought the amicus to be a more "informed source [bringing] in more empirical intellectual data" than briefs filed by the parties.

In *Bowen*, we see all of these various views represented in more specific form. Catholic Charities, U.S.A., filed because it had financial interests at stake: it had received AFLA funding. Conversely, the National Family Planning and Reproductive Health Association participated because many of its members "sought AFLA funds and had been denied because they refuse[d] to abide by the anti-abortion . . . provisions." Religious organizations submitted amicus curiae briefs for myriad, and often conflicting, reasons. One organization, representing orthodox Jews, filed in support of the act, claiming that even though none of its constituents received AFLA funds, it was "concerned because religious organizations" should be able "to participate in social

Table 13-1 Amicus Curiae Participants in *Bowen v. Kendrick*

Groups arguing to strike down the law

1. Council on Religious Freedom
2. The Committee on Public Education and Religious Liberty
3. NOW Legal Defense and Education Fund, National Abortion Rights Action League, American Association of University Women, American Humanist Association, Black Women's Agenda, B'nai B'rith Women, Inc., Center for Law and Social Policy, Committee to Defend Reproductive Rights, Equal Rights Advocates, National Emergency Civil Liberties Committee, NOW, National Women's Health Network, National Women's Political Caucus, Northwest Women's Law Center, United States Student Association, Voters for Choice, Women's Law Project, Women's Legal Defense Fund, Zero Population Growth
4. American Public Health Association, American Psychological Association, Planned Parenthood Federation of America, Inc., National Family Planning and Reproductive Health Association, Inc.
5. National Coalition for Public Education and Religious Liberty (and members of its national organization: American Ethical Union, American Humanist Association, Americans for Religious Liberty, Board of Church and Society of the United Methodist Church, Central Conference of American Rabbis, Committee for Public Education and Religious Liberty, Council for Democratic and Secular Humanism, MCPEARL, Michigan Council about Parochiaid, Missouri Baptist Christian Life Commission, Missouri PEARL, Nassau-Suffolk PEARL, National Association of Catholic Laity, National Council of Jewish Women, National Education Association, National Service Conference of the American Ethical Union, New York State United Teachers, Ohio Association for Public Association and Religious Liberty, People for the American Way, Public Funds for Public Schools of New Jersey, Union of American Hebrew Congregations, Unitarian Universalists Association), Advocates for Children of New York, Inc., Association for Supervision and Curriculum Development, National Association of Elementary School Principals, National Congress of Parents and Teachers, Sex Information and Education Council of the United States, Society for the Scientific Study of Sex
6. Anti-Defamation League of B'nai B'rith, Americans for Religious Liberty
7. Baptist Joint Committee on Public Affairs, American Jewish Committee, Americans United for Separation of Church and State
8. Unitarian Universalist Association, United Synagogues of America, Catholics for a Free Choice, and Episcopal Women's Caucus

Groups arguing to uphold the law

1. The Rutherford Institute and the Rutherford Institutes of Alabama, Arkansas, California, Colorado, Connecticut, Delaware, Florida, Georgia, Kentucky, Michigan, Minnesota, Montana, Ohio, Pennsylvania, Tennessee, Texas, Virginia, and West Virginia
2. Catholic Charities, U.S.A., Catholic Health Association of the United States
3. United States Catholic Conference
4. Catholic League for Religious and Civil Rights and Concerned Women for America
5. National Jewish Commission on Law and Public Affairs

Note: Numbers preceding group names indicate briefs filed.

Source: Adapted from BNA Microfiche Brief Series, Docket Number 87-253.

welfare programs that have legitimate secular objectives" (Brief of National Jewish Commission on Law and Public Affairs, 1988). Another Jewish group, however, argued against the law, suggesting that counseling often "occurs pursuant to overtly religious Christian curricula prepared by Churches . . . and involves proselytizing" (Brief of Anti-Defamation League of B'nai B'rith, 1988). Still other religious organizations were more concerned with the broader implications of the Court's decision on First Amendment law. So, too, women's groups presented a diverse range of reasons for participating. While the National Organization for Women (NOW) Legal Defense and Education Fund argued that the law "restricts and coerces women in their reproductive decisionmaking," Concerned Women for America claimed that the law wisely protected traditional family values.

What these examples suggest, of course, is that interest groups participate as amici curiae for many reasons. Even within the same litigation, as *Bowen* illustrates, groups attempt to advance their unique, and often divergent, perspectives.

Recent studies have attempted to sort through these seemingly idiosyncratic explanations to reach generalizations about amicus curiae participation. An important step in this direction was research reported by Gregory Caldeira and John Wright (1989b) in which they sought to explain organizational decisions to file amicus briefs on petitions for certiorari. To explore this issue, they sent surveys to all organizations ($n = 1,150$) that participated as amici during the 1982 term of the Court. In the end, they found that four factors contributed to the decision to participate: the significance of the case to the group's members, the "existence of conflict," keeping group members "satisfied," and the "perceived efficacy of the briefs" on the Court's decision. Other previously considered important indicators (such as the group's litigation budget and the number of staff attorneys) failed to contribute significantly to group decision making.

As we have already suggested, survey research is not flawless. For one thing, studies like Bruer's and Caldeira and Wright's, which paint broad pictures of group strategies and tactics, tend to lose some of the contextual and descriptive elements that made the works of Vose, Cortner, and others so intriguing. In short, just as we can criticize the case studies because they overemphasize detail and description, we can find fault with the opposite characteristics of survey research.

The discrepancy between the Bruer and Caldeira and Wright sampling frames brings another problem to light. Bruer sampled all organizations, including ones that do not litigate; Caldeira and Wright surveyed only known Court participants. Which approach is best depends on the nature of the research question. Bruer, in some ways, cast his net broader than did Caldeira and Wright, focusing on litigation as but one strategy groups use to influence the governmental process. The alternative approach, though, tells us a great deal more about litigation per se.

Despite these concerns, broad-based survey research represents an important step. Though we may lose some of the detail about specific litigation campaigns (in the style of Vose and Cortner), we can now begin to test long-held propositions about strategies and tactics, which in turn will help us to develop a more precise picture of group involvement in the judicial process.

Concluding Remarks on Strategies

In the end our knowledge about the strategies and tactics groups use to advance their objectives has expanded greatly since the early writings of Truman and Vose. We have explored in some detail group use of sponsorship and of amicus curiae briefs and we know something of why groups use them.

Much work remains, though, before we have a fully developed picture of this aspect of group litigation. For one thing, have we tapped all the strategies groups use to influence the judiciary? The external environment surrounding Court cases of the last decade or so suggests that we have not. Again, consider the Court's 1989 abortion decision, *Webster v. Reproductive Health Services.* Although groups filed seventy-eight amicus curiae briefs, their litigation strategy was far broader: after the Court announced its intention to hear the case, groups on both sides of the issue held vigils outside of the Court, marched and protested throughout the nation, and sought to influence public opinion through the media. In short, pro-life and pro-choice forces treated the Court as if it were Congress considering a piece of legislation, not a judicial body deliberating points of law. This sort of group involvement in cases—attempts at manipulating the external environment within which the Court operates—is a fascinating aspect of the litigation process. Yet, except to note that some groups attempt to garner publicity for their causes (see O'Connor 1980; Olson 1984), we have failed to include it in our discussions of group strategies and tactics.[17]

For another, we have not fully explored the kinds of tactics groups use to influence judicial decisions once they decide to sponsor a case or participate as amicus curiae. Consider again Table 13-1. One of its most striking features is the number of groups signing on to each amicus curiae brief. Such massive participation suggests that groups are attempting to build coalitions, to present the Court with united fronts. Again, coalition building as an interest group tactic has been the subject of many works that explore decision making in the elected institutions (see Wilson 1973; Hall 1969; Salisbury et al. 1987). Yet beyond acknowledging that the average brief contains multiple interest group co-signers, we have left unaddressed many questions: What kinds of groups form alliances, how do groups with generally divergent interests unify around particular legal causes, and what kinds of litigation networks have developed among various organizational types?[18]

Finally, we need to consider issues of research design and strategy. Are questions of group strategies and tactics best addressed through survey research or through case studies? Or perhaps we should blend methodologies so that we can capture all aspects of the phenomenon.

Addressing these and related questions and concerns will not be an easy task; it will require scholars to reconsider some basic issues of research design and to reopen substantive debates by plowing through fields of court briefs and opinions and group records. Yet if we are to understand fully the whys and hows of group litigation, we must turn our attention to these evolving issues.

The Frequency of Organized Participation before the U.S. Supreme Court

How much litigation engenders group participation as sponsors and amici curiae? Although this is a basic question, it is somewhat difficult to address. As we mentioned earlier, Court records may provide a less than complete picture of the extent of interest group involvement in the judiciary. Even legal briefs filed by attorneys sometimes fail to indicate group presence when some does exist. Nevertheless, in the absence of a better alternative, we can use these briefs and other case records to provide some general indication of the extent to which groups participate in litigation.

Based on our examination of Court records and briefs, we find that during the 1987 term of the U.S. Supreme Court, organized interests represented appellants in 38.2 percent of the cases and appellees in 44.2 percent.[19] Overall, they participated as sponsors in 65.4 ($n = 89$) of the 136 cases decided with full opinion. Fully 80 percent included the presence of at least one amicus curiae brief filed by organized or governmental interests; indeed, the average "amici" (that is, a case with one or more amicus briefs) attracted 4.2 briefs.[20] All in all, during the term, the justices received nearly 460 amicus curiae briefs onto which more than 1,600 groups and governmental interests signed!

As impressive as these figures might seem, they are even more so if we consider Table 13-2, which displays past and present interest group involvement as amicus curiae. Based on his data for the years between

Table 13-2   Amicus Curiae Participation before the Supreme Court

Years	Cases with amicus curiae briefs		Total number of cases
	%	N	
1928-1940	1.6	3	181
1941-1952	18.2	67	368
1953-1966	23.8	149	626
1970-1980	53.4	449	841
1988[a]	80.1	109	136

[a] Represents the 1987 term. Includes all cases, not solely those involving noncommercial issues.

Sources: For 1928-1980, Karen O'Connor and Lee Epstein, "An Appraisal of Hakman's 'Folklore,' " *Law and Society Review* 16 (1982): 701-711. (Reprinted by permission of the Law and Society Association.) For 1988, collected by the author.

1928 and 1968, it is easy to see why Hakman (1969) concluded that a view of Supreme Court litigation as "a form of political action" or "pressure group activity" was mere "scholarly folklore" (p. 199). A study (O'Connor and Epstein 1982) examining participation between 1970 and 1980 found a greater group presence, but, as we can see, far below the level reported here.

What factors might account for this rather dramatic increase in group participation before the Court? Though we can only speculate, three seem particularly relevant. First, the number of organizations dedicated to using litigation to achieve policy ends has skyrocketed over recent years. In 1976 a survey of public interest law (Council for Public Interest Law) included 92 groups; a similar one published in 1989 (O'Connor and Epstein) included more than 250. Stated simply, more organizations will inevitably generate more group-backed litigation. Second, as Schlozman and Tierney (1986) have demonstrated, more pressure group activity exists in general: "It is not simply that there are more organizations on the scene, but that these organizations are more active as well . . . [there is a] remarkable increase in the volume of organized activity" (p. 388). Overall, then, during the past decade, interest groups have moved into all arenas of government at record levels.[21]

Third, the Supreme Court itself has encouraged organized group litigants to take refuge in its corridors (see Orren 1976; O'Connor and Epstein 1984a). For one thing, the justices have freely acknowledged the special role "private attorneys general," that is, public interest law groups, can play in litigation. Writing in 1963, the Court (*NAACP v.*

Button, 371 U.S. 415 at 429) proclaimed, "Groups which find themselves unable to achieve their objectives through the ballot frequently turn to the courts. . . . Under the conditions of modern government, litigation may be the sole practicable avenue open to a minority to petition for redress of grievances" (pp. 429-431). Fifteen years later, the justices (*In re Primus,* 436 U.S. 412 [1978]) reinforced this view, acknowledging the role played by the sponsor of *Bowen,* the ACLU, "in the defense of unpopular causes" (p. 427). For another, the Court has upheld congressional legislation authorizing awards of attorneys' fees to groups defending the public interest in particular areas of the law. Such monies have allowed groups to pursue a wide range and volume of litigation (O'Connor and Epstein 1985).

Finally, the Court has taken few steps to discourage groups from participating as amicus curiae, in particular, even though its rules allow for it to do so. That is, the Court can reject motions to file third party briefs if the parties refuse to give consent.[22] Between 1969 and 1981, however, it denied only 11 percent of the 832 motions for leave to file as amicus curiae (O'Connor and Epstein 1983b).

Why the Court has allowed, even encouraged, group use of the judiciary has been the subject of a great deal of speculation. Some have suggested that the justices, like members of Congress, view groups as the fonts of important information that otherwise would not have come to their attention. Evidence of this, though, is somewhat circumstantial. Karen O'Connor and I (O'Connor and Epstein 1983b) found that justices frequently cite amicus curiae briefs in their opinions; others, conducting studies of particular cases or groups, aver that legal opinions and briefs often parallel each other. Illustrative is the case of *South Dakota v. Opperman* (428 U.S. 364 [1976]), in which the Court considered the constitutionality of car searches (inventories) pursuant to impoundment. Chief Justice Burger's majority opinion, which upheld the search, relied heavily on a survey conducted by an amicus, indicating that impoundment inventories rarely garnered criminal evidence (see Epstein 1985). Others suggest that some members of the Court, particularly those who have held political office, view interest groups as a routine part of the governmental process, including that of the judiciary. Interviews with several justices, in fact, reveal that they would be surprised if organizations did *not* try to influence their decisions (see Epstein 1989b).

Regardless of the Court's motivation, the increasing presence of organized interests in judicial proceedings has certainly transformed the environment within which it operates. Consider Hakman's (1969) conclusion about that environment in 1969: that cases "are carried to the Supreme Court primarily to resolve the immediate disputes among private adversaries" (p. 245). Surely, the converse is true today; if anything, today's cases represent the struggle of interests to etch into law their broader policy views. Virtually every brief filed in *Bowen* attested to this fact, indicating to the Court the wide-ranging effect its opinion would have on the larger body of First Amendment law. Some even pointed to the significant financial and social implications of the litigation. As Catholic Charities suggested, unless the Court upheld the act, "the delivery of important social services will be jeopardized and curtailment of these services will hurt literally tens of millions of needy persons." Hakman's second conclusion, that "contrary to some scholarly speculation, litigants in court cases are not pawns or symbols and are usually not manipulated by behind the scenes groups or organizations" (1969, 246), also may have been true twenty years ago, but now is controvertible. The vast majority of court cases attract group participation. On that score, then, Cortner's (1975) observation is far more apt: "Cases do not arrive at the Supreme Court's doorstep like abandoned orphans in the night" (p. vi). Instead, as *Bowen v. Kendrick* illustrates, a great many Court disputes exist because a group brought them to the attention of the justices.

As Table 13-2 reveals, undoubtedly, group presence in the judicial process has reached an all-time high. Pluralism is the new reality in Court, no longer a part of scholarly folklore. Indeed, the study of this particular dimension of group litigation has advanced light years since Hakman wrote in 1969. Scholars now recognize that they must dig deep into the Court's records simply to identify group participants. Even so, many important questions remain. For one, has group presence increased in other judicial forums? Research on U.S. courts of appeal (McIntosh and Parker 1986) and on state supreme courts (Epstein 1989a) indicates that groups are moving into these arenas, albeit at a slow pace. We do, however, have reason to suspect that groups will be stepping up their lobbying efforts in state supreme courts, in particular. As the U.S. Supreme Court has conferred greater authority to states in diverse legal areas, their courts of last resort will become more important and influential policy makers (see Tarr and Porter 1988). A wide range of interests might now find these forums appealing targets for their lobbying efforts.

For another, we have yet to examine the incidence of group litigation from a longitudinal perspective, asking what drove up organizational litigation rates over time. As Table 13-2 suggests, between 1928 and 1987 groups moved into the judicial arena at an astounding pace. Although several factors probably contributed (such as more groups, awards of attorneys' fees) to this phenomenon, we have not explored it systematically.

In my view, this is a particularly important research question because its answer might reveal a great deal about the Court as an evolving institution. When patterns of behavior, such as marked increases in group participation before the Court, "experience abrupt changes ... they should be treated not as idiopathic curiosities, but as perplexing phenomena worthy of systematic analysis" (Walker, Epstein, and Dixon 1988, 361). Indeed, research that examined the Court from a macro, longitudinal perspective has provided us with a richer understanding of how previously anomalous practices become norms (see Caldeira and McCrone 1982). Certainly we should try to do the same for interest group litigation.

Participants in Supreme Court Litigation

Are certain kinds of groups more likely than others to litigate in the U.S. Supreme Court? Broad-based research, using interest groups as the unit of study, suggests not. One analysis (Schlozman and Tierney 1983) found that nearly 75 percent of all organizations have litigated at least once. The Supreme Court Database Project reinforces this conclusion: between 1952 and 1986, almost 2,400 organizations, falling into twenty substantive categories (health groups, labor unions, and so on), appeared before the Court. *Bowen* again is exemplary: as Table 13-1 indicates, participating groups ranged in orientation from liberal to conservative, from religious to secular, and from overtly feminist to traditional.

If we look beyond *groups* as the units of analysis to the cases themselves, however, a slightly different picture emerges. Tables 13-3 and 13-4 display litigants, organized by the sorts of interests they represent, participating as sponsors and amicus curiae in the 1987-1988 cases.[23]

Let us first consider groups as sponsors of litigation. As Table 13-3 depicts, commercial interests (such as a chamber of commerce, Delta Airlines) dominated pressure group activity in the Court. Indeed, if we exclude governmental concerns (for example, the United States, Texas, Dallas), commercial interests sponsored more litigation than all others combined. As we might suspect, legal groups (such as the American Bar Association, Pacific Legal Foundation) also sponsored a significant number of cases. They appeared on behalf of appellants or appellees in 18 of the 136 cases.

Turning to the amicus curiae participants depicted in Table 13-4, we see that two interests dominate filings: governmental and commercial ones. Collectively, they account for nearly 50 percent of the briefs. Legal and civil liberties/criminal justice groups filed another 25 percent, with the remaining quarter scattered among the various interests.

Table 13-3   Sponsors of Supreme Court Litigation, 1987 Term

Sponsor	Appellants		Appellees	
	%	N	%	N
Governments	39.7	54	35.3	48
Commercial interests	23.5	32	27.2	37
Private counsel	22.1	30	20.6	28
Legal groups	5.9	8	7.4	10
Labor unions	2.9	4	2.2	3
Education	1.5	2	—	—
Health	1.5	2	1.5	2
Religion	1.5	2	1.5	2
Other groups	1.5	2	2.2	3
Civil liberties	—	—	2.2	3
Total		136		136

Source: Data collected by the author.

These data are of considerable interest for a number of reasons. For one, despite new research to the contrary (see Caldeira and Wright 1990; Bruer 1987), conventional wisdom certainly holds that public interest law groups and civil rights/liberties groups dominate litigation. Although they are supporting players, based on the data presented here, they are far from the leading participants. That distinction belongs to commercial groups and governmental interests.

This finding raises a second point of interest. Many scholars have tended to conceptualize court "lobbying" as something entirely different from what occurs in the legislative and executive branches. To some extent, this is a reasonable distinction—the kinds of strategies and tactics used by groups in judicial arenas, for example, are not like those employed elsewhere. On the other hand, though, the sorts of participants engaged in judicial, executive, and even legislative lobbying are monolithic. That is, contrary to conventional beliefs, the same sorts of interests that lobby other branches of government also do so in the Supreme Court. Writing in 1950, E. E. Schattschneider (1966) noted that groups representing *advantaged* interests were far more abundant and influential in the governmental process. As Schlozman and Tierney (1986) found more than three decades later, "It is clear that Schattschneider's observations . . . are apt today. Taken as a whole, the pressure community is heavily weighted in favor of business organizations" (p. 68).

Though these data reveal a great deal about the differing participants before the Court, they are more suggestive than explana-

Table 13-4 Amicus Curiae Participants in Supreme Court Litigation, 1987 Term

Amicus curiae participant	Percent of total amicus curiae filers	N
Commercial interests	24.3	111
Governments	24.3	111
Legal groups	12.9	59
Civil liberties	10.7	49
Religion	4.8	22
Public affairs	4.4	20
Women	3.7	17
Health	3.7	17
Education	3.3	15
Labor	3.3	15
Other groups	2.9	13
Consumer	1.5	7
Total		456

Note: Includes only the interest that filed the brief, not cosigners.

Source: Data collected by the author.

tory: by describing the sorts of interests currently appearing before the Court, they help us frame the kinds of questions we might ask in the future. One that clearly arises involves the role of business interests in litigation. Like other recent studies, ours found that the business community—trade and professional associations and businesses and corporations—is among the most active legal participants. To date, however, the vast majority of research has focused on public interest law firms and other legal groups. Certainly, then, the time has come for us to turn our sights to the role these business groups are playing in the litigation game and the way their participation may be affecting the legal environment.

Another issue involves our categorization of interest types: How should we classify groups appearing before the Court? This is an important question because we recognize that different kinds of groups behave in different ways. Caldeira and Wright (1990), for example, found that some groups (such as public interest law firms, citizen advocacy groups) are less likely to participate at the certiorari stage than on the merits; the converse is true of corporations. O'Connor and I (O'Connor and Epstein 1983c) demonstrated that liberal groups generally prefer to sponsor cases while conservative groups are more likely to file amicus curiae briefs (see also Bradley and Gardner 1985).

Though we recognize that different group types "manifest different" behavior "relevant to political action" (Kobylka 1987, 1065), we have not reached consensus over the most appropriate way to categorize groups. Caldeira and Wright based their classification on membership characteristics; the Supreme Court Database Project used a more substantive schema (health, education, and so on); and O'Connor and I used ideology. But certainly other possibilities exist; for example, we could adopt Jack Walker's (1983) typology, in which he classified groups by their sources of income. Or we could use Mancur Olson's (1965) and James Q. Wilson's (1973) categorization, which is based on group goal structures.

In my view, though, it is not necessary for all litigation scholars to classify groups in the same way; even students of the interest group process, generally speaking, have yet to do so. What is important, though, is that we understand the implications of our results and how they might vary solely because of the way we have classified groups. Future research ought to be sensitive to these issues, perhaps demonstrating the extent to which our findings are merely artifacts of a particular typology or classification scheme.

Issues Attracting Amicus Curiae Participation

What sorts of issues generate organizational participation? Table 13-5 depicts the percentages of sponsorship and amicus curiae participation in the different kinds of issues the Court heard during the 1987 term.[24] Let us first consider the sponsorship rates. Not surprisingly, six of the eight issues attracting more than average group attention represent topics of traditional concern to organizational litigants. As Frank J. Sorauf's (1976) work on religious cases and Lettie Wenner's (1984) on environmental campaigns make abundantly clear, these areas hold considerable interest for vast networks of group litigants. By the same token, it is not surprising to find substantial group interest in cases involving finances; after all, as shown in Table 13-4, business interests are among the most active Supreme Court litigators.

Based on other scholarly analyses, we also are less than startled by the dearth of participation in cases of criminal law and procedure. For a number of reasons, this area is not particularly ripe for group participation. As one source (O'Connor and Epstein 1984a) explains: "Indigent criminal defendants [already] enjoy constitutionally guaranteed representation. . . . While this right does not apply to all appellate stages . . . public defender offices or court appointed counsel regularly fill this void." Moreover, "because of the nature of the criminal justice process, interest groups generally are unable to foresee

Table 13-5 Participation of Groups as Sponsors of Litigation by Issue, 1987 Term

Issue	Cases sponsored by groups[a]		Cases with amicus briefs		Total number of cases[b]
	%	N	%	N	
Religion	100.0	4	100.0	4	4
Environment	100.0	8	87.5	7	8
Procedure	100.0	8	75.0	6	8
Labor relations	91.7	11	100.0	12	12
Finances	85.0	17	65.0	13	20
Freedom of expression	76.9	10	100.0	13	13
Benefits	71.4	5	85.7	6	7
Discrimination	69.2	9	92.3	12	13
Property/boundaries	66.7	2	100.0	3	3
Torts	60.0	3	60.0	3	5
Immigration/deportation	25.0	1	50.0	2	4
Federalism/institutionalism	25.0	1	100.0	4	4
Criminal law	22.6	7	64.5	20	31
Total	65.1	86	79.5	105	132

[a] Excludes governments as sponsors.

[b] Four cases did not fit compatibly into any of the above categories. Three of the four were sponsored by organized interests. All four contained at least one amicus curiae brief, raising the total percentage to 80.1.

Source: Data collected by the author.

the 'test case' quality of most criminal prosecutions and therefore do not want to risk limited resources on trivial cases" (pp. 72-73).

Turning to amicus curiae participation, we first note that most of the varying issues generated substantial levels of amicus curiae briefs; virtually all areas exceed the 50 percent mark found for the 1970-1980 years. Given that 109 of the 136 cases contained at least one brief, this is far from surprising. Interestingly, though, the overall patterns have remained rather stable since the 1970s. Our study (O'Connor and Epstein 1982) of noncommercial litigation, for example, found that cases involving labor, discrimination, and First Amendment issues generated the most participation. Today we see that those areas continue to attract group interest. Moreover, in the 1970-1980 period, groups filed amicus curiae briefs in only 36.8 percent ($n = 120$) of the 326 criminal cases; though that figure rose to 64.5 percent in 1988, criminal law remains as one of the legal areas least likely to generate group participation.

The data displayed in Table 13-5 provide some indication of interest group involvement in particular legal issues before the Court.

They reveal the presence of an active pressure group community, which has penetrated deeply into the Court's plenary docket. What they might conceal, however, are possible interactions between groups and issues, two of which seem likely. First, as we know, the Court's docket periodically undergoes an evolutionary process: it closes the window on some legal areas, while opening it to others (Pacelle 1987). What role do organized interests play in this process? Do they provide justices with the levers used to pry open some areas of the law to judicial scrutiny and with the hammers used to shut others? Previous analyses suggest that groups, in fact, do play some role in setting the Court's agenda. Case studies demonstrate that organizations brought to the Court's attention some of the following issues: capital punishment (Meltsner 1973), abortion (Rubin 1987), gender-based discrimination (O'Connor 1980; Cowan 1976), racially based discrimination (Kluger 1976; Vose 1959; Cortner 1988), and free speech (Cortner 1975). Work by Caldeira and Wright (1988) argues that briefs filed by organized interests help the Court to set its plenary docket, perhaps cuing it to important issues. Future work should combine these two approaches, focusing systematically on the particular substantive issues groups bring (and do not bring) to the justices' attention.

Another likely interaction occurs in the opposite direction—the effect of the Court's resolution of particular issues on group decision making. Joseph Kobylka's (1987) research argues that groups can respond to Court decisions in one of three ways: they can exit the arena, they can increase their efforts, or they can continue to seek redress through the legal system. Through use of an experimental design, Kobylka sought to discover which of these options libertarian groups' selected in response to a major legal shift in obscenity law. In general, he found that politically motivated organizations (such as the ACLU) opted out, while groups with material interests mobilized and accelerated their court efforts.

Kobylka's study is quite illuminating: not only does it suggest that groups play a role in setting the Court's agenda, but it also demonstrates that organizations respond to changes in the legal environment. Future research should continue along these lines, exploring specific interactions between the Court and organizations and how they might vary by type of group and legal issue.

Issues of Efficacy

The strategies and tactics, frequency, and issues of interest reveal a great deal about group litigation in the U.S. Supreme Court. The picture is less than complete, though, because it fails to provide any indication of whether groups, as sponsors or as amici, have any effect on judicial decision making. In other words, do groups matter?

In large measure, the answer to the question depends on how we define *matter*. One way is to ask whether groups influence the Court's decision to hear cases on the merits. That is, do group-backed cases stand a better chance of receiving full treatment by the Court? The answer is, unequivocally, yes. As recent research (Caldeira and Wright 1988) suggests:

> When a case involves real conflict or when the federal government is a petitioner, the addition of just one amicus curiae brief in support of certiorari increases the likelihood of plenary review by 40%-50%. Without question, then, interested parties can have a significant and positive impact on the Court's agenda by participating as amici curiae prior to the Court's decision on certiorari or jurisdiction (p. 1122).

Another way scholars explore issues of group efficacy is to look at the end of the judicial process, asking whether group-sponsored litigation has a broader impact on society. Research published in 1987 by Joseph Stewart and James Sheffield addressed this very issue, examining whether group cases affected "black mobilization in an environment most resistant to change"—counties in Mississippi. The results indicate that, in fact, litigation sponsored by civil rights organizations helped "boost black voter registration and black candidacies for public office" (pp. 780-781).

Clearly, then, groups *do* make a difference at the onset (the decision to hear cases) and at the end (the impact of decisions) of the judicial process. But what about at that important middle stage—do groups actually affect the justices' opinions? Once again, we can turn to a variety of indicators of "effect." For one, we can look at the overall success of group and nongroup litigants; this tells us whether groups are winning more cases in particular legal areas than private counsel. Past studies, relying on success rates as indicators of interest group efficacy, reveal that groups do win more cases. Susan Lawrence's (1989) analysis of the Legal Services Program (LSP), for example, discovered that it "secured victories in 62 percent of their 119 Supreme Court cases." Based on this and other findings, she concluded that "the LSP's appellate advocacy and the Court's review of its cases gave the poor a voice in Supreme Court policymaking and doctrinal development" (p. 270).

Table 13-6 depicts success rates for group- and nongroup-sponsored cases involving discrimination decided during the 1987 term. Though the number of cases is rather small, a pattern certainly emerges. Whether groups support the party alleging discrimination or

Table 13-6 Success Rates in 1987 Term Cases Involving Discrimination

	Successful cases		*Total number of cases*
	%	N	
Success of parties *alleging* discrimination	69.2	9	13
Cases sponsored by groups	80.0	4	5
Cases not sponsored by groups	62.5	5	8
Success of parties *defending* claims of discrimination	30.8	4	13
Cases sponsored by groups	50.0	2	4
Cases not sponsored by groups	22.2	2	9

Source: Data collected by the author.

defending claims of discrimination, they win at greater rates. When groups charged discrimination, they attained 11 percent greater success than their nongroup counterparts; by the same token, group defendants of discrimination won 50 percent of their cases while all defendants of discrimination won 30.8 percent.

Another way to measure effect is to determine whether the justices adopt legal arguments advanced by groups. One study exploring the percentage of opinions citing amicus curiae briefs found that 18 percent mentioned a nongovernmental friend of the court. The 1987-1988 data indicate that almost 35 percent ($n = 38$) of all decisions in which at least one amicus curiae brief was filed mentioned directly a friend of the court brief. This finding again reinforces the notion that the justices find some utility in arguments made by amici, despite the large number of participants.

Finally, scholars have conducted studies of specific cases to determine what, if any, influence groups had on the outcome. Indeed, the first rigorous study of group litigation, Vose's (1959) *Caucasians Only,* was an analysis of the NAACP LDF's role in the restrictive covenant cases. Others, including Richard Kluger's (1976) exploration of the LDF and school desegregation litigation, and David Manwaring's (1962) of the Jehovah's Witnesses and the flag salute cases, followed similar approaches. And, not surprisingly, they reached the same conclusion: groups do affect decisional outcomes.

Hence, over the years, many different kinds of analyses have depicted organizations as winners in the litigation game, participants who rarely, if ever, lose cases. Most recently, though, several challenges to this conventional view have emerged. The first was an empirical investigation, invoking an experimental design, to determine whether groups are more apt to win their cases than individuals. This study (Epstein and Rowland 1989) paired cases involving the same legal issues and decided the same year by the same judge; the only difference between the two was that one was sponsored by a group, the other by private counsel. It found no significant differences in judicial resolution of group and nongroup cases.

So, too, scholars now recognize that organizations are but one of many factors influencing the justices and that their models of group efficacy must contemplate such known determinants of judicial voting as *precedent, case facts,* and *ideology.* Again consider the ACLU's challenge in *Bowen.* On the surface, its arguments seemed to have merit—the Adolescent Family Life Act (AFLA) did involve government expenditures to religious organizations and thus might entail impermissible entanglement between church and state. Yet, only four of the nine justices adopted the ACLU's arguments; the majority voted to uphold the law.

Why did the ACLU lose *Bowen?* Though we can only speculate, the three factors specified above seem highly relevant. For one, the Court interpreted its own past decisions (that is, precedential cases) as working against the ACLU's claim. Chief Justice Rehnquist wrote for the majority that "this Court has never held that religious institutions are disabled by the First Amendment from participating in publicly sponsored social welfare programs. To the contrary in *Bradfield v. Roberts* (175 U.S. 291 [1899]), the Court upheld an agreement between the . . . District of Columbia and a religiously affiliated hospital whereby the Federal government would pay for the construction of a new building on the grounds of the hospital." [25]

Moreover, the fact situation of *Bowen* was unfavorable to the ACLU's position. That the U.S. Congress had enacted the AFLA was a particularly acute problem for it because the Court rarely overturns federal legislation, and, more pointedly, has almost never done so in cases involving federal monies to religious organizations. Had a state legislature enacted the AFLA, the ACLU's chances for victory would have improved markedly. [26]

Finally, we must consider the ideological predilection of the current Court. Scholars (see Kobylka 1989) have portrayed the Burger and Rehnquist Courts as relatively conservative in the area of church-state relations. In fact, Chief Justice Rehnquist has "adopted the position that the [First Amendment] was intended only to prevent the establishment of a national religion" and not to dissuade other forms of intermingling between church and state (Redlich 1987, 90). It is hardly surprising, then, that his opinion in *Bowen* ran directly counter to the ACLU's position.

What conclusions can we reach about the efficacy of interest group activity in the Court? On one hand, studies focusing on organizational litigants conclude that groups do, in fact, influence judicial decisions. Clearly, they affect the certiorari process and they seem to win a great proportion of their cases. On the other hand, we must temper those conclusions by considering the other forces that affect the course of judicial behavior. Seen in this light, interest groups are but one of many factors that contribute to the Court's output.

An important endeavor for future research, then, will be to determine the relative weight of this group contribution compared with other factors. This, of course, will be a difficult research challenge, and perhaps one that will force us to reconsider issues of group efficacy. For far too long, we have focused exclusively on litigation victories when, as this and other studies have indicated, groups do lose cases. Future research should seek to explore factors affecting the ability of organizations to win *as well as* those influencing defeats in the American legal system.

Conclusion

This chapter has explored the world of interest group litigation by focusing on patterns of organizational involvement during the Court's 1987 term and on a specific case decided during that term, *Bowen v. Kendrick*. Overall, this analysis has confirmed a great deal of our knowledge about group mobilization of the law. As conventional views suggest, groups are resorting to litigation in record numbers. The vast majority of court cases generate considerable interest from the pressure group community. Groups are continuing to use both tools of litigation—sponsorship and amicus curiae briefs—to influence the Court. In short, as Schlozman and Tierney observed of interest group activity in general, we find *more of the same* in the legal arena.

Conversely, there have been several changes in organizational use of the Court, which suggest interesting avenues for further research. These include:

- Other strategies groups use to influence Court decisions, such as protests and demonstrations
- Coalition building and group litigation networks
- Interest group participation in other judicial forums
- Factors driving groups into the judicial arena over time
- The role of the business community in court

- Interactions among case issues, their judicial resolution, and interest group decision making

- Interest group efficacy, with emphasis on group wins as well as group losses

Our exploration has also identified several areas, relating to the nature of scientific inquiry, which certainly deserve further consideration: classification schema and their effect on our findings, and appropriate sampling frames for survey research. In proposing these avenues of research, we recognize the many obstacles that lie ahead. If anything, this chapter has revealed that studying groups that litigate is a complex task, requiring scholars of the judicial process to explore unfamiliar terrain. Done with care, though, such analyses are bound to provide us with a greater appreciation and richer understanding of the courts, and of the governmental process more generally.

Notes

1. *Utah Public Service Commission v. El Paso Natural Gas,* 395 U.S. 464 (1969).
2. Organizations and other interests filed seventy-eight briefs in *Webster,* breaking the previous record of fifty-seven set in *Regents of the University of California v. Bakke,* 438 U.S. 265 (1978) (see Behuniak-Long 1989).
3. As Truman noted (1971), prior to Bentley scholars were concerned with formal institutional processes (how a bill becomes a law) or the output of those institutions ("the law").
4. Truman mentioned two other works (Peltason 1955; Schmidhauser 1960), neither of which focuses exclusively on group litigation.
5. As I describe later in this chapter, many studies have reached a conclusion opposite Hakman's, so that we now can apply his term to his own work—it represents scholarly folk wisdom.
6. I was fortunate to interview five members of the Supreme Court on the subject of interest group litigation. Though I found these interviews to be useful, I am still not entirely convinced about their legitimacy as primary data sources (see Epstein 1989b).
7. A third strategy is intervention. This occurs when a group "voluntarily interposes in an action ... with leave of the Court" (Black 1968, 956). Because this is a difficult strategy to pursue, presenting numerous procedural obstacles, most groups eschew it for sponsorship or participation as amicus curiae.
8. In representing these various plaintiffs, ACLU attorneys had to demonstrate that they were the appropriate parties to bring suit. According to the ACLU's briefs, the various clergy "alleged injury not only as taxpayers but also to their religious ministries." Apparently, they held views

"antithetical" to those AFLA wished to promote and thus were ineligible for funding (Brief for Appellees, 1988).

9. By obtaining its own counsel, the NCL also was ensuring that its position would be adequately represented in Court. In *People v. Williams* (189 N.Y. 131 [1906]), NCL leaders watched in horror as a state court struck down an NCL-backed maximum-hour law in part because the government's attorneys never appeared to defend the law. Afterward, an NCL leader claimed that "never again would we be caught napping. Never again would we leave the defense of a labor law to an indifferent third assistant attorney general" (Goldmark 1953, 148-149, quoted in O'Connor 1980, 68).

10. Other tactics include: continued and repeated use of the legal system (see Galanter 1974); obtaining attorneys committed to and schooled in organizational goals (see Greenberg 1974); and a sharp focus on a particular legal area (see O'Connor 1980).

11. A large body of scholarly and journalistic literature indicates that the solicitor general, a presidential appointee who represents the U.S. government in the Court, is a most successful litigator. Some even go so far as to call him the "tenth justice." For an interesting account of the role of the solicitor general in recent years, see Caplan 1987. For scholarly assessments, see Segal 1984; Krislov 1963; Puro 1971; Scigliano 1971.

12. *West Virginia State Board of Education v. Barnette,* 319 U.S. 624 (1943). For an excellent account of its litigation history, see Manwaring 1962.

13. *Adkins v. Children's Hospital,* 261 U.S. 525 (1923). For an account of the NCL's activity in *Adkins,* see Vose 1972.

14. This was not always the case. For a fascinating history of the evolution of the brief amicus curiae, see Krislov 1963.

15. The groups listed on the inside cover of this brief are constituent members of the National Coalition for Public Education and Religious Liberty.

16. For more on the ACLU's (and other groups') view of amicus curiae participation, see O'Connor and Epstein 1989.

17. O'Connor (1980, 17) stresses the importance of generating "well-timed" publicity to the legal efforts of women's rights groups. Yet, as she noted, "studying the impact of prior publicity . . . creates unique problems" for social scientists (p. 50). Indeed, disentangling the effect of publicity-oriented strategies from actual litigation campaigns presents an interesting research challenge.

18. Work by Salisbury et al. (1987) has begun to address many of these questions. Their research has moved away from a focus on specific institutions of government to one on policy areas. Unfortunately, many of the issues they chose to examine are not ones typically associated with organizational litigation.

19. I collected the data for the 1987 term reported in this chapter. Information on cases comes from the *Supreme Court Reporter* (S.Ct.); data on amicus curiae participation and on sponsorship rates come from the BNA Microfiche Brief Series. To obtain a copy of the dataset, contact me via

Bitnet at H6FR1001 @ SMUVM1 or by post at Southern Methodist University, Department of Political Science, Dallas, Texas 75275.

20. This figure excludes amicus curiae briefs filed by individuals on behalf of themselves or other individuals.

21. Hakman (1969) found that groups participated as amicus curiae in only 18.6 percent of the 1,175 noncommercial cases decided by the Court between 1969 and 1980. In replicating and updating Hakman's analysis, O'Connor and I (1982) reported amicus curiae participation in about 50 percent of noncommercial litigation occurring between 1969 and 1980.

22. According to the Court, "A Brief of an *amicus curiae* [filed on the merits] may be filed only after order of the Court or when accompanied by written consent of all parties to a case" (338 U.S. 959-960). For a concise history of the development of this rule, see Caldeira and Wright 1990.

23. The Supreme Court Database Project coded all amicus curiae participants (1952-1986) into these group types. I used the project's codebook to classify each group.

24. Cases were coded on the basis of the major legal issue resolved by the Court.

25. In cases involving questions of church-state relations, the Court applies a three-prong test, asking whether the aid (1) has a "valid secular purpose," (2) has the "primary effect of advancing religion," and (3) creates "excessive entanglement of church and state." See *Lemon v. Kurtzman*, 403 U.S. 602 (1971). The majority asserted that the AFLA passed this test; the dissenters argued that it failed to meet these requirements.

26. As Wasby notes (1988), "Throughout our history, the Court has invalidated state laws more frequently than federal laws" (p. 79). Indeed, since the early 1800s, the Court has struck down as unconstitutional more than 1,500 pieces of state legislation, while (discounting the legislative veto case, which invalidated more than 200 sections of federal laws) it has overturned fewer than 200 congressional acts.

References

Barker, Lucius. 1967. Third parties in litigation: A systematic view of the judicial function. *Journal of Politics* 29:41-69.

Baum, Lawrence. 1985. *The Supreme Court.* Washington, D.C.: CQ Press.

Behuniak-Long, Susan. 1989. Friendly fire: Amici curiae and *Webster v. Reproductive Health Services.* Paper presented at the annual meeting of the Northeastern Political Science Association, Philadelphia.

Bentley, Arthur. 1908. *The process of government.* Chicago: University of Chicago Press.

Berry, Jeffrey M. 1989. *The interest group society.* Glenview, Ill.: Scott, Foresman.

Black, Henry Campbell. 1968. *Black's law dictionary.* St. Paul, Minn.: West.

Bradley, Robert C., and Paul Gardner. 1985. Underdogs, upperdogs and the use of the amicus brief: Trends and explanations. *Justice System Journal* 10:78-96.

Bruer, Patrick. 1987. Washington organizations and public policy litigation: Explaining reliance of litigation as a strategy of influence. Paper presented at the annual meeting of the Midwest Political Science Association, Chicago.

Caldeira, Gregory A., and Donald J. McCrone. 1982. Of time and judicial activism: A study of the U.S. Supreme Court, 1800-1973. In *Supreme Court activism and restraint,* ed. Stephen C. Halpern and Charles M. Lamb. Lexington, Mass.: Lexington Books.

Caldeira, Gregory A., and John R. Wright. 1988. Interest groups and agenda-setting in the Supreme Court of the United States. *American Political Science Review* 82:1109-1127.

_____. 1989a. Agenda building in the Supreme Court: The influence of parties, sponsors, and direct representatives. Paper presented at the annual meeting of the Midwest Political Science Association, Chicago.

_____. 1989b. Why organized interests participate as amici curiae in the U.S. Supreme Court. Paper presented at the annual meeting of the Law and Society Association, Madison, Wisconsin.

_____. 1990. Amici before the Supreme Court: Who participates, when, and how much? *Journal of Politics,* forthcoming.

Caplan, Lincoln. 1987. *The tenth justice.* New York: Vintage.

Cortner, Richard C. 1964. *The Wagner Act cases.* Knoxville: University of Tennessee Press.

_____. 1968. Strategies and tactics of litigants in constitutional cases. *Journal of Public Law* 17:287-307.

_____. 1975. *The Supreme Court and civil liberties policy.* Palo Alto, Calif.: Mayfield.

_____. 1988. *A mob intent on violence.* Middletown, Conn.: Wesleyan University Press.

Council for Public Interest Law. 1976. *Balancing the scales of justice: Financing public interest law in America.* Washington, D.C.: The Council for Public Interest Law.

Cowan, Ruth B. 1976. Women's rights through litigation: An examination of the American Civil Liberties Union Women's Rights Project. *Columbia Human Rights Law Review* 8:373-412.

Epstein, Lee. 1985. *Conservatives in court.* Knoxville: University of Tennessee Press.

_____. 1989a. A comparative analysis of the evolution, rules, and usage of amicus curiae briefs in the U.S. Supreme Court and in state courts of last resort. Paper presented at the annual meeting of the Southwestern Political Science Association, Little Rock, Arkansas.

_____. 1989b. Interviewing U.S. Supreme Court justices and interest group attorneys. *Judicature* 73:196-198.

Epstein, Lee, and C. K. Rowland. 1986. Interest groups in the courts: Do groups fare better? In *Interest group politics,* 2d ed., ed. A. J. Cigler and B. A. Loomis. Washington, D.C.: CQ Press.

———. 1989. A systematic evaluation of interest group efficacy in U.S. federal courts. Paper presented at the annual meeting of the Midwest Political Science Association, Chicago.

Epstein, Lee, Joseph Kobylka, and Joseph Stewart. 1991. A theory of interest groups in court. In *Law and policy studies,* ed. Stuart A. Nagel. Greenwich, Conn.: JAI Press.

Galanter, Marc. 1974. Why the "haves" come out ahead: Speculation on the limits of legal change. *Law and Society Review* 9:95-160.

Gates, John B., and Wayne V. McIntosh. 1989. The motivations for interest group litigation. Paper presented at the annual meeting of the Law and Society Association, Madison, Wisconsin.

Goldmark, Josephine. 1953. *Impatient crusader: Florence Kelley's life story.* Urbana: University of Illinois Press.

Greenberg, Jack. 1974. Litigation for social change: Methods, limits, and role in American democracy. *Records of the Bar Association of New York* 29:9-63.

Hakman, Nathan. 1966. Lobbying the Supreme Court: An appraisal of political science "folklore." *Fordham Law Review* 35:15-50.

———. 1969. The Supreme Court's political environment: The processing of non-commercial litigation. In *Frontiers of judicial research,* ed. Joel B. Grossman and Joseph Tanenhaus. New York: Wiley.

Hall, Donald R. 1969. *Cooperative lobbying.* Tucson: University of Arizona Press.

Hrebenar, Ronald J., and Ruth Scott. 1982. *Interest group politics in America.* Englewood Cliffs, N.J.: Prentice-Hall.

Kluger, Richard. 1976. *Simple justice.* New York: Knopf.

Kobylka, Joseph F. 1987. A Court-created context for group litigation: Libertarian groups and obscenity. *Journal of Politics* 49:1061-1078.

———. 1989. Leadership on the Supreme Court: Chief Justice Burger and establishment clause litigation. *Western Political Quarterly* 42:545-568.

Krislov, Samuel. 1963. The amicus curiae brief: From friendship to advocacy. *Yale Law Journal* 72:694-721.

Lawrence, Susan E. 1989. Legal services before the Supreme Court. *Judicature* 72:266-273.

Loh, Wallace D. 1984. *Social research in the judicial process.* New York: Russell Sage Foundation.

Manwaring, David. 1962. *Render unto Caesar: The flag salute controversy.* Chicago: University of Chicago Press.

McIntosh, Wayne V., and Paul Parker. 1986. Amici curiae in the courts of appeal. Paper presented at the annual meeting of the Law and Society Association, Chicago.

Meltsner, Michael. 1973. *Cruel and unusual: The Supreme Court and capital punishment.* New York: Random House.

Newland, Chester A. 1959. Legal periodicals and the Supreme Court. *Midwest Journal of Political Science* 3:58-74.

O'Connor, Karen. 1980. *Women's organizations' use of the Court.* Lexington, Mass.: Lexington Books.

O'Connor, Karen, and Lee Epstein. 1982. An appraisal of Hakman's "folklore." *Law and Society Review* 16:701-711.

_____. 1983a. Beyond legislative lobbying: Women's rights groups and the Supreme Court. *Judicature* 67:134-143.

_____. 1983b. Court rules and workload: A case study of rules governing amicus curiae participation. *Justice System Journal* 8:35-45.

_____. 1983c. The rise of conservative interest group litigation. *Journal of Politics* 45:479-489.

_____. 1984a. Rebalancing the scales of justice: An assessment of public interest law. *Harvard Journal of Law and Public Policy* 4:483-505.

_____. 1984b. The role of interest groups in Supreme Court policy formation. In *Public policy formation,* ed. Robert Eyestone. Greenwich, Conn.: JAI Press.

_____. 1985. Bridging the gap between Congress and the Supreme Court: Interest groups and the erosion of the American rule governing awards of attorneys fees. *Western Political Quarterly* 38:238-249.

_____. 1989. *Public interest law groups.* Westport, Conn.: Greenwood Press.

Olson, Mancur. 1965. *The logic of collective action.* Chicago: University of Chicago Press.

Olson, Susan. 1984. *Clients and lawyers.* Westport, Conn.: Greenwood Press.

Orren, Karen. 1976. Standing to sue: Interest group conflict in the federal courts. *American Political Science Review* 70:723-741.

Pacelle, Richard L. 1987. The Supreme Court and the growth of civil liberties: The process and dynamics of agenda change. Paper presented at the annual meeting of the American Political Science Association, Chicago.

Peltason, Jack W. 1955. *Federal courts in the political process.* New York: Doubleday.

Puro, Steven. 1971. The role of amicus curiae in the United States Supreme Court: 1920-1966. Ph.D. dissertation, State University of New York at Buffalo.

Redlich, Norman. 1987. The separation of church and state: The Burger Court's tortuous journey. In *The Burger years,* ed. Herman Schwartz. New York: Penguin.

Rohde, David W., and Harold J. Spaeth. 1976. *Supreme Court decision making.* San Francisco: Freeman.

Rubin, Eva R. 1987. *Abortion, politics, and the courts.* Rev. ed. Westport, Conn.: Greenwood Press.

Salisbury, Robert H., John P. Heinz, Edward O. Laumann, and Robert L. Nelson. 1987. Who works with whom? *American Political Science Review* 81:1215-1234.

Schattschneider, E. E. 1966. *The semisovereign people.* New York: Holt, Rinehart and Winston.

Schlozman, Kay Lehman, and John Tierney. 1983. Washington pressure group activity in a decade of change. *Journal of Politics* 45:351-377.

———. 1986. *Organized interests and American democracy.* New York: Harper and Row.

Schmidhauser, John. 1960. *The Supreme Court.* New York: Holt, Rinehart and Winston.

Schubert, Glendon. 1959. *Quantitative analysis of judicial behavior.* New York: Free Press.

———. 1965. *The judicial mind: Attitudes and ideologies of Supreme Court justices.* Evanston, Ill.: Northwestern University Press.

Scigliano, Robert. 1971. *The Supreme Court and the presidency.* New York: Free Press.

Segal, Jeffrey A. 1984. Predicting Supreme Court cases probabilistically: The search and seizure cases, 1962-1981. *American Political Science Review* 78:891-900.

Sorauf, Frank J. 1976. *The wall of separation: Constitutional politics of church and state.* Princeton: Princeton University Press.

Spaeth, Harold J. 1963. Warren Court attitudes toward business: The "B" scale. In *Judicial decision making,* ed. Glendon A. Schubert. New York: Free Press.

Stewart, Joseph, Jr., and James F. Sheffield, Jr. 1987. Does interest group litigation matter? The case of black political mobilization in Mississippi. *Journal of Politics* 49:780-798.

Tarr, G. Alan, and Mary Cornelius Porter. 1988. *State supreme courts in nation and state.* New Haven: Yale University Press.

Truman, David B. 1951. *The governmental process.* New York: Knopf.

———. 1971. *The governmental process.* 2d ed. New York: Knopf.

Vose, Clement E. 1955. NAACP strategy in the restrictive covenant cases. *Western Reserve Law Review* 6:101-145.

———. 1957. National Consumers' League and the Brandeis brief. *Midwest Journal of Political Science* 1:178-190.

———. 1958. Litigation as a form of pressure group activity. *Annals of the American Academy of Political and Social Science* 319:20-31.

———. 1959. *Caucasians only.* Berkeley: University of California Press.

———. 1966. Interest groups, judicial review and local government. *Western Political Quarterly* 19:85-100.

———. 1972. *Constitutional change.* Lexington, Mass.: Lexington Books.

———. 1981. Interest groups and litigation. Paper presented at the annual meeting of the American Political Science Association, New York.

Walker, Jack L. 1983. The origins and maintenance of interest groups in America. *American Political Science Review* 77:390-406.

Walker, Thomas G., Lee Epstein, and William J. Dixon. 1988. On the mysterious demise of consensual norms in the United States Supreme Court. *Journal of Politics* 50:361-389.

Wasby, Stephen L. 1986. The multi-faceted elephant: Litigator perspectives on planned litigation for social change. *Capital University Law Review* 15:143-189.

———. 1988. *The Supreme Court in the federal judicial system.* Chicago: Nelson-Hall.

Wenner, Lettie. 1984. *The environmental decade in court.* Bloomington: Indiana University Press.

Wilson, James Q. 1973. *Political organizations.* New York: Basic Books.

Woodward, Bob, and Scott Armstrong. 1979. *The Brethren.* New York: Simon and Schuster.

14. COURTS, EXECUTIVES, AND LEGISLATURES

Jeffrey A. Segal

The Constitution of the United States separates powers, for as James Madison so astutely observed, "The accumulation of all powers, legislative, executive, and judiciary, in the same hands, whether of one, or few, or many, ... may justly be pronounced the very definition of tyranny" (Madison, Jay, and Hamilton 1948, 211). But the Founders were not content with separating powers. Each branch was to be checked by the others. "Ambition must be made to counteract ambition" (p. 225). So the president appoints the Supreme Court with the advice and consent of the Senate, the Congress controls the size of the Court and its appellate jurisdiction, and the Supreme Court has the power to declare actions of state and federal legislatures and executives unconstitutional. The cooperation and conflict between the judiciary and its coordinate branches of government are the focus of this chapter. I will pay particular attention to the role of the solicitor general in facilitating executive/judicial interactions and, alternatively, to the role of Congress in curbing judicial policy making.

Courts and Legislatures

The fundamental power that keeps the Supreme Court in conflict with the legislative branch of government at both the federal and the state levels is the Court's power of judicial review, the power to declare legislative acts that violate the U.S. Constitution to be void. The Supreme Court first held an act of Congress unconstitutional in *Marbury v. Madison* (1 Cranch 137 [1803]). In that case the Supreme Court, speaking through Chief Justice John Marshall, declared that Congress did not have the ability to enlarge the Supreme Court's original jurisdiction, as Congress allegedly had in Section 13 of the Judiciary Act of 1789. Article III of the Constitution specifically defines the Court's original jurisdiction and declares that in all other

This chapter is based in part on Jeffrey A. Segal, "Supreme Court Support for the Solicitor General: The Effect of Presidential Appointments." *Western Political Quarterly* 43 (1990): 137-152. Reprinted by permission of the University of Utah.

cases the Court shall have appellate jurisdiction. Thus, the relevant section of the Judiciary Act was null and void.

Many have written on the propriety of judicial review; yet a chapter dealing with judicial-legislative relations must examine the influence of judicial review. To what extent has the Court used its power to check the powers of the legislative branch? The empirical debate over judicial review began with the pathbreaking work of Robert Dahl (1957). Dahl's argument can be broken down into several parts. First, he argues that the Court has rarely attempted to overturn the wishes of contemporary lawmaking majorities. In the 167 years between the adoption of the Constitution and Dahl's study, the Court had struck down only eighty-six different provisions of federal law as unconstitutional. Of those eighty-six, only thirty-eight were declared unconstitutional within four years of passage and thus were actions in opposition to *contemporary* lawmaking majorities.[1]

Second, Dahl finds that the Court has been unsuccessful in almost every case when it has tried to thwart contemporary lawmaking majorities. This failure is ascribed to the president's ability to appoint a new justice, on average, once every twenty-two months. Democratically elected presidents, representing the national political majority, will no doubt use that power to appoint justices whose views coincide with that majority. Thus, an intransigent Court will, through turnover, soon be replaced by one more accepting of congressional authority on the issues at hand. This is exactly what Dahl finds. "Although the Court seems never to have succeeded in holding out indefinitely, in a very small number of important cases it has delayed the application of policy up to as much as twenty-five years" (p. 291).

Finally, Dahl argues that the few cases in which the Court was successful in blocking policy for an extended period of time were not cases in which the Court was protecting powerless minorities against tyranny of the majority. The cases in question involved the right of Congress to limit child labor, require workmen's compensation, or tax certain forms of income. In each case the Court ruled with the vested interests against such congressional power. If this is all the Supreme Court can or will do, why then do we tolerate such an undemocratic institution? Dahl concludes that the role of the Court in our society can be justified by its ability to "confer legitimacy on the fundamental policies of the successful [lawmaking] coalition" (p. 294).

Dahl's article is among the most influential studies of the Court's use of judicial review. Yet the preeminence of Dahl's work may have more to do with the debate it has engendered than with the correctness of his particular findings. The first significant criticism of the research was by Jonathan Casper (1976), who demonstrated that Dahl's findings were not generalizable to the period 1958-1974. The Warren Court was far more active than its predecessors in striking down national legislation. During the period studied by Casper the Court struck down thirty-two provisions of federal law in twenty-eight cases. Six of the cases were within four years of passage. Only one of the original thirty-two provisions, that lowering the voting age to eighteen in state and local elections, was reenacted. Otherwise, every one of the provisions was struck on the basis of the Bill of Rights or the Fourteenth Amendment. The Warren Court was clearly acting in a manner consistent with the Court's role of protecting powerless minorities.

Casper found even greater problems with Dahl's research design. Most troublesome was Dahl's exclusion of those cases in which the Court had struck down national legislation more than four years after it was passed. In such circumstances, the lawmaking majority was automatically presumed to be dead. Thus, more than half of the relevant cases were deleted from his substantive analysis. Finally, Casper noted the narrowness of Dahl's study, which measured responsiveness only in terms of judicial review of federal legislation. Dahl did not consider cases where the Court weakened federal legislation under the guise of statutory interpretation, nor did he consider cases in which the Court struck down state or local legislation, no matter how pervasive such legislation may have been. Under Dahl's definition, the *Roe v. Wade* (1973) decision (410 U.S. 113), which struck down abortion laws in forty-nine states, was not an example of the Court acting against a national lawmaking majority.

To Dahl, the importance of Congress-Court relations is that the Court is capable of legitimizing congressional policy, by declaring its laws to be constitutional. David Adamany (1973) critiqued this view, especially noting that the Court historically had failed to grant legitimacy to administrations when it was needed most, in the period following critical or realigning elections. This point, though, is actually consistent with Dahl's major thesis, for it is the appointment process that supposedly keeps the Court representative. A president elected by a realigning vote should not expect support from the Court until he has been able to replace several of the justices from the old regime.

Richard Funston (1975) sought to verify this proposition. Funston's reading of Dahl is that the Court is never long out of line with the dominant political coalition, except during realigning phases (p. 796). Overall, he finds the Court to be only slightly more likely to strike down federal legislation during critical periods, the eight years following the onset of realignment. Yet he finds the Court to be three times more likely to strike down federal legislation within *four years of enactment* during critical periods than during noncritical periods. Note, though, that Bradley Canon and S. Sidney Ulmer (1976) demonstrate that Funston's results are entirely due to the Court's clash with the New Deal. When the New Deal cases are eliminated the Court is significantly more likely to strike legislation in *noncritical* periods than in any of the remaining critical periods.

While the judicial/legislative responsiveness proposition has been examined most thoroughly on the federal level, scholars are beginning to examine similar questions on the state level. John Gates (1987) examined invalidation of state laws by the Supreme Court from the realignment perspective. After Reconstruction (but not before), he finds that state laws struck by the Court involve the most salient issues involving contemporary realignments. Further, laws struck by the Court were usually passed by state legislatures under partisan control different from that of the Court.

Robert Dahl's questions are among the most consequential a scholar can ask about the Supreme Court: What has been the role of the Supreme Court as a national policy maker? What justifies the existence of this undemocratic policy-making institution in a democracy? Why is the undemocratic Court nevertheless so responsive to its political environment? We now know that for much of the Court's history it did not play the role of protector of minority rights. As Casper demonstrates, there was a dramatic increase in support for minority rights during the Warren Court. Less clear is the role of the Court as legitimizer of national policy (Adamany 1973). Least clear is Dahl's assumption that to the extent that the Court is responsive to Congress, it is the appointment process that keeps it so. This assumption will surface again when we examine judicial-executive interactions.[2]

Judicial-Executive Interactions

The Solicitor General

The most frequent interaction between the executive branch of government and the Supreme Court is through the solicitor general's office. The solicitor general is *the* representative of the executive branch before the Supreme Court. The interaction between the solicitor general and the Court is so close that the solicitor general is commonly referred to as the "tenth justice" (Caplan 1987).

The powers granted to the solicitor general make the office one of the most influential in the federal judicial system. Besides being the government's attorney before the Supreme Court, the solicitor general significantly influences what cases the Court will hear. The office has complete control over Justice Department appeals to the Supreme

Court, and the solicitor general's approval is necessary for virtually all independent regulatory commission requests to petition the Court for certiorari—that is, to hear a case (28 U.S.C. section 2323 [1964]). The solicitor general also can file amicus curiae (friend of the court) briefs with the Supreme Court on his or her own initiative or at the Court's request when the United States is not a direct party to a suit. These briefs can be filed at the certiorari stage, arguing whether or not the Supreme Court should hear a case, or at the decision stage, arguing support for the government's position, and usually supporting one of the parties to the suit.

The Solicitor's Success as a Party

The success of the United States in terms of obtaining certiorari and winning on the merits has been studied extensively. The solicitor general's influence as gatekeeper was systematically examined at least as far back as the Joseph Tanenhaus and his colleagues' (1963) study of "cue theory." The authors hypothesized that the Supreme Court would pay much closer attention to petitions for certiorari when the United States favored review than it would when the United States took no position. Such attention would lead to a higher percentage of grants when the United States favored review. This is exactly what they found. The Court granted certiorari in 47 percent of the cases in which the United States favored review, versus 5.8 percent when it did not. More recent research has shown that the Court grants certiorari as often as 70 percent of the time when the United States seeks to appeal a case in which it was the losing party. For other parties, the rate is no more than 8 percent favorable (Provine 1980, Scigliano 1971, Teger and Kosinski 1980; Ulmer, Hintze, and Kirklosky 1972).

The favorable treatment given to the United States at the vote for certiorari continues when the case is decided on the merits. According to Roger Handberg and Harold Hill (1980), the United States won 62 percent of its cases before the Court between 1801 and 1958. Consistent with these findings, Harold Spaeth and Stuart Teger (1982) discovered that every justice of the Burger Court was more supportive of federal limitations on civil rights than of state limitations.[3]

The Solicitor as Amicus Curiae

As stated above, there are many cases to which the United States is not a direct party but nevertheless has a substantial interest in the outcome of the case. For instance, the United States was not a party to the famous *Brown v. Board of Education* (1954) racial desegregation suit (347 U.S. 483), but it filed a brief supporting desegregation. It was from the government's brief in the second *Brown* case that the Court found the "all deliberate speed" proposal (Caplan 1987, 31). In the *University of California Regents v. Bakke* (438 U.S. 265 [1978]) affirmative action case, the first draft of the government's brief favored Bakke's position against affirmative action. The brief was leaked to the *New York Times* and eventually caught the attention of President Carter. The brief was redrafted, with Carter giving his sign-off in the following memo to Stuart Eizenstat, head of the Domestic Policy Staff, and Robert Lipshutz, White House special counsel: "Stu-Bob, I agree: a) Strong affirmative action, b) No rigid quotas.... JC" (quoted in Caplan 1987, 44). The position adopted by Carter for the amicus brief was exactly the position adopted by the Burger Court. Affirmative action was legal, but there could not be rigid quotas.

If we look at the amicus cases more generally, it becomes quite clear that despite the government's success as a litigant, it "has an even better record as amicus curiae" (Scigliano 1971, 179). For the years 1943, 1944, 1963, and 1965, Scigliano reports that the party supported by the solicitor general won 87 percent of its cases. Such results are consistent with more recent findings of Karen O'Connor (1983) and S. Sidney Ulmer and David Willison (1985). The most comprehensive examinations of the success of the solicitor general as amicus curiae have been written by Steven Puro (1971, 1981). Between 1920 and 1973 the party supported by the solicitor general won 74 percent of the time, and over 80 percent in political cases. Success rates for every administration from Eisenhower through Reagan are presented in Table 14-1.

Although success rates vary across solicitors, presidents, and with the ideological direction of the brief (but not with the issue being adjudicated), the solicitor general typically wins as amicus regardless of these factors (Segal 1988). For instance, the solicitors general won 91 percent of their liberal briefs during the liberal Warren Court, but were also able to win 75 percent of their conservative briefs (Segal 1988). The solicitor generally wins even when siding with respondents (Segal 1990).

While studies consistently find that the solicitor general tends to be on the winning side at certiorari, as direct party, and as amicus, they typically do not demonstrate that the solicitor general in any way *influences* the Court's decisions. It could be the case, for example, that the solicitor general files amicus briefs for parties who, given the facts of the case, are likely to win anyway. Recent evidence, though, demonstrates that the solicitor general has an *independent* influence on the outcome of cases. At the certiorari stage, the solicitor general plays a crucial role even after other relevant facts, such as disagreement among lower courts, have been controlled (Caldeira and Wright 1988). On the

Table 14-1 Solicitor General Record by President, 1952-1982 Terms

Record	Eisenhower	Kennedy	Johnson	Nixon	Ford	Carter	Reagan
Percentage lost	16.7	12.5	17.1	29.1	28.9	34.9	22.0
Percentage won	83.3	87.5	82.9	70.9	71.1	65.1	78.0
n	42	48	41	79	38	86	59

Note: $X^2 = 12.80$; $p < 0.05$

Source: Jeffrey A. Segal, "Amicus Curiae Briefs by the Solicitor General during the Warren and Burger Courts," *Western Political Quarterly* 41 (1988): 135-144. Reprinted by permission of the University of Utah, copyright holder.

merits, I (Segal 1984, 1986) concluded that the Supreme Court was more supportive of federal searches and seizures than those conducted by the states, even after the precise nature of the search or seizure was controlled. For example, warrantless searches by federal officials were more likely to be upheld than similar searches by state officials. As amicus in sex discrimination cases, the solicitor general's brief strongly affects the Court's decisions even after the facts of the case are controlled (Segal and Reedy 1988). Further, the solicitor general does as well when appearing voluntarily as when appearing at the request of the Court (Ulmer and Willison 1985). If the solicitor general's office won because it was trying to inflate its winning record by picking easy victories, this would not be the case.

There is growing evidence that the solicitor general does have an independent impact on Court decisions, but this line of work needs to be replicated in other substantive areas. More important though, scholars need to pay more attention to why the solicitor general does so well. Why is it that Supreme Court justices, presumably motivated by personal policy preferences (Rohde and Spaeth 1976; Segal and Cover 1989), are influenced by the opinions of outsiders?

Well-supported answers to this question are difficult to come by. For instance, it is often argued that the solicitor general wins because of the high quality of the office's legal arguments (Caplan 1987; Puro 1971; Scigliano 1971; *Yale Law Journal* 1969), but there is no systematic evidence to support this claim. I proposed that the solicitor's success can be tied to the appointment process (see Dahl 1957). "The president appoints both the solicitor general and Supreme Court justices, and more often than not seeks persons for both positions with views similar to his" (Segal 1990, 140). Thus, the more justices a president appoints, the greater should be the solicitor's success. Nevertheless, only weak support was found for the hypothesis. Another possible explanation might be role theory (see Gibson 1978), but testing such models requires heretofore nonexistent measures of the justices' views of the importance of the solicitor general. In short, we know that the solicitor general is influential, but we still do not know why.

The Politicization of the Solicitor's Office?

In his widely publicized book *The Tenth Justice*, Lincoln Caplan (1987) argues that there has been a decrease in the success of the solicitor general under the Reagan Justice Department. The reason, according to Caplan, is the politicization, or at least the increased politicization, of the solicitor general's office. Prior to the Reagan administration, the solicitor general's office was largely independent from the powers of the president. For instance, President Nixon wanted the Court to block publication of any part of the Pentagon Papers, but Solicitor General Griswold asked the Court only to prohibit publication of one dozen sections out of forty-seven volumes (Caplan 1987, 34).

The shift from more independence to less independence began with a case involving Bob Jones University, a private fundamentalist Protestant college that did not allow blacks to enroll until 1970 (*Bob Jones University v. United States*, 461 U.S. 574 [1983]). Blacks were eventually permitted to attend if they were married to other blacks or if they promised not to date or marry outside their race. During the Nixon administration, the Internal Revenue Service drafted rules to deny Bob Jones and other segregated schools tax exemptions, on the grounds that the discrimination they practiced violated public policy. When the case reached the certiorari stage at the Supreme Court, Reagan's acting solicitor general, Lawrence Wallace, agreed with the IRS. Indeed, the Supreme Court accepted the IRS position as far back as 1971. Nevertheless, leading officials in William French Smith's Justice Department supported Bob Jones, including William Bradford Reynolds, who ironically was assistant attorney general for civil rights. President Reagan personally approved the decision to intervene on the side of Bob Jones (Caplan 1987, 56). When the Supreme Court heard the case on the merits, the Justice Department filed a brief arguing for tax exemption, undercutting the position taken by the solicitor general only four months earlier. Wallace was forced to sign the new brief but was allowed to state in a footnote that he did not completely subscribe to the government's position (pp. 58-59). The Court rejected the Reagan administration's position in an opinion written by Chief Justice Warren Burger, who compared the government's position to the separate but equal doctrine of *Plessy v. Ferguson* (163 U.S. 537 [1896]). Only William Rehnquist dissented.

In the aftermath, Wallace was relieved of all responsibilities over civil rights cases (p. 61).

Undaunted by the failure in the *Bob Jones* case, William Bradford Reynolds continued to view the solicitor's briefs as the proper forum for political manifestoes rather than legal arguments, according to Caplan. Under Reynolds's demands, the office filed a brief opposing all forms of affirmative action in a case solely about quotas in layoffs (1987, 89-91). Reynolds attempted, but failed, to get Solicitor General H. Rex Lee to support the conviction of a black man who was indicted by a grand jury from which blacks had been systematically excluded. Reynolds went so far as to urge Lee to support a lower court opinion declaring that the Fourteenth Amendment does not incorporate the Bill of Rights and, therefore, Alabama should be free to establish a state religion if it chooses (p. 100). Reynolds again backed down, but interference had become too burdensome for Lee, who soon after resigned. In an interview with Caplan, Lee declared:

> If I had done what was urged on me in a lot of cases, I would have lost those cases and the Justices wouldn't have taken me seriously in others. There has been this notion that my job is to press the Administration's policies at every turn and announce true conservative principles through the pages of my briefs. It is not. I'm the Solicitor General, not the Pamphleteer General. (p. 107)

While Lee supported the conservative position in amicus briefs far more often than had any solicitor general since the Eisenhower administration (Segal 1988), he was not sufficiently political for the Reagan administration. Reagan's new solicitor general, Charles Fried, with the backing of the new attorney general, Edwin Meese, was far more willing to push the administration's political agenda. Fried's brief in a Pennsylvania abortion case was considered by several former solicitors to be "more strident than any ever submitted by a Solicitor General" (p. 143). In a racial reapportionment case, the Court accused the solicitor's office, previously renowned for the high quality and trustworthiness of its legal opinions, of misreading legislative history and taking lower court opinions out of context (pp. 243-244).

Evidence of the politicization of the solicitor general's office is demonstrated more generally by me in Segal 1989. I found a moderate correlation, .46, between the ideology of presidents from Eisenhower through Reagan and the ideological position taken by solicitors in amicus briefs. Nevertheless, the correlation dissipates when the Reagan administration is excluded ($r = .07$) from the data. That is, prior to the Reagan administration, there was only a slight relationship between administration ideology and the positions taken by the solicitor's office.

The result of the politicization of the solicitor general's office is a decline in its influence. From all nine chambers the solicitor general's office was accused of "bad lawyering, intemperance, deceit, arrogance, extreme partisanship, and disgracing a long, great tradition" (Caplan 1987, 257). The Court granted certiorari to 57 percent of the parties who had support from the solicitor general in the 1985 term, down from 80 percent in the previous four terms (p. 257). The justices denied the solicitor general permission to argue as amicus twice as many times during the first five years of the Reagan administration as they had in the previous twenty-eight years (p. 260). We can no longer take for granted that the Court will treat the solicitor general as the tenth justice.

The President in Court

Far less frequent than interactions between the solicitor general and the judiciary are direct interactions between the president and the federal courts. These interactions, however, can make up in quality what they lack in quantity. The first such direct interaction came during the treason trial of Aaron Burr, former vice president and killer of Alexander Hamilton. Chief Justice John Marshall, an enemy of Jefferson, granted a defense motion to subpoena Jefferson to produce certain documents pertaining to the trial. After Burr was acquitted on treason charges, he was tried for waging a military attack on Mexico and Jefferson was again subpoenaed. Both times Jefferson refused to appear, but both times he made the relevant documents available to the Court (Scigliano 1971, 32).

The Supreme Court expressly recognized presidential preeminence in the field of foreign affairs in *United States v. Curtiss-Wright Export Corp* (299 U.S. 304 [1936]). The Court upheld a presidential embargo—under a broad congressional delegation of power—on arms sales to certain Latin American countries. But when the president acts unilaterally without prior congressional authority, as Truman did when he seized the steel mills during the Korean War, the Court will not typically back such actions even when foreign affairs are involved.

No doubt the most important court case to a president was *United States v. Nixon* (418 U.S. 683 [1974]). During the Senate Watergate investigation it was revealed that Nixon had secretly taped Oval Office conversations. When Watergate Special Prosecutor Archibald Cox sought to have the tapes subpoenaed, Nixon ordered Cox fired. After Attorney General Elliot Richardson and Deputy Attorney General William Ruckleshaus resigned in protest rather than fire Cox, Solicitor General Robert Bork followed Nixon's order. Because of the public outcry over the "Saturday Night Massacre," a new special prosecutor was named, Leon Jaworski. Jaworski's grand jury indicted several Nixon aides and named Nixon an "unindicted co-conspirator." Jaworski sought the tapes for the trial and was granted his request by district judge John Sirica. Nixon appealed, but when the case reached the Supreme Court, Nixon suggested that he might obey only a "definitive" Supreme Court ruling. The Supreme Court, in a *definitive* 8-0 decision, ruled that executive privilege did not counterbalance the need for evidence in criminal trials. Two weeks after the released tapes demonstrated Nixon's activity in the Watergate cover-up, Nixon resigned.

Success of the president in district courts since the end of World War II has been examined in great detail by Craig Ducat and Robert Dudley (1989). They found 198 cases that deal directly with presidential power, 61 percent of them decided in favor of the president. Lyndon Johnson was the most successful president, winning 89 percent of his cases, while Nixon was the least successful, winning but 48 percent of his. Presidents were more likely to win when their popularity was high, when the case was heard by a judge whom they appointed, and when the case involved foreign affairs. Although federal appellate judges are even more deferential to presidential power, supporting the president 74 percent of the time, the same patterns of support mentioned above hold for foreign affairs and appointing president but not for presidential popularity (Ducat and Dudley 1987).[4]

Court Curbing

The Constitution separates power but also creates checks on power so that no branch has absolute sovereignty over its sphere of influence. Thus Congress has the authority to curb the power of the federal courts in various ways: it can impeach and remove federal judges, set the number of justices on the Supreme Court, establish and disestablish lower federal courts, and limit the appellate jurisdiction of the Supreme Court. All have been used by Congress or the president as a tool against the Court, though for the most part such efforts have been unsuccessful. Where the efforts were successful, the victories were short-lived.[5]

Impeachment of Judges

Article I of the Constitution grants the House of Representatives the "sole power of impeachment" and the Senate the "sole power to try all impeachments." Presidents can be impeached only for "treason, bribery, or other high crimes and misdemeanors," but federal judges are held to higher standards. They can be impeached any time their conduct falls below the norm of "good behavior" stated in Article III.

The most serious attempt to use impeachment as a tool against the Supreme Court came during Jefferson's administration.

When Thomas Jefferson replaced John Adams as president and a Republican Congress replaced a Federalist one, the life-appointed judiciary remained in Federalist control. In 1804, as part of a continuing systematic attack against the judiciary that included dis-establishing lower courts created by Adams, the House of Represen-tatives passed eight counts of impeachment against Justice Samuel Chase for, among other things, misconduct in the trial of Republicans under the Sedition Act. The Republicans received a simple majority for removal on three counts but failed to get the requisite two-thirds majority on any count. Chase, and perhaps the future independence of the judiciary, was saved. Chief Justice Marshall, who was next on Jefferson's list, was spared any attempt at impeachment. All other impeachment attempts against Supreme Court justices have come to naught, including the attempt by Rep. Gerald Ford to impeach William O. Douglas.

Changing the Size of the Court

While Congress has successfully used its control over the size of the Court to prevent disfavored presidents from making appointments (see, for example, Andrew Johnson's administration), there has been far less success in attempts to pack the Court by adding new members. The most well known of these attempts was the Court-packing plan of Franklin D. Roosevelt.

Faced with a Supreme Court hostile to his New Deal, Roosevelt proposed legislation that would allow presidents to appoint a new justice if a justice reached the age of seventy and chose not to retire, with fifteen set as the maximum number of justices allowed. Given the age of the justices in 1937, Roosevelt would have received the full allotment of six new appointments.

Democratic party leaders were split over the plan. Chief Justice Hughes sent a letter to Congress asserting that the Court was not backlogged and that additional members would impede efficiency. Then came a series of Court decisions upholding New Deal proposals, thus eliminating the need for such a plan. Crucial to these decisions was the switch in position of Justice Roberts from conservative to liberal. Finally, conservative Justice Van Devanter announced his retirement. That day the Democratically controlled Judiciary Commit-tee voted 10-8 against the proposal. Roosevelt later declared that he had lost the battle but won the war. The same may be said of the Supreme Court, which abdicated control over the nation's economy but emerged with its independence intact.

Limiting the Court's Jurisdiction

Article III of the Constitution specifies the Supreme Court's original jurisdiction and grants the Court appellate jurisdiction "with such exceptions, and under such regulations, as the Congress shall make." Thus, a Congress dissatisfied with the Court's abortion decisions, for example, possibly could pass a law preventing the Court from hearing abortion cases. Abortion decisions would then be left to state and lower federal courts. This is obviously an enormous power over the Court. Yet there has been only one successful attempt at limiting the Supreme Court's appellate jurisdiction.

In *Ex parte Milligan* (4 Wallace 2 [1866]), the Supreme Court ruled that the military conviction of Lambdin Milligan, an officer in a secessionist organization, was unconstitutional. The Court further inflamed public opinion by striking down parts of the Reconstruction Acts. Then, in January 1886, the Court scheduled a hearing of William McCardle's appeal of his military conviction stemming from his publication of a Mississippi newspaper. McCardle brought his case to the Court through the Habeas Corpus Act of 1867. Fearing that the Court would strike all of Reconstruction, Congress passed a bill eliminating the Court's appellate jurisdiction over the Habeas Corpus Act. One year later the Court dismissed McCardle's appeal, finding that it lacked jurisdiction to hear the case (*Ex parte McCardle*, 6 Wallace 318 [1868]).

Congress similarly attempted to limit the Court's jurisdiction in the 1950s in response to the Court's protection of alleged communists. In 1956 the Court declared in *Pennsylvania v. Nelson* (350 U.S. 497 [1956]) that the Smith Act preempted the states' authority to regulate subversive activity, despite the fact that the Smith Act specifically stated that "nothing in this title shall be held to take away or impair the jurisdiction of the courts of the several States, under the laws thereof" (18 U.S.C. section 3231). Then, in *Watkins v. United States* (354 U.S. 178 [1957]), the Court overturned Watkins's conviction for refusing to testify before the House Un-American Activities Committee (HUAC). The authorizing legislation empowered the committee to investigate activities that threaten "the principle of the form of government guaranteed by our Constitution." Replied the Court, "It would be difficult to imagine a less explicit authorizing resolution" (354 U.S. 202). What could or could not be investigated would be solely up to the preferences of the committee. Such unlimited power to investigate was beyond Congress's power, so Watkins was acquitted. Then, in *Yates v. United States* (356 U.S. 363 [1958]), the Court severely limited prosecution of communists under the Smith Act.

Members of Congress sought to limit the Court's authority over subversive activities. In January 1955 Howard Smith, author of the Smith Act, introduced legislation stating that no act of Congress shall be construed by the Courts to preempt state activity unless the act expressly declares such an intent. The bill was held up in committee for over a year but belatedly managed to pass the House Judiciary Committee. The bill, known as H.R.3, eventually passed the House in July 1958.

Stronger congressional reaction surrounded the Court's attack on the HUAC. In July 1957 Sen. William Jenner, a man who at one point charged the Truman administration with being run by a "secret inner coterie which is directed by agents of the Soviet Union" (Murphy 1962, 155), introduced a bill to limit the Supreme Court's appellate jurisdiction over various antisubversive laws. The compromise bill eventually passed by committee limited the Court's jurisdiction only in bar admission cases, but also reversed the *Nelson* and *Yates* decisions. When the bill reached the Senate floor in August 1958 it was defeated by a slender 49-41 vote.

Two decisions of the Court helped reduce any further threat to the Court by Congress. In *Barenblatt v. United States* (360 U.S. 109 [1959]) the Court distinguished the *Watkins* decision and upheld the authority of the HUAC. The same day, in *Uphaus v. Wyman* (360 U.S. 72 [1959]), the Court upheld the authority of states to investigate subversive activities aimed at the states. Both cases were decided 5-4, and in both cases Harlan switched from his liberal position in *Watkins* and *Nelson*. This switch helped reduce the pressure to attack the Court, much as Owen Roberts's switch had in 1937.

Reasons for Court Curbing

Various members of Congress continue in their attempts to curb the power of the federal courts. Table 14-2 presents the number of bills introduced since 1972 that attempt to restrict the jurisdiction of the Supreme Court or all federal courts. Although none of these bills passed, they do represent a continued threat to the independence of the judiciary. The correlation between the number of bills introduced and the percentage of votes in which the "conservative coalition" appears is .36. The correlation of bills introduced with public confidence in the Supreme Court (Caldeira 1986) is predictably negative, -.157.

A more extensive study of Court curbing was conducted by Stuart Nagel (1965). Nagel examined the 165 bills introduced in Congress between 1789 and 1959 that attempted to limit substantially the powers of the Supreme Court. Periods of high frequency were 1802-1804 (Jefferson's conflict with the Federalist judges), 1823-1831 (judicial

Table 14-2   Court-curbing Bills, 1972-1985

Year	No. of bills [a]	Year	No. of bills [a]	Year	No. of bills [a]
1972	7	1977	22	1982	2
1973	7	1978	2	1983	13
1974	4	1979	13	1984	1
1975	14	1980	7	1985	6
1976	11	1981	19		

[a] Bills introduced that would limit the federal judiciary's jurisdiction.

Source: Congressional Research Service.

limits on state powers), 1858-1869 (the Civil War), 1893-1897 (income tax and economic regulation), 1922-1924 (economic regulation), 1935-1937 (the New Deal), and 1955-1959 (desegregation and internal security). According to Nagel, the Court retreated fully or in part to all of the attacks except for those of 1893-1897 and 1922-1924. For instance, the Supreme Court did not strike down another law after *Marbury* (1803) as unconstitutional until *Dred Scott* in 1857 (*Dred Scott v. Sanford*, 19 Howard 393). Yet it must be noted that this abstention in no way represented a retreat from the Federalist positions on national supremacy and judicial review.

Nagel then examined factors leading to Court curbing and factors leading to the success of these efforts. Not surprisingly, Nagel found that Court curbing periods by Congress tend to follow periods in which the Supreme Court was vigorously exercising its power of judicial review of federal legislation. Nearly sixty percent (fifty of eighty-six) of the cases in which the Court struck down federal laws were during the Court-curbing periods or within three years of their commencement; yet these periods account for less than one-third of the nation's history. The relationship still holds, though far less strongly, if the New Deal cases are excluded. Court-curbing periods were instigated by the more liberal political party in every case except the 1950s, where Republicans and Southern Democrats combined to attack the Court. Not surprisingly, every Court-curbing period occurred when the party dominating the Court was different from the party dominating Congress.

Court curbing was more likely to be successful when the cause of the action was federal-state relations or separation of powers than when the cause of the action involved economic or political rights. On the other hand, the degree of unanimity of relevant Court cases does not correlate with success, nor do the number of laws struck down.

John Schmidhauser and Larry Berg (1972) conducted an intensive roll call analysis of Court-curbing proposals starting with Franklin Roosevelt's administration. Although many scholars have argued that Roosevelt's Court-curbing proposal was defeated in large part due to deference for the institution and integrity of the Court, Schmidhauser and Berg convincingly demonstrate that members of Congress evidenced no generalized deference for the independence of the judiciary. Rather, it was the emerging conservative coalition of Republicans and Southern Democrats that defeated Roosevelt's plan. Alternatively, during the liberal Warren Court it was liberal members of Congress who defended the judiciary from Court-curbing proposals.

Less severe than attempts to curb the power and independence of the Court are attempts by Congress to reverse particular decisions of the Court. Schmidhauser and Berg (1972) find that members of Congress are generally more likely to vote for such bills than for bills to limit the actual power of the Court. Nevertheless, such attempts to overturn the Court's statutory constructions are rare, at least in the areas of antitrust and labor law (Henschen 1983).

Attempts to curb the power and independence of the Court generally fail. What, then, is the importance of studying attempted Court curbing? For one, it might give us clues as to when future attempts will be made, attempts that someday could be successful. Even if Court curbing never formally succeeds, however, the question is important, for even failed attempts may lead to self-imposed limits on judicial policy making. But with the exception of the switches of Justices Roberts and Harlan (described earlier) and some work by Nagel and by Handberg and Hill, we know almost nothing about the impact of attempted Court curbing.

A Synthesis

Three of the major themes of this chapter—democratic responsiveness of the Court, support by the Court for the United States, and Court curbing—were tied together in an article by Handberg and Hill (1980). Using support by the Court for the United States when it is a party to a suit as a measure of the Court's responsiveness to the federal government, the authors examined the interactions between the Court, Congress, and the executive branch. The general pattern following the Civil War is that low levels of Court support for the United States are associated with the inception of Court-curbing periods, especially during realignment eras. Following the Court-curbing periods, support for the United States typically increases to above average levels.

The Handberg and Hill research, while certainly interesting, leaves as many questions unanswered as answered. First, they do not show whether support for the United States as a party decreases in the periods following realignment. Rather, they show that Court curbing, which often follows low support periods, tends also to follow realignment. The direct link between low support levels and realignment is never demonstrated. Second, while they demonstrate that there tend to be increases in Court support for the United States following Court curbing, they do not allude to the cause of such increases. It certainly matters a good deal whether sitting justices change their views in response to pressure or whether support for the United States results, as Dahl (1957) hypothesized, from the appointment of new justices. These are crucial questions for future research.

Conclusion

The Founders created interbranch checks strong enough to create paralysis within the federal government. But the branches have been restrained in the use of such power. The Supreme Court, although it could cripple the legislative and executive branches through judicial review, infrequently uses such power. Even the number of state statutes declared unconstitutional is extremely small when one considers the number of ordinances passed annually. Congress has only once limited the Court's appellate jurisdiction and has never removed a Supreme Court justice through impeachment. Congress manipulated the size of the Court during Andrew Johnson's administration, but that was more of an attack on Johnson than on the Court. Franklin Roosevelt, who was one of our most popular presidents, and who had an overwhelmingly Democratic Congress and faced a decidedly unpopular Court, could not pass his infamous Court-packing scheme. The three branches of government manage to coexist with one another, despite well-known counterexamples. What we still do not know is whether it is the democratic appointment process that has kept the coexistence peaceful or rather some heretofore unexamined factor.

Notes

1. Twelve of the thirty-eight cases occurred during the New Deal. Of these twelve, two were "trivial," two were "minor," and one was about to expire anyway (Dahl 1957, 287). The remaining seven were "unceremoniously swept under the rug" (p. 287) following the Court's historic switches on substantive due process and the interstate commerce clause. Of the twenty-six cases during periods other than the New Deal, eleven were labeled "minor," fifteen "major." Thus, other than New Deal decisions that were quickly reversed, there were only fifteen major legislative

provisions representing contemporary and national lawmaking majorities that were struck.

2. Judicial-legislative interactions are not limited to the courtroom. Judges frequently lobby legislators on subjects of interest to the judiciary, including judicial budgets, and legislators actively seek the advice of judges on occasion. Chief Justice Robert Stephens of the Kentucky Supreme Court notes that legislators sometimes act as if judges do have something to trade with legislators. A frequent legislative response for a request for a raise is, "How do you feel about such-and-such case? How do you feel about this issue? " (Stephens 1989, 742).

3. These cases are a significant proportion of the Court's workload. According to data I analyzed from the Supreme Court data base collected by Harold Spaeth, they account for 34 percent of the Court's formally decided cases during the Warren Court and 29 percent of the Court's formally decided cases during the Burger Court. Furthermore, the United States won 59.4 percent of its Warren Court cases ($n = 558$), 65.4 percent of its Burger Court cases ($n = 503$), and 59.3 percent of its cases in the first two terms of the Rehnquist Court.

4. As judicial-legislative relations are not limited to the courtroom, neither are executive-legislative relations. Presidents have called on judges, and Supreme Court justices in particular, to take on quasi-judicial roles, to serve temporarily in some executive capacity, and to advise the president on political matters (see Scigliano 1971, 61-77). Five justices of the Supreme Court were called upon to help decide the disputed Hayes-Tilden presidential election of 1876. There were twenty disputed electoral votes in the 1876 election, any one of which would have given the Democrat Tilden a majority in the Electoral College. Congress created an Electoral Count Commission, consisting of five Democratic legislators, five Republican legislators, and five Supreme Court justices, three of whom were Republicans and two of whom were Democrats. Though by most fair accounts, then and now, most of the disputed votes belonged to Tilden, the commission split entirely on partisan lines and gave every disputed vote to Hayes, thus making him president.

    The most frequent off-the-Court interactions between presidents and justices have been political advising. Presidents have often placed confidants on the Court, and they have often been unwilling to sever ties after their trusted advisers have been confirmed. Abe Fortas was one of President Johnson's closest confidants and even helped plan military strategy for the Vietnam War. Fortas's continued relationship with Johnson after his confirmation was one of the factors that led to his defeat when Johnson tried to promote him to Chief Justice in 1968.

5. Sources for the historical information in this section include Abraham 1985, 1988; McCloskey 1960; Murphy 1962, 1964; Scigliano 1971; and Warren 1923.

References

Abraham, Henry J. 1985. *Justices and presidents.* 2d ed. New York: Oxford.
_____. 1988. *Freedom and the Court.* 5th ed. New York: Oxford University Press.
Adamany, David. 1973. Legitimacy, realigning elections and the Supreme Court. *Wisconsin Law Review* 1973:790-846.
Caldeira, Gregory. 1986. Neither the purse nor the sword: Dynamics of public confidence in the U.S. Supreme Court. *American Political Science Review* 80:1209-1226.
Caldeira, Gregory, and John Wright. 1988. Organized interests and agenda setting in the U.S. Supreme Court. *American Political Science Review* 82:1109-1128.
Canon, Bradley, and S. Sidney Ulmer. 1976. The Supreme Court and critical elections: A dissent. *American Political Science Review* 70:1215-1218.
Caplan, Lincoln. 1987. *The tenth justice.* New York: Knopf.
Casper, Jonathan D. 1976. The Supreme Court and national policy making. *American Political Science Review* 70:50-63.
Dahl, Robert. 1957. Decision-making in a democracy: The Supreme Court as a national policy-maker. *Journal of Public Law* 6:179-295.
Ducat, Craig, and Robert Dudley. 1989. Federal appellate judges and presidential power. Paper presented at the annual meeting of the Midwest Political Science Association, Chicago.
_____. 1989. Federal district judges and presidential power during the postwar era. *Journal of Politics* 51:98-118.
Funston, Richard. 1975. The Supreme Court and critical elections. *American Political Science Review* 69:795-811.
Gates, John. 1987. Partisan realignment, unconstitutional state policies, and the U.S. Supreme Court, 1837-1964. *American Journal of Political Science* 31:259-280.
Gibson, James. 1978. Judges' role orientations, attitudes and decisions: An interactive model. *American Political Science Review* 72:911-924.
Handberg, Roger, and Harold F. Hill, Jr. 1980. Court curbing, Court reversals, and judicial review: The Supreme Court versus Congress. *Law and Society Review* 14:309-322.
Henschen, Beth. 1983. Statutory interpretations of the Supreme Court. *American Politics Quarterly* 11:441-458.
McCloskey, Robert. 1960. *The American Supreme Court.* Chicago: University of Chicago Press.
Madison, James, John Jay, and Alexander Hamilton. 1948. *The enduring Federalist,* ed. Charles Beard. New York: Doubleday.
Murphy, Walter F. 1962. *Congress and the Court.* Chicago: University of Chicago Press.
_____. 1964. *Elements of judicial strategy.* Chicago: University of Chicago Press.
Nagel, Stuart. 1965. Court curbing periods in American history. *Vanderbilt Law Review* 18:925-944.

O'Connor, Karen. 1983. The amicus curiae role of the U.S. solicitor general in Supreme Court litigation. *Judicature* 66:256-264.

Provine, Doris M. 1980. *Case selection in the United States Supreme Court.* Chicago: University of Chicago Press.

Puro, Steven. 1971. The role of the amicus curiae in the United States Supreme Court. Ph.D. dissertation, State University of New York at Buffalo.

———. 1981. The United States as amicus curiae. In *Courts, law and judicial processes,* ed. S. Sidney Ulmer. New York: Free Press.

Rohde, David, and Harold Spaeth. 1976. *Supreme Court decision making.* San Francisco: Freeman.

Schmidhauser, John R., and Larry L. Berg. 1972. *The Supreme Court and Congress.* New York: Free Press.

Scigliano, Robert. 1971. *The Supreme Court and the presidency.* New York: Free Press.

Segal, Jeffrey A. 1984. Predicting Supreme Court decisions probabilistically: The search and seizure cases (1962-1981). *American Political Science Review* 78:891-900.

———. 1986. Supreme Court justices as human decision makers: An individual-level analysis of the search and seizure cases. *Journal of Politics* 48:938-955.

———. 1988. Amicus curiae briefs by the solicitor general during the Warren and Burger Courts. *Western Political Quarterly* 41:135-144.

———. 1989. Presidential-judicial interactions: The role of presidential ideology. Unpublished manuscript.

———. 1990. Supreme Court support for the solicitor general: The effect of presidential appointments. *Western Political Quarterly* 43:137-152.

Segal, Jeffrey A., and Albert D. Cover. 1989. Ideological values and the votes of U.S. Supreme Court justices. *American Political Science Review* 83:557-565.

Segal, Jeffrey A., and Cheryl D. Reedy. 1988. The Supreme Court and sex discrimination: The role of the solicitor general. *Western Political Quarterly* 41:553-568.

Spaeth, Harold, and Stuart Teger. 1982. Activism and restraint: A cloak for the justices' policy preferences. In *Supreme Court activism and restraint,* ed. Stephen C. Halpern and Charles M. Lamb. Lexington, Mass.: Lexington Books.

Stephens, Robert F. 1989. Commentary on state selection of judges. *Kentucky Law Journal* 77:741-746.

Tanenhaus, Joseph, Marvin Schick, Matthew Muraskin, and Daniel Rosen. 1963. The Supreme Court's certiorari jurisdiction: Cue theory. In *Judicial decision making,* ed. Glendon Schubert. Glencoe, Ill.: Free Press.

Teger, Stuart, and Douglas Kosinski. 1980. The cue theory of Supreme Court certiorari jurisdiction: A reconsideration. *Journal of Politics* 42:834-846.

Ulmer, S. Sidney, William Hintze, and Louise Kirklosky. 1972. The decision to grant or deny certiorari: Further consideration of cue theory. *Law and Society Review* 6:637-643.

Ulmer, S. Sidney, and David Willison. 1985. The solicitor general of the United States as amicus curiae in the U.S. Supreme Court, 1969-1983 terms. Paper delivered at the annual meeting of the American Political Science Association, New Orleans.

Warren, Charles. 1923. *The Supreme Court in United States history.* Boston: Little, Brown.

Yale Law Journal. 1969. Note. Government litigation in the Supreme Court: The roles of the solicitor general. *Yale Law Journal* 78:1442-1481.

15. COURTS AND CASELOADS

William P. McLauchlan

The most striking feature of court caseloads is that the number of filings in courts has increased at astronomical rates in the past century. The patterns of case filings vary considerably with particular courts, jurisdiction, and the nature of the litigating clientele. However, for federal courts, the number of aggregate filings increased from 100,000 in 1945 to 350,000 in 1985. In the late 1980s, the Supreme Court filings numbered nearly 5,000 per year; the federal courts of appeals' filings were 35,000 per year; and the federal district courts, which have original trial jurisdiction in the federal judiciary, had case filings numbering in the 300,000s in the late 1980s.

Should the dramatic growth in caseloads be of interest to us? The answer is yes for both practical and theoretical reasons. First, there has been growing concern about caseloads generally among lawyers and judges, as well as other public officials. The delay and other costs associated with presenting more cases to courts for judgments give clients and their attorneys reason to hesitate before initiating or responding to litigation. Judges are particularly concerned about growing caseloads because of the amount of work time, technical rulings, and research as well as management—that they present to the judge. In short, participants in the judicial process see increasing caseloads as a threat to the quality of justice which is expected of the court system.

Second, political scientists are concerned about increasing caseloads because they present a pressure or force to which courts are expected to respond. The pressure of caseloads influences the use that litigants (and potential litigants) make of courts. That pressure may force more litigants to resort to alternatives for resolving disputes since the courts are so burdened with cases (Goldberg, Green, and Sander 1985). In addition, caseloads are likely to stress (if not change) court procedures as a way of processing more cases in less time. Last, the product of court work—judgments—may well be altered by the press of additional cases. Courts may develop interim remedies, administrative schemes to monitor decrees (see Cooper 1988), and adaptive procedures that result in nontraditional kinds of decisions in certain cases.

The discussion that follows examines first the current state of our knowledge about caseloads and courts. This will treat the nature of that research and the kinds of questions and answers this work has provided us. The second portion of this chapter will outline an approach to exploring caseloads which may enhance our understanding of the caseload-court connection.

Our Current Understanding of Caseload

Research on Caseload Growth and Change

One category of work on caseloads considers cases as interchangeable and explores the volume or aggregate of the filings. It is the most descriptive kind of caseload research, examining how many cases have been filed and extending to questions of what changes have occurred in case filings or subcategories of cases over the years (Kagan et al. 1977, 1978). Research by Robert Kagan and his colleagues explores the patterns in the supreme courts of sixteen states from 1870 to 1970; such studies yield trends and some understanding of the patterns. Caseload studies of this type can also focus on the problems of institutional (judicial) design and process. This sort of work can have a practical element in assessing the volume (in aggregate terms) of work that cases present to the courts (McLauchlan 1984).

Other work in this genre treats the same kind of phenomenon, but from qualitative perspectives. These researchers seek to develop an appreciation for the nature of the burden that case filings present to courts. Chief Justice Warren E. Burger (1971) provides the practitioner's concerns about the caseload of his court. He argued for close attention to the problems caseloads create for the Supreme Court, and he advocated procedures and institutional remedies that he felt would relieve caseload pressures. Gerhard Casper and Richard Posner (1974), on the other hand, provide a solid, qualitative assessment of the Supreme Court's workload, based on a quantitative analysis of caseload data. Their conclusion was that the workload of the Court was not (as of 1974) excessive and that the Court was not overwhelmed. This qualitative work explores either the nature of judges' working patterns or the amount of work their cases constitute.

Focusing on the problem of case filings can quickly lead to hand wringing. If one examines the aggregate new filings before the U.S. Supreme Court over the past century, it is apparent why Chief Justice Burger called for close examination and substantial institutional and procedural remedies for the problem (Burger 1971; Freund Committee 1972). Even though these patterns exhibit a sharp increase after World War II (the rise started in about the 1947 term), there is an even greater increase in filings in the period from about 1955 onward (after *Brown v. Board of Education*). However, these kinds of patterns are not explained, the nature of the problems is not explained, and alternative explanations are not examined.

Research on Causes and Cures for Caseload Problems

It is inevitable that solutions to the problems of case filings would be forthcoming as a result of looking at the numbers (Freund Committee 1972; Hruska Commission 1975). Such solutions have certainly been offered, in terms of creating additional courts with unique functions, adding judges to existing courts to relieve the workload of individuals already serving, or changing the jurisdiction of courts to reduce or eliminate certain kinds of business from a court.

Some of these proposed solutions deal with immediate problems of ballooning caseloads and are proposed to deal specifically with case pressure. These approaches may resolve the problems for a while, but there is no certainty that such prescriptions will cure the patient because they are not concerned with the causes of filings. Stephen Wasby (1981) outlines these features of the literature by pointing out that the result is often cosmetic or superficial changes or proposals that reflect no understanding of causes.

One significant concern regarding even the raw numbers of case filings must be what factors cause or influence the rate of filings. There has been little attention paid to factors that relate to (perhaps cause) caseload development (Grossman and Sarat 1975; Heydebrand 1977; McLauchlan 1981). The findings of these kinds of studies provide only a partial picture of the kinds of variables likely to be correlated with caseload growth. We have nothing like a comprehensive understanding of these relationships. It is intuitive to expect certain variables or indicators of social, economic, and political activity to be related, generally, to caseload. Beyond this set of general relations, the precise connections are not clearly understood and are probably not uniformly related to all courts and all caseloads.

The factors that are related to case filings may depend on the court involved, the kinds of cases (issues) and litigants (parties) present, and the time (era) examined. Confounding influences such as events certainly complicate any understanding that might emerge. In fact, this work has not been a productive avenue of research because of the substantive and methodological problems that attach to this kind of causal research. Yet finding solutions to the problems may *require* a good deal *more* of this kind of research, even if it is less than satisfactory.

Certainly, courts can encourage or discourage litigation. Favorable decisions encourage other interests to challenge situations. *Brown* did not cause all of the increase in the Supreme Court filings after 1955, but it contributed to the increase in filings that raised desegregation issues. Other court decisions may discourage or deter types of litigation since they indicate a negative disposition toward various claims. Thus, for example, a court decision reconfirming an old and established antitrust doctrine may reduce the petitions seeking to reverse that policy.

One intriguing set of subjects that has received little attention involves the impact of legislation on caseloads (Boyum and Krislov 1980). The practical importance of this subject is obvious since much litigating arises over the application and interpretation of statutes. The judicial consequences of new legislation may be a crucial component of the business of some courts. The problems of undertaking such analysis are significant, as Keith Boyum and Samuel Krislov point out. As a result, such research has made little progress in enriching our understanding of courts and caseloads.

Judicial Administration

There has been a good deal of scholarly work devoted to what might be termed judicial administration. That effort is oriented to the work of individuals who are responsible for the everyday work of the court and deals with problems of administering a judicial system (see Berkson, Hays, and Carbon 1977; Friesen, Gallas, and Gallas 1971; Saari 1982; Wasby 1989; Wheeler and Whitcomb 1977; Winters 1971). This scholarship focuses on processing and managing cases. Such research can treat a court as a judicial production line and may underemphasize explanations for caseloads and courts. Nevertheless, much of this work has been of value in outlining the practical difficulties arising from case filings. In some instances, it has focused on institutional structure (Hays 1978) or issues of procedure which are important to processing caseloads, modernizing courts, and solving administrative problems.

One of the significant features of this body of work is that it places courts and their problems in the context of public administration. Although some observers would not treat courts as traditional bureaucracies, the press of added caseloads has generated a good deal of attention to the kinds of public administration problems that caseloads do cause courts.

Our understanding of courts and caseloads is haphazard, not theoretically based. It is clear that caseloads are increasing, but we have little systematic understanding of why, in what areas, for what reasons, or with what results for courts and participants in the legal process. We do not have a coherent appreciation of the relationship of cases to the operation of the court system. That is not surprising, given the connection between practitioners (lawyers and judges) and their livelihood. They are most concerned with how courts operate and what effect that operation has on the cases they bring to the judicial system. What follows is a preliminary outline for viewing cases and caseloads. From this approach to understanding cases some general appreciation of changes in caseload should be possible.[1]

An Approach to Understanding Court Caseloads

Our understanding of court caseloads is dependent on the theory we use to explain various dimensions of caseloads. This discussion suggests a theoretical perspective that could provide a comprehensive view of cases and can be used for different courts, judicial systems, or case types. My objective is to show that considering court caseloads should encompass a variety of factors, permitting the observer to appreciate significant dimensions of court caseload.

A first step in treating issues of caseload and courts is to develop a set of definitions. *Cases* can constitute different kinds and amounts of *work* for courts and judges. Although cases are often counted, they are not interchangeable; not all cases are even comparable. When judicial administrators and scholars undertake empirical or quantitative analysis of cases, they often count cases as though cases were interchangeable or identical. For some purposes, such as volume over time, they may be interchangeable. However, there may be little attention to qualitative differences among the cases or what kinds of work the case actually requires. Cases are not so easily and evenly treated for explaining caseload and courts.

Each case is a discrete and idiosyncratic decisional opportunity for a court (Krislov 1983). Each case involves unique litigants and interests, and each one constitutes different kinds of work for the judge and the judicial system. Cases at trial certainly generate a different type of work for courts than do cases (even the same cases) on appeal. That is not just because the procedural setting is so different, but also because the functions of appellate courts and trial courts differ. Furthermore, cases on appeal pose different questions for courts than they do at trial. These differences also vary from time to time (Freund Committee 1972; Hruska Commission 1975).

At the same time, cases are *artifacts* of what courts deal with. As such, they can be categorized and counted. Cases are indications of what courts do, how the courts operate, and the impact of courts on people. However, all cases are not handled by courts, and in recent times, many of the disputes and conflicts which might constitute cases have been siphoned off from court consideration to alternative dispute resolution arenas (Goldberg, Green, and Sander 1985). Furthermore, courts conduct a good deal of business that stretches the definition of cases or judging. Some of this business involves administrative or bureaucratized transactions (Friedman and Percival 1976). As a result of these considerations, it is important to consider what the case is about and what the court is being called upon to do when seeking to develop an approach to studying caseloads.

The perspective developed here views each case as a multidimensional opportunity for a court. The case represents a dispute between the litigants, and perhaps others who support one or the other side of the case. This dispute arises from a set of real-world conditions or relationships which one (or both) of the parties seek to have remedied, corrected, readjusted, or terminated. A case marks an interpersonal conflict or an intergroup contest for resources—money, prestige, political or economic advantage, even principle.

What follows is an effort to flesh out the dimensions and utility of an approach to examining caseloads. The discussion is not designed to present a complete and comprehensive view of a set of caseload data. However, it is intended to outline the variety of factors—characteristics and variables—that would provide a systematic and comprehensive approach to explaining changes in caseload and its pressure on courts and judges.

A Typology

There are several characteristics of cases and courts which appear to be central to an analytic perspective. One is a set of case types. That is, different case types require different kinds and amounts of attention by courts, and a dimension that recognizes this feature of cases is important to this effort. Cases can be typed in various ways, for different purposes. The amount or the kind of work a case presents to courts should be a determining factor. Other typologies of cases depending on the degree of idiosyncratic attention they require of courts might be used to sort cases for purposes of this analysis. Traditional substantive categories of cases—civil or criminal, tort, contract, or property—could be used if an assessment could be made of how much work such case types (rather than individual cases) require. What will be done here is impressionistic, and it is designed to be suggestive rather than definitive.

A second dimension that warrants attention in this discussion is the type of court involved. This would include appellate versus trial courts. Courts of general jurisdiction, compared with those of limited jurisdiction, may also be a valuable way of sorting through these matters. These particular categorizations are not sophisticated, and they may prove too rough or general to benefit a precise assessment of court caseload. However, it seems that this aspect of cases would influence the meaning or significance of cases for purposes of this exploration.

Although simple dichotomies of bureaucratic/idiosyncratic and trial/appellate courts are not the only ways in which cases might be treated or considered, this treatment should emphasize that cases are not identical or interchangeable in terms of analysis or consideration of court caseload. Each case could be considered individually in terms of just how routine and bureaucratic it is for the judicial system to handle, and whether it involves the trial or appellate court. Each case could then be placed on continua that permit some assessment of what kind of work or burden the case provides the judiciary. Furthermore, the relationship among different kinds of cases can be viewed on such a continuum.

Figure 15-1 provides an outline of the analytic scheme that has been roughed out above. The purpose of this is to indicate that cases and cascloads are not all interchangeable but can be compared and understood in comparative terms. It recognizes that different kinds of cases require different kinds of court work. It also illustrates how to consider the connections between court functions and caseloads. The two dimensions discussed are clearly not the only ones useful for this analysis.[2] But these will illustrate the fundamental or basic features of the judicial system and its connections to caseload. Thus, this provides an indication of how to assess the work differences among cases.[3]

The horizontal axis in Figure 15-1, "Judicial process," can be viewed as an ordinal increase (from left to right) in judicial formality. There are significant differences among courts, or even within courts, regarding the nature of the processes that are used to deal with a case. As a case or class of cases moves from left to right on the scheme, the work and attention become more individualized. Courts have to treat cases with more formality and more individuality when they are located toward the right. This is also likely to mean that the court must devote more time and more intensive attention to cases on the right.

The "Court type" axis may seem to be clearly dichotomous (nominal), but from the top to the bottom of this axis, the trial/appellate court dichotomy may gradually or ordinally increase in rigor, potential sanctions, nature of proceedings, and jurisdiction. Thus, although the federal district courts are trial courts of original, general jurisdiction, each year they treat a large number of "appeals" from Social Security Administration disability hearings.[4] Intermediate appellate courts might treat some appeals to nearly a trial de novo, while other cases within the same court's jurisdiction would be treated to very

Figure 15-1   Idealized Continua for Categorizing the Functions and Work of Courts

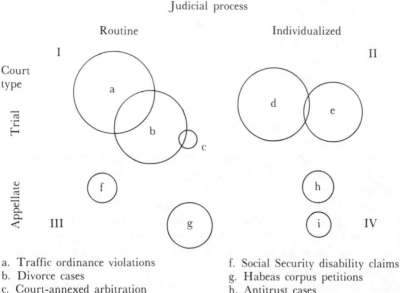

a. Traffic ordinance violations
b. Divorce cases
c. Court-annexed arbitration
d. Small claims disputes
e. Criminal prosecutions

f. Social Security disability claims
g. Habeas corpus petitions
h. Antitrust cases
i. Antitrust cases

distant (deferential) appellate review. The court of last resort in the same system might process only a very few, formal appeals from the trial courts.

Cell I of Figure 15-1 involves cases that are relatively routine and appear in trial courts (often in trial courts of limited jurisdiction).[5] These can be civil or criminal cases, although the most obvious sort of case that might fall in this category would be traffic (parking tickets) or housing ordinance (building code) violations in which there has been no personal or property damage. In most instances such cases are handled by simply paying the fine to the clerk or providing proof of compliance. A lawyer is generally not involved, and there may be no permanent record of the violation or the transaction. Such cases as these might be located in the region labeled "a" in the figure. The large circle around this category suggests that the number of these kinds of cases may well be substantial.

There are routine civil actions, such as uncontested divorces, in which the court (the judge) approves a decree which reflects the settlement that the two parties have negotiated, directly or through their attorneys. This type of case may involve attorneys, but amicable divorces barely involve the court in its traditional function. It is largely the relationship between the parties that prevents this kind of case from being litigated. The region around "b" indicates the location of this kind of case. The size of the circle is used to suggest these cases may be numerous. The location of the circle indicates these cases constitute more formal proceedings, with more court attention, than routine traffic cases.

Another set of cases in this category might be "court annexed arbitration" awards (Goldberg, Green, and Sander 1985, 225-243). This kind of proceeding may result in a case filing, but the court administratively adopts the arbitration award (or orders that the case go to arbitration) and then issues the relevant order binding the parties to what the arbitrator decides in the case. This would involve attorneys and a semi-formal proceeding (before the arbitrator) with additional expenses, but the court's attention to the issues in the case is not great and it does not constitute much work for the court.

Type I cases are the least amenable to quantitative analysis. Often courts that handle such cases do not report filings, or they do not keep permanent records of cases, once they have been disposed. If such a Type I case is not resolved routinely it may escalate to a Type II or disappear. In the first case, it would be counted (again for terms of reporting). In the second, it may not be counted at all. It is likely that this first category of cases constitutes a substantial amount of judicial business in terms of volume, but it is not clear that it involves labor-intensive efforts by courts or judges.

Type II cases are the more traditional trial court business which results in somewhat formal and individualized treatment by the court. There are at least some adversarial (pleading or pretrial) procedural stages involved in these cases. It is possible that small claims might fall in the region of point "d," at least when both parties appear, contest the allegations of the other side, and then acquiesce in the court's (judge's) resolution. This point indicates one additional factor that should be mentioned. That is, the significance of the case for a court depends in part on how the parties or the disputants relate to one another and respond to each other's claims. It also suggests that the same kind of case may fall in different regions of the figure under different circumstances, depending on the parties or matters in dispute.

The traditional trial court case, whether civil or criminal, is Type II business. Thus, a formal criminal prosecution before a jury for alleged criminal behavior would fall into the region perhaps near point "e." The case focuses clearly on the individualized, factual allegations made by the prosecutor and individual participants—defendants. Civil trials such as personal injury actions or damages could also be contained in this area. These are individualized to the point that the court could not treat the dispute routinely but rather would have to isolate the case for individual consideration.

Type III cases are an interesting but little explored kind of judicial business. These routine appeals may result in a very cursory judicial scrutiny of the issues. This kind of dispute might include the appeals from Social Security Administration determinations or tax court rulings. The cases are heard in the federal district courts (trial courts), but they generally involve judicial review of an agency's prior determination of the issues involved. There may be little judicial attention to the idiosyncrasies of each case. The decision often results in a rubber stamp or "bureaucratic" approval of what has been done. The point near "f" might indicate this kind of routine case.

Habeas corpus petitions might also fall into this same portion of the figure, near "g." Even though these are initiated as new actions in trial court (in Cell II), the petition itself is a review of the action originating at trial; the proceeding examines whether that original action was constitutionally proper. These petitions are unique, and each involves parties, facts, and circumstances that differ from any other case, but the repeated claims that are made by petitioners in most of these might convert these kinds of disputes into a routine matter of reviewing a previous court's actions.

There are other kinds of appeals that may well fall in this category. Cases of mandatory appeal, which are not viewed as important but which must be reviewed by the appellate court, might also fall in the area labeled "g" in Cell III. These may include mandatory judicial review of administrative hearings and decisions either where the reviewing court will defer to the agency's judgment or where there are a fixed set of criteria that the reviewing court applies to the review. There may not be a great volume of cases that fall in this portion of the framework, although some state appellate courts may treat a large number of these kinds of cases. It is possible, depending on the court and the history of the appellate court's operation, that such categories of cases might exist until the state legislature changes the court's jurisdiction or procedures to take care of such appeal.

Although it is worrisome to suggest this, the mandatory appeal of capital punishment cases might approach this area, if the appellate court did not view the issue as significant and worthy of individualized attention. This is not to suggest that such cases have been or are being treated routinely by appellate courts. However, the mandatory nature of the *appeal* and perhaps the number or volume of such appeals (in some states) could convert these cases into Type III cases.

The Type IV cases constitute the sort of caseloads that many scholars have examined most closely. These involve the kinds of cases the U.S. Supreme Court treats. Most state appellate courts of last resort would handle cases in this category as well. These cases involve close appellate scrutiny of the legal (and policy) questions contained in individual appeals from trial courts. There may be different regions within this area—routinized procedures and consideration of some of these cases occur. The same case could be treated twice in this region, as when a federal court of appeals reviews an antitrust action at "h," and then the Supreme Court decides it again at "i." [6]

Under this categorization scheme a case need not remain at the same point or even in the same region throughout its tenure in the system. Thus, a routine ordinance case (Type I) may move, on appeal, directly to Cell IV if it presented important constitutional statutory law interpretation.[7] There are likely to be other circumstances when a case will move from left to right or right to left on the continuum. A case could move on the routine/individualized dimension depending on the parties and their objectives a case can change its nature, and the treatment it receives in court will change accordingly. If the trial court determination is appealed, the case obviously moves down the scale into the appellate range (III or IV).

This element of change on the scale means that any analysis done is really a snapshot of an evolving situation. The movement of a case in this scheme could be due to the parties to the case, the issues involved in the case, or the perception of the dispute by the judges involved. Parties can escalate an issue to the point that the reviewing court (or even a trial court) must treat it individually or routinely This may be due to persistence or demands for such judicial attention. In addition, certain legal issues (such as constitutionality, on appeal) may change the position of the case. Major constitutional issues or matters of public concern may draw closer court attention to the issue. Courts (judges) may also categorize certain issues (not parties) as appropriate for routine consideration. The extent to which the court can accomplish this depends on the judges involved, the structure of the court system, the jurisdictional authority involved, and the political circumstances— the tolerance of judicial actors. However, the end result of this consideration is that cases are not constant commodities for the judiciary, and the result for the judicial system is a varying caseload burden for the court system.

It is obvious that the area or size of each case type in the figure will vary. The idea is to indicate that some case types constitute much larger volumes of filings and perhaps more work for courts than other kinds of cases. Thus, case category "a," traffic violations, involves more cases (although this may not mean more work) than type "f," Social Security disability cases. Certainly, this is not dependent only on the *number* of cases filed but it is a powerful indicator of work. It is also possible that case types overlap or are very close to one another in the figure. To develop these aspects of the scheme requires closer attention and better information than is now available in the study of courts and caseloads.

Utility of the Approach

One of the potential values of this approach is that it permits comparisons of a single court across time, comparisons among case types, and comparisons among courts (either within a single judicial system or across court systems). This scheme seeks to provide a framework or perspective of courts and caseload. Clearly, this scheme focuses on cases and their characteristics. While it does not ignore courts, the central focus is to explain caseload by reference to the type of case or a class of cases. This permits the analysis of caseload or the treatment of these categories by courts.

Other factors or variables influence the nature of a case and its possible significance for courts. Some cases involve complex legal issues. Thus, cases involving significant claims or issues may take longer to be considered; the long wait may affect the compliance of the parties (particularly the losing party) to the court's decision. Most important for our purposes, these cases indicate different amounts of work for courts. As the public or judicial view of the question's significance changes, the judicial treatment of the case is likely to change to reflect those views.

To make such comparisons—which we must do to make progress on our assessment of court caseloads—it will be necessary to develop and acquire adequate data sets. While the lack of adequate data can always plague research, some kinds of data have frequently not been collected with case delays (such as litigant and attorney motivations and strategies). These kinds of information should be linked to the cases, and for some purposes they are essential to assessing the nature of the caseload. Judicial role perceptions have long been of interest to judicial scholars, but role analysis has not generated very useful information to date. In connection with caseloads, it may well be quite significant because judges' perceptions of their roles will influence their treatment of cases and litigants.

Conclusion

Analysis of caseloads requires a good deal more development than can be done here. Nevertheless, the proposed model provides a valuable mechanism for evaluating the caseloads of courts. In combination with indicators of the magnitude of various types of cases or kinds of court business, this analytic method permits close examination of a single court and its caseload, exploration of the relationships among various courts and levels of courts within a jurisdiction (state or federal), and comparisons among different courts on the same level. Certainly it would be possible to compare different court systems or different kinds of cases.[8]

In the process of developing and using such a scheme as this, a close assessment of the burden of cases on courts can be made. This is particularly important since the growth of case filings seems to be such a staggering prospect. However, the added richness of our understanding of caseloads using this kind of analysis should provide a better sense of what might influence these patterns or what kinds of remedies would affect the patterns that are disclosed.

The value of this set of suggestions for considering caseloads and courts is that it recognizes the diversity of case types and court procedures. It permits the multidimensional consideration of a number of variables (only two of which were outlined in Figure 15-1 and the accompanying discussion) which are likely to influence the impact of cases on courts and judges. It is well worth continued effort to make these kinds of analyses about caseloads.

Notes

1. One deficiency in nearly all studies is the limited and inadequate data base upon which analysis is grounded. *One major focus of future effort must be the development and utilization of appropriate and comprehensive data bases.*
2. It seems as if the judges presiding in particular courts might well also be part of the dimension involving types of cases. The recruitment process by which judges are selected and the experience of the judges would influence the way in which cases are processed, the impact of court treatment, and the time involved in the handling of the case. Furthermore, the court's jurisdiction, procedures, and authority influence what a judge may do with the case. Thus, the dimension involving court types is not clear or easy to determine. Yet it is certainly important for understanding courts and caseloads.

   Another factor or dimension worth our attention involves the nature of the litigants in a case. This may entail a closer examination than just whether the government is a party, or whether one-shotters are litigating against repeat players. These are relevant, and they provide a valuable initial perspective, but they are not likely to be determinative of the analysis. Assessing the likely objectives of the plaintiff and defendant in the case, including what their motives for litigating or continuing to litigate are, would be important. This certainly has significant problems of operationalization, but these considerations will influence the impact of the cases on courts and the effect of the court on disputes.

Another dimension that should be considered is time. That is, there is a longitudinal feature to cases and to case filings that should be considered. As a case evolves during the course of litigation, the time and attention it requires change accordingly. Furthermore, cases are not equivalent over time. Divorce cases are treated much differently by courts (judges and attorneys), as well as by litigants and by society, in the 1980s than they were in the 1950s. Thus, it is significant to consider the "age" of cases in the judicial system, as well as the legal and cultural context (the times) in which litigation is occurring. This might be difficult to do, but it is well worth our research attention.

3. That is to say, depending on the location of a case or a body of cases on Figure 15-1, a qualitative, if not a quantitative, assessment of work should be possible. Eventually, it might be possible to determine the work equivalency of various case types using this kind of scheme.

It should be noted also that quantitative differences and comparisons can be noted by examining the relative size of case types on the figure. More cases equal a larger circle or area encompassed by that particular kind of caseload.

4. These are clearly treated as appellate, and it is quite rare that the court "reverses" the administrative determination, although the court would begin the process de novo. Thus, even though these cases would fall below the middle of the vertical axis, they are different cases from many others district courts handle, and they would be located very near the axis between the "Trial" and "Appellate" categories.

5. National Court Statistics Project 1981 and National Center for State Courts 1985 provide useful and detailed pictures of state court organization which suggest the variety of courts that might be included in processing each type of case, including Type I cases.

6. These two points may actually be located in the same place. This indicates, interestingly, that if an entire court system is being examined this way, the same case would count twice if considered by two appellate courts. It could also be counted a third time, if it appeared in the trial level, although this initial appearance would be located in Cell II.

Points "h" and "i" are not portrayed as identical simply to illustrate that the same case might receive somewhat separate appellate treatment by different courts. This point indicates the potential difficulties of categorizing and placing cases on this suggested scheme.

7. *Thompson v. Louisville*, 362 U.S. 199 (1960).

8. This approach is methodologically difficult to develop and use. Operationalizing some of the variables and some of the indicators that have been outlined above will be difficult. Furthermore, using more than three dimensions (sets of variables) certainly presents a significant set of

problems. Even if these problems are overcome, the acquisition of appropriate data to indicate the nature of the variables would be costly and labor intensive at least.

Certainly, this kind of approach could be criticized as being largely quantitative in nature. It focuses on the number of cases, the time it takes to process a filing, and the like. Yet it does permit a number of qualitative considerations to be accommodated and considered (such as the nature of litigants, lawyer strategies, judicial role perceptions). Furthermore, comparing courts or cases using this treatment should contribute a good deal to our qualitative or substantive understanding of courts and caseloads.

Using this framework would require a good deal of data—quantitative and qualitative—in order to make the kinds of assessments that are necessary. Even without the data, there are clearly deficiencies in the information we have about caseloads. However, there are some hopeful signs that both federal and state courts are beginning to record and publish useful sorts of data about cases. It is still possible to locate various kinds of cases on the diagram, either as points or regions. If that is done, then an assessment of the caseloads can be made in terms of the burdens they impose on courts, and the nature of the caseload for the operation of a judicial system can be estimated. Considering the jurisdiction of a court and examining the particular kinds of cases that are filed should shed a good deal of light on the nature of its caseload.

References

Berkson, Larry, Steven Hays, and Susan Carbon. 1977. *Managing the state courts: Texts and readings.* St. Paul, Minn.: West.

Boyum, Keith, and Samuel Krislov, eds. 1980. *Forecasting the impact of legislation on courts.* Washington, D.C.: National Academy Press.

Burger, Warren E. 1971. State of the federal judiciary, 1971. *American Bar Association Journal* 57:855-859.

Caldeira, Gregory. 1982. A tale of two reforms: On the work of the U.S. Supreme Court. In *The analysis of judicial reform,* ed. Philip Dubois. Lexington, Mass.: Lexington Books.

Casper, Gerhard, and Richard Posner. 1974. *The workload of the Supreme Court.* Chicago: American Bar Foundation.

Cooper, Phillip J. 1988. *Hard judicial choices: Federal district court judges and state and local officials.* New York: Oxford University Press.

Freund Committee. 1972. *Federal Judicial Center report of the Study Group on the Case Load of the Supreme Court.* Washington, D.C.: Administrative Office of the U.S. Courts.

Friedman, Lawrence, and Robert Percival. 1976. A tale of two courts: Litigation in Alameda and San Benito Counties. *Law and Society Review* 10:267-301.

Friesen, Ernest C., Jr., Edward C. Gallas, and Nesta M. Gallas. 1971. *Managing the courts.* Indianapolis: Bobbs-Merrill.

Goldberg, Steve, Eric Green, and Frank Sander. 1985. *Dispute resolution.* Boston: Little, Brown.

Grossman, Joel, and Austin Sarat. 1975. Litigation in the federal courts: A comparative study. *Law and Society Review* 9:321-346.

Hays, Steven W. 1978. *Court reform: Ideal or illusion?* Lexington, Mass.: Lexington Books.

Heydebrand, Wolf. 1977. The context of public bureaucracies: An organizational analysis of federal district courts. *Law and Society Review* 11:759-821.

Hruska Commission. 1975. *Commission on Revision of the Federal Court Appellate System, Structure and Internal Procedures: Recommendations for change.* Reprinted in 67 F.R.D. 195 (1975).

Kagan, Robert, Bliss Cartwright, Lawrence Friedman, and Stanton Wheeler. 1977. The business of state supreme courts, 1870-1970. *Stanford Law Review* 30:121-156.

———. 1978. The evolution of state supreme courts. *Michigan Law Review* 76:961-1005.

Krislov, Samuel. 1983. Theoretical perspectives on case load studies: A critique and a beginning. In *Empirical theories about courts,* ed. Keith Boyum and Lynn Mather. New York: Longman.

McLauchlan, William. 1981. Longitudinal models of the Supreme Court's caseload, 1880-1979. Paper presented at the annual meeting of the Southern Political Science Association, Memphis, Tennessee.

———. 1984. *Federal court caseloads.* New York: Praeger.

National Center for State Courts. 1985. *State court caseload statistics: Annual report.* Williamsburg, Va.: National Center for State Courts.

National Court Statistics Project. 1981. *State court organization.* Williamsburg, Va.: National Center for State Courts.

Saari, David J. 1982. *American court management: Theories and practices.* Westport, Conn.: Quorum.

Wasby, Stephen L. 1981. Appellate delay: An examination of possible remedies. *Justice System Journal* 6:325-345.

———. 1989. The bar's role in governance of the Ninth Circuit. *Willamette Law Review* 25:471-569.

Wheeler, Russell R., and Howard R. Whitcomb. 1977. *Judicial administration: Text and readings.* Englewood Cliffs, N.J.: Prentice-Hall.

Winters, Glen R., ed. 1971. *Selected readings: Court congestion and delay.* Chicago: American Judicature Society.

Part V

POLICY IMPACT AND INNOVATION

John Marshall has made his decision, now let him enforce it.

—Attributed to President Andrew Jackson

The problem is not whether the judges make the law, but when and how and how much.

—Justice Felix Frankfurter
Quoted in Alpheus T. Mason,
Harlan Fiske Stone: Pillar of the Law, 1956

One widely held view of courts in America is that they decide only winners and losers; that the decisions are based on precedent; and that the decisions themselves are obeyed by all within the court's jurisdiction. We now know that this view is narrow and uninformed. In previous parts of this book, authors have described the political nature of decision making and recruitment and how that nature affects courts' policy making. Part V discusses the related matters of judicial innovations and the impact of judicial decisions. The raison d'etre for these topics is the recognition that courts are political institutions that make new policy (that is, innovations) and that the implementation of court policy is not always automatic.

Innovative judicial decisions have been a fact of political life in the United States for some time. Chief Justice John Marshall showed remarkable inventiveness in *Marbury v. Madison* when he laid claim to the power of judicial review. That claim has been a wellspring of innovative policies from the federal judiciary. These courts have taken positive steps to create new policy in such areas as criminal law (the exclusionary rule) and the right to privacy (abortion rights). Judicial rules regarding civil matters are also often the products of judge-made innovations.

Two important issues regarding judicial innovations draw the attention of judicial scholars. First, what are the circumstances leading to the development of judicial innovations? This question quite likely requires exploration at several levels. Do certain conditions in the political and social system lead to judicial innovations? Do particular questions facing the judiciary prompt innovative decision making? Are judges with certain backgrounds, attitudes, or values more likely to render innovative policies? A second question facing judicial scholars is: What influences the spread and adoption of judicial innovations? When the state supreme court in California offers novel reasoning to resolve a difficult judicial issue, why do some courts accept that reasoning and others reject it? What influences the speed at which the reasoning is considered and adopted? What influences the modification of an innovation as it diffuses across the country? Answers to these questions are important because they tell us about judicial innovations, and they provide insights into the process of judicial decision making. Lawrence Baum is one of the few judicial scholars who have written on the topic of judicial innovations. His chapter (16) offers an overview of the brief literature in this area, poses some questions for further exploration, and ends with caveats regarding future research.

When judges innovate, they often give rights or privileges to some while limiting the rights or privileges of others. Since there are winners and losers systemwide in this process, and since the process and decisions are likely to be based on political values, innovative decisions do not often meet with widespread acceptance. Opposition may come from other judges, from bureaucrats affected by the decision, from legislatures and executives, and, sometimes, from individuals who supposedly benefit from the innovative policy.

Judicial decisions, whether innovative or not, can be viewed as the opening round of a political process affecting many in the American political system. A question driving early studies of this process was whether judges, bureaucrats, legislatures, or others were complying with judicial decisions. Were schools being desegregated? Were police officers informing suspects of their rights? Researchers found mixed answers to these questions. Sometimes compliance was not problematic, and sometimes noncompliance was the rule. The fundamental questions are: Why the variation? Why do some decisions result in widespread acceptance and others meet with overwhelming opposition? What are some of the techniques used to undercut or strengthen the implementation of a judicial policy?

Chapter 17, by Bradley C. Canon, explores the literature confronting these questions. His review of this relatively recent subfield in the judicial area reveals mixed findings. The review also discusses the decline in research in this field, a decline that leaves incomplete our understanding of the impact of judicial policies—especially the policies of recent Supreme Court decisions and decisions by lower federal and state courts.

16. COURTS AND POLICY INNOVATION

Lawrence Baum

A First Look at Judicial Innovation

The Concept of Innovation

Ordinarily, a person who brings a lawsuit for a personal injury can identify the party that is allegedly responsible for the injury. But when a woman suffers physical injury from a prescription drug that her mother used decades earlier, it usually is impossible to determine which of the many manufacturers of that drug was involved. Rejecting other approaches to this situation, in 1980 the California Supreme Court held that liability could be divided among those manufacturers primarily according to their shares of the market for the drug (*Sindell v. Abbott Laboratories*, 607 P.2d 924 [Calif. 1980]). This "market share" theory attracted wide notice. During the 1980s, courts in three other states adopted the theory altogether or in part (*Hymowitz v. Eli Lilly and Co.*, 539 N.E.2d 1069 [N.Y. 1989]), and additional adoptions may well occur in the 1990s.[1]

The market share theory is an example of innovation in the courts: one court is the first to adopt a practice or legal rule, and that practice or rule is then communicated to and adopted by other courts. We can define an innovation as a new practice or rule, diffusion as the process by which an innovation is communicated to other courts and adopted by them,[2] and innovation as the whole process of initial adoption and diffusion. Innovation is a common, even inevitable, phenomenon in the courts, as it is elsewhere in government and society.

Judicial innovations take multiple forms, ranging from a new procedure for pretrial settlement of cases (Marcotte 1987) to a novel approach to sentencing in a particular situation (*Western Legal History* 1988, 282-283). This chapter will focus on the type illustrated by the

I would like to thank Gregory Caldeira, Bradley Canon, and the editors for their comments on an earlier draft of this chapter. Many of the ideas in the chapter developed through my collaboration with Professor Canon on research concerning judicial innovation.

market share theory, doctrinal innovation. Judicial doctrines establish legal rules that can influence not only future court cases but also the practices of the legislature and executive branch and the behavior of people and institutions outside government. Thus, in a sense, they constitute the heart of judicial policy making; for that reason, it is appropriate to focus on doctrinal innovations. Courts adopt legal doctrines in interpreting both constitutions and statutes, laws made by legislatures. Courts also adopt doctrines in the "common law" fields such as property law, in which the judiciary has developed the law largely independent of the legislature. The market share theory lies in one major common law field, tort law—essentially, the law of personal injuries. The discussion of the adoption and diffusion of judicial innovations in this chapter will encompass all these types of law.

For the most part, judicial doctrines are issued by appellate courts; trial courts play a more limited role in doctrinal development, primarily applying existing rules of law to individual cases before them. Accordingly, this chapter will focus on the appellate level. But the examples of settlement procedures and approaches to sentencing are useful reminders that trial courts also engage in a great deal of innovation, and their exclusion here is not intended to suggest that the kinds of innovation that occur at the trial level are unimportant.

The Study of Innovation

During this century, social scientists in a number of disciplines have given enormous attention to innovation (Rogers 1983). Their primary subject has been the diffusion of innovations among individuals. Among their concerns have been the characteristics of innovations that influence their adoption and the characteristics of individuals that influence their readiness to adopt innovations, "innovativeness." The classic study in the field was an examination by two rural sociologists of the diffusion of a new type of seed corn among farmers (Ryan and Gross 1943). Innovation research since that time has taken a variety of forms in several academic disciplines (Rogers 1983, chap. 2).[3]

Political scientists have contributed a small but significant body of research on innovation. The primary subject of their work is policy innovation within government, most commonly in American state legislatures (Savage 1985). To a considerable extent, this work reflects the concerns of the larger social science literature on innovations and their diffusion. Probably the most important study of policy innovation was Jack Walker's (1969) analysis of states' enactment of eighty-eight types of legislation. Walker gave particular attention to the relative speed with which particular states adopted new legislation and the geographical paths by which legislation diffused from state to state. His study was followed by several others dealing with state legislation. Other scholars have extended the study of policy innovation to the local level and to diffusion across nations.[4] Political scientists also have done research on policy innovation that is less directly connected to the broader innovation literature in the social sciences (see Kingdon 1984; Polsby 1984).

Only a very small part of the scholarship on judicial policy making has focused explicitly on innovation. But a good deal of research relates to aspects of doctrinal innovation. The largest share of that research has been done by legal scholars, who have long been concerned with the development of new judicial doctrines and their successive adoption by courts in different jurisdictions (see Keeton et al. 1984). This research, however, does not analyze these phenomena as a form of innovation or make use of the scholarship on innovation; as a result, it is useful primarily in identifying innovations and diffusion processes rather than as a source of hypotheses and findings.

Within the social science literature on courts, one sizable body of work and a few small clusters of research are particularly relevant to innovation. Two studies with close connections to nonjudicial research on policy innovation are an analysis by Bradley Canon and me (Canon and Baum 1981) of the adoption and diffusion of twenty-three new tort doctrines among the states and John Domino's (1989) comparison of the extent and speed with which state supreme courts have adopted seven new privacy rights. Drawing a good deal from the social science literature on innovation, Daniel Fiorino (1976) analyzed the diffusion of Supreme Court innovations, primarily to policy makers who were responsible for implementing those innovations. His study highlights the relevance to innovation of the substantial literature which examines lower court responses to the Court's constitutional innovations in terms of the implementation and impact of judicial policies (see Johnson and Canon 1984, chap. 2, and Chapter 17 of this book, by Canon).

A few studies have examined one important element of diffusion, the communication process involved in the citation of court decisions by other courts (Caldeira 1985). Martin Shapiro's (1970) analysis of decision making in tort law is a particularly good example of other political science research that does not deal explicitly with innovation but that informs our understanding of it. Though they lie outside the scope of this chapter, the small body of studies on innovations in judicial administration and in systems for the selection of judges should also be noted.[5]

Taken together, all these sets of studies tell us a good deal about innovation. But the paucity of research focusing directly on innovation has limited our knowledge of innovation in comparison with many other topics in the judicial process. As a result, this chapter must be more speculative than most of the others in this book.

Problems in the Analysis of Judicial Innovation

In their study of policy innovation in government, political scientists have borrowed from other social scientists the concept of innovation and ideas developed in the innovation literature. By doing so, and thus analyzing innovation as a phenomenon within the policy process, they have enhanced our understanding of public policy making. Studies of the sources and flow of policy innovations, for instance, have helped to illuminate relationships among the states and between the state and federal governments (see, for instance, Light 1978; Walker 1971).

Yet there are serious drawbacks in using innovation as a distinct focus in the study of public policy making, drawbacks that stem largely from differences between government policies and the kinds of innovations that social scientists typically study.[6] At the outset, it is particularly difficult to identify innovations in public policy, because policy development typically does not take a simple and clear path. In the courts, for instance, a new doctrine may differ only marginally from an existing one; in this situation, it is unclear whether the new doctrine should be regarded (or *is* regarded by judges) as an innovation. Occasionally, in fields such as torts and constitutional law, a policy option that represents a change from the current doctrinal position of most courts also represents a return to an earlier status quo; should that option be regarded as an innovation?

Other differences affect the process of considering and adopting innovations in public policy. One such difference is that most students of innovation focus on individuals and organizations that consider and adopt innovations in order to improve their own situations. Companies, for instance, seek new technologies primarily as means to improve profits. In contrast, policy makers deal chiefly with innovations that address demands and problems in the community at large, such as a perceived deficiency in the quality of public education.

As a result of these differences, the considerations that influence decisions whether to adopt innovations (Downs and Mohr 1979, 390-401) are also likely to be quite different. Farmers who decide to plant a new type of corn seed, for instance, risk economic disaster for themselves if the innovation fails. In contrast, legislators who adopt legislation that promotes a new farming practice are creating an economic risk for other people, not themselves; the primary danger for legislators in such action is that those who suffer from a damaging piece of legislation will retaliate at the polls.

Even more important is the existence of conflicts over interests or values. Most of the scholarly work on innovation examines "technological" innovations, such as hybrid seed corn—means to help in achieving goals that are largely consensual. Because of this consensual quality, scholars tend to view decisions whether to adopt innovations as resulting primarily from attitudes toward innovation as such.

In contrast, the goals of policy innovations typically are quite nonconsensual. Civil liberties doctrines, for instance, involve perceived conflicts between values such as freedom of speech and national security. Almost surely, judges' attitudes toward these values have a far greater impact on their decisions to adopt a new doctrine than do their attitudes about innovation as such. For that reason, it is somewhat misleading to characterize choices about the adoption of such doctrines simply as responses to innovations.

Because of such differences, we need to be cautious in applying the concepts and findings of the innovation literature to policy innovation, including doctrinal innovation in the courts. Indeed, a good argument can be made that we should not even study judicial innovation as a distinct phenomenon, because doing so creates an entirely artificial distinction between judges' responses to innovations and their responses to other policy options. Yet innovation *is* an important element of judicial policy making, in that the adoption and diffusion of innovative doctrines are responsible for much of the change that occurs in judicial policy. For that reason it is useful to consider and study judicial innovation, as long as we do so carefully.

Patterns of Innovation in the Courts

I will begin this examination of judicial innovation by discussing courts as innovators in general terms. I will then turn to selected aspects of three issues: the sources of judicial innovations, the diffusion of innovations among courts, and differences among courts in innovation. In discussing judicial innovation, I will sometimes use legislatures and the literature on legislative innovation as a point of reference and comparison.

Courts as Innovators

In the past few decades, courts in the United States have engaged in a great deal of innovative policy making. They have adopted a series of novel doctrines to protect civil liberties, doctrines reflected in such decisions as the Supreme Court's requirement that police officers inform suspects of certain rights before questioning them (*Miranda v. Arizona,* 384 U.S. 436 [1966]) and the rulings by several state supreme courts that systems for financing public education were unconstitutional (for example, *Robinson v. Cahill,* 303 A.2d 273 [N.J. 1973]; *Horton v. Meskill,* 376 A.2d 359 [Conn. 1977]). Federal district judges have used an array of new remedies for constitutional defects in public institutions, such as busing and the imposition of new taxes to overcome racial segregation in school systems (see Cooper 1988). And state supreme courts have produced a series of new doctrines in tort law that expand the legal rights of people who suffer injuries, such as the market share theory for injurious drugs (Baum and Canon 1982).

This record is striking, because in some respects courts seem poorly suited for innovation. Courts operate within a structured adjudication process that makes them dependent on litigants for opportunities to adopt innovations. The principle of stare decisis generally binds judges to existing interpretations of law, so they may not be inclined to make and adopt doctrinal innovations. Judges have small staffs and essentially no additional resources for research, characteristics that limit their ability to identify and evaluate possible innovations (see Horowitz 1977). In each of these respects, legislatures appear to operate under conditions more favorable to innovation. And, far more than judges, legislators may have an incentive to offer new policies as a means to build political support (Mayhew 1974; Polsby 1984, 161-165).

On the whole, however, these disadvantages are not as significant as they initially appear. The capacities of courts to gather needed information are not necessarily inferior to those of legislatures (Reedy 1982). Stare decisis does not entirely prohibit the replacement of existing legal doctrines; in a sense, it simply creates a presumption in favor of the status quo—one that exists in legislatures as well (see Shapiro 1965). Further, courts often adopt innovations in response to new issues, issues on which directly relevant precedents do not exist; for example, technological advances such as the invention of the automobile and the computer brought to the courts many questions on which they were free—indeed, required—to establish new rules.

For their part, legislatures suffer from their own disabilities. Of particular importance is the difficulty of overcoming all the procedural roadblocks that stand in the way of adopting significant innovative legislation. In contrast, for courts to make a dramatic innovation it is necessary only that a small number of judges agree to address an issue and then agree on the new doctrine.

The issue of incentives to innovate is especially complex. Although association with innovations may allow legislators to build political support, they run the risk of being blamed for an unpopular innovation, and legislators who ordinarily can expect to be reelected with ease may be inclined to avoid blame above all else (Weaver 1986; see also Fiorina

1977, 43-46). Innovation can carry risks for judges as well, especially those who are elected. But it also can give them the satisfaction of playing a creative role, and the judges who gain the greatest recognition tend to be innovators (see White 1976).

It is difficult to reach clear conclusions about the relative propensities of legislatures and courts to engage in innovation. In any case, this very brief discussion could do no more than suggest some lines of comparison between the two kinds of policy makers.[7] But, as the wealth of doctrinal innovations in the current era suggests, courts may be suited for innovation about as well as are other institutions.

Sources of Judicial Innovations

When the first court adopts a new legal doctrine, from where does that doctrine come? Unlike the legislative arena (see Kingdon 1984; Rado 1981), there apparently are no studies that closely examine the original sources of a set of doctrines and the paths by which they reached the courts that first adopted them. In the absence of such research, a few speculations are possible.

Most generally, it is useful to think of doctrinal innovations, like new forms of legislation, as developing within "policy communities" (Walker 1981; Kingdon 1984, chap. 6). In any area of judicial policy making, such as contract law or criminal procedure, a variety of interested people discuss issues, make arguments, and formulate and recommend new policies. These people include scholars, leaders of interest groups, and policy makers throughout government. The policies that they propose ultimately can reach the attention of judges.

Litigants may be the most important channel by which potential innovations are brought to judges' attention, but they are not the only one. Judges and their law clerks often are aware of the ideas that develop in relevant policy communities, and we know that they are not entirely dependent on briefs and oral arguments for information and policy alternatives (Ulmer 1982; Miller and Barron 1975). Some judges, for instance, have their clerks range widely in searching for information relevant to cases before them.

Judges, however, are more likely to become aware of potential innovations when these ideas enter the legal subset of a policy community. Lawyers and judges talk primarily with other lawyers and judges, and probably most focus their reading primarily on legal materials. Moreover, ideas gain legitimacy for judges in part through expression and justification in legal terms. If innovations develop among nonlawyers such as economists, then, one important step is their communication to lawyers.

In the development and flow of ideas for new doctrines, legal scholarship plays a major role. Much of this scholarship is aimed at influencing doctrinal development in the courts; in a sense, law professors and other legal scholars can be viewed as doctrinal entrepreneurs. Their influence is considerable, because scholarly writing—especially in the journals published by law schools—has high visibility and carries considerable prestige for courts (see Richardson 1983). Moreover, many law clerks on appellate courts were student editors of law journals, experience that makes them attentive to legal scholarship.

Indeed, law journal articles frequently are cited in judicial opinions (Sirico and Margulies 1986; Friedman et al. 1981, 810-817). Such citations do not demonstrate influence in themselves, and courts hardly feel compelled to follow the majority view among the scholars who write articles on an issue. But some major doctrinal innovations have gained attention through law journal articles. The classic example was the right to privacy in tort law, first advocated publicly in an 1890 *Harvard Law Review* article by Samuel Warren and future Supreme Court justice Louis Brandeis. And a series of articles by Yale law professor Charles Reich (1963, 1964, 1965) helped to formulate doctrines that the Supreme Court later adopted in providing new legal rights for welfare recipients.

There are other channels of influence for legal scholarship as well. A particularly important one is the American Law Institute (Darrell and Wolkin 1980). The ALI convenes groups under the leadership of scholars to establish "model" legal rules. These model rules carry some weight with policy makers, and some sets of rules are widely adopted by courts or legislatures in the states. Thus the orientations of the members of these groups toward the areas of law they examine help to determine the likelihood that potential innovations in an area will be adopted widely.

Undoubtedly, the role of interest groups in channeling new doctrines to judges has increased as groups themselves have come to play more active parts in the judicial process (see O'Connor and Epstein 1981-1982; Epstein and Rowland 1986). Amicus curiae briefs, whose use has grown tremendously, provide groups with an opportunity to convey a wide variety of information about policy alternatives. Litigation sponsored by groups provides an even better opportunity for them to communicate a potential new doctrine to a court. One function of interest groups may be to bring ideas for new policies into the legal system from other fields.

Judges themselves often formulate the specific terms of doctrinal innovations, reshaping and making more concrete the proposals that lawyers and scholars have offered. Prominent examples from the

Supreme Court include Chief Justice Warren's rules for police warnings to suspects in *Miranda v. Arizona* (1966) and Justice Blackmun's rules for state regulation and prohibition of abortion in *Roe v. Wade* (410 U.S. 113 [1973]). This function underlines the importance of courts themselves as sources of judicial innovations.

The Diffusion of Innovations

After the first court adopts a new doctrine, the doctrine is available for adoption by other courts.[8] The possible diffusion of a judicial innovation to additional courts can be viewed as involving two stages: the communication of the innovation to those courts and their decisions whether to adopt it. I will look at a few important aspects of each stage.

The communication stage is structured by the form of the judicial process. In part because of the heavy demands on their time, judges do not generally monitor the opinions of other courts as they are issued (Frank 1958, 22). Rather, they become aware of opinions in the process of deciding cases to which those decisions are relevant. Lawyers call cases to judges' attention through written briefs and oral arguments; judges and their law clerks, primarily the latter, learn of relevant cases in the process of doing research for a decision. A study of one state supreme court by Thomas Marvell (1978, 132-135) found that about half the cases cited in opinions came from briefs or oral argument, the other half chiefly from a court's independent research. But a higher proportion of the cases emphasized in court opinions came from the lawyers.

Perhaps the key issue in the communication of doctrines is its efficiency. To what extent do judges become aware of innovative opinions from other courts? Lawyers and clerks have a large stock of tools with which to locate relevant decisions, including printed and (in recent years) computerized indexes to opinions by subject matter. A wide range of publications, including periodicals such as the *National Law Journal*, directs attention to decisions that take new positions on major issues. Marvell (1978, 135) found redundancy built into the communication process, in that clerks tend to research cases independent of the lawyers' briefs. Particularly for that reason, it seems unlikely that a novel decision by another court often would go unnoticed.

Once judges become aware of an innovation that is relevant to the case before them, they must decide whether to adopt it. The adoption decisions made by many different courts over time determine the form of the diffusion process for an innovation. One perspective from which to examine patterns of adoption decisions is in terms of influence among courts.

The most powerful basis for intercourt influence is hierarchy. Under principles that nearly all judges accept, a court ordinarily is obliged to follow the doctrinal positions of courts above it. In any relevant case, a state trial judge must adopt innovations that the state supreme court or court of appeals has approved; in the interpretation of federal law, *every* federal or state court must adopt innovations that the Supreme Court has laid down. If judges followed this obligation perfectly, then the diffusion of innovations from higher to lower courts would depend entirely on the timing of litigation: every court would adopt an innovation as soon as an appropriate case appeared.

Considerable research has been done on the responses of lower courts to doctrinal innovations by the Supreme Court, especially those that expand civil liberties (Peltason 1971; Canon 1973, 1974; Romans 1974; Tarr 1977; Gruhl 1981, 1982; Songer 1988; Reid 1988). This research demonstrates that lower court judges do not always accept the Court's lead enthusiastically, just as administrators often balk at directives from legislatures and chief executives. Yet it appears to be quite uncommon for judges flatly to reject an innovative doctrine laid down by the Supreme Court.

Far more common are subtler forms of subversion, including narrow interpretations of doctrines and the application of doctrines in ways that limit their impact. One important example concerns the rights of criminal defendants; lower court judges who were unhappy with Supreme Court decisions expanding those rights in the 1960s often responded by defining those decisions as narrowly as they could (Canon 1973, 1974).

It is not clear whether such equivocal responses should be interpreted as adoptions of the innovation in question. The ambiguity of such responses is one example of a more general phenomenon: courts, like legislatures, frequently adopt a doctrine in substantially different form from the first adopter. Such alterations in form are to be expected, but they complicate the task of analyzing the diffusion of innovations. Perhaps the key question is the impact of an equivocal response on courts still further down the judicial hierarchy. If a federal court of appeals adopts a Supreme Court innovation grudgingly, for instance, does its action deter the federal district courts in the circuit from adopting it themselves? There is some reason to think that this is the case, but we have little hard evidence on this issue. (For evidence on a related issue, see Gerstein 1982.) If grudging adoptions effectively signal lower courts to reject innovations themselves, then they probably should not be considered adoptions at all.

The diffusion of many innovative doctrines involves no element of hierarchy. An example is diffusion among the state supreme courts, fully independent of each other and operating with separate bodies of law. Despite this independence, supreme court justices are attentive to doctrinal trends in the other states, and their decisions on issues are affected by the majority view and the recent trend among other courts (Shapiro 1970). Indeed, innovative doctrines often gain a kind of momentum as courts try to keep up with a growing consensus across the states (see *Hicks v. State,* 544 P.2d 1153 [N.M. 1975]). In this respect, judges are similar to legislators and administrators who pay close attention to the activities of their counterparts in other states (Walker 1969, 888-891; Feller and Menzel 1977, 54-55).

In this nonhierarchical situation, judges are unlikely to give equal weight to the positions of all other courts. For any particular court, and for courts in general, it seems certain that some courts have greater influence than others. Although we lack direct evidence on the relative influence of courts, some indirect evidence exists on state supreme courts.

One kind of evidence derives from studies of citation patterns (Mott 1936; Merryman 1977; Caldeira 1983, 1985, 1988; Harris 1982, 1985). These studies have reached complex and sometimes inconsistent findings, but two major conclusions emerge. First, individual courts differ considerably in the numbers of times that their decisions are cited by other supreme courts as a whole, even controlling for the volume of case law produced by each state (Mott 1936; Caldeira 1983).

Second, beyond these overall differences, the frequency with which specific courts cite specific other courts is not random. Studies of state supreme courts have found that courts are most likely to cite opinions from states in their own geographical region and from states whose opinions are contained in the same "regional reporter" as their own (Caldeira 1985; Harris 1985). (The semi-official reports of state supreme court opinions published by the West Company are divided into seven separate editions, largely along regional lines.) This pattern may result from imperfect communication of decisions from distant states, due in part to limited availability of some regional reporters. But the primary cause probably is that judges prefer to cite opinions from some states more than others.

Of course, as with law review articles, citation does not necessarily mean influence. Still, the enormous differences that exist in the frequency with which various supreme courts are cited suggest that courts vary considerably in their overall influence. Indeed, such variation seems inevitable, because the reputations of courts and thus their potential influence can never be equal. Similarly, the fact that citation patterns follow regional lines suggests that judges often give greater weight to opinions from their own region. Such behavior is understandable; neighboring states are likely to be seen as particularly appropriate models because of similarities in conditions and values.[9] It is noteworthy that studies of influence among administrators in different states also have found significant inequalities of influence and regional influence patterns (Walker 1971, 378-385; Grupp and Richards 1975).

Another approach to the regionalism issue was taken in the study of tort innovation by Canon and me (Canon and Baum 1981, 983-984). This study borrowed from Walker (1969) a statistical method to analyze adoption patterns for innovations as a means to determine whether doctrines tend to diffuse within regions.[10] Unlike some studies of legislative innovations (Walker 1969; Foster 1978), ours did not find strong regional patterns. This result suggests that intercourt influence is not primarily regional; in this sense it points in a different direction from the citation studies.

This seeming conflict might be reconciled in several ways. First, it is possible—despite what I have suggested—that regional citation patterns do *not* mean that judges are most influenced by courts within their own region; such patterns might reflect, to take one example, a kind of courtesy to neighboring courts. Second, there might be a general tendency for judges to look to courts within their own region but also a more national "market" for ideas on relatively visible and controversial issues such as tort innovations.

Perhaps the most plausible explanation relates to courts' need to wait for cases to come to them before they can act. Different courts gain opportunities to adopt an innovation at different times, based on when the first relevant case reaches each of them. Suppose it is true that the state supreme courts of the Rocky Mountain region are inclined to adopt a particular innovation in rapid succession, once the most respected court in the region, or two or three Rocky Mountain courts of any sort, have adopted it. Ordinarily these courts could not do so, because some states in the region would not receive an appropriate case until much later, and on some issues there might be courts in the region that never receive such a case. This suggests that analysis of patterns of adoptions across a set of courts such as state supreme courts may be a quite imperfect means to gauge influence relationships among them. In any case, with two indirect measures of influence producing different results, the question of regionalism remains quite open.

Innovativeness as a Trait of Individual Courts

One major concern of the scholarship on innovation has been the relative innovativeness of particular individuals and organizations, the speed with which they adopt new ideas. Studies have found considerable variation in innovativeness and have shown that this variation correlates with a number of individual and organizational characteristics (Rogers 1983, chap. 7).

Similarly, studies of policy innovation have found substantial variation in the number of innovations that different states adopt and the speed with which they adopt them. Walker (1969), for instance, found that the legislatures of New York and Massachusetts had considerably higher "innovation scores" than those of Nevada and Mississippi, indicating a greater propensity to adopt the innovations he analyzed and to do so early in the diffusion process (see also Savage 1978). Large differences in innovation scores also have been found among state supreme courts in tort and privacy law (Canon and Baum 1981; Domino 1989).

Reflecting the concerns of the social science literature on innovation, these differences among states frequently are interpreted as differences in innovativeness or in other terms that refer to propensities to adopt innovations. But that interpretation is problematic, especially for courts, because of two realities that I have mentioned already.

First, opportunities to adopt judicial innovations depend heavily on when appropriate cases reach a court. This dependence on litigation creates a random element in the order in which different courts adopt a particular doctrine (see Traynor 1977, 2-3). Thus, it is not surprising that Canon and I (Canon and Baum 1981, 982-983) found generally weak relationships between the order in which state supreme courts adopted one doctrine and the order in which they adopted another— even when the two doctrines were similar in content.

More fundamentally, courts differ systematically in their opportunities to respond to innovations because of differences in the volume of litigation and in the activities of lawyers and interest groups. For these reasons the California Supreme Court undoubtedly has opportunities to adopt most new doctrines earlier than does the Wyoming Supreme Court. We (Canon and Baum 1981, 981) found that supreme courts from relatively populous states tended to adopt innovative tort doctrines earlier than courts in less populous states; the volume of litigation is probably one major reason for this difference (but see Harris 1985, 455).

Second, the content of judicial doctrines is critical in determining judges' willingness to adopt them, just as the content of legislative innovations helps determine their adoption (see Eyestone 1977). As I argued earlier, because of their own preferences and external pressures, judges undoubtedly respond to new doctrines primarily in terms of their specific content rather than in terms of the fact that they are innovations. To state the obvious, a liberal policy maker will be far more likely to support a new policy if it is liberal in content rather than conservative.

Tort policy illustrates the impact of this reality. The innovations that have diffused among state supreme courts since World War II virtually all favor the legal positions of plaintiffs (including consumers and employees) and thus weaken the positions of defendants (including manufacturers, the medical community, and insurance companies). By and large, liberals have been relatively sympathetic to plaintiff groups, conservatives to defendant groups. Not surprisingly, courts dominated by liberal judges have been more willing to adopt tort innovations than those of a more conservative tinge. When the Ohio and Texas Supreme Courts gained majorities that were sympathetic to tort plaintiffs, they quickly adopted some tort innovations that favored plaintiffs (Burka 1987; Tarr and Porter 1988, chap. 4). Is it very meaningful to say that the Ohio and Texas courts had become more innovative rather than more liberal?[11] Similarly, if we enter an era in which most judicial innovations are conservative in content, it will make more sense to label courts that readily adopt innovations as conservative rather than as innovative.[12]

There probably are some real differences among courts in innovativeness. For example, judges who are especially interested in achieving recognition from other judges and lawyers may find innovation more attractive than do other judges. Similarly, a court whose members wish to minimize internal conflict may avoid doctrinal innovation to help achieve that end (see Beiser 1973). But differences among courts in the adoption of judicial innovations—how many they adopt and how quickly they do so—almost surely reflect the timing of cases and the content of new doctrines more than they reflect inherent differences in innovativeness. For that reason, it may be appropriate to avoid the concept of innovativeness altogether in analyzing doctrinal innovation.

Conclusion

Because only a small number of studies have dealt directly with doctrinal innovation in the courts, a distinct field of research on judicial innovation does not exist. This is not necessarily a bad thing. For reasons that have been discussed in this chapter, there are drawbacks in focusing narrowly on judicial innovation as a special phenomenon and applying to it the concepts and perspectives of the scholarly literature on innovation. To treat innovativeness as a distinct trait, for instance, loses sight of the fact that decisions whether to adopt innovations are shaped by the same forces that affect judicial decisions in general. Separating the study of innovation from the study of judicial policy making as a whole may not help in developing a better understanding of either subject.

This does not mean, however, that nothing can be gained by studying judicial innovation. For one thing, doctrinal innovation is an important phenomenon in itself, so it merits some attention from scholars. Those who study doctrinal innovation for its own sake, however, are likely to learn the most if they treat it primarily as a form of judicial policy making rather than as a species of innovation. The theories that have been developed to explain judicial decisions, for instance, probably will prove more useful in understanding the adoption of doctrinal innovations than will the theories that have been developed in the social science literature on the diffusion of innovations.

Another reason to study judicial innovation is that it offers a perspective from which to approach and analyze important aspects of judicial policy making. In this respect the broader literature on innovation *is* useful, if employed carefully, because it can suggest promising lines of research. To take one example, the concern in that literature for the communication of innovations points to the value of research on the communication of doctrines among courts, and doctrinal innovations provide particularly good cases for tracing and analyzing this communication process. The same is true of influence relationships as an element in the diffusion of innovations and in judicial policy making as a whole.

Moreover, innovation provides a good focus for comparison of some aspects of policy making between courts and institutions in the other branches of government. Issues such as the speed with which new ideas diffuse and the geographic element in diffusion allow meaningful comparisons between legislatures and courts, and these comparisons in turn help to illuminate similarities and differences between these institutions. Thus the study of judicial innovation can contribute in a small way to the important goal of integrating our understanding of courts into the larger body of knowledge on public policy making.

Notes

1. The short history of the market share theory actually is more complicated than this description suggests. Two of the three adoptions of the doctrine in other states were ambiguous, with both courts proclaiming that they were rejecting the doctrine in large part (*Collins v. Eli Lilly Co.,* 342 N.W.2d 37 [Wisc. 1984]) or altogether (*Martin v. Abbott Laboratories,* 689 P.2d 368 [Wash. 1984]) even while they were adapting it to their purposes, and one court has interpreted an ambiguous decision in a fourth

state as adopting the theory (*McElhaney v. Eli Lilly & Co.*, 564 F.Supp. 265 [D.S.D. 1983]). These and other complications are quite common in policy innovation and perhaps especially so in judicial doctrine; the existence of such complications probably is one reason for the dearth of research focusing directly on doctrinal innovations and their diffusion.

2. In the most definitive analysis of the diffusion of innovations, Rogers (1983, 5) defines diffusion in terms of the communication of innovative ideas rather than their adoption, and this usage is common in studies of innovation (see, for example, Downs and Mohr 1979, 386). However, most of the literature on policy innovation in government treats diffusion as encompassing successive adoptions of innovations as well as their communication, and this usage seems appropriate for purposes of this chapter.

3. For a recent example that illustrates the development of innovation research, see Fischer and Carroll 1988.

4. Among the studies of innovation at the state level are Gray 1973; Foster 1978; Menzel and Feller 1977; Welch and Thompson 1980; and Daniels and Darcy 1985. Savage 1985 provides an overview of the state-level research. National-level studies are exemplified by Collier and Messick 1975, local-level studies by Bingham 1977 and Mohr 1969; Mohr's article is also an important theoretical contribution.

5. The studies of innovations in judicial administration include Glick 1981; Long 1974; and Scheb and Matheny 1988. Puro, Bergerson, and Puro 1985 examined successive state adoptions of the Missouri Plan for selection of judges as a diffusion process. These studies lie outside the scope of this chapter because they deal with nondoctrinal innovations. More important, these studies are not designed to probe judicial innovation as such: courts play no direct role in the adoption of judicial selection systems, and most of the administrative innovations analyzed in the studies are initiated by other policy makers, not by the courts.

   It might be useful to undertake studies that are restricted to those administrative innovations adopted by courts themselves. Such studies would provide a different perspective on judicial innovation from studies of doctrinal innovation. Administrative innovations, on the whole, do not involve conflicts in values and interests to the same extent as doctrinal innovations; for that reason, some of the problems that arise in the study of policy innovations *as innovations* (discussed later) are reduced. But, because such conflicts are not entirely absent from administrative innovations in the courts, neither are these problems.

6. Some of these drawbacks apply in part to nonpolicy innovation as well; certainly, the study of innovation in any arena encounters serious difficulties (see Rogers 1983).

7. Within the small body of work that compares legislatures and courts as policy makers, some studies are relevant to the issue of innovation. See, for instance, Howard 1969 and Dienes 1972 (pp. 5-19).

8. A new judicial doctrine also is available for adoption by other policy-making bodies to which it is relevant, particularly administrative agencies.

As Fiorino 1976 showed, the diffusion of judicial innovations to nonjudicial policy makers is a useful object of study. But there are some advantages in focusing on diffusion of judicial doctrines to courts alone. Perhaps most important, that focus makes it easier to discuss the diffusion process coherently and to work toward generalizations. Because of those advantages, this section (and the section on innovativeness that follows) will be restricted to courts as adopters of innovations.

9. If lawyers are more likely to cite cases from a state's own regional reporter, this behavior strengthens the regional element in intercourt influence.
10. The method is varimax factor analysis. See Walker 1969 (pp. 891-896).
11. To take another kind of example, over a long period the Massachusetts Supreme Court favored the interests of defendants in tort law. When new doctrines were primarily conservative, the Massachusetts court appeared to be innovative; later, when the ideological direction of tort innovations shifted, the court appeared to be noninnovative (Baum and Canon 1982, 100-101). Here, too, however, it seems more misleading than helpful to characterize the court's positions in terms of innovativeness rather than policy values.
12. There may be ways to investigate innovativeness that reduce this problem. One means to do so is to focus on doctrinal innovations whose ideological content is relatively weak —though the existence of even a weak ideological element is problematic. Another is to compare the same courts' responses to liberal and conservative innovations, to determine whether a general tendency toward innovativeness transcends ideology. The difficulty with this approach is that in any particular period either liberal or conservative innovations tend to be numerically dominant. In tort law, for instance, it would be difficult to find many innovations that diffused very far in the 1950s through 1970s whose thrust was to narrow the rights of plaintiffs— just as it might have been difficult to find many doctrines favorable to plaintiffs diffusing among courts in the late nineteenth century.

References

Baum, Lawrence, and Bradley C. Canon. 1982. State supreme courts as activists: New doctrines in the law of torts. In *State supreme courts: Policymakers in the federal system*, ed. Mary Cornelia Porter and G. Alan Tarr. Westport, Conn.: Greenwood Press.

Beiser, Edward N. 1973. The Rhode Island Supreme Court: A well-integrated political system. *Law and Society Review* 8:167-186.

Bingham, Richard D. 1977. The diffusion of innovations among local governments. *Urban Affairs Quarterly* 13:223-232.

Burka, Paul. 1987. Heads, we win, tails, you lose: How a group of trial lawyers took over the Texas Supreme Court and rewrote state law. *Texas Monthly*, May, 138-139, 206.

Caldeira, Gregory A. 1983. On the reputation of state supreme courts. *Political Behavior* 5:51-82.

_____. 1985. The transmission of legal precedent: A study of state supreme courts. *American Political Science Review* 79:178-193.

_____. 1988. Legal precedent: Structures of communication between state supreme courts. *Social Networks* 10:29-55.

Canon, Bradley C. 1973. Reactions of state supreme courts to a U.S. Supreme Court civil liberties decision. *Law and Society Review* 8:109-134.

_____. 1974. Organizational contumacy in the transmission of judicial policies: The *Mapp, Escobedo, Miranda,* and *Gault* cases. *Villanova Law Review* 20:50-79.

Canon, Bradley C., and Lawrence Baum. 1981. Patterns of adoption of tort law innovations: An application of diffusion theory to judicial doctrines. *American Political Science Review* 75:975-987.

Collier, David, and Richard E. Messick. 1975. Prerequisites versus diffusion: Testing alternative explanations of Social Security adoption. *American Political Science Review* 69:1299-1315.

Cooper, Phillip J. 1988. *Hard judicial choices: Federal district court judges and state and local officials.* New York: Oxford University Press.

Daniels, Mark R., and Robert E. Darcy. 1985. As time goes by: The arrested diffusion of the Equal Rights Amendment. *Publius* 15:51-60.

Darrell, Norris, and Paul A. Wolkin. 1980. The American Law Institute. *New York State Bar Journal* 52:99-101, 139-143.

Dienes, C. Thomas. 1972. *Law, politics and birth control.* Urbana: University of Illinois Press.

Domino, John C. 1989. State supreme court innovation in the policy area of privacy: A comparative analysis. Paper presented at the annual meeting of the Law and Society Association, Madison, Wisconsin.

Downs, George W., Jr., and Lawrence B. Mohr. 1979. Toward a theory of innovation. *Administration and Society* 10:379-408.

Epstein, Lee, and C. K. Rowland. 1986. Interest groups in the courts: Do groups fare better? In *Interest Group Politics,* ed. Allan J. Cigler and Burdett E. Loomis. Washington, D.C.: CQ Press.

Eyestone, Robert. 1977. Confusion, diffusion, and innovation. *American Political Science Review* 71:441-447.

Feller, Irwin, and Donald C. Menzel. 1977. Diffusion milieus as a focus of research on innovation in the public sector. *Policy Sciences* 8:49-68.

Fiorina, Morris P. 1977. *Congress: Keystone of the Washington establishment.* New Haven: Yale University Press.

Fiorino, Daniel J. 1976. The diffusion of judicial innovations: Court decisions as a source of change. Paper presented at the annual meeting of the International Communication Association, Portland, Oregon.

Fischer, Claude S., and Glenn R. Carroll. 1988. Telephone and automobile diffusion in the United States, 1902-1937. *American Journal of Sociology* 93:1153-1178.

Foster, John L. 1978. Regionalism and innovation in the American states. *Journal of Politics* 40:179-187.

Frank, John P. 1958. *Marble palace: The Supreme Court in American life.* New York: Knopf.

Friedman, Lawrence M., Robert A. Kagan, Bliss Cartwright, and Stanton Wheeler. 1981. State supreme courts: A century of style and citation. *Stanford Law Review* 33:773-818.

Gerstein, Robert S. 1982. Serving two masters: The California courts of appeal and criminal procedure. Paper presented at the annual meeting of the American Political Science Association, Denver.

Glick, Henry R. 1981. Innovation in state judicial administration: Effects on court management and organization. *American Politics Quarterly* 9:49-69.

Gray, Virginia. 1973. Innovation in the states: A diffusion study. *American Political Science Review* 67:1174-1185.

Gruhl, John. 1981. State supreme courts and the U.S. Supreme Court's post-Miranda rulings. *Journal of Criminal Law and Criminology* 72:886-913.

_____. 1982. Patterns of compliance with U.S. Supreme Court rulings: The case of libel in federal courts of appeals and state supreme courts. *Publius* 12:109-126.

Grupp, Fred W., Jr., and Alan R. Richards. 1975. Variations in elite perceptions of American states as referents for public policy making. *American Political Science Review* 69:850-858.

Harris, Peter. 1982. Structural change in the communication of precedent among state supreme courts, 1870-1970. *Social Networks* 4:201-212.

_____. 1985. Ecology and culture in the communication of precedent among state supreme courts, 1870-1970. *Law and Society Review* 19:449-486.

Horowitz, Donald L. 1977. *The courts and social policy.* Washington, D.C.: Brookings Institution.

Howard, J. Woodford, Jr. 1969. Adjudication considered as a process of conflict resolution: A variation on separation of powers. *Journal of Public Law* 18:339-370.

Johnson, Charles A., and Bradley C. Canon. 1984. *Judicial policies: Implementation and impact.* Washington, D.C.: CQ Press.

Keeton, W. Page, Dan B. Dobbs, Robert E. Keeton, and David G. Owen. 1984. *Prosser and Keeton on the law of torts.* St. Paul, Minn.: West.

Kingdon, John W. 1984. *Agendas, alternatives, and public policies.* Boston: Little, Brown.

Light, Alfred R. 1978. Intergovernmental sources of innovation in state administration. *American Politics Quarterly* 6:147-166.

Long, Lucinda P. 1974. Innovation in urban criminal misdemeanor courts. In *The potential for reform of criminal justice,* ed. Herbert Jacob. Beverly Hills, Calif.: Sage.

Marcotte, Paul. 1987. Summary jury trials touted. *American Bar Association Journal* 73 (April 1):27.

Marvell, Thomas B. 1978. *Appellate courts and lawyers: Information gathering in the adversary system.* Westport, Conn.: Greenwood Press.

Mayhew, David. 1974. *Congress: The electoral connection.* New Haven: Yale University Press.

Menzel, Donald C., and Irwin Feller. 1977. Leadership and interaction patterns in the diffusion of innovations among the American states. *Western Political Quarterly* 30:528-536.

Merryman, John H. 1977. Toward a theory of citations: An empirical study of the citation practice of the California Supreme Court in 1950, 1960, and 1970. *Southern California Law Review* 50:381-428.

Miller, Arthur Selwyn, and Jerome A. Barron. 1975. The Supreme Court, the adversary system, and the flow of information to the justices: A preliminary inquiry. *Virginia Law Review* 61:1187-1245.

Mohr, Lawrence B. 1969. Determinants of innovation in organizations. *American Political Science Review* 63:111-126.

Mott, Rodney. 1936. Judicial influence. *American Political Science Review* 30:295-315.

O'Connor, Karen, and Lee Epstein. 1981-1982. Amicus curiae participation in U.S. Supreme Court litigation: An appraisal of Hakman's "folklore." *Law and Society Review* 16:311-320.

Peltason, Jack W. 1971. *Fifty-eight lonely men: Southern federal judges and school desegregation.* 2d ed. Urbana: University of Illinois Press.

Polsby, Nelson W. 1984. *Political innovation in America: The politics of policy initiation.* New Haven: Yale University Press.

Puro, Marsha, Peter J. Bergerson, and Steven Puro. 1985. An analysis of judicial diffusion: Adoption of the Missouri Plan in the American states. *Publius* 15:85-97.

Rado, Leslie. 1981. Death redefined: Social and cultural influences on legislation. *Journal of Communication* 31:41-47.

Reedy, Cheryl D. 1982. The Supreme Court and Congress on abortion: An analysis of comparative institutional capacity. Paper presented at the annual meeting of the American Political Science Association, Denver.

Reich, Charles A. 1963. Midnight welfare searches and the Social Security Act. *Yale Law Journal* 72:1347-1360.

――――. 1964. The new property. *Yale Law Journal* 73:733-787.

――――. 1965. Individual rights and social welfare: The emerging legal issues. *Yale Law Journal* 74:1245-1257.

Reid, Traciel V. 1988. Judicial policy-making and implementation: An empirical examination. *Western Political Quarterly* 41:509-527.

Richardson, Frank K. 1983. Law reviews and the courts. *Whittier Law Review* 5:385-393.

Rogers, Everett M. 1983. *Diffusion of innovations.* 3d ed. New York: Free Press.

Romans, Neil T. 1974. The role of state supreme courts in judicial policy making: *Escobedo, Miranda* and the use of judicial impact analysis. *Western Political Quarterly* 27:38-59.

Ryan, Bryce, and Neal C. Gross. 1943. The diffusion of hybrid seed corn in two Iowa communities. *Rural Sociology* 8:15-24.

Savage, Robert L. 1978. Policy innovativeness as a trait of American states. *Journal of Politics* 40:212-224.

———. 1985. Diffusion research traditions and the spread of policy innovations in a federal system. *Publius* 15:1-27.

Scheb, John M. II, and Albert R. Matheny. 1988. Judicial reform and rationalization: The diffusion of court reform policies among the American states. *Law and Policy* 10:25-42.

Shapiro, Martin. 1965. Stability and change in judicial decision-making: Incrementalism or stare decisis? *Law in Transition Quarterly* 2:134-157.

———. 1970. Decentralized decision-making in the law of torts. In *Political Decision-Making*, ed. S. Sidney Ulmer. New York: Van Nostrand Reinhold.

Sirico, Louis J., Jr., and Jeffrey B. Margulies. 1986. The citation of law reviews by the Supreme Court: An empirical study. *UCLA Law Review* 34:131-147.

Songer, Donald R. 1988. Case selection in judicial impact research. *Western Political Quarterly* 41:569-582.

Tarr, G. Alan. 1977. *Judicial impact and state supreme courts.* Lexington, Mass.: Lexington Books.

Tarr, G. Alan, and Mary Cornelia Aldis Porter. 1988. *State supreme courts in state and nation.* New Haven: Yale University Press.

Traynor, Roger J. 1977. The limits of judicial creativity. *Iowa Law Review* 63:1-13.

Ulmer, S. Sidney. 1982. Issue fluidity in the U.S. Supreme Court: A conceptual analysis. In *Supreme Court activism and restraint*, ed. Stephen C. Halpern and Charles M. Lamb. Lexington, Mass.: Lexington Books.

Walker, Jack L. 1969. The diffusion of innovations among the American states. *American Political Science Review* 63:880-899.

———. 1971. Innovation in state politics. In *Politics in the American states*, 2d ed., ed. Herbert Jacob and Kenneth N. Vines. Boston: Little, Brown.

———. 1981. The diffusion of knowledge, policy communities and agenda setting. In *New strategic perspectives on social policy*, ed. John E. Tropman, Milan J. Dluhy, and Robert M. Lind. New York: Pergamon Press.

Warren, Samuel D., and Louis D. Brandeis. 1890. The right to privacy. *Harvard Law Review* 4:193-220.

Weaver, R. Kent. 1986. The politics of blame avoidance. *Journal of Public Policy* 6:371-398.

Welch, Susan, and Kay Thompson. 1980. The impact of federal incentives on state policy innovation. *American Journal of Political Science* 24:715-729.

Western Legal History. 1988. Judge Gus J. Solomon on the Vietnam-era draft. *Western Legal History* 1:280-284.

White, G. Edward. 1976. *The American judicial tradition: Profiles of leading American judges.* New York: Oxford University Press.

17. COURTS AND POLICY: COMPLIANCE, IMPLEMENTATION, AND IMPACT

Bradley C. Canon

The Development of Judicial Impact Studies

Studying court decisions, especially those of the U.S. Supreme Court, has been a major component of political science since the discipline began around 1900. Yet for over half a century political scientists in the public law subfield studied case law in a manner not very different from law professors. Almost no attention was given to judicial impact—to what happened after a decision was rendered.

Three journal articles in the late 1950s manifested the first stirrings of interest in postdecisional events. Gordon Patric (1957) and Frank Sorauf (1959) looked at episodic events following the Supreme Court's "released time" cases[1] and Walter Murphy (1959) discussed some dramatic state court refusals to handle reversals and remands as the U.S. Supreme Court intended them to do. Each of these articles focused on lower court interpretations, or misinterpretations, of Supreme Court decisions. None was theoretically oriented or even tested simple hypotheses.

Two factors contributed to the surge of interest in the impact of judicial decisions. One was the behavioral revolution that occurred within political science in the 1950s as younger scholars became more interested in explaining events based on an analysis of actual behavior.[2] The other was the realization that full compliance did not always follow court decisions. It was obvious in the 1955-1965 period that little was being done to implement *Brown v. Board of Education* (347 U.S. 483 [1954]) and that resistance—even by courts—was overt. Moreover, as the Supreme Court under Earl Warren made controversial decisions in other areas such as prayer in schools, defendants' rights, and reapportionment, it became clear that compliance problems extended well beyond *Brown*.

The 1960-1975 period was perhaps the golden age of impact studies. It produced a classic study by an established scholar (Peltason

My thanks go to the editors, John Gates and Charles Johnson, and to Lawrence A. Baum for helpful suggestions in the development of this chapter.

1961, on federal judges in the South) and numerous dissertations examining compliance by implementing agencies. Several were published (including Johnson 1967; Milner 1971; Muir 1967) and the essence of others appeared in professional journals. This and other literature led to the publication of some judicial impact readers (Becker 1969; Becker and Feeley 1973; Krislov et al. 1971). As the 1960s ended, the literature was sufficient and varied enough that Stephen Wasby could aggregate and organize it in *The Impact of the United States Supreme Court: Some Perspectives* (1970), which contained a bibliography of 108 works.[3]

Many of these studies tested, often implicitly, hypotheses about cause and effect. Indeed, Wasby extracted 135 hypotheses from the literature. Some were little more than common sense, others were very weakly supported, and a few were contradictory, reflecting opposing findings. Few worked from or toward general theories of impact.[4] However, they did point the way to organizing further research and lay groundwork for developing or testing broader theories.

In the 1970s some general theories were advanced to explain judicial impact, as I will discuss later in this chapter. They offered considerable guidance to impact research as well as a greater ability to link results with those in other subfields of political science or other disciplines, although they have inspired less research than might be hoped.

The 1980s saw Charles Johnson and my book, *Judicial Policies: Implementation and Impact* (1984), the first overview of impact research since Wasby.[5] The book was organized on a heuristic model of four impact populations (discussed in the next section). The model has proved useful, and I will use it later in this chapter. However, a careful reading of the book would have revealed a slowdown in judicial impact research. We cited more studies from before 1975 than after, and fewer from the 1980-1983 period than from the preceding four years. The situation did not change much in the rest of the 1980s. Few major impact studies have been undertaken, and no new general theories have been advanced. However, smaller scale research projects continue, as reflected in the steady production of journal articles. As this chapter proceeds, I will discuss the major gaps and opportunities in judicial impact research.

This chapter proceeds as follows. In the next section I look at how impact researchers organize their topic—how some research findings are conceptually linked to other findings in order to develop a map of what has and has not been explored. Then I move from conceptual organization to explanatory theories, focusing on the four that most commonly guide impact research. The fourth section discusses the methods used to conduct impact research. The fifth looks at the impact

Figure 17-1   Populations and Lines of Communication Involved in
the Implementation and Impact of Judicial Policies

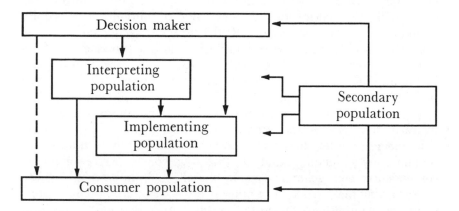

Source: Adapted from Charles A. Johnson, "The Implementation and Impact of
Judicial Policies: A Heuristic Model." In *Public Law and Public Policy,* ed. John A.
Gardiner. New York: Praeger, 1977, p. 109. Copyright © 1977 by Praeger
Publishers, Inc.

of courts other than the U.S. Supreme Court. Next I focus on the major
judicial policies that impact researchers have investigated and what
they have found. After that I look at what judicial impact research has
and has not explored in terms of functional populations (Johnson and
Canon 1984). Finally, I discuss the present state and future possibilities
of impact research.[6]

Impact Research Typologies

The linkage of research in the judicial impact field has largely
followed one of two schemes of organization. The first is explicitly
developed in some detail by Johnson and me (Johnson and Canon
1984). We offered a functional approach focusing on population sets (see
Figure 17-1). Our heuristic model suggests that appellate court decisions
are interpreted by one set of actors, implemented by another,[7] and
consumed by yet a third set. We label these sets the interpreting,
implementing, and consumer populations, respectively. For example, in
Miranda v. Arizona (384 U.S. 436 [1966]) the interpreting population
consists primarily of state and lower federal court judges, the police
constitute the implementing population, and the suspects are the
consumer population. A residual set of actors who are not directly
affected by the decision is called the secondary population (for *Miranda,*
politicians, newspaper editors, the public in general), which provides the

surrounding environment for the first three populations. Because this is a functional approach, there is considerable fluidity across populations depending on which decision is involved. For example, judges may occasionally be implementors, as when higher court decisions require them to change court procedures (Reid 1988). Legislators, often secondary actors, can also be implementors, such as for the provision of monies to reduce prison overcrowding (Lehne 1978; Moss 1985). Lawyers can be in all four categories. Put otherwise, a person may be in one population for one decision and another one for a different decision.

Johnson and I focused on two categories of responses by the actors in each set. One is the *acceptance decision,* that is, the actor's psychological reaction to the decision. This is shaped by such factors as the intensity of one's attitude toward the policy, perception of its consequences both generally and to oneself, and one's regard for the court making the decision. The other is the *behavioral response,* that is, what an actor actually does in response to a decision. Behavioral responses may be closely linked to acceptance decisions, but inertia, coercive pressures, and other demands on one's time and energy also shape this response.

The second organizational concept is a diffuse one and, perhaps excepting James Levine (1970), has not been directly articulated. It might be best envisioned as a postevent wave spreading out in time and causal space (see Figure 17-2). It organizes impact by the directness of consequences a judicial decision has, ranging from the most immediate to the more remote.

To outline this concept briefly, I will divide a decision's consequences into three broad categories: compliance, implementation, and broad impact. Keep in mind that the boundaries between these categories are not precise. Moreover, a research focus on implementation must necessarily take account of compliance while broader impact research must be cognizant of the other two.

The aim of compliance research is to learn whether lower courts or implementors such as the police abide by the decision. However, compliance is often more a continuum than an either/or condition. Also, researchers do not all use the same yardstick in measuring it, nor do they even use the same language in reporting findings. Loosely defined terms such as *evasion* and *avoidance* are not uncommon. Early research often focused exclusively on compliance. Determining compliance became less important after the 1960s, although it remains the major focus in some studies.

Implementation research investigates the degree to which agencies such as the police and school systems are taking the necessary steps to meet the decision's real goals. Put overly simply, compliance is carrying

Figure 17-2   Spread of Impact by Time and Causation

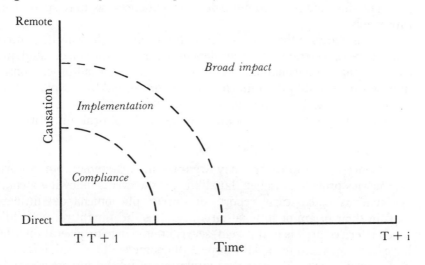

Note: The origin represents a court decision.

out the letter of the decision and implementation is fostering its spirit. The main implementation problem is that agencies usually have more central and sometimes opposite goals than those imposed by a court decision, so they can be quite reluctant to put real effort into enhancing the judicial policy.

The most sweeping concept is broad impact. In one sense broad impact encompasses every event that can be traced to a judicial decision or policy. Usually, however, researchers use it to mean what Levine (1970) calls the second-order consequences of a decision. Assuming some degree of compliance and implementation, the broad impact approach asks questions such as: Is the decision producing its intended societal goals? (For example, not Is the school system desegregated? but Is the desegregation enhancing minority learning?) What social and political reaction does a judicial policy generate? (What effect, if any, have decisions making sexually oriented material more available had on sexual behavior or family relations?) Does implementation produce additional and unexpected consequences? (Did decisions requiring legal assistance for most defendants enhance the attractiveness of the legal profession by greatly enlarging its clientele?) If so, who suffers monetary and social costs and who benefits? The very broadness of these questions makes comprehensive answers difficult to obtain, at least without large-scale research effort, but it certainly does not preclude cumulative research based upon well-designed but underfunded efforts. The clever analysis of records may give insights into second-order consequences, as may surveys or interviews.

Levine argues that the variables and even the theories that affect impact are considerably different depending on whether one is studying compliance, implementation, or broad impact. Second-order consequences are not subject to much judicial control and are explained by more general sociological and political science theories than is the behavior of those subject to judicial or related political authority.[8]

Explanatory Theories

Conceptual approaches may organize impact studies, but empirical theories provide causal explanations for the events following a court decision. As noted, early reports of impact phenomena did little to explain their origin or in what circumstances they might recur. While much later research is in this vein, several mid-range to general theories have been advanced to explain impact phenomena. This section focuses on four explanatory theories that guide much judicial impact research. The four are not mutually exclusive. They may offer competing explanations for some phenomena, but more often postdecision events are best explained in terms of two or more theories.

Utility Theory

The most comprehensive theoretical explanation of judicial impact, at least potentially, is Don Brown and Robert Stover's (1975) utility theory. The authors advanced it to explain compliance, but it can be applied to implementation as well. It can guide research on the interpreting and implementing populations and on the consumer and secondary actors in some situations. Utility theory is a variant of Jeremy Bentham's (1789/1907) pain and pleasure principle, positing obedience when the material and psychological benefits of compliance (gains minus costs) outweigh the material and psychological benefits of noncompliance. It is also a first cousin to rational choice theory, now widely used in economic and public policy analyses. The theory's practical usefulness is weakened with the inclusion of psychological variables. By their very nature such variables are extremely difficult to measure, thus tempting researchers to resort to them to explain otherwise inexplicable behavior. A theory so inclusive that it purports to explain everything loses its practical value because it cannot be tested. However, by largely restricting utility theory to measurable situations and concentrating on the behavioral response, it can be a rigorous and revealing test of the causes of variations in compliance and implementation. Where these do not occur as predicted, attention would be directed to the psychology of the acceptance decision and to other theories bearing on the behavioral response.

Although Brown and Stover did not test utility theory themselves, it has undergirded two important research projects (Rodgers and Bullock 1972, 1976a; Giles and Gatlin 1980), with positive results. The success of utility theory in explaining behavior in these projects as well as its simple logic, which can be tested in many circumstances, leads me to believe that it is one of the best vehicles for developing an empirical explanation of impact behavior. It should be a major component in building and refining a comprehensive impact theory. Of course, it is sometimes problematic to measure even nonpsychological variables as well as respondents' perception of them, but in many situations it is not particularly difficult (as when the costs and benefits are largely monetary). Unfortunately, too little research—especially in recent years—relies on utility theory.

Legitimacy Theory

Legitimacy theory is sometimes used to explain judicial impact. This theory is used in many aspects of political science, going back to Seymour Lipset's (1960) work. Several aspects of legitimacy theory apply to the courts. Here we discuss legitimacy as it directly explains acceptance decisions. Aspects related to public support for the Supreme Court, or to whether the Court or the "law" are sufficiently symbolic in themselves to legitimize controversial policies, are covered elsewhere in this book.

Legitimacy theory posits that actors will reject a decision when they do not view the political structure of society as giving the court the authority to make the decision it did. A rejection will not always lead to a negative behavioral response, especially when the costs of refusing to comply or implement are high, but it is likely to be a factor when actors decide upon a behavioral response.

Legitimacy theory is intuitively appealing, and it would be quite surprising if perceptions of legitimacy were unrelated to the acceptance decision or had no impact on the behavioral response. Nonetheless, the theory has been subject to few empirical tests. In part, this reflects the theory's somewhat inchoate and unrefined state. Although scholars have surveyed reactions to controversial decisions, no serious efforts to type or quantify perceptions of legitimacy exist, especially among the members of the interpreting and implementing populations. Likewise, there have been few attempts at sophisticated explanations of what personal and decisional factors lead people to view a decision as legitimate or illegitimate. Only a couple of studies link findings about legitimacy with the behavioral response of those specifically charged with obeying or implementing a judicial decision. William Muir (1967) used cognitive dissonance theory to explain how one can respect a Supreme Court decision yet evade its mandates. Also noteworthy is Harrell Rodgers and Charles Bullock's (1976a) reliance on two broad theories in their study of the implementation of desegregation in the Georgia schools. From legitimacy theory, they posited a personality trait called "law abidingness" and, using it in combination with utility theory, showed that the psychic costs of violating the law may constrain even economically or politically beneficial disobedience if the decision is seen as legitimate. Thomas Dalton (1985) reminds us that there are levels of legitimacy (such as federal courts, state courts, implementing agencies) to be considered in tracing impact.[9]

Communications Theory

Some impact researchers have relied on communications theory to explain impact. This is not a unified theory, but a number of related ones largely developed in the communications discipline. Using it in simple form, impact scholars posit that acceptance decisions and behavioral responses of implementors and consumers can likely be explained by whether actors have received information about the decision and to what degree, if any, it has been distorted on its journey from the originating court. In a more complex way, communications theory can be used to conduct research on the effect that a decision's clarity, ambiguous phrases (such as "all deliberate speed"), *obiter dicta,* and the justices' voting or opinion configurations[10] have on those who interpret, implement, or consume it. The prediction, of course, is that poorly written opinions, ambiguous phrasing, extraneous messages, close votes, or proliferations of complicated opinions will produce a greater variety of impact behavior, some of which will be counterproductive to compliance and the implementation of the decision's broader goals.[11] Communications theory also relates to the way recipients perceive the message. Communications and social psychology research tells us that people often misperceive even a clear policy statement, especially if it runs contrary to their own attitudes or desires; cognitive dissonance, selective perception, and other theories explain the misperception.

Several scholars, particularly Wasby (1973, 1976), have noted the obstacles to getting accurate word from the Marble Palace to the constable or magistrate in the hinterlands. As expected, lack of knowledge produces noncompliance with new policies. Ignorance of a decision, however, is usually not a lasting problem. Other research tells us that implementing agencies receive different synopses of important decisions depending upon which of several alternate channels they rely on (for example, for the police: in-service training, internal legal counsel, police academies, FBI seminars, prosecutors' bulletins). However, the only study (Milner 1971) relating differing communication routes with differences in acceptance decisions found little linkage, and no one has explored whether differing behavioral responses arise from reliance on differing communications channels. Likewise, studies of the impact of ambiguous decisions have not, contrary to expectations, shown much variation in acceptance decisions and behavioral responses, at least among the interpreting population. However, several major studies have shown that variations in perceptions of the decision help explain implementors' acceptance and behavior (Dolbeare and Hammond 1971) and that cognitive dissonance can explain misperceptions of fairly clear judicial mandates (Johnson 1967; Muir 1967).

Reliance on communications theory has diminished in the last decade. Perhaps this follows negative findings about its explanatory power. However, these studies have generally involved the interpreting population. This population, composed largely of judges, receives undistorted messages and is given to legalistic processing of information. Johnson's and Muir's studies suggest that more distortion and misperception should obtain for the other populations. Although communications theory does not offer the overarching explanatory power of utility theory, it has potent explanatory value and needs to be pursued further.

Organizational Theories

Many judicial policies (like other public policies) are implemented in an organizational context. Thus considerable implementation research relies on theories of organizational behavior, mostly borrowed from public administration or sociology. Two theories guide much of the research. Charles Johnson (1979a) developed the theory of "policy tension" out of the theoretical work of James March and Herbert Simon (1958) and Anthony Downs (1967). When an organization is strongly committed to goals (such as preventing or solving crime, for the police) that are at odds with a court decision (such as *Miranda*), policy tension occurs within the organization. The theory predicts that the organization will protect its goals as far as possible. The theory is illustrated in Figure 17-3. Variables such as the organization's resources, cost of compliance, external nonjudicial pressures for or against implementation, and the likelihood and severity of judicial sanctions will affect whether the organization implements the court decision fully, partially, or not at all. Besides Johnson's research and Martin Shapiro's (1968) work on Patent Office responses to Supreme Court decisions, little research has been done to test policy tension theory.

Figure 17-3   Organizational Policy Choices that Lead to Policy
Tensions

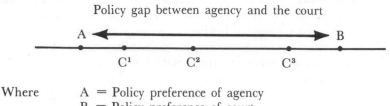

Policy gap between agency and the court

Where   A = Policy preference of agency
B = Policy preference of court
C^i = Policy alternatives after a court decision

Source: Charles A. Johnson and Bradley C. Canon, *Judicial Policies: Implementation and Impact.* Washington, D.C.: CQ Press, 1984, p. 213.

The second theory is based on organizational inertia. In addition to their policy goals, organizations develop subsidiary goals such as saving money, avoiding excess work, maintaining prestige, protecting their clientele, and generally continuing their existence without fundamental change. Thus in implementing a court decision that upsets routines or poses resource problems for the agency, there will be some resistance (except when the decision enhances the agency's policy goals). Lawrence Baum (1976, 1977), citing the work of Amitai Etzioni (1971) and others, has argued most forcefully for considering inertial theory in implementation research. In his view, we cannot expect agencies to treat judicial policies much differently from nonjudicial ones in implementation.[12]

Both policy tension and inertia have intuitive appeal and have been used to explain the implementation of nonjudicial policies. Several scholars who studied court decisions requiring bureaucratic implementation have found results compatible with the theories' expectations. The theories are certainly useful in shaping compliance and implementation research in the organizational context and, because so much implementation occurs in this context, should be further developed and used more often. For example, in *Goss v. Lopez* (419 U.S. 565 [1975]), the Supreme Court held that public schools could not suspend students without a hearing. Inertial theory predicts that because hearings are time consuming and sometimes complex, school systems will evade or minimize this requirement. Appropriate research can confirm or disconfirm this prediction.

Research Methods

Data on judicial impact are obtained in much the same way as other social science data—that is, largely from records, through surveys and interviews, and by observation. The last two types of data are self-generated, and the ability to produce them in any volume often depends on funding.

Most frequently, impact scholars rely on recorded data such as lower court opinions, the racial composition of schools, police arrest records, number of abortions, and so on. The reliability of records (that is, whether they accurately reflect what happened) can occasionally be a problem. Recently, Donald Songer (1988b) pointed out that *Shepard's Citations* is sometimes incomplete, either because of clerical errors or because of the way in which lower courts cite cases.[13] There is also a problem of validity when records are used as a surrogate for the behavior that actually interests the researcher. For instance, in studying the impact of the exclusionary rule, I (Canon 1974a, 1977) looked at arrests for crimes in which the evidence was usually obtained by police search and seizures (for example, possession of narcotics, concealed weapons), but arrest data do not indicate whether the searches were illegal. I assumed (based upon interviews and earlier police comments) that a reasonably high proportion involved illegal searches, and thus that any significant decline in arrests reflected a decline in illegal searches by the police. Finally, many records are difficult to aggregate. For example, few jurisdictions keep central records of search warrants or dismissals of libel suits.

Conclusions drawn from records are usually inferential; that is, changes in the dependent variable do not in themselves establish a casual link with the decision whose impact is under study. Other factors may have intervened. For example, in studying reapportionment's impact by noting changes in legislative outputs (Feig 1985; McCubbins and Schwartz 1988), changes in public attitudes may have affected policy changes as much as the revised geographical composition of the legislature.

When records cannot be obtained or do not exist, impact data must be generated by asking people about their behavior and attitudes. Over the last quarter century, school teachers, police officers, hospital administrators, and others have occasionally received questionnaires seeking such information in the wake of a decision affecting them (see Way 1968; Canon and Kolson 1971; Bond and Johnson 1982). Most recently, Lauren Bowen (1990) relied on a survey of small law firms in her research into how attorneys' attitudes and economic situations affect whether and how they advertise in the aftermath of *Bates v. Arizona State Bar* (433 U.S. 114 [1977]), which permitted attorney advertising. Although there are concerns about response rate and bias as well as reliability accompanying the use of survey data, surveys are a useful and inexpensive method of obtaining widespread geographical responses about acceptance decisions and behavioral responses. When carefully developed and perhaps put in the context of further illuminating hypotheses supported in case studies, they can do much to enhance our knowledge of decisional impacts.

Although they cannot reach the number of respondents that surveys can, interviews enable researchers to obtain significantly more detailed and colorful knowledge about attitudes and behavior, as well as interactions with and perceptions of others involved in the impact process. Questioning participants was the core method used in the early case studies of the impact of the school prayer and criminal justice decisions (see Muir 1967; Dolbeare and Hammond 1971). Stephen Wasby (1976) interviewed numerous police administrators in widely separated areas, showing that interviewing need not be limited to the case study approach. Because of the need for numerous respondents, interviewing consumers of judicial decisions is more problematic. Micheal Giles and Douglas Gatlin's (1980) study of responses following massive desegregation employed professional interviewers to obtain in-depth reactions of over 1,100 parents; it was, however, supported by federal money. Besides their normally limited number, the drawbacks of interview data parallel those of survey data. However, interviews can tap attitudes and nonpublic behavior as can no other technique.

Observation of relevant behavior provides the most reliable impact data. Ideally, it should be used frequently, but thorough and continuing observation is impractical, to say nothing of being financially infeasible. At best it can produce only a minute and probably nonrandom sample of the universe of impact data. Even at that, logistical difficulties abound. Nonetheless, impact researchers have occasionally used observational methods.

A few investigations relied principally on direct observation. The two major studies of *Miranda's* impact (Wald et al. 1967; Medalie, Zeitz, and Alexander 1968) observed police interrogations, as did Norman Lefstein, Vaughan Stapleton, and Lee Teitelbaum (1969) in observing juvenile judges' treatment of defendants after *In re Gault* (387 U.S. 1 [1967]). Participant observation is very difficult to arrange, but one investigator with prior experience served as a guard for several months at a maximum security penitentiary to observe the implementation of a district court prison reform decision (Marquart and Crouch 1985).[14] Levine (1970) suggested a number of methods of conducting unobtrusive observation of judicial impact (such as going to "adult" book or video stores and seeing whether constitutionally protected material is or is not available in a community), but few have put them to much use. However, Frederick Wirt's (1970) study of desegregation's impact in a rural Mississippi county partly relied on unobtrusive if nonquantitative measurement.[15]

Impact data are seldom numerous or complex enough to warrant analyses via high-powered statistics. Usually little more than cross-tabulations, correlations, or analysis of variance is used. When predecision behavior is systematically recorded or can be fairly inferred from records, researchers have attempted a before-and-after comparison. In Canon (1974a), for instance, I relied on arrest records for offenses usually revealed by police searches and used analysis of variance to discern *Mapp v. Ohio's* (367 U.S. 643 [1961]) impact on police behavior (which was mixed), and in Canon (1977) I used similar methods to determine that the rule's impact was not related to preexisting state exclusionary rules (that is, state rules had no impact). Christine Rossell (1976) used similar techniques to argue that busing was not causing "white flight" from the cities,[16] and Susan Hansen (1980) used such techniques to explain variations in the impact of the abortion decision by state. When earlier records are not available, the same techniques can help scholars track a decision's impact by stages or measure the impact of an expanding or changing judicial policy (Hanson and Crew 1973; Giles 1975; Canon and Jaros 1979). In other methodological directions, Charles Johnson (1979b, 1987) pioneered the use of content analyses to measure lower court distortion of Supreme Court decisions. Recently, Nelson Dometrius and Lee Sigelman (1988) applied an organizational regeneration model to the impact of *Wygant v. Jackson Board of Education's* (476 U.S. 267 [1986]) restrictions on layoff agreements that preserve the ratio of minority teachers. Although their model predicts a generally negligible impact, their work may well inspire further applications of quantitative modeling—a common analytical technique in other areas of political science—to judicial impact.

Level of the Court Making Policy

Most impact studies have been about U.S. Supreme Court decisions and most of this chapter discusses them.[17] However, some scholars have turned their attention to lesser appellate and even trial courts (see Glick 1971; Carp and Rowland 1983; Fino 1987), and this section will discuss these findings. Even so, studies of lower courts have not often focused directly on compliance, implementation, or broad impact. They looked at the courts' decisional processes or the decisions' substance—matters useful for understanding impact, but not in themselves explaining what happened after a decision.

One of the earliest investigations of lower court impact was Kenneth Dolbeare's (1967) study of how trial courts in a suburban

New York county affected public policy within the county. The focus was on broad impact, not compliance or implementation. Through newspaper articles and interviews, Dolbeare examined the county's most important policy disputes over a fifteen-year period and the extent to which the courts helped shape their outcome. Their greatest impact came in zoning and property policy, where local courts tended to protect the economic status quo, sometimes simply delaying change. Beyond zoning and property, the local courts had little overall impact. Dolbeare's work was thorough and revealing and remains the premier study of local court impact. In fact, no scholars have followed his lead.

No study comparable to Dolbeare's has been done on a state supreme court. The main objective has been cross-state comparison of process and policy. Susan Fino (1987) and others[18] have shown that some high courts are reasonably active in the development of state policies while others are status quo oriented or simply passive. The most systematic impact studies at the state level are those by Dean Jaros and me (Canon and Jaros 1979) and James Croyle (1979). Each used price data from all states to show a measurable economic impact of state supreme court changes in two tort law doctrines; because much economic data are collected by state, other doctrinal changes invite similar research.[19] Studies of the development of civil liberties guarantees under state constitutions (see Porter 1982) can also lead to comparative judicial impact studies, although impact data will be more diffuse and harder to aggregate.

Richard Lehne (1978) studied the aftermath of a single case, *Robinson v. Cahill* (351 A.2d 715 [1973]), New Jersey's famous school financing decision, closely tracing the major judicial and political events following the extraordinary ruling. It is a compliance and implementation study, looking at the struggle to obtain the mandated financing, not how effective the funding, once provided, was in improving education in the state. Court cases requiring massive changes in the financing of the public schools, although extraordinary in their remedies, have tremendous impact potential. About a dozen state supreme courts have rendered such decisions, and others have them on their dockets. This situation offers an excellent opportunity for comparative studies of implementation and impact.

It is more difficult to study the impact of policies developed by federal appeals and district courts because the policies they initiate are subject to considerable revision on appeal. Once in a while, however, several of the twelve appeals courts will split on substantive policy issues that the Supreme Court declines to hear (for example, in the 1970s about half struck down school dress/hair length codes while the other half upheld them). Such occasions offer a quasi experiment[20] situation for impact research: Are appellate decisions well communicated and seen as legitimate? Is the controversial policy attempted less often in circuits that constrain it?

In the last two decades many federal district judges have rendered sweeping decisions relating to prison conditions and the treatment of the mentally ill. These are areas ripe for impact research. Nathan Glazer (1978) has offered several empirically testable hypotheses about the prison decisions' impact (that they weaken prison administration authority, give greater weight to theoretical than to practical considerations, and augment the power of the legal profession in shaping prison policies), but research has not yet focused on them. However, Kathryn Moss (1985) traced the successful legislative implementation of a district court-required change in Texas's civil commitment law. James Marquart and Ben Crouch (1985) and Sheldon Ekland-Olson (1986) studied Texas prisons following one such decision, both finding that major changes in prison policies had been implemented and were producing increased tension in staff-inmate relations. George Hale (1979) and Linda Harriman and Jeffrey Straussman (1983) have found that federal prison reform decisions can significantly affect state budget allocations.[21]

Although the importance of U.S. Supreme Court decisions makes them attractive for impact research, there are good reasons to study the impact of other court decisions as well. The most important is that such study permits scholars to test the universality of explanatory theories. Legitimacy and communications theories in particular might operate quite differently at the lower court level. Further, comparative impact studies allow researchers to manipulate more variables, thus testing theories under differing conditions. In addition, a more comprehensive investigation of impact can be conducted; Lehne (1978) would simply be a study of one state if a U.S. Supreme Court decision were at issue. To strive for a more theoretical understanding of judicial impact, I believe we must pay more attention to decisions made by courts other than the U.S. Supreme Court.

Substantive Policy Impacts

Impact scholars have concentrated on a rather small number of judicial policies, mostly involving civil liberties issues. Much of it has focused on three policy areas arising from controversial Warren Court decisions: desegregation, criminal justice, and prayer in public schools. Four other areas in which the Court made major policy changes have also attracted investigation: obscenity, abortion, reapportionment, and libel law, the last largely from lawyers and journalists.

Decisions requiring or opening the way for major change naturally invite investigation of their impact, while those maintaining the
status quo have little measurable impact and are thus not worth
pursuing. Nonetheless, the impact of many important Supreme Court
decisions that made changes has gone uninvestigated. Some inattention
is no doubt due to the difficulties of collecting data on change (for
example, the frequency of symbolic protest in schools following *Tinker
v. Des Moines School District*, 393 U.S. 503 [1969]). But data collection
is not always a serious obstacle. For instance, given society's intense
interest in equal employment opportunities for minorities and women
(a topic, moreover, likely to attract outside funding), it is surprising that
there are no important studies of the impact of one or more major
Court decisions in the area. Also, major judicial changes go
unresearched because scholars in the public law subfield are not very
interested in certain policies. For example, several 1970s and 1980s
Supreme Court decisions have interpreted antitrust laws to nullify
widespread state and local policies such as fair trade laws or professional association fee schedules, but economic impact is much less
attractive than civil liberties impact.

Gaps in our knowledge also exist because compliance and
implementation studies are usually performed within a few years of
the change decision. For example, there have been no direct studies of
prayer in schools since Kenneth Dolbeare and Phillip Hammond
(1971), and research into police implementation of *Miranda* ended
around 1970. Thus we do not know whether those early findings (best
summarized in both areas as only partial compliance or implementation) have remained true for the last twenty years. Likewise, the
impact of obscenity decisions has been unattended since the mid-
1970s. To some extent, the failure to conduct further research stems
from the absence of significant court change in the policy after the
initial decision. As time passes, the decision becomes less important or
controversial, data are harder to acquire, and before-and-after compliance studies can no longer be done. But these factors are not always
operative. Twenty-five years after its pronouncement, school prayer
remains a highly visible and emotional issue—one that is yet subject
to investigation along the same theoretical paths Richard Johnson
(1967), Muir (1967), and Dolbeare and Hammond (1971) used.
Similarly, *Roe v. Wade* (410 U.S. 113 [1973]) has lost none of its
importance, and the Court has subsequently allowed important
limitations on potential impact (*Harris v. McRae*, 448 U.S. 297
[1980]; *Webster v. Reproductive Health Services*, 106 L.Ed. 2d 410
[1989]). Notably, some 1960s' decisions, such as the exclusionary rule
in search and seizure and reapportionment, have been subject in later

decades to research relying in part on old data (see Canon 1977; McCubbins and Schwartz 1988).

A more complete understanding of a decision's broad impact, not just compliance and implementation, depends upon continuing investigation of its consequences. In the absence of research, no theories of long-term impact can be developed or tested. Determining a decision's societal impact is not easy, but a number of modest investigations can contribute to larger conclusions. Little such research is conducted. For example, after twenty-five years we have little systematic knowledge about how the Court's libel decisions have affected the behavior of media reporters and editors, writers, and potential plaintiffs. Nor do we really know how the obscenity decisions such as *Miller v. California* (413 U.S. 15 [1973]), when compared with other factors, have influenced writers, publishers, book and video store owners, police and prosecutors, and customers.

Impact in two policy areas has been studied continuously. To a considerable extent this is reflective of ideological controversy in the academy surrounding the policies and their consequences.[22] One is large-scale school desegregation. Rodgers and Bullock (1976a, 1976b) conducted a sophisticated study of the implementation of integration in a sample of Georgia counties, often using a utility theory approach. The overriding conclusion is that "money talks." The threat of federal fund cutoffs was a more potent weapon for securing large-scale integration than were suits by the Justice Department or blacks or pressure from the latter, although all played some role (see also Giles 1975).

Researchers also focused on the impact of large-scale busing orders, particularly on whether white flight to the suburbs or massive transfers to private schools followed such decisions. James Coleman, Sara Kelly, and John Moore's (1975) research led them to argue that there was a causal link, while Rossell's (1976) analysis led her to urge that white flight largely occurred independently of busing. Giles, Gatlin, and Everett Cataldo (1976) determined a "tipping point" (black percentages that induce a mass exodus of white students). In later research, which also relied on a variant of utility theory, Giles and Gatlin (1980) controlled for other factors (income, moving distance to another district) to determine under what circumstances parents would avoid busing. Subsequently, researchers have found that "second generation resegregation" (segregated education within an integrated school) via policies such as tracking often occurs (Meier, Stewart, and England 1990; Wainscott and Woodward 1988).

Studies of desegregation have not addressed two broad impact questions very well. One is the extent to which types of desegregation actually improve the education of black students (or whites, for that matter), although Coleman, Kelly, and Moore (1975) argued that even high-quality desegregated schools could do little to overcome obstacles such as parental, peer group, or minority culture indifference to education. The other question is the degree to which desegregation in the schools enhances social tolerance or harmony in society in general. Obviously, these are diffuse questions and it would require considerable effort to obtain meaningful results, but the answers would tell us much about the ultimate impact of one of the most important policy changes the Supreme Court has ever initiated.

The second policy is the exclusionary rule in search and seizure (*Mapp v. Ohio*, 1961), which underwent several empirical investigations following Chief Justice Burger's assertion that the rule was not having its intended impact (dissenting in *Bivens v. Six Unknown Narcotics Agents*, 403 U.S. 388 [1971]). James Spiotto (1973), Wasby (1976), I (Canon 1974a, 1977), as well as others, did detailed work on compliance, that is, whether the police continued to conduct illegal searches. Later, Thomas Davies (1983) and I (Canon 1982) looked at the rule's impact on conviction rates. No clear pattern of police compliance emerged; compliance varied considerably depending upon the police culture in a given city as well as other factors not well understood. However, only minuscule percentages of defendants escaped conviction because illegally seized evidence was ruled inadmissible.

Notably, all the judicial policies that have attracted more than isolated impact research are two to three decades old. Yet, some more recent decisions have mandated or invited considerable change: those discouraging males-only civic organizations or clubs and those enhancing school administrators' powers regarding school newspaper content, student speech, or searches of lockers and purses. Recent decisions have seemingly reversed judicial policies, especially in the affirmative action area. Critics charge that they will have devastating effects, an assertion open to empirical verification.

Studying only the most memorable cases is unscientific. Confidence in theories supported only by research drawn from truly major cases may be significantly enhanced or diminished by impact evidence from the much greater numbers of other cases. It is also likely that the theories' explanatory power will be refined and perhaps changed when impact research reaches noncivil liberties areas such as antitrust, energy, and environmental decisions.

Functional Populations

As I have mentioned, Johnson and I (Johnson and Canon 1984) offered a conceptual framework for organizing judicial impact research based upon functional populations. This section will briefly cover impact research into each population, concentrating on that which relies upon or illuminates the four most general theories: utility theory, legitimacy theory, communications theory, and organizational theories.[23]

Interpreting Population

Scholars have paid considerable attention to lower court judges' interpretive practices. Some have found systematic interpretive differences between federal and state court judges, and some have found relationships between judges' ideology, attitudes, or partisanship and their interpretations. After interviewing southern federal district judges, Jack Peltason (1961) poignantly described the heavy cross-pressures between intense local mores of segregation and the requirements of *Brown v. Board* (1954) on them when handling desegregation suits. More recently, Frank Way and Barbara Burt (1983) and Songer (1987) have plotted lower federal court interpretive trends that reflect Supreme Court decisions in free exercise cases and in labor relations and antitrust cases, respectively.

More theoretically, G. Alan Tarr (1977) examined state supreme courts' compliance with the Supreme Court's establishment clause cases, applying several utility and communications theory hypotheses to their interpretive behavior. Utility hypotheses were supported more than were those drawn from communications theory. Studies of lower federal court interpretation of *New York Times v. Sullivan* (376 U.S. 254 [1964]), which brought libel suits under the freedom of the press clause (Gruhl 1980), and of state supreme court interpretations of U.S. Supreme Court decisions in the national security area (Jenson 1982) gave little evidence that judges' interpretations were influenced by communications factors such as lack of decisional clarity. Johnson's (1979b) study of lower federal courts' construal of three terms' worth of Supreme Court decisions showed no evidence that interpretations were related to another communications factor, divisiveness on the Court.

Research to date indicates that the interpreting population uses a personal or professional cost-benefit approach in carrying out its function, but it can be influenced by local pressures and personal attitudes as well as by a professional sense of duty. Communications theories seem to explain little about lower court behavior. However, this generalization must be very tentative. Theoretically oriented studies are not numerous; the number of cases involved in most studies is rather small; and often the hypotheses have not been rigorously defined. We need to build on existing studies with careful research which will confirm or disconfirm what we seem to know and test new hypotheses derived from utility and communications theory along with organizational theory.[24] Such research must be imaginative because the core knowledge sought is the elusive matter of what goes on in judges' minds as they engage in the interpretive process.

Implementing Population

Scholars have also explored the effect of local pressures and personal attitudes on implementors' acceptance of and behavioral responses to court decisions. At times, these can affect the implementation of controversial decisions such as those involving desegregation and school prayer.

However, most judicial policies are implemented by organizations (usually public bureaucracies), and research into organizational behavior has followed (sometimes implicitly) one or more of the broad impact theories discussed earlier. As these theories sometimes overlap (for example, often utility theory predicts the same behavior as does organizational policy tension theory, and some communications theory hypotheses closely relate to intraorganizational behavior), the separation of findings discussed below is somewhat artificial.

Organizational inertia, especially when the decision is unpopular or peripheral to organizational goals, has explained the nonimplementation of the school prayer decisions (Johnson 1967; Dolbeare and Hammond 1971) and the grudgingly limited implementation of desegregation, especially when judicial sanctions are not well suited to the situation (Giles 1975; Rodgers and Bullock 1976b). By contrast, when sanctions are direct and severe—for example, releasing prisoners unless judicially mandated reforms are implemented—change can occur quickly and thoroughly (Marquart and Crouch 1985). With regard to policy tension theory, Shapiro (1968) found the Patent Office easily able to resist Supreme Court decisions calling for a change in the office's loose patent policies, and Johnson (1979b) found that several state administrative agencies compromised differences between their own goals and court decisions. Studies of responses by police and school administrators give indications of policy tension behavior, but the theory has not been directly tested in these contexts. To date, research is insufficient to give detail to the explanatory power of policy tension theory.

Rodgers and Bullock's (1972, 1976a) large-scale examination of school desegregation in rural Georgia counties found that utility theory helped explain its successful implementation. As noted earlier, when the monetary penalties for inadequate implementation increased, implementation efforts improved. This finding gives some credence to the theory's applicability to implementors, but confidence would be greater if utility theory hypotheses were tested in more implementation contexts. Communications theory has never really been tested as an explanation of implementation behavior. Neal Milner (1971) and Wasby (1976) have noted that differences in communications procedures in police departments have produced different knowledge levels and affected attitudes on the line, but linkage to actual behavior has not been studied.

Legitimacy theory has been applied to the implementing population less frequently. However, Muir's (1967) study of a school district's decision to cease prayers found that board members and administrators' perceptions about the right of the Supreme Court to make such a decision influenced both positive and negative acceptance decisions. And Rodgers and Bullock (1976a) found that school officials' propensity to law-abidingness sometimes eased the implementation of desegregation orders.

Implementors are the population most often studied, and we have reason to believe that organization, utility, and legitimacy theory—and probably communications theory—are applicable to explaining their behavior. But the verifications are sketchy and we know little about exceptions, corollaries, and other refinements of the theories' relevance to organizational implementation. For that matter, our knowledge is largely confined to two bureaucracies, school systems and the police. Other organizations, such as the armed services and welfare agencies, have not been studied in an impact context, nor, by and large, have private implementors (but see Bond and Johnson 1982 on hospitals' abortion policies).

Consumer Population

Perhaps the ultimate measure of judicial impact lies in how those actually or potentially affected by a decision as individuals respond to it.[25] Often decisions that benefit people are permissive—that is, persons have to accept it and act positively to obtain the benefits.[26] Likewise, people can sometimes avoid the direct impact of negative judicial policies by engaging in alternate behavior, such as sending children to private schools to avoid busing. However, impact researchers have undertaken few studies of the behavior of those who consume judicial decisions.

The studies of consumer behavior have largely relied, explicitly or implicitly, on utility theory. *Miranda* researchers (Medalie, Zeitz, and Alexander 1968; Wald et al. 1967) found that suspects sometimes believed it was in their best interest to cooperate with the police even when fully aware of their right to remain silent. Many booksellers told Levine (1969) that more customers would be lost than gained if they stocked salacious books even though the courts had ruled that such books were not legally obscene. Bowen (1990) found that many attorneys chose not to advertise after prohibitions were struck down because they saw no financial advantage to it. The reverse was also true: some suspects, booksellers, and attorneys did take advantage of the courts' policies on the basis of a cost-benefit calculation. Giles and Gatlin (1980) conducted the most explicit and rigorous consumer population study relying on utility theory; they found that the behavioral decisions of parents who sought to avoid a desegregation order depended more on being able to bear the economic costs of avoidance than on even an intensely negative acceptance decision.

The *Miranda* studies (which were atheoretical in design) showed that the suspects' rights were often poorly communicated and often misunderstood, even when accurately conveyed, but communications theory hypotheses were not subsequently applied to suspects or other actors in the consumer population. Legitimacy theory seems plausible as a partial explanation for consumers' acceptance decisions, but it has received little attention. Organization theory is not often applicable to consumption decisions, although private organizations are sometimes the consuming actors affected by court decisions.

Consumers are a much neglected target of impact research; the population invites much theoretical work. It is hard to believe, for example, that there is little research and no scholarly theories about why some pregnant women choose abortion and others do not.[27] Clearly, utility theory offers a likely explanation here, as do communications and legitimacy theories. Likewise, behavior by reporters and editors in response to *New York Times v. Sullivan* (1964) (libel) and *Branzburg v. Hayes* (408 U.S. 665 [1972]) (denying claims of journalistic immunity from judicial processes) invites the testing of theoretical hypotheses. Our knowledge of the ultimate impact of many important judicial policies will be incomplete until we turn more attention to how these policies are actually consumed.

Secondary Population

Members of this population fulfill no direct impact function and need not make acceptance decisions or behavioral responses. Nonetheless, this population can influence the impact of a judicial decision in several ways. For example, judicial interpretations of federal laws can be negated when Congress passes a more explicit statute, although research by John Schmidhauser, Larry Berg, and Albert Melone (1971) and by Beth Henschen (1983) indicates that Congress seldom does this. Or Congress and legislatures can pass laws enhancing or limiting a case's impact, as happened when Congress prohibited federal Medicaid funds from being used for abortions. The president can directly or indirectly support or oppose a judicial policy; President Reagan made no secret of his dislike for the school prayer cases. Persons interested in but not directly affected by a decision (such as white liberals in the case of civil rights decisions) and the media can mobilize public opinion in support or opposition (which in turn may generate legislation and/or new court cases).[28]

Because they have no direct impact function, theoretical approaches to studying actors in this population may be somewhat different. Organizational theory is not very applicable, and, as used here, utility theory is not fruitful. Of course in a broader sense, executive or legislative reaction can reflect a political cost-benefit calculation, as when President Bush and many members of Congress rushed to support a constitutional amendment protecting the flag following *Texas v. Johnson* (105 L.Ed. 2d 342 [1989]). However, communications theory may well explain both elite and mass perceptions of a decision or the causes and influence of media attention or inattention to particular decisions. And legitimacy theory may help explain the willingness of politicians, the media, and the public to tolerate some unpopular decisions and not abide by others. (Why, for instance, does school prayer stay on the national agenda while *Miranda* is now well accepted?) Studies of congressional reaction to liberal national security decisions by C. Herman Pritchett (1961) and Walter Murphy (1962) concluded that the inherent legitimacy of the Supreme Court's judicial review function inhibited serious negative congressional action, but Harry Stumpf (1966), who looked at the same cases, argued that there was little empirical evidence that Congress views this function as sacrosanct. More abstractly, Walter Murphy and Joseph Tanenhaus (1968) have offered some legitimacy theory arguments about the impact of Supreme Court decisions and public opinion on each other.[29] Of course, theories from other subfields of political science or the social sciences dealing with legislative behavior, the executive branch, media behavior, and the formation and influence of public opinion can be useful in explaining how the secondary population reacts. Such theories have not been much used in the judicial impact context and largely lie beyond the scope of this chapter.

Conclusion

There is a slowdown—a declining enthusiasm—in judicial impact research as it enters its fourth decade. Few, if any, major impact projects are currently under way. A more theoretical understanding of impact phenomena is advancing only slowly. The major explanatory theories are decades old and have seen few recent refinements. Numerous data are still collected without even implicit theoretical guidance.

I have already suggested several causes for this stagnation. Foremost, perhaps, is the decline in judicial decisions demanding major behavioral change. Like journalists, many political scientists share the "man bites dog" syndrome of what is worthy of attention, and the halcyon days when the Warren Court bit sleeping dogs are long past. This is an unfortunate syndrome for at least two reasons. The less important one is that courts still make major decisions nowadays. The Reagan Court is significantly changing judicial policies in affirmative action, abortion, and other areas to the point that we can conduct impact research with a reasonable expectation of finding changed behavior at all population levels. Beyond that, many state courts are in an era of new activism (Porter 1982; Fino 1987). However, the more important reason for maintaining a steady research focus on judicial impact is that, unlike journalism, scientific interest must focus on the routine as well as the dramatic (Reid 1988). Theories developed and tested only in unusual circumstances may prove weak or inoperative otherwise. For political scientists to be concerned only with dramatic events is much like research chemists being concerned only with explosions.

The limited policy interests of impact researchers is another cause. The great majority of judicial decisions affect matters other than civil liberties, even defined broadly. Judicial policies redistribute wealth, improve or worsen the environment, and affect major aspects of family life. But these areas are usually of more concern to other political and social scientists than to judicial process scholars, so impact research seldom occurs in them. Impact researchers must broaden their policy horizons. Further, they must work more closely with public policy impact researchers as well as with economists, environmental scholars, social service researchers, and others who have a feel for impact but are not thinking along impact theory lines.

The cost of conducting major impact research is also an inhibiting factor. By contrast, analysis of constitutional doctrines or voting behavior on collegial courts needs little support. While funding is not as plentiful as it was two decades ago, it is available. The National Science Foundation supports good impact research proposals, and other agencies and private sources are interested in the impact of certain judicial policies. Moreover, even without funding, there are numerous opportunities to conduct important impact research. Major dissertation research (Dolbeare 1967; Tarr 1977) as well as important contributions by established scholars (Wasby 1976; Hansen 1980) have been accomplished with little or no financial support.

The point of this section—and of this chapter—is that the slowdown in impact research was not inevitable and, in fact, such research can and should be on the increase. The opportunities are there if scholars, both new and established, will but see them and act purposively to follow them up. All our knowledge about interest group judicial lobbying tactics, judges' social backgrounds, collegial court behavior, case meaning, and the like serves to little real world avail if we do not know or cannot explain what happens to individuals and to society as a result.

Notes

1. The *Illinois ex rel. McCullom v. Board of Education* (333 U.S. 203 [1948]) and *Zorach v. Clauson* (343 U.S. 306 [1952]) cases challenged the constitutionality of public school policies releasing students during the day to attend religious classes taught by members of the clergy. The Court held religious classes unconstitutional if they were taught on school grounds, but allowed them if taught off campus.
2. Behavioralism's more direct influence on public law as a subfield is found in the quantitative analyses of Supreme Court voting patterns as pioneered by Glendon Schubert (1962) in the early 1960s. However, it also produced the interest in investigating events subsequent to a court decision.
3. Many works in Wasby's bibliography did not focus on compliance or implementation, but offered insights into these phenomena.
4. As used here, theories refer to empirically testable explanations about impact behavior. General theories have universal applicability and can be tested in any circumstance. Mid-level theories are more limited in applicability and cannot be tested in some circumstances. Low-level theories are applicable only in limited circumstances.
5. Also in 1984 Jesse Choper published an article looking at the consequences of Court decisions upholding individual rights. Although it was speculative or legally oriented in parts, it showed a thorough knowledge of social science research (making it an excellent bibliographical source).
6. Political scientists are not alone in studying judicial impact. Throughout the last three decades, scholars in other disciplines, particularly law professors and sociologists, have studied institutions that implement judicial policies, most notably the legal profession, courts, and the police. In fact, studies by two law student research teams (Wald et al. 1967, and Medalie, Zeitz, and Alexander 1968) remain today the best empirical studies of how *Miranda v. Arizona* (1966) affected police interrogations. Similarly, political scientists in other subfields share in impact research, especially the effects of desegregation or the policy impact of reapportionment. Researchers in other disciplines are motivated by their own goals, as is sometimes true for political scientists not in the public law/judicial process subfield, and they are not particularly interested in developing

theories about impact. Nonetheless, their work has afforded important insights into the impact of judicial policies.

7. Not all court decisions call for implementation. Some decisions are permissive. For instance, the Supreme Court has upheld some agencies' affirmative action hiring policies, but has not required any agency to adopt one.

8. Other ways of organizing impact research have been advanced, but they do not cover the whole range of impact. Songer (1988a), for instance, divides research about the interpreting population into four approaches: searches for defiance, determination of compliance, looking at legal impact, and investigating subsequent decisional trends.

9. There is a large body of social psychology research into how children become socialized to obedience to law. While empirical linkage is difficult, at least theoretical efforts should be made to connect this research with the compliance, implementation, and consumption behavior of adults affected by court decisions.

10. The famous "reverse discrimination" case, *Regents of University of California v. Bakke* (438 U.S. 265 [1978]), is a prime example of a case where voting and opinion configurations can be important in determining its meaning.

11. Of course, it can fairly be argued that some court decisions are so ambiguous or self-contradictory that what constitutes compliance and implementation cannot reasonably be determined.

12. Inertia in general can also explain individual compliance with or consumption of judicial decisions outside the organizational context.

13. *Shepard's Citations* is an index to citations of a case by other courts. Impact scholars use it to see how lower courts have interpreted a U.S. Supreme Court decision. Songer found that when a case was very well known, lower courts sometimes would not cite it formally. For example, a court might say, "It is not clear that the Miranda warnings were given to the defendant." *Shepard's* would not cite *Miranda v. Arizona* here unless this court gave it a full citation. Songer also points out that some lower courts deliberately fail to cite a relevant case in order to mask their noncompliance. Right now, it is not clear whether the rapidly expanding electronic search systems such as Lexis and Westlaw are more or less reliable.

14. Findings from direct and sometimes from participant observation are subject to the "Hawthorne effect" (changes in behavior by those knowing they are under observation).

15. Sociologists more often use observational methods of data collection. Even law professors and students seem more adept at this than political scientists. Except for Wirt, the research reported in this paragraph was not done by political scientists. Many sociological studies, such as that of Jerome Skolnick (1966), who spent three years observing and sometimes participating with the Oakland police force, have not focused on judicial impact per se, but the findings illuminate police or prison compliance with judicial policies.

16. Both Rossell's and my inferences were enmeshed in controversy which is discussed in the section on policy impact.

17. This section discusses the impact of policies initiated by courts other than the U.S. Supreme Court. It does not focus on the role of lower courts in interpreting Supreme Court decisions.

18. Much other work is found in recent conference papers, not yet published. I have not cited these or other unpublished papers in this chapter because they are not ordinarily accessible to the average reader. I will make one exception and cite John Hagan (1986), whose tragic death in an automobile accident precludes publication of his research findings.

19. Several doctrinal changes have been recently adopted in many states, such as comparative negligence and builder-vendor implied warranty on new homes.

20. A quasi-experiment situation exists when a difference or change—not introduced by the researcher—occurs in the independent variable (here the nature of the appeals courts' decisions) which affords the researcher an opportunity to investigate to what degree the difference or change affects the dependent variable (here the number, severity, and enforcement of school dress codes).

21. For a review of the impact of prison reform decisions, see Feeley and Hansen (1990).

22. By contrast, while prayer in schools, narrow definitions of obscenity, abortion, and other judicial decisions have generated great public controversy, there is little *academic* controversy about these policies' substance or impact.

23. For a review of the literature in each population area, see Johnson and Canon (1984).

24. The judicial system is a hierarchical organization, albeit with some important dissimilarities to the organization of the executive branch. See Canon (1974b).

25. Consumption is automatic for some decisions. Antitrust decisions can lower prices for everyone while decisions upholding higher taxes leave the consumer little choice but to pay.

26. Direct and indirect consumers exist for some decisions. For decisions permitting advertising by professionals, those such as attorneys and pharmacists are the direct consumers and their clients or customers are the indirect ones. There is no impact on the latter unless at least some of the former respond positively to the decision.

27. I found the dearth of literature surprising given the centrality of abortion to American politics over the last two decades. I consulted with colleagues in other departments who were able to direct me to data about women who chose abortion (although not about those who chose to have the baby), but not to studies of reasons why pregnant women chose abortion or birth. Upon reflection, I realize that it would be difficult to conduct such a study with scientific rigor.

28. Congress and/or the president can react directly against the Supreme Court through new appointments or by such devices as limiting its jurisdiction. Such action is beyond the scope of this chapter.
29. There are numerous studies of public reaction to Supreme Court decisions and the degree to which the Court can legitimize them among the public. Although ultimately pertinent to theories of judicial impact, such studies seldom empirically link findings to actual events. Thus they are beyond the scope of this chapter, but are discussed in Chapters 1 and 12 of this book.

References

Baum, Lawrence. 1976. Implementation of judicial decisions: An organizational analysis. *American Politics Quarterly* 4:86-114.

———. 1977. Judicial impact as a form of policy implementation. In *Public law and public policy*, ed. John A. Gardiner. New York: Praeger.

Becker, Theodore L., ed. 1969. *The impact of Supreme Court decisions*. New York: Oxford University Press.

Becker, Theodore L., and Malcolm Feeley, eds. 1973. *The impact of Supreme Court decisions*. 2d ed. New York: Oxford University Press.

Bentham, Jeremy. 1789/1907. *An introduction to principles and legislation*. Oxford: Clarendon Press.

Bond, Jon, and Charles A. Johnson. 1982. Implementing a permissive policy: Hospital abortion services after *Roe v. Wade*. *American Journal of Political Science* 26:1-24.

Bowen, Lauren L. 1990. Attorney advertising in the wake of *Bates v. State Bar of Arizona:* A study of judicial impact. Ph.D. dissertation, University of Kentucky.

Brown, Don W., and Robert V. Stover. 1975. Understanding compliance and noncompliance with the law: The contributions of utility theory. *Social Science Quarterly* 56:363-375.

Canon, Bradley C. 1974a. Is the exclusionary rule in failing health? Some new data and a plea against a precipitous conclusion. *Kentucky Law Journal* 62:681-730.

———. 1974b. Organizational contumacy in the transmission of judicial policies: The *Mapp, Escobedo, Miranda,* and *Gault* cases. *Villanova Law Review* 20:50-79.

———. 1977. Testing the effectiveness of civil liberties policies at the state and federal levels: The case of the exclusionary rule. *American Politics Quarterly* 5:57-82.

———. 1982. Ideology and reality in the debate over the exclusionary rule: A conservative argument for its retention. *South Texas Law Journal* 23:558-582.

Canon, Bradley C., and Dean Jaros. 1979. The impact of changes in judicial doctrine: The abrogation of charitable immunity. *Law and Society Review* 14:969-986.

Canon, Bradley C., and Kenneth Kolson. 1971. Compliance with *Gault* in rural America: The case of Kentucky. *Journal of Family Law* 10:300-326.

Carp, Robert A., and C. K. Rowland. 1983. *Policymaking and politics in the federal district courts.* Knoxville: University of Tennessee Press.

Choper, Jesse H. 1984. Consequences of Supreme Court decisions upholding individual constitutional rights. *Michigan Law Review* 83:1-212.

Coleman, James D., Sara Kelly, and John Moore. 1975. *Recent trends in school desegregation.* Washington, D.C.: Urban Institute.

Croyle, James. 1979. The impact of judge made policies: An analysis of research strategies and an application to product liability doctrine. *Law and Society Review* 14:949-968.

Dalton, Thomas C. 1985. *The state politics of judicial and congressional reform.* Westport, Conn.: Greenwood Press.

Davies, Thomas Y. 1983. A hard look at what we know (and still need to learn) about the costs of the exclusionary rule: The NIJ study and other studies of "lost" arrests. *American Bar Foundation Research Journal* 3:611-690.

Dolbeare, Kenneth M. 1967. *Trial courts in urban politics.* New York: Wiley.

Dolbeare, Kenneth M., and Phillip E. Hammond. 1971. *The school prayer decisions: From court policy to local practice.* Chicago: University of Chicago Press.

Dometrius, Nelson C., and Lee Sigelman. 1988. Modeling the impact of Supreme Court decisions: *Wygant v. Board. Journal of Politics* 50:131-149.

Downs, Anthony. 1967. *Inside bureaucracy.* Boston: Little, Brown.

Ekland-Olson, Sheldon. 1986. Crowding, social control and prison violence: Evidence from the post-*Ruiz* years in Texas. *Law and Society Review* 21:389-422.

Etzioni, Amitai. 1971. *A comparative analysis of complex organizations.* New York: Harper and Row.

Feeley, Malcolm, and Susan B. Hansen. 1990. The impact of jail and prison conditions litigation: A review essay. In *Courts, corrections and the Constitution,* ed. John Dilulio. Princeton: Princeton University Press.

Feig, Douglas G. 1985. Looking at Supreme Court impact in context: The case of reapportionment and state spending. *American Politics Quarterly* 13:167-187.

Fino, Susan P. 1987. *The role of state supreme courts in the new judicial federalism.* Westport, Conn.: Greenwood Press.

Giles, Micheal. 1975. HEW versus the federal courts: A comparison of school desegregation enforcement. *American Politics Quarterly* 3:81-90.

Giles, Micheal, and Douglas Gatlin. 1980. Mass level compliance with public policy: The case of school desegregation. *Journal of Politics* 42:722-746.

Giles, Micheal, Douglas Gatlin, and Everett Cataldo. 1976. White flight and percent black: The tipping point reexamined. *Social Science Quarterly* 56:85-92.

Glazer, Nathan. 1978. Should judges administer social services? *The Public Interest* 50:64-80.

Glick, Henry R. 1971. *Supreme courts in state politics*. New York: Basic Books.

Gruhl, John. 1980. The Supreme Court's impact on the law of libel: Compliance by lower federal courts. *Western Political Quarterly* 33:502-519.

Hagan, John Patrick. 1986. The impact of political change and role conflict on state supreme courts: Case study of a court in transition. Paper delivered at the annual meeting of the American Political Science Association, Washington, D.C.

Hale, George E. 1979. The federal courts and the state budgetary process. *Administration and Society* 11:357-368.

Hansen, Susan B. 1980. State implementation of Supreme Court decisions: Abortion rates since *Roe v. Wade. Journal of Politics* 42:372-395.

Hanson, Roger, and Robert Crew. 1973. The policy impact of reapportionment. *Law and Society Review* 8:69-94.

Harriman, Linda, and Jeffrey D. Straussman. 1983. Do judges determine budget decisions? Federal court decisions in prison reform cases and state spending. *Public Administration Review* 43:343-351.

Henschen, Beth. 1983. Statutory interpretations of the Supreme Court: Congressional response. *American Politics Quarterly* 11:441-458.

Jenson, Carol E. 1982. *The network of control: State supreme courts and state security statutes, 1920-1970*. Westport, Conn.: Greenwood Press.

Johnson, Charles A. 1979a. Judicial decisions and organizational change. *Law and Society Review* 14:27-56.

———. 1979b. Lower court reactions to Supreme Court decisions: A quantitative examination. *American Journal of Political Science* 23:792-804.

———. 1987. Content analytic techniques and judicial research. *American Politics Quarterly* 15:169-197.

Johnson, Charles A., and Bradley C. Canon. 1984. *Judicial policies: Implementation and impact*. Washington, D.C.: CQ Press.

Johnson, Richard. 1967. *The dynamics of compliance*. Evanston, Ill.: Northwestern University Press.

Krislov, Samuel, K. O. Boyum, Jerry N. Clark, and Roger C. Shaefer, eds. 1971. *Compliance and the law: A multidisciplinary approach*. Beverly Hills, Calif.: Sage.

Lefstein, Norman, Vaughan Stapleton, and Lee Teitelbaum. 1969. In search of juvenile justice: *Gault* and its implementation. *Law and Society Review* 3:491-562.

Lehne, Richard. 1978. *The quest for justice: The politics of school finance reform*. New York: Longman.

Levine, James P. 1969. Constitutional law and obscene literature: An investigation of bookseller practices. In *The impact of Supreme Court decisions,* ed. Theodore Becker. New York: Oxford University Press.

_____. 1970. Methodological concerns in studying Supreme Court efficacy. *Law and Society Review* 4:583-611.

Lipset, Seymour M. 1960. *Political man.* New York: Doubleday.

March, James, and Herbert Simon. 1958. *Organizations.* New York: Wiley.

Marquart, James W., and Ben W. Crouch. 1985. Judicial reform and prisoner control: The impact of *Ruiz v. Estelle* on a Texas penitentiary. *Law and Society Review* 20:557-586.

McCubbins, Matthew, and Thomas Schwartz. 1988. Congress, the courts and public policy: Consequences of the one man, one vote rule. *American Journal of Political Science* 32:388-415.

Medalie, Richard, Leonard Zeitz, and Paul Alexander. 1968. Custodial interrogation in our nation's capital: The attempt to implement *Miranda. Michigan Law Review* 66:1347-1422.

Meier, Kenneth J., Joseph Stewart, Jr., and Robert E. England. 1990. *Race, class and education: The politics of second generation discrimination.* Madison: University of Wisconsin Press.

Milner, Neal A. 1971. *The court and local law enforcement.* Beverly Hills, Calif.: Sage.

Moss, Kathryn. 1985. The catalytic effect of a federal court decision on a state legislature. *Law and Society Review* 20:147-155.

Muir, William K., Jr. 1967. *Prayer in the public schools: Law and attitude change.* Chicago: University of Chicago Press.

Murphy, Walter. 1959. Lower court checks on Supreme Court power. *American Political Science Review* 53:1017-1031.

_____. 1962. *Congress and the Court.* Chicago: University of Chicago Press.

Murphy, Walter, and Joseph Tanenhaus. 1968. Public opinion and the Supreme Court: A preliminary mapping of some prerequisites for Court legitimation of regime changes. *Law and Society Review* 2:357-384.

Patric, Gordon. 1957. The impact of a court decision: Aftermath of the *McCullom* case. *Journal of Public Law* 6:455-464.

Peltason, Jack. 1961. *Fifty-eight lonely men: Southern judges and school desegregation.* New York: Harcourt, Brace and World.

Porter, Mary Cornelia. 1982. State supreme courts and the legacy of the Warren Court: Some old inquiries for a new situation. In *State supreme courts: Policymakers in the federal system,* ed. Mary Cornelia Porter and G. Alan Tarr. Westport, Conn.: Greenwood Press.

Pritchett, C. Herman. 1961. *Congress versus the Supreme Court, 1957-1960.* Minneapolis: University of Minnesota Press.

Reid, Traciel V. 1988. Judicial policy-making and implementation: An empirical examination. *Western Political Quarterly* 41:509-527.

Rodgers, Harrell, Jr., and Charles S. Bullock III. 1972. *Law and social change.* New York: McGraw-Hill.

_____. 1976a. *Coercion to compliance.* Lexington, Mass.: Heath.

_____. 1976b. School desegregation: A multivariate test of the role of law in effectuating social change. *American Politics Quarterly* 4:153-175.

Rossell, Christine H. 1976. School desegregation and white flight. *Political Science Quarterly* 90:675-695.

Schmidhauser, John, Larry L. Berg, and Albert Melone. 1971. The impact of judicial decisions: New dimensions in Supreme Court-congressional relations, 1945-1968. *Washington University Law Quarterly* 1971:209-251.

Schubert, Glendon. 1962. The 1960 term of the Supreme Court: A psychological analysis. *American Political Science Review* 56:90-107.

Shapiro, Martin. 1968. *The Supreme Court and administrative agencies.* New York: Free Press.

Skolnick, Jerome H. 1966. *Justice without trial.* New York: Wiley.

Songer, Donald. 1987. The impact of the Supreme Court on trends in economic policy making in the United States courts of appeals. *Journal of Politics* 49:830-844.

———. 1988a. Alternate approaches to the study of judicial impact: *Miranda* in five state courts. *American Politics Quarterly* 16:425-444.

———. 1988b. Case selection in judicial impact research. *Western Political Quarterly* 41:569-582.

Sorauf, Frank J. 1959. *Zorach v. Clauson:* The impact of a Supreme Court decision. *American Political Science Review* 53:777-791.

Spiotto, James E. 1973. Search and seizure: An empirical study of the exclusionary rule and its alternatives. *Journal of Legal Studies* 2:243-278.

Stumpf, Harry P. 1966. The political efficacy of judicial symbolism. *Western Political Quarterly* 19:293-303.

Tarr, G. Alan. 1977. *Judicial impact and state supreme courts.* Lexington, Mass.: Heath.

Wainscott, Stephen, and J. David Woodward. 1988. Second thoughts on second generation discrimination: Resegregation in schools. *American Politics Quarterly* 16:171-192.

Wald, Michael S., R. Ayers, D. W. Hess, M. Schantz, and C. W. Whitebread II. 1967. Interrogations in New Haven: The impact of *Miranda. Yale Law Journal* 76:1519-1648.

Wasby, Stephen. 1970. *The impact of the United States Supreme Court: Some perspectives.* Homewood, Ill.: Dorsey Press.

———. 1973. The communication of the Supreme Court's criminal procedure decisions. *Villanova Law Review* 18:1086-1118.

———. 1976. *Small town police and the Supreme Court.* Lexington, Mass.: Heath.

Way, Frank H., Jr. 1968. Survey research on judicial decisions: The prayer and Bible reading cases. *Western Political Quarterly* 21:189-205.

Way, Frank H., Jr., and Barbara J. Burt. 1983. Religious marginality and the free exercise clause. *American Political Science Review* 77:652-665.

Wirt, Frederick. 1970. *The politics of southern equality: Law and social change in a Mississippi county.* Chicago: Aldine.

Part VI

CONCLUSION

It is confessed, that the utmost effort of human reason is to reduce the principles, productive of natureal phenomena, to a greater simplicity, and to resolve the many particular effects into a few general causes, by means of reasonings from analogy, experience, and observation.

—David Hume
An Enquiry Concerning Human Understanding, 1748

The concluding chapter in this book offers a discussion of issues that are of particular interest to social scientists—theory and methods. It also addresses a new perspective in political science, which has come to be known as the new institutionalism. To students in law and political science, these topics may appear to be esoteric. Compared with the subjects of previous chapters, they are not well connected to the real world of politics, judicial decision making, or judicial policies. Nevertheless, it is important to address theory and methods.

Theories are composed of concepts that are related in some logical fashion based either on assumptions or on other relationships that are thought to be true. Their function in science is to offer explanations of why something does or does not occur, or how one set of forces influences another. Theory is important because it offers more than mere description for something of interest to us. To say that judges make decisions is an obvious descriptive fact. To say that they make decisions based on their psychological makeup is a rudimentary theory to explain why different judges may render different decisions in similar cases. Thus, the "explanation" of judicial decision making might be that a particular judge's decisions usually favor the prosecution because he or she is a conservative Republican.

Because theories force us to identify factors that explain other events, they serve the important function of offering lines of demarcation for what we know and when we will know it. Theories are good only insofar as they may be tested empirically. In previous chapters, authors have discussed research findings that confirmed (or in some instances disconfirmed) expectations about theoretical relationships. Thus, a theory will set forth the basis by which it can be evaluated. If hypothesized relationships are confirmed, then we may have confidence in the explanatory value of the theory and its potential applicability to other events or relationships.

Testing theories that involve empirical analysis requires more than passing attention to methodological issues. How one collects the data, what the data actually represent, and whether the data are potentially reproducible by someone else are important concerns. The findings reported in previous chapters are presumed not to be unique to the individual researchers who discovered them. In reporting their findings, researchers assume that anyone could have found the same relationship with the same data using the same analysis. There may be questions about whether the data were appropriate and whether the correct statistical analyses were used. If, however, the researchers pay attention to the reliability of the data, then fundamental questions about their authenticity are not likely to be raised. Indeed, the scientific process presumes sensitivity to these theoretical and methodological issues, as is discussed in Chapter 18 by John Gates.

Most theories are incomplete in that they do not explain all events or all relationships. There are exceptions to the well-established finding that judicial attitudes influence judicial decisions. Until we have a Theory of Everything Judicial, the clash of theories or the introduction of new theoretical perspectives will be welcome. Challenges to existing theories or new explanations for as yet unexplained events are important because they sharpen existing explanations and enable us to understand relationships more completely. John Gates identifies one such new perspective in this chapter: new institutionalism. This perspective introduces a new set of concerns for us to consider in explaining judicial events and behavior. Basically, the perspective calls for consideration of institutional effects and of broad-based social and historical effects when explaining political activities. This perspective challenges existing explanations of judicial behavior, for example, as being too limited and as examining too narrow a range of activities. It remains an open question whether this new perspective will ultimately broaden our understanding of things judicial, but it will at least challenge our current thinking about the research reported in this book.

18. THEORY, METHODS, AND THE NEW INSTITUTIONALISM IN JUDICIAL RESEARCH

John B. Gates

Theory and Methods: An Overview

Contemporary social science theory seeks explanation. The exact definition of social science theory remains unclear due to different views of the world and continued debate on the definition, goals, and boundaries of social scientific explanation (see Lakotos and Musgrave 1970; Suppes 1984; Graham 1986; Ricci 1984; Seidelman and Harpham 1985; MacRae 1986; Ball 1987; Dryzek and Leonard 1988). What all theories have in common is that they are made up of interrelated propositions that explain some phenomenon. Several perspectives on social science research have gained currency. These emphasize different factors, such as individual psychology, logical reasoning, organizational dynamics, socioeconomic change, or the character of institutions and rules.[1]

It is usual in the social sciences to distinguish between normative theory and empirical theory. Normative theories examine questions surrounding what should be the proper behavior of institutions and actors or the proper character of decisions and policies (see, generally, Pennock 1979, Perry 1982, Halpern and Lamb 1982, 129-270; Edelman 1984). Students of the judiciary devote considerable energy to examining the scope of rights and the meaning of justice, as well as to prescribing appropriate court behavior (Horowitz 1977; but see Neely 1981), and have focused particularly on the U.S. Supreme Court (see Berger 1977; Brigham 1987; Choper 1980; Ely 1980; Perry 1982). Normative theories are usually evaluated by methods such as logical reasoning or interpretative and historical analysis. This book has not examined normative theories directly, although many of the chapters and the findings discussed have important implications for normative

I appreciate the comments of Philip Dubois and Charles Johnson as well as their patience in subsequent discussions on many of the issues in this chapter. In addition, I would like to thank Charles Dannehl, Melinda Gann Hall, Scott Hill, and Rogers Smith for their comments on earlier drafts.

questions. Studies in areas such as judicial recruitment, policy making, and external pressures on the judicial process have significant implications for perennial debates over majority rule, accountability, and other democratic values.

The primary focus of the chapters is on empirical theories for explaining the behavior and processes of American courts.[2] Each chapter seeks to explain—and even predict—the actions, trends, and development of judicial actors and institutions. Analysts who test propositions arising from empirical theories may use qualitative methods for gathering evidence, such as interpretative and historical analysis, or quantitative methods that rely upon reliable and valid measures of the concepts of interest. Through appropriate measurement and statistical techniques quantitative analysts can often make precise estimates of relationships.[3]

In the study of judicial politics, both qualitative and quantitative scholars interested in empirical theoretical development attempt to understand and explain the norms and behavior of the actors and processes surrounding legal institutions. Unfortunately, judicial research includes many analyses divorced from either type of research. These works describe rather than prescribe or explain. As I note below, descriptive analysis is only a precursor to theory, albeit an important one. For those who seek theoretical explanation of the norms and behaviors in the judicial process, descriptive analysis is not a substitute for theory or theoretical development.[4] Some may argue that this point is obvious. The history and current state of judicial research, however, would imply otherwise (see especially Murphy and Tanenhaus 1972, 218; Gibson 1986, 146).

In recent years, there have been several assessments of theory, research, and the contemporary status of our collective knowledge of judicial politics (Baum 1983; Danelski 1983; Gibson 1983, 1986; O'Brien 1983; Provine 1988; Stumpf 1983; Shapiro 1983; Sarat 1983; Tate 1983). With few exceptions, the thinking is cautiously optimistic. In this chapter I argue that much can be learned from reflecting on the state of research on judicial politics in the United States. The following sections examine five major areas in the study of judicial politics. First, the proliferation of empirical theory appears to lag behind other fields in the discipline. Second, the field continues to emphasize the unique or idiographic character of courts, and scholars rarely employ the theoretical and conceptual perspectives that are becoming dominant in several unrelated fields of political science. Third, there have been some major methodological and conceptual developments that are distinctive to the subfield. Fourth, the field is still divided between those devoted to qualitative methodology and those seeking to develop empirical theory with more precise or quantitative methodologies. Finally, a recent and perhaps seminal attempt to reconcile the field is fraught with serious dangers (Smith 1988). This line of inquiry, the new institutionalism, is a discipline-wide movement that focuses on how institutional and long-term socioeconomic changes are part of a dynamic that is presumably ignored by current research.

The Development of Empirical Theory in Judicial Politics

Recent judicial research reflects many of the developments in the larger discipline. There has been a growing emphasis on empirical theory, increasing quantification, and the expanding use of statistical tools for precise measurement. This trend in political science generally began in the 1950s.[5]

A study of published judicial research in four prominent general political science journals from 1960 to 1987 finds that judicial research has moved toward estimating or gauging relationships more precisely (Hensley and Rhoads 1989).[6] This move consists of the quantification of theoretical concepts and the testing of probable relationships through statistical techniques which control for alternative explanations and assess the relative value of the explanatory concepts. The percentage of articles using such techniques increased from 27 percent over the decade of the 1960s to nearly 61 percent in the 1980-1987 period. In addition, the number of research projects involving more than a single researcher has grown in judicial politics and across all fields of political science. This is due, in part, to the intensive nature of data collection for most research projects that use quantitative evidence. In the 1960s, only 7 percent of the articles on judicial politics were co-authored. In the 1980-1987 period, the proportion of co-authored articles rose to nearly 30 percent. Finally, the relative attention to judicial politics in these journals did not wane: the percentage of all articles published was relatively consistent over nearly three decades (Hensley and Rhoads 1989).[7]

The researchers also found a growing number of articles based on empirical theoretical constructs. During the 1960s, such studies constituted only 13 percent of all judicial studies published in these journals, but the percentage increased to over 33 percent between 1980 and 1987. Some may take solace in this particular statistic as evidence of the congruence of the judicial politics subfield with other areas of political science; others may view the statistic with some chagrin. I estimated the percentage of articles employing empirical theoretical frameworks in nonjudicial areas of American politics because Hensley and Rhoads examined only published work on judicial politics. In the 1980-1987 period, over 80 percent of the articles on American politics employed such frameworks, compared with 33 percent for judicial articles.[8] This suggests that the study of judicial politics trails the study of American political phenomena in the attention to, and possible evolution of, empirical theory and the use of precise methodologies.

This statistical assessment is consistent with more detailed appraisals by several scholars in the 1980s. James Gibson (1983, 1986), for example, provides a thorough investigation of judicial research and argues there has been only "palpable progress" on a theoretical level (1986).[9] Moreover, he contends that the study of judicial politics is often insensitive to issues surrounding different levels of analysis. Analysts repeatedly examine the policy decisions of particular courts at the macro or aggregate level and argue that these changes are the result of changes at the individual level without examining this micro-level behavior.[10] Examining multiple or competing cross-level explanations is important because policy changes may reflect larger environmental processes such as social or economic change or changes in the individual judge. For example, relating socioeconomic change to changes in a particular court would portray the individual judges as unobtrusive conduits for such societal forces. Viewed at the individual level, however, policy changes may instead reflect changes in the judges' perceptions or philosophy, or simply changes in the composition of particular courts (see Dubois 1988). Regardless of the underlying factors and precise causal theory, greater attention to the individual-level behavior could aid in understanding macro- or aggregate-level decision making. The lack of cross-level analysis looms large in judicial research according to many analysts; it remains a problem in several other areas of political science as well (Kramer 1983).

The Focus on Idiographic Theory

A number of studies focus on how courts and participants in the judicial process are different from other actors and institutions. This emphasis on idiographic theory is particularly troubling and pervasive in the judicial field. Many would argue that the development of generalizable principles is contingent not upon emphasizing how institutions, actors, or rules are unique but instead upon discerning similarities for generalizing about political behavior. Certainly, attention to the differences between courts and other institutions is necessary. Nevertheless, the explanation and possible prediction of political behavior will develop by emphasizing how institutions and processes are similar. The chapters in this book illustrate vividly how courts are subject to the same types of institutional, social, and individual pressures as legislatures and executives. This includes such diverse areas as public opinion, socioeconomic change, and interest groups. The form and possibly the substance of such relationships may be different in the judicial arena. Nevertheless, it is perhaps most profitable to begin with the goal of drawing cross-institutional comparisons of the dynamics of political behavior.

It is also peculiar that judicial scholars devote little attention to applying or discussing some growing—and, by many accounts, major—theoretical perspectives in American politics. This is especially curious since perspectives on the judicial process are drawn from areas such as organizational, attitudinal, and group theories. For example, judicial research is less than attentive to developments in rational or public choice or variants of game theory, approaches that have a growing influence in the discipline (Brams 1985; Mueller 1979). There are exceptions in the judicial field. Walter Murphy's (1964) early work set forth many propositions consistent with the logic of a rational/public choice perspective, as did David Rohde (1972). Yet for over a decade, the rational choice perspective was applied to judicial processes only in the modeling of caseload.

The 1980s saw some renewed efforts along the path explored earlier by Murphy and Rohde. Harold Spaeth (1985) presented tests of propositions regarding Supreme Court decisions based on a rational choice perspective on decision making in committees. Jeffrey Segal (1984) borrows the concept of bounded rationality to explore how judges simplify choices in deciding cases. Nonetheless, researchers in judicial politics seem much less attentive to the potential strengths and weaknesses of these perspectives.

Methodological and Conceptual Advances

There have been some important, if little discussed, developments in the judicial field, including significant methodological and conceptual advances. First, judicial scholars have become increasingly aware of issues of reliable data; that is, information that can be recorded or collected by other analysts with identical results. For instance, it has been common to categorize judicial opinions or decisions as raising issues such as "civil liberties" and classifying the outcome in ideological terms (liberal or conservative). Recently, analysts used systematic content analysis, which can guarantee reliable data. This includes the classification of opinions, case outcomes, and off-the-bench judicial statements (Johnson 1987; Gates 1987, forthcoming; Segal and Cover 1989). Data reliability affirms that other analysts can replicate the information under similar conditions and ensures that the data constitute variations in real phenomena. The concern with reliability and the application of necessary controls in judicial studies are important and often absent in other subfields of the discipline.[11]

A second important advance is both methodological and conceptual. Lawrence Baum (1988) has presented a design and method for examining ideological change on the U.S. Supreme Court which is also applicable to other decision-making bodies (see also Segal 1986). Studies of judicial decision making often assume that any change in a judge's response to a class of cases (such as civil liberties) represents the judge's changing philosophy or values. This assumes that the types of cases are unchanging. Yet there are sound reasons for arguing that the types of cases are time bound in the sense that specific case content as well as the circumstances surrounding a class of cases changes over time. Hence, fluctuations in a justice's changing support for particular claims may come about not because of a change in the individual justice but because of differences in the content of the cases. Baum offers an important remedy that affords a comparison of individual change and changes in a broad class of cases.

In addition, recent research demonstrates a much needed focus on the analysis of judicial phenomena outside of the contemporary period (see Walker, Epstein, and Dixon 1988). Contemporary courts are tempting targets for researchers since analysts can usually avoid the pitfalls associated with limited recorded data, records, or interview sources. Nonetheless, it is necessary to apply our theoretical frameworks across a longitudinal time frame.

Moreover, there is an apparent increase in the developing and testing of hypotheses beyond American courts to the comparative context (Schmidhauser 1987), despite some formidable theoretical challenges (Tate 1987). Burton Atkins (1987) provides, for example, an analysis of British trial court success rates for different types of litigants guided by Marc Galanter's (1974) concern with the experience and resources of the litigants.

The increasing attention to issues of reliability in the collection of information, conceptual problems in the study of decision making, and a comparative and longitudinal focus are important and noteworthy developments that are distinctive to the judicial field. Writing in 1983, C. Neal Tate observed that the field had progressed on conceptual and methodological grounds but with only marginal gains. Almost a decade later, it appears that judicial scholars have made some important and significant progress on these levels. This is a sign of continued and serious reflection on the state of judicial politics.

The Separation of Quantitative and Qualitative Analysis

Despite the advances noted above, recent assessments observe continuing problems for judicial research and suggest that the study of judicial politics is alienated from the study of American politics generally. Baum describes this alienation as follows:

> Within the broader field of American politics . . . [judicial politics] seems to be unusually distinctive in that it is both more isolated and closer to unique in its characteristics than are most other fields. This was not always true; early in this century judicial politics by its various names was somewhere near the center of the study of politics, because of the legalistic approach that pervaded so many fields. But gradually the rest of political science drifted away from a concern with law, thereby severing a link with the judicial politics field. With that link gone, for several decades there has been something of a gulf between judicial politics and other fields of political science. (1983, 197)

Baum argues that the distinctive nature of the field results from attitudes engendered by the unique structural and procedural aspects of courts.[12] Also, he sees this detachment as producing certain benefits, including the development of strong interdisciplinary ties.[13]

Baum concludes his survey of the fifteen years of research preceding 1982 by stating: "Researchers do . . . need to be more self-conscious about their work and how it is building toward a general understanding of courts and of politics. Given our limited scholarly resources, we ought to use them as effectively as possible" (1983, 207).

The separation of the study of judicial politics from that of American politics is, as noted by many, unfortunate and may inhibit the development of theory in judicial research. Baum (1983, 207) argues that the slow theoretical progress is due to the sheer size of the task. I would argue that progress has been impeded by another gulf—the gulf between judicial scholars who focus on constitutional law, normative questions, and interpretive methods of inquiry and those who focus on process and behavior, empirical questions, and noninterpretive or quantitative methodologies. We can label it diversity but every judicial researcher knows that the discipline's division in the 1960s over the relative attention to qualitative and quantitative methodologies has left judicial politics particularly damaged.[14] Many other fields are more eclectic. For example, scholars of Congress or bureaucratic regulation regularly cite, discuss, and build on the work of others in their field regardless of whether qualitative or quantitative research strategies are the central focus.[15] Methodological pluralism in other fields in American politics has led to some degree of theoretical development. For whatever reason, there is much less interaction among judicial scholars using different research methods than is seen in the field of American politics generally.[16]

In a 1982 symposium on judicial research, a panel of scholars discussed this division, and many were critical. David O'Brien (1983, 561) argues, for example, that there is a need to unite normative jurisprudence with "positive political analysis." On the other hand, Martin Shapiro argues that the integration of these concerns is not necessary, and may be undesirable—the field of moral philosophy can adequately encompass normative questions. The continuing focus on jurisprudential questions could be the focus of the separate field of political theory, according to Shapiro. Moreover, he lamented the apparent increasing interest in these questions by junior judicial scholars.

Although it may be impossible to reconcile these different approaches, a sensitivity and receptivity to the diversity of approaches could aid the sharing of knowledge for explanation and theory building. The foremost drawback to implementing Shapiro's suggestion would be the continued lack of exchange between qualitative and quantitative scholars.

One example of the benefits of interaction between approaches is seen in the perennial debate over the democratic character of Supreme Court policy making. A persistent question in the study of the U.S. Supreme Court is whether Court policy making is consistent with democratic values. Since the Supreme Court established the power of judicial review in *Marbury v. Madison* (1803), unelected justices have possessed the power to overturn the actions of the popularly elected branches. Some argue that certain constitutional checks serve to reconcile the preferences of the justices with those of the majority. One of the primary constitutional checks is presidential appointment. There have been empirical studies to assess how successful presidents have been in obtaining "likeminded" justices.

David Rohde and Harold Spaeth (1976) showed that presidents were successful over 75 percent of the time in obtaining justices supportive of their policy positions as gauged by the president's party affiliation.[17] Unfortunately, normative debates that rely on examples rather than systematic evidence continue to emphasize presidential "mistakes" in discounting the political control argument. For example, John Ely argues: "It has proven hard to predict how someone in another line of work will function as a justice and sometimes one wonders whether the appointee who turns out differently from the President who appointed him expected is not the rule rather than the exception" (1980, 47). This is a mistaken premise for normative theory and its evaluation. Qualitative scholars can avoid basing their arguments on empirically falsified premises and assertions through attention to the work of scholars devoted to quantitative methods.[18]

Conversely, empirical theorists can often learn a great deal from the work of qualitative or normative scholars. This is important in the propagation of new hypotheses.[19] In addition, quantitative scholars can avoid serious and embarrassing assumptions that are disputed by the descriptive data that are part of, but by no means the end of, the best qualitative research. H. W. Perry (1990) found through interviews with several justices of the Supreme Court that conference decision-making procedures in the contemporary Court are different from the process described in textbooks. Researchers interested in explaining the votes of the justices based upon an incorrect description of conference procedures would hardly contribute to knowledge of conference behavior, despite any statistical elegance in their explanatory model.

Integrating Quantitative and Qualitative Studies through the New Institutionalism?

The complete integration of quantitative and qualitative approaches is generally thought to be impossible because each approach is more or less connected to its respective theory. Empirical theory and normative theory are fundamentally different.[20] Other fields have shown that symbiosis is both necessary and possible. Greater interaction between quantitative and qualitative judicial researchers is what Rogers Smith recently attempted to foster. He argued in a provocative essay (Smith 1988) that a new perspective on understanding politics could reconcile this gulf. Smith's analysis of the new institutionalism may be one of the most important attempts to repair the rift among judicial scholars. Although it could be read to argue for greater descriptive research, Smith's proposal has one dominant and overriding goal: the accumulation of knowledge to help us explain the judicial world. His goal is in the domain of generalization and the testing and evaluation of normative and empirical theories; it is not in the realm of particularistic description.

The New Institutionalism in Political Science

Recently, political science has seen a new theoretical perspective for understanding politics. James March and Johan Olsen (1984, 1989) label the approach "the new institutionalism." [21] This perspective focuses not so much on the pluralistic interplay of political forces as it does on how institutions and larger structures dynamically shape the choices made in the political process.

The new institutionalism developed in part as a reaction to the prevailing understanding of politics as a pluralistic process and drew additional reinforcement from perspectives that emphasize nonindividual or systemic forces for political change (March and Olsen

1989; Smith 1988, 90-97). Most contemporary American political scientists assume that understanding political choices involves the analysis of the clash of various interests, including government (such as judges on the U.S. Circuit Courts of Appeals), individuals (such as an individual filing a lawsuit in small claims court), and groups (such as the American Civil Liberties Union or the National Rifle Association). Political choices from a pluralistic perspective indicate only the result of an aggregation of preferences in the political process. These preferences or interests are givens. Although debate persists on how well this aggregation of preferences reflects the desires of the majority (Bachrach 1967; Manley 1983; Olson 1965), most political scientists continue to assume that individuals, groups, and public officials have specific, predetermined policy preferences that are independent of institutions and "deep structures" such as broad-scale social and economic change.[22] The institution or its decision is most profitably understood through understanding the structure and development of conflicts over these preferences. Institutions and their procedures and norms serve only to structure in various ways the expression of predetermined preferences (Shepsle 1979).

The new institutionalism challenges the conventional mode of political analysis by arguing that institutions as well as social and economic "structures" are not static receptacles of the battle of interests. Institutions may shape or change the preferences of the actors in the political process. Taking the preferences as a given in the process of making political choices may not capture the entire process. Institutions and their previous decisions, as well as social and economic structures, can shape the preferences in the policy-making process over time.[23] Hence, a complete picture of the policy-making process would include the institutional/structural factors that can change the form, nature, and expression of preferences. Seen through the eyes of the new institutionalism, politics involves more than the aggregation of societal interests; institutions and deep structures may affect the very nature of the preferences in a longitudinal and dynamic fashion. Smith writes:

> Ideally, then, a full account of an important political event would consider both the ways the context of "background" institutions influenced the political actions in question, and the ways in which those actions altered relevant contextual structures or institutions. (1988, 91)

This is an important point; perhaps proponents of the new institutionalism are correct. Pluralistic perspectives may neglect a potentially important dynamic in the political process. For instance, judicial decisions on standing may reflect the interaction of the types of individuals or groups seeking access to the courts, the prevailing political climate regarding such groups, or the support or lack of support for such interests by certain judges or justices. The new institutionalism would also concern itself with how these decisions possibly create societal expectations regarding standing and change the political agenda of groups outside of the specific decision or the behavior of judges. As March and Olsen (1984, 1989) argue, institutions as well as social and economic structures may influence the relative resources available to political actors as well as their sense of purpose, norms, and values. In sum, contemporary approaches to understanding politics treat political institutions as merely a reflection of exogenous or external forces that impinge on these institutions with predetermined preferences or viewpoints.

The New Institutionalism and Judicial Politics

Smith notes that judicial research should assimilate the "enduring structures of human conduct that have shaped the existing array of resources, rules, and values, instead of simply taking that array as a given" (1988, 98). The new institutionalism would not dismiss the current, essentially pluralistic, focus on political explanation, which assumes that preferences are external to the policy-making process. Smith argues that interaction and cooperation are possible. The result would be a theoretical perspective that provides fertile soil in which both qualitative and quantitative students of the judicial process could indeed grow toward an explanation of the patterns or causes of judicial affairs. Quantitative scholars would presumably reap the benefit of several new and testable hypotheses regarding judicial behavior. Qualitative scholars could build upon the expanding body of empirical theory in the uncovering and analysis of institutions and deeper structures. Smith admits at least two difficulties with such a recommendation and offers some suggestions for avoiding a theoretical impasse. First, the new institutionalism could lead analysts away from the pluralistic perspective, which has contributed a great deal to the explanation of political processes; it might produce the belief that the interplay or conflict of interests is irrelevant to understanding politics when one examines the institutional or systemic forces underlying political decisions. Smith believes that analysts need not ignore one perspective while being attentive to another.

Second, the view of policy making provided by the new institutionalism is extremely dynamic. Policy decisions purportedly reflect deeper structures, individual choices, institutional norms, group pressures, contemporary social values, and so on. Hence, "everything is somehow connected to everything else" (Smith 1988, 101). This is particularly troublesome. The testing of relationships and their relative importance to the theoretical construct becomes convoluted, and the analyst may be drawn too close to exploratory and descriptive research.

In order to allay fears that would be of concern to any analyst interested in explanation, Smith has several suggestions. Quantitative judicial scholars, for example, should add structures to their list of theoretically relevant factors. For example, students of policy change on courts should consider not only how judges' preferences affect decision making but also how institutional context and larger social changes affect these decisions. The impact of institutional structures on the rules, norms, and values of actors in the judicial process and the integration of long-term forces may be necessary.

Smith is optimistic regarding the power of the new institutionalism.

> We would not regard scholars who try to see how far ideological structures shape judicial decisions and scholars who analyze the impact of party realignments or appointive processes as engaged in sharply opposed enterprises. That sense of common endeavor might make qualitative scholars more aware of the need to connect their claims with measured patterns in actual decision making, and it might also promote quantitative studies more sensitive to the complex conceptual structures and characteristics of political beliefs. (1988, 104)

Unfortunately, empirical scholars will want to know much more regarding the parameters of these deeper structures.[24] Smith recognizes this potential problem. The definition or operationalization of these structures does not at present lend itself to the rigor demanded of a science of politics. His second recommendation is especially difficult.

Smith contends there is a need for analysts to seek a greater understanding by examining the "origins of the structures of institutions" (1988, 102). Scholars should examine the background of courts, or their social context, in order to understand the context of the institution and its choices. Given the problems qualitative and quantitative judicial scholars will confront in defining and incorporating this concept into their more precise models, this suggestion appears crucial for the new institutionalism. It is also very dangerous. This call may lead young scholars, perhaps undertaking their first major research project, to conduct purely descriptive research as a building block for future research. Such research would have only the veneer of theoretical or explanatory value. It is not moving toward explanation or the propagation of new hypotheses. Smith's proposal is worthy of future discussion and reflection, but the type of research proposed by Smith should be approached with caution.[25] Researchers should remember that Smith's purpose is the generation of specific and clearly defined hypotheses. This is essential if the new institutionalism is to foster interaction in the judicial field similar to that found in other areas of American politics.

Until the character of structures is clarified, we could witness a flurry of merely descriptive research with few advances in the generation of hypotheses regarding the relative explanatory value of choice verses the dynamics of preferences and deep structures. A careless application of this perspective to judicial politics could cast the field even further outside of the concerns of most political scientists who focus on American politics.[26]

Conclusion

Recent assessments of the judicial field reflect a continuing self-analysis, and much of this analysis is somber (but see Baum 1983). The field remains distinctive in a variety of ways (Baum 1983), and there are many lingering problems. The proliferation of empirical theory, for example, appears to lag behind other fields in the discipline, and theoretical perspectives that are growing dominant in several unrelated fields of political science are often neglected by judicial researchers. Moreover, the field continues to evidence a division that is sometimes as intense and disheartening as the debate over behavioralism in political science in the 1960s. Nevertheless, there have been some important methodological and conceptual advances for empirical theory.

C. Herman Pritchett once noted that judicial scholars should "let a thousand flowers bloom" (1968, 509). Baum concluded his assessment of judicial research by noting how this was noble and sage advice only if the field recognized that we should be very conscious of the floral arrangement we were making (1983, 207).

Smith's proposal to consider the new institutionalism as a common ground for quantitative and qualitative scholars offers one possible avenue toward reconciliation. It is, however, fraught with risks. By focusing on the origins of deep structures, there is the possibility that analysts will engage in merely descriptive research. This focus will divert, distract, and alienate judicial politics from the primary goal of generating and testing carefully grounded hypotheses. It would be wise to consider the new institutionalism as a possible common ground for scholars interested in normative and empirical theory. We should not forget, however, that scientific theory seeks explanation.

Notes

1. I am avoiding many interesting and complex questions in the philosophy of science. A good overview of the development and current status of many

of the issues in social science and political science can be found in Fiske and Shweder 1986 and Graham 1986.

2. I use the term *empirical theory* in a very broad sense, incorporating what Weisberg (1986, 3-5) labels formal theory (which seeks understanding through a set of principles), predictive theory (which emphasizes the need for our explanations to predict future behavior), and dynamic theory (which focuses upon the factors associated with change rather than the status quo).

3. Two of the most important goals in testing empirical theory are to have reliable and valid research methods. Reliable methods are those that produce data that can be replicated by other analysts—information gathered in the same way will give the same results. On the other hand, valid data are true pictures of the phenomena identified by the theory. This may seem at first to be a minor concern when one thinks of a chemist dealing with unambiguous materials. In the social sciences, questions of validity are often less than straightforward; consider the concepts "social alienation" or "policy innovation." Gibson (1986, 142-146) details other elements in the normal science perspective on judicial politics.

Underlying this perspective are some important assumptions about knowledge. Most research in political science assumes that there are regularities of behavior and we can understand these regularities with some type of causal as opposed to probabilistic explanation. This is certainly reflected in the long and continuing debate over when statistical tests of significance are necessary when one is studying the entire population versus a sample of that population. One of the most interesting and succinct summaries of this question is found in Brady 1988.

4. I am treading on admittedly controversial ground, and there are sophisticated debates in the hermeneutical school of philosophy that would suggest this position is incorrect. There are also ethnomethodological studies of the judicial process (Ryan et al. 1980). This research design is based in part on hermeneutics (see especially Mehan and Wood 1975). The goal of such research is to discover and to describe social behavior. This position turns contemporary social science on its head by arguing that behavior is not generalizable and understanding social phenomena is very individualistic. There are no agreed upon conceptions of reality and constructions of the world. Thus it is impossible to employ the scientific method to the social world.

This is an interesting position, given the fact that many of our most powerful models of political behavior cannot account or predict with the same degree of accuracy as most studies in the natural sciences. Meehl 1986 provides a different and equally intriguing perspective on the differences between the natural and social sciences. It is unusual because it takes a postpositivist intellectual stance. The dominance of a particular epistemological position for normal science is provided by Kuhn's classic analysis of the history of science (1970, 92-135.)

5. On the dynamics of scientific ideology, see Kuhn 1970 (pp. 92-135).

6. The journals used include: *American Journal of Political Science, American Political Science Review, Journal of Politics,* and *Western Political Quarterly.*

7. Moreover, the Law, Courts, and Judicial Process Section of the American Political Science Association (APSA) is currently the largest organized section of the APSA.

8. This is an estimate based upon my examination of the four journals used in the Hensley and Rhoads 1988 study. It is merely an estimate because only a brief description of an "empirical theoretical framework" was provided by the authors. Hence, this figure is probably unreliable, but the magnitude of difference is more than suggestive of the incongruence between judicial and American politics as gauged by the relative attention to empirical theory.

9. Gibson's assessment is broad and detailed. An adequate discussion is beyond the scope of this chapter.

10. It is often difficult to gauge the responses of individual judges to different cases in several appellate judicial settings. This is especially problematic for state appellate courts, which have low rates of formal dissent and hence little detectable variation in individual behavior. Dubois 1988 provides an innovative longitudinal approach which eliminates this problem and finds policy change consistent with personnel changes without individual voting data. Compare Atkins and Green 1976; Songer 1982; Epstein, Walker, and Dixon 1989; and Gibson's discussion in Chapter 10 of this book.

11. This issue is particularly relevant in the study of congressional behavior. It has been, however, a subject of much debate similar to that in the judicial arena (see Wilcox and Clausen 1989).

12. Sarat suggests that the lack of interaction between judicial politics and American politics scholars is also grounded in an attitude surrounding judicial scholars in the academic world. He writes: "When the scientists of our discipline thought of what we did they thought of constitutional law. We were for them the fake lawyers who serviced a traditional, some surely felt marginal, concern of political science, and who taught large undergraduate courses to students more interested in law school than social science theory" (1983, 552).

13. This is reflected in the publications of the *Law and Society Review* and the interdisciplinary interaction afforded by the annual meeting of the Law and Society Association. One could also argue that such interdisciplinary ties, when not connected to other fields of political science, could lead to further isolation for the study of judicial politics.

14. Why there is a lack of interaction among judicial scholars is an intriguing question. Shapiro 1983 elaborates on the connections. Smith 1988 is an important source of information on this disjunction, as noted in the discussion that follows.

15. Fenno's qualitative work (1978) on the constituency activity of members of Congress generated a great deal of more precise work including a major

empirical study of constituency service and electoral independence in the United States and Britain (Cain, Ferejohn, and Fiorina 1987).

16. This is, of course, my perception, but it is buttressed by examining how often normative studies cite empirical studies and vice versa. Epstein (1986, 1-2) also presents interesting and unsettling examples of the division from her experiences at professional meetings.

17. A more recent study shows even greater success by presidents if the presidents' preferences are measured through a content analysis of their public statements (Gates and Cohen 1988).

18. Pennock 1979 is an excellent example of normative work informed by quantitative empirical concerns.

19. Steamer's (1986) meticulous examination of the leadership styles of the chief justices of the Supreme Court is also a good example. Compare this work with an interesting diachronic study of dissent on the U.S. Supreme Court (Walker, Epstein, and Dixon 1988). Perry (1990) also discusses how quantitative scholars can benefit from greater interaction.

20. This is admittedly a modern view.

21. Shapiro (1989, 89, 98) questions the novel aspects of the new institutionalism.

22. For further elaboration on this connection, see Chapter 11, by Wayne McIntosh, in this book.

23. According to Smith, this problem is also apparent in the powerful tool of rational/public choice analysis. Here, institutions affect the expression of preferences (Shepsle 1979) but not the preferences themselves. Riker 1980 called for a return to the study of institutions and their role in politics. This was a call for an understanding of how institutions affect the expression of predetermined preferences. Riker did not discuss how institutions, norms, previous decisions, and social and economic change could affect the content of the preferences.

24. See Chapter 11 of this book.

25. Smith's essay generated serious concern by at least one normative analyst, who sees the proposal as limiting the scope of normative inquiry to certain types of questions (Barber 1989). The responses by Smith 1989 and Shapiro 1989 are also illuminating for issues outside of contemporary empirical social science theory.

26. The new institutionalism need not lead to a plethora of descriptive research. Brace and Hall 1990, for example, developed and empirically tested hypotheses on the variation of dissent rates on state courts of last resort. While premised on many assumptions derived from rational choice theory, they find that the institutional character of the courts was six times more important than the traditional explanations of the state courts' external environment (such as socioeconomic development, political party system) (p. 64). The institutional characteristics included court rules regarding the assigning of opinions, the selection process (appointive versus elective), the presence of an intermediate appellate court, and the court's voting rules.

In addition, Epstein, Walker, and Dixon (1989) focus on changes in institutional outputs by examining the voting of the Court (rather than individual justices) in cases involving the rights of criminal defendants. Factors such as the political composition of the Court and the priorities of the Court accounted for changes in support for the claims of criminally accused from 1946 through 1986. This work is quite sound in its attention to empirical theory and draws attention to institutional factors.

References

Atkins, Burton M. 1987. A cross-national perspective on the structuring of trial court outputs: The case of the English high court. In *Comparative judicial systems: Challenging frontiers in conceptual and empirical analysis,* ed. John R. Schmidhauser. London: Butterworths.

Atkins, Burton M., and Justin Green. 1976. Consensus on the United States courts of appeals: Illusion or reality? *American Journal of Political Science* 20:735-748.

Bachrach, Peter. 1967. *The theory of democratic elitism.* Boston: Little, Brown.

Ball, Terence, ed. 1987. *Idioms of inquiry: Critique and renewal in political science.* Albany: State University of New York Press.

Barber, Sotirios A. 1989. Normative theory, the "new institutionalism," and the future of public law. In *Studies in American political development,* vol. 3, ed. Karen Orren and Stephen Skowronek. New Haven: Yale University Press.

Baum, Lawrence. 1983. Judicial politics: Still a distinctive field. In *Political science: The state of the discipline,* ed. Ada W. Finifter. Washington, D.C.: American Political Science Association.

———. 1988. Measuring policy change in the U.S. Supreme Court. *American Political Science Review* 82:905-912.

Berger, Raoul. 1977. *Government by the judiciary.* Cambridge: Harvard University Press.

Brace, Paul, and Melinda Hall. 1990. Neo-institutionalism and dissent in state supreme courts. *Journal of Politics* 52:54-70.

Brady, Henry. 1988. Probability and political science. *The Political Methodologist* (newsletter of the Political Methodology Section, American Political Science Association) 2:5-8.

Brams, Steven J. 1985. *Rational politics: Decisions, games, and strategy.* Washington, D.C.: CQ Press.

Brigham, John. 1987. *The cult of the Court.* Philadelphia: Temple University Press.

Cain, Bruce, John Ferejohn, and Morris Fiorina. 1987. *The personal vote: Constituency service and electoral independence.* Cambridge, Mass.: Harvard University Press.

Choper, Jesse H. 1980. *Judicial review and the national political process.* Chicago: University of Chicago Press.

Danelski, David. 1983. Law from a political perspective. *Western Political Quarterly* 36:548-551.

Dryzek, John S., and Stephen T. Leonard. 1988. History and discipline in political science. *American Political Science Review* 82:1245-1260.

Dubois, Philip L. 1988. The illusion of judicial consensus revisited: Partisan conflict on an intermediate state court of appeals. *American Journal of Political Science* 32:946-967.

Edelman, Martin. 1984. *Democratic theories and the Constitution.* Albany: State University of New York Press.

Ely, John H. 1980. *Democracy and distrust: A theory of judicial review.* Cambridge, Mass.: Harvard University Press.

Epstein, Lee. 1986. Strategies of judicial research: Interviewing U.S. Supreme Court justices and interest group attorneys. Paper presented at the annual meeting of the Southern Political Science Association, Atlanta.

Epstein, Lee, Thomas G. Walker, and William J. Dixon. 1989. The Supreme Court and criminal justice disputes: A neo-institutional perspective. *American Journal of Political Science* 33:825-841.

Fenno, Richard. 1978. *Home style: House members and their districts.* Boston: Little, Brown.

Fiske, Donald W., and Richard A. Shweder. 1986. *Metatheory in social science: Pluralism and subjectivities.* Chicago: University of Chicago Press.

Galanter, Marc. 1974. Why the "haves" come out ahead: Speculations on the limits of legal change. *Law and Society Review* 9:95-160.

Gates, John B. 1987. Partisan realignment, unconstitutional state policies, and the U.S. Supreme Court, 1837-1964. *American Journal of Political Science* 31:259-280.

———. n.d. *The Supreme Court and partisan realignment: A macro and microlevel analysis.* Boulder, Colo.: Westview Press, forthcoming.

Gates, John B., and Jeffrey E. Cohen. 1988. Presidents, justices, and racial equality cases, 1954-1984. *Political Behavior* 10:22-36.

Gibson, James L. 1983. From simplicity to complexity: The development of theory in the study of judicial behavior. *Political Behavior* 5:7-49.

———. 1986. The social science of judicial politics. In *Political science: The science of politics,* ed. Herbert F. Weisberg. New York: Agathon Press.

Graham, George J. 1986. Philosophy of science. In *Annual review of political science,* ed. Samuel Long. Norwood, N.J.: Ablex.

Halpern, Stephen C., and Charles M. Lamb, eds. 1982. *Supreme Court activism and restraint.* Lexington, Mass.: Heath.

Hensley, Thomas R., and James C. Rhoads. 1988. Studying the studies: An assessment of judicial politics research in four major political science journals, 1960-1987. Paper presented at the annual meeting of the Southern Political Science Association, Atlanta.

Horowitz, Donald. 1977. *Courts and social policy.* Washington, D.C.: Brookings Institution.

Johnson, Charles A. 1987. Content-analytic techniques and judicial research. *American Politics Quarterly* 15:169-197.

Kramer, Gerald H. 1983. The ecological fallacy revisited: Aggregate- versus individual-level findings on economics and elections and sociotropic voting. *American Political Science Review* 77:92-112.

Kuhn, Thomas S. 1970. *The structure of scientific revolutions.* 2d ed., enlarged. Chicago: University of Chicago Press.

Lakatos, Imre, and Alan Musgrave. 1970. *Criticism and the growth of knowledge.* New York: Cambridge University Press.

MacRae, Duncan, Jr. 1986. The science of politics and its limits. In *Political science: The science of politics,* ed. Herbert Weisberg. New York: Agathon.

Manley, John. 1983. Neopluralism: A class analysis of pluralism I and pluralism II. *American Political Science Review* 77:368-384.

March, James G., and Johan P. Olsen. 1984. The new institutionalism: Organizational factors in political life. *American Political Science Review* 78:734-749.

————. 1989. *Rediscovering institutions: The organizational basis of politics.* New York: Free Press.

Meehl, P. E. 1986. What social scientists don't understand. In *Metatheory in social science: Pluralism and subjectivities,* ed. Donald W. Fiske and Richard A. Shweder. Chicago: University of Chicago Press.

Mehan, Hugh, and Houston Wood. 1975. *The reality of ethnomethodology.* New York: Wiley.

Mueller, Dennis C. 1979. *Public choice.* Cambridge: Cambridge University Press.

Murphy, Walter F. 1964. *The elements of judicial strategy.* Chicago: University of Chicago Press.

Murphy, Walter F., and Joseph Tanenhaus. 1972. *The study of public law.* New York: Random House.

Neely, Richard. 1981. *How courts govern America.* New Haven: Yale University Press.

O'Brien, David. 1983. Reconsidering whence and whither political jurisprudence. *Western Political Quarterly* 36:558-563.

Olson, Mancur. 1965. *The logic of collective action.* Cambridge, Mass.: Harvard University Press.

Pennock, J. Roland. 1979. *Democratic political theory.* Princeton: Princeton University Press.

Perry, H. W. 1990. Interviewing Supreme Court personnel. *Judicature* 73:199-200.

Perry, Michael. 1982. *The Constitution, the courts, and human rights.* New Haven: Yale University Press.

Pritchett, C. Herman. 1968. Public law and judicial behavior. *Journal of Politics* 30:480-509.

Provine, Marie. 1988. My views on Charlie's three questions. *Law, Courts, and Judicial Process Section Newsletter* (American Political Science Association) 5:11-14.

Ricci, David M. 1984. *The tragedy of political science: Politics, scholarship, and democracy.* New Haven: Yale University Press.

Riker, William H. 1980. Implications from the disequilibrium of majority rule for the study of institutions. *American Political Science Review* 74:432-436.

Rohde, David W. 1972. Policy goals and opinion coalitions. *Midwest Journal of Political Science* 16:208-224.

Rohde, David W., and Harold J. Spaeth. 1976. *Supreme Court decisionmaking.* San Francisco: Freeman.

Ryan, John Paul, Allan Ashman, Bruce D. Sales, and Sandra Shane-DuBow. 1980. *American trial judges: Their work styles and performance.* New York: Free Press.

Sarat, Austin. 1983. The maturation of political jurisprudence. *Western Political Quarterly* 36:551-558.

Schmidhauser, John R., ed. 1987. *Comparative judicial systems: Challenging frontiers in conceptual and empirical analysis.* London: Butterworths.

Segal, Jeffrey A. 1984. Predicting Supreme Court cases probabilistically: The search and seizure cases, 1962-1981. *American Political Science Review* 78:891-900.

———. 1986. Supreme Court justices as human decision makers: an individual-level analysis of the search and seizure cases. *Journal of Politics* 48:938-955.

Segal, Jeffrey A., and Albert Cover. 1989. Ideological values and the votes of U.S. Supreme Court justices. *American Political Science Review* 83:553-568.

Seidelman, Raymond, and Edward J. Harpham. 1985. *Disenchanted realists: Political science and the American crisis, 1884-1984.* Albany: State University of New York Press.

Shapiro, Martin M. 1983. Recent developments in political jurisprudence. *Western Political Quarterly* 36:541-548.

———. 1989. Political jurisprudence, public law, and post-consequentialist ethics: Comment on professors Barber and Smith. In *Studies in American political development,* vol. 3, ed. Karen Orren and Stephen Skowronek. New Haven: Yale University Press.

Shepsle, Kenneth A. 1979. Institutional arrangements and equilibrium in multi-dimensional voting models. *American Journal of Political Science* 23:27-59.

Smith, Rogers M. 1988. Political jurisprudence, the "new institutionalism," and the future of public law. *American Political Science Review* 82:89-108.

———. 1989. The new institutionalism and normative theory: Reply to professor Barber. In *Studies in American political development,* vol. 3, ed. Karen Orren and Stephen Skowronek. New Haven: Yale University Press.

Songer, Donald R. 1982. Consensual and nonconsensual decisions in unanimous opinions of the United States courts of appeals. *American Journal of Political Science* 26:225-239.

Spaeth, Harold J. 1985. On the exercise of power in a committee system: An empirical analysis of social choice models as applied to Supreme Court decision making. Paper presented at the annual meeting of the American Political Science Association, New Orleans.

Steamer, Robert J. 1986. *Chief justice: Leadership and the Supreme Court.* Columbia: University of South Carolina Press.

Stumpf, Harry P. 1983. From constitutional law to political jurisprudence. *Western Political Quarterly* 36:534-541.

Suppes, Patrick. 1984. *Probabilistic metaphysics.* New York: Basil Blackwell.

Tate, C. Neal. 1983. The methodology of judicial behavior research: A review and critique. *Political behavior* 5:51-82.

_____. 1987. Judicial institutions in cross-national perspective: Toward integrating courts into the comparative study of politics. In *Comparative judicial systems: Challenging frontiers in conceptual and empirical analysis,* ed. John R. Schmidhauser. London: Butterworths.

Walker, Thomas G., Lee Epstein, and William J. Dixon. 1988. On the mysterious demise of consensual norms in the United States Supreme Court. *Journal of Politics* 50:361-389.

Weisberg, Herbert F. 1986. Introduction: The science of politics and political change. In *Political science: The science of politics,* ed. Herbert F. Weisberg. New York: Agathon.

Wilcox, Clyde, and Aage Clausen. 1989. The dimensionality of roll-call voting reconsidered. Paper delivered at the annual meeting of the Midwest Political Science Association, Chicago.

CONTRIBUTORS

David Adamany is a professor of law and political science at Wayne State University. He received his J.D. from Harvard Law School and his Ph.D. from the University of Wisconsin. He is the author or co-author of *Financing Politics* (1969), *Campaign Finance in America* (1972), *Political Money* (1975), and *American Government: Democracy and Liberty in Balance* (1976), and co-editor of the *Borzoi Reader in American Politics* (1971). He has published articles in the *American Political Science Review, Political Science Quarterly, Western Political Quarterly, Law and Policy Quarterly,* and several law journals. Professor Adamany is currently serving as president of Wayne State University.

Lawrence Baum teaches political science at Ohio State University. He received his Ph.D. from the University of Wisconsin. He is the author of *The Supreme Court* (third edition, 1989) and *American Courts: Process and Policy* (second edition, 1990). His articles have appeared in the *American Political Science Review, American Journal of Political Science, Law and Society Review,* and many other social science and legal journals. Some of the subjects of his research have been judicial innovation, the implementation of judicial decisions, and policy change in the Supreme Court.

Gregory A. Caldeira is a professor of political science at Ohio State University. He received a Ph.D. from Princeton University in 1978. He has published articles on the courts and American politics in the *American Political Science Review, American Journal of Political Science, Journal of Politics, Law and Society Review, British Journal of Political Science,* and other journals. Currently he serves on the executive council of the American Political Science Association and the editorial boards of the *American Political Science Review, Law and Society Review,* and *American Politics Quarterly.*

Bradley C. Canon is a professor of political science at the University of Kentucky. He received his Ph.D. from the University of Wisconsin in 1967. He is the co-author of *Judicial Policies: Implementation and*

Impact (with Charles A. Johnson, 1984) and has published articles in most major political science and law and society journals as well as several law reviews. He also contributed chapters to six other books. He was a Ford Foundation Fellow in 1972-1973 and is president of the Southern Political Science Association for 1990-1991.

Lee Epstein is an associate professor of political science at Southern Methodist University. She received her Ph.D. from Emory University. She is the author of *Conservatives in Court* (1985), *Public Interest Law Groups* (1989), and articles in the *American Journal of Political Science, Journal of Politics, Western Political Quarterly,* and other professional and legal journals.

John B. Gates is an assistant professor of political science at the University of California, Davis. He received a Ph.D. from the University of Maryland. He is the author of *The Supreme Court and Partisan Realignment* (1990) and articles in the *American Journal of Political Science, Political Methodology, Social Science History,* and other social science and legal journals.

James L. Gibson is a professor of political science at the University of Houston. He received a Ph.D. from the University of Iowa. His research has appeared in the *American Political Science Review, British Journal of Political Science, American Journal of Political Science, Journal of Politics, Law and Society Review,* and in many other political science journals. He is co-author of *Party Organizations and American Politics* and *Civil Liberties and Nazis: The Skokie Free-Speech Controversy.* He is currently engaged in research on political tolerance and political freedom in the United States and Europe, and in the construction and analysis of a data base on the Warren and Burger eras of the U.S. Supreme Court.

Henry R. Glick is a professor of political science and research associate in the Institute on Aging, Florida State University. He is the author of *Supreme Courts in State Politics* and *Courts, Politics and Justice;* he is the editor of *Courts in American Politics* and co-author of *State Court Systems.* Professor Glick also has contributed numerous articles to political science and judicial journals, including the *American Political Science Review, American Journal of Political Science, Journal of Politics, American Politics Quarterly, Polity, Judicature,* and *Law and Society Review,* among others.

Sheldon Goldman is a professor of political science at the University of Massachusetts at Amherst. He received his Ph.D. from Harvard University. He is the author or co-author of eight books, including *The*

Federal Courts as a Political System (third edition, 1985), *Judicial Conflict and Consensus* (1986), *Constitutional Law: Cases and Essays* (1987), *American Court Systems* (second edition, 1989), and *American Politics and Government* (1990). He has published in several professional journals, including the *American Political Science Review* and *Judicature*.

Herbert Jacob is a professor of political science at Northwestern University. He received his Ph.D. from Yale University and has taught at Tulane University; the University of Wisconsin, Madison; and Johns Hopkins University. He has been a fellow of the Center for Advanced Study in the Behavioral Sciences and a visiting fellow at the Centre for Socio-Legal Research at Oxford University. He is past president of the Law and Society Association. He is author of sixteen books, including *Felony Justice* (with James Eisenstein, 1977), *The Frustration of Policy: Responses to Crime by American Cities* (1984), and *Silent Revolution: The Transformation of Divorce Law in the United States* (1988). He has also published articles in *Public Opinion Quarterly, Journal of Politics, Social Science Quarterly,* and *Law and Society Review,* among other journals.

Charles A. Johnson is a professor of political science and associate dean of liberal arts at Texas A&M University. He received his Ph.D. from the University of Kentucky (1977). He is co-author of *Judicial Policies: Implementation and Impact* (with Bradley C. Canon, 1984) and has published articles in such journals as the *American Journal of Political Science, Polity, Law and Society Review, Social Science Quarterly,* and *Judicature.* He is the co-founder and former chair of the American Political Science Association's Law, Courts, and Judicial Process Section and was the editor of the section's newsletter from 1983 through 1987.

Nicholas P. Lovrich, Jr., is a professor of political science and the director of the Division of Governmental Studies and Services at Washington State University. He received his Ph.D. from the University of California, Los Angeles. He is the author of articles in journals such as *Judicature, Justice System Journal, Western Political Quarterly,* and *Journalism Quarterly.*

Wayne V. McIntosh is an associate professor of government and politics at the University of Maryland. He received his Ph.D. from Washington University in St. Louis. He is the author of *The Appeal of Civil Law* (1989) and several articles in the *American Political Science Review, Journal of Politics, Law and Society Review,* and other political science and multidisciplinary journals.

William P. McLauchlan is an associate professor of political science at Purdue University. He received a Ph.D. from the University of Wisconsin and a J.D. from the University of Chicago. He is the author of *Federal Court Caseloads* (1984), *American Legal Processes* (1976), and articles in professional journals. His research interests focus on court caseload and court agendas, in addition to constitutional law.

Lynn Mather is a professor of government at Dartmouth College. She received her Ph.D. from the University of California, Irvine. She is the author of *Plea Bargaining or Trial: The Process of Criminal Case Disposition* and co-editor of *Empirical Theories about Courts*. She has also published several articles on criminal courts and dispute processing. She was elected treasurer of the Law and Society Association (1983-1987). She is currently conducting research on family law policies in the New Hampshire and Maine trial courts with a grant from the National Science Foundation.

H. W. Perry, Jr., is an assistant professor of government in the Faculty of Arts and Sciences at Harvard University. He received his Ph.D. from the University of Michigan in 1987 and was awarded the Edward S. Corwin prize by the American Political Science Association for the best dissertation in public law. His publications include articles in *Judicature* and various edited collections. He has written a book entitled *Deciding to Decide: Agenda Setting in the United States Supreme Court* (1991). His current research is on the U.S. solicitor general and the Department of Justice.

C. K. Rowland is an associate professor of political science at the University of Kansas. He received his Ph.D. from the University of Houston in 1978. He is currently completing an intra-university exchange as a visiting professor of psychology. He has previously served as a guest scholar at the Brookings Institution in Washington. He is the co-author (with Robert Carp) of *Politics and Policy Making in the Federal District Courts* (1983) and author of articles in several professional journals, including the *Journal of Politics, American Journal of Political Science,* and *Justice System Journal.*

Jeffrey A. Segal is an associate professor of political science at the State University of New York at Stony Brook. He received his Ph.D. from Michigan State University in 1983. He recently was a fellow at the Law and Social Science Program, Northwestern University. His articles have appeared in the *American Political Science Review, American Journal of Political Science,* and *Journal of Politics,* as well as other political science journals.

Charles H. Sheldon is a professor of political science at Washington State University. He received his Ph.D. from the University of Oregon and is the author of several books on the judiciary, including *The American Judicial Process: Models and Approaches* (1974); *Politicians, Judges and the People* (1980); and *A Century of Judging: A Political History of the Washington Supreme Court* (1988). Professor Sheldon also has written articles for law reviews and political science journals.

Donald R. Songer is an associate professor of political science and graduate studies director at the University of South Carolina. He received his Ph.D. from the University of North Carolina in 1975. His writing on the courts of appeals, judicial impact, and legislative behavior have appeared in a number of journals, including the *American Journal of Political Science, Journal of Politics, Western Political Quarterly, Law and Society Review,* and *Legislative Studies Quarterly.*

INDEX